Ultimate Guide to Law Schools

Fourth Edition

Anne McGrath and the Staff of *U.S.News & World Report*

Robert Morse, Director of Data Research

Brian Kelly, Series Editor

Comsewogue Public Library
170 Terryville Road
Port Jefferson Station, NY 11776

Copyright © 2010 by *U.S.News & World Report, L.P.*

Sourcebooks and the colophon are registered trademarks of Sourcebooks, Inc.

All rights reserved. No part of this book may be reproduced in any form or by any electronic or mechanical means including information storage and retrieval systems—except in the case of brief quotations embodied in critical articles or reviews—without permission in writing from its publisher, Sourcebooks, Inc.

This publication is designed to provide accurate and authoritative information in regard to the subject matter covered. It is sold with the understanding that the publisher is not engaged in rendering legal, accounting or other professional service. If legal advice or other expert assistance is required, the services of a competent professional person should be sought.

—*From a Declaration of Principles Jointly Adopted by a Committee of the American Bar Association and a Committee of Publishers and Associations*

Trademarks: All brand names and product names used in this book are trademarks, registered trademarks, or trade names of their respective holders. Sourcebooks, Inc. is not associated with any product or vendor in this book.

Published by Sourcebooks, Inc.

P.O. Box 4410

Naperville, Illinois 60567-4410

(630) 961-3900 FAX: (630) 961-2168

www.sourcebooks.com

Fourth Edition

Printed and bound in the United States of America

DR 10 9 8 7 6 5 4 3 2 1

Table of Contents

Introduction

So you want to be a lawyer.

Are you sure?

It's no idle question, given the impact choosing law will have on your life. Before walking away from three years of income (and head-on into a $100,000-plus commitment), you'd better figure out whether the reality of legal practice jibes with your vision of what your day-to-day experience will be. Many applicants, attracted by eye-popping salaries and the drama of shows such as *Law and Order*, are "woefully uninformed about what the practice of law is like," says Deborah Post, a professor at Touro College's law school in Huntington, New York, and former co-chair of the committee on admissions for the Society of American Law Teachers. Much too often, they "stumble into the law because they don't know how to find a job," says Michael Young, former dean of the George Washington University Law School in Washington, D.C., and now president of the University of Utah. "If you love it, you'll have a great life. But do you really want to spend 10 to 14 hours a day thinking about the stuff of law? If not, it might be an acceptable living, but you won't necessarily be happy."

Indeed, several studies suggest that attorneys are among the *least* happy people. A 1990 analysis of data on 104 different occupations by researchers at Johns Hopkins University, for example, found that lawyers were 3.6 times as likely as the general working population to suffer from major depression. University of Pennsylvania psychologist Martin Seligman, in his book *Authentic Happiness*,

---

"If you love law, you'll have a great life."

---

suggests three reasons: Attorneys are primed to constantly anticipate "every conceivable snare and catastrophe that might occur in any transaction"; young lawyers, in particular, often hold high-pressure jobs in which they have little voice or power to make decisions; and these days lawyering often seems more about making money and crushing opponents than offering wise counsel and finding justice.

"There's been a huge change over the last 20 years," says David Stern, an attorney and CEO of Equal Justice Works, a Washington, D.C., advocacy group that promotes public interest law. "It's no longer a profession—it's a business. The number one priority is profits per partner." That's undoubtedly a major reason for the incessant lawyer jokes you'll put up with. A 2002 survey conducted for the American Bar Association found that about 70 percent of Americans think of lawyers as "greedy and manipulative," and only 19 percent have confidence in them. (Full disclosure: Of the 10 professions and institutions covered in the survey, only the media inspire less confidence.)

Obviously, these conditions don't define every lawyer's job, and some attorneys thrive on the intrigue and competition. Moreover, graduates whose motivation is a strong commitment to social justice have plenty of opportunities to find work in public service, perhaps with the government, or maybe (more lucratively) through pro bono work for a law firm. The point is simply that you need to make this choice with both eyes open.

Those who *do* end up with a fancy paycheck—the median first-year salary at large firms is now $160,000 plus bonuses—are apt to work into the wee hours, researching case law and statutes, and then drafting memos for the partners (who are doing the interesting work). Partnership, the carrot dangled seven or eight years down the line that confers a share of the firm (and even more money), comes less easily than it once did, as the ranks of young associates have swelled and as firms have created alternative salaried partnership tracks. According to John Heinz and Robert Nelson, Northwestern professors who have studied the changing career paths of Chicago attorneys for the American Bar Foundation, only 16 percent of lawyers surveyed in 1995 who had started out at a large law firm had made full partner at the firm and stayed, compared with 35 percent in 1975, for example.

And the fact is that many lawyers end up in small or solo practices, making ends meet by taking on debt collections work or acting as public defenders. When the time comes, students who had planned a career in public interest law often find they can't pay off their debts and buy groceries on a $40,000-a-year salary—and so they end up at a big firm after all.

How can you tell if you're among those who truly belong in law school—whether the "stuff of the law," in Young's words, really "lights you up"? He advises prospective attorneys to first expose themselves to legal ideas, if not by taking an undergraduate course in law, then by talking to lawyers and following newspaper coverage of legislation and the courts. Can't make it to the end of a *New York Times* article about a Supreme Court decision without yawning? Take that as a sign.

Tom Arthur, former dean and now professor at Emory University's law school, suggests that anybody considering law first answer these questions:

Am I truly interested in public issues?

You'd better be, because you'll be working on them; typically, the law is the vehicle by which society's knotty issues are resolved. "The environment went from a movement to statutes," says Arthur. The same thing is happening now with the issues raised by Enron and the mutual fund scandal.

Do I *really* like to read and write?

If not, be prepared to suffer. "Cases, decisions, statutes, regulations—we read all the time," says Arthur. And write: "It's always, 'When can we have a draft?'"

Do I get stage fright?

Even if you never take part in a trial, a big part of your job will entail presenting your argument cogently and credibly to partners, clients, and opposing counsel, all of whom will be judging you—and some of whom will be hostile.

How good am I with details?

Partners don't tolerate mistakes. Nor do clients. Miss a filing deadline, and you might be guilty of malpractice.

Can I separate my feelings from the facts?

Whatever your own personal value system is telling you, you'll have to step back and analyze

> "*Law is no longer a profession—it's a business. The number one priority is profits per partner.*"

every situation rationally and objectively, and then act in your client's best interest—which may not be where your heart is.

Am I someone people can turn to for help?

There's a reason lawyers are called "counselors." If listening and empathizing and patiently advising confused people aren't part of your skill set, you might belong somewhere else.

Do I have good judgment?

Clients who assume you do will be trusting you—and paying you—to make the right decisions about what strategies they ought to follow and how much risk they ought to take to get the desired result.

• • •

Even if the answers to these questions point you directly to law school, consider testing your certainty by taking some time off. "I tell everybody to work for a couple years," says David Van Zandt, dean of the law school at Northwestern University in Illinois, which has adopted a policy of preferring work experience. "We feel much better about students after they've grown some, and are giving up a job and a salary," says Van Zandt. "I run into far too many 50-year-olds who were performance-oriented [in college] and got on the track seeing law school as a place where they could be rewarded. Then down the road they wake up and say, 'Why did I get on the track so fast?'"

"I think anyone who applies to both Cornell and NYU hasn't got a clue what they're doing."

Once you've studied the evidence and decided law school is indeed for you, this book will help you get there. The first chapter, "Choosing the Right School," sorts through all the factors you'll need to consider: reputation, curriculum, faculty, placement services, location, and cost, among others. As those who attend the country's most elite institutions will find themselves in demand for great jobs pretty much anywhere in the country, Chapter 2 takes you inside the law schools at Yale, Harvard, Stanford, and New York University, which regularly score near the top of the annual *U.S. News* rankings. Chapter 3 describes the attributes top schools—which have their pick of hundreds, even thousands, of qualified applicants—look for beyond grades and LSAT scores in those they accept. In Chapter 4, you'll find out how to prepare for the LSAT and put

together an outstanding application; Chapter 5 advises you on how to pay for it all. Finally, in Chapter 6, you'll read about getting that first job—and where the great opportunities are these days.

The tables that begin on page 73 allow you to compare law schools on a number of attributes key to your decision. Among them: which programs are the toughest and easiest to get into (page 75); which schools hand out the most generous financial aid (page 91); which ones leave their students with the heaviest and lightest debt loads (page 95); and which have the most success at placing graduates—and at producing new lawyers who can pass the bar exam on the first try (pages 103).

Finally, at the back of the book, you'll find detailed profiles of law schools accredited by the American Bar Association. The profiles, which are based on a comprehensive survey that *U.S. News* sends out to law schools each year, contain the most up-to-date information on everything from the academic credentials of students to programs of study and joint-degree options to the availability of financial aid and the sorts of jobs graduates land. Study it. And then go visit. Law schools are much less alike than you might think. Says Seattle-based admissions consultant Loretta DeLoggio: "I think anyone who applies to both Cornell and NYU hasn't got a clue what they're doing." This guide will clue you in.

Chapter One

Choosing the Right Law School

For many would-be attorneys, the process of picking a law school requires the coolest of calculations: apply to the most elite five or six schools within reach and enroll at the best one you can. All of those considerations that mattered so much in comparing undergraduate colleges—looking for the best campus culture, the place where you felt you fit in—get hardly a moment's thought. "I saw the choice as utilitarian—what doors will open for me for the rest of my life?—rather than as a question of how happy I'd be for the next three years," says Kimberly Parker, Harvard Law class of 1996 and now an attorney for the big corporate firm WilmerHale in Washington, D.C. "You just cannot overestimate the importance the prestige of the degree has for your life." She speaks not only as someone for whom doors have opened, but as an attorney who has recruited young lawyers to her firm.

It's undeniable that in a profession as pedigree-conscious and tradition-bound as law, the name on your diploma will have enormous influence on the trajectory of your career. "If you have a choice between a top 15 or a second-tier school, you're *crazy* not to go to the top school—the opportunities are so much better," says David Van Zandt, law dean at Northwestern University in Illinois. Graduates of the

---

"You just cannot overestimate the importance the prestige of the degree has for your life."

---

world-class institutions that sit atop the *U.S. News* rankings year after year (see table, page 14) are wooed by the most prestigious law firms, offered plum judicial clerkships, plucked for the most visible slots in government and public service, and granted entrée to ultraselective academic jobs. Degrees from these schools hold currency in every corner of the country, and they put alumni on a national stage: These are the people working on Supreme Court cases and merging the AOLs and Time Warners, while somebody else handles the contract dispute between the local restaurant and its supplier. Says Parker: "If you want to practice on the national level, being at a top 10 or top 20 school matters *a lot*."

Anybody following that most ambitious path thus starts off with a ready-made short list: Yale, Harvard, Stanford, Columbia, New York University, Chicago, and the 15 or so other truly name-brand, national institutions. What if your aspirations or LSAT scores don't point you toward the top? The quality and stature of school you choose will still be very important to your career success and your geographic flexibility—as will an exceptional performance there.

"Recruiters won't come in the same numbers," admits Patricia Adamski, former vice dean of the law school at Hofstra University in New York and now an administrator for the university. "But the top of Hofstra's class gets offers that meet those at the middle of Harvard's." Generally, she says, students who are in the top five or 10 people of their class at good but not name-brand law schools, or even the top 10 percent, can expect to find themselves in demand.

Below the top ranks, other factors besides a school's overall reputation may influence your chances for success. Someone who's bent on getting a public interest job, for example, should know that many cash-strapped nonprofit agencies are especially interested in graduates of law schools that offer students lots of hands-on experience working with Legal Aid clients, for example, because the agencies just don't have the budget to train beginners. Applicants contemplating a career in politics might be wise to opt for the law school at their state university. "You've got to be elected from somewhere," says Andrew Coats, dean of the University of Oklahoma College of Law. The people you meet in a law school like Oklahoma's—your class plus the two ahead of you and the two behind you—will hold many of the state's positions of power in business, law, and government when you're running for office, and they'll probably help a fellow grad regardless of their own political leanings, says Coats. He graduated from the law school himself in 1963 and has been a district attorney for Oklahoma County, a Democratic nominee from the state for the U.S. Senate, and the mayor of Oklahoma City.

For the same reason—a strong alumni network—those who are certain that they want to settle and practice in a given area of the country might want to pick a fine regional law school in that area rather than a more highly ranked law school elsewhere. Still, most say, if you can make it in the top 20, go for it.

No matter how high you're aiming, law deans, undergraduate pre-law advisors, and independent admissions consultants agree (as does *U.S. News*) that a decision about which school is the best one for you should never hang on its position in a numerical ranking alone. Though law schools may look much the same on paper—a standard first-year courseload, upper-level electives and clinics, lots of library time—comparable schools can have vastly different characters and areas of strength. There's large and impersonal, there's small and collegial, there's merely competitive, and there's "don't leave your notes around," says Stuart Rabinowitz, former dean of Hofstra's law school and now the university's president. Some schools emphasize legal theory (in an ideal system, how should the law work?); others emphasize actual practice (how the law works in reality).

So the experts suggest a more nuanced approach to thinking about quality: Find the most excellent *cluster* of schools that you can get into, and within the cluster, pick the school whose character and culture and curricular strengths suit you best. "There might be 15 to 30 schools for any one candidate," says Katharine Bartlett, a professor in the law school at Duke University. And within a cluster, your career opportunities are apt to be very similar. So, says George Washington University's former law dean Michael Young, you can afford to think, "Am I inter-

ested in things international? I might pick GW over Northwestern. Am I interested in policy formation through an economic perspective? Yale or Chicago." An applicant intrigued by the "countercultural view of the law" might pick Georgetown, says Young.

"Someone who is thinking of Yale, which is very small and 'all for one, one for all' might be very unhappy at Harvard, a big school of very com-

> *"If you have a choice between a top 15 or a second-tier school, you're crazy not to go to the top school."*

petitive, very motivated, Type A people," says Mark Meyerrose, a former Harvard Law admissions officer who has advised law school applicants for AdmissionsConsultants Inc. (www.admissions consultants.com), an independent Virginia-based counseling firm that helps clients get into college and graduate school. (The vast majority of law schools in the country—though not all—have been accredited by the American Bar Association, which means that they've met standards for legal education set by the profession. In many states, a lawyer who holds a JD from a nonapproved school is not eligible to sit for the bar exam.)

The *U.S. News* rankings—which measure schools by several yardsticks, including expert opinion of their programs, test scores and grades of students, placement record, and bar passage rate—are not intended to drive a decision between Nos. 3 and 4 or 5. But the rankings can help you identify your cluster. ("The difference between the [school] that ranks fourth or seventh and the one that ranks 34th or 37th? Let's not kid ourselves," says Saul Levmore, former law dean and current professor at the No. 7 University of Chicago.)

Then, as you narrow the field in search of the right fit, a number of key questions are worth thinking about.

How big is the student body—and how big is the typical class?

Harvard is home to some 1,700 students; Yale, to just under 600. George Washington University boasts some 1,600 full- and part-timers. Boalt Hall, the law school at the University of California–Berkeley, has a total enrollment of around 950; Duke, almost 700. Considering that all these numbers are pretty small compared to undergraduate colleges, why should you care? Because the size of the student body and the entering class affects law schools' personalities, the availability of professors outside of class, the extent to which you'll engage with your classmates, and, most likely, the breadth of the curriculum.

"You know everyone, and it didn't feel like we had to fight against each other," says Joe Lemon, a 2002 graduate of Stanford Law who went to work for a high-tech law firm in Menlo Park, California. "We formed study groups, shared notes, talked, created tests for each other." Stanford, one of the country's smaller law schools with some 580 students, has a first-year class of about 170. On the other hand, the roster of different classes offered after the first year may by necessity be much more limited at a small school. (For a peek inside Stanford, Harvard, and the other law schools at the very top of the newest *U.S. News* ranking, see Chapter 2 on page 15.)

The size of the first-year sections at the school you pick—the standard classes in civil procedure, constitutional law, torts, and criminal law—is apt to have a big impact on the quality of your experience. Many schools have focused recently on bringing section size down and on putting students in one small seminar their first year. At Harvard, "the resources are amazing and the professors are topnotch, but it was hard to get personal attention," recalls 1996 grad Parker. Until just a few years ago, Harvard's first-year sections numbered 140 students each. Responding to criticism that the school felt too cold and impersonal, the administration has since trimmed sections to about 80, a fairly typical size among law schools. At GW, where sections average 85 to 90 students, first-years now take at least one of their classes in a small section of 36.

At the University of Oklahoma, Dean Coats has shrunk the size of the entering class from about 225 to under 170 over the past few years, and has created four first-year sections of only 40 to 44; for instruction on legal research and writing, the class is divided into eight sections of about 20 students each. Partly as a result, the number of applicants to the school has more than doubled since 1998, and the median LSAT score and grade point average have moved higher, from 152 to 156 and from 3.28 to 3.54.

You'll also want to find out how many students will be in most of the second- and third-year classes, advises David Cohen, former dean of law at Pace University in White Plains, New York. A reasonable range would be 20 to 30, he says. A related piece of data, the student–faculty ratio, offers another clue about faculty accessibility and what the chances are that your professors will actually get to know you. At most of the top schools, the ratio is somewhere around 10 to 1 or 15 to 1. At Yale, there's a professor for every 7.3 students.

What to look for in a part-time program

Is the part-time path a route for you? "How flexible is your work schedule? Do you need to be on call or take work home with you? Law school will require every other minute of your life," warns Loretta DeLoggio, an admissions consultant based in Seattle (www.deloggio.com) who specializes in helping minority students choose a school and get in. This is because you'll have no flexibility in how long you take to earn your degree; part time means a-little-bit-less-than-full-time for four years instead of three.

Many would-be lawyers have no choice: It's their day-job salary that will pay for night school. The advantages of a full-time program—the generally much greater availability of externships, the extensive interaction with other students outside of class through study groups and extracurricular activities—don't outweigh the need for an income. Fortunately, a number of good schools offer evening programs;

you'll find detailed information about them in the directory entries at the back of this book. As you compare programs, here are the questions you should ask:

Who are the teachers? Ideally, they'll be the same people teaching the day students. At Georgetown Law, which was founded in 1870 as an evening program, part-timers are taught weekday evenings by members of the regular full-time faculty, and they're held to the same academic standards.

Are admissions yardsticks different for evening students? If the LSAT scores and grade point averages of students accepted into the part-time program are significantly lower than those of the day students, you might qualify for a law school that wouldn't otherwise take you. On the other hand, the level of discourse might be lower, too.

Will you get any hands-on experience? Many clinics are impossible to hold at night because the courts are closed, but there should be experiential learning going on. Look for simulation courses that involve role-playing or clinics that don't rely on courtroom experiences. Evening students at Pace often participate in securities arbitration and disability rights clinics, for example.

Will you get the same services as full-time students? Find out whether you'll have the same access as day students to career services programs, the financial aid office, the registrar, and the school's information-technology and library resources. What about student organizations? All opportunities afforded by the school should be available.

What does the school's location offer?

You'll care about location for a couple of reasons—okay, maybe three. ("It's beautiful all the time!" says Lemon of Stanford's relentlessly sunny weather.)

For starters, educational and externship opportunities may vary considerably according to where a law

> *"If you think you want to practice in Milwaukee, you might better go to Marquette than DePaul."*

school is situated. For example, Georgetown Law Center students, whose classes meet a mere 10-minute walk from the Supreme Court, sometimes get a chance to work on Supreme Court cases. Students at the Washington, D.C., law schools also have access to externships at a whole list of federal government agencies, while those at the University of California–Los Angeles can take courses in sports and entertainment law and find externships at television and movie studios. In Grand Forks, University of North Dakota students help Native American tribal governments develop environmental programs and offer legal assistance to the Spirit Lake Tribal Court.

Secondly, bear in mind that if you're not a candidate for a national school, your future job opportunities will certainly be shaped by where you choose to enroll. The connections students make through externships or local pro bono work often lead to the permanent offers, and a school's alumni network is apt to be much stronger in its immediate region than elsewhere. "If you think you want to practice in Milwaukee, you might better go to Marquette than DePaul," says Tom Arthur, former law dean at Emory. "If you go to

Suffolk Law School, you'll be really well placed to practice in Boston and New England, but it'll take you five or 10 years of practice to establish yourself and make the leap to San Francisco," warns admissions consultant Meyerrose.

What's the culture like?

The size of the school will tell you something about its climate, but to really get a handle on the campus culture—how intense and competitive students are, for example, or how committed to social justice or to high-paying corporate law—you're going to have to visit. Even though only a tiny fraction of law schools interview applicants, most are only too happy to entertain visitors. "We want students to figure out if this is a place that will work for them," says Hannah Arterian, dean of the College of Law at Syracuse University, which regularly hosts formal programs for prospective students that start with a group meeting with her and include breakfast, a first-year class, an introduction to the career services office, a workshop on financial planning, lunch with faculty members, and tours of the law school, Syracuse's campus, and campus housing. "Not only do prospective students get an opportunity to check out our environment; we get a chance to see how they might fit in a culture that puts a high premium on maturity and interpersonal skills," says Van Zandt of Northwestern, the only major law school that tries to interview every applicant.

Sarah Russell Vollbrecht, a native of Oklahoma and a 2003 graduate of the University of Virginia's law school, applied only to institutions ranked among the *U.S. News* top 10 in the hope that her degree would take her anywhere in the country. (It worked: She graduated into a job clerking for a judge on the U.S. Court of Appeals for the 5th Circuit in Houston, after which she planned to work for a Dallas law firm.) At the outset, she expected to enroll at the most highly ranked institution that accepted her. Once she'd visited several campuses, however, she realized that distinctions in academic excellence were small, and other qualities mattered more to her than place in the pecking order.

"Duke and UVA were very similar—their facilities were impressive, the campuses were pretty, and the students were *really* friendly; they smiled and were eager to assist me," says Vollbrecht. "At Harvard, it felt like everybody was rushing to do what they needed to do. Chicago might have been a better school academically than UVA, but the students seemed a lot more serious—I studied hard at Virginia, but also made time for softball." Accepted by Duke, Chicago, New York University, and UVA, Vollbrecht narrowed her picks to Duke and UVA, then made the "easy choice." She'd lived in Virginia and qualified for in-state tuition, so UVA was the cheapest by far.

"You need to talk to students—they're verbal and critical by nature," advises David Leebron, former dean of Columbia Law School and now president of Rice University. One good reason to quiz students in person (beyond seeking the inside dope about the place) is to gauge their capabilities and interests— and, by extension, the likely capabilities and interests of the people you'd be learning with next year. "I firmly believe that what makes a law school is the student body," says Robert Berring, a professor and former interim dean at Berkeley's Boalt Hall, whose students he describes as a "politically awake and less formal" bunch. "This isn't the same as the college

decision," says Leebron, who advises applicants to consider whether their classmates would challenge and excite them. "It's about making career choices. This is the most important group of people you will know for the rest of your life."

Check into how diverse the student population is, too—not just in terms of ethnic background, but also in work experience, education, age, gender,

> *"You need to talk to students—they're verbal and critical by nature."*

and socioeconomic background. "Much of the learning happens between students, and the more perspectives you have, the richer the discussion will be," says Evan Caminker, dean and professor of law at the University of Michigan, whose methods of factoring minority status into the admissions decision won the Supreme Court's approval (for more on the Michigan decision, see page 49). "Part of being a lawyer is seeing through others' eyes. Your clients—what's motivating them? The judge— where is he coming from?" When Leebron was at Columbia, he found the school's relatively large population of Mormons and Orthodox Jews and generally rich religious mix to be a selling point: "One of my Torts students [was] a priest—what an interesting perspective!"

What are the strengths of the curriculum?

Yes, the first-year coursework will be pretty standard wherever you go, but step back and take a look at the big picture. What are the hallmarks of the schools you're considering?

Chicago is known for its academic rigor, its examination of the law through an economics filter, and its conservative viewpoint. Boalt Hall is among the most liberal schools. Yale students, who can revel in their intellectual pursuits without obsessing over grades (they either pass with honors, pass, low pass, or fail), are steeped in the theory and philosophy of the law and not in the nuts and bolts of practice. Northwestern and Duke have made a priority of transitioning students into practice by stressing teamwork and collaboration on group projects. Georgetown is noted for its large and strong program of legal clinics in which students learn by practicing with real clients. The City University of New York is devoted to public service.

As you dig more deeply into the specifics, it's important to consider the breadth and diversity of schools' second- and third-year curricula because most students who think they've settled on a practice area before they arrive change their mind. "Law school is a transforming experience—and that's true here and at the University of Baltimore night school," says Chicago's Levmore, who advises against choosing a school based solely on its areas of specialization.

On the other hand, in what is clearly an age of specialization, most law schools *do* now have areas of strength. Each year, in addition to the general ranking of law schools, *U.S. News* also ranks specialty programs based on the opinions of faculty who teach in the field; Vermont Law School regularly gets top billing for environmental law, for example, and NYU is highly ranked for international and tax law.

"It used to be that the top schools were trying to be great in everything, but now we're setting strategic priorities," says Duke's Bartlett. Her school, for example, has paid particular attention to developing four of its programs: intellectual property, telecommunications law, health and biotech law, and international and comparative law. Syracuse boasts several "centers" (including those covering family law; indigenous law; global law; and human policy, law, and disability studies) and has launched an institute that focuses on national security. Students who complete a concentration of coursework in one of the centers receive a certificate. The University of Pittsburgh offers several certificates, including international and comparative law, environmental law, and health law; the University of Missouri–Columbia offers certificates in dispute resolution, European Union studies, and journalism.

But take note: Many schools *market* an area of specialty that isn't exactly substantive. Check what the current course offerings are. It's not unheard of for courses to appear in the catalogs that haven't been offered in years.

Investigate how much emphasis is placed on the practical skills: writing, advising clients, negotiating, arguing. Employers have complained loudly that their new hires arrive ill-prepared to practice, so now many law schools are building hands-on experience into the curriculum in the form of clinics; simulation courses that have actors or students playing the roles of opposing counsel and judge, for example; and intensive first-year classes in legal research and writing. While some schools think of the practical instruction as lesser courses and assign part-timers to teach them, ideally they'll be handled by full-time faculty members who meld the teaching of practice with theory in a child advocacy clinic, for example. Look for the student-faculty ratio to be very low. The best programs limit clinics to eight or 10 students and teach legal research and writing in small groups of 20 or 30.

"Textbooks don't tell you what clients are like or how to be in front of a judge, but that's what you need for the real world," says one graduate of the CUNY School of Law who spent 30 hours a week in the Family Law Clinic, where she represented a victim of domestic violence in a custody case, filing child-support orders, writing briefs, and arguing with opposing counsel before a judge. In Georgetown's clinics, participants represent a whole range of clients, from noncitizens seeking political asylum to victims of domestic violence to tenants in disputes with landlords to children accused of crimes. Some 60 percent of students take a clinic before graduation. One of the clinics at Northwestern puts students to work in the internationally recognized Center for Wrongful Convictions, where they work on cases involving claims of innocence.

As noted before, practical experience is especially valued by public interest employers, so anyone planning on a public service career will want to consider law schools whose clinical programs reflect a commitment to it. Several that get high marks include Georgetown, NYU, CUNY, Fordham, and Northeastern. Besides strong clinics, says Equal Justice Works CEO David Stern, good public interest programs tend to have full-time counselors who help students do career planning and find pro bono work; a selection of summer public interest internship opportunities; and a structured (and sometimes mandatory) pro bono program. (The truly committed schools also have generous loan-repay-

ment assistance programs. For more on how these plans work, see "How much will it cost?" on page 12.)

As the practice of law gets increasingly global, a growing number of students are looking for more than just a class or two in international and comparative law. Some law schools have begun to aggressively integrate discussion

> "It used to be that the top schools were trying to be great in everything, but now we're setting strategic priorities."

of other legal systems into courses throughout the curriculum, and a growing number make it possible for students to actually study law abroad. At Tulane, for example, students can spend anywhere from one week to a month in one of seven foreign countries, including Canada, England, France, Germany, and Greece; semester-abroad programs are also an option. Cornell students who are fluent in the language of the host country can study for a semester at one of several foreign law schools. Students at American University's law school can also take a semester abroad at several European, Canadian, or Mexican law schools or the City University of Hong Kong.

One advantage of choosing a school that is part of a university is the richness other programs can add to the law curriculum. At Penn, for example, with 12 schools on one campus, law students can study with Wharton business students in a small-business clinic and in a negotiation class; medical students and law students study together how to use the legal and medical systems to protect children's rights. The Institute for National

Chuck Larson Jr. went into politics before he went to law school, but it's his University of Iowa JD that really launched his career. Law school "has been the foundation of everything I do," says the 42-year-old Iowa native, who served as U.S. ambassador to Latvia and as a member of the Iowa House and Iowa Senate.

Larson had already put aside plans for a career in business back in 1992 after a conversation with some buddies. "The economy wasn't good, and we were talking about the large part of our generation that was leaving the state because we didn't have good-paying jobs," he says. By the time the chat was over, Larson had decided not only to stay in Iowa, but to get involved in running it. He campaigned by knocking on virtually every door in his district—twice.

Shortly after winning a seat in the state House of Representatives, Larson realized that "some 40 percent of the bills that land on the governor's desk move through the Judiciary Committee," and he wanted to know how the laws would affect his constituents. So he went back to school, taking his spring semester courses in the summers so as not to miss the legislative season. "I didn't have a lot of free time," he concedes, but the hard work paid off: His understanding of the intricacies of case law and constitutionality propelled him to leadership roles on first the House and then the Senate Judiciary Committees.

Day to day, Larson tackled civil issues such as the definition of marriage ("a hot topic" these days) and bankruptcy law ("it's narrow and specific and can be confusing—law school helped me put it into sharp focus"). On the criminal front, his understanding of drug laws helped when he and his colleagues drafted the nation's toughest law on methamphetamine abuse (first offense: mandatory treatment; second offense: jail).

Because of its strong alumni network in the state, the University of Iowa has been a powerful support to Larson, no small consideration when he was choosing law schools.

Many of his colleagues in government were Iowa graduates—and, perhaps most important, so were many of his constituents. "Obviously, the ties with alums across the state work politically," he says. "Iowans like their universities. Politically, it's a mark of distinction." On the other hand, he says, Iowa is "a fairly liberal school, and I'm a Republican. Some of my [professors] contributed to my opponents." He may not have raked in political contributions on campus, but he did save some money: Choosing the flagship state university allowed Larson to leave law school "relatively debt free."

As a member of the U.S. Army National Guard's Judge Advocate General corps, Larson spent a year in Iraq, where, when he wasn't handling the legal affairs of fellow soldiers, he helped build schools and water filtration systems.

Security and Counterterrorism at Syracuse University's law school will bring together students and faculty in law, journalism, history, and public affairs to study and discuss their various perspectives on how threats to national security should be handled. And at the University of Michigan, students can take up to nine credits in graduate programs outside the law school.

At the extreme, student interest in cross-disciplinary study expresses itself in the pursuit of a joint degree, which may add an extra year or two to the educational experience but (at least theoretically) offers an edge in the ultracompetitive job market. While the most common combo degree is probably law and business, there's a whole array of possible combinations, and many schools allow students to create their own dual degrees.

At Michigan, choices include a JD/master's of science in information (for those interested in the intellectual property issues created by technology) and a JD/MS in natural resources (for anyone with a particular interest in pollution and the environment). At Duke—where fully a quarter of the law school population is enrolled in a joint-degree program—students can complete a three-year-plus-one-summer combination JD/master's degree in any of some 15 academic disciplines from English to psychology to Romance studies. They can also complete longer professional joint degrees with the divinity school, the Fuqua School of Business, and the medical school, among others.

Who's doing the teaching, and are they good?

Talking to students and sitting in on first-year classes should give you a sense of the faculty as teachers, a factor that's difficult to judge from a distance. On many campuses, there's been quite a shift since the *Paper Chase* days, toward an educational experience much friendlier to students. (The noble explanation: Professors have realized that using the Socratic method to intimidate and humiliate doesn't promote learning and probably inhibits it. A more practical reason: Schools are battling one another to attract the most-qualified candidates—who happen to be a more vocal and demanding bunch of consumers than previous generations.)

The result is that many deans have put a premium on good teaching and student-faculty interaction as well as a professor's legal scholarship. Vanderbilt University law profs are expected to know every student by name from the first day and to have their doors open anytime. At the University of Pennsylvania law school, which encourages informal student-professor contact, the whole faculty pretty much lunches out with students nonstop, says Dean Michael Fitts. "We all have this irrational fear that we're going to go in [to see a professor] and our question will be stupid," says a Penn student, who remembers those fears evaporating during her first term after she and a handful of other students had lunch with each of her four professors. Pace University law school in New York has introduced a merit-based pay system in which the strength of professors' syllabi, grading methods, and student evaluations counts as 35 to 40 percent of their marks for performance, along with their records of scholarship and public service. Chicago has worked at creating an "intellectual community" by holding frequent lunchtime panel discussions by faculty and seminars at professors' homes, says Levmore.

A side effect of the reform movement has been a "huge variance in the degree to which teaching is still rigorous," says Kent Syverud, dean of the law school at Washington University in St. Louis and former president of the American Law Deans' Association. He advises prospective applicants to observe the interactions in one or two first-year classes with a critical eye. As argument and analysis are such vital legal skills, "you don't want to see a replication of Psych 101, where the professor lectures, poses rhetorical questions, and walks out," he says. It should be clear that the presentation has been carefully thought through and that the students are engaged and involved; where the Socratic method is practiced properly, students are respectfully asked to articulate and defend their arguments and are doing the talking at least a third of the time. Rather than embarrassing the unprepared by calling on students randomly, many professors now use an "on call" system that alerts those who need to be ready ahead of time.

Will your classes be led by the great legal minds who have established the school's reputation? Or are the scholars off doing their research while attorney adjuncts do the teaching? You definitely want a faculty still active out in the field and on the cutting edge of legal scholarship; the bios and vitae posted on school websites can give you some indication of professors' accomplishments and publications. Penn's Paul Robinson is a recognized scholar on criminal law who has served on the U.S. Sentencing Commission; William Banks, head of Syracuse's counterterrorism institute, is an expert in national security law who lectures around the world and has testified before the Senate Judiciary Committee on the U.S. Patriot Act.

But you also want reassurance that the scholars are the people you'll be learning from—and that they're accessible to you outside of class, too. When you quiz current students, ask them whether "when you ask to see a professor, they say 'See you in a week and a half,'" advises Andrew Popper, a professor at American University's Washington College of Law.

How much will it cost?

Take a deep breath.

Perhaps $250,000 or $300,000 or even a lot more, counting all the income you'll give up to go to school. Graduates of the top programs, where yearly tuition now runs more than $40,000, may not have to worry so much about accumulating $100,000 in debt; they can expect to be making lots of money if they choose to. But the rest of the world will need to weigh the trade-offs of choosing an in-state public institution (tuition and fees at Ohio State's law school run just a bit over $22,400 a year for state residents; in-state tuition and fees at the University of Georgia, around $14,450); apply for financial aid; investigate the availability of merit awards based on academic credentials or commitment to public service rather than need; and check out loan repayment assistance programs. (For a complete discussion on how to pay for law school, see Chapter 5 on page 51.)

One advantage of applying to school where your LSAT scores stand out is that you might well be a candidate for a scholarship. A growing number of schools now offer merit money in an effort to attract the most talented students possible. "It's amazing," says admissions consultant Mark Meyerose of the explosion of merit aid. "We can't *not* do it in this competitive environment," says Hofstra's Rabinowitz. The pool of aid money at Hofstra, which includes some need-based aid but is mostly awarded based on merit, tripled from $1.1 million to

$3.3 million between 1994 and 2002; merit aid accounted for the entire increase. Quinnipiac Law School in Connecticut, which has been working hard on attracting a student body with higher LSAT and GPA numbers, gave out some $3.4 million in 2006, up from $500,000 12 years earlier. In the past several years, the 25th/75th percentile range of LSAT scores at Quinnipiac has moved from 144–151 to 157–160. Pace University law school gave out $380,000 to first-year students in 1999; a mere four years later, the pot had grown to $1.9 million.

Pace has also joined the ranks of law schools with loan repayment assistance programs. These programs, also sometimes called loan forgiveness programs, are designed to help graduates who take public interest jobs pay back their law school loans. They now exist at more than 100 schools, according to *U.S. News* surveys (for the list, see page 60). Under the typical plan, a graduate who takes a job at a nonprofit or government agency that pays less than a certain amount, say $40,000, is either granted or loaned money each year to cover part of his yearly debt payments. If you receive the funds as a loan, the debt is forgiven after a certain number of years as long as you stay in a public interest job and your income doesn't rise too high.

What kind of help will I get finding a job?

One stop on your campus tour should be the career services office, whose assistance (or lack thereof) may mean the difference between your graduating into a job or not. Does it appear to be a professionally run operation with counselors on staff—rather than just administrative assistants who schedule interviews? In addition to arranging for scores of employers to recruit on campus, the best place-

ment services are constantly scheduling workshops on job-hunting strategies and various career paths, bringing attorneys to campus to speak about their work, sending students to recruitment fairs, and offering individual advice.

While you're there, ask how many graduates end up getting jobs after graduation, and how soon. "Most schools have extraordinarily detailed placement data that they'll share with you if asked," says Syverud of Wash U. You'll want to know the proportion of the class with a job offer at graduation and how many are working six months or nine months later; the directory entries at the back of this guide provide each school's most recent placement data. You'll want to know how many grads accepted clerkships, positions at different-size corporate law firms, and public interest slots. At Yale, for example, nearly half of the 2004 graduating class accepted judicial clerkships, and 8 to 10 percent of students typically go into teaching law.

Find out where graduates end up geographically, too, advises Syverud. "If your goal is to be a litigator in New York, does this school produce litigators in New York? If your goal is to practice employment law in San Francisco, does this school produce San Francisco lawyers?"

How much do graduates make? According to the most recent surveys by the National Association of Law Placement, the median starting pay for all JD full-time jobs has lately been $72,000; the figure for first-year associates ranged from $68,000 at small firms to $160,000 (plus bonus) at firms of 500 or more attorneys; for the class of 2004, median pay was only $43,000 for clerkships and $45,000 for government jobs and $38,000 for public interest positions.

But the actual pay packages that individuals are offered vary widely by law school and by job location.

Each year, *U.S. News & World Report* ranks the nation's accredited law schools based on such measures of excellence as the expert opinion of deans and faculty members, expenditures per student on instruction, placement success, and how well students fare on the bar exam. To see where your schools rank, check out "America's Best Graduate Schools," available on newsstands, or go to www.usnews.com. Here is this year's Top 20. Schools whose ranks are identical are tied.

1. Yale University (CT)
2. Harvard University (MA)
3. Stanford University (CA)
4. Columbia University (NY)
5. University of Chicago
6. New York University
7. University of California–Berkeley
   University of Pennsylvania
9. University of Michigan–Ann Arbor
10. University of Virginia

11. Duke University (NC)
    Northwestern University (IL)
13. Cornell University (NY)
14. Georgetown University (DC)
15. University of California–Los Angeles
    University of Texas–Austin
17. Vanderbilt University (TN)
18. University of Southern California
19. Washington University in St. Louis
20. George Washington University (DC)

The placement office can give you the data you need, and the entries in this book provide the starting salaries reported by the class of 2008.

Finally, check out how many graduates pass the bar exam on the first try. (For a look at how the schools stack up on this measure, see page 103.) Once you've decided to go into law—and committed all that time and money—you'll want to know your odds of clearing the final hurdle.

Chapter Two

Inside America's Top Law Schools

Each year, fewer than 2,000 people claim a spot in the first-year law school classes at Yale, Harvard, Stanford, and New York University—which means that, at least in terms of their career opportunities, they pretty much have it made. Are you, too, planning on gunning for the top? Here's a peek inside some of America's best law schools.

Yale Law School

New Haven, Connecticut

Things work a bit differently at Yale Law School. The traditionally grueling first term is ungraded, subsequent courses are graded on an honors, pass, low pass or fail basis, there are virtually no course requirements past first term, and professors are free to choose what they want to teach. Indeed, one former dean, Harold Koh, an international human rights expert who was tapped by the Obama administration to be legal advisor to the State Department, once took a class to a screening of Runaway Jury, during which he loudly enumerated the film's many procedural errors.

Such a freewheeling approach might be less successful if Yale weren't so small. With around 650 students, the school has a student–faculty ratio of about 7 to 1, and the hallways of its rambling Gothic building near the heart of campus are abuzz with chance meetings between students and professors. Even in crowded first-year courses, where enrollment tops 100, professors call on students by name without checking seating charts. The school's size and the absence of grades or class ranking breed a collaborative spirit and a homey informality. When Yale students express interest in a subject not accounted for in the course catalog—like maritime law or global health law—they simply draft a faculty advisor and create their own course, or "reading group."

The unrestrained air extends to classroom interaction, where students challenge professors constantly and debate one another on issues such as the legitimacy of the International Criminal Court and the limits of Supreme Court power.

Dean Robert C. Post, in an address to the incoming class in 2009, put it simply. "We educate you so that you can make the law your own," he said. "We educate you so that you might construct an intelligent, passionate, unalienated relationship to the law. We want you to discover for yourselves and in yourselves what is important to you about the law."

Classes at Yale are thus highly theoretical; this is not the place to look for a lot of attention to the nuts and bolts of practice. A recent contracts course included a long, spirited discussion over whether Pepsi could in theory be held liable for what amounts to a joke: its ad campaign offering a Harrier Jet to customers who collected 7,000,000 Pepsi points.

Given this theoretical bent, it should come as no surprise that Yale is an incubator for academics. Five years after graduation, about 13 percent of each law school class works in academia. The law school is home to a dozen research centers and projects, including the China Law Center, which aims to help the legal reform process in that country, and the Information Society Project, which studies the effect of the Internet on law and society. Each student is required to do original research and write a major paper of about 60 to 80 pages, which they might publish in one of Yale's student-run law journals.

Yale is known as an activist school, where students often fight legal battles in the larger world and a relatively large percentage pursue public interest law, which is emphasized by professors and career counselors. More than 70 percent of the class of 2009 took first-year summer jobs in public interest work, most of them unpaid (Yale provided funding).

Roughly half of Yale Law's graduating class traditionally takes judicial clerkships—and a large chunk stay with public interest work afterward. Easing their way is Yale's generous loan repayment program for graduates making less than a certain amount, recently $60,000, which covers their loan payments for up to 10 years.

While most law schools permit students to enroll in their clinics only after the first year, Yale opens clinics to students after a single term. Twenty distinct clinical projects cover areas such as immigration, tenant eviction proceedings, child advocacy, and legislative advocacy. The international human rights law clinic matches students with lawyers working on cases in federal and U.N. courts, and with regional human rights bodies in South America and Africa. Nearly 80 percent of Yale JD students take at least one clinical course, gaining experience in all aspects of lawyering, from writing and filing briefs to negotiating with opposing counsel to representing clients in court.

A burning commitment to law is practically a prerequisite for study at a school with virtually no requirements, no class rankings, and a hardly noticeable grading system. Which is not to suggest that Yalies aren't competitive: The median LSAT score and grade point average of the 2009 entering class were 173 and 3.90.

Harvard Law School

Cambridge, Massachusetts

With nearly 1,700 students, Harvard is roughly the size of the law schools at Yale, Stanford, and the University of Chicago combined. The law library, with 2 million volumes, is the largest of its kind in the world. Nearly 100 full-time professors and more than 100 part-time faculty teach 250-plus electives, providing depth in many areas—Islamic law and cyberlaw, for example—that smaller schools simply can't achieve.

Harvard's platinum reputation also rests on its biggest resource: a marquee faculty that includes defense attorney Alan Dershowitz, former U.S. Solicitor General Charles Fried, civil rights activist Lani Guinier, and constitutional scholar Laurence Tribe, to name just a few of the larger lights.

Despite the size and prestige of the school, Harvard does not ignore its students. In recent years, the school has worked to make the experience more welcoming. First-year sections—the big groups of students who take the basic courses together—shrank from 140 to about 80. And first-year students are now divided into groups, or "law colleges," that aim to promote a sense of community by sponsoring social events. The school is also home to more student groups and journals, 104 and 14, respectively, than any other law school, making it easy for students to find something of interest.

The student government organizes numerous events, including faculty luncheons and pub nights, throughout the year, and the Dean of Students Office also puts together activities, like cooking classes and movie nights, aimed at connecting students on a social level. Dean Martha Minow has organized a film series in which she chooses movies to show, followed by a panel discussion with faculty members.

While students at some smaller law schools seem uniformly bent on changing the world, many Harvard students—who in 2009 had a median 3.89 undergraduate GPA and a median 173 LSAT—proudly advertise that they're here for the renowned corporate law curriculum. The program boasts nearly 20 professors, research centers in international tax, corporate governance, and international finance, plus opportunities for interdisciplinary study through the esteemed business school.

Recently, though, the school has taken a number of steps to strengthen its focus on public interest law, adding a graduation requirement of pro bono work and increasing funds for students who do low- or nonpaying public interest work during the summer.

Harvard's "low-income protection plan" repays the loans of graduates making less than $42,000.

Slightly higher-paid grads are eligible for partial loan repayments. The school also promotes public service through 20-plus courses with clinical components that have students doing such work as helping low-income area residents with immigration, housing, and family law issues. The clinical courses also place roughly 50 JD students each year in the office of the state attorney general and in Boston's U.S. attorney's office.

In early 2010, Harvard Law School announced the creation of the Public Service Venture Fund. Each year, the fund will award $1 million in grants to help graduating students pursue careers in public service. "This new fund is inspired by our students' passion for justice," says Minow. "It's an investment that will pay dividends, not only for our students but also for the countless number of people whose lives they will touch during their public service careers." Dean

> *"The stereotype used to be that everybody wanted to come here because it was Harvard, but didn't much expect to like it."*

Minow also established 12 new Holmes fellowships for students interested in post-graduate public service work. All told, financial support for students interested in public service has increased by $2.75 million in the past year.

Alexa Shabecoff, the law school's assistant dean for public service, notes that when jobs are scarce, the fund may provide fellowships that create jobs. "It will also supplement salaries for graduates hoping to work for nonprofits that can only afford to pay for part-time positions," she says. "In this ever shifting legal job market, we will offer our students the ability to land the job of their dreams or create it."

Still, two-thirds of graduates end up taking private practice jobs—indeed, HLS attracts more than 700 private recruiters each year to its job bazaars. And students often snag a handful of offers in a single day.

Stanford Law School

Stanford, California

Academically top-notch Stanford is also easily one of the nation's most beautiful law schools, situated on an 8,000-acre campus that looks more like a Spanish-colonial country club than a college. Nearly every student has a bike (and knowledge of local hiking trails). Beaches and ski slopes are just an hour or two away.

"Looking back, I can't believe I was at all hesitant to leave the East Coast," says Connor Williams. "I've loved being part of the tight-knit community at Stanford. I've worked hard, but I've also laughed more and made stronger friendships than I ever imagined."

Last year, Stanford had more than 4,000 applicants for its entering class of 180 students. The LSAT range for the class of 2012 was 157–180 and the GPA range was 3.29–4.18.

Those who make the cut learn quickly how much size matters at the so-called Harvard of the West. With about 180 students entering this year (compared to roughly three times that at Harvard), Stanford is able to foster a level of community among students and faculty that many law schools cannot.

First-year small sections typically average no more than 30 students, and with an average student–teacher ratio of about 8 to 1, getting extra time with professors outside of class is easy. The entire law school is housed in two buildings, soon to be three, and most of the faculty's office doors are routinely open.

"I chose Stanford because I wanted a small program but didn't want to compromise on the quality of students and faculty or access to

"So many people have done really interesting non-law-related things before they come here to school."

resources and opportunities," says one student. "At Stanford, I feel that I am among the future leaders of the profession."

Decades younger than Harvard and Yale, the law school, like the West itself, is more cutting edge than traditional. Stanford is well known for its program in technology and law, for example; at the same time Stanford is also strong in more traditional areas of study, such as constitutional law, with the pre-eminent constitutional law center in the country on its campus.

"Lawyers need to be educated more broadly," says Dean Larry Kramer, "with courses beyond the traditional law school curriculum, if they are to serve their clients and society well... The idea is to utilize the rest of the university to create a more three-dimensional legal education. We realized that the rest of the university is training the people who will become our students' clients. Good lawyers need to understand what their clients do."

Students at Stanford are highly encouraged to develop a broad view of the law in several contexts, so the curriculum includes a large offering of interdisciplinary programs. And with the law

school's shift to the university's quarter system, students are better integrating with the broader campus community.

The school offers 20 joint-degree programs in a wide range of areas from bioengineering, business, computer science, and economics to history, international policy studies, and sociology. The school also has many customized joint-degree programs, including programs with Princeton's Woodrow Wilson School of Public and International Affairs and Johns Hopkins's Nitze School of Advanced International Studies. Master of laws (LL.M.), master of the science of law (J.S.M.), and doctor of the science of law (J.S.D.) degrees are offered. Ten clinical programs allow students to undertake the roles and responsibilities of practicing lawyers, and 18 programs and centers afford opportunities for research and policy-oriented study.

Not surprisingly, Stanford's proximity to Silicon Valley has made it a magnet for scholars in Internet-age intellectual property law and law and the biosciences. The school is home to the Center for Internet and Society, which examines the many constitutional and public policy legal issues raised by the Internet. Stanford's Center for E-Commerce, now in its seventh year, explores the field of electronic commerce law.

Another area of strength is the environmental law program, consistently mentioned among the top in the nation. The program relies heavily on situational case studies—much like those used in business schools—to bring disputes over resources and regulations to life and give students a crack at solving real problems, such as how to balance business interests and conservation.

The school's centers on conflict and negotiation bring together students and faculty from all parts of the university to study mediation and conflict resolution theory and practice in domestic and international settings. The Stanford Program in international and comparative law is open to grad students in law, business, engineering, and the arts and sciences, and it offers classes that explore the global nature of law, business, science, and politics, taught by faculty from several disciplines.

In the public interest arena, where the number of course offerings rivals those in technology and intellectual property, students are trained through clinics and in courses on administrative law, poverty law, racial equality, voting rights, and gender law. They also benefit from an endowed center that provides training, support, and public interest career counseling. Stanford offers a fellowship program to support third-year students or recent graduates pursuing public interest careers and guarantees at least $5,000 in summer grants for every student with financial need doing public interest work. Finally, graduates who accept public interest and government jobs can have as much as 100 percent of their law school loans forgiven.

With so many older students in Stanford's law school population—the average age is 25—count on an often unusual mix of experiences and some lively discussion. Former investment bankers, doctors, legislators, even dancers become law students; the mix is consistently mentioned by students and faculty as one of the most valuable aspects of a Stanford education. "So many people have done really interesting non-law-related things before they come here to

school," says Gabrielle Vidal, a grad of the class of 2000, which included a former Texas legislator and a coroner. "Then when they get here, they have interesting life stories to bring to the law."

Paradise, of course, comes at a price. With annual tuition now over $44,000 coupled with the San Francisco Bay Area's high cost of living,

> "Who could resist a world-class law school in paradise?"

a Stanford Law education runs over $71,000 a year. However, stop any Stanford student and you'll hear that the investment is well worth it: Stanford alumni, like graduates of the other elites, are walking away with six-figure starting salaries. And don't be surprised if the students try to interest you in a T-shirt that says "Harvard, the Stanford of the East."

New York University School of Law

New York, New York

Competitive and collegial perhaps best describe New York University School of Law.

There's no question that NYU is highly competitive: Seventy-five percent of last fall's 1Ls scored 169 or higher on their LSATs, and the same percentage boasted undergraduate GPAs of at least 3.6.

As for collegial, students report that professors, two-thirds of whom live within a five-minute walk of campus, are generally helpful and accessible. Dean Richard Revesz, an Argentine-born

Kelly Farrell had reached the midpoint of her time at Harvard Law when it happened: She realized that she didn't want to be a lawyer. Farrell hadn't figured she'd end up at Harvard initially. Wait-listed, she'd made plans to attend the University of Virginia. "I was very excited about UVA, actually," she says. But when the phone call came, "my parents were like, 'Harvard calls,' so I went," heading off to Cambridge, Massachusetts, in the autumn of 1999 with great expectations and prepared for "a really amazing experience."

And yet, she says, her time at HLS "was only so-so. My roommate was the best thing to come out of my Harvard experience." The competitiveness on campus was part of the problem. It wasn't as if people were hoarding notes, she says, or sabotaging fellow classmates. But the classes were large and populated liberally with "gunners," always at the ready with an answer. The real pressure, she says, came from the high standards people imposed on themselves. "These expectations breed a little bit more anxiety. You're told that Harvard

is the key to unlocking all of these great doors."

Which it did: After her identity crisis, Farrell took stock and decided to use her law degree to work in politics, an interest since her days as a political science major at Duke University. First, she snagged a summer internship at Verner Liipfert, which had just been named one of the most powerful firms in Washington in a survey of members of Congress, Hill staffers, and senior White House aides. Then, upon graduation, she accepted a job with the law firm. Farrell spent her days on Capitol Hill lobbying members of Congress and attending hearings that related to the public policy interests of the firm's clients, which included Lockheed Martin, Visa, and British Aerospace.

In 2002, the firm merged with a larger company—and while the merger went smoothly, Farrell says, the atmosphere changed. Then a newlywed, Farrell was much more concerned about her quality of life, which was being affected by late nights and pressure to increase billable hours. "It drains you to be working 65–70

hours a week—and my hours were even more reasonable than other associates'," she says.

She went next to the United States Maritime Administration, within the Department of Transportation, where as an attorney-advisor she followed legislation and new developments pertaining to initiatives such as the Maritime Security Program. For example, she worked on legislation allowing merchant marines to enter into agreements with private vessels during times of national emergency so that they can carry cargo for the government. Then she moved into space travel. As a legislative affairs specialist at NASA headquarters in Washington, she serves as a liaison with Congress on matters having to do with the space shuttle and the international space station. One notable effort in which she played a part: getting Discovery off the ground again after the Columbia accident.

Farrell took a pay cut when she moved to the government, but she notes that "averaged out by hours, I'm probably making about the same as I used to." The lifestyle change, of course, is just about priceless. "I was almost stunned when I didn't have to stay until 8 or 9 at night." That extra time at home has been especially precious since the birth of Jake, her first child. What's more, she loves the work. "It's kind of a nobler purpose than representing big corporations," she says. "You do your own little part for the country."

---

environmental lawyer, answers to "Ricky." Even the school's location—in a handful of brick mansions facing historic Washington Square Park in Greenwich Village, near coffee shops and bars where both the servers and the customers often know your name—has a small-town feel.

"I was four years out of college when I applied to law school, so I'd already watched many of my friends attend (and graduate from) law school," says Erin Scharff, class of 2011. "I was always struck by how happy my friends at NYU were." She recounts the story of a student who had his laptop stolen shortly before first-semester 1L exams: "Not only did his classmates share their outlines with him; we all donated money to get him a new laptop."

Perhaps the collegial atmosphere should come as no surprise—one of the strengths of the NYU curriculum is that specialty dedicated to making the world a better place: public interest law.

NYU supplements its wide variety of courses and clinics with a weekly speakers' series, a public interest career counseling center, and financial assistance for students interested in pursuing such jobs. The school's Loan Repayment Assistance Program (LRAP) is designed to provide JD graduates with greater flexibility in career choice by easing the burden of student loan repayment. Assisting JD gradu-

ates who choose careers in the public sector or other low-paying fields of law, LRAP will cover as much as 100 percent of an eligible graduate's monthly debt service from law school loans for up to 10 years after graduation, provided the graduate's qualifying income is below LRAP-established income scales. (These scales are adjusted annually to reflect changes in the cost of living and career progression.) The school also provides several thousand dollars to every first- and second-year student who takes a nonpaying summer job in a public interest organization in the United States or abroad.

Dean Revesz says the school is "truly a special place—a campus in the midst of the greatest city, where students can study in an environment that stresses academic excellence, without being cutthroat."

Another area of distinction here is international law. In addition to its star-studded American faculty, NYU maintains a "global faculty" of professors from universities abroad who visit each year to teach special classes on subjects ranging from foreign tax treaties to gender issues in Islamic law. Driven by a schoolwide sense that domestic lawyers increasingly will work on global issues, professors even outside the international arena often roll non-U.S. cases into their courses; a first-year student might study an Australian case asserting aboriginal rights in a course examining sovereignty, for example.

Many students are drawn to NYU by the opportunities it provides for students to practice before they graduate. All 1Ls take a one-year, ungraded course called Lawyering in which they role-play client interviews and negotiations, for instance, under the guidance of full-time professors. Upperclassmen may apply for admission to any of about 30 clinics in which they assist real clients in such areas as immigrant rights, child welfare, and capital defense cases.

Students also gain exposure to the real world through a faculty that features lawyers often quoted in the morning papers, like legal ethics expert Stephen Gillers or Burt Neuborne, legal director of the Brennan Center for Justice and a former legal director of the ACLU.

Revesz said the school's overarching goal is "to graduate humane people, citizen-lawyers who will be the world's leaders in business, government, and public service."

Most graduates accept jobs at private firms, but 10 to 15 percent typically join public interest organizations and government agencies—a significantly higher percentage than at peer schools. Students say they have their pick of job offers. According to the Office of Career Services, more than 650 employers interview students on campus each year, and the majority of graduates accept their first- or second-choice job. As is true at all the top schools, virtually everybody lands a job by graduation.

Chapter Three

What Law Schools Will Look For in You

The University of Chicago law school received just under 4,800 applications for 190 spots in the 2007 entering class. At the University of Pennsylvania, 5,604 people applied for about 260 slots. Georgetown fielded almost 10,690 applications last year and made 2,554 offers for 2,366 day and 188 evening spots.

And it's not only the top 20 or 25 schools that are flooded with candidates; the competition is tougher just about everywhere. American University's Washington College of Law received about 8,670 applications last year. At Quinnipiac in Connecticut, a third-tier law school that has made improving the quality of its academic program and student body a top priority, the number of applicants rose 108 percent between 2001 and 2005.

How can you possibly stand out in such a crowd? This chapter tells you what attributes the admissions committee is looking for in a candidate and how you can best convey that you've got them. Your superior qualities are going to have to shine through in your test scores, transcript, personal statement, and letters of recommendation, because only a handful of law schools offer the

that factors in LSAT score and GPA. Since schools can ask LSAC to correlate their index with the academic success of first-year law classes, the number can offer some indication of how an applicant is apt to fare during his or her first year at the school.

But contrary to popular belief about automatic acceptances and rejections, all applications generally get read—even at the very top and very bottom of the range. "In my experience, the goal of admissions is to enroll a dynamic class, and this commands a look beyond the numbers," says one person with experience both in the admissions office at an elite law school and as a private counselor. Some admissions experts believe that applications are bound to be read with even greater attention to non-numerical factors in the future. When the Supreme Court said it was legal for the University of Michigan Law School to consider race in admissions (see page 49), the justices "made clear that genuine diversity is an interest of constitutional significance—and that could include exotic languages," says Andrew Popper, a professor at American University's law school who has lots of experience reading applications himself as a member of the admissions committee. "If we're going to attempt to establish diversity, [law schools] have to really look at every file."

> *"The numbers matter, and anybody who says otherwise—that's ridiculous."*

chance to impress in person. (For more detailed advice on how to tackle the application, see Chapter 4.)

Start with strong numbers

While it's not true—as many applicants fear—that your fate will hang entirely on your LSAT score, "the numbers matter, and anybody who says otherwise—that's ridiculous," says Georgetown Dean Andy Cornblatt. Typically, grades and test scores serve as a kind of sorting mechanism, an efficient way for admissions staffers to mentally put applicants into one of three categories as they read through all the files: the probably admitted (unless something unexpected turns up to detract from the numbers), the probably denied (unless something unexpected turns up that makes them really appealing), and the ones who require considerable mulling over and discussion. Some schools do this analysis based on the LSAT, some do it based on the GPA, and some use both. Another option is to use an index number calculated by the Law School Admission Council (administrator of the LSAT)

Indeed, some of the "probably denied" may turn out to bring unique experience to the table. One admissions dean, for example, recalls a Vietnamese applicant who spent time living under a bridge before escaping to the United States. He wouldn't have made it into law school based on numbers alone. And files of the almost-certain-to-be-admitted are typically read to be sure "they're not psycho killers," says Robert Berring, formerly interim dean at UC–Berkeley's Boalt Hall—and to check for honor code violations, for example, or whether applicants reveal themselves in their personal statement as offensively arrogant or whiny.

Some schools are much more numbers-driven than others, says Seattle-based admissions consultant Loretta DeLoggio, and one way to tell is to check the variance between the 25th percentile and the 75th percentile in LSAT and GPA scores. If the bottom of the range is just a couple of points below the top, the school may well be pushing to get its numbers higher, she says. But in general, says DeLoggio, who specializes in helping minority students choose a law school and get in, applicants "grossly misuse" the 25th–75th percentile ranges in choosing schools. It's important to remember, she says, that "the 25th percentile is not a bottom. In 200 people accepted, 50 are below it!"

On the other hand, candidates who get in with scores on the low side are sure to be exceptional in some other way. In general, "someone with a 3.0 and an average LSAT score hasn't got a chance in hell of getting admitted to a top school—I'd discourage students from wasting their money" on the application, says former University of Dayton pre-law advisor Roberta Alexander, now retired.

"We have an informal sorting mechanism based on LSAT and GPA, but every applicant gets a holistic review. We're trying to find people who will be a good fit," says Derek Meeker, former associate dean for admissions and financial aid at the University of Pennsylvania law school. At the University of Chicago, applicants are admitted, denied, or held on the first reading. Those who are held might be offered the opportunity to write an additional essay or explain any puzzle in their files—really high grades and a low LSAT score, for example. "We read every single application from cover to cover," says Megan Barnett, associate dean for admissions and financial aid at Yale. The best 20 percent or so are then sent to the faculty for consideration; three faculty members read each file and rate candidates on a 2-to-4

> "In my experience, the goal of admissions is to enroll a dynamic class, and this commands a look beyond the numbers."

scale. Of a typical pool of around 12,000 that Georgetown considers to admit maybe 2,000, some "2,500 are easy 'nos' and 800 are easy 'yeses,'" says admissions head Cornblatt. "Of the rest, I get to admit 1 in 9. That's where I earn my salary." Every file at Columbia is read by at least two people from the admissions committee.

Show them you're a thinker

One characteristic of law students who succeed—the only kind admissions officers intend to accept—is that they're informed and incisive thinkers. So your application will be closely studied for evidence that you can measure up. "I try to gauge the intellectual ability of the student—who's analytically really good?" says Kate Stith, former deputy dean and professor at Yale. "I'm looking for the students who will come up with new ideas, the ones that aren't in the textbooks."

While the grades and test scores certainly indicate intellectual ability, the transcript tells a much more nuanced story. Anybody who still has maneuvering time ahead should know that grades

If your heart is set on a top school but your grades and LSAT scores won't get you there, consider enrolling elsewhere and taking another shot next year. "There are two ways to get into law school now," says Deborah Post, former co-chair of the Society of American Law Teachers' committee on admissions and a professor at Touro College's law school in Huntington, New York. "You've got the numbers, or you prove you can do the work: You go to a lower-tier school and transfer."

While they don't exactly advertise it, many highly competitive law schools rely on their transfer programs to fine-tune the composition of their student bodies and bring in appealing near-miss applicants after they've blossomed academically at another school. (Because the undergraduate grade point averages and LSAT scores of first-year students figure in the *U.S. News* law school rankings, taking less-credentialed applicants into the second-year class is also seen by many administrators as a way to avoid putting a school's rank at risk.)

"It's a terrific, terrific program," says Robert Berring, formerly interim dean at the University of California–Berkeley's Boalt Hall, which accepts about 30 transfer students each year. "We can take people from the top of lots of little law schools, and they're often [our] best students, with fire in their eyes."

It's also a good way to "do something for your legacy and donor kids—it's a better message than 'we don't have room,'" says Andrew Cornblatt, head of admissions at Georgetown University law school, who calls transfer programs "an underreported way to get into a top place."

That fire in the eye is what admissions committees will be looking to find—a position in the top 5 or 10 percent of your law school class, and, better yet, a spot on the law review, too. On the other hand, if you've *got* those credentials and are flourishing where you are, be sure to weigh the benefits of being at a higher-prestige institution against the likelihood that you'll give up star status.

"A transfer student might not make law review at the next school—you're giving up a very, very important credential and taking a risk," says Stuart Rabinowitz, president of Hofstra University in New York and formerly dean of its law school, which regularly loses top students to more prestigious places. Moreover, students at the very top of their classes at well-respected but not prestigious schools very often find themselves in contention for jobs on par with those offered to middling students at highly ranked schools. If you move, are you at risk of falling toward the bottom?

by themselves don't mean a whole lot: What matters is that you performed well in a curriculum of rigorous, challenging courses that required you to think and to write. "I want to see people who are intellectually curious and ambitious, and who have taken some courses outside their typical realm," says Meeker. "Many people have studied political science or history, and this is all fine, but it's common. A polysci major might want to take some science and math." Any patterns in your undergraduate grades will also be of great interest. "Did your grades improve over time? Is there a special explanation for a particularly weak semester?" says Evan Caminker, dean and professor of law at the University of Michigan law school.

"Some students think you have to be a polysci major—forget it!" says Cheryl Ficarra, associate dean for enrollment management at Syracuse University. "English! Or any subject that shows they've done serious analytical writing and been critiqued. These students have a serious advantage." In fact, Carol Leach, an associate professor of political science and pre-law advisor at Chicago State University, analyzed data on the undergraduate majors of the entering class at American law schools several years ago and found that the highest rates of admission were among physics majors, with history, English, economics, math, and the other sciences close behind. "I tell students to pick a major they like so they'll do well, but one that's challenging," says Leach. The bottom line, she says, is that "you have to have really good grades in hard subjects."

Put it in writing

There's no doubt about it, a bad essay speaks volumes.

The main function of the personal statement is to give the committee some insight into what kind of person you are. But your essay will also demonstrate whether you've got that all-important legal skill: the ability to marshal your arguments on paper in an articulate and persuasive fashion. So not only do you have to give information that will put you over the top, but you also must present it in a well-organized, elegant way. "Someone could have an outstanding LSAT score and GPA, and if he's not able to write compellingly or effectively, that's a *big* problem," says admissions consultant Mark Meyerrose.

"I'm looking for the students who will come up with new ideas, the ones that aren't in the textbooks."

You'll get partway there by choosing your topic well; for detailed advice on coming up with a theme, see page 44. Some general tips: It's far better to talk about yourself than about legal issues, or politics, or the state of the country today. If you try to take on the world in two pages, the result is bound to sound naïve or pseudo-intellectual. But don't just describe an experience or an achievement—go a step further and explore how it has influenced you. "What have you learned? Don't just say that you've worked at a camp for disabled children. Tell us how that's changed you," says Ann Perry, assistant dean for admissions at the University of Chicago's law school. Beware of overdoing it. Grandiose claims will certainly spur admissions officers to carefully search for the supporting evidence.

Then you need to structure your story effectively, express yourself clearly and artfully, perhaps use a bit of humor if you've got the touch. "Your personal statement is a writing sample in the most profound sense—there's no excuse for sloppy expression," says Berring of Boalt Hall. "Use crisp, clear sentences. Many people think legal writing is complex clauses—not true!"

"Is the use of language effective? Does it paint a picture? Does it make me and my colleagues stop and listen? If you've got a great story to tell and you don't tell it until the second page, I won't see it," says AU's Andrew Popper. It probably goes without saying—or should—that every comma and period better be in the right place, too.

> *"If you take on the world in two pages, it comes across as naïve, or pseudo-intellectual."*

Make the most of your experience

Once a candidate's academic abilities have been established, the committee wants to know if she'll arrive with a perspective that will make for informed and lively debate. "I'm looking for an interesting class," says Popper. At AU's Washington College of Law, the LSAC-calculated index number assigned to each candidate gives the admissions committee a sense of his or her capabilities. Each file is read by one of the committee members, who review about 50 applications a week apiece and meet regularly to discuss them and give a thumbs-up or thumbs-down.

Many kinds of experience may make a particular candidate interesting, depending on the mix of other people applying: ethnic or religious background, socioeconomic status, undergraduate major—even geographic location. "People from the West think differently about the role of government and individual rights than people in New York City do," says Michael Young, who served as dean of George Washington University law school before moving to the presidency of the University of Utah.

"People from California and Florida understand the melting pot and the importance of legal systems that work for all cultures." An applicant whose experience as a member of a minority group has been influential may want to explore that theme in the essay because most law schools value diversity for what it brings to class discussion.

One factor that has grown increasingly important in recent years is work experience. This has happened partly because the nature of the pool is changing; due to the economic downturn, the applicant pool has been rich with experienced people returning to school. "Ten years ago, 85 percent of our students came directly from college," says Lynell Cadray, dean of admission at Emory law school. This year, the share was just under 40 percent.

This is also a function of a desire on the part of law deans and professors to seed their classes with wise and seasoned students attuned to the way the world operates now. "Lawyers today are part of a team, working with people whose experience is finance or human resources—it's no longer the Abe Lincoln version of law," says David Van Zandt, dean of the law school at Northwestern University, where almost everybody arrives with at least one year of work experience, and 80 percent typically have two or more. "What we're looking for is people who have had to work with a team or lead a team to get a project done. We've turned away people with very high LSATs who've had no work experience."

"Work experience adds to the level of what we can do with them here," says Cadray. "It's fun to have young, energetic students, but it's good to have balance. People interpret the legal system differently depending on what they have done.

After five summers playing outfield for the Asheville Tourists, the Carolina Mudcats, and other minor league teams, David Feuerstein was ready for a change. He had graduated from Yale in 1995, grabbed his mitt, and begun the circuit of 14-hour bus trips to games up and down the East Coast. "That's a lot of baseball," he says. "As a minor leaguer, you make no money. And I was tired of it."

During the off-season, Feuerstein paid the bills by working as a paralegal for five months a year and discovered that he liked what he was doing. While he wasn't sure he wanted to be a lawyer, he figured that "a law degree [gives] you the most flexibility in the professional world. I knew I could do really whatever I wanted with it."

Because Feuerstein's girlfriend (now his wife) was living in New York City, he applied to the law schools at New York University, Columbia, and Yeshiva University. When he didn't get in to Columbia or NYU, he enrolled at Yeshiva's Benjamin N. Cardozo School of Law—though he worried that it didn't have the name recognition of the Ivies. "You take a risk not going to a top-name law school, and I rolled the dice a little bit," Feuerstein says. "But I thought, 'I can do well. I can make the most of it.'"

As it turned out, he loved it. Taking a position and defending it to the bitter end appealed to the athlete in him. "My time away from higher intellectual challenges may have helped, too," he adds. In his third year, he was approached by the faculty to help organize a symposium on a subject one Cardozo professor had written extensively about: the similarities between law and baseball. The symposium drew the former commissioner and deputy commissioner of baseball, the president of the Florida Marlins, a sportswriter from the *New York Times*, and, perhaps most important, the former dean of Cardozo Law School, Paul Verkuil. Later, when Feuerstein was searching for a job, it was Verkuil who introduced him to his future employer.

After graduation, Feuerstein joined Boies, Schiller, and Flexner in New York, where the majority of his clients were big corporations and the work involved such complex commercial litigations as antitrust cases and contract disputes. Many of Feuerstein's clients were sports organizations: The firm does work for the Yankees and NASCAR, for example.

Now, Feuerstein is an associate at Herrick, Feinstein, a general practice firm with offices in New York and New Jersey, where he hopes to continue combining his love of sports and the law.

And people who have worked tend to know how to work together, and want everyone to succeed."

While you might assume it's best to take a job in the legal field, perhaps as a paralegal, that's not necessarily the case. As Sandra Oakman, AU law school's late admissions director, once put it, "It really doesn't matter what it is—you could be a bartender in Vail. Go out and work beside people and learn what it's like to be a single mother making $12 an hour. As a lawyer, you'll deal with all kinds of people, and wouldn't it be nice to know something about their culture?" Joe Lemon of the Stanford Law class of 2002 wrapped up his undergraduate studies at Brown in 1992 and then managed a hotel for several years before applying to law school. In his personal statement, he wrote about how the experience taught him to handle

> "Go out and work beside people and learn what it's like to be a single mother making $12 an hour."

unexpected challenges—like the time two hours before a 200-guest wedding service when the groom had a seizure. (The wedding quickly was turned into a private affair, and the party went on as planned—except that the groom took a number of breaks to lie down.)

Remember, the point is to highlight how your background will allow you to offer something to the intellectual life at the school. "There's not one formula," says Katharine Bartlett, a former dean of the law school at Duke University, were one essay simply asks applicants to discuss what they might contribute that's different. A 37-year-old mom with three kids will certainly have an unusual perspective, says consultant DeLoggio. "People who have overcome eating disorders and drug addictions often want to hide these successes because they only see the failure they were before. But tomorrow's leaders need to understand a broad swath of society—not just the one in which they grew up," she says.

Demonstrate that you're a leader

One detail law schools can often glean from your work experience is whether or not you've got what it takes to motivate other people, solve problems, and make things happen. Ideally, your essay and your letters of recommendation will work together to paint you as the type of person who takes on responsibilities and produces results, either on the job if you've had one or in your activities as a student. "We want someone who's taken ownership of a group or a project, and made a difference," says Bartlett.

"It's very common for people to write, 'I went to college, I studied this because I wanted to do this. I was president of this,'" says Ann Perry of Chicago. "Better to tell us what challenges you faced. You needed funding? Tell us how you worked the system. We want to see that you're capable."

Prove you've got a passion— and compassion

It's definitely in your favor to show a passionate interest in something other than your schoolwork or your work. Otherwise, you might come across as a "not very active citizen," says admissions consultant Mark Meyerrose. "What have you done? I don't want someone who has just gone to class and gone home," says Cornblatt.

But no one will be impressed by a padded résumé of activities that shows breadth without any depth. Much better to be very involved in a couple of activities—perhaps you studied the environment as an undergraduate, have taken a lead role in your local community group's battle against rapid development, and have religiously biked to work for the past two years—than to be a dabbler in a whole list of organizations. That's because admissions people recognize that those who graduate and become leaders in their field are likely to be the ones who show true commitment. Keep in mind that your letters of recommendation can be very helpful here. "It would raise flags for me if someone talks about how active on campus they've been and the recommender doesn't mention it," says Cornblatt. "It's great stuff when the application and letter both say it."

Because public service is such a major focus of the legal profession (even if many lawyers can't afford to take the jobs), many law schools are impressed by evidence of heart. "We're definitely on the lookout for compassionate students who have worked in their communities. This is a profession of counseling, being altruistic, caring," says Lynell Cadray, Emory's admissions dean. One of the more memorable personal statements that Cadray has read came from an older applicant who had served in the military; he wrote about bravery and his own experience pulling an accident victim from a burning car. "If we'd only looked at the numbers, he'd have been put on the wait list," she says. "But this is the kind of character you want in the profession."

Chapter Four

The Application

Whether you've dreamed your whole life of becoming the next Thurgood Marshall or are angling to hide out in law school until the job market recovers, one thing is for sure: You're not alone. Law schools across the country are reporting record numbers of applicants, so you'll be applying during the most intensely competitive era in history.

The fact is, it's tough to get into any school, anywhere, these days.

To stand out among the overachieving, Type-A masses, you'll need to submit a virtually flawless application. The four parts of the package—your academic credentials, Law School Admission Test score, personal statement, and letters of recommendation—will demonstrate whether you're equipped (or not) with the skills you'll need to succeed in a law career: the powers of persuasion, ana-

> *It's tough to get into any school, anywhere, these days.*

lytical and critical thinking, and a mastery of clear, precise, and direct writing.

First, understand that you're playing a numbers game. Law school admission is largely about two stats: your undergraduate grade point average and your performance on the LSAT. Chances are it's too late to do very much about the former—although any opportunity to raise your GPA even just a point or two should be taken seriously. (Note that grades are generally considered in the context of who's granting them and in what subject. In other words, a B in physics from Yale may be more impressive than an A in physics from your local public college.) Even more important, you've got to kick butt on the LSAT. Together, "the numbers account for 80 percent of the decision," estimates Roberta Alexander, who served as director of the pre-law program at the University of Dayton before retiring and was a former president of the Midwest Association of Pre-Law Advisors.

The other 20 percent? You've got to prove that you're interesting and accomplished, as well as smart. "Making a law school class is a lot like making a guest list for a dinner party," says R. Michael Cassidy, associate dean for academic affairs at Boston College Law School. "We want people who will have exciting discussions." The personal statement, handled properly, will reveal something about your character that speaks to your desirability as a dinner companion, if you will—and also your abilities as an effective and fluent writer. You've also got to get your professors, bosses, ex-bosses, or anyone else who knows you well to lend credence to the impressive picture you've painted of yourself.

The advice that follows on navigating the admissions process is gleaned from interviews with dozens of people who've either been there themselves or watched it over and over, including pre-law advisors at undergraduate colleges, law school admissions officers, and students who wish they'd handled a few things differently. You still can.

Get a little guidance

If you haven't already done so, stop by your college's pre-law advising office. Though pre-law advisors, unlike high school guidance counselors, don't usually write recommendations or have any say in admissions at all, they do know a lot about the priorities of the decision makers. And sometimes, they *are* in a position to help or hurt your case: "I use pre-law advisors when we're trying to make decisions to find out about curricula and an applicant's major and colleges' grading scales," says Lynell Cadray, dean of admissions at Emory University's law school in Atlanta.

Most pre-law advisors are also professors, administrators, or career counselors with all of the multiple responsibilities of two full-time jobs. As a result, it can take some work to get a bit of face time, much less an hour-long appointment. But students who take the initiative early in their college career will find that a dedicated advisor can help them figure out which classes enhance a transcript, for example, or what major might make sense. Later on, an advisor might help you figure out which law schools are within your reach and which ones offer scholarships, and then review your personal statement before you send it off. Applicants who have been out of college for a while should feel free to tap the advising office at their alma mater—although they may be charged a fee for any services. (When you register for the LSAT, the Law School Admission Council, which administers the test, will provide you with the name and contact information of the pre-law advisor on your old campus.)

Unfortunately, many students report that overtaxed pre-law advisors are no help at all. If yours hasn't been responsive, you might consider hiring a private counselor. "Applying to law school is very much about self-assessment; this introspection really can't effectively take place unless there is another person to bounce ideas off of," argues Mark Meyerrose, a former Harvard Law School admissions officer who now works for Admissions Consultants Inc., a Virginia-based firm that offers strategy and essay editing for applicants to college and graduate schools. "Everyone needs a critical reader." The firm's soup-to-nuts packages range from $1,795 for help with three applications to $4,995 for 15 applications (www.admissionsconsultants.com).

Indeed, while seeking the feedback of a trusted friend or professor is a fine idea, applicants appear to be increasingly willing to pay for professional guidance. Test-prep behemoth Kaplan Educational

Services has seen demand for its pre-law consulting services climb rapidly in recent years. The cost for its comprehensive admissions advice, usually given over the phone or by email, is anywhere from $599 for three hours of service to $1,599 for 10 hours; check out www.kaptest.com for more details. Test Masters, at www.testmasters180.com, will help you pick a topic for your personal statement and write an outline in one hour, for $200, and will continue to lend a hand as you hone your prose for an additional $150 per hour. Full admissions counseling is also available at $200 for an initial hour and $150 for each hour after that. The 10-hour package runs $1,250.

If you're not willing or able to cough up the fees, consider contacting current law students for their insight about what qualities matter most to a school. One current 3L at the University of Pennsylvania suggests calling or emailing student organizations you may be interested in and asking a member or two how best to market yourself. Though most schools don't offer admissions interviews, deans and other faculty members also may be willing to answer questions about their school and what they value in a candidate. "I talk to every student who wants to meet with me," says David Cohen, professor and former dean at Pace University law school.

These contacts can come in handy later, after your applications are in. Randy Reliford contacted admissions officers at all of the nine law schools he applied to in late December and January of 2001–2002, and he often got put through to the dean. "I said, 'I just want to talk to you about my application, to see if I can clear up any questions you might have had,'" says Reliford, who also visited schools in Philadelphia, where he's from, and met with admissions officers, faculty members, and representatives from black student organizations. "I wanted them to have a voice to put with my application, which I think has its weight just like anything else." Reliford was accepted at six of the schools he applied to and chose the University of Wisconsin Law School, whose admissions dean had mentioned to him that graduates of the flagship institution's law school don't have to take the bar exam to become credentialed in Wisconsin.

> "I wanted them to have a voice to put with my application, which I think has its weight just like anything else."

Watch your timing

The No. 1 tip from pre-law advisors, paid and otherwise: It really helps to get your paperwork in early. Why? Better that your scintillating story about tutoring underprivileged inner-city kids be the first one a dean reads, rather than the 245th. "Earlier is always better," says Mark Meyerrose. "But there is a limit to that. I never push an applicant to get his application in by the beginning of, say, November, if that push will compromise quality. As long as the application is submitted by the December holidays, an applicant should be in good shape." See page 43 for more help with timing.

To help you stay on track, the Law School Admission Council, or LSAC—a nonprofit corporation of law schools that manages the admission process for its members—has streamlined the process of applying to multiple schools.

The LSAC administers the Law School Data Assembly Service, or LSDAS, which aggregates a report that just about every law school requires you use. For a fee, the group will compile a file that includes a summary of your undergraduate academic career, copies of all undergraduate, graduate, and law school transcripts, your LSAT score and writing sample from the test, and copies of your letters of recommendation. Registering for the LSDAS gives you access to electronic applications for all ABA-approved law schools. Save time by collecting and filling out all your applications at the same time.

Once a school receives your completed application, it will contact LSAC and request your LSDAS file, which will be sent once the report is complete and payment is received. You must pay for each report sent to a different law school.

LSDAS suggests that you register at least six weeks before you want your applications to go out, and for convenience, the organization strongly recommends you sign up for the service online at www.lsac.org. A mail-in registration option is also available.

Familiarize yourself with the LSAT

Ah, the dreaded Law School Admission Test— the bane of every future lawyer's existence. "I hate to say it's the key factor in admissions, but it certainly predominates," says one admissions officer at a top 20 school who asked not be identified. "When other things are weak and it is really strong, [it] will often make admissions officers forgive all the weaknesses." The converse can also be true, since most top schools are choosing among thousands of students with top grades *and* scores.

Why is the test so crucial? For one thing, it offers a quick and dirty way for admissions officers to compare applicants from diverse backgrounds and different schools—it's the one thing that a pottery major from State U. and a biochemical engineer from the Ivy League have in common. In addition, the test is widely considered to be a fairly reliable predictor of success during the first year of law school (as is college performance).

Part academic exercise and part endurance test, the LSAT is a half-day exam that tests skills as opposed to knowledge. It measures critical reading, verbal reasoning, analytical thinking, and writing abilities; there's no content involved whatsoever—no math or memorizing dates, in other words. "The LSAT is all about being able to pull apart arguments and understanding how evidence works," says Justin Serrano, general manager of graduate programs at Kaplan Test Prep and Admissions, who notes that these are exactly the talents you'll need in law school and, later, on the job.

The test is organized as five, 35-minute multiple-choice sections. Logical reasoning tests your capacity to understand, analyze, and complete arguments that are presented in short paragraph form; there are two logical reasoning sections that together account for half of your score. The problems in the analytical reasoning section measure your ability to understand relationships and draw conclusions about those relationships; there are four "games" with several questions apiece, and you will most likely need to sketch diagrams in your test booklet to answer them. This is by far the most feared section of the test, say veterans. It's also the most coachable, claim test-prep experts.

Reading comprehension is similar to what you experienced on the SAT; you'll have to read four long, complex passages and answer questions about them. Finally, an experimental section tests questions for future LSATs; although it appears to be a real part of the test, it doesn't count toward your score. (Unfortunately, you won't necessarily know which section is experimental when you see it on the test.) The exam wraps up with a writing sample, which doesn't count either. You'll be given two alternatives and asked to choose a posi-

> *"The LSAT is all about being able to pull apart arguments and understanding how evidence works."*

tion and advocate it. Though the essay is sent to law schools along with your LSDAS report, it's generally not considered an important part of the package, and might not even merit a glance. But complete it carefully, just in case, because some application readers find the essay revealing. "The only thing you can't get editing help with is the written essay on the LSAT," says Barbara Safriet, former associate dean at Yale's law school. "I read it for writing skills."

There's no penalty for wrong answers on the LSAT, so you should always take a guess, educated or not. The number of questions you answer correctly is your raw score, which is then converted to a scaled mark between 120 and 180. The average score is 150, but anything over 160 is considered competitive; anything over 170 puts you at or above the 98th percentile. An interesting fact: You can often miss a question or two and still nail a perfect 180.

The LSAT is offered four times a year: on a Saturday morning in October, December, and February, and on a Monday in June. (Alternatives are available for anyone who observes the Jewish

Sabbath.) You can register online at www.lsac.org, with a form from the LSAT/LSDAS Registration and Information Book, or over the phone. Be sure to sign up as soon as you can; with record numbers of test takers, popular testing sites can fill up early. (You may first want to check out www.kaptest.com/testsites, which rates various locations for the last five test dates, based on student evaluations of proctors, desk space, and the like.) Scores remain valid for five years, so anyone planning on working a year or two before applying to law school may want to tackle the exam during junior or senior year, when he or she is still in test-taking mode.

In fact, all applicants should take the test as early as possible in order to allow for further preparation and a retest, if necessary. February and June of your junior year—or one full year before you plan to matriculate—are increasingly the norm. "This is a big mindset change," says Heather Struck, pre-law advisor at Binghamton University in New York. "Students used to be able to study during the summer and take the test in October [of senior year]. But there's a lot more stress now, and it helps if you can take it in your junior year." Still, you can procrastinate until December, if necessary, and still have time to beat the final February 1 or March 1 application deadlines.

Prepare to beat the test

Though the LSAT tests for capabilities rather than knowledge, that doesn't mean you can't prepare for the exam. In fact, practicing is crucial so you'll know what types of questions and games to expect: With only 60 to 90 seconds allotted per question, there's no time for confusion. The more familiar you are with all aspects of the exam, the more confident you'll feel on test day—and the better you'll do.

Do you have enough self-discipline to set your own study schedule and stick to it? Alex Murray did. In the first week of September of his senior year at Tulane, Murray bought a test-prep book and began completing problems and taking timed practice tests on the weekends. "I started out just doing one section at a time without a time limit to get used to the questions and format," he recalls. "Then I would do one or two sections and time myself. I didn't start taking full, timed exams until about two or three weeks before the exam, because it's so time-consuming." The week before Murray sat for the exam, he took advantage of a free practice test at the local Kaplan Test Prep center, which was timed and scored for him. In the end, he raised his score from the "high 150s" on practice tests to an extremely competitive 169 on the real thing—which helped get him into the University of California–Los Angeles School of Law.

In addition to the shelves of good commercial test-prep booklets out there (those published by Kaplan and Peterson's, for example), LSAC (www.lsac.org) offers such "official" help as the $28.95 SuperPrep, which contains three previously administered LSATs, with explanations. The most recent exams are available there for $8 each, too. Applicants also can take free sample tests at websites such as www.ivyleagueadmission.com, a for-profit site run by former admissions counselors. (Print out the sample exams first in order to best approximate a real test-taking situation.)

There are less expensive online options for those who prefer to learn at their own pace, with 24-hour-a-day access to online instruction and practice tests. In fact, due to increased demand, The Princeton Review has extended its Web-based offerings with a course featuring live, real-time instruction for $1,199, a do-it-anytime online course for $999, and an express version with eight to 12 hours of lessons and two practice tests for $125.

Not everyone can do this kind of prep on his own, however. If you need additional motivation in the form of a class commitment and several hours' worth of homework a week, there are virtually endless opportunities. Many colleges and law schools offer their own test prep; the University of

The application timeline

18 months prior to enrollment

- Contact your pre-law advisor to set up a meeting; attend any related seminars offered on your college campus.
- Research schools and come up with a target list.
- Take a practice, timed LSAT to see where you stand.
- Register for the June LSAT.
- Decide on the method of test prep that suits you best and start studying.

June before applying

- Take the June LSAT, and if you don't do as well as expected, re-register for October and start studying again.
- Start visiting campuses, if possible.

August–September

- Begin crafting the "story" that will become your personal statement, then write

and rewrite it—and then rewrite it again. Get feedback from an unbiased editor.
- Put together a résumé to submit with your application.
- Figure out whom you will ask for recommendations—and whether or not each will write you a positive letter.
- Send away for or download applications.

October–November

- Continue to perfect your personal statement and résumé.
- Make sure the people writing your letters of recommendation have enough source material to draw from and remind them about deadlines.
- Take the October LSAT, if necessary.
- Subscribe to LSDAS and request transcripts from all undergraduate and graduate schools you've attended.
- Sign up for an LSAC online

account so you can obtain a copy of your master Law School Report from LSDAS. Proofread for any errors.
- Complete and mail your applications to schools—the earlier the better.

December

- Finish up any remaining applications.
- If you have not yet taken the LSAT or want to try it again, the December test is your last shot, assuming you want to be considered for the fall entering class.

January–February

- Request that any supplemental transcripts be sent to LSDAS.
- Check in with your schools to see if they need any additional information.
- Wait for the acceptance letters to start rolling in!

Arizona's law school, for example, has given free four-day classes to local students who demonstrate they can't afford a commercial one. Check with your pre-law advising center for similar opportunities in your area.

On the other end of the spectrum are intensive classes offered by companies such as Kaplan and The Princeton Review, the latter of which has boasted an average seven-point gain for its students. They offer options for everyone from the ultraorganized student who plans to spend at least three months studying to the person holding down a full-time job who only has a couple of weeks to get ready. Those seeking more personalized attention can also purchase private, one-on-one tutoring.

The quality of tutors and programs can vary from region to region, so it's a good idea to research test-prep offerings in your area before signing up for a particular company's course. Talk to different teachers and investigate their review materials to determine what approach they take, for instance, and consult friends and acquaintances who have prepped before you.

Make the most of your second time around

Didn't quite hit 175 this time? Think hard about whether you want to try again. The LSAC reports your LSAT scores (plus any decisions you make to cancel a score) over a five-year span, as well as an average score. You're also assigned a "score band" that ranges from roughly three points below to three points above your actual score—an attempt by the LSAC to recognize that there could be statistical errors, and to discourage schools from putting too much weight on single-point differentials. When applicants take the test more than once, most schools look at the average score, not just the higher one, and so only a fairly significant jump is going to have any real impact.

Admissions officers suggest sitting for the LSAT again only if practice tests taken under realistic conditions suggest that you'll get a much higher score, or if circumstances the first time—a marching band outside the testing room, say, or a nasty case of mono—had an obvious impact on your performance. If you do take the exam twice and end up with a large discrepancy between your scores, you might want to write a note of explanation countering any suspicion of cheating (and clarifying why the higher grade makes sense).

Write a mind-blowing personal statement

Here is your chance to take the admissions committee beyond the cold, hard numbers and demonstrate why you'll be an asset to the class. Think of your personal statement as the interview you probably won't have—an opportunity to showcase your personality and drive and talk about your passions and events that have made you who you are. The idea is to demonstrate that your superlative record comes with humor, an ability to reflect, and a measure of gained wisdom.

First, you need to decide on a specific topic. "Students should really home in on one thing—one activity they're involved in or one challenge that was significant," says Don Rebstock, associate dean for enrollment management and career strategy at Northwestern University School of Law in Illinois. Otherwise, there's an unappealing tendency to ramble. Rebstock suggests brainstorming for ideas by going to a bookstore and paging through a manual on hiring for questions intended to get at intervie-wees' characters. What is the defining moment of your life? What are your biggest strengths and weak-nesses? Though it might be tempting to expound on the complex legal theory du jour, an academic trea-tise won't help your case—it doesn't really address anything about *you*. "Let us know what type of voice you'll bring," says Ann Perry, assistant dean for admissions at the University of Chicago law school. "I don't want a résumé, and I don't want to know what kind of law you want to practice."

You needn't deal directly with the law at all, in fact, to show that you've got what it takes to be a lawyer. When he applied to New York University School of Law, Paul Millen wrote about scaling a difficult stretch of rock formations while hiking in Central China. "The story illustrated a method of problem solving that analyzed informa-tion to the degree possible, but recognized that the ultimate decision required a certain amount of courage and risk-acceptance," he explains. "I high-lighted my travel experiences, demonstrated my adventuresome spirit, and, in discussing the deci-sion-making process, exhibited an ability to work [with others], since the rest of my group consisted of Chinese, Israelis, and Europeans."

Another applicant wrote about organizing hotel workers in New Orleans. Although her LSAT scores were only so-so, Washington and Lee School of Law admired her pluck, commitment, and unique experience and came through with a generous financial aid package. A Naval officer accepted by an Ivy League law school described how confounded he'd felt as judge of a local beauty pageant when he'd tried to issue orders to the crowd of 17-year-old girls with absolutely no effect.

"If he'd written about the wisdom and maturity he'd gained in his naval command, he would only have put himself among everyone else with five years' work experience," says Seattle admissions consultant Loretta DeLoggio.

Many admissions officers recommend staying away from potentially inflammatory subjects such as politics or religion, as you can never be sure

> *"Students should really hone in on one thing— one activity they're involved in or one challenge that was significant."*

who your reader will be. Others counter that any topic is fine, as long as you're invested in it. But there are some definite no-no's: Unless the story is dramatic and compelling, you'll want to avoid pre-dictable themes such as "Why I've dreamed of becoming a lawyer since I was 4." It's also smart to steer clear of areas that are already well-covered in your application, like your LSAT score or your grades. (Consider an addendum to the application if you really feel there's more to say on these mat-ters, say experts.)

Writing about challenges overcome is okay, but be sure to hit the right notes. "I'm often struck by people who seem to lack perspective and who think minor hurdles overcome were extraordinary," says Sarah Zearfoss, assistant dean and director of admis-sions at the University of Michigan Law School in Ann Arbor. "It's fine and good to talk about hurdles," she says, but do not make a bigger claim for yourself than the situation warrants. And the last thing you want to seem to do is whine.

Whatever the topic, your personal statement should be well-organized and compelling because effective communication is so key to the practice of law. And make sure to proofread for any goofs in grammar, spelling, or punctuation. Or worse: You don't want to say you'd be a perfect fit at Yale on your Cornell essay, for instance (a more common occurrence than you might think). Inattention to detail is unacceptable in the field of law, so why should the application process be any different? Further, think long and hard about the tone of your personal statement, as nearly every admissions officer has a horror story about a mean-spirited or arrogant essay that doomed a candidate's application. It goes without saying that the work should be wholly your own.

One dean remembers a successful essay written as a recipe, but creative writers should generally err on the side of caution; law school, after all, is a pretty conservative place. "We're open to various styles, with one caveat: It can definitely be taken too far," says Monica Ingram, assistant dean for admissions at the University of Texas–Austin. "If you're not Charles Dickens before you write your statement, this is probably not the opportunity to take a foray into creative writing."

"No one with a rhyming essay has gotten in for at least the last five years," adds Megan Barnett, Yale's former dean of admissions and financial aid.

Get glowing recommendations

Now that you've presented your accomplishments, it's time to have a third party back you up. Ask people you've worked with closely to write your letters of recommendation—people who will offer enthusiastic support. You might assume that a letter from your senator or a local Pulitzer Prize–winning author will carry great weight, but if she doesn't know you from your next door neighbor, it's unlikely she can say anything about

you that will have any impact. Far better to have a teaching assistant who's observed you in class comment on how smart you are and how enthusiastically you participate, or to ask a former boss to describe how you went the extra mile. Then make sure each letter writer has the necessary raw material as inspiration, including a copy of your résumé and personal statement and perhaps a particularly impressive paper you wrote for class or a project you've worked on with a colleague.

"The best advice I can give to students is that they keep papers and exams so they can furnish them to letter writers," says now-retired Dayton pre-law advisor Roberta Alexander, who kept all of her grade books from 35 years of teaching and used them to write letters of recommendation for students she taught as many as 15 years earlier. Some undergraduate institutions, such as the University of California–Berkeley, will keep letters of recommendation on file for a period of years for a fee and mail them out, as needed, for an additional cost.

Most law schools allow up to three letters of recommendation, though some request only one. Be sure to follow any directions for submitting the letters: Some institutions request or require that they come through LSDAS. If so, log on to www.lsac.org to download the necessary form; anyone vouching for you will need to fill it out and return it to LSDAS along with a signed copy of the letter itself.

Interview, if you can

While most admissions officers will meet with candidates for informational meetings as time allows, only a handful of schools offer true admissions interviews. Pace University, for one, conducts up to 450 on- and off-campus interviews a year on a first-come, first-served basis; some schools make it a point to meet

Profile: The public defender

When Brian Marsicovetere enrolled in Vermont Law School, he was pretty sure he wanted to study environmental law. The school has one of the best programs in the country. But then something happened that changed his mind. "That would have been my first criminal law class," he says.

The more cases he read, the more fascinated he became with "the idea that there are limits on the government's ability to reach into people's private lives," he says. "I became really interested in the notion of privacy and of protecting people's liberty. I just really wanted to stand up for people in relation to institutions." His professor, a former prosecutor, "did a really great job of bringing out the personal elements of the cases," he says.

Vermont gave Marsicovetere the option of taking up to 18 credits of internships, so he promptly went to work in a public defender's office. By graduation, he had argued bail hearings in trial court, won his first motion to suppress an illegal search, cross-examined a police officer—and even argued an appeal before the Vermont Supreme Court. The case involved a police officer who had gone to a house to investigate a noise complaint. When the officer arrived, the homeowner refused to let him in "to the point of using force," Marsicovetere says. It was reasonably clear that it was an unlawful search, but did the homeowner have the right to resist with force?

The early immersion in the day-to-day of trial law would make Marsicovetere an attractive job candidate: Before he even began scouring the want ads, he was offered an associate position doing criminal defense with the firm of Kevin W. Griffin in White River Junction, Vermont. "I had so much experience by the time I graduated," he says. "I had this well of motions already drafted, and a whole bunch of legal research for issues that would occur in case after case. I was very much ahead of the game." He also had developed people skills. Most valuable lesson? How to ask opposing counsel for what you need without triggering a hostile response or blowing the lines of communication.

Today, the firm's name has expanded to Griffin Marsicovetere and Wilkes. Marsicovetere spends 60 percent of his time taking on assigned public defender cases—aggravated assaults, rapes, murders, and kidnappings—and the rest devoted to a thriving private practice across the state and in New Hampshire, representing plaintiffs in civil rights lawsuits and clients in criminal cases. And he loves small-town lawyering. "You really get to see the product of your work in the community—I run into past clients all the time, walking down the street, in the diner," he says. "The fact that you see these people around town really pushes you to do a better job for them." In short, he says, he doesn't miss big-city firm life at all.

their "borderline" candidates. Such meetings are used to obtain additional information about an applicant's communication skills and recent accomplishments.

Northwestern aims to interview as many candidates as possible, giving each a numerical rating and a page-long write-up. "We really feel that law is a very interactive profession, and no employer is going to hire anyone without interviewing them first," explains Don Rebstock. "I scratch my head [wondering] why other law schools aren't doing this." Rebstock says he won't admit recent college grads until he has a sense of their maturity and how well they'll interact with people who've been in the work force for several years.

It's a good idea to seek an interview if you can, and to prepare for it as carefully as you would a job interview. Bring a résumé, dress professionally, and be ready to answer questions about your studies, the value of any work experience you've had, and your interest in the law school—what attracted you to the program, for example. Rebstock recalls applicants who looked great on paper but who stared at the ground and had nothing to say and who did not get admitted as result. He has also interviewed wait-list candidates and been so impressed by their interpersonal skills that he has offered them admission on the spot.

Escape wait-list limbo

What if you land in that twilight zone between acceptance and rejection? Though it's become increasingly difficult to get into law school off of the wait list, it does still happen. Admissions deans counsel those in wait-list limbo to stay in touch over the summer about additional grades and honors, and to periodically let law schools know that they're still interested.

One Binghamton University student who found herself on the wait lists at Georgetown, Columbia, and NYU a few years ago started making plans to attend another New York law school, but stayed in touch with the admissions directors at the other three, sending an updated transcript and an additional recommendation letter, as well as an article about her role in a national mock trial competition. She also kept in phone and email contact with her pre-law advisor, who talked to several admissions staffers on her behalf. She eventually got the nod from NYU and decided to enroll there instead.

What minority students need to know

In June 2003, the Supreme Court ruled in *Grutter v. Bollinger* that the University of Michigan Law School was justified in favorably counting an underrepresented minority applicant's race when making admissions decisions. While the case concerned Michigan—whose policies were challenged by a 49-year-old white consultant and mother of two who had been rejected by the school—every other law school sat up and took note, too.

Much like other schools, Michigan has no formula for admission; deans weigh race, among other myriad factors, in a complex decision-making process. As a result, sometimes students with lower-than-average scores or grades are admitted to the school because they have other important assets such as leadership or service experience or because they are from underrepresented racial backgrounds.

In Michigan, the use of race in admissions is still in flux. In 2006, voters in the state passed a ballot initiative—similar to one in California—that again challenges the school's affirmative action policies. But the larger result of the 2003 *Grutter v. Bollinger* decision remains: Most schools will continue to consider minority status as one attribute among many that influence their choices—though not as an overriding factor, nor through a point system or quotas. And it certainly will not compensate for generally poor performance.

How should you handle the question of race in your application? "It's helpful to speak about race if it has meaning for you," advises Sarah Zearfoss, assistant dean and director of admissions at Michigan. "It's not necessary, but it is certainly additional information that we would consider positively in reviewing a file." Tamara Gustave, a graduate of the University of Baltimore School of Law, wrote in her personal statement about why she—a multilingual Haitian woman who was the first member of her family to graduate from college in the United States—wanted to be a lawyer. "I think that all of these

qualities are positive things that added to me as a person," she explains. "I talked about the fact that my family were immigrants from Haiti, my involvement with my [undergraduate] black student union, and the fact that the law sometimes doesn't apply to everybody equally, which I saw firsthand as a black woman."

"Don't think that just marking off a box indicating your racial and ethnic identity on your application is enough," says Evangeline Mitchell, author of *The African American Pre-Law School Advice Guide: Things You Really Need to Know before Applying to Law School*. She suggests students include any race-related organizations, activities, and community service work on their résumés. If you have other topics to cover in your personal statement, she also advises submitting an additional, one- to two-page "diversity statement" that covers what race means to you, how it has shaped you, and how this may have drawn you to the law—as well as how you can contribute to the incoming class.

Chapter Five

Finding the Money

Not many pieces of paper are more expensive than a law diploma. At the priciest schools—Northwestern University Law School in Illinois and Columbia Law School in New York City, to name two—the total cost of a JD degree (including living expenses and books) now tops $150,000. How do law students cover the bills? "Loans, loans, and more loans," says one assistant director of student financial aid. Debts of $80,000 are common among law school grads—and that's not counting the load that many have taken on as undergraduates.

How can you limit the damage? Most schools award at least a little financial aid based on need, and a rapidly growing number also offer merit-based scholarships to numerically attractive candidates who would enhance the student-body profile. Uncle Sam's largesse, in the form of tax credits for the cost of higher education, can also free up some extra cash. And work-study, summer employment, or tuition reimbursement from an employer can lessen your out-of-pocket expense.

Even if you do have to borrow significant sums, you can take some comfort in the fact that education debt is still pretty cheap; through your tax deductions, Uncle Sam will chip in on the interest you do pay. And if you don't wind up with a hefty salary after graduation because you're working for a government or nonprofit agency, one of a growing number of debt-forgiveness programs can help you pay off the bills (see list, page 60). Here's what you need to know to pay for your degree.

Need-based grants might help a little—very little

As you probably recall from your undergraduate days, anyone applying for financial aid funds handed out by the federal government has to fill out the Free Application for Federal Student Aid, more commonly known as the FAFSA. That's where you'll start, but the truth is that most law schools have only a modest amount of money available for need-based grants. They assume that most students will borrow to finance their degrees and will easily be able to repay their debts once they are lawyers. Even schools with more available money generally do not meet their students' full need with grants: There simply aren't enough funds available at the graduate level to fully fund the requirements of students no longer dependent on their parents. Apply early, generally before the end of January, if you hope to qualify for a need-based grant; some schools make their awards on a first-come, first-served basis.

You may find that your eligibility for need-based aid varies dramatically from school to school. That's because law schools, like undergraduate colleges and universities, use different formulas to calculate how big a discrepancy you've got between your resources and how much law school will cost. Under the formula used to disburse federal aid, for example, all graduate students are considered independent and supporting themselves, regardless of their age or whether they have financial help from their parents. Since most recent graduates have income levels in the $20,000s or $30,000, schools that use the federal methodology see quite a bit of need.

But at law schools that use their own institutional formulas—such as those at Harvard, Yale, Columbia, and Syracuse University—many students are classified as dependent, which means that financial aid officers consider Mom's and Dad's resources to be available to pay the bills. Typically, a school would call you dependent if you're under age 29 or 30, say, and don't have any dependents of your own. Other schools are stricter. At Fordham, "if the parents are alive, we look at them," says Stephen Brown, assistant dean of admissions and financial aid for the law school.

Apply with an eye on the merit money

In the past decade, many law schools have boosted the amount of merit aid they award in an effort to compete for the best students; these grants are given out not on the basis of need but to reward academic performance (and to snag top candidates). The awards are usually made based on your application for admission: High LSAT scores and undergraduate grades are the predominant criteria, but schools are also looking to lure in people with interesting work and life experience, and those who would bring geographic and racial diversity to the student body. You'll have a shot at one of these scholarships if you apply to schools where your academic credentials are above average or where you stand out in some other way. At the very top law schools, where every successful applicant is a standout student, merit awards are harder to come by. (But remember: A degree from such a school is a key credential if you hope to land a job at a prestigious corporate law firm.)

More than a dozen schools now offer scholarships specifically for students who are planning careers in public interest law and have a record of community service to prove it. Boston College's Public Service Scholarships provide full tuition each year. The University of Denver's full-tuition Chancellor's Scholarships recognize students who have a solid record of service and aspire to practice public interest law. At some schools, law students can apply for universitywide fellowships available to graduate students. Florida State University, for instance, offers a University fellowship that covers tuition for up to 12 credit hours a semester and pays a $19,000 stipend to cover living expenses. You may need to apply for the universitywide awards through the graduate school financial aid office rather than the law school, but your law school's financial aid counselor should know what's available.

Search for outside scholarships

Scholarships from foundations, associations, and civic organizations are not as plentiful for law students as they are for other graduate and professional students. Many outside awards are reserved for minority students, for residents of specific states, or for students concentrating in specific areas of the law. But it's well worth spending a few hours searching scholarship sites such as www.fastweb.com or www.collegenet.com to see if there's an award you might be eligible for. Also try the excellent listing of grants on Michigan State University's website at http://staff.lib.msu.edu/harris23/grants/3law.htm. Some examples:

- The Association of Trial Lawyers of America awards a handful of scholarships, worth $1,000 to $3,000, to students who are active ATLA student members.
- The Attorney-CPA Foundation awards several scholarships a year ($250 to $1,000) to law students who are also certified public accountants.
- Some state and local bar associations award scholarships. For instance, the Foundation of the State Bar of California makes awards of $2,500 to $7,500 to students at California law schools; it made 47 such awards in 2003.
- The American Bar Association Legal Opportunity Scholarship Fund offers 20 awards per year of $5,000 each to minority students.

Some law schools keep a binder of outside scholarship listings; others post listings on their websites. An undergraduate pre-law advisor may also be able to steer you to scholarship opportunities. Other possible sources of leads include state bar associations, unions, and civic groups

Go part time. There's nothing easy about working full time and then going to class four nights a week. But part-time study allows some students to foot the bill, at least in part, from cash flow and perhaps to take advantage of employer-paid tuition (see below). The best part-time programs are those where the same instructors teach both full-time and part-time students. (For more on choosing a part-time program, see page 5.)

Let your employer pay for it. Many large employers offer corporate tuition benefits for employees pursuing graduate degrees. But there's a catch: Most require the courses you take to be job-related. That means paralegals and legal assistants are the most likely to qualify for corporate benefits to fund a law degree. Colleges and universities also tend to be generous with their tuition benefits for employees and sometimes spouses; some prospective law students even seek out university employment for this very reason.

Live like a student. The student expense budget law schools estimate for yearly housing, food, and personal expenses is almost laughable—$12,000 to $15,000 is typical. "Food is the No. 1 budget buster," says Stephen Brown at Fordham. "It's very easy to grab a bagel and coffee out every day and spend $900 a year."

"The living expense choices that students make will affect how much they have to borrow," says Gina Soliz, director of financial aid at Syracuse University's College of Law. Those who manage to keep their debt to a minimum are the ones who say, "I don't need digital cable right now. I can get a roommate and live like a student."

Build up some savings. If you're looking ahead to law school in the next couple of years and can set aside some savings, take advantage of the tax benefits of a state-sponsored 529 plan. While most investors use these plans to save for a child's undergraduate expenses, they generally allow you to open an account and name yourself as the beneficiary. The primary benefit is that the earnings on your savings won't be taxed, and your state may throw in a deduction for your contributions. All 529 plans include investments that are appropriate for adults who will need to tap the money soon, such as bonds and money-market accounts.

While many of the broker-sold 529 plans impose upfront sales fees that would minimize or offset any tax benefits over just a year or two, many of the direct-sold plans, such as those offered by TIAA-CREF and Vanguard, do not. Several are paying a guaranteed 3 percent or so right now. Not a bad parking place for a year or two, especially when Uncle Sam isn't claiming any of the gains.

you're affiliated with, as well as honor societies, fraternities, or sororities you belonged to as an undergraduate.

Be aware that if you qualify for a need-based grant from your law school, an outside scholarship probably won't just add to your kitty; it may be used to reduce the size of your grant. At such a school, say, a $2,500 award might lighten your loan burden by $1,000 and trim a need-based grant by $1,500.

Get set to borrow

Debt is a fact of life for most law students; at many pricey private law schools, the average debt at graduation now exceeds $80,000. But low interest rates definitely help ease the sting.

Federal loans. Government-guaranteed Stafford loans made directly to students are a staple for most law students; a typical full-time student takes out the annual maximum of $20,500 per year. (Overall, you can borrow up to $138,500 in Stafford loans to finance your education, including what you've borrowed as an undergraduate.) Part of that total, up to $8,500, is often a "subsidized" loan, meaning that the federal government pays the interest while you're in school and for six months after you graduate or drop below half-time status. The rest is unsubsidized, so interest accrues while you're in school. Payments on both subsidized and unsubsidized Staffords can be deferred until after graduation.

To be eligible for a subsidized loan, your FAFSA form will have to show that you can't shoulder much of the financial burden yourself—fairly easy to do with law school costs so high. If your school participates in the Federal Direct Loan Program, you'll borrow directly from the federal government. Otherwise, you can choose your own funding source using a list of preferred lenders provided by your school. While all lenders offer Stafford loans at the same interest rate, some waive the upfront origination and guarantee fees (which can run 4 percent of the loan amount), some reduce the interest rate in repayment if you sign up for automatic payments or make a certain number of payments on time, and some do both. So it can pay to shop around. Rates on these variable-rate loans change every summer, but will not exceed a cap of 8.25 percent.

Students with high financial need—that is, the FAFSA shows that they're expected to contribute very little or nothing toward their law school education—will also qualify for a Perkins loan of up to $6,000 per year at an interest rate that's fixed at 5 percent. In addition, there are no upfront origination fees. The Perkins is a subsidized loan, so no interest accrues until nine months after you graduate or drop below half-time status.

Private loans. If the federal loan limits leave you short, private lenders stand ready to lend you as much as the full cost of your education less any financial aid. (Some law schools also have their own loan programs.) Interest rates tend to be only slightly higher than the rates on Stafford loans. However, origination and other fees can be significantly higher—running as much as 8.5 percent of the loan amount—and interest begins accruing right away. Loan programs geared specifically to law students will even lend you up to $10,000 or so on top of what you need for tuition and living expenses during the school year to help cover your costs while you study for the bar exam. Popular programs include CitiAssist from Citibank (www.studentloan.com) and Law Loans from Sallie Mae (www.salliemae.com/lawloans).

To qualify for private loans, you need a clean credit history—or a cosigner. Financial aid officers recommend that prospective students pay down their debts, close unnecessary lines of credit, and check their credit histories for errors before applying for admission. Ann Weitgenant, associate director of student financial planning at Valparaiso University Law School in Indiana, says she sometimes even counsels students to work an extra year to pay down their credit cards and car loans.

Home-equity loans. For students who own a home, a home-equity line of credit is another attractive choice. Rates are low, fees are minimal, and interest on up to $100,000 in debt is tax deductible if you itemize. If you expect to graduate into a high-paying job, home-equity debt may be a better choice than other debt because you won't qualify for tax-deductible interest on government or private student loans. Interest on regular student loans will be fully tax deductible only if your income falls below $50,000 if you're a single taxpayer and below $100,000 if you file jointly. You may be able to deduct interest you pay on a qualified student if your modified adjusted gross income does not exceed $70,000 ($145,000 if filing jointly). Remember, though, that a home-equity line of credit is secured by your home, so be certain you'll be able to make the payments regardless of where your career path leads after graduation.

Find help paying the money back

At current rates, the payment on $80,000 in debt is more than $900 a month over 10 years. Those payments may be easily manageable for newly minted lawyers who land high-paying jobs in the private sector. For those who don't, there are ways to ease the burden.

Flexible repayment options. While the standard term for repaying Stafford loans is 10 years, you can stretch the term in various ways to make your payments more affordable. With an extended repayment plan, for instance, you can lengthen the loan term to up to 25 years. Another option, a graduated repayment schedule that extends over 12 to 25 years, starts you off with lower payments than the standard plan and then ratchets them up annually. Income-contingent or income-sensitive repayment plans adjust your payment each year based on your income. In the end, you'll pay more interest over longer payback periods. But you can always boost your payments as your income rises to pay down the loan more quickly than you're asked to.

Loan consolidation. You may also be able to reduce the interest you pay on Stafford loans by consolidating them when interest rates are low. That locks in current interest rates instead of allowing them to fluctuate annually. You may even be able to consolidate your undergraduate and early law school loans to take advantage of low rates while you're still in school. For more details about student loan consolidation, you may wish to visit www.loanconsolidation.ed.gov at the Department of Education's website or www.federalconsolidation.org, a website sponsored by Access Group Inc., a private, nonprofit lender.

Student-loan interest deduction. If your income is modest, Uncle Sam will step in to help with the interest payments. You can deduct up to $2,500 a year in student-loan interest if you earn less than $50,000 as a single taxpayer or less than $100,000 if you are married and filing jointly. (You may be able to deduct interest you pay on a qualified student if your modified adjusted gross income does not exceed $70,000 or $145,000 if filing jointly.)

Note to parents: You get to take this deduction if you're legally obligated to pay back the debt and you claim the student as a dependent on your tax return.

Loan repayment assistance programs. "If you get out of here with $70,000 of debt and get a job for $30,000, it's tough to pay the debt back," says Christine Falzerano, senior campus director of the financial aid office at Pace's law school. That's why more than 70 schools, 50 employers, and a number of states now offer loan repayment assistance to lawyers who practice public interest law for a non-profit agency or who work as government prosecutors or public defenders. University of Oregon law grads earning $50,000 a year or less in a public service or public interest law job can qualify for up to $25,000 in loan-repayment assistance over five years, for instance. The university lends graduates up to $5,000 per year to make payments to the government or the bank that holds their student loans, then later forgives all or part of the debt, depending on the graduate's level of income and length of time doing public interest work. Instead of forgivable loans, a few law schools make outright grants to cover student loan debt. The University of San Diego, for one, awards grants of $2,000 to $5,000 per year for up to five years to graduates in public interest jobs.

Loan repayment programs vary dramatically from school to school. Those with meager budgets may offer help to only a handful of students, may offer relatively small loans or grants, or may cap eligibility at salaries of $35,000 or less. Institutions with ample resources, such as Harvard, Yale, Columbia, and New York University, can afford to offer loan repayment help to more graduates and to graduates with higher salaries. If you're comparing LRAPs when choosing a law school, ask how much funding is available and how many eligible students receive loans or grants. Also, be aware that you may have to repay some or all of an LRAP loan if you leave your public interest job during the course of a year, and you may cease to be eligible if your income rises over a certain amount.

Find work

While the American Bar Association recommends that first-year law students do not work during the academic year, "a lot of students feel they can handle it," says Valparaiso's Ann Weitgenant. "It lets them step away from the law for a while." In fact, students who apply for financial aid may be awarded a work-study job to meet some of their financial need; an award of $1,500 to $2,000 a year is typical, for 10 to 15 hours of work a week. Some students manage to get work-study jobs off campus providing legal services to a nonprofit organization such as Bay Area Legal Aid and the Folsom City Attorney's Office, two of the off-campus employers in UC–Berkeley's work-study program. In that case, the employer and the school, subsidized by the federal government, jointly provide the funds paid to the student.

Research assistantships are another option at some universities. At Syracuse, for instance, law students can take a graduate assistantship position anywhere in the university. "That's probably the best deal out there," says Gina Soliz, director of financial aid at Syracuse University's College of Law. "For a little bit of work, you could get part or all of your tuition paid, plus a stipend," she says. Law students would generally have to seek out such positions by knocking on faculty doors once they arrive on campus.

Theresa Owens knew when she decided on law school that she wanted to represent children. So she researched schools with specialized programs in juvenile law and settled on Whittier in Costa Mesa, California. She was swayed by Whittier's financial package and the fact that she would be eligible for summer stipends of $3,000 if she chose to do public interest work in the community. (Having grown up in New Jersey and having attended the University of Massachusetts–Amherst, Owens didn't mind the prospect of some balmy Southern California weather, either.)

Along with 20 other entering students, Owens enrolled in Whittier's children's law program, which includes courses in family law, juvenile trial advocacy, and juvenile justice in addition to the standard courses. She also took a special writing class with a focus on the research and briefs likely to be encountered in juvenile law. Monthly colloquia brought judges, doctors, and child psychologists to campus to shed light on such topics as signs of child abuse, hurdles of the adoption process, and how to interview children in court. To fulfill one of the program's requirements, she worked for one semester at the school's clinic for underprivileged families, delving into the details of domestic violence cases and restraining orders, and helping the grandparents of abandoned children file for guardianship. As the first editor-in-chief of the program's newly launched *Children and Family Law Journal* she commissioned and published articles by legal scholars on subjects that ranged from juvenile delinquency to reproductive issues such as surrogacy and custody of eggs.

As they honed their skills, Owens and her colleagues were sent into juvenile detention centers in Los Angeles to assist on civil rights cases. She recalls a talk with one child offender who was HIV positive and was having trouble getting medication because "it wasn't the sort of thing you'd want to tell any of the staff there about." Then there were the allegations of sexual abuse of children by juvenile hall staffers. To practice questioning young witnesses, Owens and her classmates took turns playing frightened 4-year-olds in mock trials.

After graduation, Owens worked frequently with the foster care system as a court-appointed lawyer helping parents get their children back. Usually, the children had been removed from their parents owing to abuse or neglect, or maybe because the home was overrun with rats or roaches. In those cases, particularly if it seemed as if the parents were doing their best, she felt as if the family were in a Catch-22. "The public financial benefits don't kick in until you have your children back with you," she says. But, understandably, "the state won't return your children until you have a home with electricity, water"—and no rodents. "You look for the cases that can bring you some joy," she says, "because a lot of them are very frustrating and very hard."

Eventually, Owens hopes to represent young people accused of juvenile offenses. Meantime, her career has taken her to California's Administrative Office of the Courts in San Francisco, where she analyzed the effectiveness of state laws and procedures for placing abused and neglected children, and to New Jersey's Office of the Public Defender in Newark, where she defends parents fighting to retain custody of their kids.

Summer jobs can be a way to rack up some serious earnings, especially for second- and third-year students at good schools, where corporate law firms recruit for summer positions that can pay $1,500 to $2,500 a week. Many students at Fordham, for instance, have summer earnings in the $32,000 range, says Stephen Brown. On the other hand, students interested in public service often pursue volunteer work, clerkships, or other public interest work that doesn't pay much at all. A job at a public interest agency may in fact pay nothing, but some law schools come up with at least some money.

Take advantage of a hand from Uncle Sam

If your household income is modest, the federal government offers help in the form of a tax credit or tax deduction for educational expenses. Law students who qualify will want to take advantage of the Lifetime Learning tax credit, worth $2,000 a year (20 percent of the first $10,000 you spend in tuition and fees each year). You qualify for the full credit if you file a single tax return and your income is $43,000 or less, and for a partial credit if you make up to $53,000. If you're married and filing jointly, the full credit is available when income is less than $87,000, and a partial credit is available up to $107,000. (A tax credit reduces your tax bill dollar for dollar.)

Most full-time law students won't exceed those thresholds. (In fact, those with little or no income won't benefit at all from the credits because they won't owe any taxes to begin with.) But if you do cross the line—perhaps as a part-time student—you may still qualify for a tax deduction for your educational expenses. For 2009, students cannot take a deduction if their adjusted gross income is between $50,000 and $60,000 ($100,000 and $120,000 if they file a joint return). Note: You can't take both the credit and the deduction.

While a law degree is obviously a major financial investment, chances are good you'll graduate knowing you've significantly boosted your earning power over your lifetime. Then you can move on to bigger worries—like passing the bar exam.

Law schools that help with the payments

According to the January 2010 listing by Equal Justice Works, a Washington, D.C.–based organization that promotes public interest law, around 100 American law schools (below) now offer or are developing loan repayment assistance programs, or LRAPs. These plans, which help graduates who take public interest jobs repay their student loans, can differ dramatically, and some schools can afford to fund only a few students each year. It's important to research the particulars by calling a school's admissions or financial aid office, or by consulting www.equaljusticeworks.org.

Albany Law School of Union University (NY)

American Univ. Washington College of Law (DC)

Arizona State Univ. Sandra Day O'Connor Coll. of Law

Boston College Law School

Boston University School of Law

Brooklyn Law School (NY)

California Western School of Law

Capital University Law School (OH)

Case Western Reserve Univ. School of Law (OH)

Catholic University of America
   Columbus School of Law (DC)

Chicago-Kent College of Law, Illinois Inst. of Tech

CUNY School of Law at Queens College

Columbia University School of Law (NY)

Cornell University Law School (NY)

Creighton University School of Law (NE)

DePaul University College of Law (IL)

Duke University School of Law (NC)

Duquesne University School of Law (PA)

Emory University School of Law (GA)

Fordham University School of Law (NY)

Franklin Pierce Law Center (NH)

George Washington University Law School (DC)

Georgetown University Law Center (DC)

Golden Gate University School of Law (CA)

Gonzaga University School of Law (WA)

Hamline University School of Law (MN)

Harvard Law School (MA)

Hofstra University School of Law (NY)

Indiana University School of Law–Bloomington

Lewis & Clark College
   Northwestern School of Law (OR)

Loyola Law School, Los Angeles

Loyola University, Chicago School of Law

Loyola University, New Orleans School of Law

Marquette University Law School (WI)

New York Law School

New York University School of Law

North Carolina Central University School of Law

Northeastern University School of Law (MA)

Northwestern University School of Law (IL)

Ohio State Univ. Michael E. Moritz College of Law

Pace University School of Law (NY)

Penn. State University Dickinson School of Law

Pepperdine University School of Law (CA)

Regent University School of Law (VA)

Roger Williams University School of Law (RI)

Rutgers University School of Law–Camden (NJ)

Rutgers University School of Law–Newark (NJ)

Santa Clara University School of Law (CA)

Seattle University School of Law

Seton Hall University School of Law (NJ)

South Texas College of Law

Southwestern University School of Law (CA)

Stanford University Law School (CA)

St. Thomas University School of Law (FL)

Suffolk University Law School (MA)

Temple Univ. James E. Beasley School of Law (PA)

Touro College Jacob D. Fuchsberg Law Center (NY)

Tulane University School of Law (LA)

Univ. of Arizona James E. Rogers College of Law

University of California–Berkeley School of Law

University of California–Davis School of Law

University of California–Hastings College of Law

University of Chicago Law School

University of Colorado Law School

University of Denver College of Law

University of Georgia School of Law

University of Illinois

University of Iowa College of Law

University of Maine School of Law

University of Maryland School of Law

University of Michigan Law School

University of Minnesota Law School

University of New Mexico School of Law

University of North Carolina School of Law

University of Notre Dame Law School (IN)

University of Oregon School of Law

Univ. of the Pacific McGeorge School of Law (CA)

University of Pennsylvania Law School

University of San Diego School of Law

University of San Francisco School of Law

University of South Carolina School of Law

University of Southern California Law School

University of St. Thomas School of Law (MN)

University of Utah College of Law

University of Virginia School of Law

University of Washington School of Law

University of Wisconsin Law School

Valparaiso University School of Law (IN)

Vanderbilt University Law School (TN)

Vermont Law School

Villanova University School of Law (PA)

Wake Forest University School of Law (NC)

Washington and Lee Univ. School of Law (VA)

Washington University in St. Louis School of Law

West Virginia University College of Law

Whittier Law School (CA)

Widener University School of Law (DE)

College of William and Mary School of Law (VA)

William Mitchell College of Law (MN)

Yale Law School (CT)

Yeshiva University

   Benjamin N. Cardozo School of Law (NY)

Chapter Six

Getting Your First Job

The past few years were tough even at prestigious law firms, many of which have handed out pink slips by the dozen. Other firms cut back their summer associate programs, which put rising third-year law students into jobs that traditionally lead to permanent offers, and have employed fewer newly minted JDs as well.

Alas, the good not-so-old days when law students were wooed by multiple firms with fancy dinners and promises of even fancier bonuses are over, at least for the moment.

"Two or three years ago, people had to work hard *not* to get a job," says a hiring partner at one top firm. "Now it's a different story." Today's third-year students will compete for fewer positions and will certainly not receive as many offers as they would have in previous years. Some students with subpar grades might not get any.

> "Two or three years ago, people had to work hard not to get a job. Now it's a different story."

But don't tear up your law school applications just yet. Even though work has been harder to come by lately, there are still opportunities to be had. And students entering law school now may find the picture much rosier by the time they're out job hunting. Indeed, many schools report the same number of recruiters showing up on campus this year as last, and experts in both career counseling offices and law firms say that with the economy on the rebound there is reason to be optimistic. Even firms that have cut back in recent years, such as Holland & Knight and Shearman & Sterling, say that the hiring picture is decidedly brighter these days.

And new JDs, by and large, do pretty well—though how well clearly depends on the type of work you're interested in. The median starting salary for 2007 graduates was $68,500, taking into account everyone from young lawyers in public interest law, where the figure is only $40,000, to those in private practice, where median base salary is $108,000. (Starting salaries at firms in big cities such as Boston, Chicago, and Los Angeles can reach $135,000–$145,000.)

To land that first job in a competitive market, you'll need impeccable credentials, and will probably have to take more initiative and be more flexible about what and where you end up practicing than young law grads of several years ago. The more prepared you are, the easier the job hunt will be. And believe it or not, the groundwork will begin almost the first day of school. That's because grades and summer work experiences play a major role in where grads end up.

Where will the jobs be?

The type of law you choose to practice clearly will have an impact on how much money you make. It may also determine how much in demand your services will be—and where. The larger the metropolis, the more specialized the law tends to be, and certain cities dominate certain practice areas. Students who specialize in corporate law may find that the best opportunities are in New York, for example, while technology centers Austin and San Francisco are still hot for intellectual property lawyers.

It's tough to predict how the employment picture might change between now, as you apply to law school, and your first round of job interviews. Consistently busy practice areas, in good times and bad, include family law and criminal law; divorce is constant, and fewer jobs and a stressed economy often equal more murders, thefts, and the like. As you look ahead for growth areas in law, here are some current winners to keep an eye on.

Litigation. It takes more than bad economic news to dampen the demand for litigators, the attorneys who argue cases in court. Litigation is the nation's favorite method for settling disputes.

Most clients—corporate and otherwise—sue whenever they perceive a wrong that needs to be addressed no matter what the economy happens to be doing, says Jackie Burt, former assistant dean of career services at the Benjamin N. Cardozo School of Law at Yeshiva University in New York. And each suit filed means an equal amount of work for the other side.

Young lawyers with visions of yelling, "Objection, Your Honor!" often gain experience in state, district, or city attorneys' offices doing legal research and preparing briefs (and may, in fact, end up settling most of their cases out of court). Starting salaries are much lower for attorneys at small- and medium-size firms, which often represent plaintiffs on a contingency basis, than for those who work in the litigation departments of big-time firms.

Intellectual property. The prospects for IP specialists are excellent over the long term because rapid innovations in science and technology continue to drive the economy. Career opportunities can be found in patent, trademark, and copyright law, as people create new gadgets, literary works, computer programs, and logos—all of which need to be protected.

"IP continues to be a growing practice area," says Sheron Hindley-Smith, former executive director of Robert Half Legal, a legal staffing firm in Menlo Park, California. "Patent prosecution is especially hot." This is particularly true in the science and technology fields, which depend so heavily on being first in research and development. As companies strive to guard their patents on new drugs, software, and the like—not to mention their brand names—law students who fully understand the technical nature of the breakthroughs as well as the applicable law will find themselves at a premium and commanding top starting salaries. A science or engineering background is widely considered essential. Patent attorneys also have to pass the patent bar exam, administered and required by the Patent and Trademark office.

> *"IP continues to be a growing practice area. Patent prosecution is especially hot."*

In IP, "you are always dealing with something complex and new," says one recent graduate of the University of Texas–Austin School of Law, who signed on with a Houston-based firm, "You are jumping from new technology to new technology." Interested graduates can work in-house for a corporation, at a firm, for a university, or for the government.

Bankruptcy. Whenever the economy sours, the demand for bankruptcy lawyers jumps. (Think Enron.) "There are some huge bankruptcies out there, and they get very complicated and very complex, and they need a lot of attorneys," says Michael Schiumo, former assistant dean for career planning at Fordham University School of Law in New York City. They can also take decades to sort out. In addition, companies fail and people lose their shirts even in the brightest of boom times.

Trust and estate. This field is expanding as the first wave of baby boomers is hitting 65. "People want to make sure their kids get their hard-earned money," says Eric Janson, an adjunct professor at Vermont Law School in South Royalton who also has his own private practice and specializes in estate planning, wills, trusts, and probate administration.

Is a clerkship right for you?

Each year, roughly 10 percent of law school grads opt to spend a year or two working with a judge in one of the nation's many courts. The median wage is just $46,450, but the payoff is far greater: A judicial clerkship is a great way to see many different aspects of the law as it unfolds—as well as have an impact on it yourself. The experience also provides a lifelong résumé boost and, often, a lifelong advisor.

Jerry Noblin Jr., for one, viewed his clerkship with Chief Judge Robin Cauthron of the U.S. District Court for the Western District of Oklahoma as the best possible way to prepare for a career as a trial lawyer—to "learn how to run a trial, without having a real client's case on the line" and to "be involved in myriad cases with all kinds of causes of action, both civil and criminal, which is something that a firm simply could not offer."

There is a range of clerkship opportunities at every court level—federal, state, and even local—and your experience will vary with each. For example, if you work for a trial court, you'll most likely be involved in every stage of a hearing, from writing jury voir dire questions and instructions to helping your judge write and edit his or her decision before it's published. The court of appeals is a more studious exercise; you'll hear oral arguments from attorneys and then help research and prepare decisions on the legal issues. Debra Strauss, author of *Behind the Bench: The Guide to Judicial Clerkships* and administrator of www.judicialclerkships.com, a site that helps students navigate the application process, suggests seeking the court that's right for you in terms of your future goals. "Federal clerkships are considered more prestigious than state, but it's great to work in the state court system if you know you want to practice law in that state, because you get to know all the attorneys and court procedures intimately," she explains. "Moreover, the highest court in a state can be just as prestigious as a federal clerkship."

Competition for all such positions is stiff. Top grades at a good school and solid writing skills are important, though some judges will pass over Ivy Leaguers in favor of in-state students who have a demonstrated interest in local legal issues. Pursuing activities such as law review and moot court can help you stand out. Strauss also suggests doing a judicial externship, like the one she oversees at the Pace University School of Law: The Federal Judicial Extern Honors Program, a yearlong course that includes a lengthy research and writing project (in which students use motion papers from federal court to write a decision, which can later serve as a writing sample for a clerkship application), places students with federal district or court of appeals judges where they act as junior clerks, of sorts.

All clerkship candidates should be proactive about the process. This includes researching what type of court you're interested in, where, as well as which judge, specifically, you'd like to work for. The recommended deadline for federal clerkship applications is now fall of the third year of law school, though that varies by court and individual judge. The cutoff date for state clerkships can be even earlier, from the spring or summer of second year on.

If you're successful, a clerkship can pay off in many ways—most ideally, in close mentorship from a judge. The post can also open doors later in your career, as firms, government agencies, and non-profits alike actively recruit former law clerks for their varied experiences and close exposure to the court system. In addition, it's seen as an essential credential if you hope to teach. One last potential advantage: Federal positions can lead to the mother of all clerkships—working for one of the nine U.S. Supreme Court justices, who typically choose clerks who have worked for peers in the U.S. Court of Appeals. Those interested should focus on working for one of the federal "feeder judges" who have sent numerous staff members to the Supreme Court in the past.

T&E lawyers, who may create living wills, plan for the eventual dispersal of billion-dollar fortunes, and arrange the transfer of long-held family businesses from one generation to the next, are needed at firms of all sizes, which handle estates of all sizes.

Employment. "Whether you are hiring or firing, a company needs lawyers," says Susan Guindi, assistant dean for career services at the University of Michigan's law school. Employment attorneys can work in-house or for a company's outside counsel, as well as for unions and government agencies. In the process, they may deal with a range of issues, including labor relations; age, race, or sex discrimination; and workplace health and safety.

Tax. Although there will almost certainly never be a sexy television show about tax attorneys, don't rule out entering this field. "Tax is always solid," says Merv Loya, former assistant dean at the University of Oregon's law school in Eugene, who notes that companies and individuals need attorneys in good and bad economic cycles who enjoy digging into financial documents and interpreting the tax code. But often, Loya adds, students need a master's degree in tax law to set them apart.

• • •

Shortly after you arrive on campus, you'll want to start getting to know the people in the career counseling office. The men and women who run on-campus recruiting programs have close contacts in the field, know the experiences of all those who've come seeking employment before, and can offer the most specific, well-tailored advice on how to make your particular career goals a reality, no matter what area of law you're interested in. Stop by early and often to get help formulating your long-term plan and attend career-oriented seminars from day one on.

Make the most of the summer

It used to be that finding a substantive legal job after the first year of law school was optional, but that is no longer the case, say many career counselors. "We recommend doing anything law-related during your first summer, even if you have to do something unrelated part time—like word processing, waiting tables, or slinging lattes at Starbucks—in order to finance some sort of volunteer gig in the legal community," says Skip Horne, former assistant dean for career services at the Santa Clara University School of Law. "The key is to get experience and not wait until your second or third year, when it will get harder and harder to overcome that initial 'I don't have any legal experience' hump."

Finding a law firm job that first summer is going to be difficult, but this is an excellent time to take advantage of opportunities in the non-profit sector. Many law schools offer scholarships that help support students who want to do low- or non-paying public interest work for a summer. The Equal Justice America fellowship, for example, is an award for first- and second-year students who work at organizations that provide civil legal services for the poor. It's offered at more than 50 schools, including Brooklyn Law School, the University of Virginia School of Law, and Stanford. Working for a judge or doing research for a professor is another common first-year choice, as is a study-abroad program. The University of Wisconsin's law school, for one, has partnered with Thammasat University Faculty of Law in Bangkok so students can study the Thai legal system firsthand while working in international law firms.

For those interested in going into private practice—that is, the vast majority of law school students—the employment process starts in the fall of the second year of law school, with interviews for summer associate positions. These eight-week jobs allow students to get firm experience for

great pay, often with the promise of future employment.

However, be forewarned: Such programs are no longer the schmooze-fests recent grads may have described, where getting to know the other young associates and partners over expense-account lunches at hip restaurants and outings to baseball games or sold-out rock concerts took precedence over real work. Many firms are now working their "summers" considerably harder than in the past and evaluating them more closely. "It used to be that summer associates really had to screw up badly in order to not get an offer," says Gihan Fernando, assistant dean for career services at Georgetown University Law Center. "In past years, behaviors of all kinds were tolerated, and not much work was accomplished. Now there's much more of a sense that you should put your best foot forward." Georgetown, for one, provides an intensive, one-day seminar to help prepare students for the experience, complete with panels of hiring partners and 3Ls and discussions about firm life, etiquette, and the kinds of basic research and writing assignments summer associates will be expected to handle.

No matter what you do on the job, try not to follow in the footsteps of one law student who, as a 2003 summer associate at Skadden, Arps in New York, mistakenly sent the following email, meant for a friend, to 40 people at the firm, including 20 partners: "I'm busy doing jack shit. Went to a nice 2hr sushi lunch today at Sushi Zen. Nice place. Spent the rest of the day typing emails and bullshitting with people. Unfortunately, I actually have work to do—I'm on some corp finance deal, under the global head of corp finance, which means I should really peruse these materials and not be a fuckup." The email slowly made its way around the firm, the city, and the rest of the country, and became a classic lesson in what not to do for summer associates everywhere, for all time. (Neither the student nor the firm will comment on what happened as a result.)

Finally, take heart: For those who maintain the appropriate level of decorum and impress associates and partners alike with their research, writing, and communication skills, many benefits remain—including the free food. "I worked really, really hard, but I gained like seven pounds," says one recent summer associate at a top New York firm. She also gained a full-time offer.

Get recruited

So how do you obtain such plum summer positions? Most students go through on-campus recruiting, which brings in employers to interview job candidates who are either prescreened using their résumés or selected in a lottery. The employers then call back those they're interested in hiring for a second interview at the office. This occurs in the fall, mostly, though there is some overflow in the spring. While recruiting schedules and procedures differ from school to school (meaning it's wise to check with your career center for details about how the process operates), it's true at most institutions that on-campus recruiting has become ever more competitive, as firms have limited the number of campuses they visit and offered fewer interview slots at those they do. Still, on-campus recruiting has rebounded along with the economy.

Needless to say, the better your law school performance is, the better your chances. Often, top firms will only interview students whose GPA falls above a certain cutoff—though they do adjust that cutoff based on the name and reputation of a school. For example, a firm may meet only candidates with a 3.7 or higher at a second-tier institution, while those at top 20 schools simply need a

> *"The key is to get experience, and not wait until your second or third year."*

3.3; grades may not matter at all for candidates from Harvard or Yale. Hiring partners say having substantial legal experience in summer positions, as noted, also helps people stand out, as does participation in clinics, which signals that you'll bring a toolbox of practical skills to the job—not just theory learned in class.

After academics, motivation and initiative matter most of all. You can no longer rely on the on-campus interview process to find a job—be prepared to do some independent outreach, too, even if it means cold calling or sending your résumé and a cover letter out to several hundred firms across the country.

"I was extraordinarily aggressive and shameless—I sent out hundreds of letters and got rejected by so many great places," recalls Alex Wellen, a graduate of Temple University's law school in Philadelphia and the author of *Barman: Ping-Pong, Pathos, & Passing the Bar*, his account of coming out of law school into the work world. Wellen says he was "crazy about Temple" but that, in his experience, aiming for a top firm out of a non–Top 20 law school (Temple is currently No. 72) was "harder at every

Like many young college grads, Stephen Sincavage applied to law school for lack of a better idea. "I never had any grand plans that I wanted to go to law school or anything like that," he says. "But...I kind of realized that I wasn't sick of school, and I knew a couple of people who'd gone to law school," he says. In fact, he'd heard some horror stories of cutthroat law schools where students hoarded notes and ripped pages out of library books to thwart the competition. "There were exceptions," says Sincavage, "but generally when I talked to other people, they'd say, 'Law school was hell.'" He knew that *that* wasn't the kind of experience he wanted.

And he figured he knew how to avoid it. Sincavage had so enjoyed being an undergraduate at the University of Virginia that the decision about where to go was easy: He'd stay in Charlottesville. "It's very social," he says. That sense of community was the key to his happy law school experience, Sincavage adds. The first week on campus, his class of 300 was divided into first-year sections

of 30 each. If someone missed a class, other students would share notes and outlines. Regular softball games "gave everybody a focus and a reason to be together." It helped that the school's grading system centered around a B mean, notes Sincavage. "That meant that, for the most part, unless you were really brilliant on an exam—or you were really just out to lunch—you were more than likely to get a B," he adds. "I don't know how you get by in an atmosphere where everyone's out for themselves."

Sincavage began to zero in on his career path during his second summer when he clerked for a circuit judge in Loudoun County, Virginia, one of the fastest-growing counties in the country. His time there made him realize he liked the courtroom experience and gave him a pretty good idea of the sort of work he *didn't* want to do— domestic relations, for example. "The rancor, the hatred—that just didn't seem like something that I'd be up for," he says. The work a friend was doing in a prosecutor's office seemed a lot

more appealing. So after graduating in 1993, he clerked for the Loudon County Circuit Court and, in 1997, went to work for the county prosecutor's office. It didn't hurt that he'd graduated from a "fairly local university known to be prestigious," had grown up in the county, and had spent time as a law clerk becoming known to the legal community around the old courthouse that still dominates the center of downtown Leesburg, Virginia, where the Loudoun County prosecutor's offices are located.

His office overlooking the green, campuslike lawn of the old Leesburg courthouse is as sociable a place as his alma mater; the county prosecutors share the fascinating cases and the not-so-scintillating work alike. "You're not just the traffic guy, or the white-collar-crime guy, or the drug guy," he says. Sincavage does tend to get a fair number of drug cases—he often carries a pager so narcotics officers can reach him 24 hours a day—but he also handles everything from juvenile cases to embezzlement and identity fraud. Some days he spends in traffic court—often the most entertaining part of his week. "The excuses you always hear are: 'All of the other cars were speeding,' or 'This guy was going faster than me, why didn't he get pulled over?'" Or, his personal favorite: "I was going downhill."

When he has to juggle hearings or be in two places at once, he relies on his colleagues—and that sense of being part of a team reminds him of law school. "I think a lot of people would say we were having too much fun," he says. "I'd do those three years again in a second if I could."

fricking step of the way—it was harder to get an interview, harder to get a callback, harder to get an offer." His determination paid off, however, and he eventually landed a job at a prestigious New York firm.

Networking is key, say many career counselors—and it should start your first year of law school. Try getting involved with a range of organizations on campus and attending local bar association and alumni events, for instance, so you can get out into the real world and interact with practicing attorneys. You never know who'll be able to lend a hand in the future, and the experience in creating and maintaining contacts will very likely help you in your future practice, as well. (One of Wellen's strategies was to identify and contact all of the Temple alumni working in midsize to large New York practices.)

No matter what happens, you should bear in mind that your first job is just that—you can always move on. Indeed, even while the hiring of first-year associates was down across the board, there's been an increase in the lateral hiring of those who have at least several years of experience.

Consider public interest law

Ironically, low-paying public interest jobs can be even more difficult to land than glamorous firm positions. Just 5.4 percent of graduates find positions in the field, which encompasses nonprofit groups such as legal aid organizations and public defender offices, as well as national, state, and local government agencies. Experts attribute this not to a lack of interest, but to a dearth of entry-level openings and graduates' huge debt loads, which make a minuscule paycheck impractical. At the same time, more JDs seem to be competing for these posts than in past years, perhaps because of the difficult firm market. "If anything, the public sector has tended to stay fairly constant," says Skip Horne. "So with similar numbers of opportunities but more students interested in them, the competition is more fierce."

Demonstrated interest and experience in the public domain are essential when you're looking for nonprofit or government jobs. Organizations and agencies with extremely tight budgets simply can't afford to train rank beginners. Committed students can increase their chances of finding employment by making their own opportunities. For example, volunteering at a local nonprofit organization may eventually turn into a full-time position.

There are quite a few fellowship openings, as well, offered through individual law schools and a range of private organizations, including the Skadden Fellowship Foundation, an arm of Skadden, Arps in New York (www.skadden fellowship.org). Such programs aim to make help-

> *"I was extraordinarily aggressive and shameless—I sent out hundreds of letters and got rejected by so many great places."*

ing others—which usually pays around $46,000, to start—a financial feasibility. For example, Equal Justice Works, a public interest advocacy group in Washington, D.C., offers fellowships for recent law graduates and experienced attorneys interested in giving back. Fellows receive up to $39,000, as well as generous student loan repayment assistance and work for such organizations as the National Housing Law Project in Oakland, California, Health Law Advocates in Boston, Alliance for Children's Rights in Los Angeles, and the Legal Assistance Foundation of Metropolitan Chicago. You can get more information at www.equal justiceworks.org.

Though the post-JD job market may be tougher than in the recent past, graduates who are determined and well prepared are clearly finding jobs. Since those are attributes that every good lawyer needs, anyway, they'll serve you well even in a new age of competing offers.

The *U.S. News* Insider's Index

How Do the Schools Stack Up?

How much competition are you facing? Here we rank schools from most to least selective based on a formula that takes into account their acceptance rates (the proportion of applicants who make the cut into the full-time program), and students' LSAT scores and grades. The 25th–75th percentile LSAT and grade-point-average ranges show you where 50 percent of enrollees fall, but remember: that means if 200 people make up the class, 50 of them fall below the bottom of the range.

Most to least selective

School	Acceptance rate	Undergraduate grade point average (25th–75th percentile)	LSAT score (25th–75th percentile)
Yale University (CT)	8%	3.82-3.96	170-176
Harvard University (MA)	11%	3.76-3.96	171-176
Stanford University (CA)	9%	3.77-3.97	167-172
University of Virginia	15%	3.54-3.92	165-171
University of California–Berkeley	10%	3.68-3.95	165-170
University of Pennsylvania	14%	3.57-3.90	166-171
Columbia University (NY)	15%	3.60-3.81	170-175
Duke University (NC)	18%	3.60-3.84	167-171
University of Chicago	18%	3.63-3.84	169-173
University of California–Los Angeles	17%	3.57-3.88	164-169
George Washington University (DC)	23%	3.45-3.86	163-168
New York University	23%	3.57-3.86	169-173
Northwestern University (IL)	18%	3.40-3.81	166-172
University of Illinois–Urbana-Champaign	29%	3.20-3.90	160-167
University of Michigan–Ann Arbor	22%	3.55-3.84	167-170
Vanderbilt University (TN)	24%	3.50-3.86	164-169
University of Texas–Austin	23%	3.54-3.87	164-168
Boston University	24%	3.50-3.83	164-167
Georgetown University (DC)	23%	3.42-3.81	168-172
University of Alabama	31%	3.42-3.91	160-166
Washington University in St. Louis	27%	3.30-3.80	161-168
Brigham Young University (Clark) (UT)	30%	3.52-3.85	160-165
College of William and Mary (Marshall-Wythe) (VA)	22%	3.42-3.77	161-166
Cornell University (NY)	21%	3.50-3.80	165-168
George Mason University (VA)	25%	3.20-3.83	158-165
University of Georgia	28%	3.40-3.80	161-165
University of Minnesota–Twin Cities	25%	3.30-3.85	160-168
Indiana University–Bloomington (Maurer)	32%	3.26-3.83	156-165
University of Southern California (Gould)	22%	3.47-3.71	165-167
University of Colorado–Boulder	23%	3.42-3.78	160-165
University of Notre Dame (IN)	25%	3.36-3.74	163-167
Fordham University (NY)	22%	3.44-3.77	164-167
University of Washington	25%	3.47-3.80	160-166
Emory University (GA)	25%	3.37-3.68	165-167
Southern Methodist University (Dedman) (TX)	23%	3.30-3.87	158-165
Boston College	20%	3.34-3.68	163-167
University of California (Hastings)	24%	3.39-3.71	161-165
University of Florida (Levin)	25%	3.42-3.85	158-163
University of North Carolina–Chapel Hill	15%	3.43-3.73	157-164

What are the hardest and easiest law schools to get into?

Most to least selective

School	Acceptance rate	Undergraduate grade point average (25th–75th percentile)	LSAT score (25th–75th percentile)
University of Wisconsin–Madison	24%	3.31-3.76	156-163
Washington and Lee University (VA)	26%	3.28-3.78	160-167
Georgia State University	16%	3.20-3.80	159-162
Ohio State University (Moritz)	34%	3.49-3.81	158-164
Pepperdine University (CA)	27%	3.43-3.79	160-163
Yeshiva University (Cardozo) (NY)	26%	3.39-3.75	161-166
Tulane University (LA)	30%	3.34-3.75	160-164
Wake Forest University (NC)	33%	3.20-3.70	160-164
Arizona State University (O'Connor)	28%	3.34-3.78	158-163
Baylor University (Umphrey) (TX)	30%	3.40-3.80	156-162
University of California–Davis	32%	3.23-3.72	160-165
University of Iowa	44%	3.43-3.81	158-164
University of Utah (Quinney)	29%	3.41-3.76	156-163
University of Tennessee–Knoxville	27%	3.28-3.77	157-161
Florida State University	26%	3.23-3.74	159-162
University of Arizona (Rogers)	33%	3.34-3.71	159-163
University of Maryland	19%	3.29-3.67	161-167
Brooklyn Law School (NY)	30%	3.26-3.64	160-164
Lewis & Clark College (Northwestern) (OR)	35%	3.21-3.72	158-164
Loyola Marymount University (CA)	32%	3.33-3.68	157-163
University of Richmond (Williams) (VA)	29%	3.19-3.63	159-163
St. John's University (NY)	39%	3.16-3.70	156-163
University of Cincinnati	50%	3.29-3.79	156-161
University of Kentucky	38%	3.33-3.82	156-161
Illinois Institute of Technology (Chicago-Kent)	44%	3.21-3.69	157-163
Rutgers, the State University of New Jersey–Camden	26%	3.21-3.70	159-162
American University (Washington) (DC)	22%	3.14-3.59	158-164
Loyola University Chicago	32%	3.29-3.62	158-162
Villanova University (PA)	43%	3.17-3.63	160-163
University of Denver (Sturm)	33%	3.27-3.69	156-161
Northeastern University (MA)	34%	3.20-3.63	155-163
University of Connecticut	26%	3.22-3.59	160-163
University of Nevada–Las Vegas (Boyd)	22%	3.19-3.67	156-160
University of Oklahoma	31%	3.29-3.72	155-161
University of San Diego	35%	3.24-3.60	158-162
Hofstra University (NY)	41%	3.27-3.70	155-159
Pennsylvania State University (Dickinson)	29%	3.28-3.68	157-160
Temple University (Beasley) (PA)	41%	3.14-3.60	160-163
University of Houston (TX)	27%	3.08-3.63	160-164
University at Buffalo–SUNY	32%	3.19-3.73	153-159
Chapman University (CA)	32%	3.11-3.56	156-159
University of Kansas	35%	3.25-3.71	155-160
University of Pittsburgh	37%	3.18-3.63	157-161
University of South Carolina	37%	3.14-3.70	156-160
Case Western Reserve University (OH)	42%	3.21-3.64	157-161
University of Missouri	44%	3.24-3.70	156-161
University of San Francisco	37%	3.15-3.57	156-160
Louisiana State University–Baton Rouge (Hebert)	37%	3.22-3.66	155-159
Rutgers, the State University of New Jersey–Newark	30%	3.13-3.60	155-161
University of Hawaii–Manoa (Richardson)	20%	3.21-3.68	155-160
University of Louisville (Brandeis) (KY)	37%	3.15-3.75	154-159
University of New Mexico	24%	3.12-3.67	152-158

What are the hardest and easiest law schools to get into?

Most to least selective

School	Acceptance rate	Undergraduate grade point average (25th–75th percentile)	LSAT score (25th–75th percentile)
Wayne State University (MI)	39%	3.25-3.69	153-159
Indiana University–Indianapolis	38%	3.23-3.73	154-160
University of Nebraska–Lincoln	52%	3.29-3.82	154-158
Catholic University of America (Columbus) (DC)	34%	3.17-3.55	157-160
Santa Clara University (CA)	45%	3.11-3.61	157-161
Seton Hall University (NJ)	52%	3.21-3.68	158-161
University of Arkansas–Fayetteville	34%	3.16-3.74	153-158
University of Miami (FL)	52%	3.25-3.66	155-159
University of Oregon	42%	3.12-3.56	157-161
Cleveland State University (Cleveland-Marshall)	36%	3.19-3.68	153-158
DePaul University (IL)	38%	3.11-3.57	158-162
Stetson University (FL)	39%	3.21-3.65	153-158
Texas Tech University	37%	3.13-3.62	153-158
University of Memphis (Humphreys)	32%	3.17-3.68	153-158
Marquette University (WI)	46%	3.09-3.61	155-159
Mercer University (George) (GA)	38%	3.13-3.67	153-158
University of the Pacific (McGeorge) (CA)	43%	3.07-3.60	155-160
Campbell University (Wiggins) (NC)	30%	3.12-3.59	154-159
Seattle University	38%	3.16-3.63	155-160
Ohio Northern University (Pettit)	36%	2.96-3.65	149-157
University of Mississippi	41%	3.27-3.71	151-157
Quinnipiac University (CT)	41%	3.10-3.63	156-160
University of St. Thomas (MN)	51%	3.07-3.59	153-161
Florida International University	26%	3.18-3.67	152-156
Drake University (IA)	54%	3.12-3.64	153-158
St. Louis University	48%	3.21-3.64	154-160
University of Montana	50%	3.26-3.69	151-157
Hamline University (MN)	47%	3.27-3.68	151-159
Michigan State University	48%	3.09-3.61	153-159
Syracuse University (NY)	38%	3.13-3.51	153-157
University of Wyoming	34%	3.25-3.68	150-157
William Mitchell College of Law (MN)	47%	3.29-3.67	154-159
Pace University (NY)	41%	3.20-3.61	152-157
Suffolk University (MA)	51%	3.30-3.50	154-159
Albany Law School (NY)	44%	3.03-3.56	153-157
Gonzaga University (WA)	43%	3.05-3.51	153-157
University of Baltimore	40%	3.03-3.67	153-158
University of Maine	48%	3.06-3.61	152-158
Samford University (Cumberland) (AL)	52%	3.01-3.59	153-157
University of Akron (OH)	38%	3.16-3.70	152-159
University of Idaho	48%	2.85-3.58	152-157
Creighton University (NE)	57%	3.15-3.64	151-156
CUNY–Queens College	27%	3.10-3.54	151-156
Southwestern Law School (CA)	31%	3.10-3.56	153-157
West Virginia University	50%	3.12-3.70	151-156
Northern Kentucky University (Chase)	43%	3.16-3.64	152-157
University of Arkansas–Little Rock (Bowen)	24%	2.92-3.70	150-158
University of Missouri–Kansas City	48%	3.03-3.58	152-156
Vermont Law School	67%	3.05-3.57	152-158
Washburn University (KS)	47%	2.95-3.68	152-157
Regent University (VA)	45%	3.00-3.71	150-157
University of South Dakota	57%	3.13-3.65	149-155

What are the hardest and easiest law schools to get into?

Most to least selective

School	Acceptance rate	Undergraduate grade point average (25th–75th percentile)	LSAT I Verbal (25th–75th percentile)
Northern Illinois University	40%	2.93-3.51	153-156
University of Tulsa (OK)	51%	2.83-3.55	152-157
Willamette University (Collins) (OR)	39%	3.05-3.51	153-157
Duquesne University (PA)	47%	3.25-3.67	152-155
Howard University (DC)	21%	2.92-3.51	150-156
University of North Dakota	35%	3.30-3.73	149-155
California Western School of Law	48%	3.05-3.50	150-155
Franklin Pierce Law Center (NH)	50%	3.06-3.62	149-155
New York Law School	57%	3.02-3.48	152-157
South Texas College of Law	48%	3.04-3.56	151-156
St. Mary's University (TX)	43%	2.88-3.50	151-156
Loyola University New Orleans	49%	3.05-3.52	151-155
Southern Illinois University–Carbondale	48%	3.01-3.52	151-157
John Marshall Law School (IL)	49%	3.00-3.53	150-156
Capital University (OH)	59%	2.96-3.51	151-156
Roger Williams University (RI)	58%	3.00-3.50	150-157
Texas Wesleyan University	47%	2.93-3.46	151-156
University of Toledo (OH)	57%	3.07-3.59	152-158
Western New England College (MA)	54%	2.94-3.55	151-156
Golden Gate University (CA)	52%	2.88-3.43	151-155
New England School of Law (MA)	60%	3.00-3.45	151-154
Valparaiso University (IN)	62%	3.08-3.59	148-152
Mississippi College	57%	3.01-3.53	148-153
Ave Maria School of Law (FL)	50%	2.91-3.53	147-155
Touro College (Fuchsberg) (NY)	49%	2.88-3.41	149-153
University of the District of Columbia (Clarke)	21%	2.83-3.28	149-153
Western State University (CA)	52%	2.83-3.40	149-154
Whittier College (CA)	47%	2.82-3.35	149-153
Nova Southeastern University (Broad) (FL)	46%	3.02-3.47	147-152
Oklahoma City University	56%	2.90-3.47	148-152
University of Dayton (OH)	58%	2.87-3.40	148-153
University of Detroit Mercy	45%	2.93-3.38	147-154
Widener University (DE)	57%	2.82-3.44	150-154
Florida Coastal School of Law	66%	2.95-3.42	147-153
North Carolina Central University	18%	2.99-3.43	142-148
Atlanta's John Marshall Law School	40%	2.67-3.26	149-153
Thomas Jefferson School of Law (CA)	52%	2.71-3.22	149-153
Faulkner University (Jones) (AL)	54%	2.76-3.33	147-152
Florida A&M University	30%	2.78-3.36	144-149
Barry University (FL)	57%	2.58-3.26	148-152
Appalachian School of Law (VA)	48%	2.61-3.31	147-152
Texas Southern University (Marshall)	34%	2.66-3.21	144-148

As you compare schools, you'll want to pay attention to the total enrollment, the size of first-year sections, the availability of small classes, and the student-faculty ratio. All will have an impact on the schools' personalities, the availability of professors outside of class, the extent to which you engage with your classmates, and the breadth of the curriculum. Schools are ranked here by total enrollment.

School	Total full- and part-time enrollment	Full-time enrollment	Part-time enrollment	Size of first-year class	Typical first-year section size	Public or private	Student to faculty ratio	% classes under 25	% classes 25–100	% classes over 100	Number of course offerings after first year
Georgetown University (DC)	1,982	1,628	354	593	117	Private	12.4	55%	39%	6%	407
New York Law School	1,856	1,408	448	727	114	Private	23.6	48%	37%	15%	245
Harvard University (MA)	1,771	1,771	N/A	565	80	Private	11.0	47%	47%	6%	N/A
Suffolk University (MA)	1,682	1,079	603	537	89	Private	16.5	51%	43%	6%	281
George Washington Univ. (DC)	1,632	1,328	304	520	103	Private	14.2	61%	35%	4%	213
Florida Coastal School of Law	1,605	1,539	66	664	82	Private	20.9	48%	51%	0%	129
American Univ. (DC)	1,485	1,195	290	480	98	Private	13.4	64%	36%	0%	295
Fordham University (NY)	1,469	1,160	309	476	80	Private	13.6	32%	64%	4%	247
Brooklyn Law School (NY)	1,458	1,278	180	496	45	Private	18.4	60%	33%	7%	189
Widener University (DE)	1,436	970	466	559	69	Private	19.0	70%	30%	1%	198
New York University	1,427	1,427	N/A	449	89	Private	9.4	47%	47%	6%	326
University of Miami (FL)	1,384	1,351	33	525	100	Private	16.5	30%	57%	13%	82
John Marshall Law School (IL)	1,377	1,038	339	497	75	Private	14.4	69%	31%	0%	270
Columbia University (NY)	1,310	1,309	1	398	95	Private	10.1	51%	39%	9%	237
Univ. of California (Hastings)	1,292	1,292	N/A	470	95	Public	16.5	61%	38%	1%	161
Loyola Marymount Univ. (CA)	1,287	1,002	285	400	86	Private	14.8	62%	33%	5%	162
South Texas College of Law	1,278	973	305	628	95	Private	20.0	64%	36%	0%	163
Northern Illinois University	1,183	1,169	14	109	49	Public	18.7	62%	38%	0%	59
University of Texas–Austin	1,182	1,182	N/A	384	99	Public	11.3	69%	26%	5%	158
University of Virginia	1,122	1,122	N/A	365	72	Public	12.6	58%	38%	4%	233
Yeshiva Univ. (Cardozo) (NY)	1,121	1,020	101	346	49	Private	15.6	46%	44%	10%	156
Univ. of Michigan–Ann Arbor	1,117	1,117	N/A	371	91	Public	11.3	51%	44%	5%	191
Hofstra University (NY)	1,109	939	170	393	97	Private	15.4	48%	50%	2%	131
University of Florida (Levin)	1,106	1,106	N/A	306	105	Public	15.4	49%	46%	5%	166
University of Baltimore	1,103	672	431	423	58	Public	15.8	73%	27%	N/A	150
New England School of Law (MA)	1,096	737	359	400	110	Private	23.1	55%	44%	2%	121
Nova Southeastern Univ. (FL)	1,092	903	189	453	63	Private	16.7	63%	37%	0%	119
Seton Hall University (NJ)	1,090	723	367	356	70	Private	15.4	71%	29%	0%	138
Stetson University (FL)	1,084	876	208	395	68	Private	15.8	75%	25%	0%	172
Southwestern Law School (CA)	1,052	729	323	388	76	Private	14.3	62%	38%	0%	151
Univ. of the Pacific (CA)	1,037	660	377	329	79	Private	14.0	66%	31%	3%	176
Seattle University	1,036	808	228	330	85	Private	12.3	62%	38%	0%	160
DePaul University (IL)	1,027	772	255	364	90	Private	13.3	68%	31%	1%	156
University of Denver (Sturm)	1,018	786	232	296	80	Private	15.5	66%	34%	0%	171
Univ. of California–Los Angeles	1,011	1,011	N/A	319	80	Public	11.3	49%	45%	6%	188
Santa Clara University (CA)	1,001	749	252	319	73	Private	17.8	66%	34%	0%	179
University of San Diego	1,000	816	184	323	80	Private	14.2	76%	24%	0%	133
William Mitchell Coll. of Law (MN)	977	603	374	301	80	Private	20.4	60%	40%	0%	149
Temple University (Beasley) (PA)	976	784	192	304	60	Public	13.0	70%	29%	1%	185

What are the largest and smallest law schools?

School	Total full- and part-time enrollment	Full-time enrollment	Part-time enrollment	Size of first-year class	Typical first-year section size	Public or private	Student to faculty ratio	% classes under 25	% classes 25–100	% classes over 100	Number of course offerings after first year
St. Louis University	967	771	196	327	75	Private	17.0	70%	26%	4%	150
Michigan State University	957	892	65	283	74	Private	16.6	63%	32%	5%	175
University of Maryland	953	723	230	301	78	Public	11.7	79%	19%	1%	223
Illinois Inst. of Tech (Kent)	948	769	179	304	54	Private	10.9	74%	25%	1%	145
Indiana University–Indianapolis	944	625	319	389	90	Public	17.7	52%	47%	1%	126
St. John's University (NY)	915	737	178	312	85	Private	14.6	65%	34%	1%	184
Southern Methodist Univ. (TX)	903	524	379	253	82	Private	14.9	48%	50%	2%	134
University of Houston (TX)	898	715	183	254	70	Public	11.8	65%	34%	2%	196
California Western School of Law	892	791	101	313	87	Private	18.3	69%	26%	5%	114
University of California–Berkeley	892	892	N/A	290	90	Public	11.4	31%	53%	16%	252
Catholic Univ. of America (DC)	890	574	316	263	60	Private	12.8	64%	36%	N/A	120
Thomas Jefferson School of Law (CA)	889	648	241	306	85	Private	17.9	70%	29%	1%	95
Loyola University New Orleans	882	726	156	326	74	Private	17.1	37%	62%	1%	102
St. Mary's University (TX)	863	681	182	366	80	Private	20.9	51%	49%	0%	115
Washington University in St. Louis	856	851	5	261	96	Private	10.7	60%	39%	1%	154
Loyola University Chicago	840	652	188	270	65	Private	14.3	67%	32%	0%	183
Rutgers–Newark (NJ)	835	593	242	257	60	Public	17.6	49%	47%	4%	109
Boston University	830	827	3	271	90	Private	12.1	62%	36%	2%	195
University of Wisconsin–Madison	825	792	33	275	71	Public	12.7	62%	35%	3%	167
Boston College	814	814	N/A	266	88	Private	13.2	57%	42%	2%	149
Northwestern University (IL)	814	814	N/A	271	65	Private	8.8	61%	39%	0%	217
Rutgers–Camden (NJ)	810	619	191	270	56	Public	11.8	69%	31%	0%	139
Texas Wesleyan University	793	522	271	413	95	Private	21.0	61%	37%	2%	94
University of Pennsylvania	790	790	N/A	253	85	Private	10.7	45%	51%	4%	172
Touro College (Fuchsberg) (NY)	786	553	233	311	70	Private	15.9	63%	36%	1%	91
Tulane University (LA)	774	771	3	283	83	Private	14.1	57%	40%	3%	193
Barry University (FL)	771	609	162	257	100	Private	26.7	67%	30%	3%	172
Univ. of Minnesota–Twin Cities	766	766	N/A	213	96	Public	11.9	55%	43%	2%	178
Univ. of N. Carolina–Chapel Hill	765	765	N/A	258	85	Public	15.4	53%	43%	4%	117
Florida State University	763	763	N/A	245	83	Public	14.2	61%	38%	1%	119
Villanova University (PA)	754	754	N/A	258	85	Private	17.0	61%	37%	1%	117
Albany Law School (NY)	749	712	37	257	65	Private	13.1	56%	41%	3%	129
Pace University (NY)	747	562	185	261	52	Private	12.7	71%	29%	0%	148
Marquette University (WI)	743	563	180	219	81	Private	19.1	55%	45%	0%	153
University of Detroit Mercy	730	586	144	281	58	Private	14.1	65%	35%	0%	96
University at Buffalo–SUNY	726	718	8	208	65	Public	15.3	71%	29%	0%	220
Emory University (GA)	715	715	N/A	248	75	Private	10.5	66%	33%	1%	165
Lewis & Clark College (NW) (OR)	715	521	194	230	70	Private	10.0	64%	36%	1%	131
University of San Francisco	706	574	132	268	97	Private	15.2	60%	40%	0%	101
Duquesne University (PA)	704	446	258	235	83	Private	19.4	52%	48%	0%	85
George Mason University (VA)	697	480	217	247	48	Public	13.2	74%	26%	N/A	133
University of Georgia	694	694	N/A	242	80	Public	12.2	61%	39%	N/A	124
University of South Carolina	685	685	N/A	239	82	Public	14.8	51%	48%	1%	116
University of Pittsburgh	682	682	N/A	233	82	Public	12.9	70%	27%	3%	192
Georgia State University	673	480	193	212	70	Public	10.7	65%	35%	0%	112
Ohio State University (Moritz)	669	669	N/A	224	75	Public	13.3	56%	44%	0%	123
Pepperdine University (CA)	667	667	N/A	231	75	Private	16.0	67%	30%	3%	125
Duke University (NC)	661	626	35	229	68	Private	9.7	66%	30%	3%	184
Charleston School of Law (SC)	659	459	200	239	62	Private	18.2	65%	35%	0%	77
Hamline University (MN)	650	468	182	205	58	Private	14.8	57%	43%	N/A	134
Capital University (OH)	648	461	187	247	85	Private	15.8	67%	33%	0%	184

What are the largest and smallest law schools?

School	Total full- and part-time enrollment	Full-time enrollment	Part-time enrollment	Size of first-year class	Typical first-year section size	Public or private	Student to faculty ratio	% classes under 25	% classes 25–100	% classes over 100	Number of course offerings after first year
University of Connecticut	641	450	191	182	62	Public	11.4	68%	32%	0%	147
Case Western Reserve Univ. (OH)	640	618	22	211	70	Private	12.2	66%	34%	N/A	162
Cleveland State Univ. (Marshall)	639	482	157	201	52	Public	13.1	64%	36%	0%	95
Golden Gate University (CA)	637	529	108	247	70	Private	15.2	77%	23%	0%	122
Texas Tech University	637	637	N/A	228	51	Public	15.3	60%	34%	5%	95
Coll. of William and Mary (VA)	626	626	N/A	212	70	Public	15.7	71%	26%	3%	129
Florida International University	623	294	329	237	80	Public	16.2	67%	33%	0%	66
Oklahoma City University	623	533	90	229	70	Private	17.6	71%	29%	0%	128
Cornell University (NY)	622	622	N/A	205	99	Private	10.0	51%	45%	4%	137
Indiana Univ.–Bloomington	620	620	N/A	218	72	Public	9.5	68%	30%	2%	138
Univ. of S. California (Gould)	618	618	N/A	212	70	Private	12.4	67%	30%	3%	107
Univ. of Illinois–Urbana-Champaign	617	617	N/A	229	63	Public	13.1	55%	45%	0%	128
Florida A&M University	613	385	228	233	60	Public	18.5	56%	44%	0%	134
Yale University (CT)	613	613	N/A	213	58	Private	7.3	56%	41%	3%	163
Northern Kentucky Univ. (Chase)	609	374	235	190	70	Public	15.1	51%	49%	0%	50
University of California–Davis	606	606	N/A	214	72	Public	11.6	52%	44%	4%	75
Syracuse University (NY)	603	598	5	220	68	Private	10.9	73%	27%	0%	129
Northeastern University (MA)	602	602	N/A	214	70	Private	15.4	47%	52%	1%	93
North Carolina Central University	601	480	121	206	65	Public	16.5	50%	47%	3%	77
Louisiana St. Univ.–Baton Rouge	598	587	11	235	78	Public	17.5	64%	36%	0%	77
Pennsylvania St. Univ. (Dickinson)	597	586	11	205	50	Public	9.4	79%	21%	0%	124
Vanderbilt University (TN)	594	594	N/A	196	97	Private	14.4	64%	34%	2%	151
Whittier College (CA)	591	450	141	305	85	Private	17.6	80%	20%	0%	112
University of Chicago	590	590	N/A	191	93	Private	9.5	41%	56%	3%	193
University of Iowa	590	590	N/A	195	75	Public	15.5	54%	46%	0%	65
Valparaiso University (IN)	582	541	41	213	72	Private	15.8	66%	31%	3%	100
Arizona State Univ. (O'Connor)	576	576	N/A	187	63	Public	8.5	75%	25%	0%	121
Wayne State University (MI)	569	457	112	180	90	Public	14.4	66%	34%	0%	75
Vermont Law School	567	567	N/A	232	65	Private	13.5	60%	40%	0%	128
Stanford University (CA)	557	557	N/A	180	60	Private	8.0	81%	19%	1%	160
Atlanta's John Marshall Law School	555	371	184	233	49	Private	12.9	69%	31%	0%	51
Roger Williams University (RI)	550	550	N/A	219	60	Private	16.7	59%	40%	1%	110
University of Oklahoma	550	550	N/A	195	44	Public	14.2	49%	51%	0%	108
University of Notre Dame (IN)	548	548	N/A	184	64	Private	10.9	64%	35%	1%	128
University of Alabama	547	527	20	205	63	Public	10.2	65%	33%	1%	149
University of Colorado–Boulder	547	547	N/A	165	84	Public	11.5	63%	38%	0%	105
University of Oregon	544	544	N/A	183	61	Public	16.4	66%	34%	0%	103
Texas Southern Univ. (Marshall)	542	542	N/A	232	60	Public	12.8	65%	34%	1%	74
Western New England Coll. (MA)	538	389	149	182	46	Private	12.7	46%	54%	0%	95
Chapman University (CA)	536	499	37	181	60	Private	8.9	72%	28%	0%	152
Mississippi College	536	521	15	198	87	Private	18.2	63%	36%	1%	84
University of Washington	530	530	N/A	181	52	Public	10.0	49%	51%	0%	126
Gonzaga University (WA)	526	516	10	186	70	Private	15.3	43%	57%	0%	94
University of Akron (OH)	517	279	238	203	41	Public	11.2	57%	43%	1%	92
Univ. of Missouri–Kansas City	515	489	26	187	56	Public	14.1	67%	33%	0%	114
University of Dayton (OH)	500	500	N/A	204	90	Private	16.7	58%	41%	1%	70
University of Kansas	499	499	N/A	161	67	Public	12.4	68%	32%	0%	93
University of Mississippi	495	495	N/A	173	57	Public	18.2	55%	44%	1%	89
Samford Univ. (Cumberland) (AL)	493	493	N/A	179	55	Private	18.0	56%	44%	0%	105
University of Toledo (OH)	493	346	147	209	55	Public	13.4	69%	31%	0%	88
Creighton University (NE)	484	471	13	183	83	Private	17.6	74%	26%	0%	84

What are the largest and smallest law schools?

School	Total full- and part-time enrollment	Full-time enrollment	Part-time enrollment	Size of first-year class	Typical first-year section size	Public or private	Student to faculty ratio	% classes under 25	% classes 25–100	% classes over 100	Number of course offerings after first year
Univ. of Nevada–Las Vegas (Boyd)	484	366	118	159	65	Public	16.8	73%	27%	0%	79
Charlotte School of Law (NC)	481	380	101	276	75	Private	19.7	56%	44%	N/A	43
Wake Forest University (NC)	476	463	13	151	38	Private	9.8	55%	45%	0%	108
University of Arizona (Rogers)	475	475	N/A	155	77	Public	10.6	81%	17%	2%	120
Univ. of Arkansas–Little Rock	471	316	155	165	93	Public	16.2	60%	39%	1%	83
Univ. of Tennessee–Knoxville	471	471	N/A	158	55	Public	13.9	70%	30%	0%	130
Howard University (DC)	468	468	N/A	165	50	Private	16.5	69%	31%	0%	120
Drake University (IA)	467	451	16	167	81	Private	14.5	69%	31%	0%	98
Baylor University (Umphrey) (TX)	465	465	N/A	191	66	Private	15.1	61%	39%	N/A	81
Univ. of Richmond (Williams) (VA)	465	465	N/A	150	55	Private	13.8	73%	27%	0%	104
University of St. Thomas (MN)	457	457	N/A	170	75	Private	17.7	77%	23%	N/A	76
Brigham Young Univ. (Clark) (UT)	447	447	N/A	143	100	Private	17.3	61%	39%	0%	109
University of Missouri	445	441	4	154	73	Public	16.8	66%	34%	0%	119
Washburn University (KS)	441	441	N/A	163	76	Public	12.9	66%	34%	0%	97
Univ. of Louisville (Brandeis) (KY)	435	368	67	147	62	Public	15.4	52%	48%	0%	67
Mercer University (George) (GA)	431	431	N/A	160	73	Private	13.0	75%	25%	0%	112
Franklin Pierce Law Center (NH)	429	429	N/A	153	80	Private	14.2	75%	25%	0%	107
Willamette Univ. (Collins) (OR)	426	421	5	147	80	Private	15.0	67%	32%	1%	N/A
University of Tulsa (OK)	422	382	40	138	45	Private	11.9	73%	27%	0%	132
Univ. of Memphis (Humphreys)	420	392	28	160	75	Public	17.7	41%	58%	1%	62
West Virginia University	418	412	6	154	70	Public	12.9	53%	47%	0%	79
Regent University (VA)	417	394	23	162	72	Private	16.2	74%	26%	0%	88
Western State University (CA)	417	276	141	181	52	Private	22.6	74%	26%	0%	48
Quinnipiac University (CT)	415	291	124	158	75	Private	11.2	86%	14%	0%	106
Drexel University (Mack) (PA)	410	410	N/A	156	78	Private	16.4	57%	43%	N/A	84
CUNY–Queens College	406	406	N/A	165	80	Public	10.0	59%	38%	3%	N/A
University of Kentucky	406	406	N/A	151	56	Public	16.8	49%	51%	0%	72
Campbell Univ. (Wiggins) (NC)	405	405	N/A	159	40	Private	17.9	21%	76%	2%	90
University of Utah (Quinney)	400	381	19	127	39	Public	8.1	78%	22%	0%	120
Univ. of Arkansas–Fayetteville	398	398	N/A	138	70	Public	12.2	75%	25%	0%	88
University of Nebraska–Lincoln	394	394	N/A	137	70	Public	13.6	64%	36%	0%	91
University of Cincinnati	391	391	N/A	138	54	Public	9.9	57%	42%	1%	103
Washington and Lee Univ. (VA)	390	390	N/A	134	51	Private	9.4	74%	25%	1%	81
S. Illinois Univ.–Carbondale	383	382	1	135	56	Public	11.7	70%	30%	N/A	70
Ave Maria School of Law (FL)	375	375	N/A	208	63	Private	17.5	74%	26%	0%	77
University of New Mexico	351	351	N/A	124	56	Public	11.3	66%	34%	0%	81
Faulkner University (Jones) (AL)	341	323	18	150	60	Private	14.0	63%	37%	N/A	43
Appalachian School of Law (VA)	334	334	N/A	128	129	Private	15.8	43%	36%	21%	46
Univ. of Hawaii–Manoa	326	285	41	151	97	Public	7.8	79%	21%	0%	87
Elon University (NC)	315	315	N/A	120	30	Private	17.3	29%	63%	9%	54
Ohio Northern University (Pettit)	307	307	N/A	114	60	Private	12.7	62%	38%	0%	78
Univ. of the District of Columbia	293	266	27	122	96	Public	12.2	60%	40%	0%	44
University of Maine	264	264	N/A	90	91	Public	14.2	70%	30%	0%	73
University of Montana	252	252	N/A	84	42	Public	14.3	67%	31%	3%	N/A
University of North Dakota	247	247	N/A	86	85	Public	16.8	55%	45%	N/A	53
University of Wyoming	225	225	N/A	83	75	Public	12.3	70%	30%	0%	61
University of South Dakota	202	202	N/A	80	61	Public	12.3	67%	33%	N/A	52
University of Idaho	114	114	N/A	114	53	Public	16.5	74%	25%	1%	96

What are the most and least diverse law schools?

If you're looking for a law school culture that features students from a wealth of backgrounds, the *U.S. News* diversity index can point you to institutions with both a significant proportion of minority students and a mix of different ethnic groups. The closer the index number is to 1.0, the more likely you are to interact with people of a different ethnicity than you.

School	Diversity index	American Indian	Asian	Black	Hispanic	White	International	Men	Women	Minority faculty	Male faculty	Female faculty
Florida A&M University	0.66	0.8%	3.6%	40.6%	16.5%	38.5%	0.0%	45.4%	54.6%	69.0%	50.0%	50.0%
Texas Southern University (Marshall)	0.64	0.4%	6.5%	50.2%	23.8%	16.8%	2.4%	47.6%	52.4%	78.3%	43.5%	56.5%
Univ. of the District of Columbia (Clarke)	0.64	1.0%	7.8%	29.4%	11.3%	50.5%	0.0%	42.3%	57.7%	54.1%	54.1%	45.9%
Florida International University	0.60	0.8%	2.1%	9.0%	43.8%	43.8%	0.5%	52.3%	47.7%	45.8%	50.0%	50.0%
University of New Mexico	0.60	10.0%	2.8%	3.7%	28.2%	55.3%	0.0%	45.9%	54.1%	36.2%	48.9%	51.1%
Santa Clara University (CA)	0.58	1.6%	30.0%	2.9%	8.6%	56.9%	0.0%	55.2%	44.8%	20.8%	54.5%	45.5%
Univ. of Southern California (Gould)	0.58	0.6%	20.6%	7.1%	11.0%	58.9%	1.8%	49.7%	50.3%	21.5%	63.4%	36.6%
Loyola Marymount University (CA)	0.57	0.5%	22.5%	4.3%	12.9%	59.9%	0.0%	50.4%	49.6%	26.4%	63.6%	36.4%
Northwestern University (IL)	0.57	1.1%	17.3%	8.4%	8.7%	57.0%	7.5%	53.8%	46.2%	9.3%	64.0%	36.0%
American University (Washington) (DC)	0.56	1.1%	11.2%	9.6%	13.9%	61.3%	2.8%	44.6%	55.4%	14.7%	65.4%	34.6%
North Carolina Central University	0.56	0.7%	3.3%	48.8%	3.0%	40.9%	3.3%	39.4%	60.6%	53.7%	46.3%	53.7%
Rutgers–Newark (NJ)	0.56	0.2%	10.4%	15.1%	11.0%	61.4%	1.8%	57.0%	43.0%	19.5%	64.4%	35.6%
Stanford University (CA)	0.56	2.2%	12.6%	10.8%	10.2%	62.3%	2.0%	52.8%	47.2%	14.9%	62.1%	37.9%
Southwestern Law School (CA)	0.54	0.7%	15.1%	6.7%	13.4%	63.9%	0.2%	46.1%	53.9%	20.8%	64.9%	35.1%
University of San Francisco	0.54	1.0%	16.3%	7.6%	10.2%	62.9%	2.0%	45.2%	54.8%	25.3%	62.7%	37.3%
University of California–Berkeley	0.53	1.7%	17.5%	4.8%	10.7%	65.4%	0.0%	48.4%	51.6%	8.6%	67.2%	32.8%
Western State University (CA)	0.53	0.7%	17.0%	3.8%	12.5%	64.3%	1.7%	50.1%	49.9%	26.5%	67.6%	32.4%
Cornell University (NY)	0.52	1.3%	13.7%	6.1%	9.3%	60.5%	9.2%	48.2%	51.8%	8.0%	70.7%	29.3%
Thomas Jefferson School of Law (CA)	0.52	1.0%	11.5%	6.7%	13.7%	66.3%	0.8%	54.6%	45.4%	12.9%	64.5%	35.5%
University of California–Davis	0.52	0.3%	26.7%	1.7%	7.1%	62.5%	1.7%	46.7%	53.3%	37.7%	54.1%	45.9%
Univ. of Hawaii–Manoa (Richardson)	0.52	0.6%	56.7%	1.8%	1.8%	37.1%	1.8%	42.3%	57.7%	44.7%	51.1%	48.9%
Emory University (GA)	0.51	1.1%	10.1%	9.1%	10.3%	65.2%	4.2%	52.2%	47.8%	15.2%	63.6%	36.4%
University of California–Los Angeles	0.51	1.2%	18.0%	4.5%	8.8%	65.5%	2.0%	51.5%	48.5%	12.2%	72.2%	27.8%
Northeastern University (MA)	0.50	1.3%	8.6%	10.3%	11.3%	68.4%	0.0%	40.5%	59.5%	19.0%	54.4%	45.6%
St. Mary's University (TX)	0.50	0.9%	4.6%	3.6%	25.3%	65.5%	0.1%	57.2%	42.8%	15.2%	60.8%	39.2%
University of California (Hastings)	0.50	0.9%	20.5%	2.6%	8.2%	65.9%	1.8%	48.8%	51.2%	18.6%	62.0%	38.0%
University of Maryland	0.50	0.4%	10.8%	12.6%	7.7%	67.3%	1.3%	50.1%	49.9%	14.9%	55.3%	44.7%
Columbia University (NY)	0.49	0.2%	15.1%	8.0%	5.4%	62.4%	8.9%	51.5%	48.5%	9.2%	69.4%	30.6%
CUNY–Queens College	0.49	0.0%	10.6%	8.1%	12.1%	68.2%	1.0%	37.4%	62.6%	33.3%	42.9%	57.1%
Golden Gate University (CA)	0.48	1.1%	20.3%	2.7%	6.8%	67.3%	1.9%	43.5%	56.5%	16.5%	53.6%	46.4%
Harvard University (MA)	0.48	0.6%	10.6%	11.5%	6.5%	68.7%	2.0%	52.7%	47.3%	11.4%	79.0%	21.0%
Nova Southeastern Univ. (Broad) (FL)	0.48	0.4%	5.1%	5.3%	19.5%	68.3%	1.4%	46.1%	53.9%	18.2%	64.6%	35.4%
University of Chicago	0.47	0.3%	11.5%	6.3%	10.2%	69.3%	2.4%	55.3%	44.7%	10.8%	71.1%	28.9%
University of Houston (TX)	0.47	0.4%	10.2%	8.0%	9.8%	70.0%	1.4%	56.0%	44.0%	16.0%	71.3%	28.7%
Univ. of Nevada–Las Vegas (Boyd)	0.47	2.3%	11.2%	5.6%	9.9%	70.7%	0.4%	53.7%	46.3%	11.8%	55.9%	44.1%
University of Texas–Austin	0.47	0.6%	6.8%	6.0%	15.7%	70.4%	0.6%	55.4%	44.6%	14.0%	66.4%	33.6%
Yale University (CT)	0.47	0.2%	11.6%	7.5%	8.5%	68.2%	4.1%	52.2%	47.8%	12.8%	76.0%	24.0%
Northern Illinois University	0.46	0.6%	9.4%	12.6%	6.3%	71.2%	0.0%	63.1%	36.9%	30.0%	60.0%	40.0%
University of Pennsylvania	0.46	0.3%	13.9%	7.3%	6.5%	69.6%	2.4%	52.8%	47.2%	13.1%	69.7%	30.3%

What are the most and least diverse law schools?

School	Diversity index	American Indian	Asian	Black	Hispanic	White	International	Men	Women	Minority faculty	Male faculty	Female faculty
California Western School of Law	0.45	0.8%	14.3%	3.3%	9.5%	71.2%	0.9%	45.0%	55.0%	11.8%	61.3%	38.7%
Hofstra University (NY)	0.45	0.4%	9.8%	8.3%	8.4%	70.2%	3.0%	51.3%	48.7%	17.2%	78.8%	21.2%
Loyola University New Orleans	0.45	0.6%	4.0%	14.6%	8.4%	72.0%	0.5%	51.1%	48.9%	19.7%	65.6%	34.4%
University of Arizona (Rogers)	0.45	6.3%	8.6%	3.2%	8.6%	72.2%	1.1%	52.6%	47.4%	14.1%	57.8%	42.2%
Univ. of the Pacific (McGeorge) (CA)	0.45	1.1%	14.9%	3.2%	9.0%	71.9%	0.0%	49.7%	50.3%	14.7%	64.0%	36.0%
Whittier College (CA)	0.45	0.3%	13.5%	2.7%	11.0%	72.1%	0.3%	45.5%	54.5%	20.0%	62.9%	37.1%
Florida Coastal School of Law	0.44	1.2%	6.0%	9.7%	10.0%	73.0%	0.0%	52.4%	47.6%	9.2%	56.3%	43.7%
University of San Diego	0.44	1.1%	16.8%	1.5%	8.0%	72.2%	0.4%	54.5%	45.5%	8.0%	70.0%	30.0%
Brooklyn Law School (NY)	0.43	0.1%	15.5%	4.8%	5.8%	73.1%	0.6%	51.3%	48.7%	8.6%	65.6%	34.4%
South Texas College of Law	0.43	1.2%	10.1%	3.8%	10.9%	73.8%	0.2%	51.6%	48.4%	13.2%	64.8%	35.2%
Seattle University	0.42	1.1%	14.6%	4.3%	5.2%	74.0%	0.8%	49.1%	50.9%	18.9%	60.4%	39.6%
Washington University in St. Louis	0.42	0.7%	10.9%	10.5%	2.1%	69.2%	6.7%	58.2%	41.8%	9.1%	64.3%	35.7%
Atlanta's John Marshall Law School	0.41	0.5%	3.6%	18.7%	2.9%	74.1%	0.2%	48.8%	51.2%	16.7%	52.4%	47.6%
DePaul University (IL)	0.41	0.3%	6.1%	7.0%	10.7%	74.3%	1.6%	49.2%	50.8%	11.6%	63.6%	36.4%
St. John's University (NY)	0.41	0.0%	9.2%	6.3%	8.5%	74.6%	1.3%	53.0%	47.0%	10.6%	67.3%	32.7%
Texas Tech University	0.41	0.9%	4.4%	3.8%	15.9%	75.0%	0.0%	58.2%	41.8%	19.0%	68.3%	31.7%
Texas Wesleyan University	0.41	1.5%	6.9%	6.3%	10.0%	75.3%	0.0%	49.4%	50.6%	10.6%	66.0%	34.0%
Univ. of North Carolina–Chapel Hill	0.41	2.5%	6.8%	7.6%	7.1%	75.9%	0.1%	47.2%	52.8%	12.4%	64.8%	35.2%
University of Wisconsin–Madison	0.41	2.4%	7.4%	7.0%	6.9%	73.6%	2.7%	53.9%	46.1%	22.9%	54.1%	45.9%
Boston University	0.40	0.2%	11.6%	5.3%	5.7%	73.6%	3.6%	50.2%	49.8%	11.9%	60.7%	39.3%
New York University	0.40	0.2%	10.5%	6.2%	6.4%	73.7%	3.1%	56.0%	44.0%	23.1%	69.7%	30.3%
Southern Methodist Univ. (Dedman) (TX)	0.40	1.4%	7.6%	5.1%	9.6%	75.7%	0.4%	53.2%	46.8%	11.8%	76.5%	23.5%
University of Florida (Levin)	0.40	0.7%	6.8%	6.2%	9.7%	74.8%	1.8%	52.0%	48.0%	14.8%	55.7%	44.3%
Univ. of Illinois–Urbana-Champaign	0.40	0.8%	8.9%	7.6%	5.2%	72.3%	5.2%	57.9%	42.1%	15.3%	70.8%	29.2%
University of Miami (FL)	0.40	0.3%	4.4%	6.8%	11.7%	72.5%	4.3%	56.9%	43.1%	19.5%	68.6%	31.4%
University of Michigan–Ann Arbor	0.40	1.5%	12.1%	5.1%	4.2%	73.7%	3.4%	56.5%	43.5%	7.9%	69.3%	30.7%
University of Notre Dame (IN)	0.40	1.3%	8.4%	5.1%	8.6%	75.9%	0.7%	57.8%	42.2%	9.6%	67.5%	32.5%
Boston College	0.39	0.7%	11.5%	3.6%	6.8%	75.9%	1.5%	52.9%	47.1%	11.6%	66.3%	33.7%
Duke University (NC)	0.39	0.2%	8.3%	8.6%	5.3%	76.1%	1.5%	57.0%	43.0%	9.8%	70.7%	29.3%
Georgetown University (DC)	0.39	0.3%	8.9%	8.6%	4.6%	74.4%	3.2%	54.7%	45.3%	6.6%	73.2%	26.8%
John Marshall Law School (IL)	0.39	0.9%	5.6%	7.9%	8.3%	76.3%	1.1%	54.6%	45.4%	11.5%	67.8%	32.2%
Temple University (Beasley) (PA)	0.39	0.9%	9.6%	7.1%	5.0%	76.5%	0.8%	53.8%	46.2%	18.4%	57.1%	42.9%
Fordham University (NY)	0.38	0.3%	6.9%	5.9%	9.1%	75.9%	2.0%	51.3%	48.7%	14.5%	61.2%	38.8%
Touro College (Fuchsberg) (NY)	0.38	0.3%	6.2%	8.9%	6.2%	76.6%	1.8%	51.9%	48.1%	13.1%	62.3%	37.7%
University of Washington	0.38	2.6%	13.2%	2.1%	4.2%	74.9%	3.0%	45.1%	54.9%	13.0%	62.0%	38.0%
Arizona State University (O'Connor)	0.37	6.4%	3.3%	2.1%	9.2%	77.1%	1.9%	56.6%	43.4%	10.1%	73.4%	26.6%
George Washington University (DC)	0.37	0.8%	9.4%	5.1%	6.0%	76.7%	2.1%	58.0%	42.0%	13.6%	63.9%	36.1%
Ohio State University (Moritz)	0.37	0.3%	7.8%	8.1%	5.2%	77.9%	0.7%	57.2%	42.8%	12.3%	70.2%	29.8%
Syracuse University (NY)	0.37	0.5%	11.9%	3.6%	4.8%	74.8%	4.3%	58.5%	41.5%	22.2%	66.7%	33.3%
University of Detroit Mercy	0.37	0.5%	4.0%	10.7%	2.5%	62.1%	20.3%	54.1%	45.9%	5.4%	62.2%	37.8%
Baylor University (Umphrey) (TX)	0.36	0.2%	9.0%	2.6%	9.0%	79.1%	0.0%	52.9%	47.1%	10.0%	80.0%	20.0%
University of Connecticut	0.36	0.6%	8.0%	5.8%	6.2%	78.2%	1.2%	54.6%	45.4%	12.5%	73.9%	26.1%
University of Oklahoma	0.36	8.5%	4.5%	4.2%	3.6%	78.7%	0.4%	56.7%	43.3%	8.2%	63.3%	36.7%
Yeshiva University (Cardozo) (NY)	0.36	0.3%	9.2%	4.6%	6.4%	76.9%	2.6%	49.9%	50.1%	8.3%	66.2%	33.8%
Chapman University (CA)	0.35	0.6%	14.2%	1.1%	5.0%	78.5%	0.6%	50.6%	49.4%	41.9%	73.3%	26.7%
Lewis & Clark College (NW) (OR)	0.35	2.4%	9.0%	3.1%	5.2%	77.8%	2.7%	51.5%	48.5%	9.2%	63.3%	36.7%
Pennsylvania State Univ. (Dickinson)	0.35	0.3%	8.4%	5.5%	6.2%	79.6%	0.0%	60.0%	40.0%	11.8%	55.9%	44.1%
Univ. of Arkansas–Little Rock (Bowen)	0.35	1.1%	2.5%	12.1%	4.2%	77.9%	2.1%	52.4%	47.6%	10.8%	65.7%	34.3%
University of Colorado–Boulder	0.35	3.1%	7.1%	2.7%	7.3%	79.2%	0.5%	50.1%	49.9%	16.1%	66.1%	33.9%
University of Tennessee–Knoxville	0.35	0.8%	4.2%	11.9%	3.4%	78.8%	0.8%	52.9%	47.1%	4.3%	66.7%	33.3%
University of Virginia	0.35	1.4%	8.4%	5.3%	4.5%	79.4%	0.9%	55.9%	44.1%	7.3%	76.8%	23.2%

What are the most and least diverse law schools?

School	Diversity index	American Indian	Asian	Black	Hispanic	White	International	Men	Women	Minority faculty	Male faculty	Female faculty
Catholic Univ. of America (DC)	0.34	0.4%	10.6%	4.6%	3.1%	77.5%	3.7%	48.7%	51.3%	9.2%	64.2%	35.8%
Georgia State University	0.34	0.6%	7.4%	9.1%	2.5%	80.4%	0.0%	52.7%	47.3%	19.0%	56.9%	43.1%
Illinois Inst. of Tech (Chicago-Kent)	0.34	0.3%	9.3%	5.2%	4.4%	78.3%	2.5%	54.0%	46.0%	9.9%	71.7%	28.3%
New York Law School	0.34	0.2%	5.0%	6.1%	8.6%	80.1%	0.0%	49.6%	50.4%	11.8%	64.6%	35.4%
Stetson University (FL)	0.34	0.8%	3.3%	6.8%	8.7%	79.9%	0.5%	47.4%	52.6%	10.4%	61.3%	38.7%
Washington and Lee University (VA)	0.34	1.5%	5.4%	7.9%	3.8%	79.0%	2.3%	56.9%	43.1%	10.7%	82.1%	17.9%
Franklin Pierce Law Center (NH)	0.33	0.2%	9.3%	5.4%	3.5%	76.9%	4.7%	62.2%	37.8%	4.3%	60.9%	39.1%
Rutgers–Camden (NJ)	0.33	0.1%	8.4%	5.6%	4.8%	80.7%	0.4%	59.5%	40.5%	8.1%	62.6%	37.4%
Drexel University (Mack) (PA)	0.32	1.0%	3.7%	6.6%	6.6%	79.8%	2.4%	52.4%	47.6%	12.2%	55.1%	44.9%
Indiana Univ.–Bloomington (Maurer)	0.32	0.0%	6.0%	7.4%	4.7%	81.9%	0.0%	58.5%	41.5%	11.6%	75.4%	24.6%
University of Oregon	0.32	2.0%	9.6%	2.9%	3.7%	81.1%	0.7%	55.3%	44.7%	25.0%	48.1%	51.9%
Ave Maria School of Law (FL)	0.31	0.5%	4.5%	3.5%	8.5%	80.5%	2.4%	57.3%	42.7%	0.0%	77.4%	22.6%
Howard University (DC)	0.31	1.1%	5.1%	78.2%	2.8%	7.5%	5.3%	39.3%	60.7%	72.4%	56.6%	43.4%
Pace University (NY)	0.31	0.1%	6.8%	4.1%	6.4%	81.4%	1.1%	41.5%	58.5%	7.3%	63.4%	36.6%
University of Arkansas–Fayetteville	0.31	2.8%	2.5%	9.3%	2.8%	82.4%	0.3%	59.0%	41.0%	8.7%	63.0%	37.0%
University of Denver (Sturm)	0.31	2.0%	5.7%	2.7%	7.4%	82.3%	0.0%	52.8%	47.2%	7.4%	70.5%	29.5%
University of Georgia	0.31	0.1%	4.5%	12.0%	1.3%	81.8%	0.3%	52.6%	47.4%	8.9%	67.9%	32.1%
University of Kansas	0.31	3.8%	5.4%	3.0%	4.2%	79.2%	4.4%	60.1%	39.9%	10.9%	60.9%	39.1%
Vanderbilt University (TN)	0.31	0.5%	3.5%	9.1%	3.9%	80.1%	2.9%	51.5%	48.5%	12.1%	59.1%	40.9%
Villanova University (PA)	0.31	0.4%	8.6%	2.0%	6.2%	82.0%	0.8%	56.0%	44.0%	12.9%	72.3%	27.7%
Charlotte School of Law (NC)	0.30	1.2%	1.2%	8.5%	6.2%	82.7%	0.0%	50.1%	49.9%	40.0%	51.4%	48.6%
Florida State University	0.30	0.4%	1.8%	8.4%	6.6%	82.7%	0.1%	58.8%	41.2%	11.3%	64.8%	35.2%
George Mason University (VA)	0.30	0.4%	10.5%	2.6%	3.6%	81.6%	1.3%	58.2%	41.8%	8.2%	75.9%	24.1%
Loyola University Chicago	0.30	0.5%	4.9%	5.6%	5.5%	82.5%	1.1%	47.1%	52.9%	8.7%	57.1%	42.9%
Oklahoma City University	0.30	5.3%	3.0%	3.4%	4.7%	82.7%	1.0%	59.4%	40.6%	8.3%	60.4%	39.6%
Tulane University (LA)	0.30	1.4%	2.5%	7.2%	5.2%	81.5%	2.2%	59.4%	40.6%	9.6%	75.3%	24.7%
Wake Forest University (NC)	0.30	0.8%	3.4%	8.8%	4.0%	82.8%	0.2%	58.2%	41.8%	8.8%	66.7%	33.3%
Willamette University (Collins) (OR)	0.30	1.4%	7.5%	1.6%	6.1%	82.9%	0.5%	57.3%	42.7%	14.3%	68.6%	31.4%
Barry University (FL)	0.29	0.0%	4.2%	3.8%	8.7%	83.4%	0.0%	55.1%	44.9%	12.9%	67.7%	32.3%
Mercer University (George) (GA)	0.29	0.7%	5.1%	9.0%	1.6%	83.5%	0.0%	53.4%	46.6%	8.7%	69.6%	30.4%
Pepperdine University (CA)	0.29	0.4%	8.4%	3.6%	3.9%	83.7%	0.0%	50.4%	49.6%	6.9%	46.3%	53.8%
University of Cincinnati	0.29	0.3%	7.7%	5.9%	2.3%	83.9%	0.0%	57.8%	42.2%	10.8%	60.0%	40.0%
University of Iowa	0.29	1.0%	6.1%	3.6%	4.7%	81.4%	3.2%	55.8%	44.2%	10.3%	69.2%	30.8%
Univ. of Minnesota–Twin Cities	0.29	1.4%	8.2%	2.9%	3.4%	81.3%	2.7%	58.4%	41.6%	5.4%	57.0%	43.0%
Univ. of Richmond (Williams) (VA)	0.29	0.9%	6.0%	9.0%	0.6%	82.8%	0.6%	52.3%	47.7%	6.2%	69.1%	30.9%
University of Tulsa (OK)	0.29	9.5%	2.8%	0.9%	2.8%	83.6%	0.2%	61.1%	38.9%	13.2%	58.5%	41.5%
Valparaiso University (IN)	0.29	0.7%	2.7%	7.4%	5.5%	82.5%	1.2%	52.4%	47.6%	10.5%	63.2%	36.8%
Brigham Young Univ. (Clark) (UT)	0.28	1.1%	7.8%	1.6%	5.1%	83.4%	0.9%	65.3%	34.7%	10.0%	71.7%	28.3%
College of William and Mary (VA)	0.28	0.0%	2.9%	12.1%	0.8%	83.2%	1.0%	50.8%	49.2%	13.9%	68.4%	31.6%
Indiana University–Indianapolis	0.28	0.3%	4.3%	7.5%	3.0%	80.6%	4.2%	55.1%	44.9%	6.9%	64.6%	35.4%
Seton Hall University (NJ)	0.28	0.1%	7.2%	3.3%	4.9%	83.4%	1.1%	54.4%	45.6%	11.1%	56.3%	43.7%
St. Louis University	0.28	0.6%	5.2%	6.9%	3.0%	84.0%	0.3%	52.8%	47.2%	16.7%	63.3%	36.7%
University of Pittsburgh	0.28	0.1%	6.3%	6.7%	2.6%	84.2%	0.0%	54.4%	45.6%	10.2%	65.9%	34.1%
Wayne State University (MI)	0.28	1.1%	4.2%	7.7%	2.3%	81.7%	3.0%	49.7%	50.3%	8.6%	70.7%	29.3%
Marquette University (WI)	0.27	0.9%	3.6%	4.6%	5.5%	85.3%	0.0%	56.0%	44.0%	11.1%	68.5%	31.5%
Regent University (VA)	0.27	1.4%	4.8%	6.7%	2.2%	83.9%	1.0%	51.3%	48.7%	12.0%	76.0%	24.0%
University at Buffalo–SUNY	0.27	0.6%	5.6%	4.7%	4.0%	85.1%	0.0%	54.4%	45.6%	12.5%	70.5%	29.5%
Cleveland State Univ. (Marshall)	0.26	0.3%	2.8%	8.8%	2.7%	84.5%	0.9%	58.5%	41.5%	14.1%	62.0%	38.0%
Michigan State University	0.26	1.5%	3.8%	5.3%	2.7%	79.0%	7.7%	60.9%	39.1%	15.1%	70.9%	29.1%
Suffolk University (MA)	0.26	0.4%	7.1%	2.5%	4.1%	84.1%	1.8%	52.7%	47.3%	10.7%	67.9%	32.1%
University of Akron (OH)	0.26	0.6%	3.5%	7.0%	3.5%	85.5%	0.0%	54.5%	45.5%	9.6%	65.4%	34.6%

What are the most and least diverse law schools?

School	Diversity index	American Indian	Asian	Black	Hispanic	White	International	Men	Women	Minority faculty	Male faculty	Female faculty
University of Alabama	0.26	0.7%	2.7%	9.1%	1.8%	85.6%	0.0%	58.0%	42.0%	12.1%	75.8%	24.2%
University of Baltimore	0.26	0.3%	5.6%	6.2%	2.3%	85.0%	0.6%	48.4%	51.6%	14.3%	63.9%	36.1%
University of Dayton (OH)	0.26	0.6%	2.6%	7.4%	3.4%	85.0%	1.0%	58.0%	42.0%	8.9%	64.3%	35.7%
Louisiana State Univ.–Baton Rouge	0.25	1.2%	2.3%	4.3%	5.5%	86.1%	0.5%	55.0%	45.0%	5.8%	78.8%	21.2%
University of Kentucky	0.25	0.7%	2.2%	8.9%	2.0%	86.0%	0.2%	55.7%	44.3%	8.9%	75.6%	24.4%
University of Memphis (Humphreys)	0.25	0.7%	2.1%	9.5%	1.7%	85.7%	0.2%	57.9%	42.1%	11.4%	65.9%	34.1%
University of Mississippi	0.25	0.8%	0.8%	12.1%	0.8%	85.5%	0.0%	56.6%	43.4%	14.7%	67.6%	32.4%
University of Missouri	0.25	0.7%	3.6%	6.5%	2.9%	86.1%	0.2%	61.6%	38.4%	11.5%	73.1%	26.9%
University of St. Thomas (MN)	0.25	0.2%	6.3%	4.2%	2.8%	86.4%	0.0%	54.5%	45.5%	14.6%	64.6%	35.4%
Case Western Reserve University (OH)	0.24	0.9%	7.0%	3.4%	1.3%	83.4%	3.9%	57.7%	42.3%	4.2%	67.6%	32.4%
Hamline University (MN)	0.24	0.8%	4.9%	3.4%	4.0%	85.8%	1.1%	46.3%	53.7%	8.8%	56.3%	43.8%
Ohio Northern University (Pettit)	0.24	0.7%	3.6%	7.2%	2.0%	86.6%	0.0%	58.0%	42.0%	10.3%	65.5%	34.5%
Quinnipiac University (CT)	0.24	0.7%	5.1%	3.1%	3.9%	84.6%	2.7%	48.9%	51.1%	5.0%	68.3%	31.7%
University of Utah (Quinney)	0.24	2.0%	3.5%	1.8%	6.0%	86.8%	0.0%	59.0%	41.0%	9.7%	67.7%	32.3%
Washburn University (KS)	0.24	1.4%	2.9%	4.1%	4.5%	86.6%	0.5%	59.4%	40.6%	6.0%	60.7%	39.3%
Albany Law School (NY)	0.23	0.7%	4.8%	2.4%	4.1%	86.6%	2.0%	56.1%	43.9%	15.8%	56.6%	43.4%
University of Idaho	0.23	2.6%	0.9%	0.9%	7.9%	86.8%	0.9%	66.7%	33.3%	5.3%	55.3%	44.7%
University of Missouri–Kansas City	0.23	0.8%	2.5%	6.0%	3.3%	86.0%	1.4%	59.6%	40.4%	8.7%	65.2%	34.8%
Widener University (DE)	0.23	0.5%	4.5%	4.8%	2.8%	87.3%	0.1%	54.6%	45.4%	7.6%	65.5%	34.5%
Capital University (OH)	0.21	0.2%	2.3%	8.0%	1.2%	88.3%	0.0%	54.5%	45.5%	10.7%	69.6%	30.4%
Elon University (NC)	0.21	0.3%	3.2%	5.7%	1.9%	88.9%	0.0%	54.9%	45.1%	7.1%	64.3%	35.7%
Faulkner University (Jones) (AL)	0.21	1.5%	1.5%	7.0%	1.5%	88.6%	0.0%	62.2%	37.8%	16.7%	70.8%	29.2%
Mississippi College	0.21	0.4%	1.3%	9.3%	0.7%	88.1%	0.2%	58.0%	42.0%	12.8%	54.1%	45.9%
University of South Carolina	0.21	0.1%	1.9%	8.5%	1.3%	88.2%	0.0%	58.4%	41.6%	10.4%	62.5%	37.5%
Western New England College (MA)	0.21	0.4%	4.5%	3.2%	3.5%	87.9%	0.6%	47.4%	52.6%	10.9%	60.9%	39.1%
Campbell University (Wiggins) (NC)	0.20	0.2%	2.2%	3.7%	4.4%	88.9%	0.5%	50.4%	49.6%	5.1%	76.9%	23.1%
University of North Dakota	0.20	3.6%	1.2%	2.4%	2.8%	82.6%	7.3%	54.7%	45.3%	9.5%	57.1%	42.9%
Creighton University (NE)	0.19	0.2%	3.9%	2.3%	3.7%	89.7%	0.2%	57.6%	42.4%	6.7%	71.1%	28.9%
Drake University (IA)	0.19	0.2%	1.5%	6.4%	2.1%	88.2%	1.5%	55.5%	44.5%	6.5%	67.4%	32.6%
New England School of Law (MA)	0.19	0.2%	5.4%	1.9%	2.5%	90.1%	0.0%	44.5%	55.5%	13.6%	62.1%	37.9%
Roger Williams University (RI)	0.19	0.5%	2.4%	2.4%	5.1%	88.7%	0.9%	49.1%	50.9%	9.3%	70.4%	29.6%
University of Toledo (OH)	0.19	0.0%	3.0%	3.9%	2.8%	88.2%	2.0%	59.8%	40.2%	8.7%	63.0%	37.0%
University of Wyoming	0.19	0.9%	3.1%	0.9%	5.3%	89.3%	0.4%	52.0%	48.0%	11.1%	66.7%	33.3%
Appalachian School of Law (VA)	0.18	0.6%	1.8%	4.8%	2.4%	89.8%	0.6%	62.9%	37.1%	19.0%	71.4%	28.6%
Northern Kentucky University (Chase)	0.18	0.3%	2.5%	5.4%	1.5%	90.3%	0.0%	53.5%	46.5%	7.9%	73.7%	26.3%
William Mitchell College of Law (MN)	0.18	1.0%	4.8%	2.3%	1.5%	90.0%	0.4%	50.3%	49.7%	24.5%	57.4%	42.6%
Charleston School of Law (SC)	0.16	0.2%	0.9%	6.4%	0.9%	91.7%	0.0%	55.5%	44.5%	9.3%	61.1%	38.9%
Gonzaga University (WA)	0.16	1.1%	4.0%	0.4%	2.9%	91.6%	0.0%	60.5%	39.5%	3.4%	63.8%	36.2%
Southern Illinois Univ.–Carbondale	0.16	0.5%	2.3%	3.4%	2.1%	91.4%	0.3%	62.4%	37.6%	8.1%	56.8%	43.2%
University of Louisville (Brandeis) (KY)	0.16	0.0%	2.3%	3.9%	2.1%	90.3%	1.4%	54.7%	45.3%	8.3%	58.3%	41.7%
University of Maine	0.16	1.5%	2.7%	1.9%	2.3%	90.5%	1.1%	57.6%	42.4%	0.0%	72.4%	27.6%
Vermont Law School	0.16	0.4%	2.8%	2.8%	2.6%	90.3%	1.1%	49.9%	50.1%	10.4%	60.4%	39.6%
Samford University (Cumberland) (AL)	0.15	1.0%	0.8%	5.3%	0.8%	91.5%	0.6%	54.8%	45.2%	11.6%	67.4%	32.6%
West Virginia University	0.15	0.2%	1.7%	5.7%	0.2%	92.1%	0.0%	69.8%		11.3%	69.8%	30.2%
University of Nebraska–Lincoln	0.14	0.5%	1.8%	2.8%	2.3%	92.1%	0.5%	60.2%	39.8%	2.1%	72.3%	27.7%
Duquesne University (PA)	0.12	0.1%	2.1%	3.0%	1.1%	93.2%	0.4%	48.6%	51.4%	8.3%	66.7%	33.3%
University of South Dakota	0.12	4.0%	0.5%	1.5%	1.5%	93.6%	0.0%	49.0%	51.0%	0.0%	68.8%	31.3%

The total cost of a JD degree can easily top $150,000 at the most expensive schools, once you factor in living expenses. (And that's not counting lost income, since you won't be working full-time while you're in school.) Private law schools are listed here by tuition and fees for the 2009-2010 academic year, with the most expensive on top. Public institutions follow, sorted by in-state tuition so you can easily see what you might save by sticking close to home.

Private Schools

School	Total tuition and fees	Room and board	Books	Other expenses
Cornell University (NY)	$48,950	$11,000	$850	$6,450
Yale University (CT)	$48,340	$16,000	$1,100	$1,800
Columbia University (NY)	$48,004	$16,190	$1,448	$3,625
Northwestern University (IL)	$47,472	$12,376	$1,418	$6,555
University of Pennsylvania	$46,514	$12,654	$1,225	$5,217
University of Southern California (Gould)	$46,264	$15,842	$1,664	$4,148
Duke University (NC)	$45,271	$10,304	$1,260	$5,128
Yeshiva University (Cardozo) (NY)	$45,170	$18,400	$1,200	$4,771
Fordham University (NY)	$44,996	$17,690	$1,600	$5,204
Syracuse University (NY)	$44,856	$11,830	$1,300	$5,394
New York University	$44,820	$20,914	$1,370	$2,946
New York Law School	$44,800	$16,840	$1,300	$4,215
University of Chicago	$44,757	$13,455	$1,650	$7,194
Stanford University (CA)	$44,121	$18,603	$1,815	$3,321
Vanderbilt University (TN)	$44,074	$12,900	$1,720	$7,328
Brooklyn Law School (NY)	$43,990	$16,420	$1,100	$4,825
Harvard University (MA)	$43,900	$18,457	$1,100	$3,317
Georgetown University (DC)	$43,750	$16,240	$1,025	$4,985
Seton Hall University (NJ)	$42,980	$13,050	$1,200	$5,355
Washington University in St. Louis	$42,330	$11,000	$2,000	$6,600
George Washington University (DC)	$42,205	$14,200	$1,295	$7,200
St. John's University (NY)	$42,200	$16,677	$1,400	$4,140
Hofstra University (NY)	$41,780	$13,772	$1,400	$5,401
American University (Washington) (DC)	$41,406	$14,623	$1,038	$5,724
Emory University (GA)	$41,376	$17,748	$3,126	$3,588
Quinnipiac University (CT)	$40,780	$8,949	$1,200	$9,315
Tulane University (LA)	$40,644	$12,100	$1,500	$5,770
Loyola Marymount University (CA)	$40,530	$15,806	$1,050	$9,052
Vermont Law School	$40,420	$10,080	$1,500	$9,480
University of San Diego	$40,014	$12,080	$1,129	$7,391
Northeastern University (MA)	$39,866	$15,414	$1,500	$2,875
Pace University (NY)	$39,794	$15,720	$1,800	$2,154
Suffolk University (MA)	$39,670	$8,950	$900	$5,844
Boston University	$39,658	$11,808	$1,374	$4,394
Boston College	$39,490	$12,785	$1,300	$4,971
Pepperdine University (CA)	$39,340	$16,366	$980	$5,100
University of Notre Dame (IN)	$39,320	$8,500	$1,400	$6,500
Touro College (Fuchsberg) (NY)	$39,130	$18,691	$1,500	$3,369
Albany Law School (NY)	$39,050	$10,100	$1,100	$7,100

Who's the priciest? Who's the cheapest?

Private Schools

School	Total tuition and fees	Room and board	Books	Other expenses
Case Western Reserve University (OH)	$38,679	$16,405	$1,525	$1,320
University of the Pacific (McGeorge) (CA)	$38,629	$9,738	$1,600	$11,720
New England School of Law (MA)	$38,580	$11,950	$1,250	$4,925
Baylor University (Umphrey) (TX)	$38,408	$9,273	$2,007	$5,541
Southern Methodist University (Dedman) (TX)	$38,406	$14,000	$1,800	$2,600
California Western School of Law	$38,400	$11,600	$1,300	$9,098
Illinois Institute of Technology (Chicago-Kent)	$38,152	$14,400	$1,200	$4,509
Washington and Lee University (VA)	$38,062	$10,315	$2,000	$6,728
University of Miami (FL)	$38,012	$13,302	$1,200	$7,161
DePaul University (IL)	$37,975	$20,907	$1,500	N/A
Chapman University (CA)	$37,950	$15,300	$1,560	$8,082
Catholic University of America (Columbus) (DC)	$37,850	$15,800	$1,750	$8,500
University of San Francisco	$37,310	$13,500	$1,500	$5,660
Whittier College (CA)	$37,060	$16,944	$1,740	$8,376
Franklin Pierce Law Center (NH)	$36,980	$11,250	$1,400	$7,014
Southwestern Law School (CA)	$36,950	$19,620	$1,250	$5,949
Loyola University Chicago	$36,770	$13,200	$1,300	$5,498
Golden Gate University (CA)	$36,600	$14,400	$1,200	$7,915
Thomas Jefferson School of Law (CA)	$36,300	N/A	N/A	N/A
University of Denver (Sturm)	$35,700	$9,963	$1,749	$4,825
Western New England College (MA)	$35,612	$13,400	$1,528	$6,465
Wake Forest University (NC)	$35,450	$8,810	$1,200	$6,600
Seattle University	$35,406	$11,448	$1,258	$5,137
Ave Maria School of Law (FL)	$35,380	$13,131	$900	$6,368
John Marshall Law School (IL)	$35,380	$15,230	$2,226	$7,448
Villanova University (PA)	$35,250	$14,850	$1,400	$3,445
Valparaiso University (IN)	$35,230	$8,800	$1,200	$2,760
University of St. Thomas (MN)	$34,756	N/A	N/A	N/A
Charleston School of Law (SC)	$34,568	$7,700	$1,020	$4,300
St. Louis University	$34,362	$11,988	$1,660	$5,764
Mercer University (George) (GA)	$34,330	$9,630	$1,380	$4,990
Loyola University New Orleans	$34,166	$13,200	$1,550	$5,550
Widener University (DE)	$33,540	$9,900	$1,200	$5,364
Charlotte School of Law (NC)	$33,166	$11,415	$1,925	$5,273
Western State University (CA)	$32,870	$14,018	$1,500	$7,299
Michigan State University	$32,828	$10,886	$1,368	$1,736
University of Dayton (OH)	$32,684	$13,000	$1,500	$0
Florida Coastal School of Law	$32,662	$9,819	$1,300	$8,460
University of Richmond (Williams) (VA)	$32,450	$10,530	$1,300	$3,440
Marquette University (WI)	$32,410	$11,735	$1,345	$6,160
William Mitchell College of Law (MN)	$32,340	$14,500	$1,550	$800
Drexel University (Mack) (PA)	$32,200	N/A	N/A	N/A
University of Detroit Mercy	$32,090	$11,340	$1,920	$7,496
Hamline University (MN)	$32,014	$15,360	$1,200	N/A
Lewis & Clark College (Northwestern) (OR)	$31,934	$11,250	$1,050	$5,400
Samford University (Cumberland) (AL)	$31,733	$13,500	$2,000	$6,720
Barry University (FL)	$31,700	$13,340	$1,800	$8,590
Gonzaga University (WA)	$31,460	$8,775	$1,000	$4,629
Stetson University (FL)	$31,420	$10,248	$1,800	$8,774
Drake University (IA)	$31,186	$10,000	$1,300	$6,710
Nova Southeastern University (Broad) (FL)	$31,172	$16,281	$2,626	$6,318

Who's the priciest? Who's the cheapest?

Private Schools

School	Total tuition and fees	Room and board	Books	Other expenses
Duquesne University (PA)	$30,866	$9,858	$1,100	$1,150
Campbell University (Wiggins) (NC)	$30,850	$15,370	$1,400	$2,500
Elon University (NC)	$30,750	$12,000	$1,600	$8,400
Faulkner University (Jones) (AL)	$30,500	$14,000	$3,000	$5,400
Creighton University (NE)	$30,294	$13,500	$3,085	$4,070
Willamette University (Collins) (OR)	$29,680	$14,510	$1,460	$80
University of Tulsa (OK)	$29,040	$7,000	$1,500	$6,810
Ohio Northern University (Pettit)	$28,600	$9,880	$1,200	$2,500
St. Mary's University (TX)	$27,404	$8,225	$1,385	$5,834
Appalachian School of Law (VA)	$27,025	$13,900	$900	$1,400
Mississippi College	$26,300	$12,000	$1,200	$7,650
Texas Wesleyan University	$26,000	$10,521	$1,740	$2,114
South Texas College of Law	$25,710	$9,500	$2,000	$7,200
Howard University (DC)	$24,490	$13,247	$2,000	$6,494
Brigham Young University (Clark) (UT)	$9,980	$8,400	$1,850	$4,690

Public Schools

School	In-state tuition and fees	Out-of-state tuition and fees	Room and board	Books	Other expenses
University of Michigan–Ann Arbor	$43,250	$46,250	$11,386	$1,050	$5,064
University of Virginia	$38,800	$43,800	$14,050	$1,800	$3,350
University of Illinois–Urbana-Champaign	$36,420	$43,420	$10,964	$1,750	$2,760
University of California–Berkeley	$35,907	$48,152	$15,485	$1,495	$4,741
University of California–Los Angeles	$35,327	$45,967	$13,968	$1,941	$5,160
Pennsylvania State University (Dickinson)	$34,462	$34,462	$10,674	$1,360	$8,892
University of California–Davis	$33,949	$44,895	$11,584	$1,014	$3,734
University of California (Hastings)	$32,468	$43,693	$14,040	$1,150	$4,708
University of Minnesota–Twin Cities	$28,203	$37,605	$1,666	$9,612	$2,750
University of Texas–Austin	$27,177	$42,814	$9,980	$1,076	$4,020
University of Colorado–Boulder	$25,399	$33,463	$8,478	$1,749	$5,570
University of Pittsburgh	$25,098	$33,094	$15,054	$1,530	$730
Indiana University–Bloomington (Maurer)	$24,891	$40,691	$9,407	$1,800	$4,709
University of Baltimore	$23,992	$35,988	$13,100	$1,600	$6,380
Rutgers–Camden (NJ)	$23,860	$34,360	$11,465	$1,313	$2,383
University of Maryland	$23,762	$35,041	$19,350	$1,725	$7,484
Wayne State University (MI)	$23,713	$25,919	$12,350	$1,240	$9,090
Rutgers–Newark (NJ)	$23,676	$33,740	$11,465	$1,313	$3,286
Ohio State University (Moritz)	$22,433	$37,383	$8,172	$3,860	$6,080
University of Oregon	$22,328	$27,818	$10,260	$1,050	$2,556
University of Washington	$22,267	$32,777	$12,876	$1,206	$3,789
Coll. of William and Mary (Marshall-Wythe) (VA)	$21,646	$31,846	$8,882	$1,250	$2,836
University of Iowa	$21,432	$39,138	$9,900	$2,300	$4,530
University of Houston (TX)	$21,029	$28,439	$9,234	$1,100	$5,122
University of Arizona (Rogers)	$20,895	$35,807	$11,840	$816	$8,094
University of Maine	$20,702	$31,202	$10,444	$1,400	$3,628

Who's the priciest? Who's the cheapest?

Public Schools

School	In-state tuition and fees	Out-of-state tuition and fees	Room and board	Books	Other expenses
George Mason University (VA)	$20,556	$34,220	$16,220	$1,100	$5,400
University of Connecticut	$20,374	$42,094	$11,800	$1,200	$4,300
University of Cincinnati	$19,942	$34,776	$10,596	$1,275	$4,575
University of Akron (OH)	$19,570	$30,850	$14,247	$1,157	N/A
Arizona State University (O'Connor)	$19,225	$32,619	$10,660	$1,850	$7,534
University of Toledo (OH)	$19,137	$29,553	$10,440	$1,164	$4,784
University of South Carolina	$19,034	$38,014	$11,661	$936	$4,070
University of Nevada–Las Vegas (Boyd)	$18,838	$30,838	$15,925	$1,700	$250
Indiana University–Indianapolis	$18,163	$38,478	$11,296	$1,700	$8,128
University of Utah (Quinney)	$17,948	$34,044	$9,360	$2,784	$4,950
Temple University (Beasley) (PA)	$17,226	$29,516	$11,416	$1,500	$7,138
University of Oklahoma	$16,976	$26,904	$11,781	$1,235	$3,658
Cleveland State University (Cleveland-Marshall)	$16,764	$22,995	$13,000	$1,500	$4,300
University of Wisconsin–Madison	$16,426	$36,350	$8,740	$2,250	$6,000
Texas Tech University	$16,200	$23,610	$8,110	$1,000	$4,366
University of Kentucky	$16,020	$27,758	$11,050	$900	$3,192
University of Missouri	$16,017	$30,519	$8,590	$1,550	$6,884
University of North Carolina–Chapel Hill	$16,014	$29,332	$12,920	$1,000	$4,012
University at Buffalo–SUNY	$16,010	$24,260	$10,980	$1,627	$3,381
University of Hawaii–Manoa (Richardson)	$15,581	$28,565	$12,802	$1,123	$1,674
Northern Illinois University	$14,847	$27,351	$10,032	$1,500	$4,080
Northern Kentucky University (Chase)	$14,812	$32,232	$9,956	$1,000	$0
University of Louisville (Brandeis) (KY)	$14,632	$29,172	$8,490	$1,000	$7,240
University of Kansas	$14,478	$25,375	$10,002	$900	$5,284
University of Alabama	$14,450	$26,785	$10,400	$1,400	$4,667
University of Georgia	$14,448	$30,226	$10,600	$1,400	$3,320
Louisiana State Univ.–Baton Rouge (Hebert)	$14,350	$25,446	$13,377	$2,500	$2,204
University of Missouri–Kansas City	$14,242	$27,262	$8,970	$4,470	$7,350
Florida State University	$14,239	$31,250	$10,000	$1,300	$7,000
University of Florida (Levin)	$14,228	$33,593	$8,170	$990	$3,940
Southern Illinois University–Carbondale	$14,137	$33,040	$10,458	$1,150	$2,520
University of Memphis (Humphreys)	$13,710	$35,582	$8,731	$1,700	$4,401
Texas Southern University (Marshall)	$13,235	$16,985	$12,380	$1,918	$4,394
University of Tennessee–Knoxville	$13,118	$31,862	$10,060	$1,606	$3,676
University of New Mexico	$12,620	$28,235	$8,180	$1,082	$4,884
Florida International University	$12,450	$26,250	$16,532	$2,652	$4,832
University of Nebraska–Lincoln	$12,154	$26,600	$7,900	$1,340	$3,538
Georgia State University	$11,838	$32,862	$9,000	$1,500	$4,084
University of Idaho	$11,776	$21,856	$9,292	$1,474	$4,038
University of Arkansas–Little Rock (Bowen)	$11,456	$23,538	$7,726	$1,250	$4,160
University of South Dakota	$10,695	$20,575	$6,970	$1,400	$4,838
West Virginia University	$10,644	$24,010	$8,900	$1,250	$2,840
University of Montana	$10,620	$24,333	$12,000	$1,200	$486
CUNY–Queens College	$10,612	$16,512	$7,425	$1,711	$8,691
University of Wyoming	$9,966	$21,156	$10,919	$1,200	$2,200
University of North Dakota	$9,461	$20,476	$8,750	$1,100	$4,950
University of Mississippi	$9,350	$20,440	$12,800	$1,300	$4,660
Florida A&M University	$9,036	$28,302	$10,450	$1,000	$6,000
North Carolina Central University	$8,097	$20,835	$17,095	$2,100	$600
University of the District of Columbia (Clarke)	$7,350	$14,700	N/A	N/A	N/A

What schools award the most and the least financial aid?

Compared to what you're going to need, you may be surprised at how little you get: Law schools assume that their students can afford to borrow to pay the bills because they'll easily make enough after graduation to manage the loan payments. However, students whose LSAT scores and undergraduate grades put them near the top of a law school's applicant pool may find a generous merit award on the table.

Private Schools

School	Median grant	% of students receiving grants	Grants range (25th–75th percentile)	Grants of full tuition	Grants of more than full tuition
Chapman University (CA)	$28,760	45%	$14,380-$35,950	9%	5%
Drexel University (Mack) (PA)	$24,347	91%	$14,775-$30,800	11%	N/A
Michigan State University	$23,814	31%	$15,232-$31,552	14%	0%
St. John's University (NY)	$22,500	43%	$12,500-$40,600	13%	1%
Stanford University (CA)	$22,178	48%	$12,749-$33,380	2%	1%
Yale University (CT)	$21,410	51%	$11,300-$28,300	0%	0%
University of San Diego	$21,000	43%	$17,000-$29,000	2%	4%
Loyola Marymount University (CA)	$20,500	33%	$15,000-$27,000	N/A	2%
Illinois Inst. of Tech (Chicago-Kent)	$20,000	60%	$9,121-$20,000	7%	3%
Mercer University (George) (GA)	$20,000	31%	$10,000-$33,190	8%	5%
New York University	$20,000	35%	$10,000-$25,000	8%	0%
Northwestern University (IL)	$20,000	34%	$15,000-$30,000	0%	0%
Ohio Northern University (Pettit)	$20,000	54%	$15,000-$23,000	3%	0%
Quinnipiac University (CT)	$20,000	71%	$6,000-$25,000	9%	0%
Samford University (Cumberland) (AL)	$20,000	34%	$3,539-$29,556	9%	5%
Seton Hall University (NJ)	$20,000	50%	$10,000-$30,000	0%	0%
University of Miami (FL)	$20,000	31%	$10,000-$23,000	1%	1%
University of St. Thomas (MN)	$20,000	59%	$8,000-$28,233	21%	N/A
Washington University in St. Louis	$20,000	61%	$12,000-$25,000	6%	3%
Yeshiva University (Cardozo) (NY)	$20,000	58%	$10,000-$30,000	7%	1%
William Mitchell College of Law (MN)	$19,923	41%	$13,793-$23,813	1%	0%
California Western School of Law	$18,120	41%	$9,060-$36,240	5%	4%
Hamline University (MN)	$18,058	59%	$12,038-$30,096	16%	1%
Albany Law School (NY)	$18,000	32%	$10,000-$25,000	3%	0%
Cornell University (NY)	$18,000	35%	$10,450-$25,000	0%	0%
Emory University (GA)	$18,000	68%	$18,000-$30,000	1%	2%
Southern Methodist Univ. (Dedman) (TX)	$18,000	96%	$4,996-$22,996	2%	4%
University of San Francisco	$18,000	39%	$7,500-$23,000	0%	0%
St. Louis University	$17,740	47%	$8,870-$26,610	5%	0%
University of Denver (Sturm)	$17,600	37%	$10,000-$21,900	5%	N/A
Brooklyn Law School (NY)	$17,164	75%	$8,960-$31,064	0%	7%
Boston College	$16,678	50%	$10,000-$20,000	0%	0%
Valparaiso University (IN)	$16,250	26%	$8,125-$24,375	6%	4%
Hofstra University (NY)	$16,000	42%	$8,000-$25,000	4%	0%
Appalachian School of Law (VA)	$15,582	26%	$7,791-$23,373	11%	N/A
Harvard University (MA)	$15,490	46%	$7,598-$25,995	1%	0%
Stetson University (FL)	$15,250	20%	$5,000-$30,500	4%	4%
Ave Maria School of Law (FL)	$15,000	51%	$10,000-$25,000	7%	0%
Boston University	$15,000	60%	$10,000-$25,000	N/A	2%
Georgetown University (DC)	$15,000	37%	$7,800-$24,800	1%	0%

What schools award the most and the least financial aid?

Private Schools

School	Median grant	% of students receiving grants	Grants range (25th–75th percentile)	Grants of full tuition	Grants of more than full tuition
Southwestern Law School (CA)	$15,000	35%	$9,500-$21,000	1%	4%
Tulane University (LA)	$15,000	60%	$7,500-$20,000	N/A	N/A
Vanderbilt University (TN)	$15,000	69%	$10,000-$22,000	1%	2%
Villanova University (PA)	$15,000	21%	$10,000-$20,000	1%	0%
Washington and Lee University (VA)	$15,000	63%	$10,000-$23,000	2%	0%
Whittier College (CA)	$15,000	35%	$5,000-$29,120	7%	1%
Duquesne University (PA)	$14,813	34%	$3,126-$29,406	10%	2%
Campbell University (Wiggins) (NC)	$14,250	24%	$7,130-$14,260	0%	0%
Drake University (IA)	$14,035	59%	$7,500-$18,000	4%	3%
Duke University (NC)	$14,000	69%	$10,000-$18,000	1%	0%
Faulkner University (Jones) (AL)	$14,000	25%	$8-$18,480	4%	0%
Nova Southeastern University (Broad) (FL)	$14,000	11%	$9,181-$29,972	4%	0%
University of Pennsylvania	$14,000	40%	$10,000-$20,900	2%	0%
DePaul University (IL)	$13,000	68%	$7,000-$18,000	0%	0%
George Washington University (DC)	$13,000	54%	$9,000-$30,000	6%	6%
Loyola University New Orleans	$13,000	44%	$5,000-$22,446	1%	1%
Oklahoma City University	$13,000	38%	$8,000-$18,000	0%	2%
University of Notre Dame (IN)	$13,000	80%	$10,000-$15,400	0%	0%
Western New England College (MA)	$13,000	67%	$10,000-$21,000	2%	0%
Loyola University Chicago	$12,600	71%	$8,000-$21,000	1%	0%
Roger Williams University (RI)	$12,500	39%	$7,500-$28,990	11%	1%
Santa Clara University (CA)	$12,500	33%	$9,000-$16,000	2%	0%
Thomas Jefferson School of Law (CA)	$12,500	42%	$8,000-$17,000	1%	0%
American University (Washington) (DC)	$12,000	30%	$8,000-$16,000	2%	0%
Gonzaga University (WA)	$12,000	72%	$8,500-$15,000	3%	N/A
University of Southern California (Gould)	$12,000	67%	$8,000-$18,000	2%	1%
University of Tulsa (OK)	$12,000	50%	$8,000-$18,000	3%	3%
Wake Forest University (NC)	$12,000	52%	$7,000-$33,950	13%	2%
Western State University (CA)	$12,000	49%	$5,000-$24,000	7%	2%
Willamette University (Collins) (OR)	$12,000	55%	$8,000-$16,000	0%	0%
University of Chicago	$10,800	56%	$7,200-$18,000	1%	N/A
Columbia University (NY)	$10,250	53%	$4,000-$22,062	2%	2%
Case Western Reserve University (OH)	$10,179	59%	$9,333-$16,333	0%	0%
Capital University (OH)	$10,000	57%	$5,000-$12,000	0%	0%
Catholic Univ. of America (Columbus) (DC)	$10,000	29%	$7,000-$16,000	0%	0%
Charlotte School of Law (NC)	$10,000	17%	$7,500-$12,000	0%	0%
Fordham University (NY)	$10,000	40%	$5,000-$15,000	0%	0%
Howard University (DC)	$10,000	54%	$7,500-$18,200	1%	4%
Lewis & Clark College (Northwestern) (OR)	$10,000	51%	$6,000-$20,000	2%	0%
New York Law School	$10,000	31%	$5,000-$20,000	0%	0%
Suffolk University (MA)	$10,000	51%	$5,000-$15,000	1%	0%
University of Dayton (OH)	$10,000	45%	$7,000-$14,000	N/A	0%
University of the Pacific (McGeorge) (CA)	$10,000	58%	$6,433-$15,000	0%	0%
Creighton University (NE)	$9,796	48%	$4,898-$14,694	3%	0%
Widener University (DE)	$9,612	32%	$3,000-$15,500	2%	0%
Northeastern University (MA)	$9,200	79%	$7,629-$11,637	0%	N/A
Seattle University	$9,000	53%	$6,000-$11,500	1%	0%
John Marshall Law School (IL)	$8,000	52%	$4,500-$9,000	1%	1%
Marquette University (WI)	$8,000	43%	$3,500-$16,500	4%	N/A
Pace University (NY)	$8,000	69%	$4,000-$15,000	2%	0%
Vermont Law School	$8,000	65%	$5,000-$13,000	1%	0%

What schools award the most and the least financial aid?

Private Schools

School	Median grant	% of students receiving grants	Grants range (25th–75th percentile)	Grants of full tuition	Grants of more than full tuition
Charleston School of Law (SC)	$7,500	44%	$5,000-$10,000	0%	0%
Golden Gate University (CA)	$7,500	42%	$4,600-$15,000	2%	0%
Texas Wesleyan University	$7,500	47%	$2,500-$10,000	0%	0%
University of Richmond (Williams) (VA)	$7,500	74%	$4,000-$15,000	0%	0%
Florida Coastal School of Law	$7,000	38%	$5,000-$12,000	0%	N/A
Franklin Pierce Law Center (NH)	$6,500	58%	$4,000-$12,000	1%	0%
Syracuse University (NY)	$6,500	78%	$4,100-$15,000	0%	0%
Barry University (FL)	$6,000	87%	$4,000-$9,000	0%	0%
Elon University (NC)	$6,000	69%	$3,000-$10,000	1%	N/A
Regent University (VA)	$6,000	80%	$3,000-$16,000	6%	0%
University of Detroit Mercy	$5,500	25%	$2,500-$8,826	0%	0%
Mississippi College	$5,000	35%	$300-$15,100	3%	5%
New England School of Law (MA)	$5,000	52%	$3,500-$14,975	5%	0%
Brigham Young University (Clark) (UT)	$4,620	32%	$2,210-$9,240	9%	0%
Pepperdine University (CA)	$4,300	80%	$2,000-$23,000	0%	4%
Touro College (Fuchsberg) (NY)	$4,000	63%	$500-$9,096	1%	0%
South Texas College of Law	$3,400	37%	$1,900-$4,500	0%	0%
Baylor University (Umphrey) (TX)	$3,331	82%	$3,000-$21,649	12%	4%
St. Mary's University (TX)	$1,824	37%	$1,017-$3,327	0%	0%
Atlanta's John Marshall Law School	$0	2%	$0-$0	0%	0%

Public Schools

School	Median grant	% of students receiving grants	Grants range (25th–75th percentile)	Grants of full tuition	Grants of more than full tuition
University of Iowa	$16,758	34%	$5,000-$16,758	19%	0%
University of Toledo (OH)	$15,216	63%	$7,714-$17,336	13%	18%
University of Virginia	$15,000	59%	$12,000-$18,000	1%	0%
University of California–Berkeley	$14,349	46%	$7,517-$21,600	1%	3%
University of Akron (OH)	$14,006	42%	$3,500-$23,965	0%	20%
University of Baltimore	$14,000	20%	$3,400-$20,591	0%	2%
University of Alabama	$12,564	43%	$2,500-$15,000	12%	7%
Indiana University–Bloomington (Maurer)	$12,000	77%	$6,240-$24,038	8%	14%
Northern Kentucky University (Chase)	$12,000	35%	$10,000-$13,344	13%	0%
University of Wisconsin–Madison	$12,000	28%	$6,000-$21,067	1%	5%
University of California–Davis	$11,991	60%	$9,100-$20,000	0%	1%
University of Illinois–Urbana-Champaign	$11,500	85%	$8,500-$16,000	9%	0%
University of Michigan–Ann Arbor	$11,300	60%	$7,731-$18,000	3%	1%
University of Arizona (Rogers)	$10,000	68%	$7,000-$15,000	3%	8%
University of Connecticut	$10,000	74%	$7,650-$14,900	3%	6%
University of Nebraska–Lincoln	$10,000	41%	$5,000-$12,000	0%	9%
University of Pittsburgh	$10,000	58%	$6,000-$18,000	1%	1%
University of Colorado–Boulder	$9,838	66%	$2,300-$20,056	14%	8%
University of California–Los Angeles	$9,557	61%	$4,000-$15,416	0%	6%
University of South Carolina	$8,912	50%	$5,000-$16,408	1%	1%
University of Memphis (Humphreys)	$8,891	29%	$3,563-$10,376	3%	2%
University of Texas–Austin	$8,320	80%	$4,520-$10,895	0%	2%
University of Minnesota–Twin Cities	$8,150	65%	$5,000-$12,000	1%	3%
George Mason University (VA)	$8,000	14%	$8,000-$16,000	0%	1%
Temple University (Beasley) (PA)	$7,500	53%	$5,000-$15,000	10%	0%

What schools award the most and the least financial aid?

Public Schools

School	Median grant	% of students receiving grants	Grants range (25th–75th percentile)	Grants of full tuition	Grants of more than full tuition
University of California (Hastings)	$7,500	72%	$7,000-$8,500	N/A	N/A
Washburn University (KS)	$7,500	46%	$2,500-$13,000	0%	6%
Texas Tech University	$7,000	54%	$1,400-$14,420	0%	20%
University of Cincinnati	$7,000	66%	$4,000-$10,000	2%	0%
University of Nevada–Las Vegas (Boyd)	$7,000	38%	$5,000-$10,300	13%	N/A
Pennsylvania State University (Dickinson)	$6,500	53%	$3,000-$10,000	N/A	N/A
University of New Mexico	$6,498	23%	$4,775-$11,593	8%	1%
University of Missouri–Kansas City	$6,023	36%	$3,000-$13,950	4%	2%
College of William and Mary (Marshall-Wythe)	$6,000	41%	$5,000-$10,000	0%	0%
Rutgers–Newark (NJ)	$6,000	41%	$4,000-$8,000	1%	1%
University of Arkansas–Fayetteville	$6,000	40%	$2,250-$10,000	0%	2%
University of Washington	$6,000	49%	$5,000-$11,000	0%	7%
University of Oregon	$5,941	49%	$3,000-$8,000	0%	1%
Northern Illinois University	$5,846	12%	$2,000-$11,892	2%	2%
Ohio State University (Moritz)	$5,500	84%	$3,000-$10,500	0%	3%
University of Utah (Quinney)	$5,406	52%	$1,900-$10,812	N/A	4%
West Virginia University	$5,322	50%	$2,661-$7,983	6%	6%
University of Hawaii–Manoa (Richardson)	$5,223	33%	$5,223-$7,212	0%	0%
Florida A&M University	$5,000	10%	$2,250-$7,600	2%	0%
Florida International University	$5,000	43%	$5,000-$5,412	3%	4%
Indiana University–Indianapolis	$5,000	47%	$2,500-$7,500	0%	1%
Rutgers–Camden (NJ)	$5,000	30%	$2,500-$6,000	0%	0%
Southern Illinois University–Carbondale	$5,000	46%	$4,500-$7,500	3%	4%
University of Georgia	$5,000	61%	$2,000-$15,778	1%	0%
University of Houston (TX)	$5,000	65%	$2,200-$7,200	1%	0%
North Carolina Central University	$4,536	61%	$3,764-$6,242	24%	0%
Cleveland State Univ. (Cleveland-Marshall)	$4,070	45%	$3,610-$13,911	8%	0%
University of Missouri	$4,025	59%	$3,000-$7,000	N/A	2%
University of Kentucky	$4,000	63%	$1,000-$11,178	0%	2%
University of Louisville (Brandeis) (KY)	$4,000	44%	$3,000-$6,000	N/A	N/A
University of North Dakota	$4,000	33%	$1,000-$6,550	N/A	3%
University of Tennessee–Knoxville	$4,000	62%	$2,000-$7,438	2%	4%
Wayne State University (MI)	$4,000	70%	$2,000-$11,000	5%	5%
Louisiana State Univ.–Baton Rouge (Hebert)	$3,913	65%	$2,000-$10,096	7%	8%
University of North Carolina–Chapel Hill	$3,900	80%	$900-$6,400	0%	3%
University of the District of Columbia (Clarke)	$3,800	56%	$2,900-$6,300	14%	0%
University of Maryland	$3,571	57%	$3,571-$10,000	0%	0%
University of Kansas	$3,450	79%	$1,700-$7,500	1%	3%
University of Maine	$3,133	30%	$2,000-$6,000	0%	1%
Arizona State University (O'Connor)	$3,000	47%	$2,000-$8,122	1%	4%
Texas Southern University (Marshall)	$3,000	43%	$1,500-$3,500	6%	0%
University of Florida (Levin)	$3,000	31%	$1,285-$4,100	1%	0%
University of Oklahoma	$3,000	74%	$1,250-$6,964	0%	3%
University of Arkansas–Little Rock (Bowen)	$2,750	40%	$1,000-$9,979	7%	1%
Georgia State University	$2,500	20%	$1,000-$11,683	10%	0%
CUNY–Queens College	$2,362	28%	$1,181-$3,543	13%	N/A
University of Montana	$2,200	N/A	$1,000-$4,950	N/A	N/A
Florida State University	$2,000	36%	$1,200-$6,000	2%	1%
University of Wyoming	$2,000	56%	$1,000-$3,000	0%	0%
University of South Dakota	$1,305	42%	$653-$1,958	N/A	0%
University of Mississippi	$1,000	29%	$850-$5,000	1%	4%
University at Buffalo–SUNY	$550	78%	$550-$3,000	17%	1%

Whose graduates have the most debt? The least?

How much should you expect to borrow? Debts of $70,000 to $80,000 are common for law school grads—and that's not counting any college loans. This table shows the average amount of debt incurred by borrowers in the class of 2009, as well as the proportion of the class that took out loans.

School	Average amount of law school debt	% of grads with debt
Thomas Jefferson School of Law (CA)	$131,800	95%
New York Law School	$129,410	87%
Columbia University (NY)	$128,425	77%
American University (Washington) (DC)	$128,258	84%
Northwestern University (IL)	$127,242	80%
New York University	$125,504	81%
Loyola Marymount University (CA)	$125,264	86%
George Washington University (DC)	$125,200	82%
Georgetown University (DC)	$125,174	82%
University of the Pacific (McGeorge) (CA)	$124,488	90%
John Marshall Law School (IL)	$124,015	59%
University of Chicago	$123,904	88%
Vermont Law School	$122,475	89%
Duke University (NC)	$122,296	78%
Albany Law School (NY)	$120,722	82%
University of Southern California (Gould)	$120,161	81%
Pepperdine University (CA)	$120,148	87%
Roger Williams University (RI)	$119,558	91%
California Western School of Law	$119,345	86%
Syracuse University (NY)	$119,076	84%
Golden Gate University (CA)	$118,429	88%
Vanderbilt University (TN)	$118,220	82%
Villanova University (PA)	$116,878	89%
Stetson University (FL)	$116,184	78%
Franklin Pierce Law Center (NH)	$115,376	81%
Charleston School of Law (SC)	$114,941	76%
Atlanta's John Marshall Law School	$114,933	82%
Tulane University (LA)	$114,266	85%
Hofstra University (NY)	$114,154	78%
Harvard University (MA)	$113,432	81%
Catholic University of America (Columbus) (DC)	$112,945	94%
Emory University (GA)	$112,383	77%
Creighton University (NE)	$110,036	79%
Cornell University (NY)	$109,700	80%
University of San Francisco	$109,696	89%
University of San Diego	$109,657	84%
Nova Southeastern University (Broad) (FL)	$109,575	85%
Florida Coastal School of Law	$109,528	90%
Regent University (VA)	$109,025	81%
Elon University (NC)	$108,663	92%
Campbell University (Wiggins) (NC)	$108,627	79%
University of Pennsylvania	$108,601	84%
Suffolk University (MA)	$108,557	87%
Chapman University (CA)	$108,465	86%
Pennsylvania State University (Dickinson)	$108,383	84%
Southwestern Law School (CA)	$107,383	83%

Whose graduates have the most debt? The least?

School	Average amount of law school debt	% of grads with debt
Valparaiso University (IN)	$107,313	89%
Barry University (FL)	$107,175	84%
University of Detroit Mercy	$107,139	81%
St. John's University (NY)	$107,137	85%
New England School of Law (MA)	$106,632	85%
Washington University in St. Louis	$106,614	71%
DePaul University (IL)	$106,412	90%
Yeshiva University (Cardozo) (NY)	$105,067	75%
University of Denver (Sturm)	$104,926	84%
Howard University (DC)	$104,787	92%
Santa Clara University (CA)	$104,546	88%
University of Virginia	$103,645	76%
Northeastern University (MA)	$103,311	82%
University of Michigan–Ann Arbor	$103,251	85%
Fordham University (NY)	$103,213	79%
Marquette University (WI)	$102,727	84%
Oklahoma City University	$102,125	85%
Samford University (Cumberland) (AL)	$102,106	80%
Boston University	$101,285	84%
Widener University (DE)	$100,849	92%
Washington and Lee University (VA)	$100,670	91%
Seton Hall University (NJ)	$100,371	86%
Yale University (CT)	$99,989	77%
Baylor University (Umphrey) (TX)	$99,371	81%
Mercer University (George) (GA)	$99,038	92%
St. Louis University	$99,000	80%
Capital University (OH)	$98,531	92%
Western State University (CA)	$97,530	89%
University of California–Los Angeles	$97,140	80%
Boston College	$96,806	83%
Stanford University (CA)	$96,533	81%
Whittier College (CA)	$96,506	94%
Quinnipiac University (CT)	$95,691	85%
Lewis & Clark College (Northwestern) (OR)	$95,608	88%
Seattle University	$95,572	91%
Touro College (Fuchsberg) (NY)	$94,680	92%
Western New England College (MA)	$94,496	62%
University of Minnesota–Twin Cities	$94,087	85%
Gonzaga University (WA)	$94,074	91%
Brooklyn Law School (NY)	$93,666	80%
South Texas College of Law	$93,494	87%
University of Richmond (Williams) (VA)	$93,200	72%
University of Notre Dame (IN)	$92,955	86%
Hamline University (MN)	$92,794	83%
University of St. Thomas (MN)	$92,637	95%
University of California (Hastings)	$92,327	87%
St. Mary's University (TX)	$91,518	85%
Southern Methodist University (Dedman) (TX)	$91,210	84%
Indiana University–Bloomington (Maurer)	$91,142	92%
Case Western Reserve University (OH)	$90,529	95%
University of California–Berkeley	$90,164	88%
Mississippi College	$89,906	82%
George Mason University (VA)	$89,857	85%
Loyola University Chicago	$89,796	75%
Appalachian School of Law (VA)	$89,340	90%
Ave Maria School of Law (FL)	$87,436	78%

Whose graduates have the most debt? The least?

School	Average amount of law school debt	% of grads with debt
University of Miami (FL)	$87,272	77%
Ohio Northern University (Pettit)	$87,230	93%
University of Illinois–Urbana-Champaign	$87,194	97%
University of the District of Columbia (Clarke)	$86,297	90%
University of Baltimore	$86,133	84%
Drake University (IA)	$85,905	91%
Illinois Institute of Technology (Chicago-Kent)	$85,503	90%
University of Pittsburgh	$83,826	88%
Wake Forest University (NC)	$83,700	97%
Pace University (NY)	$83,515	87%
Texas Wesleyan University	$82,913	65%
University of Maryland	$81,872	88%
University of Iowa	$81,735	84%
Florida A&M University	$81,601	87%
William Mitchell College of Law (MN)	$81,532	96%
Indiana University–Indianapolis	$80,718	87%
University of Texas–Austin	$80,322	73%
Ohio State University (Moritz)	$79,855	84%
Temple University (Beasley) (PA)	$78,502	84%
Willamette University (Collins) (OR)	$78,393	89%
University of Oregon	$77,571	89%
College of William and Mary (Marshall-Wythe) (VA)	$76,155	85%
University of Missouri–Kansas City	$75,093	85%
University of Colorado–Boulder	$74,916	84%
University of Arizona (Rogers)	$74,678	88%
Faulkner University (Jones) (AL)	$74,674	86%
University of Toledo (OH)	$74,167	88%
Arizona State University (O'Connor)	$73,317	82%
Rutgers–Newark (NJ)	$73,244	90%
University of California–Davis	$72,959	72%
University of Maine	$72,627	90%
Northern Kentucky University (Chase)	$72,376	75%
Duquesne University (PA)	$72,124	92%
University of Akron (OH)	$71,836	93%
Washburn University (KS)	$71,661	85%
University of Dayton (OH)	$71,525	91%
University of Houston (TX)	$70,575	79%
University of Washington	$69,945	78%
University of Tulsa (OK)	$68,642	70%
University of Wisconsin–Madison	$67,655	87%
University of North Dakota	$67,236	83%
North Carolina Central University	$66,394	77%
University of Oklahoma	$65,775	87%
West Virginia University	$65,602	84%
CUNY–Queens College	$65,328	88%
Louisiana State University–Baton Rouge (Hebert)	$65,324	80%
Michigan State University	$65,292	83%
University of Connecticut	$65,224	81%
University of Georgia	$65,047	78%
University of North Carolina–Chapel Hill	$63,621	84%
University of Florida (Levin)	$63,509	80%
Southern Illinois University–Carbondale	$63,223	90%
Cleveland State University (Cleveland-Marshall)	$61,500	80%
Wayne State University (MI)	$61,180	90%
University of Mississippi	$60,121	73%
University of Montana	$58,962	96%

Whose graduates have the most debt? The least?

School	Average amount of law school debt	% of grads with debt
University of Cincinnati	$58,376	86%
Florida International University	$58,119	83%
University at Buffalo–SUNY	$56,880	100%
University of Utah (Quinney)	$56,685	91%
University of Alabama	$56,643	76%
University of Arkansas–Little Rock (Bowen)	$56,585	76%
University of South Dakota	$56,112	90%
University of Nevada–Las Vegas (Boyd)	$55,944	86%
University of Kentucky	$55,870	81%
University of Arkansas–Fayetteville	$55,305	90%
University of Missouri	$54,896	99%
Texas Tech University	$54,373	86%
University of Tennessee–Knoxville	$53,751	80%
University of Hawaii–Manoa (Richardson)	$53,569	74%
Florida State University	$52,969	83%
University of New Mexico	$51,685	94%
Northern Illinois University	$50,880	86%
Loyola University New Orleans	$50,103	100%
University of Nebraska–Lincoln	$49,946	82%
University of Memphis (Humphreys)	$49,737	80%
Brigham Young University (Clark) (UT)	$44,035	87%
University of South Carolina	$41,612	87%
University of Kansas	$39,099	82%
Charlotte School of Law (NC)	$36,682	72%
University of Wyoming	$36,016	90%
Rutgers–Camden (NJ)	$28,767	84%
University of Louisville (Brandeis) (KY)	$26,177	87%
University of Idaho	$25,268	94%
Drexel University (Mack) (PA)	$23,171	80%
Georgia State University	$22,129	69%
Texas Southern University (Marshall)	$20,429	100%

Whose students are the most and least likely to drop out?

If the schools you're considering have a seemingly high attrition rate, you'll want to investigate why. The reasons students leave run the gamut, of course, from an inhospitable culture and dissatisfaction with the program to personal or family problems or a lack of money. The dropout rates shown here are for students who discontinued their law school education in the 2008-2009 academic year.

School	% not returning after 1st year	% not returning after 2nd year
Florida A&M University	38%	7%
Western State University (CA)	33%	9%
Ave Maria School of Law (FL)	31%	3%
Faulkner University (Jones) (AL)	30%	2%
Widener University (DE)	29%	2%
University of Detroit Mercy	26%	0%
Golden Gate University (CA)	22%	2%
Capital University (OH)	20%	5%
Florida Coastal School of Law	20%	13%
New England School of Law (MA)	20%	5%
University of Akron (OH)	20%	4%
California Western School of Law	19%	2%
Ohio Northern University (Pettit)	19%	0%
Gonzaga University (WA)	18%	1%
Oklahoma City University	18%	6%
Charlotte School of Law (NC)	17%	5%
Cleveland State University (Cleveland-Marshall)	17%	1%
Atlanta's John Marshall Law School	16%	3%
George Mason University (VA)	16%	2%
Texas Southern University (Marshall)	16%	1%
Hofstra University (NY)	15%	1%
Louisiana State University–Baton Rouge (Hebert)	15%	0%
Michigan State University	15%	1%
Mississippi College	15%	2%
Mercer University (George) (GA)	14%	0%
North Carolina Central University	14%	1%
Regent University (VA)	14%	2%
Roger Williams University (RI)	14%	2%
Syracuse University (NY)	14%	8%
University of Richmond (Williams) (VA)	14%	0%
Pace University (NY)	13%	2%
Southern Illinois University–Carbondale	13%	3%
University of Missouri–Kansas City	13%	1%
University of San Francisco	13%	2%
University of the District of Columbia (Clarke)	13%	2%
Valparaiso University (IN)	13%	0%
Washburn University (KS)	13%	1%
Florida International University	12%	1%
Franklin Pierce Law Center (NH)	12%	1%
Loyola Marymount University (CA)	12%	2%
Nova Southeastern University (Broad) (FL)	12%	2%
Pennsylvania State University (Dickinson)	12%	2%
University of San Diego	12%	1%
Western New England College (MA)	12%	2%

Whose students are the most and least likely to drop out?

School	% not returning after 1st year	% not returning after 2nd year
Campbell University (Wiggins) (NC)	11%	3%
New York Law School	11%	0%
University of Baltimore	11%	1%
Willamette University (Collins) (OR)	11%	9%
Catholic University of America (Columbus) (DC)	10%	1%
Hamline University (MN)	10%	2%
Loyola University New Orleans	10%	2%
Quinnipiac University (CT)	10%	1%
Rutgers–Camden (NJ)	10%	2%
Thomas Jefferson School of Law (CA)	10%	2%
University of Cincinnati	10%	1%
University of Maine	10%	0%
Whittier College (CA)	10%	4%
Baylor University (Umphrey) (TX)	9%	4%
Florida State University	9%	N/A
Marquette University (WI)	9%	0%
Northern Kentucky University (Chase)	9%	10%
Pepperdine University (CA)	9%	0%
Samford University (Cumberland) (AL)	9%	2%
University of Missouri	9%	1%
University of Nebraska–Lincoln	9%	3%
University of Nevada–Las Vegas (Boyd)	9%	3%
William Mitchell College of Law (MN)	9%	1%
Case Western Reserve University (OH)	8%	1%
Georgia State University	8%	1%
Howard University (DC)	8%	4%
Seton Hall University (NJ)	8%	7%
University of California–Davis	8%	1%
University of Miami (FL)	8%	0%
University of the Pacific (McGeorge) (CA)	8%	11%
University of Toledo (OH)	8%	8%
West Virginia University	8%	0%
Appalachian School of Law (VA)	7%	9%
Boston University	7%	1%
Brooklyn Law School (NY)	7%	0%
Chapman University (CA)	7%	1%
CUNY–Queens College	7%	0%
DePaul University (IL)	7%	0%
Drexel University (Mack) (PA)	7%	2%
Duquesne University (PA)	7%	1%
Elon University (NC)	7%	1%
Indiana University–Indianapolis	7%	4%
John Marshall Law School (IL)	7%	2%
Lewis & Clark College (Northwestern) (OR)	7%	2%
Loyola University Chicago	7%	1%
Rutgers–Newark (NJ)	7%	3%
Seattle University	7%	1%
Texas Wesleyan University	7%	0%
Touro College (Fuchsberg) (NY)	7%	2%
University of Denver (Sturm)	7%	2%
University of Idaho	7%	1%
University of Mississippi	7%	1%
University of Tulsa (OK)	7%	9%
University of Utah (Quinney)	7%	1%
George Washington University (DC)	6%	0%
Santa Clara University (CA)	6%	0%

Whose students are the most and least likely to drop out?

School	% not returning after 1st year	% not returning after 2nd year
Southwestern Law School (CA)	6%	10%
Suffolk University (MA)	6%	3%
University of Alabama	6%	0%
University of Louisville (Brandeis) (KY)	6%	1%
University of Minnesota–Twin Cities	6%	3%
Washington University in St. Louis	6%	2%
American University (Washington) (DC)	5%	N/A
Boston College	5%	0%
Indiana University–Bloomington (Maurer)	5%	0%
Northern Illinois University	5%	1%
South Texas College of Law	5%	2%
Stetson University (FL)	5%	2%
University of California–Los Angeles	5%	1%
University of Hawaii–Manoa (Richardson)	5%	2%
University of Illinois–Urbana-Champaign	5%	1%
University of Oklahoma	5%	0%
University of Oregon	5%	0%
University of Pittsburgh	5%	0%
University of South Dakota	5%	2%
Arizona State University (O'Connor)	4%	4%
Barry University (FL)	4%	6%
College of William and Mary (Marshall-Wythe) (VA)	4%	0%
St. Mary's University (TX)	4%	0%
University of Arkansas–Little Rock (Bowen)	4%	9%
University of Iowa	4%	2%
University of Maryland	4%	1%
University of North Carolina–Chapel Hill	4%	0%
University of Wisconsin–Madison	4%	0%
Vermont Law School	4%	1%
Wayne State University (MI)	4%	8%
Illinois Institute of Technology (Chicago-Kent)	3%	2%
University of Arkansas–Fayetteville	3%	N/A
University of California–Berkeley	3%	N/A
University of Dayton (OH)	3%	3%
University of New Mexico	3%	0%
University of Southern California (Gould)	3%	1%
Yeshiva University (Cardozo) (NY)	3%	1%
Albany Law School (NY)	2%	0%
Cornell University (NY)	2%	N/A
Creighton University (NE)	2%	N/A
Drake University (IA)	2%	0%
Emory University (GA)	2%	4%
Georgetown University (DC)	2%	0%
Northeastern University (MA)	2%	6%
Northwestern University (IL)	2%	N/A
Ohio State University (Moritz)	2%	1%
St. John's University (NY)	2%	5%
St. Louis University	2%	0%
Temple University (Beasley) (PA)	2%	4%
University at Buffalo–SUNY	2%	5%
University of Memphis (Humphreys)	2%	2%
University of Virginia	2%	1%
University of Washington	2%	0%
Vanderbilt University (TN)	2%	0%
Villanova University (PA)	2%	N/A
Wake Forest University (NC)	2%	4%

Whose students are the most and least likely to drop out?

School	% not returning after 1st year	% not returning after 2nd year
Yale University (CT)	2%	1%
Charleston School of Law (SC)	1%	3%
Fordham University (NY)	1%	5%
New York University	1%	1%
University of Arizona (Rogers)	1%	0%
University of California (Hastings)	1%	0%
University of Chicago	1%	4%
University of Houston (TX)	1%	3%
University of Kansas	1%	3%
University of Kentucky	1%	0%
University of North Dakota	1%	0%
University of Notre Dame (IN)	1%	2%
University of South Carolina	1%	0%
University of St. Thomas (MN)	1%	9%
University of Tennessee–Knoxville	1%	4%
University of Texas–Austin	1%	4%
University of Wyoming	1%	0%
Brigham Young University (Clark) (UT)	N/A	N/A
Columbia University (NY)	N/A	N/A
Duke University (NC)	0%	5%
Harvard University (MA)	0%	0%
Southern Methodist University (Dedman) (TX)	N/A	4%
Stanford University (CA)	0%	2%
Texas Tech University	0%	1%
Tulane University (LA)	0%	1%
University of Colorado–Boulder	0%	1%
University of Connecticut	N/A	N/A
University of Florida (Levin)	0%	0%
University of Georgia	0%	0%
University of Michigan–Ann Arbor	0%	1%
University of Montana	0%	0%
University of Pennsylvania	0%	0%
Washington and Lee University (VA)	N/A	7%

What schools have the best first-time bar passage rate?

How well do the schools you're considering prepare students for the bar exam? To judge, you'll need to know not only how many grads pass on their first try, but also how that compares with the overall pass rate of everybody taking the test in the same state. Schools appear under the state in which most 2008 grads sat for the bar and are then organized by their individual passage rates.

State	State's overall bar passage rate	School	School's pass rate
Alabama	79%	University of Alabama	97%
Alabama	79%	Samford University (Cumberland) (AL)	96%
Alabama	79%	Faulkner University (Jones) (AL)	93%
Arizona	84%	University of Arizona (Rogers)	92%
Arizona	84%	Arizona State University (O'Connor)	90%
Arkansas	83%	University of Arkansas–Fayetteville	82%
Arkansas	83%	University of Arkansas–Little Rock (Bowen)	81%
California	71%	Stanford University (CA)	96%
California	71%	University of Southern California (Gould)	90%
California	71%	University of California–Los Angeles	89%
California	71%	University of California–Berkeley	88%
California	71%	Pepperdine University (CA)	87%
California	71%	Loyola Marymount University (CA)	86%
California	71%	University of San Francisco	86%
California	71%	California Western School of Law	84%
California	71%	Whittier College (CA)	83%
California	71%	University of California–Davis	80%
California	71%	University of California (Hastings)	80%
California	71%	University of the Pacific (McGeorge) (CA)	80%
California	71%	Santa Clara University (CA)	79%
California	71%	University of San Diego	79%
California	71%	Chapman University (CA)	75%
California	71%	Golden Gate University (CA)	72%
California	71%	Southwestern Law School (CA)	70%
California	71%	Thomas Jefferson School of Law (CA)	70%
California	71%	Western State University (CA)	65%
Colorado	83%	University of Colorado–Boulder	93%
Colorado	83%	University of Denver (Sturm)	80%
Connecticut	87%	Quinnipiac University (CT)	93%
Connecticut	87%	University of Connecticut	92%
Connecticut	87%	Western New England College (MA)	77%
Florida	81%	University of Miami (FL)	91%
Florida	81%	University of Florida (Levin)	89%
Florida	81%	Florida International University	88%
Florida	81%	Florida State University	87%
Florida	81%	Nova Southeastern University (Broad) (FL)	84%
Florida	81%	Florida Coastal School of Law	83%
Florida	81%	Stetson University (FL)	82%
Florida	81%	Barry University (FL)	77%
Florida	81%	Florida A&M University	66%
Georgia	89%	University of Georgia	99%
Georgia	89%	Mercer University (George) (GA)	96%
Georgia	89%	Emory University (GA)	94%
Georgia	89%	Georgia State University	94%
Georgia	89%	Atlanta's John Marshall Law School	84%

What schools have the best first-time bar passage rate?

State	State's overall bar passage rate	School	School's pass rate
Hawaii	88%	University of Hawaii–Manoa (Richardson)	87%
Idaho	80%	University of Idaho	81%
Illinois	91%	University of Notre Dame (IN)	100%
Illinois	91%	Northwestern University (IL)	98%
Illinois	91%	Illinois Institute of Technology (Chicago-Kent)	96%
Illinois	91%	Northern Illinois University	96%
Illinois	91%	Southern Illinois University–Carbondale	95%
Illinois	91%	University of Chicago	95%
Illinois	91%	Loyola University Chicago	94%
Illinois	91%	University of Illinois–Urbana-Champaign	91%
Illinois	91%	DePaul University (IL)	89%
Illinois	91%	John Marshall Law School (IL)	88%
Indiana	84%	Indiana University–Bloomington (Maurer)	95%
Indiana	84%	Indiana University–Indianapolis	84%
Indiana	84%	Valparaiso University (IN)	83%
Iowa	90%	University of Iowa	94%
Iowa	90%	Drake University (IA)	90%
Kansas	89%	University of Kansas	94%
Kansas	89%	Washburn University (KS)	89%
Kentucky	83%	University of Kentucky	94%
Kentucky	83%	University of Louisville (Brandeis) (KY)	88%
Louisiana	66%	Louisiana State University–Baton Rouge (Hebert)	81%
Louisiana	66%	Tulane University (LA)	76%
Louisiana	66%	Loyola University New Orleans	67%
Maine	91%	University of Maine	92%
Maryland	85%	University of the District of Columbia (Clarke)	92%
Maryland	85%	University of Maryland	90%
Maryland	85%	Catholic University of America (Columbus) (DC)	88%
Maryland	85%	University of Baltimore	85%
Maryland	85%	Howard University (DC)	64%
Massachusetts	89%	Boston University	98%
Massachusetts	89%	Boston College	94%
Massachusetts	89%	Northeastern University (MA)	94%
Massachusetts	89%	Suffolk University (MA)	93%
Massachusetts	89%	New England School of Law (MA)	91%
Massachusetts	89%	Roger Williams University (RI)	86%
Michigan	82%	Wayne State University (MI)	96%
Michigan	82%	Michigan State University	84%
Michigan	82%	Ave Maria School of Law (FL)	80%
Michigan	82%	University of Detroit Mercy	71%
Minnesota	91%	University of Minnesota–Twin Cities	97%
Minnesota	91%	Hamline University (MN)	93%
Minnesota	91%	University of St. Thomas (MN)	90%
Minnesota	91%	William Mitchell College of Law (MN)	90%
Mississippi	88%	Mississippi College	94%
Mississippi	88%	University of Mississippi	90%
Missouri	91%	Washington University in St. Louis	100%
Missouri	91%	University of Missouri–Kansas City	98%
Missouri	91%	St. Louis University	94%
Missouri	91%	University of Missouri	92%
Montana	93%	University of Montana	88%
Nebraska	89%	University of Nebraska–Lincoln	91%
Nebraska	89%	Creighton University (NE)	88%
Nevada	77%	University of Nevada–Las Vegas (Boyd)	82%
New Hampshire	88%	Franklin Pierce Law Center (NH)	93%
New Jersey	85%	Seton Hall University (NJ)	89%

What schools have the best first-time bar passage rate?

State	State's overall bar passage rate	School	School's pass rate
New Jersey	85%	Rutgers–Newark	87%
New Jersey	85%	Rutgers–Camden	85%
New Mexico	92%	University of New Mexico	92%
New York	81%	Cornell University (NY)	99%
New York	81%	Harvard University (MA)	98%
New York	81%	University of Pennsylvania	98%
New York	81%	University of Virginia	98%
New York	81%	Columbia University (NY)	97%
New York	81%	Georgetown University (DC)	97%
New York	81%	New York University	97%
New York	81%	Yale University (CT)	97%
New York	81%	Duke University (NC)	96%
New York	81%	George Washington University (DC)	95%
New York	81%	Fordham University (NY)	94%
New York	81%	American University (Washington) (DC)	92%
New York	81%	Yeshiva University (Cardozo) (NY)	92%
New York	81%	New York Law School	91%
New York	81%	St. John's University (NY)	91%
New York	81%	University of Michigan–Ann Arbor	91%
New York	81%	Brooklyn Law School (NY)	89%
New York	81%	Hofstra University (NY)	87%
New York	81%	Syracuse University (NY)	84%
New York	81%	Pace University (NY)	83%
New York	81%	Vermont Law School	83%
New York	81%	CUNY–Queens College	82%
New York	81%	Albany Law School (NY)	81%
New York	81%	University at Buffalo–SUNY	81%
New York	81%	Touro College (Fuchsberg) (NY)	79%
North Carolina	83%	Wake Forest University (NC)	96%
North Carolina	83%	Campbell University (Wiggins) (NC)	95%
North Carolina	83%	University of North Carolina–Chapel Hill	90%
North Carolina	83%	North Carolina Central University	81%
North Dakota	86%	University of North Dakota	92%
Ohio	88%	Capital University (OH)	95%
Ohio	88%	Ohio Northern University (Pettit)	94%
Ohio	88%	University of Dayton (OH)	92%
Ohio	88%	Cleveland State University (Cleveland-Marshall)	90%
Ohio	88%	Ohio State University (Moritz)	90%
Ohio	88%	University of Akron (OH)	90%
Ohio	88%	Case Western Reserve University (OH)	88%
Ohio	88%	University of Toledo (OH)	88%
Ohio	88%	Northern Kentucky University (Chase)	86%
Ohio	88%	University of Cincinnati	82%
Oklahoma	93%	University of Oklahoma	96%
Oklahoma	93%	University of Tulsa (OK)	93%
Oklahoma	93%	Oklahoma City University	90%
Oregon	79%	University of Oregon	85%
Oregon	79%	Willamette University (Collins) (OR)	84%
Oregon	79%	Lewis & Clark College (Northwestern) (OR)	81%
Pennsylvania	87%	Duquesne University (PA)	96%
Pennsylvania	87%	Villanova University (PA)	92%
Pennsylvania	87%	University of Pittsburgh	91%
Pennsylvania	87%	Temple University (Beasley) (PA)	89%
Pennsylvania	87%	Widener University (DE)	88%
Pennsylvania	87%	Pennsylvania State University (Dickinson)	85%
South Carolina	82%	University of South Carolina	91%

What schools have the best first-time bar passage rate?

State	State's overall bar passage rate	School	School's pass rate
South Dakota	95%	University of South Dakota	95%
Tennessee	83%	Vanderbilt University (TN)	96%
Tennessee	83%	University of Memphis (Humphreys)	93%
Tennessee	83%	University of Tennessee–Knoxville	90%
Texas	84%	Southern Methodist University (Dedman) (TX)	94%
Texas	84%	Baylor University (Umphrey) (TX)	93%
Texas	84%	University of Houston (TX)	91%
Texas	84%	South Texas College of Law	89%
Texas	84%	University of Texas–Austin	89%
Texas	84%	St. Mary's University (TX)	87%
Texas	84%	Texas Tech University	87%
Texas	84%	Texas Wesleyan University	78%
Texas	84%	Texas Southern University (Marshall)	60%
Utah	87%	Brigham Young University (Clark) (UT)	92%
Utah	87%	University of Utah (Quinney)	87%
Virginia	82%	University of Richmond (Williams) (VA)	91%
Virginia	82%	College of William and Mary (Marshall-Wythe)	89%
Virginia	82%	George Mason University (VA)	87%
Virginia	82%	Washington and Lee University (VA)	84%
Virginia	82%	Appalachian School of Law (VA)	83%
Virginia	82%	Regent University (VA)	73%
Washington	74%	University of Washington	85%
Washington	74%	Gonzaga University (WA)	82%
Washington	74%	Seattle University	79%
West Virginia	79%	West Virginia University	76%
Wisconsin	92%	Marquette University (WI)	100%
Wisconsin	92%	University of Wisconsin–Madison	99%
Wyoming	67%	University of Wyoming	76%

Whose graduates are the most and least likely to land a job?

While economic turmoil impacted employment, many law schools in 2008 could boast that virtually the entire class had accepted a job offer by the time they'd been given their diplomas. (The schools that didn't provide information about how many graduates were immediately working appear at the end of the list, so that prospective students can see the proportion of students who were employed nine months out.)

School	% employed at graduation	% employed at 9 months	School	% employed at graduation	% employed at 9 months
Duke University (NC)	100%	100%	University of Iowa	85%	100%
Columbia University (NY)	99%	100%	Rutgers–Newark (NJ)	84%	96%
New York University	99%	99%	University of Minnesota–Twin Cities	84%	97%
Northwestern University (IL)	98%	100%	University of New Mexico	82%	96%
Stanford University (CA)	98%	98%	Washington and Lee University (VA)	82%	89%
University of Michigan–Ann Arbor	98%	100%	DePaul University (IL)	81%	94%
University of Pennsylvania	98%	100%	Seton Hall University (NJ)	81%	97%
Cornell University (NY)	97%	98%	University of Wisconsin–Madison	81%	98%
Emory University (GA)	97%	95%	Brooklyn Law School (NY)	80%	92%
Harvard University (MA)	97%	99%	University of Colorado–Boulder	80%	96%
University of California–Berkeley	97%	99%	Case Western Reserve University (OH)	79%	95%
University of California–Davis	97%	98%	Santa Clara University (CA)	79%	93%
University of California–Los Angeles	97%	99%	St. John's University (NY)	78%	96%
University of Chicago	97%	99%	University of Miami (FL)	78%	96%
University of Texas–Austin	97%	98%	University of Arizona (Rogers)	77%	97%
Vanderbilt University (TN)	97%	98%	Cleveland State Univ. (Marshall)	76%	91%
George Mason University (VA)	96%	99%	Florida State University	76%	98%
University of Virginia	96%	100%	Pepperdine University (CA)	76%	97%
Georgetown University (DC)	94%	97%	Southern Methodist Univ. (Dedman)	76%	99%
Yale University (CT)	94%	98%	University at Buffalo–SUNY	76%	91%
George Washington University (DC)	93%	99%	University of Florida (Levin)	76%	97%
University of Baltimore	93%	96%	University of Houston (TX)	76%	97%
Univ. of Southern California (Gould)	92%	97%	University of Kentucky	76%	98%
University of Utah (Quinney)	92%	100%	Rutgers–Camden (NJ)	75%	90%
Arizona State University (O'Connor)	91%	100%	Univ. of North Carolina–Chapel Hill	75%	95%
Boston University	91%	99%	Wake Forest University (NC)	75%	96%
Chapman University (CA)	91%	97%	Yeshiva University (Cardozo) (NY)	75%	94%
University of Washington	91%	98%	University of Akron (OH)	74%	88%
University of Georgia	90%	98%	University of Cincinnati	74%	96%
University of Notre Dame (IN)	90%	99%	Howard University (DC)	72%	86%
Indiana Univ.–Bloomington (Maurer)	89%	96%	Indiana University–Indianapolis	72%	96%
University of Maryland	89%	95%	University of Connecticut	72%	94%
University of Toledo (OH)	89%	96%	University of Pittsburgh	72%	94%
Washington University in St. Louis	89%	95%	University of Tennessee–Knoxville	72%	95%
College of William and Mary	88%	97%	Illinois Inst. of Tech (Chicago-Kent)	71%	90%
Ohio State University (Moritz)	88%	98%	Tulane University (LA)	71%	91%
American University (Washington) (DC)	87%	96%	University of Denver (Sturm)	71%	94%
Brigham Young University (Clark) (UT)	87%	99%	Univ. of Hawaii–Manoa (Richardson)	71%	100%
University of Nevada–Las Vegas (Boyd)	87%	98%	Loyola University Chicago	70%	94%
Boston College	86%	97%	St. Louis University	70%	93%
St. Mary's University (TX)	86%	91%	University of California (Hastings)	70%	93%
Fordham University (NY)	85%	95%	West Virginia University	70%	98%
Southwestern Law School (CA)	85%	96%	University of Kansas	69%	94%
Univ. of Illinois–Urbana-Champaign	85%	97%	Catholic Univ. of America (Columbus)	68%	92%

Whose graduates are the most and least likely to land a job?

School	% employed at graduation	% employed at 9 months
Louisiana St. Univ.–Baton Rouge (Hebert)	68%	96%
Regent University (VA)	68%	94%
Temple University (Beasley) (PA)	66%	91%
University of Louisville (Brandeis) (KY)	65%	95%
Villanova University (PA)	65%	94%
John Marshall Law School (IL)	64%	89%
University of Nebraska–Lincoln	64%	94%
Marquette University (WI)	61%	93%
University of Oklahoma	61%	96%
University of Richmond (Williams) (VA)	61%	91%
Loyola University New Orleans	60%	95%
Vermont Law School	60%	95%
Seattle University	59%	97%

School	% employed at graduation	% employed at 9 months
University of Wyoming	59%	89%
University of Oregon	58%	90%
Texas Wesleyan University	57%	76%
University of South Carolina	56%	91%
Widener University (DE)	55%	84%
University of Mississippi	54%	90%
University of South Dakota	54%	94%
University of Missouri	51%	90%
Whittier College (CA)	51%	96%
Creighton University (NE)	50%	92%
Atlanta's John Marshall Law School	45%	96%
University of Memphis (Humphreys)	41%	93%
Univ. of Arkansas–Little Rock (Bowen)	38%	96%

School	% employed at 9 months
Georgia State University	99%
University of San Diego	98%
Drake University (IA)	97%
Loyola Marymount University (CA)	97%
University of Alabama	97%
William Mitchell College of Law (MN)	97%
Hofstra University (NY)	96%
Quinnipiac University (CT)	96%
University of Arkansas–Fayetteville	96%
University of Missouri–Kansas City	96%
University of the Pacific (McGeorge) (CA)	96%
Baylor University (Umphrey) (TX)	95%
Faulkner University (Jones) (AL)	95%
Florida Coastal School of Law	95%
Stetson University (FL)	95%
Syracuse University (NY)	95%
Albany Law School (NY)	94%
Campbell University (Wiggins) (NC)	94%
Franklin Pierce Law Center (NH)	94%
Gonzaga University (WA)	94%
Lewis & Clark College (Northwestern) (OR)	94%
Mississippi College	94%
Northeastern University (MA)	94%
Samford University (Cumberland) (AL)	94%
Washburn University (KS)	94%
New York Law School	93%
Northern Kentucky University (Chase)	93%
Ohio Northern University (Pettit)	93%
University of San Francisco	93%
Mercer University (George) (GA)	92%
Michigan State University	92%
Oklahoma City University	92%
Pace University (NY)	92%
Thomas Jefferson School of Law (CA)	92%
University of Dayton (OH)	92%
University of Maine	92%

School	% employed at 9 months
University of Montana	92%
University of Tulsa (OK)	92%
Pennsylvania State University (Dickinson)	91%
University of St. Thomas (MN)	91%
Willamette University (Collins) (OR)	91%
Golden Gate University (CA)	90%
Hamline University (MN)	90%
Suffolk University (MA)	90%
University of North Dakota	90%
Florida International University	89%
Northern Illinois University	89%
Valparaiso University (IN)	89%
Roger Williams University (RI)	88%
Texas Tech University	88%
University of Idaho	88%
Wayne State University (MI)	88%
Florida A&M University	87%
Nova Southeastern University (Broad) (FL)	86%
Duquesne University (PA)	85%
Southern Illinois University–Carbondale	85%
South Texas College of Law	85%
California Western School of Law	84%
Texas Southern University (Marshall)	83%
Ave Maria School of Law (FL)	82%
CUNY–Queens College	82%
New England School of Law (MA)	81%
North Carolina Central University	81%
Western New England College (MA)	81%
Univ. of the District of Columbia (Clarke)	80%
University of Detroit Mercy	78%
Capital University (OH)	77%
Touro College (Fuchsberg) (NY)	72%
Barry University (FL)	71%
Western State University (CA)	71%
Appalachian School of Law (VA)	66%

Whose graduates earn the most? The least?

According to the most recent surveys by the National Association for Law Placement, the median salary for first-year associates at law firms ranges from $40,000 in small firms to $160,000 at firms with 500 lawyers or more. But, as this table of median starting salaries for the class of 2008 shows, many make considerably more—or, if they go into the public sector, considerably less.

School	Private sector starting salary (median)	Private sector starting salary (25th–75th percentile)	Public sector starting salary (median)
American University (Washington) (DC)	$160,000	$120,000-$160,000	$52,000
Boston College	$160,000	$160,000-$160,000	$49,423
Boston University	$160,000	$160,000-$160,000	$48,000
Columbia University (NY)	$160,000	$95,000-$168,000	$54,000
Cornell University (NY)	$160,000	$160,000-$160,000	$58,206
Duke University (NC)	$160,000	$145,000-$160,000	$53,500
Fordham University (NY)	$160,000	$150,000-$160,000	$52,900
Georgetown University (DC)	$160,000	$160,000-$160,000	$57,800
George Washington University (DC)	$160,000	$145,000-$160,000	$55,731
Harvard University (MA)	$160,000	$160,000-$160,000	$55,000
Hofstra University (NY)	$160,000	$67,500-$160,000	$52,000
Howard University (DC)	$160,000	$105,000-$160,000	$52,000
New York Law School	$160,000	$71,250-$160,000	$53,500
New York University	$160,000	$160,000-$160,000	$57,354
Northwestern University (IL)	$160,000	$160,000-$160,000	$46,500
Stanford University (CA)	$160,000	$160,000-$160,000	$57,845
University of California–Berkeley	$160,000	$160,000-$160,000	$51,000
University of California (Hastings)	$160,000	$85,000-$160,000	$56,000
University of California–Los Angeles	$160,000	$145,000-$160,000	$59,800
University of Chicago	$160,000	$160,000-$160,000	$50,000
University of Michigan–Ann Arbor	$160,000	$160,000-$160,000	$56,386
University of Pennsylvania	$160,000	$160,000-$160,000	$53,626
University of Southern California (Gould)	$160,000	$145,000-$160,000	$45,000
University of Texas–Austin	$160,000	$125,000-$160,000	$51,617
University of Virginia	$160,000	$160,000-$160,000	$52,500
Yale University (CT)	$160,000	$160,000-$160,000	$59,631
University of California–Davis	$152,500	$85,000-$160,000	$54,494
Washington University in St. Louis	$152,500	$110,000-$160,000	$39,750
University of Notre Dame (IN)	$150,000	$120,000-$160,000	$52,500
Brooklyn Law School (NY)	$145,000	$70,000-$160,000	$55,000
Emory University (GA)	$145,000	$85,000-$160,000	$52,000
George Mason University (VA)	$145,000	$70,000-$160,000	$55,000
Santa Clara University (CA)	$145,000	$80,000-$160,000	$56,000
University of Illinois–Urbana-Champaign	$145,000	$70,000-$160,000	$52,000
Vanderbilt University (TN)	$145,000	$112,500-$160,000	$50,000
College of William and Mary (Marshall-Wythe) (VA)	$140,000	$110,000-$160,000	$53,635
Yeshiva University (Cardozo) (NY)	$137,500	$75,000-$160,000	$53,000
Catholic University of America (Columbus) (DC)	$135,000	$75,000-$160,000	$52,549
St. John's University (NY)	$130,000	$70,000-$160,000	$53,000

Whose graduates earn the most? The least?

School	Private sector starting salary (median)	Private sector starting salary (25th–75th percentile)	Public sector starting salary (median)
University of Georgia	$130,000	$80,000–$145,000	$55,000
University of North Carolina–Chapel Hill	$130,000	$90,000–$160,000	$46,000
Washington and Lee University (VA)	$128,500	$80,000–$160,000	$50,000
Rutgers–Camden (NJ)	$125,000	$75,000–$145,000	$40,746
Seton Hall University (NJ)	$125,000	$92,500–$145,000	$39,179
Temple University (Beasley) (PA)	$125,000	$69,000–$145,000	$45,000
University of Washington	$125,000	$80,000–$160,000	$49,000
University of Wisconsin–Madison	$125,000	$67,625–$160,000	$47,500
Brigham Young University (Clark) (UT)	$120,000	$90,000–$160,000	$50,250
Franklin Pierce Law Center (NH)	$120,000	$75,000–$142,500	$48,500
Rutgers–Newark (NJ)	$120,000	$95,000–$160,000	$41,000
University of Connecticut	$120,000	$95,000–$160,000	$52,125
University of Minnesota–Twin Cities	$120,000	$80,000–$140,000	$50,000
Wake Forest University (NC)	$120,000	$73,000–$145,000	$45,742
University of Arizona (Rogers)	$115,000	$80,000–$125,000	$52,000
Case Western Reserve University (OH)	$110,000	$76,000–$145,000	$49,000
Hamline University (MN)	$110,000	$65,000–$160,000	$50,000
University of Maryland	$109,999	$65,000–$150,000	$45,000
University of Pittsburgh	$102,500	$56,500–$145,000	$47,000
University of Miami (FL)	$102,000	$70,000–$135,000	$44,000
Villanova University (PA)	$101,250	$55,781–$108,750	$49,000
Loyola University Chicago	$100,433	$60,521–$144,238	$50,922
Arizona State University (O'Connor)	$100,000	$75,000–$125,000	$54,000
Illinois Institute of Technology (Chicago-Kent)	$100,000	$60,000–$160,000	$55,339
Loyola Marymount University (CA)	$100,000	$70,000–$160,000	$61,800
Ohio State University (Moritz)	$100,000	$75,000–$120,000	$46,500
Pace University (NY)	$100,000	$65,000–$160,000	$53,500
Indiana University–Bloomington (Maurer)	$97,000	$71,000–$107,500	$55,000
University of Houston (TX)	$95,000	$60,000–$160,000	$47,400
University of Iowa	$92,500	$65,000–$145,000	$47,750
Loyola University New Orleans	$90,000	N/A	$61,000
Pepperdine University (CA)	$90,000	$72,000–$150,000	$60,000
Tulane University (LA)	$90,000	$70,000–$145,000	$38,000
University of Alabama	$90,000	$63,000–$102,000	$43,750
University of Richmond (Williams) (VA)	$90,000	$70,000–$127,000	$48,000
DePaul University (IL)	$87,500	$55,000–$145,000	$55,000
Northeastern University (MA)	$85,000	$55,000–$160,000	$47,000
Southern Methodist University (Dedman) (TX)	$85,000	$70,000–$160,000	$51,334
University of Florida (Levin)	$85,000	$70,000–$130,000	$44,500
University of San Diego	$85,000	$65,000–$135,000	$60,000
Stetson University (FL)	$84,442	$65,000–$95,000	$45,545
University of San Francisco	$83,000	$61,000–$128,000	$48,000
University of Colorado–Boulder	$82,500	$60,000–$120,000	$47,000
University of Mississippi	$81,500	$56,250–$100,000	$52,000
Indiana University–Indianapolis	$80,500	$52,000–$100,000	$46,112
Lewis & Clark College (Northwestern) (OR)	$80,370	$65,000–$105,000	$50,000
Cleveland State University (Cleveland-Marshall)	$80,000	$60,000–$120,000	$49,000
Georgia State University	$80,000	$55,000–$120,000	$51,000
Golden Gate University (CA)	$80,000	$62,500–$95,000	$60,000
Syracuse University (NY)	$80,000	$55,000–$110,000	$49,500
University of Cincinnati	$80,000	$56,250–$115,000	$47,436
University of Utah (Quinney)	$80,000	$60,000–$110,000	$53,961

Whose graduates earn the most? The least?

School	Private sector starting salary (median)	Private sector starting salary (25th–75th percentile)	Public sector starting salary (median)
Capital University (OH)	$79,000	$55,000-$118,500	$44,250
Suffolk University (MA)	$79,000	$57,500-$130,000	$47,800
Widener University (DE)	$79,000	$50,000-$135,000	$42,000
University of Nevada–Las Vegas (Boyd)	$78,000	$62,000-$105,000	$56,000
Southwestern Law School (CA)	$77,000	$66,000-$87,500	$61,000
University of Tennessee–Knoxville	$76,250	$66,250-$88,750	$48,750
Baylor University (Umphrey) (TX)	$75,000	$60,000-$105,000	$52,730
California Western School of Law	$75,000	$65,000-$80,000	$58,552
Chapman University (CA)	$75,000	$60,000-$85,000	$66,500
John Marshall Law School (IL)	$75,000	$56,500-$120,000	$55,316
Louisiana State University–Baton Rouge (Hebert)	$75,000	$50,500-$92,250	$44,687
Mississippi College	$75,000	$48,000-$90,000	$51,500
Quinnipiac University (CT)	$75,000	$60,000-$95,000	$40,789
Seattle University	$75,000	$59,742-$100,000	$48,925
University at Buffalo–SUNY	$75,000	$55,000-$160,000	$55,000
University of South Carolina	$75,000	$51,000-$107,500	$39,000
Wayne State University (MI)	$75,000	$50,000-$100,000	$48,000
University of Oregon	$72,500	$48,000-$97,000	$47,000
University of the Pacific (McGeorge) (CA)	$72,000	$60,000-$90,000	$56,400
Pennsylvania State University (Dickinson)	$71,000	$50,000-$115,000	$48,000
South Texas College of Law	$71,000	$55,000-$120,000	$52,000
University of Hawaii–Manoa (Richardson)	$71,000	$55,000-$80,000	$55,200
Appalachian School of Law (VA)	$70,689	N/A	$46,057
Florida State University	$70,000	$58,000-$105,000	$42,000
Michigan State University	$70,000	$45,000-$100,000	$43,750
University of Denver (Sturm)	$70,000	$51,000-$105,000	$49,400
University of Toledo (OH)	$70,000	$55,000-$105,000	$42,500
University of Tulsa (OK)	$70,000	$55,000-$95,000	$47,500
Whittier College (CA)	$70,000	$60,000-$80,000	$65,000
Gonzaga University (WA)	$67,500	$51,500-$90,000	$54,500
University of St. Thomas (MN)	$66,000	$50,000-$120,000	$48,229
West Virginia University	$66,000	$55,000-$73,000	$42,612
Drake University (IA)	$65,375	$5,000-$85,000	$49,000
Duquesne University (PA)	$65,000	$50,000-$80,000	$43,500
Samford University (Cumberland) (AL)	$65,000	$55,000-$95,000	$46,000
Thomas Jefferson School of Law (CA)	$65,000	$50,000-$80,000	$60,000
University of Baltimore	$65,000	$55,000-$83,000	$43,000
Vermont Law School	$65,000	$50,000-$80,000	$43,000
Albany Law School (NY)	$63,000	$50,000-$105,000	$50,500
University of Akron (OH)	$63,000	$49,500-$81,250	$49,210
Atlanta's John Marshall Law School	$62,500	$50,000-$67,500	$44,000
University of Kansas	$62,500	$50,000-$105,000	$46,000
University of Missouri–Kansas City	$62,500	$50,000-$100,000	$43,800
New England School of Law (MA)	$61,750	$50,625-$95,000	$46,983
Texas Wesleyan University	$61,000	$50,000-$90,000	$50,000
University of New Mexico	$61,000	$52,000-$70,000	$44,000
Ave Maria School of Law (FL)	$60,000	$45,300-$81,000	$57,500
Creighton University (NE)	$60,000	$50,000-$80,000	$56,475
Mercer University (George) (GA)	$60,000	$50,000-$125,000	$48,000
Nova Southeastern University (Broad) (FL)	$60,000	$45,000-$75,000	$42,000
Ohio Northern University (Pettit)	$60,000	$47,500-$87,500	$42,500
University of Kentucky	$60,000	$45,000-$92,000	$35,000

Whose graduates earn the most? The least?

School	Private sector starting salary (median)	Private sector starting salary (25th–75th percentile)	Public sector starting salary (median)
University of Maine	$60,000	$45,000-$68,000	$41,000
University of Missouri	$60,000	$52,500-$92,000	$44,000
Western New England College (MA)	$60,000	$50,000-$75,000	$47,000
William Mitchell College of Law (MN)	$60,000	$47,500-$85,000	$45,000
Willamette University (Collins) (OR)	$59,625	$45,800-$76,000	$45,000
St. Louis University	$59,500	$50,000-$80,500	$39,000
University of Memphis (Humphreys)	$59,281	$50,000-$80,000	$47,000
University of Dayton (OH)	$58,900	$47,500-$65,000	$45,000
Touro College (Fuchsberg) (NY)	$57,500	$51,250-$66,500	$47,500
Marquette University (WI)	$56,325	$48,000-$107,000	$49,000
Western State University (CA)	$55,640	$39,250-$90,000	$60,000
Barry University (FL)	$55,000	$45,000-$68,000	$44,000
Charleston School of Law (SC)	$55,000	$48,000-$72,000	$40,000
Northern Kentucky University (Chase)	$55,000	$40,000-$80,000	$40,000
St. Mary's University (TX)	$55,000	$40,000-$70,872	$54,250
Texas Southern University (Marshall)	$55,000	$47,250-$70,000	$55,000
Texas Tech University	$55,000	$50,000-$72,500	$50,000
University of Arkansas–Little Rock (Bowen)	$55,000	$42,000-$70,000	$47,635
University of Louisville (Brandeis) (KY)	$55,000	$45,000-$90,000	$44,000
University of Nebraska–Lincoln	$55,000	$48,000-$75,000	$44,100
Valparaiso University (IN)	$55,000	$50,000-$80,000	N/A
Washburn University (KS)	$55,000	$45,000-$64,000	$45,600
Florida International University	$54,000	$50,000-$75,000	$42,000
Florida Coastal School of Law	$53,750	$47,250-$70,000	$40,062
CUNY–Queens College	$53,524	$41,600-$70,000	$58,090
University of Montana	$53,500	$43,500-$60,000	$45,000
University of Idaho	$52,500	$42,500-$60,000	$45,000
University of Oklahoma	$52,250	$45,500-$80,000	$45,040
Campbell University (Wiggins) (NC)	$52,000	$45,300-$72,000	$43,000
Oklahoma City University	$52,000	$46,000-$65,000	$42,000
University of Arkansas–Fayetteville	$52,000	$42,500-$70,000	$42,000
Roger Williams University (RI)	$51,000	$43,500-$65,000	$45,000
University of Detroit Mercy	$50,500	$42,500-$80,000	$48,500
Southern Illinois University–Carbondale	$50,000	$40,000-$60,000	$42,000
University of South Dakota	$49,000	$42,500-$55,000	$42,422
University of North Dakota	$48,000	$36,000-$71,000	$47,100
University of Wyoming	$48,000	$40,000-$54,000	$46,000
Northern Illinois University	$45,250	$42,000-$52,000	$44,435
Regent University (VA)	$45,000	$40,000-$53,500	$48,000

Where do graduates work?

You can tell a great deal about a law school by looking at where its newly minted JDs go to work. Harvard, whose corporate law program is one of its great strengths, launched 66 percent of its 2006 graduating class into law firms, for example. Yale sent 35 percent to judicial clerkships and 13 percent into government and public service. Schools are sorted by the percentage of graduates who took jobs at law firms.

School	% employed by law firms	% employed in business and industry	% employed in government	% employed in public interest jobs	% employed in judicial clerkships	% employed in academia	% employed in law school's state	% employed in foreign countries
Cornell University (NY)	85%	0%	2%	4%	10%	1%	60%	2%
University of Chicago	82%	3%	2%	1%	13%	0%	35%	1%
Columbia University (NY)	81%	2%	2%	3%	11%	1%	66%	3%
University of Pennsylvania	77%	4%	0%	3%	17%	0%	16%	2%
University of Virginia	77%	1%	5%	4%	14%	0%	11%	2%
Fordham University (NY)	76%	10%	5%	3%	4%	1%	84%	0%
Univ. of Southern California (Gould)	76%	7%	4%	6%	5%	3%	86%	0%
Western State University (CA)	76%	13%	6%	1%	0%	4%	81%	0%
Duke University (NC)	75%	3%	2%	3%	16%	1%	9%	0%
New York University	75%	2%	2%	9%	11%	1%	69%	3%
Georgetown University (DC)	74%	5%	6%	5%	8%	1%	35%	2%
Northwestern University (IL)	74%	5%	2%	5%	12%	2%	41%	1%
Vanderbilt University (TN)	74%	3%	6%	2%	15%	0%	19%	2%
Samford University (Cumberland) (AL)	73%	11%	11%	0%	3%	2%	58%	1%
University of Michigan–Ann Arbor	73%	5%	3%	5%	14%	1%	10%	2%
University of California–Berkeley	72%	4%	5%	10%	9%	0%	69%	2%
Emory University (GA)	70%	10%	4%	2%	9%	0%	42%	1%
University of Memphis (Humphreys)	70%	11%	9%	4%	5%	2%	88%	0%
Wake Forest University (NC)	70%	6%	9%	N/A	9%	3%	56%	N/A
Boston University	69%	5%	5%	6%	6%	7%	46%	1%
Faulkner University (Jones) (AL)	69%	7%	11%	4%	7%	2%	91%	N/A
Nova Southeastern Univ. (Broad) (FL)	68%	10%	10%	7%	3%	1%	88%	1%
Boston College	67%	5%	7%	3%	14%	4%	50%	1%
Campbell University (Wiggins) (NC)	67%	5%	22%	1%	3%	1%	91%	0%
George Washington University (DC)	66%	7%	12%	4%	9%	2%	52%	0%
Harvard University (MA)	66%	4%	4%	6%	19%	1%	11%	4%
Mercer University (George) (GA)	66%	5%	18%	3%	8%	0%	81%	0%
Pepperdine University (CA)	66%	17%	6%	4%	5%	3%	81%	1%
Southern Methodist Univ. (Dedman) (TX)	66%	23%	5%	1%	2%	3%	94%	N/A
University of Miami (FL)	66%	10%	10%	3%	5%	1%	66%	1%
Wayne State University (MI)	66%	13%	12%	6%	2%	2%	90%	0%
Baylor University (Umphrey) (TX)	65%	9%	12%	1%	10%	2%	90%	0%
University of Florida (Levin)	65%	8%	13%	5%	5%	3%	75%	1%
Atlanta's John Marshall Law School	64%	15%	10%	4%	5%	2%	82%	1%
Marquette University (WI)	64%	14%	10%	5%	4%	3%	74%	1%
University of California–Los Angeles	64%	7%	8%	9%	11%	2%	87%	0%
University of California (Hastings)	63%	8%	9%	6%	6%	8%	87%	0%
University of North Carolina–Chapel Hill	63%	9%	7%	9%	10%	1%	55%	0%
University of Texas–Austin	63%	10%	10%	3%	13%	1%	67%	1%

Where do graduates work?

School	% employed by law firms	% employed in business and industry	% employed in government	% employed in public interest jobs	% employed in judicial clerkships	% employed in academia	% employed in law school's state	% employed in foreign countries
Appalachian School of Law (VA)	62%	11%	11%	6%	6%	0%	21%	0%
Loyola University Chicago	62%	17%	13%	4%	3%	1%	82%	1%
Loyola University New Orleans	62%	11%	12%	4%	10%	1%	69%	3%
Oklahoma City University	62%	14%	15%	6%	0%	3%	66%	1%
South Texas College of Law	62%	17%	13%	3%	5%	1%	93%	0%
St. Louis University	62%	17%	7%	11%	3%	0%	62%	0%
St. Mary's University (TX)	62%	11%	18%	2%	5%	2%	89%	0%
University of Arkansas–Fayetteville	62%	17%	11%	5%	3%	2%	64%	0%
University of Pittsburgh	62%	17%	10%	4%	7%	1%	63%	1%
Washington University in St. Louis	62%	10%	11%	2%	11%	2%	23%	4%
Whittier College (CA)	62%	22%	8%	3%	2%	3%	86%	4%
Stanford University (CA)	61%	5%	4%	6%	23%	1%	44%	2%
Stetson University (FL)	61%	11%	11%	7%	3%	3%	81%	2%
University at Buffalo–SUNY	61%	11%	11%	7%	5%	4%	82%	1%
University of Notre Dame (IN)	61%	6%	12%	7%	14%	1%	7%	0%
California Western School of Law	60%	13%	14%	7%	5%	1%	76%	1%
College of William and Mary	60%	7%	15%	4%	14%	0%	36%	1%
Florida International University	60%	18%	15%	0%	1%	1%	98%	0%
Southwestern Law School (CA)	60%	19%	9%	4%	2%	3%	91%	0%
Univ. of Illinois–Urbana-Champaign	60%	14%	14%	3%	7%	3%	64%	1%
University of Minnesota–Twin Cities	60%	8%	11%	4%	17%	0%	52%	1%
University of Utah (Quinney)	60%	7%	15%	5%	10%	3%	78%	1%
Valparaiso University (IN)	60%	13%	12%	0%	12%	3%	45%	0%
Franklin Pierce Law Center (NH)	59%	16%	6%	7%	9%	3%	21%	1%
Loyola Marymount University (CA)	59%	18%	7%	12%	2%	1%	95%	0%
University of Tennessee–Knoxville	59%	6%	16%	4%	13%	2%	68%	1%
University of Tulsa (OK)	59%	21%	11%	5%	1%	3%	57%	1%
Barry University (FL)	58%	16%	15%	7%	1%	3%	84%	0%
Northern Illinois University	58%	13%	19%	5%	2%	2%	81%	2%
St. John's University (NY)	58%	15%	17%	3%	4%	3%	90%	0%
Texas Wesleyan University	58%	29%	10%	1%	2%	0%	89%	0%
Touro College (Fuchsberg) (NY)	58%	14%	19%	3%	5%	1%	90%	0%
University of Connecticut	58%	14%	10%	2%	13%	2%	66%	1%
University of Dayton (OH)	58%	13%	13%	4%	9%	3%	62%	0%
University of Georgia	58%	7%	11%	6%	17%	1%	77%	1%
University of Houston (TX)	58%	21%	10%	4%	4%	2%	90%	1%
University of Kentucky	58%	7%	9%	5%	19%	1%	69%	0%
University of Missouri–Kansas City	58%	8%	17%	5%	11%	1%	76%	1%
University of Wisconsin–Madison	58%	12%	15%	7%	6%	2%	51%	3%
Yeshiva University (Cardozo) (NY)	58%	19%	8%	10%	5%	0%	81%	2%
Brooklyn Law School (NY)	57%	12%	18%	6%	6%	1%	86%	2%
Capital University (OH)	57%	17%	20%	4%	1%	2%	87%	0%
Chapman University (CA)	57%	9%	11%	1%	3%	20%	90%	0%
Duquesne University (PA)	57%	17%	11%	1%	12%	2%	72%	0%
Georgia State University	57%	18%	10%	6%	3%	4%	92%	1%
Santa Clara University (CA)	57%	26%	9%	4%	2%	1%	90%	0%
Texas Southern University (Marshall)	57%	24%	10%	1%	1%	3%	64%	1%
Tulane University (LA)	57%	10%	10%	9%	12%	2%	38%	2%
University of Detroit Mercy	57%	22%	5%	5%	6%	5%	58%	17%
University of Louisville (Brandeis) (KY)	57%	16%	11%	8%	5%	3%	79%	3%
University of Oklahoma	57%	15%	20%	2%	3%	3%	76%	0%

Where do graduates work?

School	% employed by law firms	% employed in business and industry	% employed in government	% employed in public interest jobs	% employed in judicial clerkships	% employed in academia	% employed in law school's state	% employed in foreign countries
Washington and Lee University (VA)	57%	7%	9%	6%	20%	1%	27%	2%
Brigham Young University (Clark) (UT)	56%	13%	13%	1%	16%	1%	40%	3%
Florida A&M University	56%	8%	15%	8%	1%	5%	90%	0%
University of Kansas	56%	15%	18%	4%	7%	1%	45%	2%
University of San Diego	56%	18%	13%	6%	4%	2%	88%	1%
Villanova University (PA)	56%	17%	6%	6%	15%	0%	60%	1%
DePaul University (IL)	55%	20%	13%	3%	2%	6%	81%	0%
Illinois Inst. of Tech (Chicago-Kent)	55%	17%	13%	8%	5%	2%	80%	0%
John Marshall Law School (IL)	55%	23%	15%	2%	2%	3%	84%	0%
Texas Tech University	55%	17%	21%	3%	5%	1%	85%	1%
University of Maine	55%	11%	11%	7%	16%	N/A	70%	2%
University of Nevada–Las Vegas (Boyd)	55%	12%	10%	4%	16%	2%	83%	1%
Ohio State University (Moritz)	54%	14%	18%	3%	6%	5%	63%	1%
University of Alabama	54%	13%	15%	4%	12%	1%	61%	2%
University of Missouri	54%	11%	14%	5%	13%	2%	80%	1%
University of Washington	54%	7%	14%	8%	16%	1%	62%	2%
Arizona State University (O'Connor)	53%	10%	17%	9%	7%	3%	73%	0%
Cleveland State Univ. (Marshall)	53%	24%	12%	3%	5%	3%	89%	1%
Indiana University–Indianapolis	53%	19%	18%	5%	1%	4%	80%	1%
North Carolina Central University	53%	6%	22%	7%	6%	1%	68%	0%
University of California–Davis	53%	7%	11%	12%	7%	3%	87%	0%
University of Richmond (Williams) (VA)	53%	8%	12%	2%	17%	0%	72%	0%
Golden Gate University (CA)	52%	12%	15%	7%	4%	9%	86%	1%
Gonzaga University (WA)	52%	12%	15%	7%	8%	2%	62%	1%
Mississippi College	52%	20%	15%	0%	12%	1%	66%	1%
Northern Kentucky University (Chase)	52%	21%	10%	7%	8%	1%	44%	0%
University of Denver (Sturm)	52%	17%	14%	4%	10%	1%	77%	1%
University of Iowa	52%	14%	16%	3%	12%	3%	34%	0%
William Mitchell College of Law (MN)	52%	26%	8%	3%	9%	1%	84%	0%
Drake University (IA)	51%	20%	12%	6%	9%	2%	63%	0%
Louisiana St. Univ.–Baton Rouge (Hebert)	51%	11%	15%	2%	18%	2%	80%	0%
Univ. of Arkansas–Little Rock (Bowen)	51%	14%	13%	4%	13%	5%	85%	0%
University of South Carolina	51%	9%	15%	4%	19%	1%	73%	1%
Howard University (DC)	50%	10%	16%	3%	16%	0%	36%	0%
Ohio Northern University (Pettit)	50%	5%	27%	2%	3%	4%	38%	0%
University of Cincinnati	50%	13%	12%	13%	6%	5%	68%	0%
University of Mississippi	50%	11%	14%	5%	17%	3%	60%	0%
University of the Pacific (McGeorge) (CA)	50%	9%	25%	9%	3%	3%	90%	0%
Creighton University (NE)	49%	21%	23%	2%	5%	0%	49%	0%
University of San Francisco	49%	24%	10%	10%	1%	1%	85%	0%
Western New England College (MA)	49%	17%	10%	8%	16%	2%	36%	1%
Willamette University (Collins) (OR)	49%	20%	19%	5%	6%	1%	67%	0%
Albany Law School (NY)	48%	18%	16%	5%	9%	2%	81%	0%
American University (Washington) (DC)	48%	12%	14%	12%	13%	1%	44%	1%
Florida Coastal School of Law	48%	14%	15%	18%	3%	2%	74%	0%
Florida State University	48%	10%	25%	11%	2%	4%	80%	0%
Hofstra University (NY)	48%	26%	13%	3%	6%	3%	84%	0%
Michigan State University	48%	23%	10%	3%	9%	6%	55%	4%
University of Akron (OH)	48%	23%	19%	5%	4%	1%	80%	0%
University of Arizona (Rogers)	48%	9%	21%	2%	18%	2%	65%	1%
Case Western Reserve University (OH)	47%	17%	17%	11%	5%	2%	46%	2%

Where do graduates work?

School	% employed by law firms	% employed in business and industry	% employed in government	% employed in public interest jobs	% employed in judicial clerkships	% employed in academia	% employed in law school's state	% employed in foreign countries
George Mason University (VA)	47%	10%	17%	8%	13%	5%	43%	1%
Southern Illinois University–Carbondale	47%	14%	27%	7%	2%	4%	67%	0%
Thomas Jefferson School of Law (CA)	47%	22%	9%	3%	6%	3%	71%	1%
Ave Maria School of Law (FL)	46%	19%	18%	7%	7%	2%	38%	1%
Rutgers–Newark (NJ)	46%	16%	11%	5%	21%	1%	62%	1%
Syracuse University (NY)	46%	24%	14%	6%	9%	1%	40%	1%
Temple University (Beasley) (PA)	46%	15%	14%	7%	16%	3%	69%	1%
University of Montana	46%	4%	10%	10%	25%	0%	72%	0%
Indiana Univ.–Bloomington (Maurer)	45%	17%	17%	6%	11%	4%	32%	1%
Lewis & Clark Coll. (Northwestern) (OR)	45%	20%	17%	11%	6%	1%	64%	2%
Seattle University	45%	30%	12%	5%	7%	1%	84%	1%
University of Oregon	45%	11%	16%	11%	14%	4%	62%	1%
West Virginia University	45%	23%	8%	5%	16%	3%	73%	0%
Pace University (NY)	44%	17%	17%	7%	5%	7%	62%	0%
Roger Williams University (RI)	44%	21%	13%	8%	13%	1%	43%	1%
University of North Dakota	44%	17%	10%	6%	22%	1%	64%	0%
University of St. Thomas (MN)	44%	21%	12%	6%	14%	2%	72%	0%
Charleston School of Law (SC)	43%	7%	14%	4%	31%	2%	89%	0%
New York Law School	43%	23%	14%	6%	4%	4%	71%	1%
Regent University (VA)	43%	11%	19%	9%	11%	5%	44%	1%
University of Colorado–Boulder	43%	6%	14%	7%	25%	4%	80%	2%
University of Toledo (OH)	43%	13%	25%	8%	4%	5%	62%	1%
Washburn University (KS)	43%	13%	24%	9%	9%	1%	65%	0%
Catholic Univ. of America (Columbus)	42%	13%	27%	2%	12%	2%	47%	0%
Widener University (DE)	42%	20%	12%	4%	20%	2%	16%	0%
Hamline University (MN)	41%	27%	8%	7%	15%	1%	74%	1%
Rutgers–Camden (NJ)	41%	9%	7%	2%	40%	0%	55%	0%
University of Nebraska–Lincoln	41%	15%	26%	4%	11%	4%	66%	0%
University of Wyoming	41%	16%	16%	7%	14%	2%	57%	2%
Yale University (CT)	41%	7%	5%	8%	35%	3%	6%	3%
Seton Hall University (NJ)	40%	13%	6%	1%	39%	1%	70%	0%
Suffolk University (MA)	40%	28%	13%	3%	11%	3%	81%	0%
University of Maryland	40%	15%	15%	6%	18%	6%	58%	0%
New England School of Law (MA)	39%	27%	15%	4%	13%	2%	63%	0%
Pennsylvania State University (Dickinson)	39%	11%	22%	3%	20%	3%	46%	1%
University of Hawaii–Manoa (Richardson)	37%	9%	19%	4%	24%	7%	85%	3%
University of Idaho	37%	6%	21%	8%	24%	2%	64%	0%
University of New Mexico	35%	14%	17%	16%	13%	3%	79%	1%
Vermont Law School	35%	19%	16%	15%	15%	1%	15%	1%
Northeastern University (MA)	34%	26%	8%	16%	13%	3%	69%	2%
University of South Dakota	32%	14%	22%	8%	18%	4%	64%	N/A
University of Baltimore	31%	18%	20%	7%	21%	3%	83%	0%
Quinnipiac University (CT)	30%	25%	21%	2%	10%	1%	63%	0%
Univ. of the District of Columbia (Clarke)	27%	17%	19%	19%	11%	5%	55%	0%
CUNY–Queens College	22%	7%	17%	35%	18%	2%	63%	0%

The *U.S.News & World Report*

Ultimate Law School Directory

How to use the directory

In the following pages, you'll find exhaustive profiles of the country's American Bar Association–accredited law schools, based on a survey that *U.S. News* conducts each year. The directory is organized alphabetically. The online version of the directory at www.usnews.com allows you to do a customized search of our database. Want to know which law schools specialize in tax law and are located within 100 miles of your home? Enter those criteria and pull up a list.

The vital statistics shown in each directory entry are explained below. The data were collected from the schools during late 2009 and early 2010. If a law school did not supply the data requested, you'll see a N/A, for "not available." If a school did not return the full *U.S. News* questionnaire, it appears at the end of the directory on page 498 with limited information, gathered by calling the schools and consulting their websites.

Addresses and Essential Stats

In addition to the law school's address and the year the school was founded, you'll find key facts and figures here.

Website: Use the website to research the law school's programs.

Tuition: Figures cited for tuition are for the 2009–2010 academic year.

Enrollment: The number represents full-time students during the 2009–2010 academic year.

U.S. News ranking: A school's overall rank, shown in the lower-right-hand corner of the gray box, indicates where it sits among its peers in the

2011 ranking of law schools published by *U.S. News* at www.usnews.com and in its annual guide "America's Best Graduate Schools." Law schools among the top 100 are ranked numerically. Other schools are grouped in tiers. The school's ranking in various specialty areas (clinical training, dispute resolution, environmental law, healthcare law, intellectual property law, international law, tax law, and trial advocacy) is presented as well.

GPA and LSAT: The Law School Admission Test scores and grade point averages shown are for the Fall 2009 entering class and represent the range within which half of the students scored. In other words, 25 percent of students scored at or below the lower end of the range, and 25 percent scored at or above the upper end of the range.

Acceptance rate: The percentage of applicants accepted is provided for the full-time class entering in Fall 2009.

Admissions

Use the admissions phone number or the admissions email address to request information or an application. Many law schools also allow you to complete and submit an application online.

Application deadline: The application deadline for Fall 2011 admission is reported. Some schools allow students to enter at times other than the fall term; those entry points are also listed.

Applicants and acceptees: The admissions statistics provided—numbers of applicants and people accepted, and their credentials—are for the fall 2009 entering class. If the law school has a part-time option, the admissions data is presented for both full-time and part-time programs.

Financial Aid

Call the financial aid office with questions or requests for applications. Note that the deadlines for a school's financial aid form may not be the same as deadlines to apply for federal and state aid.

Tuition and other expenses: The tuition figures are for the 2009–2010 academic year. For public schools, we list both in-state and out-of-state tuition and the estimated cost of books and other miscellaneous living expenses. Whether or not the university offers student housing for law students is also noted.

Financial aid profile: The data on financial aid packages are for the 2008–2009 academic year. Grants are awarded by the university to full- or part-time students who either show need or have excellent academic records. We also list here the average amount of law-school debt borrowers in the Class of 2009 graduated with, and the proportion of students who took out at least one loan.

Academic Programs

Calendar: We tell you whether the school operates on a traditional semester schedule or a quarter system.

Joint degrees awarded: Many law students pursue a second degree in another university department to marry their interests or gain an edge in the job market. One common joint degree, the JD/MBA, combines law and business. Some people get a JD and master's or PhD degree in any of a number of arts or humanities or science disciplines. Other degree combos include the JD/MD (medicine) and the JD/MPH (public health).

Curricular offerings: What are the classes like? This section provides information on the size of both first-year and upper-level classes as well as the breadth of the curriculum during the 2008–2009 academic year. (If the school has a part-time program, its data is broken out.) If first-year students have the opportunity to take a class other than Legal Writing in a small section, that fact is noted. While the first-year curriculum is standard at most schools, the offerings in the second and third year vary widely. The number of course titles refers only to classroom courses offered, not to clinical or field placement offerings. Class-size figures include full- and part-time programs and exclude seminars.

Areas of specialization: A school listed any of the following: appellate advocacy, clinical training, dispute resolution, environmental law, healthcare law, intellectual property law, international law, tax law, and trial advocacy.

Faculty profile: Here, you'll find the total number of full-time tenured or tenure-track faculty (not including professors on leave or on sabbatical) plus part-time faculty during 2009–2010, as well as a breakdown. Part-timers include adjuncts, permanent part-time, and emeritus part-time. The student/faculty ratio (for Fall 2009) gives some indication of how accessible professors are likely to be.

Special programs: The text describing special programs was written by the schools. *U.S. News* edited this text for style but did not verify the information.

Student Body

What will your classmates be like? This section supplies the breakdown of full-time and part-time students, the male and female enrollments, and the ethnic makeup of the student body. All figures are for the 2009–2010 academic year. Note that students who did not identify themselves as members of any demographic group are classified by schools as "White" and that numbers may not add up to 100 percent because of rounding.

Attrition rates: The attrition rates indicate the percentage of students who chose not to come back to the law school during the 2008–2009 academic year. Students who transferred or left for health or financial reasons are included in the count. The percentage of full- and part-time students who left the law school during the 2008–2009 academic year is broken down by gender and by their year in school.

Library resources: In this section, you'll find key stats about the size of the library's collection at the end of the 2008–2009 academic year. Titles are those items that have their own bibliographic record. Total volumes includes any printed, typewritten, mimeographed, or processed work including microforms that are contained in a single binding. The total number of seats includes carrel and non-carrel seats.

Information technology: How many wired network connections are available to students? Is there a wireless network? How many users can access the wireless network at the same time? Are students required to lease or own a computer? These questions are answered in this section.

Employment and Salaries

This section provides data on the employment status of the 2008 graduating class both at the time of their graduation and nine months later. (Some schools did not know the status or location of all graduates, so the data may not be a complete reflection of the graduating class.) Salary information is provided for graduates working in the private sector, which includes law firms and any for-profit company. We also list the median salary and the 25th–75th percentile salary range. Salary figures are also listed for the public service sector, which includes government, judicial clerkships, academic posts, and non-profit jobs.

Occupational breakdown by type: The employment data listed here includes both part-time and full-time jobs. Graduates working in the government are employed by federal, state, or local entities. Public interest work includes Legal Aid groups and other non-profits. The unknown category includes graduates who reported to the school that they were employed but did not note the type of employment.

Employment location: We show the percentage of 2008 employed graduates who are employed in the same state as the law school, the percentage whose jobs are located outside of the United States, and the number of states in which the remaining graduates work. We also show the percentage employed in each of the following geographic areas: New England (Connecticut, Maine, Massachusetts, New Hampshire, Rhode Island, Vermont); Middle Atlantic (New York, New Jersey, and Pennsylvania); East North Central (Illinois, Indiana, Michigan, Ohio, and Wisconsin); South Atlantic (Delaware, District of Columbia, Florida, Georgia, Maryland, North Carolina, South Carolina, Virginia, and West Virginia); East South Central (Alabama, Kentucky, Mississippi, and Tennessee); West South Central (Arkansas, Louisiana, Oklahoma, and Texas); Mountain (Arizona, Colorado, Idaho, Montana, Nevada, New Mexico, Utah, and

Wyoming); and Pacific (Alaska, California, Hawaii, Oregon, and Washington).

Bar Passage Rates

Bar passage statistics are based on 2008 graduates taking either the Summer 2008 or Winter 2009 bar exams. Schools reported the bar passage rates and state in which the largest number of their 2008 graduates took the bar exam. So that you can see how a school's graduates fared compared to all first-time test-takers in the state, we also show the state's overall pass rates.

Albany Law School

- 80 New Scotland Avenue, Albany, NY, 12208-3494
- http://www.albanylaw.edu
- Private
- Year founded: 1851
- 2009-2010 tuition: full-time: $39,050; part-time: $29,325
- Enrollment 2009-10 academic year: full-time: 712; part-time: 37
- U.S. News 2010 law specialty ranking: N/A

3.03-3.56 GPA, 25TH-75TH PERCENTILE

153-157 LSAT, 25TH-75TH PERCENTILE

44% ACCEPTANCE RATE

Tier 3 2011 U.S. NEWS LAW SCHOOL RANKING

ADMISSIONS

Admissions phone number: (518) 445-2326
Admissions email address: admissions@albanylaw.edu
Application website: N/A
Application deadline for Fall 2011 admission: rolling

Admissions statistics:
Number of applicants for Fall 2009: 2,215
Number of acceptances: 972
Number enrolled: 255
Acceptance rate: 44%
GPA, 25th-75th percentile, entering class Fall 2009: 3.03-3.56
LSAT, 25th-75th percentile, entering class Fall 2009: 153-157

FINANCIAL AID

Financial aid phone number: (518) 445-2357
Financial aid application deadline:
Tuition 2009-2010 academic year: **full-time: $39,050; part-time: $29,325**
Room and board: $10,100 ; books: $1,100 ; miscellaneous expenses: $7,100
Total of room/board/books/miscellaneous expenses: $18,300
University does not offer graduate student housing for which law students are eligible.

Financial aid profile
Percent of students that received grants for the 2008-2009 academic year: full-time: 32%; part-time 24%
Median grant amount: full-time: $18,000 ; part-time: $13,500
The average law-school debt of those in the Class of 2009 who borrowed: $120,722 . Proportion who borrowed: 82%

ACADEMIC PROGRAMS

Calendar: **semester**
Joint degrees awarded: **N/A**
Typical first-year section size: Full-time: **65**

Is there typically a "small section" of the first year class, other than Legal Writing, taught by full-time faculty?:
Full-time: **no**
Number of course titles, beyond the first year curriculum, offered last year: **129**
Percentages of upper division course sections, excluding seminars, with an enrollment of:
Under 25: **56%**   25 to 49: **22%**
50 to 74: **15%**   75 to 99: **4%**
100+: **3%**
Areas of specialization: appellate advocacy, clinical training, dispute resolution, environmental law, health care law, intellectual property law, international law, tax law, trial advocacy

Fall 2009 faculty profile
Total teaching faculty: **76**. Full-time: **61%**; 50% men, 50% women, 20% minorities. Part-time: **39%**; 67% men, 33% women, 10% minorities
Student-to-faculty ratio: **13.1**

SPECIAL PROGRAMS *(as provided by law school):*
The Law Clinic & Justice Center and the Government Law Center offer students the chance to participate in representing clients in five in-house clinics and more than 140 placements. Students can spend a full semester working in a government agency in Albany, NY or in Washington, D.C. through the Semester in Government Program, a joint project of the Justice Center and the Government Law Center.

STUDENT BODY
Fall 2009 full-time enrollment: 712
Men: **56%**   Women: **44%**
African-American: **2.20%**   American Indian: **0.70%**
Asian-American: **4.90%**   Mexican-American: **0.40%**
Puerto Rican: **0.80%**   Other Hisp-Amer: **2.90%**
White: **75.00%**   International: **2.00%**
Unknown: **11.00%**

Fall 2009 part-time enrollment: 37
Men: **51%**   Women: **49%**

African-American: 5.40% American Indian: 0.00%
Asian-American: 2.70% Mexican-American: 0.00%
Puerto Rican: 2.70% Other Hisp-Amer: 0.00%
White: 81.10% International: 2.70%
Unknown: 5.40%

Attrition rates for 2008-2009 full-time students
Percent of students discontinuing law school:
Men: 0% Women: 1%
First-year students: 2% Second-year students: N/A
Third-year students: N/A Fourth-year students: N/A

LIBRARY RESOURCES
Total titles: 202,323
Total volumes: 707,090
Total seats available for library users: 432

INFORMATION TECHNOLOGY
Number of wired network connections available to students: 1,142 total (in the law library, excluding computer labs: 112; in classrooms: 989; in computer labs: 2; elsewhere in the law school: 39)
Law school has a wireless network.
Students are not required to own a computer.

EMPLOYMENT AND SALARIES
Proportion of 2008 graduates employed at graduation: N/A
Employed 9 months later, as of February 15, 2009: 94%
Salaries in the private sector (law firms, business, industry): $50,000 –$105,000 (25th-75th percentile)

Median salary in the private sector: $63,000
Percentage in the private sector who reported salary information: 55%
Median salary in public service (government, judicial clerkships, academic posts, non-profits): $50,500

Percentage of 2008 graduates in:
Law firms: 48% Government: 16%
Bus./industry: 18% Judicial clerkship: 9%
Public interest: 5% Unknown: 1%
Academia : 2%

2008 graduates employed in-state: 81%
2008 graduates employed in foreign countries: 0%
Number of states where graduates are employed: 16
Percentage of 2008 graduates working in: New England: 3%, Middle Atlantic: 86%, East North Central: 1%, West North Central: 0%, South Atlantic: 4%, East South Central: 0%, West South Central: 3%, Mountain: 1%, Pacific: 1%, Unknown: 1%

BAR PASSAGE RATES
Based on 2008 graduates taking Summer 2008 or Winter 2009 exams. Most of the school's first-time test takers took the bar in New York.

81%

School's bar passage rate for first-time test takers

81%

Statewide bar passage rate for first-time test takers

American University (Washington)

- 4801 Massachusetts Avenue NW, Washington, DC, 20016-8192
- http://www.wcl.american.edu
- Private
- Year founded: 1896
- 2009-2010 tuition: full-time: $41,406; part-time: $29,027
- Enrollment 2009-10 academic year: full-time: 1,195; part-time: 290
- U.S. News 2010 law specialty ranking: clinical training: 2, intellectual property law: 16, international law: 8

3.14-3.59 GPA, 25TH-75TH PERCENTILE

158-164 LSAT, 25TH-75TH PERCENTILE

22% ACCEPTANCE RATE

48 2011 U.S. NEWS LAW SCHOOL RANKING

ADMISSIONS

Admissions phone number: **(202) 274-4101**
Admissions email address: **wcladmit@wcl.american.edu**
Application website:
   http://www.wcl.american.edu/admiss/
Application deadline for Fall 2011 admission: **1-Mar**

Admissions statistics:
Number of applicants for Fall 2009: **7,649**
Number of acceptances: **1,715**
Number enrolled: **385**
Acceptance rate: **22%**
GPA, 25th-75th percentile, entering class Fall 2009: **3.14-3.59**
LSAT, 25th-75th percentile, entering class Fall 2009: **158-164**

Part-time program:
Number of applicants for Fall 2009: **1,018**
Number of acceptances: **216**
Number enrolled: **96**
Acceptance rate: **21%**
GPA, 25th-75th percentile, entering class Fall 2009: **3.06-3.52**
LSAT, 25th-75th percentile, entering class Fall 2009: **159-162**

FINANCIAL AID

Financial aid phone number: **(202) 274-4040**
Financial aid application deadline: **1-Mar**
Tuition 2009-2010 academic year: **full-time: $41,406; part-time: $29,027**
Room and board: **$14,623** ; books: **$1,038** ; miscellaneous expenses: **$5,724**
Total of room/board/books/miscellaneous expenses: **$21,385**
University offers graduate student housing for which law students are eligible.

Financial aid profile
Percent of students that received grants for the 2008-2009 academic year: full-time: **30%**; part-time **4%**

Median grant amount: full-time: **$12,000** ; part-time: **$3,675**
The average law-school debt of those in the Class of 2009 who borrowed: **$128,258** . Proportion who borrowed: **84%**

ACADEMIC PROGRAMS

Calendar: **semester**
Joint degrees awarded: **J.D./M.A.; J.D./M.B.A.; J.D./M.S.; J.D./M.P.A.; J.D./M.P.P.; J.D./LL.M.**
Typical first-year section size: Full-time: **98**; Part-time: **93**
Is there typically a "small section" of the first year class, other than Legal Writing, taught by full-time faculty?: Full-time: **yes**; Part-time: **no**
Number of course titles, beyond the first year curriculum, offered last year: **295**
Percentages of upper division course sections, excluding seminars, with an enrollment of:
   Under 25: **64%**   25 to 49: **21%**
   50 to 74: **11%**   75 to 99: **4%**
   100+: **0%**
Areas of specialization: appellate advocacy, clinical training, dispute resolution, environmental law, health care law, intellectual property law, international law, tax law, trial advocacy

Fall 2009 faculty profile
Total teaching faculty: **266**. Full-time: **35%**; **57%** men, **43%** women, **22%** minorities. Part-time: **65%**; **70%** men, **30%** women, **11%** minorities
Student-to-faculty ratio: **13.4**

SPECIAL PROGRAMS *(as provided by law school):*
Clinic: Gen Practice, Community Econ Dev, Crim, Disability, Women&Law, Dom Vio, Tax, IP, Human Rts. Center: Human Rts, Envt, ADR, Intl Law, Law&Gov, Gender, Innocence Proj. Study Abroad: Aus, Can, Chile, Fra, Hong Kong, Holland, Spain, Turkey, UK. Summer Inst: Human Rts, Intl Comm Arb, Envt Law, Health. Internships: US/Intl NGOs. Special: UNCAT, UNROW, Impact Litigation. Degrees: J.D. w/ M.B.A., M.A., LL.M.

STUDENT BODY

Fall 2009 full-time enrollment: 1,195

Men: 44%	Women: 56%
African-American: 8.50%	American Indian: 1.20%
Asian-American: 11.10%	Mexican-American: 2.60%
Puerto Rican: 0.90%	Other Hisp-Amer: 11.00%
White: 55.40%	International: 3.00%
Unknown: 6.20%	

Fall 2009 part-time enrollment: 290

Men: 46%	Women: 54%
African-American: 14.10%	American Indian: 1.00%
Asian-American: 11.70%	Mexican-American: 1.40%
Puerto Rican: 1.00%	Other Hisp-Amer: 8.60%
White: 50.30%	International: 2.10%
Unknown: 9.70%	

Attrition rates for 2008-2009 full-time students
Percent of students discontinuing law school:

Men: 3%	Women: 1%
First-year students: 5%	Second-year students: N/A
Third-year students: N/A	Fourth-year students: N/A

LIBRARY RESOURCES

Total titles: 273,971
Total volumes: 608,899
Total seats available for library users: 596

INFORMATION TECHNOLOGY

Number of wired network connections available to students: 2160 total (in the law library, excluding computer labs: 350; in classrooms: 1,500; in computer labs: 60; elsewhere in the law school: 250)
Law school has a wireless network.
Students are not required to own a computer.

EMPLOYMENT AND SALARIES

Proportion of 2008 graduates employed at graduation: 87%
Employed 9 months later, as of February 15, 2009: 96%
Salaries in the private sector (law firms, business, industry): $120,000 –$160,000 (25th-75th percentile)
Median salary in the private sector: $160,000
Percentage in the private sector who reported salary information: 71%
Median salary in public service (government, judicial clerkships, academic posts, non-profits): $52,000

Percentage of 2008 graduates in:

Law firms: 48%	Government: 14%
Bus./industry: 12%	Judicial clerkship: 13%
Public interest: 12%	Unknown: 1%
Academia : 1%	

2008 graduates employed in-state: 44%
2008 graduates employed in foreign countries: 1%
Number of states where graduates are employed: 31
Percentage of 2008 graduates working in: New England: 2%, Middle Atlantic: 15%, East North Central: 2%, West North Central: 1%, South Atlantic: 67%, East South Central: 1%, West South Central: 1%, Mountain: 2%, Pacific: 3%, Unknown: 6%

BAR PASSAGE RATES

Based on 2008 graduates taking Summer 2008 or Winter 2009 exams. Most of the school's first-time test takers took the bar in New York.

92%
School's bar passage rate for first-time test takers

81%
Statewide bar passage rate for first-time test takers

Appalachian School of Law

- PO Box 2825, Grundy, VA, 24614-2825
- http://www.asl.edu
- Private
- Year founded: 1994
- 2009-2010 tuition: full-time: $27,025; part-time: N/A
- Enrollment 2009-10 academic year: full-time: 334
- U.S. News 2010 law specialty ranking: N/A

2.61-3.31 GPA, 25TH-75TH PERCENTILE

147-152 LSAT, 25TH-75TH PERCENTILE

48% ACCEPTANCE RATE

Tier 4 2011 U.S. NEWS LAW SCHOOL RANKING

ADMISSIONS
Admissions phone number: **(800) 895-7411**
Admissions email address: **aslinfo@asl.edu**
Application website:
   http://os.lsac.org/Release/Logon/Access.aspx
Application deadline for Fall 2011 admission: **rolling**

Admissions statistics:
Number of applicants for Fall 2009: **1,617**
Number of acceptances: **784**
Number enrolled: **129**
Acceptance rate: **48%**
GPA, 25th-75th percentile, entering class Fall 2009: **2.61-3.31**
LSAT, 25th-75th percentile, entering class Fall 2009: **147-152**

FINANCIAL AID
Financial aid phone number: **(800) 895-7411**
Financial aid application deadline: **1-Jul**
Tuition 2009-2010 academic year: **full-time: $27,025; part-time: N/A**
Room and board: **$13,900** ; books: **$900** ; miscellaneous expenses: **$1,400**
Total of room/board/books/miscellaneous expenses: **$16,200**
University does not offer graduate student housing for which law students are eligible.

Financial aid profile
Percent of students that received grants for the 2008-2009 academic year: full-time: **26%**
Median grant amount: full-time: **$15,582**
The average law-school debt of those in the Class of 2009 who borrowed: **$89,340** . Proportion who borrowed: **90%**

ACADEMIC PROGRAMS
Calendar: **semester**
Joint degrees awarded: **N/A**
Typical first-year section size: Full-time: **129**

Is there typically a "small section" of the first year class, other than Legal Writing, taught by full-time faculty?:
   Full-time: **yes**
Number of course titles, beyond the first year curriculum, offered last year: **46**
Percentages of upper division course sections, excluding seminars, with an enrollment of:
   Under 25: **43%**   25 to 49: **17%**
   50 to 74: **19%**   75 to 99: **N/A**
   100+: **21%**
Areas of specialization: appellate advocacy, dispute resolution, environmental law, intellectual property law, international law, tax law, trial advocacy

Fall 2009 faculty profile
Total teaching faculty: **21**. Full-time: **90%**; **68%** men, **32%** women, **21%** minorities. Part-time: **10%**; **100%** men, **0%** women, **0%** minorities
Student-to-faculty ratio: **15.8**

SPECIAL PROGRAMS (as provided by law school):
Externships (required) for all rising 2L students; Community Service required (all students); Certificate–Lawyer as a Problem Solver (optional)

STUDENT BODY
Fall 2009 full-time enrollment: 334
Men: **63%**	Women: **37%**
African-American: **4.80%**	American Indian: **0.60%**
Asian-American: **1.80%**	Mexican-American: **0.00%**
Puerto Rican: **0.00%**	Other Hisp-Amer: **2.40%**
White: **79.30%**	International: **0.60%**
Unknown: **10.50%**	

Attrition rates for 2008-2009 full-time students
Percent of students discontinuing law school:
Men: **5%**	Women: **6%**
First-year students: **7%**	Second-year students: **9%**
Third-year students: **N/A**	Fourth-year students: **N/A**

LIBRARY RESOURCES

Total titles: 136,099
Total volumes: 220,298
Total seats available for library users: 232

INFORMATION TECHNOLOGY

Number of wired network connections available to students: 730 total (in the law library, excluding computer labs: 213; in classrooms: 379; in computer labs: 50; elsewhere in the law school: 88)
Law school has a wireless network.
Students are not required to own a computer.

EMPLOYMENT AND SALARIES

Proportion of 2008 graduates employed at graduation: N/A
Employed 9 months later, as of February 15, 2009: 66%
Salaries in the private sector (law firms, business, industry): N/A–N/A (25th-75th percentile)
Median salary in the private sector: $70,689
Percentage in the private sector who reported salary information: 56%
Median salary in public service (government, judicial clerkships, academic posts, non-profits): $46,057

Percentage of 2008 graduates in:

Law firms: 62%   Government: 11%
Bus./industry: 11%   Judicial clerkship: 6%
Public interest: 6%   Unknown: 4%
Academia : 0%

2008 graduates employed in-state: 21%
2008 graduates employed in foreign countries: 0%
Number of states where graduates are employed: 17
Percentage of 2008 graduates working in: New England: N/A, Middle Atlantic: N/A, East North Central: N/A, West North Central: N/A, South Atlantic: N/A, East South Central: N/A, West South Central: N/A, Mountain: N/A, Pacific: N/A, Unknown: 5%

BAR PASSAGE RATES

Based on 2008 graduates taking Summer 2008 or Winter 2009 exams. Most of the school's first-time test takers took the bar in Virginia.

83%

School's bar passage rate for first-time test takers

82%

Statewide bar passage rate for first-time test takers

Arizona State University (O'Connor)

- 1100 S. McAllister Avenue, Tempe, AZ, 85287-7906
- http://www.law.asu.edu
- Public
- Year founded: 1967
- 2009-2010 tuition: full-time: $19,225; part-time: N/A
- Enrollment 2009-10 academic year: full-time: 576
- U.S. News 2010 law specialty ranking: dispute resolution: 15

3.34-3.78 GPA, 25TH-75TH PERCENTILE

158-163 LSAT, 25TH-75TH PERCENTILE

28% ACCEPTANCE RATE

38 2011 U.S. NEWS LAW SCHOOL RANKING

ADMISSIONS

Admissions phone number: **(480) 965-1474**
Admissions email address: **law.admissions@asu.edu**
Application website:
https://www4.lsac.org/lsacd_on_the_web/login/openfirst.aspx?ID=KE934007A1489MO
Application deadline for Fall 2011 admission: **1-Feb**

Admissions statistics:

Number of applicants for Fall 2009: **2,400**
Number of acceptances: **667**
Number enrolled: **184**
Acceptance rate: **28%**
GPA, 25th-75th percentile, entering class Fall 2009: **3.34-3.78**
LSAT, 25th-75th percentile, entering class Fall 2009: **158-163**

FINANCIAL AID

Financial aid phone number: **(480) 965-1474**
Financial aid application deadline: **15-Mar**
Tuition 2009-2010 academic year: **full-time: $19,225; part-time: N/A**
Room and board: **$10,660** ; books: **$1,850** ; miscellaneous expenses: **$7,534**
Total of room/board/books/miscellaneous expenses: **$20,044**
University offers graduate student housing for which law students are eligible.

Financial aid profile

Percent of students that received grants for the 2008-2009 academic year: full-time: **47%**
Median grant amount: full-time: **$3,000**
The average law-school debt of those in the Class of 2009 who borrowed: **$73,317** . Proportion who borrowed: **82%**

ACADEMIC PROGRAMS

Calendar: **semester**
Joint degrees awarded: **J.D./M.B.A.; J.D./M.D. (Mayo Clinic); J.D./Ph.D. Psychology; J.D./Ph.D. Justice and Social Inquiry; J.D./M.H.S.A.**

Typical first-year section size: Full-time: **63**
Is there typically a "small section" of the first year class, other than Legal Writing, taught by full-time faculty?:
Full-time: **yes**
Number of course titles, beyond the first year curriculum, offered last year: **121**
Percentages of upper division course sections, excluding seminars, with an enrollment of:
Under 25: **75%**   25 to 49: **18%**
50 to 74: **4%**   75 to 99: **3%**
100+: **0%**
Areas of specialization: appellate advocacy, clinical training, dispute resolution, environmental law, health care law, intellectual property law, international law, tax law, trial advocacy

Fall 2009 faculty profile

Total teaching faculty: **79**. Full-time: **65%**; **71%** men, **29%** women, **16%** minorities. Part-time: **35%**; **79%** men, **21%** women, **N/A** minorities
Student-to-faculty ratio: **8.5**

SPECIAL PROGRAMS (as provided by law school):

The Center for Law, Science and Innovation is the largest and most comprehensive in the country. The Indian Legal Program is nationally renowned. Joint Degrees include J.D./MD (Mayo Medical School) and J.D./PhD in Psychology. The College has two LL.M.'s: Biotechnology and Genomics; and Tribal Policy, Law and Government. The Master of Legal Studies familiarizes non-lawyers with the law.

STUDENT BODY

Fall 2009 full-time enrollment: 576

Men: **57%**   Women: **43%**
African-American: **2.10%**   American Indian: **6.40%**
Asian-American: **3.30%**   Mexican-American: **4.20%**
Puerto Rican: **0.30%**   Other Hisp-Amer: **4.70%**
White: **68.20%**   International: **1.90%**
Unknown: **8.90%**

Attrition rates for 2008-2009 full-time students

Percent of students discontinuing law school:

Men: **2%**   Women: **3%**

First-year students: **4%**   Second-year students: **4%**

Third-year students: **1%**   Fourth-year students: **N/A**

LIBRARY RESOURCES

Total titles: **123,391**

Total volumes: **428,093**

Total seats available for library users: **570**

INFORMATION TECHNOLOGY

Number of wired network connections available to students: **186** total (in the law library, excluding computer labs: **170**; in classrooms: **10**; in computer labs: **3**; elsewhere in the law school: **3**)

Law school has a wireless network.

Students are not required to own a computer.

EMPLOYMENT AND SALARIES

Proportion of 2008 graduates employed at graduation: **91%**

Employed 9 months later, as of February 15, 2009: **100%**

Salaries in the private sector (law firms, business, industry): **$75,000 –$125,000** (25th-75th percentile)

Median salary in the private sector: **$100,000**

Percentage in the private sector who reported salary information: **55%**

Median salary in public service (government, judicial clerkships, academic posts, non-profits): **$54,000**

Percentage of 2008 graduates in:

Law firms: **53%**   Government: **17%**

Bus./industry: **10%**   Judicial clerkship: **7%**

Public interest: **9%**   Unknown: **1%**

Academia : **3%**

2008 graduates employed in-state: **73%**

2008 graduates employed in foreign countries: **0%**

Number of states where graduates are employed: **21**

Percentage of 2008 graduates working in: New England: **1%**, Middle Atlantic: **2%**, East North Central: **4%**, West North Central: **1%**, South Atlantic: **3%**, East South Central: **1%**, West South Central: **2%**, Mountain: **76%**, Pacific: **12%**, Unknown: **0%**

BAR PASSAGE RATES

Based on 2008 graduates taking Summer 2008 or Winter 2009 exams. Most of the school's first-time test takers took the bar in Arizona.

90%

School's bar passage rate for first-time test takers

84%

Statewide bar passage rate for first-time test takers

Atlanta's John Marshall Law School

- 1422 W. Peachtree Street, NW, Atlanta, GA, 30309
- http://www.johnmarshall.edu
- Private
- **Year founded:** 1933
- **2009-2010 tuition:** full-time: $1,024/credit hour; part-time: $1,024/credit hour
- **Enrollment 2009-10 academic year:** full-time: 371; part-time: 184
- **U.S. News 2010 law specialty ranking:** N/A

2.67-3.26 GPA, 25TH-75TH PERCENTILE

149-153 LSAT, 25TH-75TH PERCENTILE

40% ACCEPTANCE RATE

Tier 4 2011 U.S. NEWS LAW SCHOOL RANKING

ADMISSIONS
Admissions phone number: **(404) 872-3593**
Admissions email address: **admissions@johnmarshall.edu**
Application website: **http://www.johnmarshall.edu**
Application deadline for Fall 2011 admission: **rolling**

Admissions statistics:
Number of applicants for Fall 2009: **1,436**
Number of acceptances: **580**
Number enrolled: **145**
Acceptance rate: **40%**
GPA, 25th-75th percentile, entering class Fall 2009: **2.67-3.26**
LSAT, 25th-75th percentile, entering class Fall 2009: **149-153**

Part-time program:
Number of applicants for Fall 2009: **353**
Number of acceptances: **132**
Number enrolled: **66**
Acceptance rate: **37%**
GPA, 25th-75th percentile, entering class Fall 2009: **2.64-3.31**
LSAT, 25th-75th percentile, entering class Fall 2009: **149-153**

FINANCIAL AID
Financial aid phone number: **(404) 872-3593**
Financial aid application deadline:
Tuition 2009-2010 academic year: **full-time: $1,024/credit hour; part-time: $1,024/credit hour**
Room and board: **$10,400** ; books: **$2,400** ; miscellaneous expenses: **$8,200**
Total of room/board/books/miscellaneous expenses: **$21,000**
University does not offer graduate student housing for which law students are eligible.

Financial aid profile
Percent of students that received grants for the 2008-2009 academic year: full-time: **2%**; part-time **2%**
Median grant amount: full-time: **$0** ; part-time: **$0**

The average law-school debt of those in the Class of 2009 who borrowed: **$114,933** . Proportion who borrowed: **82%**

ACADEMIC PROGRAMS
Calendar: **semester**
Joint degrees awarded: **N/A**
Typical first-year section size: Full-time: **49**; Part-time: **45**
Is there typically a "small section" of the first year class, other than Legal Writing, taught by full-time faculty?:
Full-time: **no**; Part-time: **no**
Number of course titles, beyond the first year curriculum, offered last year: **51**
Percentages of upper division course sections, excluding seminars, with an enrollment of:
Under 25: **69%**   25 to 49: **26%**
50 to 74: **4%**   75 to 99: **0%**
100+: **0%**
Areas of specialization: appellate advocacy, dispute resolution, environmental law, health care law, intellectual property law, international law, tax law, trial advocacy

Fall 2009 faculty profile
Total teaching faculty: **42**. Full-time: **71%**; **40%** men, **60%** women, **20%** minorities. Part-time: **29%**; **83%** men, **17%** women, **8%** minorities
Student-to-faculty ratio: **12.9**

SPECIAL PROGRAMS *(as provided by law school)*:
The Externship Program provides the opportunity to integrate substantive knowledge learned in class with the practice of law. Second and third year students earn academic credit while working in legal placements in corporate legal departments, governmental agencies, and pro bono organizations. Full-time students may and part-time students must register for classes in the Summer Session.

STUDENT BODY
Fall 2009 full-time enrollment: **371**
Men: **51%**   Women: **49%**
African-American: **14.00%**   American Indian: **0.80%**
Asian-American: **3.00%**   Mexican-American: **0.00%**
Puerto Rican: **3.00%**   Other Hisp-Amer: **0.00%**

White: 72.50%   International: 0.30%
Unknown: 6.50%

Fall 2009 part-time enrollment: 184

Men: 43%   Women: 57%
African-American: 28.30%   American Indian: 0.00%
Asian-American: 4.90%   Mexican-American: 0.00%
Puerto Rican: 2.70%   Other Hisp-Amer: 0.00%
White: 62.00%   International: 0.00%
Unknown: 2.20%

Attrition rates for 2008-2009 full-time students
Percent of students discontinuing law school:
Men: 6%   Women: 6%
First-year students: 16%   Second-year students: 3%
Third-year students: N/A   Fourth-year students: N/A

LIBRARY RESOURCES
Total titles: 168,663
Total volumes: 260,616
Total seats available for library users: 212

INFORMATION TECHNOLOGY
Number of wired network connections available to stu-
    dents: 181 total (in the law library, excluding computer
    labs: 94; in classrooms: 59; in computer labs: 24; else-
    where in the law school: 4)
Law school has a wireless network.
Students are not required to own a computer.

EMPLOYMENT AND SALARIES
Proportion of 2008 graduates employed at graduation:
    45%
Employed 9 months later, as of February 15, 2009: 96%

Salaries in the private sector (law firms, business, indus-
    try): $50,000 –$67,500 (25th-75th percentile)
Median salary in the private sector: $62,500
Percentage in the private sector who reported salary
    information: 31%
Median salary in public service (government, judicial clerk-
    ships, academic posts, non-profits): $44,000

Percentage of 2008 graduates in:
Law firms: 64%   Government: 10%
Bus./industry: 15%   Judicial clerkship: 5%
Public interest: 4%   Unknown: 0%
Academia : 2%

2008 graduates employed in-state: 82%
2008 graduates employed in foreign countries: 1%
Number of states where graduates are employed: 15
Percentage of 2008 graduates working in: New England:
    N/A, Middle Atlantic: 1%, East North Central: N/A, West
    North Central: N/A, South Atlantic: 87%, East South
    Central: 7%, West South Central: 2%, Mountain: 1%,
    Pacific: 1%, Unknown: 0%

BAR PASSAGE RATES
Based on 2008 graduates taking Summer 2008 or
Winter 2009 exams. Most of the school's first-time test
takers took the bar in Georgia.

| 84% |
School's bar passage rate for first-time test takers

| 89% |
Statewide bar passage rate for first-time test takers

Ave Maria School of Law

- 1025 Commons Circle, Naples, FL, 34119
- http://www.avemarialaw.edu
- Private
- Year founded: 2000
- 2009-2010 tuition: full-time: $35,380; part-time: N/A
- Enrollment 2009-10 academic year: full-time: 375
- U.S. News 2010 law specialty ranking: N/A

2.91-3.53 GPA, 25TH-75TH PERCENTILE

147-155 LSAT, 25TH-75TH PERCENTILE

50% ACCEPTANCE RATE

Tier 4 2011 U.S. NEWS LAW SCHOOL RANKING

ADMISSIONS

Admissions phone number: **(239) 687-5420**
Admissions email address: **info@avemarialaw.edu**
Application website: **http://www.avemarialaw.edu/apply**
Application deadline for Fall 2011 admission: **10-Jun**

Admissions statistics:
Number of applicants for Fall 2009: **1,775**
Number of acceptances: **885**
Number enrolled: **210**
Acceptance rate: **50%**
GPA, 25th-75th percentile, entering class Fall 2009: **2.91-3.53**
LSAT, 25th-75th percentile, entering class Fall 2009: **147-155**

FINANCIAL AID

Financial aid phone number: **(239) 687-5335**
Financial aid application deadline: **1-Jun**
Tuition 2009-2010 academic year: **full-time: $35,380; part-time: N/A**
Room and board: **$13,131** ; books: **$900** ; miscellaneous expenses: **$6,368**
Total of room/board/books/miscellaneous expenses: **$20,399**
University does not offer graduate student housing for which law students are eligible.

Financial aid profile
Percent of students that received grants for the 2008-2009 academic year: full-time: **51%**
Median grant amount: full-time: **$15,000**
The average law-school debt of those in the Class of 2009 who borrowed: **$87,436** . Proportion who borrowed: **78%**

ACADEMIC PROGRAMS

Calendar: **semester**
Joint degrees awarded: **N/A**
Typical first-year section size: Full-time: **63**
Is there typically a "small section" of the first year class, other than Legal Writing, taught by full-time faculty?:
Full-time: **no**
Number of course titles, beyond the first year curriculum, offered last year: **77**
Percentages of upper division course sections, excluding seminars, with an enrollment of:
Under 25: **74%**   25 to 49: **19%**
50 to 74: **8%**   75 to 99: **0%**
100+: **0%**
Areas of specialization: appellate advocacy, clinical training, dispute resolution, environmental law, health care law, intellectual property law, international law, tax law, trial advocacy

Fall 2009 faculty profile
Total teaching faculty: **31**. Full-time: **55%**; **76%** men, **24%** women, **0%** minorities. Part-time: **45%**; **79%** men, **21%** women, **0%** minorities
Student-to-faculty ratio: **17.5**

SPECIAL PROGRAMS *(as provided by law school)*:
Our rigorous academic program provides students with the doctrinal knowledge and practical skills needed to excel in the practice of law. Traditional courses are complemented by classes, programs, and clinical programs that hone and develop essential legal skills, thereby helping ensure that students successfully transition to the practice of law.

STUDENT BODY
Fall 2009 full-time enrollment: **375**
Men: **57%**   Women: **43%**
African-American: **3.50%**   American Indian: **0.50%**
Asian-American: **4.50%**   Mexican-American: **3.70%**
Puerto Rican: **0.50%**   Other Hisp-Amer: **4.30%**
White: **79.50%**   International: **2.40%**
Unknown: **1.10%**

Attrition rates for 2008-2009 full-time students
Percent of students discontinuing law school:
Men: **15%**   Women: **13%**
First-year students: **31%**   Second-year students: **3%**
Third-year students: **N/A**   Fourth-year students: **N/A**

LIBRARY RESOURCES

Total titles: **59,959**
Total volumes: **69,149**
Total seats available for library users: **103**

INFORMATION TECHNOLOGY

Number of wired network connections available to students: **20** total (in the law library, excluding computer labs: **0**; in classrooms: **0**; in computer labs: **20**; elsewhere in the law school: **0**)
Law school has a wireless network.
Students are not required to own a computer.

EMPLOYMENT AND SALARIES

Proportion of 2008 graduates employed at graduation: **N/A**
Employed 9 months later, as of February 15, 2009: **82%**
Salaries in the private sector (law firms, business, industry): **$45,300 –$81,000** (25th-75th percentile)
Median salary in the private sector: **$60,000**
Percentage in the private sector who reported salary information: **29%**
Median salary in public service (government, judicial clerkships, academic posts, non-profits): **$57,500**

Percentage of 2008 graduates in:

Law firms: **46%**   Government: **18%**
Bus./industry: **19%**   Judicial clerkship: **7%**
Public interest: **7%**   Unknown: **0%**
Academia : **2%**

2008 graduates employed in-state: **38%**
2008 graduates employed in foreign countries: **1%**
Number of states where graduates are employed: **25**
Percentage of 2008 graduates working in: New England: **3%**, Middle Atlantic: **7%**, East North Central: **46%**, West North Central: **4%**, South Atlantic: **19%**, East South Central: **6%**, West South Central: **0%**, Mountain: **10%**, Pacific: **5%**, Unknown: **0%**

BAR PASSAGE RATES

Based on 2008 graduates taking Summer 2008 or Winter 2009 exams. Most of the school's first-time test takers took the bar in Michigan.

80%

School's bar passage rate for first-time test takers

82%

Statewide bar passage rate for first-time test takers

Barry University

- 6441 E. Colonial Drive, Orlando, FL, 32807
- http://www.barry.edu/law/
- Private
- Year founded: 1995
- 2009-2010 tuition: full-time: $31,700; part-time: $23,920
- Enrollment 2009-10 academic year: full-time: 609; part-time: 162
- U.S. News 2010 law specialty ranking: N/A

2.58-3.26 GPA, 25TH-75TH PERCENTILE

148-152 LSAT, 25TH-75TH PERCENTILE

57% ACCEPTANCE RATE

Tier 4 2011 U.S. NEWS LAW SCHOOL RANKING

ADMISSIONS
Admissions phone number: **(866) 532-2779**
Admissions email address: **lawinfo@mail.barry.edu**
Application website:
  http://www.barry.edu/law/pdf/application.pdf
Application deadline for Fall 2011 admission: **1-Apr**

Admissions statistics:
Number of applicants for Fall 2009: **1,773**
Number of acceptances: **1,019**
Number enrolled: **214**
Acceptance rate: **57%**
GPA, 25th-75th percentile, entering class Fall 2009: **2.58-3.26**
LSAT, 25th-75th percentile, entering class Fall 2009: **148-152**

Part-time program:
Number of applicants for Fall 2009: **216**
Number of acceptances: **98**
Number enrolled: **39**
Acceptance rate: **45%**
GPA, 25th-75th percentile, entering class Fall 2009: **2.57-3.25**
LSAT, 25th-75th percentile, entering class Fall 2009: **149-154**

FINANCIAL AID
Financial aid phone number: **(321) 206-5621**
Financial aid application deadline: **1-Apr**
Tuition 2009-2010 academic year: **full-time: $31,700; part-time: $23,920**
Room and board: **$13,340** ; books: **$1,800** ; miscellaneous expenses: **$8,590**
Total of room/board/books/miscellaneous expenses: **$23,730**
University does not offer graduate student housing for which law students are eligible.

Financial aid profile
Percent of students that received grants for the 2008-2009 academic year: full-time: **87%**; part-time **72%**
Median grant amount: full-time: **$6,000** ; part-time: **$6,500**
The average law-school debt of those in the Class of 2009 who borrowed: **$107,175** . Proportion who borrowed: **84%**

ACADEMIC PROGRAMS
Calendar: **semester**
Joint degrees awarded: **N/A**
Typical first-year section size: Full-time: **100**; Part-time: **55**
Is there typically a "small section" of the first year class, other than Legal Writing, taught by full-time faculty?:
  Full-time: **no**; Part-time: **no**
Number of course titles, beyond the first year curriculum, offered last year: **172**
Percentages of upper division course sections, excluding seminars, with an enrollment of:
  Under 25: **67%**   25 to 49: **13%**
  50 to 74: **12%**   75 to 99: **5%**
  100+: **3%**
Areas of specialization: appellate advocacy, clinical training, dispute resolution, environmental law, health care law, intellectual property law, international law, tax law, trial advocacy

Fall 2009 faculty profile
Total teaching faculty: **62**. Full-time: **39%**; **54%** men, **46%** women, **17%** minorities. Part-time: **61%**; **76%** men, **24%** women, **11%** minorities
Student-to-faculty ratio: **26.7**

SPECIAL PROGRAMS *(as provided by law school):*
Barry University Dwayne O. Andreas School of Law offers clinical programs focusing on Children and Families, Earth Advocacy, and Immigration. We also offer classes in intellectual property such as Trademarks, Patents, Copyrights, Sports Law, Internet Law and Entertainment Law.

STUDENT BODY
Fall 2009 full-time enrollment: **609**
Men: **55%**   Women: **45%**

African-American: 3.40% American Indian: 0.00%
Asian-American: 4.90% Mexican-American: 0.00%
Puerto Rican: 0.00% Other Hisp-Amer: 8.90%
White: 65.50% International: 0.00%
Unknown: 17.20%

Fall 2009 part-time enrollment: 162
Men: 54% Women: 46%
African-American: 4.90% American Indian: 0.00%
Asian-American: 1.20% Mexican-American: 0.00%
Puerto Rican: 0.00% Other Hisp-Amer: 8.00%
White: 69.80% International: 0.00%
Unknown: 16.00%

Attrition rates for 2008-2009 full-time students
Percent of students discontinuing law school:
Men: 4% Women: 4%
First-year students: 4% Second-year students: 6%
Third-year students: 2% Fourth-year students: N/A

LIBRARY RESOURCES
Total titles: 117,550
Total volumes: 273,067
Total seats available for library users: 338

INFORMATION TECHNOLOGY
Number of wired network connections available to students: 0 total (in the law library, excluding computer labs: 0; in classrooms: 0; in computer labs: 0; elsewhere in the law school: 0)
Law school has a wireless network.
Students are not required to own a computer.

EMPLOYMENT AND SALARIES
Proportion of 2008 graduates employed at graduation: N/A

Employed 9 months later, as of February 15, 2009: 71%
Salaries in the private sector (law firms, business, industry): $45,000 –$68,000 (25th-75th percentile)
Median salary in the private sector: $55,000
Percentage in the private sector who reported salary information: 73%
Median salary in public service (government, judicial clerkships, academic posts, non-profits): $44,000

Percentage of 2008 graduates in:
Law firms: 58% Government: 15%
Bus./industry: 16% Judicial clerkship: 1%
Public interest: 7% Unknown: N/A
Academia : 3%

2008 graduates employed in-state: 84%
2008 graduates employed in foreign countries: 0%
Number of states where graduates are employed: 13
Percentage of 2008 graduates working in: New England: 0%, Middle Atlantic: 4%, East North Central: 0%, West North Central: 1%, South Atlantic: 87%, East South Central: 2%, West South Central: 2%, Mountain: 1%, Pacific: 2%, Unknown: 1%

BAR PASSAGE RATES
Based on 2008 graduates taking Summer 2008 or Winter 2009 exams. Most of the school's first-time test takers took the bar in Florida.

77%
School's bar passage rate for first-time test takers

81%
Statewide bar passage rate for first-time test takers

Baylor University (Umphrey)

- 1114 S. University Parks Drive, 1 Bear Place # 97288, Waco, TX, 76798-7288
- http://law.baylor.edu
- Private
- Year founded: 1857
- 2009-2010 tuition: full-time: $38,408; part-time: N/A
- Enrollment 2009-10 academic year: full-time: 465
- U.S. News 2010 law specialty ranking: trial advocacy: 4

3.40-3.80 GPA, 25TH-75TH PERCENTILE

156-162 LSAT, 25TH-75TH PERCENTILE

30% ACCEPTANCE RATE

64 2011 U.S. NEWS LAW SCHOOL RANKING

ADMISSIONS

Admissions phone number: **(254) 710-1911**
Admissions email address: **Becky_Beck@baylor.edu**
Application website:
http://law.baylor.edu/ProspectiveStudents/PS_appinstructions.html
Application deadline for Fall 2011 admission: **1-Mar**

Admissions statistics:
Number of applicants for Fall 2009: **3,659**
Number of acceptances: **1,090**
Number enrolled: **197**
Acceptance rate: **30%**
GPA, 25th-75th percentile, entering class Fall 2009: **3.40-3.80**
LSAT, 25th-75th percentile, entering class Fall 2009: **156-162**

FINANCIAL AID

Financial aid phone number: **(254) 710-2611**
Financial aid application deadline: **1-Feb**
Tuition 2009-2010 academic year: **full-time: $38,408; part-time: N/A**
Room and board: **$9,273** ; books: **$2,007** ; miscellaneous expenses: **$5,541**
Total of room/board/books/miscellaneous expenses: **$16,821**
University offers graduate student housing for which law students are eligible.

Financial aid profile
Percent of students that received grants for the 2008-2009 academic year: full-time: **82%**
Median grant amount: full-time: **$3,331**
The average law-school debt of those in the Class of 2009 who borrowed: **$99,371** . Proportion who borrowed: **81%**

ACADEMIC PROGRAMS

Calendar: **quarter**
Joint degrees awarded: **J.D./M.P.P.A.; J.D./M.B.A.; J.D./M.Tax**

Typical first-year section size: Full-time: **66**
Is there typically a "small section" of the first year class, other than Legal Writing, taught by full-time faculty?: Full-time: **yes**
Number of course titles, beyond the first year curriculum, offered last year: **81**
Percentages of upper division course sections, excluding seminars, with an enrollment of:
Under 25: **61%**   25 to 49: **22%**
50 to 74: **10%**   75 to 99: **7%**
100+: **N/A**
Areas of specialization: appellate advocacy, clinical training, dispute resolution, environmental law, health care law, intellectual property law, international law, tax law, trial advocacy

Fall 2009 faculty profile
Total teaching faculty: **40**. Full-time: **68%**; **78%** men, **22%** women, **11%** minorities. Part-time: **33%**; **85%** men, **15%** women, **8%** minorities
Student-to-faculty ratio: **15.1**

SPECIAL PROGRAMS *(as provided by law school):*
Baylor's rigorous & unique curriculum is described at law.baylor.edu/curriculum/curriculum.htm. Seven areas of concentration (General Civil Litigation, Business Litigation, Criminal Practice, Business Transactions, Estate Planning, Administrative Practice & Intellectual Property); 3 joint degree programs (JD/MBA, JD/MTax, & JD/MPPA) and a 2 week summer program in Guadalajara, Mexico.

STUDENT BODY
Fall 2009 full-time enrollment: **465**
Men: **53%**   Women: **47%**
African-American: **2.60%**   American Indian: **0.20%**
Asian-American: **9.00%**   Mexican-American: **2.60%**
Puerto Rican: **0.00%**   Other Hisp-Amer: **6.50%**
White: **79.10%**   International: **0.00%**
Unknown: **0.00%**

Attrition rates for 2008-2009 full-time students
Percent of students discontinuing law school:

Men: **3%** Women: **8%**
First-year students: **9%** Second-year students: **4%**
Third-year students: **1%** Fourth-year students: **N/A**

LIBRARY RESOURCES

Total titles: **55,471**
Total volumes: **241,927**
Total seats available for library users: **279**

INFORMATION TECHNOLOGY

Number of wired network connections available to students: **733** total (in the law library, excluding computer labs: **125**; in classrooms: **564**; in computer labs: **12**; elsewhere in the law school: **32**)
Law school has a wireless network.
Students are not required to own a computer.

EMPLOYMENT AND SALARIES

Proportion of 2008 graduates employed at graduation: **N/A**
Employed 9 months later, as of February 15, 2009: **95%**
Salaries in the private sector (law firms, business, industry): **$60,000 –$105,000** (25th-75th percentile)
Median salary in the private sector: **$75,000**
Percentage in the private sector who reported salary information: **69%**

Median salary in public service (government, judicial clerkships, academic posts, non-profits): **$52,730**

Percentage of 2008 graduates in:

Law firms: **65%** Government: **12%**
Bus./industry: **9%** Judicial clerkship: **10%**
Public interest: **1%** Unknown: **1%**
Academia : **2%**

2008 graduates employed in-state: **90%**
2008 graduates employed in foreign countries: **0%**
Number of states where graduates are employed: **12**
Percentage of 2008 graduates working in: New England: **0%**, Middle Atlantic: **0%**, East North Central: **0%**, West North Central: **1%**, South Atlantic: **1%**, East South Central: **1%**, West South Central: **91%**, Mountain: **4%**, Pacific: **2%**, Unknown: **0%**

BAR PASSAGE RATES

Based on 2008 graduates taking Summer 2008 or Winter 2009 exams. Most of the school's first-time test takers took the bar in Texas.

93%

School's bar passage rate for first-time test takers

84%

Statewide bar passage rate for first-time test takers

Boston College

- 885 Centre Street, Newton, MA, 02459-1154
- http://www.bc.edu/lawschool
- Private
- Year founded: 1929
- 2009-2010 tuition: full-time: $39,490; part-time: N/A
- Enrollment 2009-10 academic year: full-time: 814
- U.S. News 2010 law specialty ranking: tax law: 18

3.34-3.68 GPA, 25TH-75TH PERCENTILE

163-167 LSAT, 25TH-75TH PERCENTILE

20% ACCEPTANCE RATE

28 2011 U.S. NEWS LAW SCHOOL RANKING

ADMISSIONS
Admissions phone number: **(617) 552-4351**
Admissions email address: **bclawadm@bc.edu**
Application website:
  http://www.bc.edu/schools/law/admission
Application deadline for Fall 2011 admission: **1-Mar**

Admissions statistics:
Number of applicants for Fall 2009: **7,166**
Number of acceptances: **1,431**
Number enrolled: **264**
Acceptance rate: **20%**
GPA, 25th-75th percentile, entering class Fall 2009: **3.34-3.68**
LSAT, 25th-75th percentile, entering class Fall 2009: **163-167**

FINANCIAL AID
Financial aid phone number: **(617) 552-4243**
Financial aid application deadline:
Tuition 2009-2010 academic year: **full-time: $39,490; part-time: N/A**
Room and board: **$12,785** ; books: **$1,300** ; miscellaneous expenses: **$4,971**
Total of room/board/books/miscellaneous expenses: **$19,056**
University offers graduate student housing for which law students are eligible.

Financial aid profile
Percent of students that received grants for the 2008-2009 academic year: full-time: **50%**
Median grant amount: full-time: **$16,678**
The average law-school debt of those in the Class of 2009 who borrowed: **$96,806** . Proportion who borrowed: **83%**

ACADEMIC PROGRAMS
Calendar: **semester**
Joint degrees awarded: **J.D./M.B.A.; J.D./M.A. Education; J.D./M.S.W.; J.D./M.A.**
Typical first-year section size: Full-time: **88**

Is there typically a "small section" of the first year class, other than Legal Writing, taught by full-time faculty?:
  Full-time: **yes**
Number of course titles, beyond the first year curriculum, offered last year: **149**
Percentages of upper division course sections, excluding seminars, with an enrollment of:
  Under 25: **57%**   25 to 49: **25%**
  50 to 74: **9%**   75 to 99: **8%**
  100+: **2%**
Areas of specialization: appellate advocacy, clinical training, dispute resolution, environmental law, health care law, intellectual property law, international law, tax law, trial advocacy

Fall 2009 faculty profile
Total teaching faculty: **86**. Full-time: **59%**; **59%** men, **41%** women, **18%** minorities. Part-time: **41%**; **77%** men, **23%** women, **3%** minorities
Student-to-faculty ratio: **13.2**

SPECIAL PROGRAMS *(as provided by law school)*:
Clinic/Program subjects include: immigration, civil litigation, criminal justice, homelessness, juvenile rights, women & the law, Attorney General, International Criminal Tribunal, London semester, semester in practice, judge & community courts, judicial process. Also offered: dual degree programs, cross-registration, and studying abroad.

STUDENT BODY
Fall 2009 full-time enrollment: 814
Men: **53%**   Women: **47%**
African-American: **3.60%**   American Indian: **0.70%**
Asian-American: **11.50%**   Mexican-American: **1.00%**
Puerto Rican: **0.50%**   Other Hisp-Amer: **5.30%**
White: **66.10%**   International: **1.50%**
Unknown: **9.80%**

Attrition rates for 2008-2009 full-time students
Percent of students discontinuing law school:
Men: **2%**   Women: **2%**

First-year students: **5%**   Second-year students: **N/A**
Third-year students: **N/A**   Fourth-year students: **N/A**

LIBRARY RESOURCES

Total titles: **117,055**
Total volumes: **481,235**
Total seats available for library users: **673**

INFORMATION TECHNOLOGY

Number of wired network connections available to students: **1014** total (in the law library, excluding computer labs: **227**; in classrooms: **608**; in computer labs: **0**; elsewhere in the law school: **179**)
Law school has a wireless network.
Students are not required to own a computer.

EMPLOYMENT AND SALARIES

Proportion of 2008 graduates employed at graduation: **86%**
Employed 9 months later, as of February 15, 2009: **97%**
Salaries in the private sector (law firms, business, industry): **$160,000 –$160,000** (25th-75th percentile)
Median salary in the private sector: **$160,000**
Percentage in the private sector who reported salary information: **87%**
Median salary in public service (government, judicial clerkships, academic posts, non-profits): **$49,423**

Percentage of 2008 graduates in:

Law firms: **67%**   Government: **7%**
Bus./industry: **5%**   Judicial clerkship: **14%**
Public interest: **3%**   Unknown: **0%**
Academia : **4%**

2008 graduates employed in-state: **50%**
2008 graduates employed in foreign countries: **1%**
Number of states where graduates are employed: **24**
Percentage of 2008 graduates working in: New England: **57%**, Middle Atlantic: **24%**, East North Central: **2%**, West North Central: **0%**, South Atlantic: **9%**, East South Central: **0%**, West South Central: **0%**, Mountain: **2%**, Pacific: **6%**, Unknown: **0%**

BAR PASSAGE RATES

Based on 2008 graduates taking Summer 2008 or Winter 2009 exams. Most of the school's first-time test takers took the bar in Massachusetts.

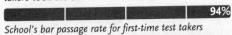

94%

School's bar passage rate for first-time test takers

89%

Statewide bar passage rate for first-time test takers

Boston University

- 765 Commonwealth Avenue, Boston, MA, 2215
- http://www.bu.edu/law/
- Private
- **Year founded:** 1872
- **2009-2010 tuition:** full-time: $39,658; part-time: N/A
- **Enrollment 2009-10 academic year:** full-time: 827; part-time: 3
- **U.S. News 2010 law specialty ranking:** healthcare law: 4, intellectual property law: 4, tax law: 6

3.50-3.83 GPA, 25TH-75TH PERCENTILE

164-167 LSAT, 25TH-75TH PERCENTILE

24% ACCEPTANCE RATE

22 2011 U.S. NEWS LAW SCHOOL RANKING

ADMISSIONS

Admissions phone number: **(617) 353-3100**
Admissions email address: **bulawadm@bu.edu**
Application website:
  http://www.bu.edu/law/prospective/apply
Application deadline for Fall 2011 admission: **1-Mar**

Admissions statistics:
Number of applicants for Fall 2009: **7,659**
Number of acceptances: **1,801**
Number enrolled: **271**
Acceptance rate: **24%**
GPA, 25th-75th percentile, entering class Fall 2009: **3.50-3.83**
LSAT, 25th-75th percentile, entering class Fall 2009: **164-167**

FINANCIAL AID

Financial aid phone number: **(617) 353-3160**
Financial aid application deadline: **1-Mar**
Tuition 2009-2010 academic year: **full-time: $39,658; part-time: N/A**
Room and board: **$11,808** ; books: **$1,374** ; miscellaneous expenses: **$4,394**
Total of room/board/books/miscellaneous expenses: **$17,576**
University offers graduate student housing for which law students are eligible.

Financial aid profile
Percent of students that received grants for the 2008-2009 academic year: full-time: **60%**
Median grant amount: full-time: **$15,000**
The average law-school debt of those in the Class of 2009 who borrowed: **$101,285** . Proportion who borrowed: **84%**

ACADEMIC PROGRAMS

Calendar: **semester**
Joint degrees awarded: **J.D./M.S.W.; J.D./M.B.A.; J.D./M.P.H.; J.D./M.S.; J.D./M.A. International Relations; J.D./LL.M . Tax; J.D./M.A. Historic** Preservation; **J.D./M.A. Philosophy; J.D./LL.M. Banking**
Typical first-year section size: Full-time: **90**
Is there typically a "small section" of the first year class, other than Legal Writing, taught by full-time faculty?: Full-time: **yes**
Number of course titles, beyond the first year curriculum, offered last year: **195**
Percentages of upper division course sections, excluding seminars, with an enrollment of:
  Under 25: **62%**   25 to 49: **23%**
  50 to 74: **9%**   75 to 99: **4%**
  100+: **2%**
Areas of specialization: appellate advocacy, clinical training, dispute resolution, environmental law, health care law, intellectual property law, international law, tax law, trial advocacy

Fall 2009 faculty profile
Total teaching faculty: **135.** Full-time: **41%**; **57%** men, **43%** women, **7%** minorities. Part-time: **59%**; **63%** men, **37%** women, **15%** minorities
Student-to-faculty ratio: **12.1**

SPECIAL PROGRAMS *(as provided by law school):*
We offer three clinical programs (civil, criminal, legislative) and three internship/externship programs. We have thirteen academic-year programs that allow students to study at leading universities in Oxford, Paris, Florence, Hong Kong, Buenos Aires, Tel Aviv, Leiden, Lyon, Hamburg, Beijing, Madrid, Singapore, and Geneva.

STUDENT BODY
Fall 2009 full-time enrollment: **827**
Men: **50%**   Women: **50%**
African-American: **5.30%**   American Indian: **0.20%**
Asian-American: **11.60%**   Mexican-American: **1.20%**
Puerto Rican: **1.10%**   Other Hisp-Amer: **3.40%**
White: **65.70%**   International: **3.60%**
Unknown: **7.90%**

Fall 2009 part-time enrollment: 3

Men: **67%** Women: **33%**
African-American: **0.00%** American Indian: **0.00%**
Asian-American: **0.00%** Mexican-American: **0.00%**
Puerto Rican: **0.00%** Other Hisp-Amer: **0.00%**
White: **100.00%** International: **0.00%**
Unknown: **0.00%**

Attrition rates for 2008-2009 full-time students
Percent of students discontinuing law school:
Men: **3%** Women: **2%**
First-year students: **7%** Second-year students: **1%**
Third-year students: **N/A** Fourth-year students: **N/A**

LIBRARY RESOURCES
Total titles: **590,508**
Total volumes: **659,182**
Total seats available for library users: **600**

INFORMATION TECHNOLOGY
Number of wired network connections available to students: **22** total (in the law library, excluding computer labs: **0**; in classrooms: **0**; in computer labs: **0**; elsewhere in the law school: **22**)
Law school has a wireless network.
Students are not required to own a computer.

EMPLOYMENT AND SALARIES
Proportion of 2008 graduates employed at graduation: **91%**
Employed 9 months later, as of February 15, 2009: **99%**
Salaries in the private sector (law firms, business, industry): **$160,000 –$160,000** (25th-75th percentile)

Median salary in the private sector: **$160,000**
Percentage in the private sector who reported salary information: **82%**
Median salary in public service (government, judicial clerkships, academic posts, non-profits): **$48,000**

Percentage of 2008 graduates in:
Law firms: **69%** Government: **5%**
Bus./industry: **5%** Judicial clerkship: **6%**
Public interest: **6%** Unknown: **2%**
Academia : **7%**

2008 graduates employed in-state: **46%**
2008 graduates employed in foreign countries: **1%**
Number of states where graduates are employed: **24**
Percentage of 2008 graduates working in: New England: **49%**, Middle Atlantic: **24%**, East North Central: **3%**, West North Central: **1%**, South Atlantic: **7%**, East South Central: **1%**, West South Central: **1%**, Mountain: **1%**, Pacific: **10%**, Unknown: **2%**

BAR PASSAGE RATES
Based on 2008 graduates taking Summer 2008 or Winter 2009 exams. Most of the school's first-time test takers took the bar in Massachusetts.

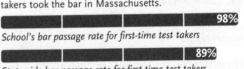

School's bar passage rate for first-time test takers

Statewide bar passage rate for first-time test takers

Brigham Young University (Clark)

- 340 JRCB, Provo, UT, 84602-8000
- http://www.law.byu.edu
- Private
- Year founded: 1972
- 2009-2010 tuition: full-time: $9,980; part-time: N/A
- Enrollment 2009-10 academic year: full-time: 447
- U.S. News 2010 law specialty ranking: N/A

3.52-3.85 GPA, 25TH-75TH PERCENTILE

160-165 LSAT, 25TH-75TH PERCENTILE

30% ACCEPTANCE RATE

42 2011 U.S. NEWS LAW SCHOOL RANKING

ADMISSIONS

Admissions phone number: **(801) 422-4277**
Admissions email address: **kucharg@lawgate.byu.edu**
Application website:
   http://www.law2.byu.edu/admissions/pdf_documents/current_application.pdf
Application deadline for Fall 2011 admission: **rolling**

Admissions statistics:

Number of applicants for Fall 2009: **733**
Number of acceptances: **218**
Number enrolled: **147**
Acceptance rate: **30%**
GPA, 25th-75th percentile, entering class Fall 2009: **3.52-3.85**
LSAT, 25th-75th percentile, entering class Fall 2009: **160-165**

FINANCIAL AID

Financial aid phone number: **(801) 422-6386**
Financial aid application deadline:
Tuition 2009-2010 academic year: **full-time: $9,980; part-time: N/A**
Room and board: **$8,400** ; books: **$1,850** ; miscellaneous expenses: **$4,690**
Total of room/board/books/miscellaneous expenses: **$14,940**
University offers graduate student housing for which law students are eligible.

Financial aid profile

Percent of students that received grants for the 2008-2009 academic year: full-time: **32%**
Median grant amount: full-time: **$4,620**
The average law-school debt of those in the Class of 2009 who borrowed: **$44,035** . Proportion who borrowed: **87%**

ACADEMIC PROGRAMS

Calendar: **semester**
Joint degrees awarded: **J.D./M.B.A.; J.D./M.A.C.C.; J.D./M.A. Education; J.D./M.P.A.**

Typical first-year section size: Full-time: **100**
Is there typically a "small section" of the first year class, other than Legal Writing, taught by full-time faculty?: Full-time: **yes**
Number of course titles, beyond the first year curriculum, offered last year: **109**
Percentages of upper division course sections, excluding seminars, with an enrollment of:

Under 25: **61%**	25 to 49: **18%**
50 to 74: **14%**	75 to 99: **6%**
100+: **0%**	

Areas of specialization: appellate advocacy, clinical training, dispute resolution, environmental law, health care law, intellectual property law, international law, tax law, trial advocacy

Fall 2009 faculty profile

Total teaching faculty: **60**. Full-time: **37%**; **77%** men, **23%** women, **9%** minorities. Part-time: **63%**; **68%** men, **32%** women, **11%** minorities
Student-to-faculty ratio: **17.3**

SPECIAL PROGRAMS (as provided by law school):

The Law and Religion Center works with scholars, government leaders, and NGOs in promoting religious liberty.
Approximately 90 percent of BYU law students participate in externships prior to graduation.

STUDENT BODY

Fall 2009 full-time enrollment: 447

Men: **65%**	Women: **35%**
African-American: **1.60%**	American Indian: **1.10%**
Asian-American: **7.80%**	Mexican-American: **0.40%**
Puerto Rican: **0.00%**	Other Hisp-Amer: **4.70%**
White: **81.70%**	International: **0.90%**
Unknown: **1.80%**	

Attrition rates for 2008-2009 full-time students

Percent of students discontinuing law school:

Men: **N/A**	Women: **N/A**
First-year students: **N/A**	Second-year students: **N/A**

Third-year students: **N/A**   Fourth-year students: **N/A**

LIBRARY RESOURCES
Total titles: 215,494
Total volumes: 514,373
Total seats available for library users: 906

INFORMATION TECHNOLOGY
Number of wired network connections available to students: 533 total (in the law library, excluding computer labs: 505; in classrooms: 28; in computer labs: 0; elsewhere in the law school: 0)
Law school has a wireless network.
Students are required to own a computer.

EMPLOYMENT AND SALARIES
Proportion of 2008 graduates employed at graduation: 87%
Employed 9 months later, as of February 15, 2009: 99%
Salaries in the private sector (law firms, business, industry): $90,000 –$160,000 (25th-75th percentile)
Median salary in the private sector: $120,000
Percentage in the private sector who reported salary information: 56%
Median salary in public service (government, judicial clerkships, academic posts, non-profits): $50,250

Percentage of 2008 graduates in:

Law firms: 56%   Government: 13%
Bus./industry: 13%   Judicial clerkship: 16%
Public interest: 1%   Unknown: 1%
Academia : 1%

2008 graduates employed in-state: 40%
2008 graduates employed in foreign countries: 3%
Number of states where graduates are employed: 27
Percentage of 2008 graduates working in: New England: 1%, Middle Atlantic: 4%, East North Central: 4%, West North Central: 3%, South Atlantic: 6%, East South Central: 1%, West South Central: 5%, Mountain: 56%, Pacific: 16%, Unknown: 1%

BAR PASSAGE RATES
Based on 2008 graduates taking Summer 2008 or Winter 2009 exams. Most of the school's first-time test takers took the bar in Utah.

92%

School's bar passage rate for first-time test takers

87%

Statewide bar passage rate for first-time test takers

Brooklyn Law School

- 250 Joralemon Street, Brooklyn, NY, 11201
- http://www.brooklaw.edu
- Private
- Year founded: 1901
- 2009-2010 tuition: full-time: $43,990; part-time: $33,074
- Enrollment 2009-10 academic year: full-time: 1,278; part-time: 180
- U.S. News 2010 law specialty ranking: clinical training: 28

3.26-3.64 GPA, 25TH-75TH PERCENTILE

160-164 LSAT, 25TH-75TH PERCENTILE

30% ACCEPTANCE RATE

67 2011 U.S. NEWS LAW SCHOOL RANKING

ADMISSIONS
Admissions phone number: **(718) 780-7906**
Admissions email address: **admitq@brooklaw.edu**
Application website: **http://www.brooklaw.edu/howtoapply**
Application deadline for Fall 2011 admission: **rolling**

Admissions statistics:
Number of applicants for Fall 2009: **4,909**
Number of acceptances: **1,470**
Number enrolled: **406**
Acceptance rate: **30%**
GPA, 25th-75th percentile, entering class Fall 2009: **3.26-3.64**
LSAT, 25th-75th percentile, entering class Fall 2009: **160-164**

Part-time program:
Number of applicants for Fall 2009: **977**
Number of acceptances: **182**
Number enrolled: **90**
Acceptance rate: **19%**
GPA, 25th-75th percentile, entering class Fall 2009: **3.28-3.55**
LSAT, 25th-75th percentile, entering class Fall 2009: **157-160**

FINANCIAL AID
Financial aid phone number: **(718) 780-7915**
Financial aid application deadline:
Tuition 2009-2010 academic year: **full-time: $43,990; part-time: $33,074**
Room and board: **$16,420** ; books: **$1,100** ; miscellaneous expenses: **$4,825**
Total of room/board/books/miscellaneous expenses: **$22,345**
University does not offer graduate student housing for which law students are eligible.

Financial aid profile
Percent of students that received grants for the 2008-2009 academic year: full-time: **75%**; part-time **29%**

Median grant amount: full-time: **$17,164** ; part-time: **$13,400**
The average law-school debt of those in the Class of 2009 who borrowed: **$93,666** . Proportion who borrowed: **80%**

ACADEMIC PROGRAMS
Calendar: **semester**
Joint degrees awarded: **J.D./M.A. Political Science; J.D./M.B.A. ; J.D./M.S. Library & Information Science; J.D./M.S. City & Regional Planning; J.D./M.U.P.**
Typical first-year section size: Full-time: **45**; Part-time: **31**
Is there typically a "small section" of the first year class, other than Legal Writing, taught by full-time faculty?: Full-time: **yes**; Part-time: **no**
Number of course titles, beyond the first year curriculum, offered last year: **189**
Percentages of upper division course sections, excluding seminars, with an enrollment of:

Under 25: **60%**	25 to 49: **19%**
50 to 74: **8%**	75 to 99: **6%**
100+: **7%**	

Areas of specialization: appellate advocacy, clinical training, dispute resolution, environmental law, health care law, intellectual property law, international law, tax law, trial advocacy

Fall 2009 faculty profile
Total teaching faculty: **151**. Full-time: **45%**; **53%** men, **47%** women, **9%** minorities. Part-time: **55%**; **76%** men, **24%** women, **8%** minorities
Student-to-faculty ratio: **18.4**

SPECIAL PROGRAMS *(as provided by law school):*
Nationally renowned clinics: criminal justice, individual client and group/business representation, dispute resolution. Fellowships: international business, public interest, human rights, bankruptcy law. Centers: international business law; health, science and public policy; law, language and cognition. One of best Legal Writing Programs in nation. Study abroad: China, Italy, Germany and England.

STUDENT BODY

Fall 2009 full-time enrollment: 1,278

Men: 52%	Women: 48%
African-American: 3.90%	American Indian: 0.20%
Asian-American: 15.90%	Mexican-American: 0.50%
Puerto Rican: 1.00%	Other Hisp-Amer: 4.40%
White: 69.90%	International: 0.70%
Unknown: 3.50%	

Fall 2009 part-time enrollment: 180

Men: 43%	Women: 57%
African-American: 11.10%	American Indian: 0.00%
Asian-American: 12.80%	Mexican-American: 0.00%
Puerto Rican: 1.70%	Other Hisp-Amer: 3.30%
White: 67.80%	International: 0.00%
Unknown: 3.30%	

Attrition rates for 2008-2009 full-time students
Percent of students discontinuing law school:

Men: 2%	Women: 3%
First-year students: 7%	Second-year students: N/A
Third-year students: N/A	Fourth-year students: N/A

LIBRARY RESOURCES

Total titles: 206,927
Total volumes: 580,994
Total seats available for library users: 665

INFORMATION TECHNOLOGY

Number of wired network connections available to students: 1984 total (in the law library, excluding computer labs: 216; in classrooms: 1,584; in computer labs: 110; elsewhere in the law school: 74)
Law school has a wireless network.
Students are not required to own a computer.

EMPLOYMENT AND SALARIES

Proportion of 2008 graduates employed at graduation: 80%
Employed 9 months later, as of February 15, 2009: 92%
Salaries in the private sector (law firms, business, industry): $70,000 –$160,000 (25th-75th percentile)
Median salary in the private sector: $145,000
Percentage in the private sector who reported salary information: 63%
Median salary in public service (government, judicial clerkships, academic posts, non-profits): $55,000

Percentage of 2008 graduates in:

Law firms: 57%	Government: 18%
Bus./industry: 12%	Judicial clerkship: 6%
Public interest: 6%	Unknown: 0%
Academia : 1%	

2008 graduates employed in-state: 86%
2008 graduates employed in foreign countries: 2%
Number of states where graduates are employed: 21
Percentage of 2008 graduates working in: New England: 1%, Middle Atlantic: 90%, East North Central: 0%, West North Central: 1%, South Atlantic: 3%, East South Central: 0%, West South Central: 1%, Mountain: 1%, Pacific: 2%, Unknown: 0%

BAR PASSAGE RATES

Based on 2008 graduates taking Summer 2008 or Winter 2009 exams. Most of the school's first-time test takers took the bar in New York.

89%
School's bar passage rate for first-time test takers

81%
Statewide bar passage rate for first-time test takers

California Western School of Law

- 225 Cedar Street, San Diego, CA, 92101-3090
- http://www.cwsl.edu
- Private
- Year founded: 1924
- 2009-2010 tuition: full-time: $38,400; part-time: $27,000
- Enrollment 2009-10 academic year: full-time: 791; part-time: 101
- U.S. News 2010 law specialty ranking: N/A

3.05-3.50 GPA, 25TH-75TH PERCENTILE

150-155 LSAT, 25TH-75TH PERCENTILE

48% ACCEPTANCE RATE

Tier 4 2011 U.S. NEWS LAW SCHOOL RANKING

ADMISSIONS

Admissions phone number: (619) 525-1401
Admissions email address: **admissions@cwsl.edu**
Application website:
**http://www.cwsl.edu/main/default.asp?nav=admissions.
asp&body=admissions/application.asp**
Application deadline for Fall 2011 admission: **4-Jan**

Admissions statistics:

Number of applicants for Fall 2009: **2,683**
Number of acceptances: **1,276**
Number enrolled: **322**
Acceptance rate: **48%**
GPA, 25th-75th percentile, entering class Fall 2009: **3.05-3.50**
LSAT, 25th-75th percentile, entering class Fall 2009: **150-155**

Part-time program:

Number of applicants for Fall 2009: **239**
Number of acceptances: **72**
Number enrolled: **18**
Acceptance rate: **30%**
GPA, 25th-75th percentile, entering class Fall 2009: **2.93-3.56**
LSAT, 25th-75th percentile, entering class Fall 2009: **148-154**

FINANCIAL AID

Financial aid phone number: (619) 525-7060
Financial aid application deadline: **1-Apr**
Tuition 2009-2010 academic year: **full-time: $38,400; part-time: $27,000**
Room and board: **$11,600** ; books: **$1,300** ; miscellaneous expenses: **$9,098**
Total of room/board/books/miscellaneous expenses: **$21,998**
University does not offer graduate student housing for which law students are eligible.

Financial aid profile

Percent of students that received grants for the 2008-2009 academic year: full-time: **41%**; part-time **25%**
Median grant amount: full-time: **$18,120** ; part-time: **$11,667**
The average law-school debt of those in the Class of 2009 who borrowed: **$119,345** . Proportion who borrowed: **86%**

ACADEMIC PROGRAMS

Calendar: **semester**
Joint degrees awarded: **J.D./M.S.W.; J.D./Ph.D. History; J.D./M.B.A.; J.D./Ph.D. Political Science; Health Law Masters in Advanced Studies**
Typical first-year section size: Full-time: **87**
Is there typically a "small section" of the first year class, other than Legal Writing, taught by full-time faculty?: Full-time: **no**; Part-time: **no**
Number of course titles, beyond the first year curriculum, offered last year: **114**
Percentages of upper division course sections, excluding seminars, with an enrollment of:

Under 25: **69%**	25 to 49: **13%**
50 to 74: **5%**	75 to 99: **7%**
100+: **5%**	

Areas of specialization: appellate advocacy, clinical training, dispute resolution, environmental law, health care law, intellectual property law, international law, tax law, trial advocacy

Fall 2009 faculty profile

Total teaching faculty: **119**. Full-time: **67%**; **63%** men, **38%** women, **13%** minorities. Part-time: **33%**; **59%** men, **41%** women, **10%** minorities
Student-to-faculty ratio: **18.3**

SPECIAL PROGRAMS *(as provided by law school):*

Special programs include California Innocence Project, Proyecto ACCESO, Street Law and Community Law Project. Areas of concentration are Health, International, Intellectual Property, Family, Employment Law and Creative Problem

Solving. Other programs are study abroad, dual-degree programs with UCSD and SDSU, and clinical internships.
www.cwsl.edu/specialprograms

STUDENT BODY

Fall 2009 full-time enrollment: 791

Men: 46%	Women: 54%
African-American: 3.00%	American Indian: 0.90%
Asian-American: 14.80%	Mexican-American: 7.50%
Puerto Rican: 0.30%	Other Hisp-Amer: 1.50%
White: 61.30%	International: 1.00%
Unknown: 9.70%	

Fall 2009 part-time enrollment: 101

Men: 39%	Women: 61%
African-American: 5.00%	American Indian: 0.00%
Asian-American: 10.90%	Mexican-American: 7.90%
Puerto Rican: 0.00%	Other Hisp-Amer: 4.00%
White: 61.40%	International: 0.00%
Unknown: 10.90%	

Attrition rates for 2008-2009 full-time students
Percent of students discontinuing law school:

Men: 9%	Women: 8%
First-year students: 19%	Second-year students: 2%
Third-year students: 1%	Fourth-year students: N/A

LIBRARY RESOURCES

Total titles: 186,505
Total volumes: 345,342
Total seats available for library users: 438

INFORMATION TECHNOLOGY

Number of wired network connections available to students: 540 total (in the law library, excluding computer labs: 355; in classrooms: 122; in computer labs: 41; elsewhere in the law school: 22)
Law school has a wireless network.
Students are not required to own a computer.

EMPLOYMENT AND SALARIES

Proportion of 2008 graduates employed at graduation:
N/A
Employed 9 months later, as of February 15, 2009: 84%
Salaries in the private sector (law firms, business, industry): $65,000 –$80,000 (25th-75th percentile)
Median salary in the private sector: $75,000
Percentage in the private sector who reported salary information: 36%
Median salary in public service (government, judicial clerkships, academic posts, non-profits): $58,552

Percentage of 2008 graduates in:

Law firms: 60%	Government: 14%
Bus./industry: 13%	Judicial clerkship: 5%
Public interest: 7%	Unknown: 0%
Academia : 1%	

2008 graduates employed in-state: 76%
2008 graduates employed in foreign countries: 1%
Number of states where graduates are employed: 15
Percentage of 2008 graduates working in: New England: N/A, Middle Atlantic: 1%, East North Central: 1%, West North Central: 1%, South Atlantic: 4%, East South Central: N/A, West South Central: 1%, Mountain: 13%, Pacific: 78%, Unknown: 0%

BAR PASSAGE RATES

Based on 2008 graduates taking Summer 2008 or Winter 2009 exams. Most of the school's first-time test takers took the bar in California.

84%
School's bar passage rate for first-time test takers

71%
Statewide bar passage rate for first-time test takers

Campbell University (Wiggins)

- 225 Hillsborough Street, Suite 401, Raleigh, NC, 27603
- http://www.law.campbell.edu
- Private
- Year founded: 1976
- 2009-2010 tuition: full-time: $30,850; part-time: N/A
- Enrollment 2009-10 academic year: full-time: 405
- U.S. News 2010 law specialty ranking: N/A

3.12-3.59 GPA, 25TH-75TH PERCENTILE

154-159 LSAT, 25TH-75TH PERCENTILE

30% ACCEPTANCE RATE

Tier 4 2011 U.S. NEWS LAW SCHOOL RANKING

ADMISSIONS
Admissions phone number: **(919) 865-5989**
Admissions email address: **admissions@law.campbell.edu**
Application website:
  http://www.applyweb.com/apply/camplaw/index.html
Application deadline for Fall 2011 admission: **1-Apr**

Admissions statistics:
Number of applicants for Fall 2009: **1,514**
Number of acceptances: **460**
Number enrolled: **159**
Acceptance rate: **30%**
GPA, 25th-75th percentile, entering class Fall 2009: **3.12-3.59**
LSAT, 25th-75th percentile, entering class Fall 2009: **154-159**

FINANCIAL AID
Financial aid phone number: **(910) 893-1310**
Financial aid application deadline: **15-Jun**
Tuition 2009-2010 academic year: **full-time: $30,850; part-time: N/A**
Room and board: **$15,370** ; books: **$1,400** ; miscellaneous expenses: **$2,500**
Total of room/board/books/miscellaneous expenses: **$19,270**
University does not offer graduate student housing for which law students are eligible.

Financial aid profile
Percent of students that received grants for the 2008-2009 academic year: full-time: **24%**
Median grant amount: full-time: **$14,250**
The average law-school debt of those in the Class of 2009 who borrowed: **$108,627** . Proportion who borrowed: **79%**

ACADEMIC PROGRAMS
Calendar: **semester**
Joint degrees awarded: **J.D./M.B.A. ; J.D./M.T.I.M.**
Typical first-year section size: Full-time: **40**

Is there typically a "small section" of the first year class, other than Legal Writing, taught by full-time faculty?: Full-time: **yes**
Number of course titles, beyond the first year curriculum, offered last year: **90**
Percentages of upper division course sections, excluding seminars, with an enrollment of:
  Under 25: **21%**   25 to 49: **38%**
  50 to 74: **31%**   75 to 99: **7%**
  100+: **2%**
Areas of specialization: appellate advocacy, clinical training, dispute resolution, environmental law, health care law, intellectual property law, international law, tax law, trial advocacy

Fall 2009 faculty profile
Total teaching faculty: **39**. Full-time: **51%**; **75%** men, **25%** women, **10%** minorities. Part-time: **49%**; **79%** men, **21%** women, **0%** minorities
Student-to-faculty ratio: **17.9**

SPECIAL PROGRAMS (as provided by law school):
The law school offers two options for clinical experiences. The Juvenile Justice Project exposes our students to both the theoretical and the practical aspects of the mediation process in the context of restorative justice. The newly added Senior Law Clinic allows for our students to assist low-income senior citizens through offering services that are specific to this population.

STUDENT BODY
Fall 2009 full-time enrollment: 405
Men: **50%**   Women: **50%**
African-American: **3.70%**   American Indian: **0.20%**
Asian-American: **2.20%**   Mexican-American: **2.00%**
Puerto Rican: **0.00%**   Other Hisp-Amer: **2.50%**
White: **88.90%**   International: **0.50%**
Unknown: **0.00%**

Attrition rates for 2008-2009 full-time students
Percent of students discontinuing law school:

Men: **6%**   Women: **5%**
First-year students: **11%**   Second-year students: **3%**
Third-year students: **1%**   Fourth-year students: **N/A**

LIBRARY RESOURCES
Total titles: **87,152**
Total volumes: **193,633**
Total seats available for library users: **395**

INFORMATION TECHNOLOGY
Number of wired network connections available to students: **59** total (in the law library, excluding computer labs: **4**; in classrooms: **6**; in computer labs: **47**; elsewhere in the law school: **2**)
Law school has a wireless network.
Students are not required to own a computer.

EMPLOYMENT AND SALARIES
Proportion of 2008 graduates employed at graduation: **N/A**
Employed 9 months later, as of February 15, 2009: **94%**
Salaries in the private sector (law firms, business, industry): **$45,300 –$72,000** (25th-75th percentile)
Median salary in the private sector: **$52,000**
Percentage in the private sector who reported salary information: **70%**
Median salary in public service (government, judicial clerkships, academic posts, non-profits): **$43,000**

Percentage of 2008 graduates in:
Law firms: **67%**   Government: **22%**
Bus./industry: **5%**   Judicial clerkship: **3%**
Public interest: **1%**   Unknown: **1%**
Academia : **1%**

2008 graduates employed in-state: **91%**
2008 graduates employed in foreign countries: **0%**
Number of states where graduates are employed: **6**
Percentage of 2008 graduates working in: New England: **N/A**, Middle Atlantic: **N/A**, East North Central: **N/A**, West North Central: **N/A**, South Atlantic: **98%**, East South Central: **N/A**, West South Central: **1%**, Mountain: **1%**, Pacific: **N/A**, Unknown: **0%**

BAR PASSAGE RATES
Based on 2008 graduates taking Summer 2008 or Winter 2009 exams. Most of the school's first-time test takers took the bar in North Carolina.

95%
School's bar passage rate for first-time test takers

83%
Statewide bar passage rate for first-time test takers

Capital University

- 303 E. Broad Street, Columbus, OH, 43215-3200
- http://www.law.capital.edu
- Private
- Year founded: 1903
- 2009-2010 tuition: full-time: $1,074/credit hour; part-time: $1,074/credit hour
- Enrollment 2009-10 academic year: full-time: 461; part-time: 187
- U.S. News 2010 law specialty ranking: N/A

2.96-3.51 GPA, 25TH-75TH PERCENTILE

151-156 LSAT, 25TH-75TH PERCENTILE

59% ACCEPTANCE RATE

Tier 4 2011 U.S. NEWS LAW SCHOOL RANKING

ADMISSIONS
Admissions phone number: **(614) 236-6310**
Admissions email address: **admissions@law.capital.edu**
Application website:
 https://secure.law.capital.edu/application/
Application deadline for Fall 2011 admission: **1-May**

Admissions statistics:
Number of applicants for Fall 2009: **1,174**
Number of acceptances: **693**
Number enrolled: **182**
Acceptance rate: **59%**
GPA, 25th-75th percentile, entering class Fall 2009: **2.96-3.51**
LSAT, 25th-75th percentile, entering class Fall 2009: **151-156**

Part-time program:
Number of applicants for Fall 2009: **260**
Number of acceptances: **120**
Number enrolled: **66**
Acceptance rate: **46%**
GPA, 25th-75th percentile, entering class Fall 2009: **2.86-3.47**
LSAT, 25th-75th percentile, entering class Fall 2009: **150-155**

FINANCIAL AID
Financial aid phone number: **(614) 236-6350**
Financial aid application deadline: **1-Apr**
Tuition 2009-2010 academic year: **full-time: $1,074/credit hour; part-time: $1,074/credit hour**
Room and board: **$13,514** ; books: **$1,501** ; miscellaneous expenses: **$271**
Total of room/board/books/miscellaneous expenses: **$15,286**
University does not offer graduate student housing for which law students are eligible.

Financial aid profile
Percent of students that received grants for the 2008-2009 academic year: full-time: **57%**; part-time **36%**
Median grant amount: full-time: **$10,000** ; part-time: **$5,000**
The average law-school debt of those in the Class of 2009 who borrowed: **$98,531** . Proportion who borrowed: **92%**

ACADEMIC PROGRAMS
Calendar: **semester**
Joint degrees awarded: **J.D./LL.M. Business; J.D./LL.M. Tax; J.D./LL.M. Tax & Business; J.D./M.B.A.; J.D./M.T.S.; J.D./M.S.A.; J.D./M.S.N.**
Typical first-year section size: Full-time: **85**; Part-time: **70**
Is there typically a "small section" of the first year class, other than Legal Writing, taught by full-time faculty?: Full-time: **yes**; Part-time: **yes**
Number of course titles, beyond the first year curriculum, offered last year: **184**
Percentages of upper division course sections, excluding seminars, with an enrollment of:

Under 25: **67%**	25 to 49: **20%**
50 to 74: **6%**	75 to 99: **6%**
100+: **0%**	

Areas of specialization: appellate advocacy, clinical training, dispute resolution, environmental law, health care law, intellectual property law, international law, tax law, trial advocacy

Fall 2009 faculty profile
Total teaching faculty: **56**. Full-time: **52%**; **66%** men, **34%** women, **10%** minorities. Part-time: **48%**; **74%** men, **26%** women, **11%** minorities
Student-to-faculty ratio: **15.8**

SPECIAL PROGRAMS *(as provided by law school):*
Concentrations in governmental affairs, labor/employment, small-business entities, publicly held companies, dispute resolution, environmental law, children & family law, criminal & civil litigation. Joint degrees in tax, business, nursing, sports admin, theological studies. Nat'l Ctr. for Adoption Law & Policy, Legal Clinics, Externships, Legal Res/Writing program, Bar & Academic Success programs.

STUDENT BODY

Fall 2009 full-time enrollment: 461

Men: 53%	Women: 47%
African-American: 7.20%	American Indian: 0.20%
Asian-American: 2.00%	Mexican-American: 0.00%
Puerto Rican: 0.00%	Other Hisp-Amer: 1.10%
White: 80.50%	International: 0.00%
Unknown: 9.10%	

Fall 2009 part-time enrollment: 187

Men: 57%	Women: 43%
African-American: 10.20%	American Indian: 0.00%
Asian-American: 3.20%	Mexican-American: 0.00%
Puerto Rican: 0.00%	Other Hisp-Amer: 1.60%
White: 73.80%	International: 0.00%
Unknown: 11.20%	

Attrition rates for 2008-2009 full-time students
Percent of students discontinuing law school:

Men: 9%	Women: 9%
First-year students: 20%	Second-year students: 5%
Third-year students: 1%	Fourth-year students: N/A

LIBRARY RESOURCES

Total titles: 52,144
Total volumes: 263,714
Total seats available for library users: 460

INFORMATION TECHNOLOGY

Number of wired network connections available to students: 113 total (in the law library, excluding computer labs: 113; in classrooms: 0; in computer labs: 0; elsewhere in the law school: 0)
Law school has a wireless network.
Students are not required to own a computer.

EMPLOYMENT AND SALARIES

Proportion of 2008 graduates employed at graduation: N/A
Employed 9 months later, as of February 15, 2009: 77%
Salaries in the private sector (law firms, business, industry): $55,000 –$118,500 (25th-75th percentile)
Median salary in the private sector: $79,000
Percentage in the private sector who reported salary information: 39%
Median salary in public service (government, judicial clerkships, academic posts, non-profits): $44,250

Percentage of 2008 graduates in:

Law firms: 57%	Government: 20%
Bus./industry: 17%	Judicial clerkship: 1%
Public interest: 4%	Unknown: 0%
Academia : 2%	

2008 graduates employed in-state: 87%
2008 graduates employed in foreign countries: 0%
Number of states where graduates are employed: 12
Percentage of 2008 graduates working in: New England: 0%, Middle Atlantic: 2%, East North Central: 91%, West North Central: 2%, South Atlantic: 2%, East South Central: 0%, West South Central: 2%, Mountain: 0%, Pacific: 2%, Unknown: 0%

BAR PASSAGE RATES

Based on 2008 graduates taking Summer 2008 or Winter 2009 exams. Most of the school's first-time test takers took the bar in Ohio.

95%
School's bar passage rate for first-time test takers

88%
Statewide bar passage rate for first-time test takers

Case Western Reserve University

- 11075 E. Boulevard, Cleveland, OH, 44106-7148
- http://www.law.case.edu
- Private
- Year founded: 1892
- 2009-2010 tuition: full-time: $38,679; part-time: N/A
- Enrollment 2009-10 academic year: full-time: 618; part-time: 22
- U.S. News 2010 law specialty ranking: healthcare law: 3

3.21-3.64 GPA, 25TH-75TH PERCENTILE

157-161 LSAT, 25TH-75TH PERCENTILE

42% ACCEPTANCE RATE

56 2011 U.S. NEWS LAW SCHOOL RANKING

ADMISSIONS
Admissions phone number: **(800) 756-0036**
Admissions email address: lawadmissions@case.edu
Application website: http://www.law.case.edu/admissions/
Application deadline for Fall 2011 admission: **1-Apr**

Admissions statistics:
Number of applicants for Fall 2009: **2,667**
Number of acceptances: **1,126**
Number enrolled: **195**
Acceptance rate: **42%**
GPA, 25th-75th percentile, entering class Fall 2009: **3.21-3.64**
LSAT, 25th-75th percentile, entering class Fall 2009: **157-161**

Part-time program:
Number of applicants for Fall 2009: **275**
Number of acceptances: **38**
Number enrolled: **15**
Acceptance rate: **14%**
GPA, 25th-75th percentile, entering class Fall 2009: **3.20-3.57**
LSAT, 25th-75th percentile, entering class Fall 2009: **150-157**

FINANCIAL AID
Financial aid phone number: **(877) 889-4279**
Financial aid application deadline: **1-May**
Tuition 2009-2010 academic year: **full-time: $38,679**; part-time: N/A
Room and board: **$16,405** ; books: **$1,525** ; miscellaneous expenses: **$1,320**
Total of room/board/books/miscellaneous expenses: **$19,250**
University does not offer graduate student housing for which law students are eligible.

Financial aid profile
Percent of students that received grants for the 2008-2009 academic year: full-time: **59%**

Median grant amount: full-time: **$10,179**
The average law-school debt of those in the Class of 2009 who borrowed: **$90,529** . Proportion who borrowed: **95%**

ACADEMIC PROGRAMS
Calendar: semester
Joint degrees awarded: **J.D./M.B.A.; J.D./M.S.S.A. Social Work; J.D./M.P.H. Public Health; J.D./M.N.O. Nonprofit Management; J.D./M.A. Bioethics; J.D./M.D. Medicine; J.D./M.S. Biochemistry; J.D./M.A. Legal History; J.D./Certificate in Nonprofit Management; J.D./M.A. Political Science; J.D./M.S. Engineering**
Typical first-year section size: Full-time: **70**
Is there typically a "small section" of the first year class, other than Legal Writing, taught by full-time faculty?: Full-time: **no**
Number of course titles, beyond the first year curriculum, offered last year: **162**
Percentages of upper division course sections, excluding seminars, with an enrollment of:

Under 25: **66%**	25 to 49: **23%**
50 to 74: **8%**	75 to 99: **3%**
100+: **N/A**	

Areas of specialization: appellate advocacy, clinical training, dispute resolution, environmental law, health care law, intellectual property law, international law, tax law, trial advocacy

Fall 2009 faculty profile
Total teaching faculty: **71**. Full-time: **58%**; **66%** men, **34%** women, **5%** minorities. Part-time: **42%**; **70%** men, **30%** women, **3%** minorities
Student-to-faculty ratio: **12.2**

SPECIAL PROGRAMS *(as provided by law school):*
Capstone experiences: seven Labs, four Clinics, twelve Externships. Concentration Options: Law & Technology; Law & the Arts; Criminal Law; Business Organizations; Litigation; Health Law; International Law; Individual Rights & Social Reform; and Public & Regulatory Institutions. Each year, we

fund extensive international summer internships and post-graduate fellowships for work abroad.

STUDENT BODY

Fall 2009 full-time enrollment: 618

Men: 58%	Women: 42%
African-American: 3.20%	American Indian: 1.00%
Asian-American: 7.10%	Mexican-American: 0.00%
Puerto Rican: 0.00%	Other Hisp-Amer: 1.30%
White: 74.40%	International: 4.00%
Unknown: 8.90%	

Fall 2009 part-time enrollment: 22

Men: 50%	Women: 50%
African-American: 9.10%	American Indian: 0.00%
Asian-American: 4.50%	Mexican-American: 0.00%
Puerto Rican: 0.00%	Other Hisp-Amer: 0.00%
White: 86.40%	International: 0.00%
Unknown: 0.00%	

Attrition rates for 2008-2009 full-time students
Percent of students discontinuing law school:

Men: 3%	Women: 3%
First-year students: 8%	Second-year students: 1%
Third-year students: 0%	Fourth-year students: N/A

LIBRARY RESOURCES

Total titles: 117,275
Total volumes: 414,846
Total seats available for library users: 354

INFORMATION TECHNOLOGY

Number of wired network connections available to students: 100 total (in the law library, excluding computer labs: 68; in classrooms: 32; in computer labs: 0; elsewhere in the law school: 0)
Law school has a wireless network.
Students are not required to own a computer.

EMPLOYMENT AND SALARIES

Proportion of 2008 graduates employed at graduation: 79%
Employed 9 months later, as of February 15, 2009: 95%
Salaries in the private sector (law firms, business, industry): $76,000 –$145,000 (25th-75th percentile)
Median salary in the private sector: $110,000
Percentage in the private sector who reported salary information: 68%
Median salary in public service (government, judicial clerkships, academic posts, non-profits): $49,000

Percentage of 2008 graduates in:

Law firms: 47%	Government: 17%
Bus./industry: 17%	Judicial clerkship: 5%
Public interest: 11%	Unknown: 1%
Academia : 2%	

2008 graduates employed in-state: 46%
2008 graduates employed in foreign countries: 2%
Number of states where graduates are employed: 28
Percentage of 2008 graduates working in: New England: 2%, Middle Atlantic: 14%, East North Central: 52%, West North Central: 1%, South Atlantic: 16%, East South Central: 1%, West South Central: 3%, Mountain: 3%, Pacific: 6%, Unknown: 0%

BAR PASSAGE RATES

Based on 2008 graduates taking Summer 2008 or Winter 2009 exams. Most of the school's first-time test takers took the bar in Ohio.

88%
School's bar passage rate for first-time test takers

88%
Statewide bar passage rate for first-time test takers

Catholic University of America

- 3600 John McCormack Road NE, Washington, DC, 20064
- http://www.law.edu
- Private
- Year founded: 1925
- 2009-2010 tuition: full-time: $37,850; part-time: $1,375/credit hour
- Enrollment 2009-10 academic year: full-time: 574; part-time: 316
- U.S. News 2010 law specialty ranking: clinical training: 17

3.17-3.55 GPA, 25TH-75TH PERCENTILE

157-160 LSAT, 25TH-75TH PERCENTILE

34% ACCEPTANCE RATE

98 2011 U.S. NEWS LAW SCHOOL RANKING

ADMISSIONS
Admissions phone number: (202) 319-5151
Admissions email address: **admissions@law.edu**
Application website: **http://law.cua.edu/admissions/CSL**
Application deadline for Fall 2011 admission: **11-Mar**

Admissions statistics:
Number of applicants for Fall 2009: **2,517**
Number of acceptances: **845**
Number enrolled: **172**
Acceptance rate: **34%**
GPA, 25th-75th percentile, entering class Fall 2009: **3.17-3.55**
LSAT, 25th-75th percentile, entering class Fall 2009: **157-160**

Part-time program:
Number of applicants for Fall 2009: **782**
Number of acceptances: **233**
Number enrolled: **90**
Acceptance rate: **30%**
GPA, 25th-75th percentile, entering class Fall 2009: **3.03-3.48**
LSAT, 25th-75th percentile, entering class Fall 2009: **154-158**

FINANCIAL AID
Financial aid phone number: (202) 319-5143
Financial aid application deadline: **1-Aug**
Tuition 2009-2010 academic year: **full-time: $37,850; part-time: $1,375/credit hour**
Room and board: **$15,800** ; books: **$1,750** ; miscellaneous expenses: **$8,500**
Total of room/board/books/miscellaneous expenses: **$26,050**
University offers graduate student housing for which law students are eligible.

Financial aid profile
Percent of students that received grants for the 2008-2009 academic year: full-time: **29%**; part-time **19%**

Median grant amount: full-time: **$10,000** ; part-time: **$7,000**
The average law-school debt of those in the Class of 2009 who borrowed: **$112,945** . Proportion who borrowed: **94%**

ACADEMIC PROGRAMS
Calendar: **semester**
Joint degrees awarded: **J.D./M.S.W. (Social Work); J.D./M.A. Politics; J.D./M.A. Psychology; J.D./M.S. Library & Information Science; J.D./JCL (Canon Law); J.D./M.A. History; J.D./M.A. Philosophy**
Typical first-year section size: Full-time: **60**; Part-time: **45**
Is there typically a "small section" of the first year class, other than Legal Writing, taught by full-time faculty?: Full-time: **yes**; Part-time: **yes**
Number of course titles, beyond the first year curriculum, offered last year: **120**
Percentages of upper division course sections, excluding seminars, with an enrollment of:

Under 25: **64%**	25 to 49: **23%**
50 to 74: **12%**	75 to 99: **1%**
100+: **N/A**	

Areas of specialization: appellate advocacy, clinical training, dispute resolution, environmental law, health care law, intellectual property law, international law, tax law, trial advocacy

Fall 2009 faculty profile
Total teaching faculty: **109**. Full-time: **42%**; 48% men, 52% women, 13% minorities. Part-time: **58%**; 76% men, 24% women, 6% minorities
Student-to-faculty ratio: **12.8**

SPECIAL PROGRAMS *(as provided by law school):*
Clinics: General Practice; Families and Law; Advocacy for the Elderly; Criminal Prosecution; DC Law Students in Court; Externships; Innocence Project Clinic; SEC Student Observer Program; Institutes: Communications; International; Public Policy; Securities; Interdisciplinary Program, Law and Religion;

Center for Law, Philosophy and Culture; Int'l Business/Trade Summer Law Program, Cracow, Poland.

STUDENT BODY

Fall 2009 full-time enrollment: 574

Men: 44%	Women: 56%
African-American: 3.00%	American Indian: 0.30%
Asian-American: 9.60%	Mexican-American: 0.20%
Puerto Rican: 0.20%	Other Hisp-Amer: 3.50%
White: 59.20%	International: 3.30%
Unknown: 20.70%	

Fall 2009 part-time enrollment: 316

Men: 56%	Women: 44%
African-American: 7.60%	American Indian: 0.60%
Asian-American: 12.30%	Mexican-American: 0.00%
Puerto Rican: 0.00%	Other Hisp-Amer: 1.90%
White: 53.80%	International: 4.40%
Unknown: 19.30%	

Attrition rates for 2008-2009 full-time students
Percent of students discontinuing law school:

Men: 4%	Women: 4%
First-year students: 10%	Second-year students: 1%
Third-year students: 0%	Fourth-year students: N/A

LIBRARY RESOURCES
Total titles: 178,445
Total volumes: 435,073
Total seats available for library users: 502

INFORMATION TECHNOLOGY
Number of wired network connections available to students: 294 total (in the law library, excluding computer labs: 166; in classrooms: 128; in computer labs: 0; elsewhere in the law school: 0)
Law school has a wireless network.
Students are not required to own a computer.

EMPLOYMENT AND SALARIES
Proportion of 2008 graduates employed at graduation: 68%
Employed 9 months later, as of February 15, 2009: 92%
Salaries in the private sector (law firms, business, industry): $75,000 –$160,000 (25th-75th percentile)
Median salary in the private sector: $135,000
Percentage in the private sector who reported salary information: 55%
Median salary in public service (government, judicial clerkships, academic posts, non-profits): $52,549

Percentage of 2008 graduates in:

Law firms: 42%	Government: 27%
Bus./industry: 13%	Judicial clerkship: 12%
Public interest: 2%	Unknown: 1%
Academia : 2%	

2008 graduates employed in-state: 47%
2008 graduates employed in foreign countries: 0%
Number of states where graduates are employed: 23
Percentage of 2008 graduates working in: New England: 3%, Middle Atlantic: 10%, East North Central: 2%, West North Central: 0%, South Atlantic: 81%, East South Central: 1%, West South Central: 1%, Mountain: 1%, Pacific: 2%, Unknown: 0%

BAR PASSAGE RATES
Based on 2008 graduates taking Summer 2008 or Winter 2009 exams. Most of the school's first-time test takers took the bar in Maryland.

88%

School's bar passage rate for first-time test takers

85%

Statewide bar passage rate for first-time test takers

Chapman University

- 1 University Drive, Orange, CA, 92866
- http://www.chapman.edu/law
- Private
- Year founded: 1995
- 2009-2010 tuition: full-time: $37,950; part-time: $30,240
- Enrollment 2009-10 academic year: full-time: 499; part-time: 37
- U.S. News 2010 law specialty ranking: N/A

3.11-3.56	GPA, 25TH-75TH PERCENTILE
156-159	LSAT, 25TH-75TH PERCENTILE
32%	ACCEPTANCE RATE
93	2011 U.S. NEWS LAW SCHOOL RANKING

ADMISSIONS

Admissions phone number: **(714) 628-2500**
Admissions email address: **lawadm@chapman.edu**
Application website:
  http://www.chapman.edu/admission/law/application.asp
Application deadline for Fall 2011 admission: **15-Apr**

Admissions statistics:

Number of applicants for Fall 2009: **2,615**
Number of acceptances: **839**
Number enrolled: **178**
Acceptance rate: **32%**
GPA, 25th-75th percentile, entering class Fall 2009: **3.11-3.56**
LSAT, 25th-75th percentile, entering class Fall 2009: **156-159**

Part-time program:

Number of applicants for Fall 2009: **268**
Number of acceptances: **52**
Number enrolled: **3**
Acceptance rate: **19%**
GPA, 25th-75th percentile, entering class Fall 2009: **2.85-3.82**
LSAT, 25th-75th percentile, entering class Fall 2009: **151-160**

FINANCIAL AID

Financial aid phone number: **(714) 628-2510**
Financial aid application deadline: **1-Mar**
Tuition 2009-2010 academic year: **full-time: $37,950; part-time: $30,240**
Room and board: **$15,300** ; books: **$1,560** ; miscellaneous expenses: **$8,082**
Total of room/board/books/miscellaneous expenses: **$24,942**
University offers graduate student housing for which law students are eligible.

Financial aid profile

Percent of students that received grants for the 2008-2009 academic year: full-time: **45%**
Median grant amount: full-time: **$28,760** ; part-time: **$0**
The average law-school debt of those in the Class of 2009 who borrowed: **$108,465** . Proportion who borrowed: **86%**

ACADEMIC PROGRAMS

Calendar: **semester**
Joint degrees awarded: **J.D./M.B.A.; J.D./M.F.A.**
Typical first-year section size: Full-time: **60**; Part-time: **60**
Is there typically a "small section" of the first year class, other than Legal Writing, taught by full-time faculty?: Full-time: **yes**; Part-time: **no**
Number of course titles, beyond the first year curriculum, offered last year: **152**
Percentages of upper division course sections, excluding seminars, with an enrollment of:
  Under 25: **72%**   25 to 49: **16%**
  50 to 74: **11%**   75 to 99: **1%**
  100+: **0%**
Areas of specialization: appellate advocacy, clinical training, dispute resolution, environmental law, intellectual property law, international law, tax law, trial advocacy

Fall 2009 faculty profile

Total teaching faculty: **86**. Full-time: **60%**; **67%** men, **33%** women, **48%** minorities. Part-time: **40%**; **82%** men, **18%** women, **32%** minorities
Student-to-faculty ratio: **8.9**

SPECIAL PROGRAMS (as provided by law school):

Certificate programs: Tax; Env'l, Land Use & Real Estate; ADR; Entertainment Law; and Internat'l Law. We have joint J.D./M.B.A. and J.D./M.F.A. programs, and clinical programs in elder law, tax, constitutional litigation, domestic violence, 9th Circuit Appellate Law Clinic, Military Personnel/AMVETS law clinic, Working with Filmmakers clinic, and Mediation Clinic. We co-sponsor a summer law program in England.

STUDENT BODY

Fall 2009 full-time enrollment: 499

Men: 51%	Women: 49%
African-American: 0.80%	American Indian: 0.60%
Asian-American: 13.20%	Mexican-American: 2.40%
Puerto Rican: 0.00%	Other Hisp-Amer: 2.20%
White: 56.90%	International: 0.60%
Unknown: 23.20%	

Fall 2009 part-time enrollment: 37

Men: 49%	Women: 51%
African-American: 5.40%	American Indian: 0.00%
Asian-American: 27.00%	Mexican-American: 10.80%
Puerto Rican: 0.00%	Other Hisp-Amer: 0.00%
White: 35.10%	International: 0.00%
Unknown: 21.60%	

Attrition rates for 2008-2009 full-time students
Percent of students discontinuing law school:

Men: 3%	Women: 3%
First-year students: 7%	Second-year students: 1%
Third-year students: N/A	Fourth-year students: N/A

LIBRARY RESOURCES

Total titles: 180,973
Total volumes: 303,464
Total seats available for library users: 286

INFORMATION TECHNOLOGY

Number of wired network connections available to students: 587 total (in the law library, excluding computer labs: 215; in classrooms: 288; in computer labs: 30; elsewhere in the law school: 54)
Law school has a wireless network.
Students are not required to own a computer.

EMPLOYMENT AND SALARIES

Proportion of 2008 graduates employed at graduation: 91%
Employed 9 months later, as of February 15, 2009: 97%
Salaries in the private sector (law firms, business, industry): $60,000 –$85,000 (25th-75th percentile)
Median salary in the private sector: $75,000
Percentage in the private sector who reported salary information: 54%
Median salary in public service (government, judicial clerkships, academic posts, non-profits): $66,500

Percentage of 2008 graduates in:

Law firms: 57%	Government: 11%
Bus./industry: 9%	Judicial clerkship: 3%
Public interest: 1%	Unknown: 1%
Academia : 20%	

2008 graduates employed in-state: 90%
2008 graduates employed in foreign countries: 0%
Number of states where graduates are employed: 12
Percentage of 2008 graduates working in: New England: 0%, Middle Atlantic: 0%, East North Central: 0%, West North Central: 0%, South Atlantic: 4%, East South Central: 1%, West South Central: 1%, Mountain: 3%, Pacific: 92%, Unknown: 0%

BAR PASSAGE RATES

Based on 2008 graduates taking Summer 2008 or Winter 2009 exams. Most of the school's first-time test takers took the bar in California.

75%
School's bar passage rate for first-time test takers

71%
Statewide bar passage rate for first-time test takers

Charleston School of Law

- PO Box 535, Charleston, SC, 29402
- http://www.charlestonlaw.edu
- Private
- Year founded: 2003
- 2009-2010 tuition: full-time: $34,568; part-time: $27,774
- Enrollment 2009-10 academic year: full-time: 459; part-time: 200
- U.S. News 2010 law specialty ranking: N/A

2.95-3.43 GPA, 25TH-75TH PERCENTILE

151-156 LSAT, 25TH-75TH PERCENTILE

46% ACCEPTANCE RATE

Unranked 2011 U.S. NEWS LAW SCHOOL RANKING

ADMISSIONS

Admissions phone number: (843) 377-2143
Admissions email address: info@charlestonlaw.edu
Application website: http://www.charlestonlaw.edu
Application deadline for Fall 2011 admission: 1-Mar

Admissions statistics:
Number of applicants for Fall 2009: 1,710
Number of acceptances: 785
Number enrolled: 189
Acceptance rate: 46%
GPA, 25th-75th percentile, entering class Fall 2009: 2.95-3.43
LSAT, 25th-75th percentile, entering class Fall 2009: 151-156

Part-time program:
Number of applicants for Fall 2009: 352
Number of acceptances: 110
Number enrolled: 52
Acceptance rate: 31%
GPA, 25th-75th percentile, entering class Fall 2009: 2.51-3.30
LSAT, 25th-75th percentile, entering class Fall 2009: 147-152

FINANCIAL AID

Financial aid phone number: (843) 377-4901
Financial aid application deadline: 1-Apr
Tuition 2009-2010 academic year: **full-time:** $34,568; **part-time:** $27,774
Room and board: $7,700 ; books: $1,020 ; miscellaneous expenses: $4,300
Total of room/board/books/miscellaneous expenses: $13,020
University does not offer graduate student housing for which law students are eligible.

Financial aid profile
Percent of students that received grants for the 2008-2009 academic year: full-time: 44%; part-time 12%

Median grant amount: full-time: $7,500 ; part-time: $5,000
The average law-school debt of those in the Class of 2009 who borrowed: $114,941 . Proportion who borrowed: 76%

ACADEMIC PROGRAMS

Calendar: **semester**
Joint degrees awarded: **N/A**
Typical first-year section size: Full-time: **62**; Part-time: **53**
Is there typically a "small section" of the first year class, other than Legal Writing, taught by full-time faculty?: Full-time: **no**; Part-time: **no**
Number of course titles, beyond the first year curriculum, offered last year: **77**
Percentages of upper division course sections, excluding seminars, with an enrollment of:
Under 25: **65%**   25 to 49: **17%**
50 to 74: **12%**   75 to 99: **6%**
100+: **0%**
Areas of specialization: appellate advocacy, dispute resolution, environmental law, health care law, intellectual property law, international law, tax law, trial advocacy

Fall 2009 faculty profile
Total teaching faculty: 54. Full-time: **46%**; **56%** men, **44%** women, **20%** minorities. Part-time: **54%**; **66%** men, **34%** women, **0%** minorities
Student-to-faculty ratio: **18.2**

SPECIAL PROGRAMS *(as provided by law school)*:
The Charleston School of Law offers an extensive externship program providing students with practical experience in more than 110 placement sites. The school is developing a Maritime Law Institute. All students are required to complete a minimum of 30 hours of pro bono work prior to graduation.

STUDENT BODY
Fall 2009 full-time enrollment: 459
Men: 55%   Women: 45%
African-American: 5.40%   American Indian: 0.00%
Asian-American: 0.90%   Mexican-American: 0.00%
Puerto Rican: 0.00%   Other Hisp-Amer: 0.90%

White: 87.80%   International: 0.00%
Unknown: 5.00%

Fall 2009 part-time enrollment: 200
Men: 57%   Women: 43%
African-American: 8.50% American Indian: 0.50%
Asian-American: 1.00%   Mexican-American: 0.00%
Puerto Rican: 0.00%   Other Hisp-Amer: 1.00%
White: 84.00%   International: 0.00%
Unknown: 5.00%

Attrition rates for 2008-2009 full-time students
Percent of students discontinuing law school:
Men: 2%   Women: 1%
First-year students: 1% Second-year students: 3%
Third-year students: N/A Fourth-year students: N/A

LIBRARY RESOURCES
Total titles: 584,901
Total volumes: 27,575
Total seats available for library users: 354

INFORMATION TECHNOLOGY
Number of wired network connections available to students: **6** total (in the law library, excluding computer labs: **2**; in classrooms: **0**; in computer labs: **0**; elsewhere in the law school: **4**)
Law school has a wireless network.
Students are required to own a computer.

EMPLOYMENT AND SALARIES
Proportion of 2008 graduates employed at graduation: N/A
Employed 9 months later, as of February 15, 2009: N/A

Salaries in the private sector (law firms, business, industry): **$48,000 –$72,000** (25th-75th percentile)
Median salary in the private sector: **$55,000**
Percentage in the private sector who reported salary information: **50%**
Median salary in public service (government, judicial clerkships, academic posts, non-profits): **$40,000**

Percentage of 2008 graduates in:
Law firms: 43%   Government: 14%
Bus./industry: 7%   Judicial clerkship: 31%
Public interest: 4%   Unknown: 0%
Academia : 2%

2008 graduates employed in-state: **89%**
2008 graduates employed in foreign countries: **0%**
Number of states where graduates are employed: **9**
Percentage of 2008 graduates working in: New England: 0%, Middle Atlantic: **2%**, East North Central: **N/A**, West North Central: **N/A**, South Atlantic: **96%**, East South Central: **2%**, West South Central: **N/A**, Mountain: **N/A**, Pacific: **N/A**, Unknown: **0%**

BAR PASSAGE RATES
Based on 2008 graduates taking Summer 2008 or Winter 2009 exams. Most of the school's first-time test takers took the bar in South Carolina.

N/A
School's bar passage rate for first-time test takers

N/A
Statewide bar passage rate for first-time test takers

Charlotte School of Law

- 2145 Suttle Avenue, Charlotte, NC, 28208
- http://www.charlottelaw.edu/
- Private
- Year founded: 2005
- 2009-2010 tuition: full-time: $33,166; part-time: $26,816
- Enrollment 2009-10 academic year: full-time: 380; part-time: 101
- U.S. News 2010 law specialty ranking: N/A

2.76-3.40 GPA, 25TH-75TH PERCENTILE

149-153 LSAT, 25TH-75TH PERCENTILE

55% ACCEPTANCE RATE

Unranked 2011 U.S. NEWS LAW SCHOOL RANKING

ADMISSIONS

Admissions phone number: **(704) 971-8500**
Admissions email address: **admissions@charlottelaw.edu**
Application website:
 http://www.charlottelaw.edu/admissions/default.asp?PageID=12
Application deadline for Fall 2011 admission: **rolling**

Admissions statistics:
Number of applicants for Fall 2009: **2,025**
Number of acceptances: **1,118**
Number enrolled: **234**
Acceptance rate: **55%**
GPA, 25th-75th percentile, entering class Fall 2009: **2.76-3.40**
LSAT, 25th-75th percentile, entering class Fall 2009: **149-153**

Part-time program:
Number of applicants for Fall 2009: **257**
Number of acceptances: **91**
Number enrolled: **42**
Acceptance rate: **35%**
GPA, 25th-75th percentile, entering class Fall 2009: **2.73-3.40**
LSAT, 25th-75th percentile, entering class Fall 2009: **147-153**

FINANCIAL AID

Financial aid phone number: () -
Financial aid application deadline:
Tuition 2009-2010 academic year: **full-time: $33,166; part-time: $26,816**
Room and board: **$11,415** ; books: **$1,925** ; miscellaneous expenses: **$5,273**
Total of room/board/books/miscellaneous expenses: **$18,613**
University does not offer graduate student housing for which law students are eligible.

Financial aid profile
Percent of students that received grants for the 2008-2009 academic year: full-time: **17%**; part-time **19%**
Median grant amount: full-time: **$10,000** ; part-time: **$4,000**
The average law-school debt of those in the Class of 2009 who borrowed: **$36,682** . Proportion who borrowed: **72%**

ACADEMIC PROGRAMS

Calendar: **semester**
Joint degrees awarded: N/A
Typical first-year section size: Full-time: **75**; Part-time: **40**
Is there typically a "small section" of the first year class, other than Legal Writing, taught by full-time faculty?: Full-time: **no**; Part-time: **no**
Number of course titles, beyond the first year curriculum, offered last year: **43**
Percentages of upper division course sections, excluding seminars, with an enrollment of:
 Under 25: **56%**   25 to 49: **26%**
 50 to 74: **14%**   75 to 99: **4%**
 100+: **N/A**
Areas of specialization: appellate advocacy, clinical training, dispute resolution, environmental law, health care law, intellectual property law, international law, tax law, trial advocacy

Fall 2009 faculty profile
Total teaching faculty: **35**. Full-time: **54%**; 47% men, 53% women, 42% minorities. Part-time: **46%**; 56% men, 44% women, 38% minorities
Student-to-faculty ratio: **19.7**

SPECIAL PROGRAMS *(as provided by law school):*
We provide a student-centered education to produce practice-ready lawyers and to serve the underserved. Students learn in context with practice-based simulations and real world law experiences. Externships, clinical labs, practicums, and mandatory pro bono, allow students to apply knowledge to a range of community legal problems. Our academic support program bolsters student learning.

STUDENT BODY

Fall 2009 full-time enrollment: 380

Men: 50%	Women: 50%
African-American: 7.10%	American Indian: 1.10%
Asian-American: 1.30%	Mexican-American: 2.10%
Puerto Rican: 0.50%	Other Hisp-Amer: 3.20%
White: 82.10%	International: 0.00%
Unknown: 2.60%	

Fall 2009 part-time enrollment: 101

Men: 51%	Women: 49%
African-American: 13.90%	American Indian: 2.00%
Asian-American: 1.00%	Mexican-American: 1.00%
Puerto Rican: 1.00%	Other Hisp-Amer: 5.90%
White: 71.30%	International: 0.00%
Unknown: 4.00%	

Attrition rates for 2008-2009 full-time students
Percent of students discontinuing law school:

Men: 12%	Women: 7%
First-year students: 17%	Second-year students: 5%
Third-year students: N/A	Fourth-year students: N/A

LIBRARY RESOURCES

Total titles: 111,608
Total volumes: 113,717
Total seats available for library users: 368

INFORMATION TECHNOLOGY

Number of wired network connections available to students: 0 total (in the law library, excluding computer labs: 0; in classrooms: 0; in computer labs: 0; elsewhere in the law school: 0)
Law school has a wireless network.
Students are required to own a computer.

EMPLOYMENT AND SALARIES

Proportion of 2008 graduates employed at graduation: N/A
Employed 9 months later, as of February 15, 2009: N/A
Salaries in the private sector (law firms, business, industry): N/A–N/A (25th-75th percentile)
Median salary in the private sector: N/A
Percentage in the private sector who reported salary information: N/A
Median salary in public service (government, judicial clerkships, academic posts, non-profits): N/A

Percentage of 2008 graduates in:

Law firms: N/A	Government: N/A
Bus./industry: N/A	Judicial clerkship: N/A
Public interest: N/A	Unknown: N/A
Academia : N/A	

2008 graduates employed in-state: N/A
2008 graduates employed in foreign countries: N/A
Number of states where graduates are employed: N/A
Percentage of 2008 graduates working in: New England: N/A, Middle Atlantic: N/A, East North Central: N/A, West North Central: N/A, South Atlantic: N/A, East South Central: N/A, West South Central: N/A, Mountain: N/A, Pacific: N/A, Unknown: N/A

BAR PASSAGE RATES

Based on 2008 graduates taking Summer 2008 or Winter 2009 exams.

N/A
School's bar passage rate for first-time test takers

N/A
Statewide bar passage rate for first-time test takers

Cleveland State University (Marshall)

- 2121 Euclid Avenue, LB 138, Cleveland, OH, 44115-2214
- http://www.law.csuohio.edu
- Public
- Year founded: 1897
- 2009-2010 tuition: full-time: $16,764; part-time: $12,895
- Enrollment 2009-10 academic year: full-time: 482; part-time: 157
- U.S. News 2010 law specialty ranking: N/A

3.19-3.68 GPA, 25TH-75TH PERCENTILE

153-158 LSAT, 25TH-75TH PERCENTILE

36% ACCEPTANCE RATE

Tier 3 2011 U.S. NEWS LAW SCHOOL RANKING

ADMISSIONS

Admissions phone number: (216) 687-2304
Admissions email address: admissions@law.csuohio.edu
Application website:
   http://www.law.csuohio.edu/prospectivestudents/apply/
Application deadline for Fall 2011 admission: 1-May

Admissions statistics:
Number of applicants for Fall 2009: 1,513
Number of acceptances: 543
Number enrolled: 158
Acceptance rate: 36%
GPA, 25th-75th percentile, entering class Fall 2009: 3.19-3.68
LSAT, 25th-75th percentile, entering class Fall 2009: 153-158

Part-time program:
Number of applicants for Fall 2009: 309
Number of acceptances: 79
Number enrolled: 45
Acceptance rate: 26%
GPA, 25th-75th percentile, entering class Fall 2009: 3.25-3.59
LSAT, 25th-75th percentile, entering class Fall 2009: 151-158

FINANCIAL AID

Financial aid phone number: (216) 687-2304
Financial aid application deadline: 1-May
Tuition 2009-2010 academic year: **full-time: $16,764; part-time: $12,895**
Room and board: $13,000 ; books: $1,500 ; miscellaneous expenses: $4,300
Total of room/board/books/miscellaneous expenses: $18,800
University offers graduate student housing for which law students are eligible.

Financial aid profile
Percent of students that received grants for the 2008-2009 academic year: full-time: 45%; part-time 19%
Median grant amount: full-time: $4,070 ; part-time: $1,805
The average law-school debt of those in the Class of 2009 who borrowed: $61,500 . Proportion who borrowed: 80%

ACADEMIC PROGRAMS

Calendar: **semester**
Joint degrees awarded: **J.D./M.B.A.; J.D./M.P.A.; J.D./M.U.P.D.D.; J.D./M.A.E.S.; J.D./M.S.E.S.**
Typical first-year section size: Full-time: **52**; Part-time: **38**
Is there typically a "small section" of the first year class, other than Legal Writing, taught by full-time faculty?:
   Full-time: **no**; Part-time: **no**
Number of course titles, beyond the first year curriculum, offered last year: **95**
Percentages of upper division course sections, excluding seminars, with an enrollment of:
   Under 25: **64%**   25 to 49: **27%**
   50 to 74: **8%**   75 to 99: **1%**
   100+: **0%**
Areas of specialization: appellate advocacy, clinical training, dispute resolution, environmental law, health care law, intellectual property law, international law, tax law, trial advocacy

Fall 2009 faculty profile
Total teaching faculty: **71**. Full-time: **52%**; **54%** men, **46%** women, **16%** minorities. Part-time: **48%**; **71%** men, **29%** women, **12%** minorities
Student-to-faculty ratio: **13.1**

SPECIAL PROGRAMS *(as provided by law school)*:

Clinics (Commun.Health Adv.Law,Emp.Law, Envir.Law, Fair Housing, Urban Dvlp.); Externships (Judicial, Pub.Int., US Atty. and Indep.(student-designed); Summer Law Inst. in St.Petersburg; concentrations (Bus., Civ. Litig. & Dispute Resolution, Crim. Law, Int'l & Comp. Law, and Emp. & Labor Law); Joint Degree Programs: MBA, MPA, MUPDD (planning/design), MAES & MSES (Environmental); Pro Bono Program.

STUDENT BODY

Fall 2009 full-time enrollment: 482

Men: 60%	Women: 40%
African-American: 6.80%	American Indian: 0.40%
Asian-American: 2.50%	Mexican-American: 0.00%
Puerto Rican: 0.40%	Other Hisp-Amer: 2.30%
White: 85.70%	International: 1.20%
Unknown: 0.60%	

Fall 2009 part-time enrollment: 157

Men: 54%	Women: 46%
African-American: 14.60%	American Indian: 0.00%
Asian-American: 3.80%	Mexican-American: 0.00%
Puerto Rican: 0.00%	Other Hisp-Amer: 2.50%
White: 78.30%	International: 0.00%
Unknown: 0.60%	

Attrition rates for 2008-2009 full-time students
Percent of students discontinuing law school:

Men: 6%	Women: 5%
First-year students: 17%	Second-year students: 1%
Third-year students: 0%	Fourth-year students: N/A

LIBRARY RESOURCES

Total titles: 170,146
Total volumes: 538,989
Total seats available for library users: 493

INFORMATION TECHNOLOGY

Number of wired network connections available to students: 183 total (in the law library, excluding computer labs: 148; in classrooms: 0; in computer labs: 0; elsewhere in the law school: 35)
Law school has a wireless network.
Students are not required to own a computer.

EMPLOYMENT AND SALARIES

Proportion of 2008 graduates employed at graduation: 76%
Employed 9 months later, as of February 15, 2009: 91%
Salaries in the private sector (law firms, business, industry): $60,000 –$120,000 (25th-75th percentile)
Median salary in the private sector: $80,000
Percentage in the private sector who reported salary information: 43%
Median salary in public service (government, judicial clerkships, academic posts, non-profits): $49,000

Percentage of 2008 graduates in:

Law firms: 53%	Government: 12%
Bus./industry: 24%	Judicial clerkship: 5%
Public interest: 3%	Unknown: 0%
Academia : 3%	

2008 graduates employed in-state: 89%
2008 graduates employed in foreign countries: 1%
Number of states where graduates are employed: 15
Percentage of 2008 graduates working in: New England: 0%, Middle Atlantic: 2%, East North Central: 90%, West North Central: 0%, South Atlantic: 3%, East South Central: 1%, West South Central: 1%, Mountain: 1%, Pacific: 1%, Unknown: 0%

BAR PASSAGE RATES

Based on 2008 graduates taking Summer 2008 or Winter 2009 exams. Most of the school's first-time test takers took the bar in Ohio.

90%
School's bar passage rate for first-time test takers

88%
Statewide bar passage rate for first-time test takers

College of William and Mary

- PO Box 8795, Williamsburg, VA, 23187-8795
- http://www.wm.edu/law
- Public
- Year founded: 1779
- 2009-2010 tuition: full-time: $21,646; part-time: N/A
- Enrollment 2009-10 academic year: full-time: 626
- U.S. News 2010 law specialty ranking: N/A

3.42-3.77 GPA, 25TH-75TH PERCENTILE

161-166 LSAT, 25TH-75TH PERCENTILE

22% ACCEPTANCE RATE

28 2011 U.S. NEWS LAW SCHOOL RANKING

ADMISSIONS

Admissions phone number: **(757) 221-3785**
Admissions email address: **lawadm@wm.edu**
Application website:
  http://law.wm.edu/admissions/documents/firstyearappo
  9-10.pdf
Application deadline for Fall 2011 admission: **1-Mar**

Admissions statistics:
Number of applicants for Fall 2009: **4,980**
Number of acceptances: **1,109**
Number enrolled: **209**
Acceptance rate: **22%**
GPA, 25th-75th percentile, entering class Fall 2009: **3.42-3.77**
LSAT, 25th-75th percentile, entering class Fall 2009: **161-166**

FINANCIAL AID

Financial aid phone number: **(757) 221-2420**
Financial aid application deadline: **15-Feb**
Tuition 2009-2010 academic year: **full-time: $21,646; part-time: N/A**
Room and board: **$8,882** ; books: **$1,250** ; miscellaneous expenses: **$2,836**
Total of room/board/books/miscellaneous expenses: **$12,968**
University offers graduate student housing for which law students are eligible.

Financial aid profile
Percent of students that received grants for the 2008-2009 academic year: full-time: **41%**
Median grant amount: full-time: **$6,000**
The average law-school debt of those in the Class of 2009 who borrowed: **$76,155** . Proportion who borrowed: **85%**

ACADEMIC PROGRAMS

Calendar: **semester**
Joint degrees awarded: **J.D./M.B.A.; J.D./M.P.P.; J.D./M.A.**
Typical first-year section size: Full-time: **70**

Is there typically a "small section" of the first year class, other than Legal Writing, taught by full-time faculty?:
  Full-time: **yes**
Number of course titles, beyond the first year curriculum, offered last year: **129**
Percentages of upper division course sections, excluding seminars, with an enrollment of:
  Under 25: **71%**   25 to 49: **18%**
  50 to 74: **7%**   75 to 99: **1%**
  100+: **3%**
Areas of specialization: appellate advocacy, clinical training, dispute resolution, environmental law, health care law, intellectual property law, international law, tax law, trial advocacy

Fall 2009 faculty profile
Total teaching faculty: **79**. Full-time: **44%**; **66%** men, **34%** women, **20%** minorities. Part-time: **56%**; **70%** men, **30%** women, **9%** minorities
Student-to-faculty ratio: **15.7**

SPECIAL PROGRAMS *(as provided by law school):*
Our law students select from numerous externship and clinical opportunities. Students actively participate in our programs including: Institute of Bill of Rights Law; Center for Legal & Court Technology; Human Rights & National Security Law; Summer Abroad in Madrid, Spain. We offer the joint degrees: JD/MBA, JD/MPP, JD/MA in American Culture.

STUDENT BODY
Fall 2009 full-time enrollment: 626
Men: **51%**   Women: **49%**
African-American: **12.10%**   American Indian: **0.00%**
Asian-American: **2.90%**   Mexican-American: **0.00%**
Puerto Rican: **0.00%**   Other Hisp-Amer: **0.80%**
White: **64.50%**   International: **1.00%**
Unknown: **18.70%**

Attrition rates for 2008-2009 full-time students
Percent of students discontinuing law school:
Men: **3%**   Women: **1%**

First-year students: **4%** Second-year students: **0%**
Third-year students: **1%** Fourth-year students: **N/A**

LIBRARY RESOURCES
Total titles: **215,835**
Total volumes: **406,004**
Total seats available for library users: **568**

INFORMATION TECHNOLOGY
Number of wired network connections available to students: total (in the law library, excluding computer labs: **28**; in classrooms: **N/A**; in computer labs: **25**; elsewhere in the law school: **15**)
Law school has a wireless network.
Students are not required to own a computer.

EMPLOYMENT AND SALARIES
Proportion of 2008 graduates employed at graduation: **88%**
Employed 9 months later, as of February 15, 2009: **97%**
Salaries in the private sector (law firms, business, industry): **$110,000 –$160,000** (25th-75th percentile)
Median salary in the private sector: **$140,000**
Percentage in the private sector who reported salary information: **81%**
Median salary in public service (government, judicial clerkships, academic posts, non-profits): **$53,635**

Percentage of 2008 graduates in:
Law firms: **60%** Government: **15%**
Bus./industry: **7%** Judicial clerkship: **14%**
Public interest: **4%** Unknown: **0%**
Academia : **0%**

2008 graduates employed in-state: **36%**
2008 graduates employed in foreign countries: **1%**
Number of states where graduates are employed: **25**
Percentage of 2008 graduates working in: New England: **1%**, Middle Atlantic: **14%**, East North Central: **6%**, West North Central: **1%**, South Atlantic: **65%**, East South Central: **1%**, West South Central: **2%**, Mountain: **3%**, Pacific: **2%**, Unknown: **4%**

BAR PASSAGE RATES
Based on 2008 graduates taking Summer 2008 or Winter 2009 exams. Most of the school's first-time test takers took the bar in Virginia.

| **89%** |
School's bar passage rate for first-time test takers

| **82%** |
Statewide bar passage rate for first-time test takers

Columbia University

- 435 W. 116th Street, New York, NY, 10027
- http://www.law.columbia.edu
- Private
- Year founded: 1858
- 2009-2010 tuition: full-time: $48,004; part-time: N/A
- Enrollment 2009-10 academic year: full-time: 1,309; part-time: 1
- U.S. News 2010 law specialty ranking: clinical training: 14, dispute resolution: 14, intellectual property law: 6, international law: 2, tax law: 14

3.60-3.81 GPA, 25TH-75TH PERCENTILE

170-175 LSAT, 25TH-75TH PERCENTILE

15% ACCEPTANCE RATE

4 2011 U.S. NEWS LAW SCHOOL RANKING

ADMISSIONS

Admissions phone number: (212) 854-2670
Admissions email address: admissions@law.columbia.edu
Application website:
    http://www.law.columbia.edu/jd_applicants/jd_application
Application deadline for Fall 2011 admission: 15-Feb

Admissions statistics:

Number of applicants for Fall 2009: 8,505
Number of acceptances: 1,235
Number enrolled: 400
Acceptance rate: 15%
GPA, 25th-75th percentile, entering class Fall 2009: 3.60-3.81
LSAT, 25th-75th percentile, entering class Fall 2009: 170-175

FINANCIAL AID

Financial aid phone number: (212) 854-7730
Financial aid application deadline: 1-Mar
Tuition 2009-2010 academic year: **full-time: $48,004; part-time: N/A**
Room and board: $16,190 ; books: $1,448 ; miscellaneous expenses: $3,625
Total of room/board/books/miscellaneous expenses: $21,263
University offers graduate student housing for which law students are eligible.

Financial aid profile

Percent of students that received grants for the 2008-2009 academic year: full-time: 53%
Median grant amount: full-time: $10,250
The average law-school debt of those in the Class of 2009 who borrowed: $128,425 . Proportion who borrowed: 77%

ACADEMIC PROGRAMS

Calendar: **semester**
Joint degrees awarded: J.D./M.A. Economics; J.D./M.A. History; J.D./M.A. Philosophy; J.D./M.A. Politics;
J.D./M.A. Psychology; J.D./M.A. Sociology; J.D./M.B.A.; J.D./M.F.A.; J.D./M.I.A.; J.D./M.P.A.; J.D./M.P.H.; J.D./M.S. Journalism; J.D./M.U.P.; J.D./M.S.W.; J.D./PH.D. Anthropology; J.D./PH.D. History; J.D./PH.D. Philosophy; J.D./PH.D. Politics; J.D./PH.D. Sociology; J.D./PH.D. Economics; J.D./M.P.H.I.L.; J.D./PH.D. Engineering; J.D./PH.D. Religion; J.D./M.A. Anthropology
Typical first-year section size: Full-time: **95**
Is there typically a "small section" of the first year class, other than Legal Writing, taught by full-time faculty?: Full-time: **yes**
Number of course titles, beyond the first year curriculum, offered last year: **237**
Percentages of upper division course sections, excluding seminars, with an enrollment of:

Under 25: **51%**	25 to 49: **21%**
50 to 74: **11%**	75 to 99: **8%**
100+: **9%**	

Areas of specialization: appellate advocacy, clinical training, dispute resolution, environmental law, health care law, intellectual property law, international law, tax law, trial advocacy

Fall 2009 faculty profile

Total teaching faculty: **196**. Full-time: 54%; 70% men, 30% women, 11% minorities. Part-time: 46%; 69% men, 31% women, 7% minorities
Student-to-faculty ratio: **10.1**

SPECIAL PROGRAMS (as provided by law school):

For information regarding specialty programs, visit http://www.law.columbia.edu... Clinics:.../focusareas/clinics; Centers:.../center_program; Externships:.../programs/social-justice/externships;
JointDegree:.../jd_applicants/curriculum/jointdegree; DualDegree:.../careers/career_services/employers/About_Columbia_/Academic_Progra#4422; SemesterAbroad: .../center_program/intl_progs/Semesterstudy

STUDENT BODY

Fall 2009 full-time enrollment: 1,309

Men: 52%	Women: 48%
African-American: 8.00%	American Indian: 0.20%
Asian-American: 15.10%	Mexican-American: 2.80%
Puerto Rican: 1.50%	Other Hisp-Amer: 1.10%
White: 59.20%	International: 8.90%
Unknown: 3.20%	

Fall 2009 part-time enrollment: 1

Men: N/A	Women: 100%
African-American: 0.00%	American Indian: 0.00%
Asian-American: 0.00%	Mexican-American: 0.00%
Puerto Rican: 0.00%	Other Hisp-Amer: 0.00%
White: 100.00%	International: 0.00%
Unknown: 0.00%	

Attrition rates for 2008-2009 full-time students
Percent of students discontinuing law school:

Men: N/A	Women: N/A
First-year students: N/A	Second-year students: N/A
Third-year students: N/A	Fourth-year students: N/A

LIBRARY RESOURCES

Total titles: 444,351
Total volumes: 1,181,317
Total seats available for library users: 369

INFORMATION TECHNOLOGY

Number of wired network connections available to students: 3028 total (in the law library, excluding computer labs: 42; in classrooms: 2,504; in computer labs: 150; elsewhere in the law school: 332)
Law school has a wireless network.
Students are not required to own a computer.

EMPLOYMENT AND SALARIES

Proportion of 2008 graduates employed at graduation: 99%
Employed 9 months later, as of February 15, 2009: 100%
Salaries in the private sector (law firms, business, industry): $95,000 –$168,000 (25th-75th percentile)
Median salary in the private sector: $160,000
Percentage in the private sector who reported salary information: 98%
Median salary in public service (government, judicial clerkships, academic posts, non-profits): $54,000

Percentage of 2008 graduates in:

Law firms: 81%	Government: 2%
Bus./industry: 2%	Judicial clerkship: 11%
Public interest: 3%	Unknown: 0%
Academia : 1%	

2008 graduates employed in-state: 66%
2008 graduates employed in foreign countries: 3%
Number of states where graduates are employed: 23
Percentage of 2008 graduates working in: New England: 3%, Middle Atlantic: 67%, East North Central: 1%, West North Central: 1%, South Atlantic: 10%, East South Central: 1%, West South Central: 3%, Mountain: 1%, Pacific: 10%, Unknown: 0%

BAR PASSAGE RATES

Based on 2008 graduates taking Summer 2008 or Winter 2009 exams. Most of the school's first-time test takers took the bar in New York.

97%

School's bar passage rate for first-time test takers

81%

Statewide bar passage rate for first-time test takers

Cornell University

- Myron Taylor Hall, Ithaca, NY, 14853-4901
- http://www.lawschool.cornell.edu
- Private
- Year founded: 1887
- 2009-2010 tuition: full-time: $48,950; part-time: N/A
- Enrollment 2009-10 academic year: full-time: 622
- U.S. News 2010 law specialty ranking: N/A

3.50-3.80 GPA, 25TH-75TH PERCENTILE

165-168 LSAT, 25TH-75TH PERCENTILE

21% ACCEPTANCE RATE

13 2011 U.S. NEWS LAW SCHOOL RANKING

ADMISSIONS

Admissions phone number: **(607) 255-5141**
Admissions email address: **lawad-mit@lawschool.cornell.edu**
Application website:
http://www.lawschool.cornell.edu/admissions
Application deadline for Fall 2011 admission: **1-Feb**

Admissions statistics:

Number of applicants for Fall 2009: **4,207**
Number of acceptances: **900**
Number enrolled: **205**
Acceptance rate: **21%**
GPA, 25th-75th percentile, entering class Fall 2009: **3.50-3.80**
LSAT, 25th-75th percentile, entering class Fall 2009: **165-168**

FINANCIAL AID

Financial aid phone number: **(607) 255-5141**
Financial aid application deadline: **15-Mar**
Tuition 2009-2010 academic year: **full-time: $48,950; part-time: N/A**
Room and board: **$11,000** ; books: **$850** ; miscellaneous expenses: **$6,450**
Total of room/board/books/miscellaneous expenses: **$18,300**
University offers graduate student housing for which law students are eligible.

Financial aid profile

Percent of students that received grants for the 2008-2009 academic year: full-time: **35%**
Median grant amount: full-time: **$18,000**
The average law-school debt of those in the Class of 2009 who borrowed: **$109,700** . Proportion who borrowed: **80%**

ACADEMIC PROGRAMS

Calendar: **semester**
Joint degrees awarded: **J.D./LL.M. International Legal Studies; JD/Master en Droit French Law Degree; JD/M. Global Business Law ; J.D./M.LL.P. German Law Degree; J.D./M.B.A.; J.D./M.P.A.; J.D./M.A.; J.D./I.L.A. (Intn'l Legal Affairs); J.D./Ph.D.**
Typical first-year section size: Full-time: **99**
Is there typically a "small section" of the first year class, other than Legal Writing, taught by full-time faculty?: Full-time: **yes**
Number of course titles, beyond the first year curriculum, offered last year: **137**
Percentages of upper division course sections, excluding seminars, with an enrollment of:

Under 25: **51%**	25 to 49: **25%**
50 to 74: **11%**	75 to 99: **10%**
100+: **4%**	

Areas of specialization: appellate advocacy, clinical training, dispute resolution, environmental law, health care law, intellectual property law, international law, tax law, trial advocacy

Fall 2009 faculty profile

Total teaching faculty: **75.** Full-time: **61%**; **67%** men, **33%** women, **13%** minorities. Part-time: **39%**; **76%** men, **24%** women, **N/A** minorities
Student-to-faculty ratio: **10**

SPECIAL PROGRAMS *(as provided by law school):*

Students benefit not only from the small class size and well-known collegial learning environment, but also from exchange programs with 17 foreign law schools, a summer program in Paris, a very large array of externships, numerous live-client clinics, and various centers and institutes. Get more info at www.lawschool.cornell.edu

STUDENT BODY

Fall 2009 full-time enrollment: 622

Men: **48%**	Women: **52%**
African-American: **6.10%**	American Indian: **1.30%**
Asian-American: **13.70%**	Mexican-American: **3.40%**
Puerto Rican: **1.60%**	Other Hisp-Amer: **4.30%**

White: **60.50%**   International: **9.20%**
Unknown: **0.00%**

Attrition rates for 2008-2009 full-time students
Percent of students discontinuing law school:
Men: **1%**   Women: **0%**
First-year students: **2%**   Second-year students: **N/A**
Third-year students: **N/A**   Fourth-year students: **N/A**

LIBRARY RESOURCES
Total titles: **260,127**
Total volumes: **762,179**
Total seats available for library users: **419**

INFORMATION TECHNOLOGY
Number of wired network connections available to students: **105** total (in the law library, excluding computer labs: **0**; in classrooms: **34**; in computer labs: **45**; elsewhere in the law school: **26**)
Law school has a wireless network.
Students are not required to own a computer.

EMPLOYMENT AND SALARIES
Proportion of 2008 graduates employed at graduation: **97%**
Employed 9 months later, as of February 15, 2009: **98%**
Salaries in the private sector (law firms, business, industry): **$160,000 –$160,000** (25th-75th percentile)
Median salary in the private sector: **$160,000**

Percentage in the private sector who reported salary information: **82%**
Median salary in public service (government, judicial clerkships, academic posts, non-profits): **$58,206**

Percentage of 2008 graduates in:
Law firms: **85%**   Government: **2%**
Bus./industry: **0%**   Judicial clerkship: **10%**
Public interest: **4%**   Unknown: **0%**
Academia : **1%**

2008 graduates employed in-state: **60%**
2008 graduates employed in foreign countries: **2%**
Number of states where graduates are employed: **21**
Percentage of 2008 graduates working in: New England: **9%**, Middle Atlantic: **60%**, East North Central: **6%**, West North Central: **1%**, South Atlantic: **11%**, East South Central: **0%**, West South Central: **2%**, Mountain: **0%**, Pacific: **10%**, Unknown: **0%**

BAR PASSAGE RATES
Based on 2008 graduates taking Summer 2008 or Winter 2009 exams. Most of the school's first-time test takers took the bar in New York.

| | | | | **99%** |

School's bar passage rate for first-time test takers

| | | | **81%** |

Statewide bar passage rate for first-time test takers

Creighton University

■ 2500 California Plaza, Omaha, NE, 68178
■ http://www.creighton.edu/law
■ Private
■ Year founded: 1904
■ 2009-2010 tuition: full-time: $30,294; part-time: $17,670
■ Enrollment 2009-10 academic year: full-time: 471; part-time: 13
■ U.S. News 2010 law specialty ranking: N/A

3.15-3.64 GPA, 25TH-75TH PERCENTILE

151-156 LSAT, 25TH-75TH PERCENTILE

57% ACCEPTANCE RATE

Tier 3 2011 U.S. NEWS LAW SCHOOL RANKING

ADMISSIONS

Admissions phone number: (800) 282-5835
Admissions email address: lawadmit@creighton.edu
Application website:
   http://www.creighton.edu/law/admissions/applyingtocreightonlaw/index.php
Application deadline for Fall 2011 admission: 1-May

Admissions statistics:
Number of applicants for Fall 2009: 1,314
Number of acceptances: 753
Number enrolled: 173
Acceptance rate: 57%
GPA, 25th-75th percentile, entering class Fall 2009: 3.15-3.64
LSAT, 25th-75th percentile, entering class Fall 2009: 151-156

Part-time program:
Number of applicants for Fall 2009: 52
Number of acceptances: 18
Number enrolled: 4
Acceptance rate: 35%
GPA, 25th-75th percentile, entering class Fall 2009: 2.79-3.10
LSAT, 25th-75th percentile, entering class Fall 2009: 147-152

FINANCIAL AID

Financial aid phone number: (402) 280-2352
Financial aid application deadline: 1-Jul
Tuition 2009-2010 academic year: **full-time: $30,294; part-time: $17,670**
Room and board: $13,500 ; books: $3,085 ; miscellaneous expenses: $4,070
Total of room/board/books/miscellaneous expenses: $20,655
University does not offer graduate student housing for which law students are eligible.

Financial aid profile
Percent of students that received grants for the 2008-2009 academic year: full-time: 48%
Median grant amount: full-time: $9,796
The average law-school debt of those in the Class of 2009 who borrowed: $110,036 . Proportion who borrowed: 79%

ACADEMIC PROGRAMS

Calendar: semester
Joint degrees awarded: **J.D./M.B.A.; J.D./M.S. Information Tech. Management; J.D./M.S. Negotiation/Dispute Resolution; J.D./M.A. International Relations**
Typical first-year section size: Full-time: 83
Is there typically a "small section" of the first year class, other than Legal Writing, taught by full-time faculty?: Full-time: no
Number of course titles, beyond the first year curriculum, offered last year: 84
Percentages of upper division course sections, excluding seminars, with an enrollment of:

Under 25: **74%**		25 to 49: **19%**
50 to 74: **5%**		75 to 99: **1%**
100+: **0%**		

Areas of specialization: appellate advocacy, clinical training, dispute resolution, environmental law, health care law, intellectual property law, international law, tax law, trial advocacy

Fall 2009 faculty profile
Total teaching faculty: 45. Full-time: 49%; 77% men, 23% women, 14% minorities. Part-time: 51%; 65% men, 35% women, 0% minorities
Student-to-faculty ratio: 17.6

SPECIAL PROGRAMS (as provided by law school):
Abrahams Legal Clinic for civil matters; Community Economic Development Clinic advising non-profits. Externships with governmental and public interest organizations. Interdisciplinary combined degree programs: MBA, MS in Information Technology, MS in Dispute Resolution, and MS in International

Relations. Opportunity for semester's study in Spain at Universidad Pontifica Comillias de Madrid.

STUDENT BODY

Fall 2009 full-time enrollment: 471
Men: 58%	Women: 42%
African-American: 1.90%	American Indian: 0.20%
Asian-American: 4.00%	Mexican-American: 1.10%
Puerto Rican: 0.20%	Other Hisp-Amer: 2.30%
White: 89.80%	International: 0.20%
Unknown: 0.20%	

Fall 2009 part-time enrollment: 13
Men: 38%	Women: 62%
African-American: 15.40%	American Indian: 0.00%
Asian-American: 0.00%	Mexican-American: 0.00%
Puerto Rican: 0.00%	Other Hisp-Amer: 7.70%
White: 69.20%	International: 0.00%
Unknown: 7.70%	

Attrition rates for 2008-2009 full-time students
Percent of students discontinuing law school:
Men: 0%	Women: 2%
First-year students: 2%	Second-year students: N/A
Third-year students: N/A	Fourth-year students: N/A

LIBRARY RESOURCES
Total titles: 186,739
Total volumes: 384,395
Total seats available for library users: 371

INFORMATION TECHNOLOGY
Number of wired network connections available to students: 174 total (in the law library, excluding computer labs: 38; in classrooms: 116; in computer labs: 8; elsewhere in the law school: 12)
Law school has a wireless network.
Students are not required to own a computer.

EMPLOYMENT AND SALARIES
Proportion of 2008 graduates employed at graduation: 50%
Employed 9 months later, as of February 15, 2009: 92%
Salaries in the private sector (law firms, business, industry): $50,000 –$80,000 (25th-75th percentile)
Median salary in the private sector: $60,000
Percentage in the private sector who reported salary information: 60%
Median salary in public service (government, judicial clerkships, academic posts, non-profits): $56,475

Percentage of 2008 graduates in:
Law firms: 49%	Government: 23%
Bus./industry: 21%	Judicial clerkship: 5%
Public interest: 2%	Unknown: 1%
Academia : 0%	

2008 graduates employed in-state: 49%
2008 graduates employed in foreign countries: 0%
Number of states where graduates are employed: 27
Percentage of 2008 graduates working in: New England: 0%, Middle Atlantic: 1%, East North Central: 4%, West North Central: 61%, South Atlantic: 3%, East South Central: 1%, West South Central: 4%, Mountain: 15%, Pacific: 8%, Unknown: 5%

BAR PASSAGE RATES
Based on 2008 graduates taking Summer 2008 or Winter 2009 exams. Most of the school's first-time test takers took the bar in Nebraska.

88%
School's bar passage rate for first-time test takers

89%
Statewide bar passage rate for first-time test takers

CUNY–Queens College

■ 65-21 Main Street, Flushing, NY, 11367
■ http://www.law.cuny.edu/
■ Public
■ Year founded: 1983
■ 2009-2010 tuition: full-time: $10,612; part-time: N/A
■ Enrollment 2009-10 academic year: full-time: 406
■ U.S. News 2010 law specialty ranking: clinical training: 3

3.10-3.54 GPA, 25TH-75TH PERCENTILE

151-156 LSAT, 25TH-75TH PERCENTILE

27% ACCEPTANCE RATE

Tier 4 2011 U.S. NEWS LAW SCHOOL RANKING

ADMISSIONS

Admissions phone number: (718) 340-4210
Admissions email address: admissions@mail.law.cuny.edu
Application website: N/A
Application deadline for Fall 2011 admission: 15-Mar

Admissions statistics:
Number of applicants for Fall 2009: 2,165
Number of acceptances: 575
Number enrolled: 158
Acceptance rate: 27%
GPA, 25th-75th percentile, entering class Fall 2009: 3.10-3.54
LSAT, 25th-75th percentile, entering class Fall 2009: 151-156

FINANCIAL AID

Financial aid phone number: (718) 340-4284
Financial aid application deadline: 3-May
Tuition 2009-2010 academic year: **full-time: $10,612; part-time: N/A**
Room and board: **$7,425** ; books: **$1,711** ; miscellaneous expenses: **$8,691**
Total of room/board/books/miscellaneous expenses: **$17,827**
University does not offer graduate student housing for which law students are eligible.

Financial aid profile
Percent of students that received grants for the 2008-2009 academic year: full-time: **28%**
Median grant amount: full-time: **$2,362**
The average law-school debt of those in the Class of 2009 who borrowed: **$65,328** . Proportion who borrowed: **88%**

ACADEMIC PROGRAMS

Calendar: **semester**
Joint degrees awarded: **N/A**
Typical first-year section size: Full-time: **80**
Is there typically a "small section" of the first year class, other than Legal Writing, taught by full-time faculty?: Full-time: **yes**

Number of course titles, beyond the first year curriculum, offered last year: **N/A**
Percentages of upper division course sections, excluding seminars, with an enrollment of:
Under 25: **59%**   25 to 49: **28%**
50 to 74: **9%**   75 to 99: **2%**
100+: **3%**
Areas of specialization: appellate advocacy, clinical training, dispute resolution, environmental law, health care law, intellectual property law, international law, trial advocacy

Fall 2009 faculty profile
Total teaching faculty: **42**. Full-time: **76%**; **44%** men, **56%** women, **31%** minorities. Part-time: **24%**; **40%** men, **60%** women, **40%** minorities
Student-to-faculty ratio: **10**

SPECIAL PROGRAMS (as provided by law school):

Unlike other law schools, CUNY Law's nationally-ranked clinical program requires every third year student to fulfill 12-16 credits of supervised live-client representation. In-house clinics and external placements include Battered Women's Rights, Criminal Defense, Immigrant and Refugees' Rights, International Women's Human Rights, Elder Law, Mediation, Equality, and Health Law.

STUDENT BODY

Fall 2009 full-time enrollment: 406
Men: **37%**   Women: **63%**
African-American: **8.10%**   American Indian: **0.00%**
Asian-American: **10.60%**   Mexican-American: **0.70%**
Puerto Rican: **2.20%**   Other Hisp-Amer: **9.10%**
White: **61.60%**   International: **1.00%**
Unknown: **6.70%**

Attrition rates for 2008-2009 full-time students
Percent of students discontinuing law school:
Men: **2%**   Women: **3%**
First-year students: **7%**   Second-year students: **N/A**
Third-year students: **N/A**   Fourth-year students: **N/A**

LIBRARY RESOURCES

Total titles: **45,613**
Total volumes: **291,162**
Total seats available for library users: **223**

INFORMATION TECHNOLOGY

Number of wired network connections available to students: **62** total (in the law library, excluding computer labs: **0**; in classrooms: **20**; in computer labs: **6**; elsewhere in the law school: **36**)
Law school has a wireless network.
Students are not required to own a computer.

EMPLOYMENT AND SALARIES

Proportion of 2008 graduates employed at graduation: **N/A**
Employed 9 months later, as of February 15, 2009: **82%**
Salaries in the private sector (law firms, business, industry): **$41,600 –$70,000** (25th-75th percentile)
Median salary in the private sector: **$53,524**
Percentage in the private sector who reported salary information: **29%**
Median salary in public service (government, judicial clerkships, academic posts, non-profits): **$58,090**

Percentage of 2008 graduates in:

Law firms: **22%**   Government: **17%**
Bus./industry: **7%**   Judicial clerkship: **18%**
Public interest: **35%**   Unknown: **0%**
Academia : **2%**

2008 graduates employed in-state: **63%**
2008 graduates employed in foreign countries: **0%**
Number of states where graduates are employed: **15**
Percentage of 2008 graduates working in: New England: **5%**, Middle Atlantic: **72%**, East North Central: **0%**, West North Central: **1%**, South Atlantic: **5%**, East South Central: **0%**, West South Central: **5%**, Mountain: **2%**, Pacific: **9%**, Unknown: **1%**

BAR PASSAGE RATES

Based on 2008 graduates taking Summer 2008 or Winter 2009 exams. Most of the school's first-time test takers took the bar in New York.

82%

School's bar passage rate for first-time test takers

81%

Statewide bar passage rate for first-time test takers

DePaul University

- 25 E. Jackson Boulevard, Chicago, IL, 60604
- http://www.law.depaul.edu
- Private
- Year founded: 1912
- 2009-2010 tuition: full-time: $37,975; part-time: $24,830
- Enrollment 2009-10 academic year: full-time: 772; part-time: 255
- U.S. News 2010 law specialty ranking: healthcare law: 13, intellectual property law: 16

3.11-3.57 GPA, 25TH-75TH PERCENTILE

158-162 LSAT, 25TH-75TH PERCENTILE

38% ACCEPTANCE RATE

98 2011 U.S. NEWS LAW SCHOOL RANKING

ADMISSIONS

Admissions phone number: (312) 362-6831
Admissions email address: lawinfo@depaul.edu
Application website: http://www.law.depaul.edu/apply
Application deadline for Fall 2011 admission: 3-Jan

Admissions statistics:

Number of applicants for Fall 2009: 4,366
Number of acceptances: 1,658
Number enrolled: 252
Acceptance rate: 38%
GPA, 25th-75th percentile, entering class Fall 2009: 3.11-3.57
LSAT, 25th-75th percentile, entering class Fall 2009: 158-162

Part-time program:

Number of applicants for Fall 2009: 702
Number of acceptances: 330
Number enrolled: 112
Acceptance rate: 47%
GPA, 25th-75th percentile, entering class Fall 2009: 3.04-3.41
LSAT, 25th-75th percentile, entering class Fall 2009: 154-157

FINANCIAL AID

Financial aid phone number: (312) 362-8091
Financial aid application deadline: 1-Apr
Tuition 2009-2010 academic year: full-time: $37,975; part-time: $24,830
Room and board: $20,907 ; books: $1,500 ; miscellaneous expenses: N/A
Total of room/board/books/miscellaneous expenses: $22,407
University offers graduate student housing for which law students are eligible.

Financial aid profile

Percent of students that received grants for the 2008-2009 academic year: full-time: 68%; part-time 40%

Median grant amount: full-time: $13,000 ; part-time: $4,000
The average law-school debt of those in the Class of 2009 who borrowed: $106,412 . Proportion who borrowed: 90%

ACADEMIC PROGRAMS

Calendar: semester
Joint degrees awarded: J.D./M.B.A.; J.D./M.S. Public Service Management; J.D./M.A. International Studies; J.D./M.A. Computer Science; J.D./M.S. Computer Science
Typical first-year section size: Full-time: 90; Part-time: 97
Is there typically a "small section" of the first year class, other than Legal Writing, taught by full-time faculty?: Full-time: no; Part-time: no
Number of course titles, beyond the first year curriculum, offered last year: 156
Percentages of upper division course sections, excluding seminars, with an enrollment of:

Under 25: 68%	25 to 49: 18%
50 to 74: 8%	75 to 99: 5%
100+: 1%	

Areas of specialization: appellate advocacy, clinical training, dispute resolution, environmental law, health care law, intellectual property law, international law, tax law, trial advocacy

Fall 2009 faculty profile

Total teaching faculty: 121. Full-time: 50%; 57% men, 43% women, 13% minorities. Part-time: 50%; 70% men, 30% women, 10% minorities
Student-to-faculty ratio: 13.3

SPECIAL PROGRAMS (as provided by law school):

DePaul is home to 13 academic research centers and institutes that focus on major legal issues of national and international scope. Additionally, DePaul offers 8 legal clinics, 11 certificate programs, 5 joint degree programs and 7 study abroad programs. For further information, visit: http://www.law.depaul.edu

STUDENT BODY

Fall 2009 full-time enrollment: 772

Men: 51%	Women: 49%
African-American: 7.00%	American Indian: 0.30%
Asian-American: 5.70%	Mexican-American: 1.20%
Puerto Rican: 0.30%	Other Hisp-Amer: 9.30%
White: 72.20%	International: 1.60%
Unknown: 2.60%	

Fall 2009 part-time enrollment: 255

Men: 45%	Women: 55%
African-American: 7.10%	American Indian: 0.40%
Asian-American: 7.50%	Mexican-American: 0.40%
Puerto Rican: 0.00%	Other Hisp-Amer: 10.20%
White: 69.80%	International: 1.60%
Unknown: 3.10%	

Attrition rates for 2008-2009 full-time students
Percent of students discontinuing law school:

Men: 1%	Women: 3%
First-year students: 7%	Second-year students: N/A
Third-year students: 0%	Fourth-year students: 2%

LIBRARY RESOURCES

Total titles: 110,581
Total volumes: 401,828
Total seats available for library users: 446

INFORMATION TECHNOLOGY

Number of wired network connections available to students: 70 total (in the law library, excluding computer labs: 40; in classrooms: 0; in computer labs: 10; elsewhere in the law school: 20)
Law school has a wireless network.
Students are not required to own a computer.

EMPLOYMENT AND SALARIES

Proportion of 2008 graduates employed at graduation: 81%
Employed 9 months later, as of February 15, 2009: 94%
Salaries in the private sector (law firms, business, industry): $55,000 –$145,000 (25th-75th percentile)
Median salary in the private sector: $87,500
Percentage in the private sector who reported salary information: 75%
Median salary in public service (government, judicial clerkships, academic posts, non-profits): $55,000

Percentage of 2008 graduates in:

Law firms: 55%	Government: 13%
Bus./industry: 20%	Judicial clerkship: 2%
Public interest: 3%	Unknown: 2%
Academia : 6%	

2008 graduates employed in-state: 81%
2008 graduates employed in foreign countries: 0%
Number of states where graduates are employed: 21
Percentage of 2008 graduates working in: New England: 0%, Middle Atlantic: 2%, East North Central: 86%, West North Central: 1%, South Atlantic: 5%, East South Central: 0%, West South Central: 0%, Mountain: 2%, Pacific: 1%, Unknown: 3%

BAR PASSAGE RATES

Based on 2008 graduates taking Summer 2008 or Winter 2009 exams. Most of the school's first-time test takers took the bar in Illinois.

89%

School's bar passage rate for first-time test takers

91%

Statewide bar passage rate for first-time test takers

Drake University

- 2507 University Avenue, Des Moines, IA, 50311
- http://www.law.drake.edu/
- Private
- Year founded: 1881
- 2009-2010 tuition: full-time: $31,186; part-time: $1,070/credit hour
- Enrollment 2009-10 academic year: full-time: 451; part-time: 16
- U.S. News 2010 law specialty ranking: intellectual property law: 25

3.12-3.64 GPA, 25TH-75TH PERCENTILE

153-158 LSAT, 25TH-75TH PERCENTILE

54% ACCEPTANCE RATE

Tier 3 2011 U.S. NEWS LAW SCHOOL RANKING

ADMISSIONS
Admissions phone number: **(515) 271-2782**
Admissions email address: **lawadmit@drake.edu**
Application website:
  http://www.law.drake.edu/admissions/
Application deadline for Fall 2011 admission: **1-Apr**

Admissions statistics:
Number of applicants for Fall 2009: **1,069**
Number of acceptances: **575**
Number enrolled: **150**
Acceptance rate: **54%**
GPA, 25th-75th percentile, entering class Fall 2009: **3.12-3.64**
LSAT, 25th-75th percentile, entering class Fall 2009: **153-158**

Part-time program:
Number of applicants for Fall 2009: **36**
Number of acceptances: **9**
Number enrolled: **6**
Acceptance rate: **25%**
GPA, 25th-75th percentile, entering class Fall 2009: **3.10-3.93**
LSAT, 25th-75th percentile, entering class Fall 2009: **155-159**

FINANCIAL AID
Financial aid phone number: **(515) 271-2782**
Financial aid application deadline: **1-Mar**
Tuition 2009-2010 academic year: **full-time: $31,186; part-time: $1,070/credit hour**
Room and board: **$10,000** ; books: **$1,300** ; miscellaneous expenses: **$6,710**
Total of room/board/books/miscellaneous expenses: **$18,010**
University offers graduate student housing for which law students are eligible.

Financial aid profile
Percent of students that received grants for the 2008-2009

academic year: full-time: **59%**
Median grant amount: full-time: **$14,035** ; part-time: **$0**
The average law-school debt of those in the Class of 2009 who borrowed: **$85,905** . Proportion who borrowed: **91%**

ACADEMIC PROGRAMS
Calendar: **semester**
Joint degrees awarded: **J.D./M.B.A.; J.D./M.P.A.**
Typical first-year section size: Full-time: **81**
Is there typically a "small section" of the first year class, other than Legal Writing, taught by full-time faculty?:
  Full-time: **no**; Part-time: **no**
Number of course titles, beyond the first year curriculum, offered last year: **98**
Percentages of upper division course sections, excluding seminars, with an enrollment of:

Under 25: **69%**	25 to 49: **21%**
50 to 74: **8%**	75 to 99: **1%**
100+: **0%**	

Areas of specialization: appellate advocacy, clinical training, dispute resolution, environmental law, health care law, intellectual property law, international law, tax law, trial advocacy

Fall 2009 faculty profile
Total teaching faculty: **46**. Full-time: **59%**; **63%** men, **37%** women, **11%** minorities. Part-time: **41%**; **74%** men, **26%** women, **0%** minorities
Student-to-faculty ratio: **14.5**

SPECIAL PROGRAMS *(as provided by law school):*
Drake offers live-client clinics in civil practice, criminal defense, mediation, elder law, and children's rights. It has five centers: Constitutional Law, Children's Rights, Agricultural Law, Legislative Practice and Intellectual Property Law. It offers a unique First-Year Trial Practicum; a Summer in France Program; nearly 20 internships; and more than 30 paid Summer Public Interest Internships.

STUDENT BODY

Fall 2009 full-time enrollment: 451

Men: 57%	Women: 43%
African-American: 6.70%	American Indian: 0.20%
Asian-American: 1.60%	Mexican-American: 1.10%
Puerto Rican: 0.20%	Other Hisp-Amer: 0.90%
White: 73.60%	International: 0.90%
Unknown: 14.90%	

Fall 2009 part-time enrollment: 16

Men: 19%	Women: 81%
African-American: 0.00%	American Indian: 0.00%
Asian-American: 0.00%	Mexican-American: 0.00%
Puerto Rican: 0.00%	Other Hisp-Amer: 0.00%
White: 81.30%	International: 18.80%
Unknown: 0.00%	

Attrition rates for 2008-2009 full-time students

Percent of students discontinuing law school:

Men: 2%	Women: N/A
First-year students: 2%	Second-year students: N/A
Third-year students: N/A	Fourth-year students: N/A

LIBRARY RESOURCES

Total titles: 73,968
Total volumes: 333,281
Total seats available for library users: 705

INFORMATION TECHNOLOGY

Number of wired network connections available to students: 180 total (in the law library, excluding computer labs: 160; in classrooms: 0; in computer labs: 20; elsewhere in the law school: 0)

Law school has a wireless network.

Students are not required to own a computer.

EMPLOYMENT AND SALARIES

Proportion of 2008 graduates employed at graduation: N/A

Employed 9 months later, as of February 15, 2009: 97%

Salaries in the private sector (law firms, business, industry): $5,000 –$85,000 (25th-75th percentile)

Median salary in the private sector: $65,375

Percentage in the private sector who reported salary information: 27%

Median salary in public service (government, judicial clerkships, academic posts, non-profits): $49,000

Percentage of 2008 graduates in:

Law firms: 51%	Government: 12%
Bus./industry: 20%	Judicial clerkship: 9%
Public interest: 6%	Unknown: 0%
Academia : 2%	

2008 graduates employed in-state: 63%

2008 graduates employed in foreign countries: 0%

Number of states where graduates are employed: 21

Percentage of 2008 graduates working in: New England: 0%, Middle Atlantic: 1%, East North Central: 11%, West North Central: 70%, South Atlantic: 4%, East South Central: 0%, West South Central: 2%, Mountain: 8%, Pacific: 4%, Unknown: 0%

BAR PASSAGE RATES

Based on 2008 graduates taking Summer 2008 or Winter 2009 exams. Most of the school's first-time test takers took the bar in Iowa.

90%

School's bar passage rate for first-time test takers

90%

Statewide bar passage rate for first-time test takers

Drexel University (Mack)

- 3320 Market Street, Suite 400, Philadelphia, PA, 19104
- http://www.drexel.edu/law/admissions-home.asp
- Private
- Year founded: 2006
- 2009-2010 tuition: full-time: $32,200; part-time: N/A
- Enrollment 2009-10 academic year: full-time: 410
- U.S. News 2010 law specialty ranking: healthcare law: 12

3.09-3.70 GPA, 25TH-75TH PERCENTILE

156-163 LSAT, 25TH-75TH PERCENTILE

33% ACCEPTANCE RATE

Unranked 2011 U.S. NEWS LAW SCHOOL RANKING

ADMISSIONS

Admissions phone number: **(215) 895-1529**
Admissions email address: **lawadmissions@drexel.edu**
Application website: **http://www.drexel.edu/law/apply**
Application deadline for Fall 2011 admission: **rolling**

Admissions statistics:
Number of applicants for Fall 2009: **2,862**
Number of acceptances: **937**
Number enrolled: **156**
Acceptance rate: **33%**
GPA, 25th-75th percentile, entering class Fall 2009: **3.09-3.70**
LSAT, 25th-75th percentile, entering class Fall 2009: **156-163**

FINANCIAL AID

Financial aid phone number: **(215) 895-6395**
Financial aid application deadline:
Tuition 2009-2010 academic year: **full-time: $32,200; part-time: N/A**
Room and board: **N/A**; books: **N/A**; miscellaneous expenses: **N/A**
Total of room/board/books/miscellaneous expenses: **$21,435**
University offers graduate student housing for which law students are eligible.

Financial aid profile
Percent of students that received grants for the 2008-2009 academic year: full-time: **91%**
Median grant amount: full-time: **$24,347**
The average law-school debt of those in the Class of 2009 who borrowed: **$23,171** . Proportion who borrowed: **80%**

ACADEMIC PROGRAMS

Calendar: **quarter**
Joint degrees awarded: **J.D./Ph.D Psychology; J.D./M.B.A; B.S.- B.A./J.D.**
Typical first-year section size: Full-time: **78**
Is there typically a "small section" of the first year class, other than Legal Writing, taught by full-time faculty?: Full-time: **no**
Number of course titles, beyond the first year curriculum, offered last year: **84**
Percentages of upper division course sections, excluding seminars, with an enrollment of:
Under 25: **57%**   25 to 49: **34%**
50 to 74: **7%**   75 to 99: **2%**
100+: **N/A**
Areas of specialization: appellate advocacy, clinical training, dispute resolution, environmental law, health care law, intellectual property law, international law, tax law, trial advocacy

Fall 2009 faculty profile
Total teaching faculty: **49**. Full-time: **45%; 55%** men, **45%** women, **23%** minorities. Part-time: **55%; 56%** men, **44%** women, **4%** minorities
Student-to-faculty ratio: **16.4**

SPECIAL PROGRAMS (as provided by law school):

The law school offers a comprehensive experiential education program. The centerpiece of the program is the Drexel Co-op, which gives students significant academic credit for immersion in a wide variety of for-profit, public interest and governmental settings. The law school also offers three academic concentrations: business law, intellectual property and health law.

STUDENT BODY

Fall 2009 full-time enrollment: 410
Men: **52%**   Women: **48%**
African-American: **6.60%**   American Indian: **1.00%**
Asian-American: **3.70%**   Mexican-American: **1.20%**
Puerto Rican: **1.20%**   Other Hisp-Amer: **4.10%**
White: **71.20%**   International: **2.40%**
Unknown: **8.50%**

Attrition rates for 2008-2009 full-time students
Percent of students discontinuing law school:
Men: **3%**   Women: **3%**
First-year students: **7%**   Second-year students: **2%**
Third-year students: **N/A**   Fourth-year students: **N/A**

LIBRARY RESOURCES

Total titles: 152,753
Total volumes: 48,148
Total seats available for library users: 283

INFORMATION TECHNOLOGY

Number of wired network connections available to students: 731 total (in the law library, excluding computer labs: 189; in classrooms: 530; in computer labs: 0; elsewhere in the law school: 12)
Law school has a wireless network.
Students are required to own a computer.

EMPLOYMENT AND SALARIES

Proportion of 2008 graduates employed at graduation: N/A
Employed 9 months later, as of February 15, 2009: N/A
Salaries in the private sector (law firms, business, industry): N/A–N/A (25th-75th percentile)
Median salary in the private sector: N/A
Percentage in the private sector who reported salary information: N/A
Median salary in public service (government, judicial clerkships, academic posts, non-profits): N/A

Percentage of 2008 graduates in:

Law firms: **N/A**   Government: **N/A**
Bus./industry: **N/A**   Judicial clerkship: **N/A**
Public interest: **N/A**   Unknown: **N/A**
Academia : **N/A**

2008 graduates employed in-state: **N/A**
2008 graduates employed in foreign countries: **N/A**
Number of states where graduates are employed: **N/A**
Percentage of 2008 graduates working in: New England: **N/A**, Middle Atlantic: **N/A**, East North Central: **N/A**, West North Central: **N/A**, South Atlantic: **N/A**, East South Central: **N/A**, West South Central: **N/A**, Mountain: **N/A**, Pacific: **N/A**, Unknown: **N/A**

BAR PASSAGE RATES

Based on 2008 graduates taking Summer 2008 or Winter 2009 exams.

N/A

School's bar passage rate for first-time test takers

N/A

Statewide bar passage rate for first-time test takers

Duke University

■ Towerview and Science Drive, Box 90362, Durham, NC, 27708-0362
■ http://www.law.duke.edu
■ Private
■ Year founded: 1930
■ 2009-2010 tuition: full-time: $45,271; part-time: N/A
■ Enrollment 2009-10 academic year: full-time: 626; part-time: 35
■ U.S. News 2010 law specialty ranking: environmental law: 12, health-care law: 19, intellectual property law: 9, international law: 10

3.60-3.84 GPA, 25TH-75TH PERCENTILE

167-171 LSAT, 25TH-75TH PERCENTILE

18% ACCEPTANCE RATE

11 2011 U.S. NEWS LAW SCHOOL RANKING

ADMISSIONS

Admissions phone number: **(919) 613-7020**
Admissions email address: **admissions@law.duke.edu**
Application website:
  https://admissions.law.duke.edu/admis/apply.html
Application deadline for Fall 2011 admission: **15-Feb**

Admissions statistics:

Number of applicants for Fall 2009: **6,334**
Number of acceptances: **1,161**
Number enrolled: **228**
Acceptance rate: **18%**
GPA, 25th-75th percentile, entering class Fall 2009: **3.60-3.84**
LSAT, 25th-75th percentile, entering class Fall 2009: **167-171**

FINANCIAL AID

Financial aid phone number: **(919) 613-7026**
Financial aid application deadline: **15-Mar**
Tuition 2009-2010 academic year: **full-time: $45,271; part-time: N/A**
Room and board: **$10,304** ; books: **$1,260** ; miscellaneous expenses: **$5,128**
Total of room/board/books/miscellaneous expenses: **$16,692**
University does not offer graduate student housing for which law students are eligible.

Financial aid profile

Percent of students that received grants for the 2008-2009 academic year: full-time: **69%**
Median grant amount: full-time: **$14,000**
The average law-school debt of those in the Class of 2009 who borrowed: **$122,296** . Proportion who borrowed: **78%**

ACADEMIC PROGRAMS

Calendar: **semester**
Joint degrees awarded: **J.D./M.A. Cultural Anthropology; J.D./M.A. East Asian Studies; J.D./M.A. Environmental** Science/Policy; J.D./M.A. Economics; J.D./M.A. History; J.D./M.A. Humanities; J.D./LL.M Int'l and Comparative Law; J.D./M.B.A.; J.D./M.D.; J.D./M.S. Engineering; J.D./M.P.P. ; J.D./M.T.S. ; J.D./M.A. Philosophy; J.D./M.A. Political Science; J.D./M.A. Int'l Development Policy; J.D./M.A. Psychology; J.D./M.S. Biomedical Engineering; J.D./M.A. Romance Studies; J.D./M.A. Sociology; J.D./M.A. Religion; J.D./M.A. English; J.D./Ph.D History; J.D./Ph.D Political Science; J.D./M.A. Literature; J.D./M.A. Art & Art History; J.D./M.S. Cellular/Molecular Biology; J.D. MEM
Typical first-year section size: Full-time: **68**
Is there typically a "small section" of the first year class, other than Legal Writing, taught by full-time faculty?: Full-time: **yes**
Number of course titles, beyond the first year curriculum, offered last year: **184**
Percentages of upper division course sections, excluding seminars, with an enrollment of:
  Under 25: **66%**   25 to 49: **22%**
  50 to 74: **7%**   75 to 99: **2%**
  100+: **3%**
Areas of specialization: appellate advocacy, clinical training, dispute resolution, environmental law, health care law, intellectual property law, international law, tax law, trial advocacy

Fall 2009 faculty profile

Total teaching faculty: **82**. Full-time: **66%**; **74%** men, **26%** women, **11%** minorities. Part-time: **34%**; **64%** men, **36%** women, **7%** minorities
Student-to-faculty ratio: **9.7**

SPECIAL PROGRAMS (as provided by law school):

Duke leads in interdisciplinary study with almost 25% of students in joint-degrees; interdisciplinary centers offer conferences, research and teaching; leading in clinical education, Duke operates eight clinics; Duke in DC and capstone projects integrate academics and hands-on practice; international opportunities include externships, foreign exchanges, and summer institutes in Geneva & Hong Kong.

STUDENT BODY

Fall 2009 full-time enrollment: 626

Men: 58%	Women: 42%
African-American: 8.80%	American Indian: 0.20%
Asian-American: 8.30%	Mexican-American: 0.80%
Puerto Rican: 0.50%	Other Hisp-Amer: 4.20%
White: 62.50%	International: 1.40%
Unknown: 13.40%	

Fall 2009 part-time enrollment: 35

Men: 46%	Women: 54%
African-American: 5.70%	American Indian: 0.00%
Asian-American: 8.60%	Mexican-American: 0.00%
Puerto Rican: 0.00%	Other Hisp-Amer: 2.90%
White: 68.60%	International: 2.90%
Unknown: 11.40%	

Attrition rates for 2008-2009 full-time students
Percent of students discontinuing law school:

Men: 2%	Women: 1%
First-year students: N/A	Second-year students: 5%
Third-year students: N/A	Fourth-year students: N/A

LIBRARY RESOURCES

Total titles: 251,594
Total volumes: 658,918
Total seats available for library users: 585

INFORMATION TECHNOLOGY

Number of wired network connections available to students: 894 total (in the law library, excluding computer labs: 174; in classrooms: 680; in computer labs: 0; elsewhere in the law school: 40)
Law school has a wireless network.
Students are not required to own a computer.

EMPLOYMENT AND SALARIES

Proportion of 2008 graduates employed at graduation: 100%
Employed 9 months later, as of February 15, 2009: 100%
Salaries in the private sector (law firms, business, industry): $145,000 –$160,000 (25th-75th percentile)
Median salary in the private sector: $160,000
Percentage in the private sector who reported salary information: 96%
Median salary in public service (government, judicial clerkships, academic posts, non-profits): $53,500

Percentage of 2008 graduates in:

Law firms: 75%	Government: 2%
Bus./industry: 3%	Judicial clerkship: 16%
Public interest: 3%	Unknown: 0%
Academia : 1%	

2008 graduates employed in-state: 9%
2008 graduates employed in foreign countries: 0%
Number of states where graduates are employed: 30
Percentage of 2008 graduates working in: New England: 2%, Middle Atlantic: 24%, East North Central: 5%, West North Central: 1%, South Atlantic: 42%, East South Central: 3%, West South Central: 7%, Mountain: 2%, Pacific: 14%, Unknown: 0%

BAR PASSAGE RATES

Based on 2008 graduates taking Summer 2008 or Winter 2009 exams. Most of the school's first-time test takers took the bar in New York.

96%
School's bar passage rate for first-time test takers

81%
Statewide bar passage rate for first-time test takers

Duquesne University

- 600 Forbes Avenue, Pittsburgh, PA, 15282
- http://www.duq.edu/law
- Private
- Year founded: 1911
- 2009-2010 tuition: full-time: $30,866; part-time: $23,874
- Enrollment 2009-10 academic year: full-time: 446; part-time: 258
- U.S. News 2010 law specialty ranking: N/A

3.25-3.67 GPA, 25TH-75TH PERCENTILE

152-155 LSAT, 25TH-75TH PERCENTILE

47% ACCEPTANCE RATE

Tier 4 2011 U.S. NEWS LAW SCHOOL RANKING

ADMISSIONS
Admissions phone number: (412) 396-6296
Admissions email address: campion@duq.edu
Application website: N/A
Application deadline for Fall 2011 admission: 1-Apr

Admissions statistics:
Number of applicants for Fall 2009: 852
Number of acceptances: 397
Number enrolled: 161
Acceptance rate: 47%
GPA, 25th-75th percentile, entering class Fall 2009: 3.25-3.67
LSAT, 25th-75th percentile, entering class Fall 2009: 152-155

Part-time program:
Number of applicants for Fall 2009: 212
Number of acceptances: 99
Number enrolled: 63
Acceptance rate: 47%
GPA, 25th-75th percentile, entering class Fall 2009: 3.13-3.59
LSAT, 25th-75th percentile, entering class Fall 2009: 149-154

FINANCIAL AID
Financial aid phone number: (412) 396-6607
Financial aid application deadline: 1-May
Tuition 2009-2010 academic year: full-time: $30,866; part-time: $23,874
Room and board: $9,858 ; books: $1,100 ; miscellaneous expenses: $1,150
Total of room/board/books/miscellaneous expenses: $12,108
University offers graduate student housing for which law students are eligible.

Financial aid profile
Percent of students that received grants for the 2008-2009 academic year: full-time: 34%; part-time 6%

Median grant amount: full-time: $14,813 ; part-time: $8,147
The average law-school debt of those in the Class of 2009 who borrowed: $72,124 . Proportion who borrowed: 92%

ACADEMIC PROGRAMS
Calendar: semester
Joint degrees awarded: J.D./M.B.A.; J.D./M.S.E.S.M.; J.D./M.Div.; J.D./M.S.T.
Typical first-year section size: Full-time: 83; Part-time: 60
Is there typically a "small section" of the first year class, other than Legal Writing, taught by full-time faculty?: Full-time: yes; Part-time: no
Number of course titles, beyond the first year curriculum, offered last year: 85
Percentages of upper division course sections, excluding seminars, with an enrollment of:

Under 25: 52%   25 to 49: 17%
50 to 74: 15%   75 to 99: 16%
100+: 0%

Areas of specialization: appellate advocacy, clinical training, dispute resolution, environmental law, health care law, intellectual property law, international law, tax law, trial advocacy

Fall 2009 faculty profile
Total teaching faculty: 60. Full-time: 43%; 69% men, 31% women, 15% minorities. Part-time: 57%; 65% men, 35% women, 3% minorities
Student-to-faculty ratio: 19.4

SPECIAL PROGRAMS *(as provided by law school):*
Summer programs: Beijing, Rome, Dublin. Clinics: low income taxation, securities, family justice, economic/community development, post conviction DNA. Center: The Legal Research and Writing Program was recently ranked in the top 17 of all the law schools in the nation. A new Legal Research and Writing Center opened in Fall 2009.

STUDENT BODY
Fall 2009 full-time enrollment: 446
Men: 49%   Women: 51%

African-American: 3.10%   American Indian: 0.00%
Asian-American: 1.80%   Mexican-American: 0.00%
Puerto Rican: 0.00%   Other Hisp-Amer: 1.30%
White: 89.00%   International: 0.20%
Unknown: 4.50%

Fall 2009 part-time enrollment: 258
Men: 48%   Women: 52%
African-American: 2.70%   American Indian: 0.40%
Asian-American: 2.70%   Mexican-American: 0.00%
Puerto Rican: 0.00%   Other Hisp-Amer: 0.80%
White: 90.30%   International: 0.80%
Unknown: 2.30%

Attrition rates for 2008-2009 full-time students
Percent of students discontinuing law school:
Men: 2%   Women: 4%
First-year students: 7%   Second-year students: 1%
Third-year students: N/A   Fourth-year students: N/A

LIBRARY RESOURCES
Total titles: 90,921
Total volumes: 302,036
Total seats available for library users: 411

INFORMATION TECHNOLOGY
Number of wired network connections available to stu-
    dents: 26 total (in the law library, excluding computer
    labs: 26; in classrooms: 0; in computer labs: 0; else-
    where in the law school: 0)
Law school has a wireless network.
Students are not required to own a computer.

EMPLOYMENT AND SALARIES
Proportion of 2008 graduates employed at graduation:
    N/A

Employed 9 months later, as of February 15, 2009: 85%
Salaries in the private sector (law firms, business, indus-
    try): $50,000 –$80,000 (25th-75th percentile)
Median salary in the private sector: $65,000
Percentage in the private sector who reported salary
    information: 74%
Median salary in public service (government, judicial clerk-
    ships, academic posts, non-profits): $43,500

Percentage of 2008 graduates in:
Law firms: 57%   Government: 11%
Bus./industry: 17%   Judicial clerkship: 12%
Public interest: 1%   Unknown: 0%
Academia : 2%

2008 graduates employed in-state: 72%
2008 graduates employed in foreign countries: 0%
Number of states where graduates are employed: 18
Percentage of 2008 graduates working in: New England:
    1%, Middle Atlantic: 75%, East North Central: 2%, West
    North Central: 0%, South Atlantic: 11%, East South
    Central: 1%, West South Central: 0%, Mountain: 2%,
    Pacific: 1%, Unknown: 7%

BAR PASSAGE RATES
Based on 2008 graduates taking Summer 2008 or
Winter 2009 exams. Most of the school's first-time test
takers took the bar in Pennsylvania.

96%
School's bar passage rate for first-time test takers

87%
Statewide bar passage rate for first-time test takers

Elon University

- 201 N. Greene Street, Greensboro, NC, 27401
- http://law.elon.edu
- Private
- Year founded: 2006
- 2009-2010 tuition: full-time: $30,750; part-time: N/A
- Enrollment 2009-10 academic year: full-time: 315
- U.S. News 2010 law specialty ranking: N/A

2.99-3.49 GPA, 25TH-75TH PERCENTILE

152-156 LSAT, 25TH-75TH PERCENTILE

42% ACCEPTANCE RATE

Unranked 2011 U.S. NEWS LAW SCHOOL RANKING

ADMISSIONS

Admissions phone number: **(336) 279-9200**
Admissions email address: **law@elon.edu**
Application website: **http://www.elon.edu/e-web/law/admissions/howtoapply.xhtml**
Application deadline for Fall 2011 admission: **31-Jul**

Admissions statistics:
Number of applicants for Fall 2009: **761**
Number of acceptances: **316**
Number enrolled: **121**
Acceptance rate: **42%**
GPA, 25th-75th percentile, entering class Fall 2009: **2.99-3.49**
LSAT, 25th-75th percentile, entering class Fall 2009: **152-156**

FINANCIAL AID

Financial aid phone number: **(336) 278-2000**
Financial aid application deadline:
Tuition 2009-2010 academic year: **full-time: $30,750; part-time: N/A**
Room and board: **$12,000** ; books: **$1,600** ; miscellaneous expenses: **$8,400**
Total of room/board/books/miscellaneous expenses: **$22,000**
University does not offer graduate student housing for which law students are eligible.

Financial aid profile
Percent of students that received grants for the 2008-2009 academic year: full-time: **69%**
Median grant amount: full-time: **$6,000**
The average law-school debt of those in the Class of 2009 who borrowed: **$108,663** . Proportion who borrowed: **92%**

ACADEMIC PROGRAMS
Calendar: **semester**
Joint degrees awarded: **N/A**
Typical first-year section size: Full-time: **30**

Is there typically a "small section" of the first year class, other than Legal Writing, taught by full-time faculty?:
Full-time: **yes**
Number of course titles, beyond the first year curriculum, offered last year: **54**
Percentages of upper division course sections, excluding seminars, with an enrollment of:
Under 25: **29%**   25 to 49: **20%**
50 to 74: **34%**   75 to 99: **9%**
100+: **9%**
Areas of specialization: appellate advocacy, clinical training, dispute resolution, environmental law, health care law, intellectual property law, international law, tax law, trial advocacy

Fall 2009 faculty profile
Total teaching faculty: **28**. Full-time: **50%**; **64%** men, **36%** women, **14%** minorities. Part-time: **50%**; **64%** men, **36%** women, **0%** minorities
Student-to-faculty ratio: **17.3**

SPECIAL PROGRAMS *(as provided by law school):*
Elon's leadership emphasis incorporates the best of leadership education through courses, community activities and capstone experiences. Students participate in a Legal Aid Housing and Domestic Relations Clinic and a Juvenile Justice Mediation and Intervention Clinic. The Center for Engaged Learning in the Law provides dialogue between Elon and other law schools about improving legal education.

STUDENT BODY
Fall 2009 full-time enrollment: 315
Men: **55%**   Women: **45%**
African-American: **5.70%**   American Indian: **0.30%**
Asian-American: **3.20%**   Mexican-American: **0.00%**
Puerto Rican: **0.00%**   Other Hisp-Amer: **1.90%**
White: **84.80%**   International: **0.00%**
Unknown: **4.10%**

Attrition rates for 2008-2009 full-time students
Percent of students discontinuing law school:

Men: **2%**   Women: **4%**
First-year students: **7%**   Second-year students: **1%**
Third-year students: **N/A**   Fourth-year students: **N/A**

LIBRARY RESOURCES

Total titles: **120,985**
Total volumes: **172,815**
Total seats available for library users: **333**

INFORMATION TECHNOLOGY

Number of wired network connections available to students: **102** total (in the law library, excluding computer labs: **79**; in classrooms: **13**; in computer labs: **2**; elsewhere in the law school: **8**)
Law school has a wireless network.
Students are not required to own a computer.

EMPLOYMENT AND SALARIES

Proportion of 2008 graduates employed at graduation: **N/A**
Employed 9 months later, as of February 15, 2009: **N/A**
Salaries in the private sector (law firms, business, industry): **N/A–N/A** (25th-75th percentile)
Median salary in the private sector: **N/A**
Percentage in the private sector who reported salary information: **N/A**
Median salary in public service (government, judicial clerkships, academic posts, non-profits): **N/A**

Percentage of 2008 graduates in:
Law firms: **N/A**   Government: **N/A**
Bus./industry: **N/A**   Judicial clerkship: **N/A**
Public interest: **N/A**   Unknown: **N/A**
Academia : **N/A**

2008 graduates employed in-state: **N/A**
2008 graduates employed in foreign countries: **N/A**
Number of states where graduates are employed: **N/A**
Percentage of 2008 graduates working in: New England: **N/A**, Middle Atlantic: **N/A**, East North Central: **N/A**, West North Central: **N/A**, South Atlantic: **N/A**, East South Central: **N/A**, West South Central: **N/A**, Mountain: **N/A**, Pacific: **N/A**, Unknown: **N/A**

BAR PASSAGE RATES

Based on 2008 graduates taking Summer 2008 or Winter 2009 exams.

N/A
School's bar passage rate for first-time test takers

N/A
Statewide bar passage rate for first-time test takers

Emory University

- 1301 Clifton Road, Atlanta, GA, 30322-2770
- http://www.law.emory.edu
- Private
- Year founded: 1916
- 2009-2010 tuition: full-time: $41,376; part-time: N/A
- Enrollment 2009-10 academic year: full-time: 715
- U.S. News 2010 law specialty ranking: N/A

3.37-3.68 GPA, 25TH-75TH PERCENTILE

165-167 LSAT, 25TH-75TH PERCENTILE

25% ACCEPTANCE RATE

22 2011 U.S. NEWS LAW SCHOOL RANKING

ADMISSIONS
Admissions phone number: **(404) 727-6802**
Admissions email address: **lawinfo@law.emory.edu**
Application website:
  http://www.law.emory.edu/admissions/application.html
Application deadline for Fall 2011 admission: **1-Mar**

Admissions statistics:
Number of applicants for Fall 2009: **4,558**
Number of acceptances: **1,149**
Number enrolled: **248**
Acceptance rate: **25%**
GPA, 25th-75th percentile, entering class Fall 2009: **3.37-3.68**
LSAT, 25th-75th percentile, entering class Fall 2009: **165-167**

FINANCIAL AID
Financial aid phone number: **(404) 727-6039**
Financial aid application deadline: **1-Mar**
Tuition 2009-2010 academic year: **full-time: $41,376; part-time: N/A**
Room and board: **$17,748** ; books: **$3,126** ; miscellaneous expenses: **$3,588**
Total of room/board/books/miscellaneous expenses: **$24,462**
University offers graduate student housing for which law students are eligible.

Financial aid profile
Percent of students that received grants for the 2008-2009 academic year: full-time: **68%**
Median grant amount: full-time: **$18,000**
The average law-school debt of those in the Class of 2009 who borrowed: **$112,383** . Proportion who borrowed: **77%**

ACADEMIC PROGRAMS
Calendar: **semester**
Joint degrees awarded: **J.D./M.B.A.; J.D./M.Div.; J.D./M.T.S.; J.D./M.P.H.; J.D./R.E.E.S.; J.D./Ph.D.; J.D./M.A.**

Typical first-year section size: Full-time: **75**
Is there typically a "small section" of the first year class, other than Legal Writing, taught by full-time faculty?:
  Full-time: **yes**
Number of course titles, beyond the first year curriculum, offered last year: **165**
Percentages of upper division course sections, excluding seminars, with an enrollment of:

Under 25: **66%**	25 to 49: **19%**
50 to 74: **6%**	75 to 99: **8%**
100+: **1%**	

Areas of specialization: appellate advocacy, clinical training, dispute resolution, environmental law, health care law, intellectual property law, international law, tax law, trial advocacy

Fall 2009 faculty profile
Total teaching faculty: **99**. Full-time: **58%**; **56%** men, **44%** women, **12%** minorities. Part-time: **42%**; **74%** men, **26%** women, **19%** minorities
Student-to-faculty ratio: **10.5**

SPECIAL PROGRAMS *(as provided by law school):*
Interdisciplinary programs of study; Centers of Excellence in Law and Religion; International Law; Feminist Jurisprudence; Health Law; Federalism; Trial Techniques program; Extensive Field Placement program; Clinics-Barton Child Law and Policy; Juvenile Defender; Indigent Criminal Defense; Turner Environmental Law Clinic; TI:GER program of technology and business law co-sponsored with GA Tech.

STUDENT BODY
Fall 2009 full-time enrollment: **715**

Men: **52%**	Women: **48%**
African-American: **9.10%**	American Indian: **1.10%**
Asian-American: **10.10%**	Mexican-American: **0.00%**
Puerto Rican: **0.00%**	Other Hisp-Amer: **10.30%**
White: **56.20%**	International: **4.20%**
Unknown: **9.00%**	

Attrition rates for 2008-2009 full-time students
Percent of students discontinuing law school:

Men: 2%	Women: 2%
First-year students: 2%	Second-year students: 4%
Third-year students: N/A	Fourth-year students: N/A

LIBRARY RESOURCES

Total titles: 203,954
Total volumes: 415,878
Total seats available for library users: 516

INFORMATION TECHNOLOGY

Number of wired network connections available to students: **64** total (in the law library, excluding computer labs: **37**; in classrooms: **20**; in computer labs: **0**; elsewhere in the law school: **7**)
Law school has a wireless network.
Students are not required to own a computer.

EMPLOYMENT AND SALARIES

Proportion of 2008 graduates employed at graduation: **97%**
Employed 9 months later, as of February 15, 2009: **95%**
Salaries in the private sector (law firms, business, industry): **$85,000 –$160,000** (25th-75th percentile)
Median salary in the private sector: **$145,000**
Percentage in the private sector who reported salary information: **83%**

Median salary in public service (government, judicial clerkships, academic posts, non-profits): **$52,000**

Percentage of 2008 graduates in:

Law firms: 70%	Government: 4%
Bus./industry: 10%	Judicial clerkship: 9%
Public interest: 2%	Unknown: 4%
Academia : 0%	

2008 graduates employed in-state: **42%**
2008 graduates employed in foreign countries: **1%**
Number of states where graduates are employed: **29**
Percentage of 2008 graduates working in: New England: **3%**, Middle Atlantic: **22%**, East North Central: **4%**, West North Central: **0%**, South Atlantic: **57%**, East South Central: **4%**, West South Central: **3%**, Mountain: **0%**, Pacific: **5%**, Unknown: **1%**

BAR PASSAGE RATES

Based on 2008 graduates taking Summer 2008 or Winter 2009 exams. Most of the school's first-time test takers took the bar in Georgia.

94%
School's bar passage rate for first-time test takers

89%
Statewide bar passage rate for first-time test takers

Faulkner University (Jones)

■ 5345 Atlanta Highway, Montgomery, AL, 36109
■ http://www.faulkner.edu/admissions/jonesLaw.asp
■ Private
■ Year founded: 1928
■ 2009-2010 tuition: full-time: $30,500; part-time: N/A
■ Enrollment 2009-10 academic year: full-time: 323; part-time: 18
■ U.S. News 2010 law specialty ranking: N/A

2.76-3.33 GPA, 25TH-75TH PERCENTILE

147-152 LSAT, 25TH-75TH PERCENTILE

54% ACCEPTANCE RATE

Tier 4 2011 U.S. NEWS LAW SCHOOL RANKING

ADMISSIONS

Admissions phone number: **(334) 386-7210**
Admissions email address: **law@faulkner.edu**
Application website: **N/A**
Application deadline for Fall 2011 admission: **15-Jun**

Admissions statistics:
Number of applicants for Fall 2009: **747**
Number of acceptances: **405**
Number enrolled: **150**
Acceptance rate: **54%**
GPA, 25th-75th percentile, entering class Fall 2009: **2.76-3.33**
LSAT, 25th-75th percentile, entering class Fall 2009: **147-152**

FINANCIAL AID

Financial aid phone number: **(334) 386-7197**
Financial aid application deadline:
Tuition 2009-2010 academic year: **full-time: $30,500; part-time: N/A**
Room and board: **$14,000** ; books: **$3,000** ; miscellaneous expenses: **$5,400**
Total of room/board/books/miscellaneous expenses: **$22,400**
University does not offer graduate student housing for which law students are eligible.

Financial aid profile
Percent of students that received grants for the 2008-2009 academic year: full-time: **25%**
Median grant amount: full-time: **$14,000**
The average law-school debt of those in the Class of 2009 who borrowed: **$74,674** . Proportion who borrowed: **86%**

ACADEMIC PROGRAMS

Calendar: **semester**
Joint degrees awarded: **N/A**
Typical first-year section size: Full-time: **60**
Is there typically a "small section" of the first year class, other than Legal Writing, taught by full-time faculty?:

Full-time: **no**; Part-time: **no**
Number of course titles, beyond the first year curriculum, offered last year: **43**
Percentages of upper division course sections, excluding seminars, with an enrollment of:
Under 25: **63%**   25 to 49: **24%**
50 to 74: **13%**   75 to 99: **N/A**
100+: **N/A**
Areas of specialization: appellate advocacy, clinical training, dispute resolution, environmental law, health care law, intellectual property law, international law, tax law, trial advocacy

Fall 2009 faculty profile
Total teaching faculty: **24**. Full-time: **83%**; **75%** men, **25%** women, **15%** minorities. Part-time: **17%**; **50%** men, **50%** women, **25%** minorities
Student-to-faculty ratio: **14**

SPECIAL PROGRAMS *(as provided by law school)*:
Clinics: Elder Law Clinic, Family Violence Clinic and Mediation Clinic; Programs: Academic Success Program, Advocacy Programs, Alternative Dispute Resolution Program, Externship Program and Public Interest Program

STUDENT BODY
Fall 2009 full-time enrollment: **323**

Men: **62%**	Women: **38%**
African-American: **7.40%**	American Indian: **1.50%**
Asian-American: **1.20%**	Mexican-American: **0.00%**
Puerto Rican: **0.00%**	Other Hisp-Amer: **1.50%**
White: **87.30%**	International: **0.00%**
Unknown: **0.90%**	

Fall 2009 part-time enrollment: **18**

Men: **61%**	Women: **39%**
African-American: **0.00%**	American Indian: **0.00%**
Asian-American: **5.60%**	Mexican-American: **0.00%**
Puerto Rican: **0.00%**	Other Hisp-Amer: **0.00%**
White: **94.40%**	International: **0.00%**
Unknown: **0.00%**	

Attrition rates for 2008-2009 full-time students
Percent of students discontinuing law school:

Men: **16%** Women: **9%**

First-year students: **30%** Second-year students: **2%**

Third-year students: **N/A** Fourth-year students: **N/A**

LIBRARY RESOURCES

Total titles: **N/A**

Total volumes: **N/A**

Total seats available for library users: **218**

INFORMATION TECHNOLOGY

Number of wired network connections available to students: **205** total (in the law library, excluding computer labs: **151**; in classrooms: **54**; in computer labs: **0**; elsewhere in the law school: **0**)

Law school has a wireless network.

Students are not required to own a computer.

EMPLOYMENT AND SALARIES

Proportion of 2008 graduates employed at graduation: **N/A**

Employed 9 months later, as of February 15, 2009: **95%**

Salaries in the private sector (law firms, business, industry): **N/A–N/A** (25th-75th percentile)

Median salary in the private sector: **N/A**

Percentage in the private sector who reported salary information: **N/A**

Median salary in public service (government, judicial clerkships, academic posts, non-profits): **N/A**

Percentage of 2008 graduates in:

Law firms: **69%** Government: **11%**

Bus./industry: **7%** Judicial clerkship: **7%**

Public interest: **4%** Unknown: **0%**

Academia : **2%**

2008 graduates employed in-state: **91%**

2008 graduates employed in foreign countries: **N/A**

Number of states where graduates are employed: **2**

Percentage of 2008 graduates working in: New England: **N/A**, Middle Atlantic: **N/A**, East North Central: **N/A**, West North Central: **N/A**, South Atlantic: **N/A**, East South Central: **N/A**, West South Central: **N/A**, Mountain: **N/A**, Pacific: **N/A**, Unknown: **N/A**

BAR PASSAGE RATES

Based on 2008 graduates taking Summer 2008 or Winter 2009 exams. Most of the school's first-time test takers took the bar in Alabama.

93%

School's bar passage rate for first-time test takers

79%

Statewide bar passage rate for first-time test takers

Florida A&M University

- 201 Beggs Avenue, Orlando, FL, 32801
- http://www.famu.edu/index.cfm?a=law
- Public
- **Year founded:** 2002
- **2009-2010 tuition:** full-time: $9,036; part-time: $6,627
- **Enrollment 2009-10 academic year:** full-time: 385; part-time: 228
- **U.S. News 2010 law specialty ranking:** N/A

2.78-3.36 GPA, 25TH-75TH PERCENTILE

144-149 LSAT, 25TH-75TH PERCENTILE

30% ACCEPTANCE RATE

Tier 4 2011 U.S. NEWS LAW SCHOOL RANKING

ADMISSIONS
Admissions phone number: **(407) 254-3263**
Admissions email address: **famu-law.admissions@famu.edu**
Application website: **N/A**
Application deadline for Fall 2011 admission: **15-May**

Admissions statistics:
Number of applicants for Fall 2009: **1,519**
Number of acceptances: **452**
Number enrolled: **165**
Acceptance rate: **30%**
GPA, 25th-75th percentile, entering class Fall 2009: **2.78-3.36**
LSAT, 25th-75th percentile, entering class Fall 2009: **144-149**

Part-time program:
Number of applicants for Fall 2009: **288**
Number of acceptances: **107**
Number enrolled: **69**
Acceptance rate: **37%**
GPA, 25th-75th percentile, entering class Fall 2009: **2.67-3.25**
LSAT, 25th-75th percentile, entering class Fall 2009: **145-150**

FINANCIAL AID
Financial aid phone number: **(850) 599-3730**
Financial aid application deadline:
Tuition 2009-2010 academic year: **full-time: $9,036; part-time: $6,627**
Room and board: **$10,450** ; books: **$1,000** ; miscellaneous expenses: **$6,000**
Total of room/board/books/miscellaneous expenses: **$17,450**
University does not offer graduate student housing for which law students are eligible.

Financial aid profile
Percent of students that received grants for the 2008-2009

academic year: full-time: **10%**; part-time **13%**
Median grant amount: full-time: **$5,000** ; part-time: **$2,000**
The average law-school debt of those in the Class of 2009 who borrowed: **$81,601** . Proportion who borrowed: **87%**

ACADEMIC PROGRAMS
Calendar: **semester**
Joint degrees awarded: **N/A**
Typical first-year section size: Full-time: **60**; Part-time: **60**
Is there typically a "small section" of the first year class, other than Legal Writing, taught by full-time faculty?: Full-time: **no**; Part-time: **no**
Number of course titles, beyond the first year curriculum, offered last year: **134**
Percentages of upper division course sections, excluding seminars, with an enrollment of:

Under 25: **56%**	25 to 49: **24%**
50 to 74: **19%**	75 to 99: **0%**
100+: **0%**	

Areas of specialization: clinical training, dispute resolution, environmental law, health care law, intellectual property law, international law, tax law, trial advocacy

Fall 2009 faculty profile
Total teaching faculty: **42**. Full-time: **83%**; **43%** men, **57%** women, **71%** minorities. Part-time: **17%**; **86%** men, **14%** women, **57%** minorities
Student-to-faculty ratio: **18.5**

SPECIAL PROGRAMS *(as provided by law school):*
The College of Law's practical skills training program has been recognized by National Jurist and Pre-Law Magazines. The College of Law offers four (4) in-house clinics, four (4) external clinics and judicial externships. Students are required to take a clinic or complete 20 hours of pro bono service. Students may participate in International Study Programs.

STUDENT BODY
Fall 2009 full-time enrollment: 385
Men: **44%**   Women: **56%**

African-American: 45.20%   American Indian: 0.50%
Asian-American: 4.20%   Mexican-American: 0.80%
Puerto Rican: 0.80%   Other Hisp-Amer: 12.70%
White: 33.20%   International: 0.00%
Unknown: 2.60%

Fall 2009 part-time enrollment: 228
Men: 47%   Women: 53%
African-American: 32.90%   American Indian: 1.30%
Asian-American: 2.60%   Mexican-American: 0.00%
Puerto Rican: 2.20%   Other Hisp-Amer: 18.00%
White: 41.70%   International: 0.00%
Unknown: 1.30%

Attrition rates for 2008-2009 full-time students
Percent of students discontinuing law school:
Men: 21%   Women: 14%
First-year students: 38%   Second-year students: 7%
Third-year students: 1%   Fourth-year students: N/A

LIBRARY RESOURCES
Total titles: 156,274
Total volumes: 367,704
Total seats available for library users: 416

INFORMATION TECHNOLOGY
Number of wired network connections available to students: 37 total (in the law library, excluding computer labs: 7; in classrooms: 7; in computer labs: 18; elsewhere in the law school: 5)
Law school has a wireless network.
Students are not required to own a computer.

EMPLOYMENT AND SALARIES
Proportion of 2008 graduates employed at graduation: N/A

Employed 9 months later, as of February 15, 2009: 87%
Salaries in the private sector (law firms, business, industry): N/A–N/A (25th-75th percentile)
Median salary in the private sector: N/A
Percentage in the private sector who reported salary information: N/A
Median salary in public service (government, judicial clerkships, academic posts, non-profits): N/A

Percentage of 2008 graduates in:
Law firms: 56%   Government: 15%
Bus./industry: 8%   Judicial clerkship: 1%
Public interest: 8%   Unknown: 7%
Academia : 5%

2008 graduates employed in-state: 90%
2008 graduates employed in foreign countries: 0%
Number of states where graduates are employed: 6
Percentage of 2008 graduates working in: New England: 0%, Middle Atlantic: 1%, East North Central: 0%, West North Central: 0%, South Atlantic: 97%, East South Central: 0%, West South Central: 0%, Mountain: 1%, Pacific: 0%, Unknown: 0%

BAR PASSAGE RATES
Based on 2008 graduates taking Summer 2008 or Winter 2009 exams. Most of the school's first-time test takers took the bar in Florida.

66%
School's bar passage rate for first-time test takers

81%
Statewide bar passage rate for first-time test takers

Florida Coastal School of Law

- 8787 Baypine Road, Jacksonville, FL, 32256
- http://www.fcsl.edu
- Private
- Year founded: 1996
- 2009-2010 tuition: full-time: $32,662; part-time: $26,442
- Enrollment 2009-10 academic year: full-time: 1,539; part-time: 66
- U.S. News 2010 law specialty ranking: N/A

2.95-3.42 GPA, 25TH-75TH PERCENTILE

147-153 LSAT, 25TH-75TH PERCENTILE

66% ACCEPTANCE RATE

Tier 4 2011 U.S. NEWS LAW SCHOOL RANKING

ADMISSIONS

Admissions phone number: **(904) 680-7710**
Admissions email address: **admissions@fcsl.edu**
Application website: **N/A**
Application deadline for Fall 2011 admission: **rolling**

Admissions statistics:
Number of applicants for Fall 2009: **6,274**
Number of acceptances: **4,118**
Number enrolled: **702**
Acceptance rate: **66%**
GPA, 25th-75th percentile, entering class Fall 2009: **2.95-3.42**
LSAT, 25th-75th percentile, entering class Fall 2009: **147-153**

Part-time program:
Number of applicants for Fall 2009: **57**
Number of acceptances: **33**
Number enrolled: **20**
Acceptance rate: **58%**
GPA, 25th-75th percentile, entering class Fall 2009: **2.57-3.38**
LSAT, 25th-75th percentile, entering class Fall 2009: **147-153**

FINANCIAL AID

Financial aid phone number: **(904) 680-7717**
Financial aid application deadline:
Tuition 2009-2010 academic year: **full-time: $32,662; part-time: $26,442**
Room and board: **$9,819** ; books: **$1,300** ; miscellaneous expenses: **$8,460**
Total of room/board/books/miscellaneous expenses: **$19,579**
University does not offer graduate student housing for which law students are eligible.

Financial aid profile
Percent of students that received grants for the 2008-2009 academic year: full-time: **38%**

Median grant amount: full-time: **$7,000** ; part-time: **$4,000**
The average law-school debt of those in the Class of 2009 who borrowed: **$109,528** . Proportion who borrowed: **90%**

ACADEMIC PROGRAMS

Calendar: **semester**
Joint degrees awarded: **N/A**
Typical first-year section size: Full-time: **82**
Is there typically a "small section" of the first year class, other than Legal Writing, taught by full-time faculty?: Full-time: **no**; Part-time: **no**
Number of course titles, beyond the first year curriculum, offered last year: **129**
Percentages of upper division course sections, excluding seminars, with an enrollment of:

Under 25: **48%**	25 to 49: **31%**
50 to 74: **20%**	75 to 99: **0%**
100+: **0%**	

Areas of specialization: appellate advocacy, clinical training, dispute resolution, environmental law, health care law, intellectual property law, international law, tax law, trial advocacy

Fall 2009 faculty profile
Total teaching faculty: **119**. Full-time: **51%**; **44%** men, **56%** women, **11%** minorities. Part-time: **49%**; **69%** men, **31%** women, **7%** minorities
Student-to-faculty ratio: **20.9**

SPECIAL PROGRAMS *(as provided by law school):*
FCSL has five clinical programs, as well as externships for over 100 students per semester. In addition, it has certificate programs in sports law, international law, family law, environmental law, and legal writing.

STUDENT BODY
Fall 2009 full-time enrollment: **1,539**

Men: **52%**	Women: **48%**
African-American: **9.70%**	American Indian: **1.20%**

Asian-American: **6.20%** Mexican-American: **1.00%**
Puerto Rican: **0.90%** Other Hisp-Amer: **8.00%**
White: **62.60%** International: **0.00%**
Unknown: **10.40%**

Fall 2009 part-time enrollment: **66**
Men: **56%** Women: **44%**
African-American: **10.60%** American Indian: **1.50%**
Asian-American: **1.50%** Mexican-American: **0.00%**
Puerto Rican: **3.00%** Other Hisp-Amer: **10.60%**
White: **57.60%** International: **0.00%**
Unknown: **15.20%**

Attrition rates for 2008-2009 full-time students
Percent of students discontinuing law school:
Men: **11%** Women: **13%**
First-year students: **20%** Second-year students: **13%**
Third-year students: **0%** Fourth-year students: **N/A**

LIBRARY RESOURCES
Total titles: **129,160**
Total volumes: **224,583**
Total seats available for library users: **516**

INFORMATION TECHNOLOGY
Number of wired network connections available to students: **3780** total (in the law library, excluding computer
labs: **500**; in classrooms: **2,180**; in computer labs: **60**;
elsewhere in the law school: **1,040**)
Law school has a wireless network.
Students are not required to own a computer.

EMPLOYMENT AND SALARIES
Proportion of 2008 graduates employed at graduation:
N/A

Employed 9 months later, as of February 15, 2009: **95%**
Salaries in the private sector (law firms, business, indus-
try): **$47,250 –$70,000** (25th-75th percentile)
Median salary in the private sector: **$53,750**
Percentage in the private sector who reported salary
information: **28%**
Median salary in public service (government, judicial clerk-
ships, academic posts, non-profits): **$40,062**

Percentage of 2008 graduates in:
Law firms: **48%** Government: **15%**
Bus./industry: **14%** Judicial clerkship: **3%**
Public interest: **18%** Unknown: **0%**
Academia : **2%**

2008 graduates employed in-state: **74%**
2008 graduates employed in foreign countries: **0%**
Number of states where graduates are employed: **33**
Percentage of 2008 graduates working in: New England:
2%, Middle Atlantic: **4%**, East North Central: **4%**, West
North Central: **N/A**, South Atlantic: **85%**, East South
Central: **1%**, West South Central: **1%**, Mountain: **2%**,
Pacific: **1%**, Unknown: **0%**

BAR PASSAGE RATES
Based on 2008 graduates taking Summer 2008 or
Winter 2009 exams. Most of the school's first-time test
takers took the bar in Florida.

| 83% |
School's bar passage rate for first-time test takers

| 81% |
Statewide bar passage rate for first-time test takers

Florida International University

- Modesto A. Maidique Campus, RDB 2015, Miami, FL, 33199
- http://www.fiu.edu/law
- Public
- Year founded: 2002
- 2009-2010 tuition: full-time: $12,450; part-time: $9,337
- Enrollment 2009-10 academic year: full-time: 294; part-time: 329
- U.S. News 2010 law specialty ranking: N/A

3.18-3.67	GPA, 25TH-75TH PERCENTILE
152-156	LSAT, 25TH-75TH PERCENTILE
26%	ACCEPTANCE RATE
Tier 4	2011 U.S. NEWS LAW SCHOOL RANKING

ADMISSIONS

Admissions phone number: (305) 348-8006
Admissions email address: lawadmit@fiu.edu
Application website:
   http://law.lawnet.fiu.edu/images/docs/application_2010.
   pdf
Application deadline for Fall 2011 admission: 1-May

Admissions statistics:
Number of applicants for Fall 2009: 1,957
Number of acceptances: 515
Number enrolled: 168
Acceptance rate: 26%
GPA, 25th-75th percentile, entering class Fall 2009: 3.18-3.67
LSAT, 25th-75th percentile, entering class Fall 2009: 152-156

Part-time program:
Number of applicants for Fall 2009: 486
Number of acceptances: 117
Number enrolled: 82
Acceptance rate: 24%
GPA, 25th-75th percentile, entering class Fall 2009: 2.90-3.48
LSAT, 25th-75th percentile, entering class Fall 2009: 150-155

FINANCIAL AID

Financial aid phone number: (305) 348-8006
Financial aid application deadline: 1-Mar
Tuition 2009-2010 academic year: **full-time: $12,450; part-time: $9,337**
Room and board: $16,532 ; books: $2,652 ; miscellaneous expenses: $4,832
Total of room/board/books/miscellaneous expenses: $24,016
University offers graduate student housing for which law students are eligible.

Financial aid profile
Percent of students that received grants for the 2008-2009 academic year: full-time: 43%; part-time 6%
Median grant amount: full-time: $5,000 ; part-time: $5,000
The average law-school debt of those in the Class of 2009 who borrowed: $58,119 . Proportion who borrowed: 83%

ACADEMIC PROGRAMS

Calendar: **semester**
Joint degrees awarded: **J.D./M.B.A.; J.D./M.S.W.; J.D./M.A. Latin Amer.Caribbean Studies; J.D./M.A. International Business; J.D./M.P.A.; J.D./M.S. Psychology; J.D./M.S. Criminal Justice; J.D./M.S. Environmental Studies**
Typical first-year section size: Full-time: **80**; Part-time: **77**
Is there typically a "small section" of the first year class, other than Legal Writing, taught by full-time faculty?: Full-time: **no**; Part-time: **no**
Number of course titles, beyond the first year curriculum, offered last year: **66**
Percentages of upper division course sections, excluding seminars, with an enrollment of:

Under 25: **67%**	25 to 49: **24%**
50 to 74: **9%**	75 to 99: **1%**
100+: **0%**	

Areas of specialization: appellate advocacy, clinical training, dispute resolution, environmental law, health care law, intellectual property law, international law, tax law, trial advocacy

Fall 2009 faculty profile
Total teaching faculty: 48. Full-time: 56%; 48% men, 52% women, 48% minorities. Part-time: 44%; 52% men, 48% women, 43% minorities
Student-to-faculty ratio: 16.2

SPECIAL PROGRAMS (as provided by law school):
We offer extensive programming in international and comparative law, community service, and a clinical program that specializes in Human Rights, Immigrant Children Justice, Community Development, Judicial Externship, Juvenile Justice,

Education Law, and Criminal Law. We have a summer study program in Seville, Spain and also offer externships to increase student contact with the bar.

STUDENT BODY

Fall 2009 full-time enrollment: 294

Men: 53%	Women: 47%
African-American: 6.10%	American Indian: 0.70%
Asian-American: 2.40%	Mexican-American: 0.00%
Puerto Rican: 0.00%	Other Hisp-Amer: 40.50%
White: 47.30%	International: 0.70%
Unknown: 2.40%	

Fall 2009 part-time enrollment: 329

Men: 51%	Women: 49%
African-American: 11.60%	American Indian: 0.90%
Asian-American: 1.80%	Mexican-American: 0.00%
Puerto Rican: 0.00%	Other Hisp-Amer: 46.80%
White: 35.60%	International: 0.30%
Unknown: 3.00%	

Attrition rates for 2008-2009 full-time students
Percent of students discontinuing law school:

Men: 5%	Women: 5%
First-year students: 12%	Second-year students: 1%
Third-year students: 1%	Fourth-year students: N/A

LIBRARY RESOURCES

Total titles: 103,002
Total volumes: 214,879
Total seats available for library users: 322

INFORMATION TECHNOLOGY

Number of wired network connections available to students: 35 total (in the law library, excluding computer labs: 9; in classrooms: 16; in computer labs: 10; elsewhere in the law school: 0)
Law school has a wireless network.
Students are not required to own a computer.

EMPLOYMENT AND SALARIES

Proportion of 2008 graduates employed at graduation: N/A
Employed 9 months later, as of February 15, 2009: 89%
Salaries in the private sector (law firms, business, industry): $50,000 –$75,000 (25th-75th percentile)
Median salary in the private sector: $54,000
Percentage in the private sector who reported salary information: N/A
Median salary in public service (government, judicial clerkships, academic posts, non-profits): $42,000

Percentage of 2008 graduates in:

Law firms: 60%	Government: 15%
Bus./industry: 18%	Judicial clerkship: 1%
Public interest: 0%	Unknown: 5%
Academia : 1%	

2008 graduates employed in-state: 98%
2008 graduates employed in foreign countries: 0%
Number of states where graduates are employed: 3
Percentage of 2008 graduates working in: New England: N/A, Middle Atlantic: N/A, East North Central: N/A, West North Central: 1%, South Atlantic: 99%, East South Central: N/A, West South Central: N/A, Mountain: N/A, Pacific: N/A, Unknown: 0%

BAR PASSAGE RATES

Based on 2008 graduates taking Summer 2008 or Winter 2009 exams. Most of the school's first-time test takers took the bar in Florida.

88%

School's bar passage rate for first-time test takers

81%

Statewide bar passage rate for first-time test takers

Florida State University

- 425 W. Jefferson Street, Tallahassee, FL, 32306-1601
- http://www.law.fsu.edu
- Public
- Year founded: 1966
- 2009-2010 tuition: full-time: $14,239; part-time: N/A
- Enrollment 2009-10 academic year: full-time: 763
- U.S. News 2010 law specialty ranking: environmental law: 5

3.23-3.74 GPA, 25TH-75TH PERCENTILE

159-162 LSAT, 25TH-75TH PERCENTILE

26% ACCEPTANCE RATE

54 2011 U.S. NEWS LAW SCHOOL RANKING

ADMISSIONS
Admissions phone number: **(850) 644-3787**
Admissions email address: **admissions@law.fsu.edu**
Application website:
   http://www.law.fsu.edu/prospective_students/index.htm
   l
Application deadline for Fall 2011 admission: **1-Apr**

Admissions statistics:
Number of applicants for Fall 2009: **3,316**
Number of acceptances: **860**
Number enrolled: **244**
Acceptance rate: **26%**
GPA, 25th-75th percentile, entering class Fall 2009: **3.23-3.74**
LSAT, 25th-75th percentile, entering class Fall 2009: **159-162**

FINANCIAL AID
Financial aid phone number: **(850) 644-5716**
Financial aid application deadline: **1-Feb**
Tuition 2009-2010 academic year: **full-time: $14,239; part-time: N/A**
Room and board: **$10,000** ; books: **$1,300** ; miscellaneous expenses: **$7,000**
Total of room/board/books/miscellaneous expenses: **$18,300**
University offers graduate student housing for which law students are eligible.

Financial aid profile
Percent of students that received grants for the 2008-2009 academic year: full-time: **36%**
Median grant amount: full-time: **$2,000**
The average law-school debt of those in the Class of 2009 who borrowed: **$52,969** . Proportion who borrowed: **83%**

ACADEMIC PROGRAMS
Calendar: **semester**
Joint degrees awarded: **J.D./M.B.A.; J.D./M.S. International Affairs; J.D./M.P.A.; J.D./M.S. Economics; J.D./M.URP.;**
J.D./M.S.W.; J.D./M.S. Library & Information Science; J.D./M.S. Family and Child Sciences
Typical first-year section size: Full-time: **83**
Is there typically a "small section" of the first year class, other than Legal Writing, taught by full-time faculty?: Full-time: **no**
Number of course titles, beyond the first year curriculum, offered last year: **119**
Percentages of upper division course sections, excluding seminars, with an enrollment of:
   Under 25: **61%**   25 to 49: **26%**
   50 to 74: **7%**   75 to 99: **5%**
   100+: **1%**
Areas of specialization: appellate advocacy, clinical training, dispute resolution, environmental law, health care law, intellectual property law, international law, tax law, trial advocacy

Fall 2009 faculty profile
Total teaching faculty: **71**. Full-time: **61%**; **56%** men, **44%** women, **14%** minorities. Part-time: **39%**; **79%** men, **21%** women, **7%** minorities
Student-to-faculty ratio: **14.2**

SPECIAL PROGRAMS *(as provided by law school):*
Florida State Law has strong programs in environmental law, international law, business, criminal law and tax. Students may earn certificates in two of these: environmental law and international law. Additionally, the law school offers joint-degree programs, an extensive clinical externship program with domestic and foreign placements, an in-house legal clinic, and an Oxford Summer Program.

STUDENT BODY
Fall 2009 full-time enrollment: 763
Men: **59%**	Women: **41%**
African-American: **8.40%**	American Indian: **0.40%**
Asian-American: **1.80%**	Mexican-American: **0.40%**
Puerto Rican: **0.30%**	Other Hisp-Amer: **5.90%**
White: **80.70%**	International: **0.10%**
Unknown: **2.00%**	

Attrition rates for 2008-2009 full-time students
Percent of students discontinuing law school:

Men: **3%**   Women: **4%**
First-year students: **9%**   Second-year students: **N/A**
Third-year students: **1%**   Fourth-year students: **N/A**

LIBRARY RESOURCES
Total titles: **226,886**
Total volumes: **525,173**
Total seats available for library users: **420**

INFORMATION TECHNOLOGY
Number of wired network connections available to students: **0** total (in the law library, excluding computer labs: **0**; in classrooms: **0**; in computer labs: **0**; elsewhere in the law school: **0**)
Law school has a wireless network.
Students are required to own a computer.

EMPLOYMENT AND SALARIES
Proportion of 2008 graduates employed at graduation: **76%**
Employed 9 months later, as of February 15, 2009: **98%**
Salaries in the private sector (law firms, business, industry): **$58,000 –$105,000** (25th-75th percentile)
Median salary in the private sector: **$70,000**
Percentage in the private sector who reported salary information: **48%**

Median salary in public service (government, judicial clerkships, academic posts, non-profits): **$42,000**

Percentage of 2008 graduates in:
Law firms: **48%**   Government: **25%**
Bus./industry: **10%**   Judicial clerkship: **2%**
Public interest: **11%**   Unknown: **0%**
Academia : **4%**

2008 graduates employed in-state: **80%**
2008 graduates employed in foreign countries: **0%**
Number of states where graduates are employed: **19**
Percentage of 2008 graduates working in: New England: **1%**, Middle Atlantic: **1%**, East North Central: **2%**, West North Central: **0%**, South Atlantic: **90%**, East South Central: **2%**, West South Central: **2%**, Mountain: **1%**, Pacific: **1%**, Unknown: **0%**

BAR PASSAGE RATES
Based on 2008 graduates taking Summer 2008 or Winter 2009 exams. Most of the school's first-time test takers took the bar in Florida.

87%
School's bar passage rate for first-time test takers

81%
Statewide bar passage rate for first-time test takers

Fordham University

- 140 W. 62nd Street, New York, NY, 10023-7485
- http://law.fordham.edu
- Private
- Year founded: 1905
- 2009-2010 tuition: full-time: $44,996; part-time: $33,816
- Enrollment 2009-10 academic year: full-time: 1,160; part-time: 309
- U.S. News 2010 law specialty ranking: clinical training: 13, dispute resolution: 8, intellectual property law: 15

3.44-3.77 GPA, 25TH-75TH PERCENTILE

164-167 LSAT, 25TH-75TH PERCENTILE

22% ACCEPTANCE RATE

34 2011 U.S. NEWS LAW SCHOOL RANKING

ADMISSIONS

Admissions phone number: **(212) 636-6810**
Admissions email address: **lawadmissions@law.fordham.edu**
Application website: **http://law.fordham.edu/admissions**
Application deadline for Fall 2011 admission: **1-Mar**

Admissions statistics:

Number of applicants for Fall 2009: **7,294**
Number of acceptances: **1,635**
Number enrolled: **318**
Acceptance rate: **22%**
GPA, 25th-75th percentile, entering class Fall 2009: **3.44-3.77**
LSAT, 25th-75th percentile, entering class Fall 2009: **164-167**

Part-time program:

Number of applicants for Fall 2009: **1,549**
Number of acceptances: **269**
Number enrolled: **158**
Acceptance rate: **17%**
GPA, 25th-75th percentile, entering class Fall 2009: **3.28-3.66**
LSAT, 25th-75th percentile, entering class Fall 2009: **161-165**

FINANCIAL AID

Financial aid phone number: **(212) 636-6815**
Financial aid application deadline: **1-Apr**
Tuition 2009-2010 academic year: **full-time: $44,996; part-time: $33,816**
Room and board: **$17,690** ; books: **$1,600** ; miscellaneous expenses: **$5,204**
Total of room/board/books/miscellaneous expenses: **$24,494**
University offers graduate student housing for which law students are eligible.

Financial aid profile

Percent of students that received grants for the 2008-2009 academic year: full-time: **40%**; part-time **17%**
Median grant amount: full-time: **$10,000** ; part-time: **$6,600**
The average law-school debt of those in the Class of 2009 who borrowed: **$103,213** . Proportion who borrowed: **79%**

ACADEMIC PROGRAMS

Calendar: **semester**
Joint degrees awarded: **J.D./M.B.A.; J.D./M.S.W.; J.D./M.A.**
Typical first-year section size: Full-time: **80**; Part-time: **80**
Is there typically a "small section" of the first year class, other than Legal Writing, taught by full-time faculty?: Full-time: **yes**; Part-time: **yes**
Number of course titles, beyond the first year curriculum, offered last year: **247**
Percentages of upper division course sections, excluding seminars, with an enrollment of:

Under 25: **32%**	25 to 49: **31%**
50 to 74: **16%**	75 to 99: **17%**
100+: **4%**	

Areas of specialization: appellate advocacy, clinical training, dispute resolution, environmental law, health care law, intellectual property law, international law, tax law, trial advocacy

Fall 2009 faculty profile

Total teaching faculty: **227**. Full-time: **35%**; **59%** men, **41%** women, **18%** minorities. Part-time: **65%**; **63%** men, **37%** women, **13%** minorities
Student-to-faculty ratio: **13.6**

SPECIAL PROGRAMS *(as provided by law school):*

Center: M. Trial Ad; L.& Info Pol.-CLIP; Compet. L; Conf. Resol & ADR; Corp. L.; E.U. L.; Soc Just & Disp. Res; L., Cult. & Soc.; Relig. L. & L. Wk; Fam & Child Adv; L. & Just; L. & Ethic. Clinics: Comm. Devel.; Crim. Def.; Fed. Litig.; Housng; Immigr; Intl Just; Intl Sust Devlp; Mediation; Sec. Arbitr; Soc. Just.; Tax & Consmr Litg.; Urban Policy; Intl Human Rts. Summer study: Ireland, S. Korea.

STUDENT BODY

Fall 2009 full-time enrollment: 1,160

Men: 51%	Women: 49%
African-American: 6.00%	American Indian: 0.30%
Asian-American: 6.40%	Mexican-American: 0.50%
Puerto Rican: 1.10%	Other Hisp-Amer: 8.90%
White: 54.10%	International: 2.50%
Unknown: 20.30%	

Fall 2009 part-time enrollment: 309

Men: 52%	Women: 48%
African-American: 5.20%	American Indian: 0.30%
Asian-American: 8.70%	Mexican-American: 0.00%
Puerto Rican: 0.60%	Other Hisp-Amer: 2.90%
White: 56.30%	International: 0.30%
Unknown: 25.60%	

Attrition rates for 2008-2009 full-time students
Percent of students discontinuing law school:

Men: 2%	Women: 2%
First-year students: 1%	Second-year students: 5%
Third-year students: 0%	Fourth-year students: N/A

LIBRARY RESOURCES

Total titles: 310,985
Total volumes: 651,568
Total seats available for library users: 442

INFORMATION TECHNOLOGY

Number of wired network connections available to students: 601 total (in the law library, excluding computer labs: 282; in classrooms: 287; in computer labs: 0; elsewhere in the law school: 32)
Law school has a wireless network.
Students are not required to own a computer.

EMPLOYMENT AND SALARIES

Proportion of 2008 graduates employed at graduation: 85%
Employed 9 months later, as of February 15, 2009: 95%
Salaries in the private sector (law firms, business, industry): $150,000 –$160,000 (25th-75th percentile)
Median salary in the private sector: $160,000
Percentage in the private sector who reported salary information: 89%
Median salary in public service (government, judicial clerkships, academic posts, non-profits): $52,900

Percentage of 2008 graduates in:

Law firms: 76%	Government: 5%
Bus./industry: 10%	Judicial clerkship: 4%
Public interest: 3%	Unknown: 1%
Academia : 1%	

2008 graduates employed in-state: 84%
2008 graduates employed in foreign countries: 0%
Number of states where graduates are employed: 14
Percentage of 2008 graduates working in: New England: 3%, Middle Atlantic: 88%, East North Central: 1%, West North Central: 0%, South Atlantic: 1%, East South Central: 0%, West South Central: 1%, Mountain: 1%, Pacific: 3%, Unknown: 4%

BAR PASSAGE RATES

Based on 2008 graduates taking Summer 2008 or Winter 2009 exams. Most of the school's first-time test takers took the bar in New York.

94%

School's bar passage rate for first-time test takers

81%

Statewide bar passage rate for first-time test takers

Franklin Pierce Law Center

- 2 White Street, Concord, NH, 3301
- http://www.piercelaw.edu
- Private
- Year founded: 1973
- 2009-2010 tuition: full-time: $36,980; part-time: N/A
- Enrollment 2009-10 academic year: full-time: 429
- U.S. News 2010 law specialty ranking: intellectual property law: 9

3.06-3.62 GPA, 25ᵀᴴ-75ᵀᴴ PERCENTILE

149-155 LSAT, 25ᵀᴴ-75ᵀᴴ PERCENTILE

50% ACCEPTANCE RATE

Tier 3 2011 U.S. NEWS LAW SCHOOL RANKING

ADMISSIONS

Admissions phone number: (603) 228-9217
Admissions email address: admissions@piercelaw.edu
Application website: http://www.piercelaw.edu/apply/
Application deadline for Fall 2011 admission: 1-Apr

Admissions statistics:
Number of applicants for Fall 2009: 1,336
Number of acceptances: 671
Number enrolled: 158
Acceptance rate: 50%
GPA, 25th-75th percentile, entering class Fall 2009: 3.06-3.62
LSAT, 25th-75th percentile, entering class Fall 2009: 149-155

FINANCIAL AID

Financial aid phone number: (603) 228-1541
Financial aid application deadline:
Tuition 2009-2010 academic year: **full-time: $36,980; part-time: N/A**
Room and board: $11,250 ; books: $1,400 ; miscellaneous expenses: $7,014
Total of room/board/books/miscellaneous expenses: $19,664
University offers graduate student housing for which law students are eligible.

Financial aid profile
Percent of students that received grants for the 2008-2009 academic year: full-time: 58%
Median grant amount: full-time: $6,500
The average law-school debt of those in the Class of 2009 who borrowed: $115,376 . Proportion who borrowed: 81%

ACADEMIC PROGRAMS

Calendar: semester
Joint degrees awarded: **JD/Master of Commerce & Tech. Law; JD/Master of Int'l Crim Law & Justice; JD/Master of IP Law; JD/LLM in Commerce & Tech. Law; JD/LLM in Int'l Crim. Law & Justice; JD/LLM in IP Law**

Typical first-year section size: Full-time: **80**
Is there typically a "small section" of the first year class, other than Legal Writing, taught by full-time faculty?: Full-time: **yes**
Number of course titles, beyond the first year curriculum, offered last year: **107**
Percentages of upper division course sections, excluding seminars, with an enrollment of:

Under 25: **75%**   25 to 49: **12%**
50 to 74: **7%**   75 to 99: **6%**
100+: **0%**

Areas of specialization: appellate advocacy, clinical training, dispute resolution, environmental law, health care law, intellectual property law, international law, tax law, trial advocacy

Fall 2009 faculty profile
Total teaching faculty: **46**. Full-time: **54%**; **56%** men, **44%** women, **8%** minorities. Part-time: **46%**; **67%** men, **33%** women, **0%** minorities
Student-to-faculty ratio: **14.2**

SPECIAL PROGRAMS *(as provided by law school):*
Students enroll in clinics focused on IP, commercial, and criminal law or spend a semester working in an externship in the US or abroad. Public interest projects are open to students. Summer programs in IP and e-Law are available in China, Ireland, and NH and a course in International Criminal Law and Justice is offered in Washington, DC. An honors program offers an alternative to the NH bar exam.

STUDENT BODY
Fall 2009 full-time enrollment: 429
Men: 62%   Women: 38%
African-American: 5.40%   American Indian: 0.20%
Asian-American: 9.30%   Mexican-American: 0.90%
Puerto Rican: 0.20%   Other Hisp-Amer: 2.30%
White: 70.90%   International: 4.70%
Unknown: 6.10%

Attrition rates for 2008-2009 full-time students
Percent of students discontinuing law school:

Men: **5%**   Women: **4%**

First-year students: **12%**   Second-year students: **1%**

Third-year students: **N/A**   Fourth-year students: **N/A**

LIBRARY RESOURCES

Total titles: **108,068**

Total volumes: **307,364**

Total seats available for library users: **306**

INFORMATION TECHNOLOGY

Number of wired network connections available to students: **307** total (in the law library, excluding computer labs: **108**; in classrooms: **140**; in computer labs: **31**; elsewhere in the law school: **28**)

Law school has a wireless network.

Students are not required to own a computer.

EMPLOYMENT AND SALARIES

Proportion of 2008 graduates employed at graduation: **N/A**

Employed 9 months later, as of February 15, 2009: **94%**

Salaries in the private sector (law firms, business, industry): **$75,000 –$142,500** (25th-75th percentile)

Median salary in the private sector: **$120,000**

Percentage in the private sector who reported salary information: **75%**

Median salary in public service (government, judicial clerkships, academic posts, non-profits): **$48,500**

Percentage of 2008 graduates in:

Law firms: **59%**   Government: **6%**

Bus./industry: **16%**   Judicial clerkship: **9%**

Public interest: **7%**   Unknown: **1%**

Academia : **3%**

2008 graduates employed in-state: **21%**

2008 graduates employed in foreign countries: **1%**

Number of states where graduates are employed: **24**

Percentage of 2008 graduates working in: New England: **43%**, Middle Atlantic: **15%**, East North Central: **3%**, West North Central: **1%**, South Atlantic: **21%**, East South Central: **1%**, West South Central: **6%**, Mountain: **6%**, Pacific: **5%**, Unknown: **0%**

BAR PASSAGE RATES

Based on 2008 graduates taking Summer 2008 or Winter 2009 exams. Most of the school's first-time test takers took the bar in New Hampshire.

93%

School's bar passage rate for first-time test takers

88%

Statewide bar passage rate for first-time test takers

George Mason University

■ 3301 Fairfax Drive, Arlington, VA, 22201-4426
■ http://www.law.gmu.edu
■ Public
■ Year founded: 1980
■ 2009-2010 tuition: full-time: $20,556; part-time: $727/credit hour
■ Enrollment 2009-10 academic year: full-time: 480; part-time: 217
■ U.S. News 2010 law specialty ranking: intellectual property law: 23

3.20-3.83 GPA, 25TH-75TH PERCENTILE

158-165 LSAT, 25TH-75TH PERCENTILE

25% ACCEPTANCE RATE

42 2011 U.S. NEWS LAW SCHOOL RANKING

ADMISSIONS

Admissions phone number: **(703) 993-8010**
Admissions email address: **lawadmit@gmu.edu**
Application website:
  http://www.law.gmu.edu/assets/files/admissions/JD_Appl_09FORM.pdf
Application deadline for Fall 2011 admission: **1-Apr**

Admissions statistics:

Number of applicants for Fall 2009: **4,624**
Number of acceptances: **1,144**
Number enrolled: **190**
Acceptance rate: **25%**
GPA, 25th-75th percentile, entering class Fall 2009: **3.20-3.83**
LSAT, 25th-75th percentile, entering class Fall 2009: **158-165**

Part-time program:

Number of applicants for Fall 2009: **1,787**
Number of acceptances: **156**
Number enrolled: **56**
Acceptance rate: **9%**
GPA, 25th-75th percentile, entering class Fall 2009: **3.25-3.81**
LSAT, 25th-75th percentile, entering class Fall 2009: **157-163**

FINANCIAL AID

Financial aid phone number: **(703) 993-2353**
Financial aid application deadline: **1-Mar**
Tuition 2009-2010 academic year: **full-time: $20,556; part-time: $727/credit hour**
Room and board: **$16,220** ; books: **$1,100** ; miscellaneous expenses: **$5,400**
Total of room/board/books/miscellaneous expenses: **$22,720**
University does not offer graduate student housing for which law students are eligible.

Financial aid profile

Percent of students that received grants for the 2008-2009 academic year: full-time: **14%**; part-time **6%**
Median grant amount: full-time: **$8,000** ; part-time: **$8,000**
The average law-school debt of those in the Class of 2009 who borrowed: **$89,857** . Proportion who borrowed: **85%**

ACADEMIC PROGRAMS

Calendar: **semester**
Joint degrees awarded: **J.D./M.A. Economics; J.D./Ph.D. Economics; J.D./M.P.P.**
Typical first-year section size: Full-time: **48**; Part-time: **60**
Is there typically a "small section" of the first year class, other than Legal Writing, taught by full-time faculty?: Full-time: **no**; Part-time: **no**
Number of course titles, beyond the first year curriculum, offered last year: **133**
Percentages of upper division course sections, excluding seminars, with an enrollment of:

Under 25: **74%**	25 to 49: **19%**
50 to 74: **5%**	75 to 99: **2%**
100+: **N/A**	

Areas of specialization: appellate advocacy, clinical training, dispute resolution, environmental law, health care law, intellectual property law, international law, tax law, trial advocacy

Fall 2009 faculty profile

Total teaching faculty: **170**. Full-time: **22%**; **82%** men, **18%** women, **16%** minorities. Part-time: **78%**; **74%** men, **26%** women, **6%** minorities
Student-to-faculty ratio: **13.2**

SPECIAL PROGRAMS (as provided by law school):

Mason integrates economic and quantitative methods and requires extensive research and writing. Field programs include the Clinic for Legal Assistance to Service members and regulatory, patent, immigration, mental health and Virginia litigation practice programs. Mason academic centers and initiatives include the Patent Law Program, Law & Economics Center & Center for Infrastructure Protection.

STUDENT BODY

Fall 2009 full-time enrollment: 480

Men: 58%	Women: 43%
African-American: 2.50%	American Indian: 0.40%
Asian-American: 10.80%	Mexican-American: 0.00%
Puerto Rican: 0.00%	Other Hisp-Amer: 4.20%
White: 70.80%	International: 1.70%
Unknown: 9.60%	

Fall 2009 part-time enrollment: 217

Men: 60%	Women: 40%
African-American: 2.80%	American Indian: 0.50%
Asian-American: 9.70%	Mexican-American: 0.00%
Puerto Rican: 0.00%	Other Hisp-Amer: 2.30%
White: 80.60%	International: 0.50%
Unknown: 3.70%	

Attrition rates for 2008-2009 full-time students
Percent of students discontinuing law school:

Men: 4%	Women: 6%
First-year students: 16%	Second-year students: 2%
Third-year students: 1%	Fourth-year students: N/A

LIBRARY RESOURCES
Total titles: 214,168
Total volumes: 469,833
Total seats available for library users: 369

INFORMATION TECHNOLOGY
Number of wired network connections available to students: 888 total (in the law library, excluding computer labs: 216; in classrooms: 637; in computer labs: 0; elsewhere in the law school: 35)
Law school has a wireless network.
Students are not required to own a computer.

EMPLOYMENT AND SALARIES
Proportion of 2008 graduates employed at graduation: 96%
Employed 9 months later, as of February 15, 2009: 99%
Salaries in the private sector (law firms, business, industry): $70,000 –$160,000 (25th-75th percentile)
Median salary in the private sector: $145,000
Percentage in the private sector who reported salary information: 57%
Median salary in public service (government, judicial clerkships, academic posts, non-profits): $55,000

Percentage of 2008 graduates in:

Law firms: 47%	Government: 17%
Bus./industry: 10%	Judicial clerkship: 13%
Public interest: 8%	Unknown: 0%
Academia : 5%	

2008 graduates employed in-state: 43%
2008 graduates employed in foreign countries: 1%
Number of states where graduates are employed: 18
Percentage of 2008 graduates working in: New England: 1%, Middle Atlantic: 4%, East North Central: 1%, West North Central: 0%, South Atlantic: 87%, East South Central: 1%, West South Central: 2%, Mountain: 1%, Pacific: 2%, Unknown: 0%

BAR PASSAGE RATES
Based on 2008 graduates taking Summer 2008 or Winter 2009 exams. Most of the school's first-time test takers took the bar in Virginia.

87%
School's bar passage rate for first-time test takers

82%
Statewide bar passage rate for first-time test takers

George Washington University

- 2000 H Street NW, Washington, DC, 20052
- http://www.law.gwu.edu
- Private
- Year founded: 1865
- 2009-2010 tuition: full-time: $42,205; part-time: $32,648
- Enrollment 2009-10 academic year: full-time: 1,328; part-time: 304
- U.S. News 2010 law specialty ranking: clinical training: 25, environmental law: 16, intellectual property law: 3, international law: 6

3.45-3.86 GPA, 25TH-75TH PERCENTILE

163-168 LSAT, 25TH-75TH PERCENTILE

23% ACCEPTANCE RATE

20 2011 U.S. NEWS LAW SCHOOL RANKING

ADMISSIONS

Admissions phone number: **(202) 994-7230**
Admissions email address: **jdadmit@law.gwu.edu**
Application website: **http://www.law.gwu.edu/admissions/**
Application deadline for Fall 2011 admission: **31-Mar**

Admissions statistics:

Number of applicants for Fall 2009: **8,906**
Number of acceptances: **2,029**
Number enrolled: **456**
Acceptance rate: **23%**
GPA, 25th-75th percentile, entering class Fall 2009: **3.45-3.86**
LSAT, 25th-75th percentile, entering class Fall 2009: **163-168**

Part-time program:

Number of applicants for Fall 2009: **686**
Number of acceptances: **116**
Number enrolled: **50**
Acceptance rate: **17%**
GPA, 25th-75th percentile, entering class Fall 2009: **3.16-3.83**
LSAT, 25th-75th percentile, entering class Fall 2009: **162-167**

FINANCIAL AID

Financial aid phone number: **(202) 994-6592**
Financial aid application deadline: **15-May**
Tuition 2009-2010 academic year: **full-time: $42,205; part-time: $32,648**
Room and board: **$14,200** ; books: **$1,295** ; miscellaneous expenses: **$7,200**
Total of room/board/books/miscellaneous expenses: **$22,695**
University offers graduate student housing for which law students are eligible.

Financial aid profile

Percent of students that received grants for the 2008-2009 academic year: full-time: **54%**; part-time **16%**

Median grant amount: full-time: **$13,000** ; part-time: **$8,968**
The average law-school debt of those in the Class of 2009 who borrowed: **$125,200** . Proportion who borrowed: **82%**

ACADEMIC PROGRAMS

Calendar: **semester**
Joint degrees awarded: **J.D./M.A.; J.D./M.B.A.; J.D./M.P.H.; J.D./M.P.A.; J.D./M.P.P.; LL.M./M.A.; LL.M./M.P.H.**
Typical first-year section size: Full-time: **103**; Part-time: **127**
Is there typically a "small section" of the first year class, other than Legal Writing, taught by full-time faculty?: Full-time: **yes**; Part-time: **no**
Number of course titles, beyond the first year curriculum, offered last year: **213**
Percentages of upper division course sections, excluding seminars, with an enrollment of:

Under 25: **61%**	25 to 49: **21%**
50 to 74: **10%**	75 to 99: **4%**
100+: **4%**	

Areas of specialization: appellate advocacy, clinical training, dispute resolution, environmental law, health care law, intellectual property law, international law, tax law, trial advocacy

Fall 2009 faculty profile

Total teaching faculty: **280**. Full-time: **37%**; **55%** men, **45%** women, **16%** minorities. Part-time: **63%**; **69%** men, **31%** women, **12%** minorities
Student-to-faculty ratio: **14.2**

SPECIAL PROGRAMS *(as provided by law school):*

14 clinics: cases argued before international courts/Supreme Court; 7 research centers/exchanges; summer session; Germany/UK study abroad (European/international economic law, IP, international human rights); Canadian/Mexican partner programs (NACLE); career office: internships, externships, clerkships; student-faculty Public Interest Committee; joint degrees (four schools); legal writing program.

STUDENT BODY

Fall 2009 full-time enrollment: **1,328**

Men: **56%**	Women: **44%**
African-American: **4.70%**	American Indian: **0.80%**
Asian-American: **8.40%**	Mexican-American: **0.00%**
Puerto Rican: **0.00%**	Other Hisp-Amer: **6.40%**
White: **61.40%**	International: **2.30%**
Unknown: **16.00%**	

Fall 2009 part-time enrollment: **304**

Men: **65%**	Women: **35%**
African-American: **6.90%**	American Indian: **0.70%**
Asian-American: **13.80%**	Mexican-American: **0.00%**
Puerto Rican: **0.00%**	Other Hisp-Amer: **4.30%**
White: **61.20%**	International: **1.30%**
Unknown: **11.80%**	

Attrition rates for 2008-2009 full-time students
Percent of students discontinuing law school:

Men: **3%**	Women: **2%**
First-year students: **6%**	Second-year students: **0%**
Third-year students: **0%**	Fourth-year students: **N/A**

LIBRARY RESOURCES

Total titles: **1,324,716**
Total volumes: **659,242**
Total seats available for library users: **637**

INFORMATION TECHNOLOGY

Number of wired network connections available to students: **54** total (in the law library, excluding computer labs: **54**; in classrooms: **0**; in computer labs: **0**; elsewhere in the law school: **0**)
Law school has a wireless network.
Students are required to own a computer.

EMPLOYMENT AND SALARIES

Proportion of 2008 graduates employed at graduation: **93%**
Employed 9 months later, as of February 15, 2009: **99%**
Salaries in the private sector (law firms, business, industry): **$145,000 –$160,000** (25th-75th percentile)
Median salary in the private sector: **$160,000**
Percentage in the private sector who reported salary information: **87%**
Median salary in public service (government, judicial clerkships, academic posts, non-profits): **$55,731**

Percentage of 2008 graduates in:

Law firms: **66%**	Government: **12%**
Bus./industry: **7%**	Judicial clerkship: **9%**
Public interest: **4%**	Unknown: **0%**
Academia : **2%**	

2008 graduates employed in-state: **52%**
2008 graduates employed in foreign countries: **0%**
Number of states where graduates are employed: **26**
Percentage of 2008 graduates working in: New England: **3%**, Middle Atlantic: **17%**, East North Central: **3%**, West North Central: **0%**, South Atlantic: **64%**, East South Central: **1%**, West South Central: **1%**, Mountain: **2%**, Pacific: **6%**, Unknown: **3%**

BAR PASSAGE RATES

Based on 2008 graduates taking Summer 2008 or Winter 2009 exams. Most of the school's first-time test takers took the bar in New York.

95%
School's bar passage rate for first-time test takers

81%
Statewide bar passage rate for first-time test takers

Georgetown University

- 600 New Jersey Avenue NW, Washington, DC, 20001-2075
- http://www.law.georgetown.edu
- Private
- Year founded: 1870
- 2009-2010 tuition: full-time: $43,750; part-time: $38,280
- Enrollment 2009-10 academic year: full-time: 1,628; part-time: 354
- U.S. News 2010 law specialty ranking: clinical training: 1, environmental law: 6, healthcare law: 7, intellectual property law: 11, international law: 3, tax law: 2, trial advocacy: 5

3.42-3.81 GPA, 25TH-75TH PERCENTILE

168-172 LSAT, 25TH-75TH PERCENTILE

23% ACCEPTANCE RATE

14 2011 U.S. NEWS LAW SCHOOL RANKING

ADMISSIONS
Admissions phone number: (202) 662-9015
Admissions email address: admis@law.georgetown.edu
Application website:
 http://www.law.georgetown.edu/admissions
Application deadline for Fall 2011 admission: 1-Mar

Admissions statistics:
Number of applicants for Fall 2009: 10,731
Number of acceptances: 2,459
Number enrolled: 463
Acceptance rate: 23%
GPA, 25th-75th percentile, entering class Fall 2009: 3.42-3.81
LSAT, 25th-75th percentile, entering class Fall 2009: 168-172

Part-time program:
Number of applicants for Fall 2009: 922
Number of acceptances: 186
Number enrolled: 127
Acceptance rate: 20%
GPA, 25th-75th percentile, entering class Fall 2009: 3.42-3.78
LSAT, 25th-75th percentile, entering class Fall 2009: 163-168

FINANCIAL AID
Financial aid phone number: (202) 662-9210
Financial aid application deadline: 1-Mar
Tuition 2009-2010 academic year: full-time: $43,750; part-time: $38,280
Room and board: $16,240 ; books: $1,025 ; miscellaneous expenses: $4,985
Total of room/board/books/miscellaneous expenses: $22,250
University does not offer graduate student housing for which law students are eligible.

Financial aid profile
Percent of students that received grants for the 2008-2009 academic year: full-time: 37%; part-time 2%
Median grant amount: full-time: $15,000 ; part-time: $9,730
The average law-school debt of those in the Class of 2009 who borrowed: $125,174 . Proportion who borrowed: 82%

ACADEMIC PROGRAMS
Calendar: semester
Joint degrees awarded: J.D./M.S.F.S.; J.D./M.B.A.; J.D./M.P.H.; J.D./M.P.P.; J.D./M.A. Government; J.D./M.A. Philosophy; J.D./M.A. Arab Studies; J.D./M.A. Russian & E. European Studies; J.D./M.A. Latin American Studies; J.D./M.A. Security Studies; J.D./PhD Philosophy; J.D./M.A. German and European Studies
Typical first-year section size: Full-time: 117; Part-time: 129
Is there typically a "small section" of the first year class, other than Legal Writing, taught by full-time faculty?: Full-time: yes; Part-time: yes
Number of course titles, beyond the first year curriculum, offered last year: 407
Percentages of upper division course sections, excluding seminars, with an enrollment of:

Under 25: 55%	25 to 49: 27%
50 to 74: 9%	75 to 99: 3%
100+: 6%	

Areas of specialization: appellate advocacy, clinical training, dispute resolution, environmental law, health care law, intellectual property law, international law, tax law, trial advocacy

Fall 2009 faculty profile
Total teaching faculty: 377. Full-time: 40%; 63% men, 38% women, 11% minorities. Part-time: 60%; 80% men, 20% women, 4% minorities
Student-to-faculty ratio: 12.4

SPECIAL PROGRAMS (as provided by law school):
With more than 150 full time faculty who have a broad range of scholarly interests and legal backgrounds, Georgetown is able to offer a comprehensive legal curriculum with more than 350 courses, seminars, and other programs including the largest in-

house clinical program of any law school in the nation, the Public Interest Law Scholars program, and The Global Law Scholars program.

STUDENT BODY

Fall 2009 full-time enrollment: 1,628

Men: 54%	Women: 46%
African-American: 8.90%	American Indian: 0.10%
Asian-American: 9.00%	Mexican-American: 0.50%
Puerto Rican: 0.00%	Other Hisp-Amer: 4.10%
White: 67.70%	International: 3.30%
Unknown: 6.40%	

Fall 2009 part-time enrollment: 354

Men: 57%	Women: 43%
African-American: 7.10%	American Indian: 1.10%
Asian-American: 8.80%	Mexican-American: 0.80%
Puerto Rican: 0.30%	Other Hisp-Amer: 3.70%
White: 64.10%	International: 2.80%
Unknown: 11.30%	

Attrition rates for 2008-2009 full-time students
Percent of students discontinuing law school:

Men: 1%	Women: 0%
First-year students: 2%	Second-year students: 0%
Third-year students: 0%	Fourth-year students: 3%

LIBRARY RESOURCES

Total titles: 414,717
Total volumes: 1,185,910
Total seats available for library users: 1,083

INFORMATION TECHNOLOGY

Number of wired network connections available to students: 840 total (in the law library, excluding computer labs: 150; in classrooms: 350; in computer labs: 20; elsewhere in the law school: 320)
Law school has a wireless network.
Students are required to own a computer.

EMPLOYMENT AND SALARIES

Proportion of 2008 graduates employed at graduation: 94%
Employed 9 months later, as of February 15, 2009: 97%
Salaries in the private sector (law firms, business, industry): $160,000 –$160,000 (25th-75th percentile)
Median salary in the private sector: $160,000
Percentage in the private sector who reported salary information: 90%
Median salary in public service (government, judicial clerkships, academic posts, non-profits): $57,800

Percentage of 2008 graduates in:

Law firms: 74%	Government: 6%
Bus./industry: 5%	Judicial clerkship: 8%
Public interest: 5%	Unknown: 1%
Academia : 1%	

2008 graduates employed in-state: 35%
2008 graduates employed in foreign countries: 2%
Number of states where graduates are employed: 33
Percentage of 2008 graduates working in: New England: 4%, Middle Atlantic: 25%, East North Central: 4%, West North Central: 2%, South Atlantic: 45%, East South Central: 1%, West South Central: 3%, Mountain: 2%, Pacific: 8%, Unknown: 5%

BAR PASSAGE RATES

Based on 2008 graduates taking Summer 2008 or Winter 2009 exams. Most of the school's first-time test takers took the bar in New York.

97%
School's bar passage rate for first-time test takers

81%
Statewide bar passage rate for first-time test takers

Georgia State University

- PO Box 4049, Atlanta, GA, 30302-4049
- http://law.gsu.edu
- Public
- Year founded: 1982
- 2009-2010 tuition: full-time: $11,838; part-time: $10,980
- Enrollment 2009-10 academic year: full-time: 480; part-time: 193
- U.S. News 2010 law specialty ranking: healthcare law: 4

3.20-3.80 GPA, 25TH-75TH PERCENTILE

159-162 LSAT, 25TH-75TH PERCENTILE

16% ACCEPTANCE RATE

60 2011 U.S. NEWS LAW SCHOOL RANKING

ADMISSIONS

Admissions phone number: **(404) 651-2048**
Admissions email address: **admissions@gsulaw.gsu.edu**
Application website:
 https://www.applyweb.com/aw?gsulaw
Application deadline for Fall 2011 admission: **15-Mar**

Admissions statistics:
Number of applicants for Fall 2009: **2,493**
Number of acceptances: **410**
Number enrolled: **168**
Acceptance rate: **16%**
GPA, 25th-75th percentile, entering class Fall 2009: **3.20-3.80**
LSAT, 25th-75th percentile, entering class Fall 2009: **159-162**

Part-time program:
Number of applicants for Fall 2009: **321**
Number of acceptances: **81**
Number enrolled: **49**
Acceptance rate: **25%**
GPA, 25th-75th percentile, entering class Fall 2009: **3.10-3.73**
LSAT, 25th-75th percentile, entering class Fall 2009: **158-161**

FINANCIAL AID

Financial aid phone number: **(404) 651-2227**
Financial aid application deadline: **1-Apr**
Tuition 2009-2010 academic year: **full-time: $11,838; part-time: $10,980**
Room and board: **$9,000** ; books: **$1,500** ; miscellaneous expenses: **$4,084**
Total of room/board/books/miscellaneous expenses: **$14,584**
University offers graduate student housing for which law students are eligible.

Financial aid profile
Percent of students that received grants for the 2008-2009 academic year: full-time: **20%**; part-time **23%**
Median grant amount: full-time: **$2,500** ; part-time: **$2,500**
The average law-school debt of those in the Class of 2009 who borrowed: **$22,129** . Proportion who borrowed: **69%**

ACADEMIC PROGRAMS

Calendar: **semester**
Joint degrees awarded: **J.D./M.S.H.A.; J.D./M.B.A.; J.D./M.P.A.; J.D./M.A. Philosophy; J.D./M.C.R.P.**
Typical first-year section size: Full-time: **70**; Part-time: **70**
Is there typically a "small section" of the first year class, other than Legal Writing, taught by full-time faculty?: Full-time: **no**; Part-time: **no**
Number of course titles, beyond the first year curriculum, offered last year: **112**
Percentages of upper division course sections, excluding seminars, with an enrollment of:

Under 25: **65%**	25 to 49: **24%**
50 to 74: **10%**	75 to 99: **1%**
100+: **0%**	

Areas of specialization: appellate advocacy, clinical training, dispute resolution, environmental law, health care law, intellectual property law, international law, tax law, trial advocacy

Fall 2009 faculty profile
Total teaching faculty: **58**. Full-time: **79%**; **57%** men, **43%** women, **15%** minorities. Part-time: **21%**; **58%** men, **42%** women, **33%** minorities
Student-to-faculty ratio: **10.7**

SPECIAL PROGRAMS *(as provided by law school)*:
The College of Law offers several special programs including: an Externship Program; 5 joint degree programs; the Consortium on Negotiation and Conflict Resolution, three international programs; two accredited foreign law programs; Trial Advocacy Program; Litigation Workshop; national mock trial competitions; Appellate Advocacy Program; Moot Court; and a Legislation Clinic and Practicum.

STUDENT BODY

Fall 2009 full-time enrollment: 480

Men: 52%	Women: 48%
African-American: 7.70%	American Indian: 0.60%
Asian-American: 8.10%	Mexican-American: 0.00%
Puerto Rican: 0.00%	Other Hisp-Amer: 2.30%
White: 70.40%	International: 0.00%
Unknown: 10.80%	

Fall 2009 part-time enrollment: 193

Men: 54%	Women: 46%
African-American: 12.40%	American Indian: 0.50%
Asian-American: 5.70%	Mexican-American: 0.00%
Puerto Rican: 0.00%	Other Hisp-Amer: 3.10%
White: 68.90%	International: 0.00%
Unknown: 9.30%	

Attrition rates for 2008-2009 full-time students
Percent of students discontinuing law school:

Men: 4%	Women: 1%
First-year students: 8%	Second-year students: 1%
Third-year students: N/A	Fourth-year students: N/A

LIBRARY RESOURCES

Total titles: 107,132
Total volumes: 378,065
Total seats available for library users: 335

INFORMATION TECHNOLOGY

Number of wired network connections available to students: 926 total (in the law library, excluding computer labs: 200; in classrooms: 700; in computer labs: 6; elsewhere in the law school: 20)
Law school has a wireless network.
Students are not required to own a computer.

EMPLOYMENT AND SALARIES

Proportion of 2008 graduates employed at graduation:
N/A
Employed 9 months later, as of February 15, 2009: 99%
Salaries in the private sector (law firms, business, industry): $55,000 –$120,000 (25th-75th percentile)
Median salary in the private sector: $80,000
Percentage in the private sector who reported salary information: 74%
Median salary in public service (government, judicial clerkships, academic posts, non-profits): $51,000

Percentage of 2008 graduates in:

Law firms: 57%	Government: 10%
Bus./industry: 18%	Judicial clerkship: 3%
Public interest: 6%	Unknown: 2%
Academia : 4%	

2008 graduates employed in-state: 92%
2008 graduates employed in foreign countries: 1%
Number of states where graduates are employed: 9
Percentage of 2008 graduates working in: New England: 0%, Middle Atlantic: 1%, East North Central: 1%, West North Central: 1%, South Atlantic: 94%, East South Central: 2%, West South Central: 2%, Mountain: 0%, Pacific: 0%, Unknown: N/A

BAR PASSAGE RATES

Based on 2008 graduates taking Summer 2008 or Winter 2009 exams. Most of the school's first-time test takers took the bar in Georgia.

94%
School's bar passage rate for first-time test takers

89%
Statewide bar passage rate for first-time test takers

Golden Gate University

- 536 Mission Street, San Francisco, CA, 94105
- http://www.ggu.edu/law/
- Private
- **Year founded:** 1901
- **2009-2010 tuition:** full-time: $36,600; part-time: $25,620
- **Enrollment 2009-10 academic year:** full-time: 529; part-time: 108
- **U.S. News 2010 law specialty ranking:** N/A

2.88-3.43 GPA, 25TH-75TH PERCENTILE

151-155 LSAT, 25TH-75TH PERCENTILE

52% ACCEPTANCE RATE

Tier 4 2011 U.S. NEWS LAW SCHOOL RANKING

ADMISSIONS

Admissions phone number: **(415) 442-6630**
Admissions email address: **lawadmit@ggu.edu**
Application website: **http://www.lsac.org**
Application deadline for Fall 2011 admission: **1-Apr**

Admissions statistics:
Number of applicants for Fall 2009: **2,419**
Number of acceptances: **1,257**
Number enrolled: **199**
Acceptance rate: **52%**
GPA, 25th-75th percentile, entering class Fall 2009: **2.88-3.43**
LSAT, 25th-75th percentile, entering class Fall 2009: **151-155**

Part-time program:
Number of applicants for Fall 2009: **350**
Number of acceptances: **115**
Number enrolled: **44**
Acceptance rate: **33%**
GPA, 25th-75th percentile, entering class Fall 2009: **2.63-3.18**
LSAT, 25th-75th percentile, entering class Fall 2009: **151-155**

FINANCIAL AID

Financial aid phone number: **(415) 442-6635**
Financial aid application deadline:
Tuition 2009-2010 academic year: **full-time: $36,600; part-time: $25,620**
Room and board: **$14,400** ; books: **$1,200** ; miscellaneous expenses: **$7,915**
Total of room/board/books/miscellaneous expenses: **$23,515**
University does not offer graduate student housing for which law students are eligible.

Financial aid profile
Percent of students that received grants for the 2008-2009 academic year: full-time: **42%**; part-time **26%**

Median grant amount: full-time: **$7,500** ; part-time: **$5,000**
The average law-school debt of those in the Class of 2009 who borrowed: **$118,429** . Proportion who borrowed: **88%**

ACADEMIC PROGRAMS

Calendar: **semester**
Joint degrees awarded: **J.D./M.B.A.; J.D./Ph.D.**
Typical first-year section size: Full-time: **70**; Part-time: **46**
Is there typically a "small section" of the first year class, other than Legal Writing, taught by full-time faculty?: Full-time: **no**; Part-time: **no**
Number of course titles, beyond the first year curriculum, offered last year: **122**
Percentages of upper division course sections, excluding seminars, with an enrollment of:

Under 25: **77%**	25 to 49: **18%**
50 to 74: **4%**	75 to 99: **1%**
100+: **0%**	

Areas of specialization: appellate advocacy, clinical training, dispute resolution, environmental law, intellectual property law, international law, tax law, trial advocacy

Fall 2009 faculty profile
Total teaching faculty: **97**. Full-time: **35%**; **59%** men, **41%** women, **21%** minorities. Part-time: **65%**; **51%** men, **49%** women, **14%** minorities
Student-to-faculty ratio: **15.2**

SPECIAL PROGRAMS *(as provided by law school)*:
GGU Law students study a practice-oriented curriculum that enables them to understand legal theory and provide meaningful legal assistance both during and after law school. Through simulation exercises, clinics, externships, trial practice teams, specialization programs and our competitive Honors Lawyering Program, GGU students start thinking and working like lawyers from the day they arrive.

STUDENT BODY
Fall 2009 full-time enrollment: 529
Men: **43%**   Women: **57%**

African-American: **1.90%**   American Indian: **1.30%**
Asian-American: **19.80%**   Mexican-American: **2.30%**
Puerto Rican: **0.20%**   Other Hisp-Amer: **4.00%**
White: **54.10%**   International: **2.10%**
Unknown: **14.40%**

Fall 2009 part-time enrollment: 108
Men: **48%**   Women: **52%**
African-American: **6.50%**   American Indian: **0.00%**
Asian-American: **22.20%**   Mexican-American: **3.70%**
Puerto Rican: **0.00%**   Other Hisp-Amer: **4.60%**
White: **53.70%**   International: **0.90%**
Unknown: **8.30%**

Attrition rates for 2008-2009 full-time students
Percent of students discontinuing law school:
Men: **13%**   Women: **7%**
First-year students: **22%**   Second-year students: **2%**
Third-year students: **1%**   Fourth-year students: **N/A**

LIBRARY RESOURCES
Total titles: **84,568**
Total volumes: **383,876**
Total seats available for library users: **463**

INFORMATION TECHNOLOGY
Number of wired network connections available to students: **572** total (in the law library, excluding computer labs: **145**; in classrooms: **427**; in computer labs: **0**; elsewhere in the law school: **0**)
Law school has a wireless network.
Students are not required to own a computer.

EMPLOYMENT AND SALARIES
Proportion of 2008 graduates employed at graduation: **N/A**

Employed 9 months later, as of February 15, 2009: **90%**
Salaries in the private sector (law firms, business, industry): **$62,500 –$95,000** (25th-75th percentile)
Median salary in the private sector: **$80,000**
Percentage in the private sector who reported salary information: **35%**
Median salary in public service (government, judicial clerkships, academic posts, non-profits): **$60,000**

Percentage of 2008 graduates in:
Law firms: **52%**   Government: **15%**
Bus./industry: **12%**   Judicial clerkship: **4%**
Public interest: **7%**   Unknown: **1%**
Academia : **9%**

2008 graduates employed in-state: **86%**
2008 graduates employed in foreign countries: **1%**
Number of states where graduates are employed: **11**
Percentage of 2008 graduates working in: New England: **0%**, Middle Atlantic: **1%**, East North Central: **0%**, West North Central: **0%**, South Atlantic: **2%**, East South Central: **0%**, West South Central: **0%**, Mountain: **6%**, Pacific: **88%**, Unknown: **2%**

BAR PASSAGE RATES
Based on 2008 graduates taking Summer 2008 or Winter 2009 exams. Most of the school's first-time test takers took the bar in California.

| 72% |

School's bar passage rate for first-time test takers

| 71% |

Statewide bar passage rate for first-time test takers

Gonzaga University

- PO Box 3528, Spokane, WA, 99220-3528
- http://www.law.gonzaga.edu
- Private
- Year founded: 1912
- 2009-2010 tuition: full-time: $31,460; part-time: N/A
- Enrollment 2009-10 academic year: full-time: 516; part-time: 10
- U.S. News 2010 law specialty ranking: N/A

3.05-3.51 GPA, 25TH-75TH PERCENTILE

153-157 LSAT, 25TH-75TH PERCENTILE

43% ACCEPTANCE RATE

Tier 3 2011 U.S. NEWS LAW SCHOOL RANKING

ADMISSIONS

Admissions phone number: **(800) 793-1710**

Admissions email address: **admissions@lawschool.gonzaga.edu**

Application website:
http://www.law.gonzaga.edu/admissions/Application_Information/

Application deadline for Fall 2011 admission: **15-Apr**

Admissions statistics:

Number of applicants for Fall 2009: **1,513**

Number of acceptances: **649**

Number enrolled: **188**

Acceptance rate: **43%**

GPA, 25th-75th percentile, entering class Fall 2009: **3.05-3.51**

LSAT, 25th-75th percentile, entering class Fall 2009: **153-157**

FINANCIAL AID

Financial aid phone number: **(800) 448-2138**

Financial aid application deadline: **1-Feb**

Tuition 2009-2010 academic year: **full-time: $31,460; part-time: N/A**

Room and board: **$8,775** ; books: **$1,000** ; miscellaneous expenses: **$4,629**

Total of room/board/books/miscellaneous expenses: **$14,404**

University offers graduate student housing for which law students are eligible.

Financial aid profile

Percent of students that received grants for the 2008-2009 academic year: full-time: **72%**

Median grant amount: full-time: **$12,000**

The average law-school debt of those in the Class of 2009 who borrowed: **$94,074** . Proportion who borrowed: **91%**

ACADEMIC PROGRAMS

Calendar: **semester**

Joint degrees awarded: **J.D./M.B.A.; J.D./M.A.C.C.; J.D./M.S.W.**

Typical first-year section size: Full-time: **70**

Is there typically a "small section" of the first year class, other than Legal Writing, taught by full-time faculty?: Full-time: **no**

Number of course titles, beyond the first year curriculum, offered last year: **94**

Percentages of upper division course sections, excluding seminars, with an enrollment of:

Under 25: **43%**	25 to 49: **32%**
50 to 74: **22%**	75 to 99: **3%**
100+: **0%**	

Areas of specialization: appellate advocacy, clinical training, dispute resolution, environmental law, health care law, intellectual property law, international law, tax law, trial advocacy

Fall 2009 faculty profile

Total teaching faculty: **58**. Full-time: **48%**; 50% men, 50% women, 7% minorities. Part-time: **52%**; 77% men, 23% women, 0% minorities

Student-to-faculty ratio: **15.3**

SPECIAL PROGRAMS (as provided by law school):

Gonzaga students receive experiential training through innovative labs the first year and two years of extensive training in legal research and writing. Programs include the legal clinic where students work with practicing attorneys in one of seven focus areas(including the Indian Law program), a robust externship program, a summer law program in Florence Italy, and three joint degree programs.

STUDENT BODY

Fall 2009 full-time enrollment: 516

Men: **61%**	Women: **39%**
African-American: **0.40%**	American Indian: **1.20%**
Asian-American: **3.90%**	Mexican-American: **0.80%**
Puerto Rican: **0.00%**	Other Hisp-Amer: **2.10%**
White: **81.60%**	International: **0.00%**
Unknown: **10.10%**	

Fall 2009 part-time enrollment: 10

Men: **30%**	Women: **70%**
African-American: **0.00%**	American Indian: **0.00%**
Asian-American: **10.00%**	Mexican-American: **0.00%**
Puerto Rican: **0.00%**	Other Hisp-Amer: **0.00%**
White: **90.00%**	International: **0.00%**
Unknown: **0.00%**	

Attrition rates for 2008-2009 full-time students
Percent of students discontinuing law school:

Men: **9%**	Women: **3%**
First-year students: **18%**	Second-year students: **1%**
Third-year students: **N/A**	Fourth-year students: **N/A**

LIBRARY RESOURCES
Total titles: **81,636**
Total volumes: **308,615**
Total seats available for library users: **507**

INFORMATION TECHNOLOGY
Number of wired network connections available to students: **140** total (in the law library, excluding computer labs: **87**; in classrooms: **18**; in computer labs: **10**; elsewhere in the law school: **25**)
Law school has a wireless network.
Students are not required to own a computer.

EMPLOYMENT AND SALARIES
Proportion of 2008 graduates employed at graduation: **N/A**
Employed 9 months later, as of February 15, 2009: **94%**
Salaries in the private sector (law firms, business, industry): **$51,500 –$90,000** (25th-75th percentile)

Median salary in the private sector: **$67,500**
Percentage in the private sector who reported salary information: **30%**
Median salary in public service (government, judicial clerkships, academic posts, non-profits): **$54,500**

Percentage of 2008 graduates in:

Law firms: **52%**	Government: **15%**
Bus./industry: **12%**	Judicial clerkship: **8%**
Public interest: **7%**	Unknown: **4%**
Academia : **2%**	

2008 graduates employed in-state: **62%**
2008 graduates employed in foreign countries: **1%**
Number of states where graduates are employed: **13**
Percentage of 2008 graduates working in: New England: **0%**, Middle Atlantic: **1%**, East North Central: **1%**, West North Central: **0%**, South Atlantic: **0%**, East South Central: **1%**, West South Central: **0%**, Mountain: **22%**, Pacific: **70%**, Unknown: **4%**

BAR PASSAGE RATES
Based on 2008 graduates taking Summer 2008 or Winter 2009 exams. Most of the school's first-time test takers took the bar in Washington.

82%
School's bar passage rate for first-time test takers

74%
Statewide bar passage rate for first-time test takers

Hamline University

- 1536 Hewitt Avenue, St. Paul, MN, 55104-1284
- http://www.hamline.edu/law
- Private
- Year founded: 1973
- 2009-2010 tuition: full-time: $32,014; part-time: $23,078
- Enrollment 2009-10 academic year: full-time: 468; part-time: 182
- U.S. News 2010 law specialty ranking: dispute resolution: 2, health-care law: 18

3.27-3.68 GPA, 25TH-75TH PERCENTILE

151-159 LSAT, 25TH-75TH PERCENTILE

47% ACCEPTANCE RATE

Tier 4 2011 U.S. NEWS LAW SCHOOL RANKING

ADMISSIONS

Admissions phone number: **(651) 523-2461**
Admissions email address: **lawadm@hamline.edu**
Application website:
http://law.hamline.edu/admissions/application-require-ments-and-procedures.html
Application deadline for Fall 2011 admission: **1-Apr**

Admissions statistics:

Number of applicants for Fall 2009: **1,331**
Number of acceptances: **628**
Number enrolled: **147**
Acceptance rate: **47%**
GPA, 25th-75th percentile, entering class Fall 2009: **3.27-3.68**
LSAT, 25th-75th percentile, entering class Fall 2009: **151-159**

Part-time program:

Number of applicants for Fall 2009: **175**
Number of acceptances: **116**
Number enrolled: **60**
Acceptance rate: **66%**
GPA, 25th-75th percentile, entering class Fall 2009: **2.95-3.51**
LSAT, 25th-75th percentile, entering class Fall 2009: **147-155**

FINANCIAL AID

Financial aid phone number: **(651) 523-3000**
Financial aid application deadline: **1-Apr**
Tuition 2009-2010 academic year: **full-time: $32,014; part-time: $23,078**
Room and board: **$15,360** ; books: **$1,200** ; miscellaneous expenses: **N/A**
Total of room/board/books/miscellaneous expenses: **$16,560**
University offers graduate student housing for which law students are eligible.

Financial aid profile

Percent of students that received grants for the 2008-2009 academic year: full-time: **59%**; part-time **34%**
Median grant amount: full-time: **$18,058** ; part-time: **$10,834**
The average law-school debt of those in the Class of 2009 who borrowed: **$92,794** . Proportion who borrowed: **83%**

ACADEMIC PROGRAMS

Calendar: **semester**
Joint degrees awarded: **J.D./M.A.P.A.; J.D./M.A.O.L.; J.D./M.A.M.; J.D./M.A.N.M.; J.D./M.F.A; J.D./M.B.A**
Typical first-year section size: Full-time: **58**; Part-time: **46**
Is there typically a "small section" of the first year class, other than Legal Writing, taught by full-time faculty?: Full-time: **no**; Part-time: **no**
Number of course titles, beyond the first year curriculum, offered last year: **134**
Percentages of upper division course sections, excluding seminars, with an enrollment of:

Under 25: **57%**	25 to 49: **33%**	
50 to 74: **9%**	75 to 99: **1%**	
100+: **N/A**		

Areas of specialization: appellate advocacy, clinical training, dispute resolution, environmental law, health care law, intellectual property law, international law, tax law, trial advocacy

Fall 2009 faculty profile

Total teaching faculty: **80**. Full-time: **44%**; **57%** men, **43%** women, **17%** minorities. Part-time: **56%**; **56%** men, **44%** women, **2%** minorities
Student-to-faculty ratio: **14.8**

SPECIAL PROGRAMS *(as provided by law school)*:

Hamline offers 11 clinics, 6 study abroad programs, & externships in 8 substantive fields. Hamline is home to the nationally recognized Dispute Resolution Institute & the Health Law Institute, offering courses, research opportunities, & other programming for students & the community. Joint degree/dual degree options are available in business, management, and a new JD/MFA.

STUDENT BODY

Fall 2009 full-time enrollment: 468

Men: 45%	Women: 55%
African-American: 3.60%	American Indian: 0.20%
Asian-American: 5.30%	Mexican-American: 0.00%
Puerto Rican: 0.00%	Other Hisp-Amer: 3.00%
White: 76.10%	International: 1.30%
Unknown: 10.50%	

Fall 2009 part-time enrollment: 182

Men: 51%	Women: 49%
African-American: 2.70%	American Indian: 2.20%
Asian-American: 3.80%	Mexican-American: 0.00%
Puerto Rican: 0.00%	Other Hisp-Amer: 6.60%
White: 75.80%	International: 0.50%
Unknown: 8.20%	

Attrition rates for 2008-2009 full-time students
Percent of students discontinuing law school:

Men: 4%	Women: 4%
First-year students: 10%	Second-year students: 2%
Third-year students: 0%	Fourth-year students: N/A

LIBRARY RESOURCES

Total titles: 164,899
Total volumes: 285,374
Total seats available for library users: 335

INFORMATION TECHNOLOGY

Number of wired network connections available to students: 506 total (in the law library, excluding computer labs: 42; in classrooms: 457; in computer labs: 0; elsewhere in the law school: 7)
Law school has a wireless network.
Students are required to own a computer.

EMPLOYMENT AND SALARIES

Proportion of 2008 graduates employed at graduation: N/A
Employed 9 months later, as of February 15, 2009: 90%
Salaries in the private sector (law firms, business, industry): $65,000 –$160,000 (25th-75th percentile)
Median salary in the private sector: $110,000
Percentage in the private sector who reported salary information: 45%
Median salary in public service (government, judicial clerkships, academic posts, non-profits): $50,000

Percentage of 2008 graduates in:

Law firms: 41%	Government: 8%
Bus./industry: 27%	Judicial clerkship: 15%
Public interest: 7%	Unknown: 1%
Academia : 1%	

2008 graduates employed in-state: 74%
2008 graduates employed in foreign countries: 1%
Number of states where graduates are employed: 18
Percentage of 2008 graduates working in: New England: 0%, Middle Atlantic: 2%, East North Central: 12%, West North Central: 76%, South Atlantic: 2%, East South Central: 0%, West South Central: 1%, Mountain: 6%, Pacific: 1%, Unknown: 1%

BAR PASSAGE RATES

Based on 2008 graduates taking Summer 2008 or Winter 2009 exams. Most of the school's first-time test takers took the bar in Minnesota.

93%
School's bar passage rate for first-time test takers

91%
Statewide bar passage rate for first-time test takers

Harvard University

- 1563 Massachusetts Avenue, Cambridge, MA, 2138
- http://www.law.harvard.edu
- Private
- Year founded: 1817
- 2009-2010 tuition: full-time: $43,900; part-time: N/A
- Enrollment 2009-10 academic year: full-time: 1,771
- U.S. News 2010 law specialty ranking: clinical training: 20, dispute resolution: 4, healthcare law: 13, intellectual property law: 11, international law: 4, tax law: 8

3.76-3.96 GPA, 25TH-75TH PERCENTILE

171-176 LSAT, 25TH-75TH PERCENTILE

11% ACCEPTANCE RATE

2 2011 U.S. NEWS LAW SCHOOL RANKING

ADMISSIONS

Admissions phone number: **(617) 495-3109**
Admissions email address: **jdadmiss@law.harvard.edu**
Application website:
  http://www.law.harvard.edu/Admissions/JD/apply.php
Application deadline for Fall 2011 admission: **1-Feb**

Admissions statistics:

Number of applicants for Fall 2009: **7,391**
Number of acceptances: **833**
Number enrolled: **559**
Acceptance rate: **11%**
GPA, 25th-75th percentile, entering class Fall 2009: **3.76-3.96**
LSAT, 25th-75th percentile, entering class Fall 2009: **171-176**

FINANCIAL AID

Financial aid phone number: **(617) 495-4606**
Financial aid application deadline: **1-Apr**
Tuition 2009-2010 academic year: **full-time: $43,900; part-time: N/A**
Room and board: **$18,457** ; books: **$1,100** ; miscellaneous expenses: **$3,317**
Total of room/board/books/miscellaneous expenses: **$22,874**
University offers graduate student housing for which law students are eligible.

Financial aid profile

Percent of students that received grants for the 2008-2009 academic year: full-time: **46%**
Median grant amount: full-time: **$15,490**
The average law-school debt of those in the Class of 2009 who borrowed: **$113,432** . Proportion who borrowed: **81%**

ACADEMIC PROGRAMS

Calendar: **semester**
Joint degrees awarded: **J.D./M.B.A.; J.D./M.P.P.; J.D./M.A.L.D.; J.D./Ph.D.; J.D./M.P.H.; J.D./M.U.P.; J.D./LL.M.**

Typical first-year section size: Full-time: **80**
Is there typically a "small section" of the first year class, other than Legal Writing, taught by full-time faculty?: Full-time: **no**
Number of course titles, beyond the first year curriculum, offered last year: **N/A**
Percentages of upper division course sections, excluding seminars, with an enrollment of:
  Under 25: **47%**   25 to 49: **27%**
  50 to 74: **16%**   75 to 99: **4%**
  100+: **6%**
Areas of specialization: appellate advocacy, clinical training, dispute resolution, environmental law, health care law, intellectual property law, international law, tax law, trial advocacy

Fall 2009 faculty profile

Total teaching faculty: **105**. Full-time: **100%**; **79%** men, **21%** women, **11%** minorities. Part-time: **N/A**; **N/A** men, **N/A** women, **N/A** minorities
Student-to-faculty ratio: **11**

SPECIAL PROGRAMS (as provided by law school):

Harvard Law School is the world's premier center for legal education and research. At the center of the HLS experience is learning from and working with teachers who shape the landscape of the law. Each year, HLS offers more than 200 seminars and classes with fewer than 25 students, an extensive clinical program, study abroad, joint degree programs, and is home to more than 15 research centers.

STUDENT BODY

Fall 2009 full-time enrollment: 1,771

Men: **53%**   Women: **47%**
African-American: **11.50%**   American Indian: **0.60%**
Asian-American: **10.60%**   Mexican-American: **1.60%**
Puerto Rican: **0.60%**   Other Hisp-Amer: **4.40%**
White: **53.50%**   International: **2.00%**
Unknown: **15.20%**

Attrition rates for 2008-2009 full-time students

Percent of students discontinuing law school:

Men: **N/A**   Women: **N/A**

First-year students: **N/A**   Second-year students: **N/A**

Third-year students: **N/A**   Fourth-year students: **N/A**

LIBRARY RESOURCES

Total titles: **882,895**

Total volumes: **2,312,217**

Total seats available for library users: **802**

INFORMATION TECHNOLOGY

Number of wired network connections available to students: **2750** total (in the law library, excluding computer labs: **1,000**; in classrooms: **800**; in computer labs: **100**; elsewhere in the law school: **850**)

Law school has a wireless network.

Students are not required to own a computer.

EMPLOYMENT AND SALARIES

Proportion of 2008 graduates employed at graduation: **97%**

Employed 9 months later, as of February 15, 2009: **99%**

Salaries in the private sector (law firms, business, industry): **$160,000** – **$160,000** (25th-75th percentile)

Median salary in the private sector: **$160,000**

Percentage in the private sector who reported salary information: **N/A**

Median salary in public service (government, judicial clerkships, academic posts, non-profits): **$55,000**

Percentage of 2008 graduates in:

Law firms: **66%**   Government: **4%**

Bus./industry: **4%**   Judicial clerkship: **19%**

Public interest: **6%**   Unknown: **0%**

Academia : **1%**

2008 graduates employed in-state: **11%**

2008 graduates employed in foreign countries: **4%**

Number of states where graduates are employed: **35**

Percentage of 2008 graduates working in: New England: **12%**, Middle Atlantic: **33%**, East North Central: **7%**, West North Central: **1%**, South Atlantic: **18%**, East South Central: **1%**, West South Central: **4%**, Mountain: **2%**, Pacific: **17%**, Unknown: **0%**

BAR PASSAGE RATES

Based on 2008 graduates taking Summer 2008 or Winter 2009 exams. Most of the school's first-time test takers took the bar in New York.

98%

School's bar passage rate for first-time test takers

81%

Statewide bar passage rate for first-time test takers

Hofstra University

- 121 Hofstra University, Hempstead, NY, 11549
- http://law.hofstra.edu
- Private
- Year founded: 1970
- 2009-2010 tuition: full-time: $41,780; part-time: $31,259
- Enrollment 2009-10 academic year: full-time: 939; part-time: 170
- U.S. News 2010 law specialty ranking: N/A

3.27-3.70 GPA, 25TH-75TH PERCENTILE

155-159 LSAT, 25TH-75TH PERCENTILE

41% ACCEPTANCE RATE

86 2011 U.S. NEWS LAW SCHOOL RANKING

ADMISSIONS

Admissions phone number: **(516) 463-5916**
Admissions email address: **lawadmissions@hofstra.edu**
Application website:
   https://law.hofstra.edu/pdf/apply_jd_application.pdf
Application deadline for Fall 2011 admission: **15-Apr**

Admissions statistics:

Number of applicants for Fall 2009: **4,573**
Number of acceptances: **1,853**
Number enrolled: **391**
Acceptance rate: **41%**
GPA, 25th-75th percentile, entering class Fall 2009: **3.27-3.70**
LSAT, 25th-75th percentile, entering class Fall 2009: **155-159**

Part-time program:

Number of applicants for Fall 2009: **328**
Number of acceptances: **38**
Number enrolled: **10**
Acceptance rate: **12%**
GPA, 25th-75th percentile, entering class Fall 2009: **3.08-3.67**
LSAT, 25th-75th percentile, entering class Fall 2009: **152-158**

FINANCIAL AID

Financial aid phone number: **(516) 463-5929**
Financial aid application deadline: **1-Apr**
Tuition 2009-2010 academic year: **full-time: $41,780; part-time: $31,259**
Room and board: **$13,772** ; books: **$1,400** ; miscellaneous expenses: **$5,401**
Total of room/board/books/miscellaneous expenses: **$20,573**
University offers graduate student housing for which law students are eligible.

Financial aid profile

Percent of students that received grants for the 2008-2009 academic year: full-time: **42%**; part-time **26%**
Median grant amount: full-time: **$16,000** ; part-time: **$12,000**
The average law-school debt of those in the Class of 2009 who borrowed: **$114,154** . Proportion who borrowed: **78%**

ACADEMIC PROGRAMS

Calendar: **semester**
Joint degrees awarded: **J.D./M.B.A.; J.D./M.A. in Applied Social Research**
Typical first-year section size: Full-time: **97**; Part-time: **81**
Is there typically a "small section" of the first year class, other than Legal Writing, taught by full-time faculty?: Full-time: **yes**; Part-time: **yes**
Number of course titles, beyond the first year curriculum, offered last year: **131**
Percentages of upper division course sections, excluding seminars, with an enrollment of:
   Under 25: **48%**   25 to 49: **31%**
   50 to 74: **7%**   75 to 99: **11%**
   100+: **2%**
Areas of specialization: appellate advocacy, clinical training, dispute resolution, environmental law, health care law, intellectual property law, international law, tax law, trial advocacy

Fall 2009 faculty profile

Total teaching faculty: **99**. Full-time: **61%**; **72%** men, **28%** women, **17%** minorities. Part-time: **39%**; **90%** men, **10%** women, **18%** minorities
Student-to-faculty ratio: **15.4**

SPECIAL PROGRAMS (as provided by law school):

Fellowships in Child and Family Advocacy, LGBT Rights and Health Law; 7 clinics (Criminal Justice, Child Advocacy, Community & Econ. Development, Asylum, Securities Arbitration, Law Reform Advocacy and Mediation); summer programs in Germany, Italy and Australia; winter program in Curacao, Dutch Antilles; Summer Skills Institute; advanced degree programs in international and family law.

STUDENT BODY

Fall 2009 full-time enrollment: 939

Men: **50%**	Women: **50%**
African-American: **7.30%**	American Indian: **0.40%**
Asian-American: **9.80%**	Mexican-American: **0.90%**
Puerto Rican: **1.20%**	Other Hisp-Amer: **6.10%**
White: **64.50%**	International: **3.30%**
Unknown: **6.50%**	

Fall 2009 part-time enrollment: **170**

Men: **56%**	Women: **44%**
African-American: **13.50%**	American Indian: **0.00%**
Asian-American: **10.00%**	Mexican-American: **0.00%**
Puerto Rican: **2.40%**	Other Hisp-Amer: **7.60%**
White: **54.70%**	International: **1.20%**
Unknown: **10.60%**	

Attrition rates for 2008-2009 full-time students
Percent of students discontinuing law school:

Men: **5%**	Women: **5%**
First-year students: **15%**	Second-year students: **1%**
Third-year students: **0%**	Fourth-year students: **N/A**

LIBRARY RESOURCES

Total titles: **171,329**
Total volumes: **583,435**
Total seats available for library users: **490**

INFORMATION TECHNOLOGY

Number of wired network connections available to students: **170** total (in the law library, excluding computer labs: **120**; in classrooms: **40**; in computer labs: **0**; elsewhere in the law school: **10**)
Law school has a wireless network.
Students are not required to own a computer.

EMPLOYMENT AND SALARIES

Proportion of 2008 graduates employed at graduation:
N/A
Employed 9 months later, as of February 15, 2009: **96%**
Salaries in the private sector (law firms, business, industry): **$67,500 –$160,000** (25th-75th percentile)
Median salary in the private sector: **$160,000**
Percentage in the private sector who reported salary information: **29%**
Median salary in public service (government, judicial clerkships, academic posts, non-profits): **$52,000**

Percentage of 2008 graduates in:

Law firms: **48%**	Government: **13%**
Bus./industry: **26%**	Judicial clerkship: **6%**
Public interest: **3%**	Unknown: **1%**
Academia : **3%**	

2008 graduates employed in-state: **84%**
2008 graduates employed in foreign countries: **0%**
Number of states where graduates are employed: **18**
Percentage of 2008 graduates working in: New England: **1%**, Middle Atlantic: **88%**, East North Central: **0%**, West North Central: **0%**, South Atlantic: **4%**, East South Central: **0%**, West South Central: **1%**, Mountain: **0%**, Pacific: **3%**, Unknown: **2%**

BAR PASSAGE RATES

Based on 2008 graduates taking Summer 2008 or Winter 2009 exams. Most of the school's first-time test takers took the bar in New York.

87%
School's bar passage rate for first-time test takers

81%
Statewide bar passage rate for first-time test takers

Howard University

- 2900 Van Ness Street NW, Washington, DC, 20008
- http://www.law.howard.edu
- Private
- Year founded: 1869
- 2009-2010 tuition: full-time: $24,490; part-time: N/A
- Enrollment 2009-10 academic year: full-time: 468
- U.S. News 2010 law specialty ranking: N/A

2.92-3.51 GPA, 25TH-75TH PERCENTILE

150-156 LSAT, 25TH-75TH PERCENTILE

21% ACCEPTANCE RATE

Tier 3 2011 U.S. NEWS LAW SCHOOL RANKING

ADMISSIONS

Admissions phone number: (202) 806-8009
Admissions email address: admissions@law.howard.edu
Application website: http://www.law.howard.edu/660
Application deadline for Fall 2011 admission: 15-Mar

Admissions statistics:
Number of applicants for Fall 2009: 2,132
Number of acceptances: 443
Number enrolled: 160
Acceptance rate: 21%
GPA, 25th-75th percentile, entering class Fall 2009: 2.92-3.51
LSAT, 25th-75th percentile, entering class Fall 2009: 150-156

FINANCIAL AID

Financial aid phone number: (202) 806-8005
Financial aid application deadline: 15-Feb
Tuition 2009-2010 academic year: **full-time: $24,490; part-time: N/A**
Room and board: **$13,247** ; books: **$2,000** ; miscellaneous expenses: **$6,494**
Total of room/board/books/miscellaneous expenses: **$21,741**
University offers graduate student housing for which law students are eligible.

Financial aid profile
Percent of students that received grants for the 2008-2009 academic year: full-time: **54%**
Median grant amount: full-time: **$10,000**
The average law-school debt of those in the Class of 2009 who borrowed: **$104,787** . Proportion who borrowed: **92%**

ACADEMIC PROGRAMS

Calendar: **semester**
Joint degrees awarded: **J.D./M.B.A.**
Typical first-year section size: Full-time: **50**
Is there typically a "small section" of the first year class, other than Legal Writing, taught by full-time faculty?: Full-time: **no**
Number of course titles, beyond the first year curriculum, offered last year: **120**
Percentages of upper division course sections, excluding seminars, with an enrollment of:
Under 25: **69%**   25 to 49: **19%**
50 to 74: **12%**   75 to 99: **0%**
100+: **0%**
Areas of specialization: appellate advocacy, clinical training, dispute resolution, environmental law, health care law, intellectual property law, international law, tax law, trial advocacy

Fall 2009 faculty profile
Total teaching faculty: **76**. Full-time: **38%**; **52%** men, **48%** women, **90%** minorities. Part-time: **62%**; **60%** men, **40%** women, **62%** minorities
Student-to-faculty ratio: **16.5**

SPECIAL PROGRAMS *(as provided by law school):*
The Clinical Law Center (CLC) offers students the opportunity to gain professional skills training and practical lawyering experiences in Criminal Justice, Fair Housing, Alternative Dispute Resolution, Civil Rights, and a civil clinic. There are many externships that permit students to work for credit, a pro bono honors program, South African Summer Aboard Program, and a J.D./M.B.A. degree program.

STUDENT BODY
Fall 2009 full-time enrollment: 468
Men: **39%**   Women: **61%**
African-American: **78.20%**   American Indian: **1.10%**
Asian-American: **5.10%**   Mexican-American: **0.60%**
Puerto Rican: **0.90%**   Other Hisp-Amer: **1.30%**
White: **6.20%**   International: **5.30%**
Unknown: **1.30%**

Attrition rates for 2008-2009 full-time students
Percent of students discontinuing law school:
Men: **5%**   Women: **4%**

First-year students: **8%**   Second-year students: **4%**
Third-year students: **1%**   Fourth-year students: **N/A**

LIBRARY RESOURCES
Total titles: **32,858**
Total volumes: **632,218**
Total seats available for library users: **374**

INFORMATION TECHNOLOGY
Number of wired network connections available to students: **607** total (in the law library, excluding computer labs: **319**; in classrooms: **145**; in computer labs: **78**; elsewhere in the law school: **65**)
Law school has a wireless network.
Students are required to own a computer.

EMPLOYMENT AND SALARIES
Proportion of 2008 graduates employed at graduation: **72%**
Employed 9 months later, as of February 15, 2009: **86%**
Salaries in the private sector (law firms, business, industry): **$105,000 –$160,000** (25th-75th percentile)
Median salary in the private sector: **$160,000**
Percentage in the private sector who reported salary information: **60%**
Median salary in public service (government, judicial clerkships, academic posts, non-profits): **$52,000**

Percentage of 2008 graduates in:
Law firms: **50%**   Government: **16%**
Bus./industry: **10%**   Judicial clerkship: **16%**
Public interest: **3%**   Unknown: **5%**
Academia : **0%**

2008 graduates employed in-state: **36%**
2008 graduates employed in foreign countries: **0%**
Number of states where graduates are employed: **21**
Percentage of 2008 graduates working in: New England: **2%**, Middle Atlantic: **23%**, East North Central: **4%**, West North Central: **2%**, South Atlantic: **61%**, East South Central: **1%**, West South Central: **2%**, Mountain: **2%**, Pacific: **5%**, Unknown: **0%**

BAR PASSAGE RATES
Based on 2008 graduates taking Summer 2008 or Winter 2009 exams. Most of the school's first-time test takers took the bar in Maryland.

64%
School's bar passage rate for first-time test takers

85%
Statewide bar passage rate for first-time test takers

Illinois Institute of Technology

- 565 W. Adams Street, Chicago, IL, 60661-3691
- http://www.kentlaw.edu/
- Private
- Year founded: 1888
- 2009-2010 tuition: full-time: $38,152; part-time: $27,910
- Enrollment 2009-10 academic year: full-time: 769; part-time: 179
- U.S. News 2010 law specialty ranking: intellectual property law: 23, trial advocacy: 7

3.21-3.69 GPA, 25TH-75TH PERCENTILE

157-163 LSAT, 25TH-75TH PERCENTILE

44% ACCEPTANCE RATE

80 2011 U.S. NEWS LAW SCHOOL RANKING

ADMISSIONS

Admissions phone number: (312) 906-5020
Admissions email address: **admit@kentlaw.edu**
Application website:
  https://www.kentlaw.edu/admissions/jd_application.html
Application deadline for Fall 2011 admission: **1-Mar**

Admissions statistics:

Number of applicants for Fall 2009: **3,141**
Number of acceptances: **1,383**
Number enrolled: **246**
Acceptance rate: **44%**
GPA, 25th-75th percentile, entering class Fall 2009: **3.21-3.69**
LSAT, 25th-75th percentile, entering class Fall 2009: **157-163**

Part-time program:

Number of applicants for Fall 2009: **348**
Number of acceptances: **133**
Number enrolled: **52**
Acceptance rate: **38%**
GPA, 25th-75th percentile, entering class Fall 2009: **2.96-3.59**
LSAT, 25th-75th percentile, entering class Fall 2009: **155-160**

FINANCIAL AID

Financial aid phone number: (312) 906-5180
Financial aid application deadline: **15-Mar**
Tuition 2009-2010 academic year: **full-time: $38,152; part-time: $27,910**
Room and board: **$14,400** ; books: **$1,200** ; miscellaneous expenses: **$4,509**
Total of room/board/books/miscellaneous expenses: **$20,109**
University offers graduate student housing for which law students are eligible.

Financial aid profile

Percent of students that received grants for the 2008-2009 academic year: full-time: **60%**; part-time **58%**
Median grant amount: full-time: **$20,000** ; part-time: **$5,000**
The average law-school debt of those in the Class of 2009 who borrowed: **$85,503** . Proportion who borrowed: **90%**

ACADEMIC PROGRAMS

Calendar: **semester**
Joint degrees awarded: **J.D./M.B.A.; J.D./LL.M. Taxation; J.D./M.S. Financial Markets; J.D./LL.M. Financial Services Law; J.D./M.S. Environmental Management; J.D./M.P.A.; J.D./M.P.H.; JD/LL.M. Family Law**
Typical first-year section size: Full-time: **54**; Part-time: **54**
Is there typically a "small section" of the first year class, other than Legal Writing, taught by full-time faculty?: Full-time: **no**; Part-time: **no**
Number of course titles, beyond the first year curriculum, offered last year: **145**
Percentages of upper division course sections, excluding seminars, with an enrollment of:

Under 25: **74%**	25 to 49: **19%**
50 to 74: **4%**	75 to 99: **2%**
100+: **1%**	

Areas of specialization: appellate advocacy, clinical training, dispute resolution, environmental law, health care law, intellectual property law, international law, tax law, trial advocacy

Fall 2009 faculty profile

Total teaching faculty: **152**. Full-time: **43%**; **62%** men, **38%** women, **14%** minorities. Part-time: **57%**; **79%** men, **21%** women, **7%** minorities
Student-to-faculty ratio: **10.9**

SPECIAL PROGRAMS (as provided by law school):

Clinical: Criminal, Employment, Family, Health/Disability, IP, Immigration, Low Inc Taxpayer, Meditation/ADR, Business Transactions, Open Government, Legal and Judicial Externships. Certificates: IP, Criminal Litigation, Labor/Empl,

Intl/Comparative, Environmental, Public Int, Litigation/ADR.
Centers/Institutes: Law & Human, Law & Workplace, Science.
Study Abroad: 12 partner law schools.

STUDENT BODY

Fall 2009 full-time enrollment: 769

Men: 54%	Women: 46%
African-American: 4.90%	American Indian: 0.40%
Asian-American: 8.70%	Mexican-American: 0.90%
Puerto Rican: 0.50%	Other Hisp-Amer: 3.10%
White: 70.10%	International: 2.30%
Unknown: 9.00%	

Fall 2009 part-time enrollment: 179

Men: 56%	Women: 44%
African-American: 6.10%	American Indian: 0.00%
Asian-American: 11.70%	Mexican-American: 1.10%
Puerto Rican: 0.60%	Other Hisp-Amer: 2.20%
White: 64.20%	International: 3.40%
Unknown: 10.60%	

Attrition rates for 2008-2009 full-time students
Percent of students discontinuing law school:

Men: 1%	Women: 2%
First-year students: 3%	Second-year students: 2%
Third-year students: N/A	Fourth-year students: N/A

LIBRARY RESOURCES

Total titles: 192,150
Total volumes: 558,433
Total seats available for library users: 459

INFORMATION TECHNOLOGY

Number of wired network connections available to students: 1800 total (in the law library, excluding computer labs: 175; in classrooms: 1,048; in computer labs: 62; elsewhere in the law school: 515)
Law school has a wireless network.
Students are required to own a computer.

EMPLOYMENT AND SALARIES

Proportion of 2008 graduates employed at graduation: 71%
Employed 9 months later, as of February 15, 2009: 90%
Salaries in the private sector (law firms, business, industry): $60,000 –$160,000 (25th-75th percentile)
Median salary in the private sector: $100,000
Percentage in the private sector who reported salary information: 59%
Median salary in public service (government, judicial clerkships, academic posts, non-profits): $55,339

Percentage of 2008 graduates in:

Law firms: 55%	Government: 13%
Bus./industry: 17%	Judicial clerkship: 5%
Public interest: 8%	Unknown: N/A
Academia : 2%	

2008 graduates employed in-state: 80%
2008 graduates employed in foreign countries: 0%
Number of states where graduates are employed: 23
Percentage of 2008 graduates working in: New England: N/A, Middle Atlantic: 1%, East North Central: 85%, West North Central: 2%, South Atlantic: 7%, East South Central: 0%, West South Central: 2%, Mountain: 0%, Pacific: 2%, Unknown: N/A

BAR PASSAGE RATES

Based on 2008 graduates taking Summer 2008 or Winter 2009 exams. Most of the school's first-time test takers took the bar in Illinois.

96%
School's bar passage rate for first-time test takers

91%
Statewide bar passage rate for first-time test takers

Indiana University–Bloomington

- 211 S. Indiana Avenue, Bloomington, IN, 47405-1001
- http://www.law.indiana.edu
- Public
- Year founded: 1842
- 2009-2010 tuition: full-time: $24,891; part-time: N/A
- Enrollment 2009-10 academic year: full-time: 620
- U.S. News 2010 law specialty ranking: healthcare law: 19

3.26-3.83 GPA, 25TH-75TH PERCENTILE

156-165 LSAT, 25TH-75TH PERCENTILE

32% ACCEPTANCE RATE

27 2011 U.S. NEWS LAW SCHOOL RANKING

ADMISSIONS

Admissions phone number: **(812) 855-4765**
Admissions email address: **lawadmis@indiana.edu**
Application website:
  http://www.law.indiana.edu/degrees/jd/apply/index.sht
  ml
Application deadline for Fall 2011 admission: **rolling**

Admissions statistics:

Number of applicants for Fall 2009: **2,524**
Number of acceptances: **805**
Number enrolled: **220**
Acceptance rate: **32%**
GPA, 25th-75th percentile, entering class Fall 2009: **3.26-3.83**
LSAT, 25th-75th percentile, entering class Fall 2009: **156-165**

FINANCIAL AID

Financial aid phone number: **(812) 855-7746**
Financial aid application deadline: **1-Mar**
Tuition 2009-2010 academic year: **full-time: $24,891; part-time: N/A**
Room and board: **$9,407** ; books: **$1,800** ; miscellaneous expenses: **$4,709**
Total of room/board/books/miscellaneous expenses: **$15,916**
University offers graduate student housing for which law students are eligible.

Financial aid profile

Percent of students that received grants for the 2008-2009 academic year: full-time: **77%**
Median grant amount: full-time: **$12,000**
The average law-school debt of those in the Class of 2009 who borrowed: **$91,142** . Proportion who borrowed: **92%**

ACADEMIC PROGRAMS

Calendar: **semester**
Joint degrees awarded: **J.D./M.P.A. Public Affairs; J.D./M.P.A. Accounting; J.D./M.A. Telecommunications;**
J.D./M.B.A.; J.D./M.L.S.; Ph.D. Law & Social Science; J.D./M.S.E.S. Pub./Environmental Affairs; J.D./M.A. Journalism
Typical first-year section size: Full-time: **72**
Is there typically a "small section" of the first year class, other than Legal Writing, taught by full-time faculty?: Full-time: **no**
Number of course titles, beyond the first year curriculum, offered last year: **138**
Percentages of upper division course sections, excluding seminars, with an enrollment of:
  Under 25: **68%**   25 to 49: **18%**
  50 to 74: **8%**   75 to 99: **5%**
  100+: **2%**
Areas of specialization: appellate advocacy, clinical training, dispute resolution, environmental law, health care law, intellectual property law, international law, tax law, trial advocacy

Fall 2009 faculty profile

Total teaching faculty: **69**. Full-time: **80%**; **71%** men, **29%** women, **15%** minorities. Part-time: **20%**; **93%** men, **7%** women, **0%** minorities
Student-to-faculty ratio: **9.5**

SPECIAL PROGRAMS *(as provided by law school)*:

Joint degrees are offered in business, public affairs, journalism, communications, and library science; special joint degrees may be arranged. Clinics include family law, mediation, business law, environmental law, criminal law, elder law, and disability law. Study abroad in Poland, Germany, France, Spain, England, Hong Kong, China, or New Zealand. Summer start is available.

STUDENT BODY

Fall 2009 full-time enrollment: 620

Men: **59%**	Women: **41%**
African-American: **7.40%**	American Indian: **0.00%**
Asian-American: **6.00%**	Mexican-American: **4.70%**
Puerto Rican: **0.00%**	Other Hisp-Amer: **0.00%**
White: **81.30%**	International: **0.00%**
Unknown: **0.60%**	

Attrition rates for 2008-2009 full-time students
Percent of students discontinuing law school:

Men: **2%**	Women: **2%**
First-year students: **5%**	Second-year students: **N/A**
Third-year students: **N/A**	Fourth-year students: **N/A**

LIBRARY RESOURCES

Total titles: **284,772**
Total volumes: **768,164**
Total seats available for library users: **684**

INFORMATION TECHNOLOGY

Number of wired network connections available to students: **164** total (in the law library, excluding computer labs: **149**; in classrooms: **15**; in computer labs: **0**; elsewhere in the law school: **0**)
Law school has a wireless network.
Students are required to own a computer.

EMPLOYMENT AND SALARIES

Proportion of 2008 graduates employed at graduation: **89%**
Employed 9 months later, as of February 15, 2009: **96%**
Salaries in the private sector (law firms, business, industry): **$71,000 –$107,500** (25th-75th percentile)
Median salary in the private sector: **$97,000**
Percentage in the private sector who reported salary information: **62%**

Median salary in public service (government, judicial clerkships, academic posts, non-profits): **$55,000**

Percentage of 2008 graduates in:

Law firms: **45%**	Government: **17%**
Bus./industry: **17%**	Judicial clerkship: **11%**
Public interest: **6%**	Unknown: **0%**
Academia : **4%**	

2008 graduates employed in-state: **32%**
2008 graduates employed in foreign countries: **1%**
Number of states where graduates are employed: **31**
Percentage of 2008 graduates working in: New England: **3%**, Middle Atlantic: **2%**, East North Central: **50%**, West North Central: **2%**, South Atlantic: **19%**, East South Central: **6%**, West South Central: **2%**, Mountain: **3%**, Pacific: **10%**, Unknown: **2%**

BAR PASSAGE RATES

Based on 2008 graduates taking Summer 2008 or Winter 2009 exams. Most of the school's first-time test takers took the bar in Indiana.

95%
School's bar passage rate for first-time test takers

84%
Statewide bar passage rate for first-time test takers

Indiana University–Indianapolis

- 530 W. New York Street, Indianapolis, IN, 46202-3225
- http://www.indylaw.indiana.edu
- Public
- Year founded: 1894
- 2009-2010 tuition: full-time: $18,163; part-time: $14,065
- Enrollment 2009-10 academic year: full-time: 625; part-time: 319
- U.S. News 2010 law specialty ranking: healthcare law: 11

3.23-3.73 GPA, 25TH-75TH PERCENTILE

154-160 LSAT, 25TH-75TH PERCENTILE

38% ACCEPTANCE RATE

86 2011 U.S. NEWS LAW SCHOOL RANKING

ADMISSIONS

Admissions phone number: (317) 274-2459
Admissions email address: pkkinney@iupui.edu
Application website:
  http://www.indylaw.indiana.edu/admissions/app.htm
Application deadline for Fall 2011 admission: 1-Mar

Admissions statistics:
Number of applicants for Fall 2009: 1,513
Number of acceptances: 570
Number enrolled: 195
Acceptance rate: 38%
GPA, 25th-75th percentile, entering class Fall 2009: 3.23-3.73
LSAT, 25th-75th percentile, entering class Fall 2009: 154-160

Part-time program:
Number of applicants for Fall 2009: 253
Number of acceptances: 140
Number enrolled: 102
Acceptance rate: 55%
GPA, 25th-75th percentile, entering class Fall 2009: 3.04-3.56
LSAT, 25th-75th percentile, entering class Fall 2009: 147-155

FINANCIAL AID

Financial aid phone number: (317) 278-2862
Financial aid application deadline: 10-Mar
Tuition 2009-2010 academic year: full-time: $18,163; part-time: $14,065
Room and board: $11,296 ; books: $1,700 ; miscellaneous expenses: $8,128
Total of room/board/books/miscellaneous expenses: $21,124
University offers graduate student housing for which law students are eligible.

Financial aid profile
Percent of students that received grants for the 2008-2009 academic year: full-time: 47%; part-time 26%
Median grant amount: full-time: $5,000 ; part-time: $2,000
The average law-school debt of those in the Class of 2009 who borrowed: $80,718 . Proportion who borrowed: 87%

ACADEMIC PROGRAMS
Calendar: semester
Joint degrees awarded: J.D./M.B.A.; J.D./M.P.A.; J.D./M.H.A.; J.D./M.P.H.; J.D./M.L.S.; J.D./M.Phil; J.D./M.S.W.
Typical first-year section size: Full-time: 90; Part-time: 102
Is there typically a "small section" of the first year class, other than Legal Writing, taught by full-time faculty?: Full-time: no; Part-time: no
Number of course titles, beyond the first year curriculum, offered last year: 126
Percentages of upper division course sections, excluding seminars, with an enrollment of:

Under 25: 52%	25 to 49: 28%
50 to 74: 10%	75 to 99: 9%
100+: 1%	

Areas of specialization: appellate advocacy, clinical training, dispute resolution, environmental law, health care law, intellectual property law, international law, tax law, trial advocacy

Fall 2009 faculty profile
Total teaching faculty: 130. Full-time: 41%; 57% men, 43% women, 9% minorities. Part-time: 59%; 70% men, 30% women, 5% minorities
Student-to-faculty ratio: 17.7

SPECIAL PROGRAMS (as provided by law school):
IU School of Law–Indianapolis has three in-house clinics (Civil, Disability, and Criminal) each providing students with real-world experience under the supervision of faculty. We have the nationally recognized Hall Center for Law and Health, the Center for Intellectual Property Law and Innovation, the Center for International and Comparative Law and the Program in International Human Rights Law.

STUDENT BODY

Fall 2009 full-time enrollment: 625

Men: 55%	Women: 45%
African-American: 5.60%	American Indian: 0.20%
Asian-American: 4.50%	Mexican-American: 1.00%
Puerto Rican: 0.30%	Other Hisp-Amer: 1.80%
White: 81.80%	International: 5.00%
Unknown: 0.00%	

Fall 2009 part-time enrollment: 319

Men: 55%	Women: 45%
African-American: 11.30%	American Indian: 0.60%
Asian-American: 4.10%	Mexican-American: 0.30%
Puerto Rican: 0.90%	Other Hisp-Amer: 1.60%
White: 78.40%	International: 2.80%
Unknown: 0.00%	

Attrition rates for 2008-2009 full-time students

Percent of students discontinuing law school:

Men: 5%	Women: 3%
First-year students: 7%	Second-year students: 4%
Third-year students: N/A	Fourth-year students: N/A

LIBRARY RESOURCES

Total titles: 227,479
Total volumes: 609,151
Total seats available for library users: 470

INFORMATION TECHNOLOGY

Number of wired network connections available to students: 1140 total (in the law library, excluding computer labs: 325; in classrooms: 686; in computer labs: 0; elsewhere in the law school: 129)
Law school has a wireless network.
Students are not required to own a computer.

EMPLOYMENT AND SALARIES

Proportion of 2008 graduates employed at graduation: 72%
Employed 9 months later, as of February 15, 2009: 96%
Salaries in the private sector (law firms, business, industry): $52,000 –$100,000 (25th-75th percentile)
Median salary in the private sector: $80,500
Percentage in the private sector who reported salary information: 43%
Median salary in public service (government, judicial clerkships, academic posts, non-profits): $46,112

Percentage of 2008 graduates in:

Law firms: 53%	Government: 18%
Bus./industry: 19%	Judicial clerkship: 1%
Public interest: 5%	Unknown: 0%
Academia : 4%	

2008 graduates employed in-state: 80%
2008 graduates employed in foreign countries: 1%
Number of states where graduates are employed: 22
Percentage of 2008 graduates working in: New England: 0%, Middle Atlantic: 1%, East North Central: 90%, West North Central: 0%, South Atlantic: 3%, East South Central: 2%, West South Central: 2%, Mountain: 2%, Pacific: 1%, Unknown: 0%

BAR PASSAGE RATES

Based on 2008 graduates taking Summer 2008 or Winter 2009 exams. Most of the school's first-time test takers took the bar in Indiana.

84%

School's bar passage rate for first-time test takers

84%

Statewide bar passage rate for first-time test takers

John Marshall Law School

- 315 S. Plymouth Court, Chicago, IL, 60604
- http://www.jmls.edu
- Private
- Year founded: 1899
- 2009-2010 tuition: full-time: $35,380; part-time: $25,300
- Enrollment 2009-10 academic year: full-time: 1,038; part-time: 339
- U.S. News 2010 law specialty ranking: intellectual property law: 19

3.00-3.53 GPA, 25TH-75TH PERCENTILE

150-156 LSAT, 25TH-75TH PERCENTILE

49% ACCEPTANCE RATE

Tier 4 2011 U.S. NEWS LAW SCHOOL RANKING

ADMISSIONS

Admissions phone number: **(800) 537-4280**
Admissions email address: **admission@jmls.edu**
Application website:
  http://jmls.edu/admission/jdonlineapplicationbridgepage.shtml
Application deadline for Fall 2011 admission: **rolling**

Admissions statistics:
Number of applicants for Fall 2009: **2,738**
Number of acceptances: **1,328**
Number enrolled: **394**
Acceptance rate: **49%**
GPA, 25th-75th percentile, entering class Fall 2009: **3.00-3.53**
LSAT, 25th-75th percentile, entering class Fall 2009: **150-156**

Part-time program:
Number of applicants for Fall 2009: **617**
Number of acceptances: **225**
Number enrolled: **125**
Acceptance rate: **36%**
GPA, 25th-75th percentile, entering class Fall 2009: **2.88-3.44**
LSAT, 25th-75th percentile, entering class Fall 2009: **149-154**

FINANCIAL AID

Financial aid phone number: **(800) 537-4280**
Financial aid application deadline:
Tuition 2009-2010 academic year: **full-time: $35,380; part-time: $25,300**
Room and board: **$15,230** ; books: **$2,226** ; miscellaneous expenses: **$7,448**
Total of room/board/books/miscellaneous expenses: **$24,904**
University does not offer graduate student housing for which law students are eligible.

Financial aid profile
Percent of students that received grants for the 2008-2009 academic year: full-time: **52%**; part-time **37%**
Median grant amount: full-time: **$8,000** ; part-time: **$6,000**
The average law-school debt of those in the Class of 2009 who borrowed: **$124,015** . Proportion who borrowed: **59%**

ACADEMIC PROGRAMS
Calendar: **semester**
Joint degrees awarded: **J.D./M.B.A.; J.D./M.P.A.; J.D./M.A.; J.D./LL.M. Employee Benefits Law; J.D./LL.M. Intellectual Property Law; J.D./LL.M. Information Technology Law; J.D./LL.M. International Business/Trade ; J.D./LL.M. Real Estate Law; J.D./LL.M. Tax Law**
Typical first-year section size: Full-time: **75**; Part-time: **60**
Is there typically a "small section" of the first year class, other than Legal Writing, taught by full-time faculty?: Full-time: **no**; Part-time: **no**
Number of course titles, beyond the first year curriculum, offered last year: **270**
Percentages of upper division course sections, excluding seminars, with an enrollment of:

Under 25: **69%**	25 to 49: **17%**
50 to 74: **9%**	75 to 99: **4%**
100+: **0%**	

Areas of specialization: appellate advocacy, clinical training, dispute resolution, environmental law, health care law, intellectual property law, international law, tax law, trial advocacy

Fall 2009 faculty profile
Total teaching faculty: **183**. Full-time: **40%**; **64%** men, **36%** women, **15%** minorities. Part-time: **60%**; **70%** men, **30%** women, **9%** minorities
Student-to-faculty ratio: **14.4**

SPECIAL PROGRAMS (as provided by law school):
We offer the nation's only Fair Housing Legal Clinic (2009 marks its 16th year); a Veterans Legal Support Clinic; 17

externship programs (some in Washington, DC) in areas like tax, real estate, and immigration, with placements in enforcement agencies, public defender offices, and local government; a Czech student exchange; a summer program in China; and joint J.D./LL.M. degrees in six specialty areas.

STUDENT BODY

Fall 2009 full-time enrollment: 1,038

Men: 55%	Women: 45%
African-American: 6.20%	American Indian: 0.90%
Asian-American: 5.70%	Mexican-American: 2.70%
Puerto Rican: 0.80%	Other Hisp-Amer: 4.70%
White: 70.80%	International: 1.00%
Unknown: 7.30%	

Fall 2009 part-time enrollment: 339

Men: 52%	Women: 48%
African-American: 13.30%	American Indian: 0.90%
Asian-American: 5.30%	Mexican-American: 3.50%
Puerto Rican: 0.30%	Other Hisp-Amer: 4.70%
White: 63.70%	International: 1.50%
Unknown: 6.80%	

Attrition rates for 2008-2009 full-time students
Percent of students discontinuing law school:

Men: 2%	Women: 4%
First-year students: 7%	Second-year students: 2%
Third-year students: N/A	Fourth-year students: N/A

LIBRARY RESOURCES

Total titles: 99,008
Total volumes: 409,154
Total seats available for library users: 750

INFORMATION TECHNOLOGY

Number of wired network connections available to students: 0 total (in the law library, excluding computer labs: 0; in classrooms: 0; in computer labs: 0; elsewhere in the law school: 0)
Law school has a wireless network.
Students are not required to own a computer.

EMPLOYMENT AND SALARIES

Proportion of 2008 graduates employed at graduation: 64%
Employed 9 months later, as of February 15, 2009: 89%
Salaries in the private sector (law firms, business, industry): $56,500 –$120,000 (25th-75th percentile)
Median salary in the private sector: $75,000
Percentage in the private sector who reported salary information: 42%
Median salary in public service (government, judicial clerkships, academic posts, non-profits): $55,316

Percentage of 2008 graduates in:

Law firms: 55%	Government: 15%
Bus./industry: 23%	Judicial clerkship: 2%
Public interest: 2%	Unknown: 0%
Academia : 3%	

2008 graduates employed in-state: 84%
2008 graduates employed in foreign countries: 0%
Number of states where graduates are employed: 23
Percentage of 2008 graduates working in: New England: 1%, Middle Atlantic: 1%, East North Central: 87%, West North Central: 1%, South Atlantic: 4%, East South Central: 1%, West South Central: 0%, Mountain: 2%, Pacific: 3%, Unknown: 0%

BAR PASSAGE RATES

Based on 2008 graduates taking Summer 2008 or Winter 2009 exams. Most of the school's first-time test takers took the bar in Illinois.

88%
School's bar passage rate for first-time test takers

91%
Statewide bar passage rate for first-time test takers

Lewis & Clark College (Northwestern)

- 10015 S.W. Terwilliger Boulevard, Portland, OR, 97219
- http://law.lclark.edu
- Private
- Year founded: 1884
- 2009-2010 tuition: full-time: $31,934; part-time: $23,948
- Enrollment 2009-10 academic year: full-time: 521; part-time: 194
- U.S. News 2010 law specialty ranking: environmental law: 2

3.21-3.72 GPA, 25TH-75TH PERCENTILE

158-164 LSAT, 25TH-75TH PERCENTILE

35% ACCEPTANCE RATE

64 2011 U.S. NEWS LAW SCHOOL RANKING

ADMISSIONS

Admissions phone number: (503) 768-6613
Admissions email address: lawadmss@lclark.edu
Application website:
  http://law.lclark.edu/dept/lawadmss/requirements.html
Application deadline for Fall 2011 admission: 1-Mar

Admissions statistics:
Number of applicants for Fall 2009: **2,946**
Number of acceptances: **1,034**
Number enrolled: **176**
Acceptance rate: **35%**
GPA, 25th-75th percentile, entering class Fall 2009: **3.21-3.72**
LSAT, 25th-75th percentile, entering class Fall 2009: **158-164**

Part-time program:
Number of applicants for Fall 2009: **235**
Number of acceptances: **73**
Number enrolled: **55**
Acceptance rate: **31%**
GPA, 25th-75th percentile, entering class Fall 2009: **3.12-3.68**
LSAT, 25th-75th percentile, entering class Fall 2009: **153-160**

FINANCIAL AID

Financial aid phone number: (503) 768-7090
Financial aid application deadline: 1-Mar
Tuition 2009-2010 academic year: **full-time: $31,934;** part-time: $23,948
Room and board: **$11,250** ; books: **$1,050** ; miscellaneous expenses: **$5,400**
Total of room/board/books/miscellaneous expenses: **$17,700**
University does not offer graduate student housing for which law students are eligible.

Financial aid profile
Percent of students that received grants for the 2008-2009

academic year: full-time: **51%**; part-time **22%**
Median grant amount: full-time: **$10,000** ; part-time: **$9,000**
The average law-school debt of those in the Class of 2009 who borrowed: **$95,608** . Proportion who borrowed: **88%**

ACADEMIC PROGRAMS

Calendar: **semester**
Joint degrees awarded: **JD/LL.M. in Environmental Law**
Typical first-year section size: Full-time: **70**; Part-time: **67**
Is there typically a "small section" of the first year class, other than Legal Writing, taught by full-time faculty?:
  Full-time: **yes**; Part-time: **yes**
Number of course titles, beyond the first year curriculum, offered last year: **131**
Percentages of upper division course sections, excluding seminars, with an enrollment of:

Under 25: **64%**	25 to 49: **25%**
50 to 74: **7%**	75 to 99: **3%**
100+: **1%**	

Areas of specialization: appellate advocacy, clinical training, dispute resolution, environmental law, health care law, intellectual property law, international law, tax law, trial advocacy

Fall 2009 faculty profile
Total teaching faculty: **120**. Full-time: **44%**; **57%** men, **43%** women, **11%** minorities. Part-time: **56%**; **69%** men, **31%** women, **7%** minorities
Student-to-faculty ratio: **10**

SPECIAL PROGRAMS *(as provided by law school):*

Certificates in environmental, criminal, intellectual property, business, tax, pubic interest. Six clinics. Externships around the world. Internships in many practice areas. Summer courses in environmental, Indian law. Summer abroad partnerships with U. of San Diego, & U. of MO K.C. China program. Law Centers=Environmental, international env, crime victims, animal law

STUDENT BODY

Fall 2009 full-time enrollment: 521

Men: 51%	Women: 49%
African-American: 2.30%	American Indian: 1.50%
Asian-American: 8.80%	Mexican-American: 1.70%
Puerto Rican: 0.00%	Other Hisp-Amer: 2.90%
White: 73.30%	International: 2.70%
Unknown: 6.70%	

Fall 2009 part-time enrollment: 194

Men: 52%	Women: 48%
African-American: 5.20%	American Indian: 4.60%
Asian-American: 9.30%	Mexican-American: 1.50%
Puerto Rican: 1.00%	Other Hisp-Amer: 4.10%
White: 64.40%	International: 2.60%
Unknown: 7.20%	

Attrition rates for 2008-2009 full-time students
Percent of students discontinuing law school:

Men: 2%	Women: 4%
First-year students: 7%	Second-year students: 2%
Third-year students: 0%	Fourth-year students: N/A

LIBRARY RESOURCES

Total titles: 363,280
Total volumes: 535,270
Total seats available for library users: 385

INFORMATION TECHNOLOGY

Number of wired network connections available to students: 943 total (in the law library, excluding computer labs: 269; in classrooms: 292; in computer labs: 15; elsewhere in the law school: 367)
Law school has a wireless network.
Students are not required to own a computer.

EMPLOYMENT AND SALARIES

Proportion of 2008 graduates employed at graduation:
N/A
Employed 9 months later, as of February 15, 2009: 94%
Salaries in the private sector (law firms, business, industry): $65,000 –$105,000 (25th-75th percentile)
Median salary in the private sector: $80,370
Percentage in the private sector who reported salary information: 65%
Median salary in public service (government, judicial clerkships, academic posts, non-profits): $50,000

Percentage of 2008 graduates in:

Law firms: 45%	Government: 17%
Bus./industry: 20%	Judicial clerkship: 6%
Public interest: 11%	Unknown: 0%
Academia : 1%	

2008 graduates employed in-state: 64%
2008 graduates employed in foreign countries: 2%
Number of states where graduates are employed: 19
Percentage of 2008 graduates working in: New England: 1%, Middle Atlantic: 1%, East North Central: 4%, West North Central: 0%, South Atlantic: 5%, East South Central: 1%, West South Central: 1%, Mountain: 6%, Pacific: 82%, Unknown: 0%

BAR PASSAGE RATES

Based on 2008 graduates taking Summer 2008 or Winter 2009 exams. Most of the school's first-time test takers took the bar in Oregon.

81%
School's bar passage rate for first-time test takers

79%
Statewide bar passage rate for first-time test takers

Louisiana State Univ.–Baton Rouge

■ 400 Paul M. Hebert Law Center, Baton Rouge, LA, 70803
■ http://www.law.lsu.edu
■ Public
■ Year founded: 1906
■ 2009-2010 tuition: full-time: $14,350; part-time: N/A
■ Enrollment 2009-10 academic year: full-time: 587; part-time: 11
■ U.S. News 2010 law specialty ranking: N/A

3.22-3.66 GPA, 25TH-75TH PERCENTILE

155-159 LSAT, 25TH-75TH PERCENTILE

37% ACCEPTANCE RATE

80 2011 U.S. NEWS LAW SCHOOL RANKING

ADMISSIONS

Admissions phone number: **(225) 578-8646**
Admissions email address: **admissions@law.lsu.edu**
Application website:
  http://appl030.lsu.edu/admissions/lawappl.nsf/OpenDatabase?OpenAgent
Application deadline for Fall 2011 admission: **1-Mar**

Admissions statistics:
Number of applicants for Fall 2009: **1,408**
Number of acceptances: **527**
Number enrolled: **233**
Acceptance rate: **37%**
GPA, 25th-75th percentile, entering class Fall 2009: **3.22-3.66**
LSAT, 25th-75th percentile, entering class Fall 2009: **155-159**

FINANCIAL AID

Financial aid phone number: **(225) 578-3103**
Financial aid application deadline: **1-Jul**
Tuition 2009-2010 academic year: **full-time: $14,350; part-time: N/A**
Room and board: **$13,377** ; books: **$2,500** ; miscellaneous expenses: **$2,204**
Total of room/board/books/miscellaneous expenses: **$18,081**
University does not offer graduate student housing for which law students are eligible.

Financial aid profile
Percent of students that received grants for the 2008-2009 academic year: full-time: **65%**
Median grant amount: full-time: **$3,913** ; part-time: **$0**
The average law-school debt of those in the Class of 2009 who borrowed: **$65,324** . Proportion who borrowed: **80%**

ACADEMIC PROGRAMS

Calendar: **semester**
Joint degrees awarded: **Juris Doctor/Graduate Diploma in Civil L**

Typical first-year section size: Full-time: **78**
Is there typically a "small section" of the first year class, other than Legal Writing, taught by full-time faculty?:
  Full-time: **yes**; Part-time: **no**
Number of course titles, beyond the first year curriculum, offered last year: **77**
Percentages of upper division course sections, excluding seminars, with an enrollment of:
  Under 25: **64%**   25 to 49: **24%**
  50 to 74: **8%**   75 to 99: **4%**
  100+: **0%**
Areas of specialization: appellate advocacy, clinical training, dispute resolution, environmental law, health care law, intellectual property law, international law, tax law, trial advocacy

Fall 2009 faculty profile
Total teaching faculty: 52. Full-time: **52%**; **74%** men, **26%** women, **7%** minorities. Part-time: **48%**; **84%** men, **16%** women, **4%** minorities
Student-to-faculty ratio: **17.5**

SPECIAL PROGRAMS *(as provided by law school):*
The LSU Law Center has a summer program in Lyon, France. In Fall 2009, these live client clinics were offered: Domestic Violence; Immigration; Juvenile Representation. Externships available are the Judicial and Attorney General Externships as well as the opportunity to work with government agencies, local prosecutors and public defenders, and state and federal revenue offices.

STUDENT BODY
Fall 2009 full-time enrollment: 587
Men: **55%**   Women: **45%**
African-American: **4.30%**   American Indian: **1.20%**
Asian-American: **2.40%**   Mexican-American: **0.00%**
Puerto Rican: **0.00%**   Other Hisp-Amer: **5.50%**
White: **76.50%**   International: **0.50%**
Unknown: **9.70%**

Fall 2009 part-time enrollment: 11

Men: **64%**   Women: **36%**
African-American: **9.10%**   American Indian: **0.00%**
Asian-American: **0.00%**   Mexican-American: **0.00%**
Puerto Rican: **0.00%**   Other Hisp-Amer: **9.10%**
White: **72.70%**   International: **0.00%**
Unknown: **9.10%**

Attrition rates for 2008-2009 full-time students
Percent of students discontinuing law school:
Men: **6%**   Women: **5%**
First-year students: **15%**   Second-year students: **N/A**
Third-year students: **N/A**   Fourth-year students: **N/A**

LIBRARY RESOURCES

Total titles: **348,545**
Total volumes: **870,402**
Total seats available for library users: **468**

INFORMATION TECHNOLOGY

Number of wired network connections available to students: **60** total (in the law library, excluding computer labs: **60**; in classrooms: **0**; in computer labs: **0**; elsewhere in the law school: **0**)
Law school has a wireless network.
Students are not required to own a computer.

EMPLOYMENT AND SALARIES

Proportion of 2008 graduates employed at graduation: **68%**
Employed 9 months later, as of February 15, 2009: **96%**
Salaries in the private sector (law firms, business, industry): **$50,500 –$92,250** (25th-75th percentile)

Median salary in the private sector: **$75,000**
Percentage in the private sector who reported salary information: **100%**
Median salary in public service (government, judicial clerkships, academic posts, non-profits): **$44,687**

Percentage of 2008 graduates in:
Law firms: **51%**   Government: **15%**
Bus./industry: **11%**   Judicial clerkship: **18%**
Public interest: **2%**   Unknown: **1%**
Academia : **2%**

2008 graduates employed in-state: **80%**
2008 graduates employed in foreign countries: **0%**
Number of states where graduates are employed: **13**
Percentage of 2008 graduates working in: New England: **1%**, Middle Atlantic: **1%**, East North Central: **1%**, West North Central: **0%**, South Atlantic: **5%**, East South Central: **1%**, West South Central: **92%**, Mountain: **0%**, Pacific: **1%**, Unknown: **0%**

BAR PASSAGE RATES

Based on 2008 graduates taking Summer 2008 or Winter 2009 exams. Most of the school's first-time test takers took the bar in Louisiana.

81%
School's bar passage rate for first-time test takers

66%
Statewide bar passage rate for first-time test takers

Loyola Marymount University

- 919 Albany Street, Los Angeles, CA, 90015-1211
- http://www.lls.edu
- Private
- Year founded: 1920
- 2009-2010 tuition: full-time: $40,530; part-time: $27,165
- Enrollment 2009-10 academic year: full-time: 1,002; part-time: 285
- U.S. News 2010 law specialty ranking: tax law: 9

3.33-3.68 GPA, 25TH-75TH PERCENTILE

157-163 LSAT, 25TH-75TH PERCENTILE

32% ACCEPTANCE RATE

56 2011 U.S. NEWS LAW SCHOOL RANKING

ADMISSIONS
Admissions phone number: **(213) 736-1074**
Admissions email address: **Admissions@lls.edu**
Application website: http://www.lls.edu/admissions
Application deadline for Fall 2011 admission: **1-Feb**

Admissions statistics:
Number of applicants for Fall 2009: **4,994**
Number of acceptances: **1,602**
Number enrolled: **339**
Acceptance rate: **32%**
GPA, 25th-75th percentile, entering class Fall 2009: **3.33-3.68**
LSAT, 25th-75th percentile, entering class Fall 2009: **157-163**

Part-time program:
Number of applicants for Fall 2009: **2,485**
Number of acceptances: **110**
Number enrolled: **57**
Acceptance rate: **4%**
GPA, 25th-75th percentile, entering class Fall 2009: **3.20-3.66**
LSAT, 25th-75th percentile, entering class Fall 2009: **155-163**

FINANCIAL AID
Financial aid phone number: **(213) 736-1140**
Financial aid application deadline: **14-Mar**
Tuition 2009-2010 academic year: **full-time: $40,530; part-time: $27,165**
Room and board: **$15,806** ; books: **$1,050** ; miscellaneous expenses: **$9,052**
Total of room/board/books/miscellaneous expenses: **$25,908**
University does not offer graduate student housing for which law students are eligible.

Financial aid profile
Percent of students that received grants for the 2008-2009 academic year: full-time: **33%**; part-time **12%**

Median grant amount: full-time: **$20,500** ; part-time: **$16,500**
The average law-school debt of those in the Class of 2009 who borrowed: **$125,264** . Proportion who borrowed: **86%**

ACADEMIC PROGRAMS
Calendar: **semester**
Joint degrees awarded: **J.D./M.B.A.**
Typical first-year section size: Full-time: **86**; Part-time: **58**
Is there typically a "small section" of the first year class, other than Legal Writing, taught by full-time faculty?: Full-time: **no**; Part-time: **no**
Number of course titles, beyond the first year curriculum, offered last year: **162**
Percentages of upper division course sections, excluding seminars, with an enrollment of:
Under 25: **62%**   25 to 49: **24%**
50 to 74: **4%**   75 to 99: **6%**
100+: **5%**
Areas of specialization: appellate advocacy, clinical training, dispute resolution, environmental law, health care law, intellectual property law, international law, tax law, trial advocacy

Fall 2009 faculty profile
Total teaching faculty: **129**. Full-time: **53%**; 53% men, 47% women, **16%** minorities. Part-time: **47%**; 75% men, 25% women, **38%** minorities
Student-to-faculty ratio: **14.8**

SPECIAL PROGRAMS *(as provided by law school):*
Academic Support Programs. Externships with federal, state & local governments, public interest and entertainment firms, and District Attorney. Clinics: Juvenile Justice, Disability Rights, Conflict Resolution, State Board of Equalization, Nonprofit Tax and Transactions. Study Abroad: Italy, Costa Rica, London, China. Ethical Advocacy Center, Alumni Mentor Program, and Public Interest Program.

STUDENT BODY

Fall 2009 full-time enrollment: 1,002

Men: 47%	Women: 53%
African-American: 4.10%	American Indian: 0.20%
Asian-American: 23.20%	Mexican-American: 9.00%
Puerto Rican: 0.60%	Other Hisp-Amer: 4.50%
White: 51.80%	International: 0.00%
Unknown: 6.70%	

Fall 2009 part-time enrollment: 285

Men: 61%	Women: 39%
African-American: 4.90%	American Indian: 1.40%
Asian-American: 20.00%	Mexican-American: 5.60%
Puerto Rican: 0.70%	Other Hisp-Amer: 2.50%
White: 57.20%	International: 0.00%
Unknown: 7.70%	

Attrition rates for 2008-2009 full-time students
Percent of students discontinuing law school:

Men: 4%	Women: 5%
First-year students: 12%	Second-year students: 2%
Third-year students: 0%	Fourth-year students: N/A

LIBRARY RESOURCES

Total titles: 294,882
Total volumes: 605,739
Total seats available for library users: 550

INFORMATION TECHNOLOGY

Number of wired network connections available to students: 930 total (in the law library, excluding computer labs: 620; in classrooms: 0; in computer labs: 100; elsewhere in the law school: 210)
Law school has a wireless network.
Students are not required to own a computer.

EMPLOYMENT AND SALARIES

Proportion of 2008 graduates employed at graduation: N/A
Employed 9 months later, as of February 15, 2009: 97%
Salaries in the private sector (law firms, business, industry): $70,000 –$160,000 (25th-75th percentile)
Median salary in the private sector: $100,000
Percentage in the private sector who reported salary information: 59%
Median salary in public service (government, judicial clerkships, academic posts, non-profits): $61,800

Percentage of 2008 graduates in:

Law firms: 59%	Government: 7%
Bus./industry: 18%	Judicial clerkship: 2%
Public interest: 12%	Unknown: 1%
Academia : 1%	

2008 graduates employed in-state: 95%
2008 graduates employed in foreign countries: 0%
Number of states where graduates are employed: 9
Percentage of 2008 graduates working in: New England: 0%, Middle Atlantic: 0%, East North Central: 1%, West North Central: 0%, South Atlantic: 1%, East South Central: 0%, West South Central: 1%, Mountain: 0%, Pacific: 95%, Unknown: 1%

BAR PASSAGE RATES

Based on 2008 graduates taking Summer 2008 or Winter 2009 exams. Most of the school's first-time test takers took the bar in California.

86%
School's bar passage rate for first-time test takers

71%
Statewide bar passage rate for first-time test takers

Loyola University Chicago

- 25 E. Pearson Street, Chicago, IL, 60611
- http://www.luc.edu/law/
- Private
- **Year founded:** 1908
- **2009-2010 tuition:** full-time: $36,770; part-time: $27,720
- **Enrollment 2009-10 academic year:** full-time: 652; part-time: 188
- **U.S. News 2010 law specialty ranking:** healthcare law: 9

3.29-3.62 GPA, 25ᵀᴴ-75ᵀᴴ PERCENTILE

158-162 LSAT, 25ᵀᴴ-75ᵀᴴ PERCENTILE

32% ACCEPTANCE RATE

78 2011 U.S. NEWS LAW SCHOOL RANKING

ADMISSIONS
Admissions phone number: (312) 915-7170
Admissions email address: **law-admissions@luc.edu**
Application website:
  http://www.luc.edu/law/admission/index.html
Application deadline for Fall 2011 admission: **1-Apr**

Admissions statistics:
Number of applicants for Fall 2009: **3,565**
Number of acceptances: **1,133**
Number enrolled: **203**
Acceptance rate: **32%**
GPA, 25th-75th percentile, entering class Fall 2009: **3.29-3.62**
LSAT, 25th-75th percentile, entering class Fall 2009: **158-162**

Part-time program:
Number of applicants for Fall 2009: **671**
Number of acceptances: **151**
Number enrolled: **65**
Acceptance rate: **23%**
GPA, 25th-75th percentile, entering class Fall 2009: **3.06-3.50**
LSAT, 25th-75th percentile, entering class Fall 2009: **153-158**

FINANCIAL AID
Financial aid phone number: (312) 915-7170
Financial aid application deadline: **1-Mar**
Tuition 2009-2010 academic year: **full-time: $36,770; part-time: $27,720**
Room and board: **$13,200** ; books: **$1,300** ; miscellaneous expenses: **$5,498**
Total of room/board/books/miscellaneous expenses: **$19,998**
University offers graduate student housing for which law students are eligible.

Financial aid profile
Percent of students that received grants for the 2008-2009

academic year: full-time: **71%**; part-time **55%**
Median grant amount: full-time: **$12,600** ; part-time: **$4,783**
The average law-school debt of those in the Class of 2009 who borrowed: **$89,796** . Proportion who borrowed: **75%**

ACADEMIC PROGRAMS
Calendar: **semester**
Joint degrees awarded: **J.D./M.S.W.; J.D./M.B.A.; J.D./M.A.**
Typical first-year section size: Full-time: **65**; Part-time: **75**
Is there typically a "small section" of the first year class, other than Legal Writing, taught by full-time faculty?:
  Full-time: **yes**; Part-time: **no**
Number of course titles, beyond the first year curriculum, offered last year: **183**
Percentages of upper division course sections, excluding seminars, with an enrollment of:

Under 25: **67%**	25 to 49: **19%**
50 to 74: **11%**	75 to 99: **2%**
100+: **0%**	

Areas of specialization: appellate advocacy, clinical training, dispute resolution, environmental law, health care law, intellectual property law, international law, tax law, trial advocacy

Fall 2009 faculty profile
Total teaching faculty: **161.** Full-time: **30%**; **63%** men, **38%** women, **13%** minorities. Part-time: **70%**; **55%** men, **45%** women, **7%** minorities
Student-to-faculty ratio: **14.3**

SPECIAL PROGRAMS *(as provided by law school):*
Loyola's clinics include the Community Law Center, ChildLaw Clinic, Tax Clinic, and Business Law Clinic. Centers of excellence include the Beazley Health Law Institute, Civitas ChildLaw Center, Advocacy Center and the Institute for Consumer Antitrust Studies. Annual overseas programs include Rome; Strasbourg; Oxford, London and Santiago, Chile.

STUDENT BODY

Fall 2009 full-time enrollment: 652

Men: 45%	Women: 55%
African-American: 5.20%	American Indian: 0.60%
Asian-American: 4.80%	Mexican-American: 3.40%
Puerto Rican: 0.20%	Other Hisp-Amer: 2.10%
White: 79.30%	International: 1.20%
Unknown: 3.20%	

Fall 2009 part-time enrollment: 188

Men: 53%	Women: 47%
African-American: 6.90%	American Indian: 0.00%
Asian-American: 5.30%	Mexican-American: 2.10%
Puerto Rican: 1.60%	Other Hisp-Amer: 1.10%
White: 78.20%	International: 0.50%
Unknown: 4.30%	

Attrition rates for 2008-2009 full-time students
Percent of students discontinuing law school:

Men: 3%	Women: 2%
First-year students: 7%	Second-year students: 1%
Third-year students: N/A	Fourth-year students: 2%

LIBRARY RESOURCES

Total titles: 70,663
Total volumes: 398,495
Total seats available for library users: 436

INFORMATION TECHNOLOGY

Number of wired network connections available to students: 328 total (in the law library, excluding computer labs: 180; in classrooms: 148; in computer labs: 0; elsewhere in the law school: 0)
Law school has a wireless network.
Students are not required to own a computer.

EMPLOYMENT AND SALARIES

Proportion of 2008 graduates employed at graduation: 70%
Employed 9 months later, as of February 15, 2009: 94%
Salaries in the private sector (law firms, business, industry): $60,521 –$144,238 (25th-75th percentile)
Median salary in the private sector: $100,433
Percentage in the private sector who reported salary information: 50%
Median salary in public service (government, judicial clerkships, academic posts, non-profits): $50,922

Percentage of 2008 graduates in:

Law firms: 62%	Government: 13%
Bus./industry: 17%	Judicial clerkship: 3%
Public interest: 4%	Unknown: 0%
Academia : 1%	

2008 graduates employed in-state: 82%
2008 graduates employed in foreign countries: 1%
Number of states where graduates are employed: 22
Percentage of 2008 graduates working in: New England: 1%, Middle Atlantic: 2%, East North Central: 87%, West North Central: 1%, South Atlantic: 4%, East South Central: 2%, West South Central: 1%, Mountain: 2%, Pacific: 3%, Unknown: 0%

BAR PASSAGE RATES

Based on 2008 graduates taking Summer 2008 or Winter 2009 exams. Most of the school's first-time test takers took the bar in Illinois.

94%

School's bar passage rate for first-time test takers

91%

Statewide bar passage rate for first-time test takers

Loyola University New Orleans

- 7214 St. Charles Avenue, PO Box 901, New Orleans, LA, 70118
- http://law.loyno.edu/
- Private
- Year founded: 1931
- 2009-2010 tuition: full-time: $34,166; part-time: $23,096
- Enrollment 2009-10 academic year: full-time: 726; part-time: 156
- U.S. News 2010 law specialty ranking: N/A

3.05-3.52 GPA, 25TH-75TH PERCENTILE

151-155 LSAT, 25TH-75TH PERCENTILE

49% ACCEPTANCE RATE

Tier 3 2011 U.S. NEWS LAW SCHOOL RANKING

ADMISSIONS

Admissions phone number: **(504) 861-5575**
Admissions email address: **ladmit@loyno.edu**
Application website: **http://law.loyno.edu/apply-now**
Application deadline for Fall 2011 admission: **rolling**

Admissions statistics:

Number of applicants for Fall 2009: **1,671**
Number of acceptances: **825**
Number enrolled: **254**
Acceptance rate: **49%**
GPA, 25th-75th percentile, entering class Fall 2009: **3.05-3.52**
LSAT, 25th-75th percentile, entering class Fall 2009: **151-155**

Part-time program:

Number of applicants for Fall 2009: **156**
Number of acceptances: **103**
Number enrolled: **69**
Acceptance rate: **66%**
GPA, 25th-75th percentile, entering class Fall 2009: **2.84-3.46**
LSAT, 25th-75th percentile, entering class Fall 2009: **149-155**

FINANCIAL AID

Financial aid phone number: **(504) 865-3231**
Financial aid application deadline:
Tuition 2009-2010 academic year: **full-time: $34,166; part-time: $23,096**
Room and board: **$13,200** ; books: **$1,550** ; miscellaneous expenses: **$5,550**
Total of room/board/books/miscellaneous expenses: **$20,300**
University offers graduate student housing for which law students are eligible.

Financial aid profile

Percent of students that received grants for the 2008-2009 academic year: full-time: **44%**; part-time **22%**

Median grant amount: full-time: **$13,000** ; part-time: **$2,525**
The average law-school debt of those in the Class of 2009 who borrowed: **$50,103** . Proportion who borrowed: **100%**

ACADEMIC PROGRAMS

Calendar: **semester**
Joint degrees awarded: **J.D./M.B.A.; J.D./M.U.R.P.; J.D./M.P.A.**
Typical first-year section size: Full-time: **74**; Part-time: **48**
Is there typically a "small section" of the first year class, other than Legal Writing, taught by full-time faculty?: Full-time: **no**; Part-time: **no**
Number of course titles, beyond the first year curriculum, offered last year: **102**
Percentages of upper division course sections, excluding seminars, with an enrollment of:

Under 25: **37%**	25 to 49: **32%**
50 to 74: **19%**	75 to 99: **12%**
100+: **1%**	

Areas of specialization: appellate advocacy, clinical training, dispute resolution, environmental law, intellectual property law, international law, tax law, trial advocacy

Fall 2009 faculty profile

Total teaching faculty: **61**. Full-time: **64%**; **56%** men, **44%** women, **28%** minorities. Part-time: **36%**; **82%** men, **18%** women, **5%** minorities
Student-to-faculty ratio: **17.1**

SPECIAL PROGRAMS (as provided by law school):

Loyola offers programs in civil and common law; Summer programs in Vienna, Moscow, Budapest, Mexico, Brazil, Costa Rica; Certificate in international legal studies; Joint degrees JD/MBA and JD/MA in several disciplines; Law Clinic students represent clients in civil, criminal and other cases; loan forgiveness for public service employment; Externships with federal and state courts/agencies.

STUDENT BODY

Fall 2009 full-time enrollment: 726

Men: 52%	Women: 48%
African-American: 14.30%	American Indian: 0.30%
Asian-American: 4.40%	Mexican-American: 1.50%
Puerto Rican: 0.80%	Other Hisp-Amer: 6.10%
White: 65.60%	International: 0.60%
Unknown: 6.50%	

Fall 2009 part-time enrollment: 156

Men: 46%	Women: 54%
African-American: 16.00%	American Indian: 1.90%
Asian-American: 1.90%	Mexican-American: 0.60%
Puerto Rican: 1.90%	Other Hisp-Amer: 5.80%
White: 68.60%	International: 0.00%
Unknown: 3.20%	

Attrition rates for 2008-2009 full-time students
Percent of students discontinuing law school:

Men: 4%	Women: 4%
First-year students: 10%	Second-year students: 2%
Third-year students: 1%	Fourth-year students: N/A

LIBRARY RESOURCES

Total titles: 148,349
Total volumes: 404,868
Total seats available for library users: 366

INFORMATION TECHNOLOGY

Number of wired network connections available to students: 40 total (in the law library, excluding computer labs: 28; in classrooms: 0; in computer labs: 0; elsewhere in the law school: 12)
Law school has a wireless network.
Students are not required to own a computer.

EMPLOYMENT AND SALARIES

Proportion of 2008 graduates employed at graduation: 60%
Employed 9 months later, as of February 15, 2009: 95%
Salaries in the private sector (law firms, business, industry): N/A–N/A (25th-75th percentile)
Median salary in the private sector: $90,000
Percentage in the private sector who reported salary information: N/A
Median salary in public service (government, judicial clerkships, academic posts, non-profits): $61,000

Percentage of 2008 graduates in:

Law firms: 62%	Government: 12%
Bus./industry: 11%	Judicial clerkship: 10%
Public interest: 4%	Unknown: N/A
Academia : 1%	

2008 graduates employed in-state: 69%
2008 graduates employed in foreign countries: 3%
Number of states where graduates are employed: 19
Percentage of 2008 graduates working in: New England: 0%, Middle Atlantic: 2%, East North Central: 1%, West North Central: 1%, South Atlantic: 7%, East South Central: 3%, West South Central: 80%, Mountain: 2%, Pacific: 2%, Unknown: 0%

BAR PASSAGE RATES

Based on 2008 graduates taking Summer 2008 or Winter 2009 exams. Most of the school's first-time test takers took the bar in Louisiana.

67%
School's bar passage rate for first-time test takers

66%
Statewide bar passage rate for first-time test takers

Marquette University

■ Sensenbrenner Hall, PO Box 1881, Milwaukee, WI, 53201-1881
■ http://law.marquette.edu
■ Private
■ Year founded: 1892
■ 2009-2010 tuition: full-time: $32,410; part-time: $19,425
■ Enrollment 2009-10 academic year: full-time: 563; part-time: 180
■ U.S. News 2010 law specialty ranking: dispute resolution: 6

3.09-3.61 GPA, 25TH-75TH PERCENTILE

155-159 LSAT, 25TH-75TH PERCENTILE

46% ACCEPTANCE RATE

Tier 3 2011 U.S. NEWS LAW SCHOOL RANKING

ADMISSIONS
Admissions phone number: **(414) 288-6767**
Admissions email address: **law.admission@marquette.edu**
Application website: **N/A**
Application deadline for Fall 2011 admission: **1-Apr**

Admissions statistics:
Number of applicants for Fall 2009: **1,905**
Number of acceptances: **868**
Number enrolled: **185**
Acceptance rate: **46%**
GPA, 25th-75th percentile, entering class Fall 2009: **3.09-3.61**
LSAT, 25th-75th percentile, entering class Fall 2009: **155-159**

Part-time program:
Number of applicants for Fall 2009: **179**
Number of acceptances: **59**
Number enrolled: **34**
Acceptance rate: **33%**
GPA, 25th-75th percentile, entering class Fall 2009: **2.88-3.60**
LSAT, 25th-75th percentile, entering class Fall 2009: **151-158**

FINANCIAL AID
Financial aid phone number: **(414) 288-7390**
Financial aid application deadline: **1-Mar**
Tuition 2009-2010 academic year: **full-time: $32,410; part-time: $19,425**
Room and board: **$11,735** ; books: **$1,345** ; miscellaneous expenses: **$6,160**
Total of room/board/books/miscellaneous expenses: **$19,240**
University does not offer graduate student housing for which law students are eligible.

Financial aid profile
Percent of students that received grants for the 2008-2009 academic year: full-time: **43%**; part-time **29%**

Median grant amount: full-time: **$8,000** ; part-time: **$3,500**
The average law-school debt of those in the Class of 2009 who borrowed: **$102,727** . Proportion who borrowed: **84%**

ACADEMIC PROGRAMS
Calendar: **semester**
Joint degrees awarded: **J.D./M.B.A.; J.D./M.A. Political Science; J.D./M.A. International Affairs; J.D./M.A. History of Philosophy; J.D./M.A. Philosophy; J.D./Certificate in Dispute Resolution; J.D./M.B.A. Sports Business**
Typical first-year section size: Full-time: **81**; Part-time: **35**
Is there typically a "small section" of the first year class, other than Legal Writing, taught by full-time faculty?: Full-time: **yes**; Part-time: **yes**
Number of course titles, beyond the first year curriculum, offered last year: **153**
Percentages of upper division course sections, excluding seminars, with an enrollment of:
Under 25: **55%** 25 to 49: **31%**
50 to 74: **9%** 75 to 99: **5%**
100+: **0%**
Areas of specialization: appellate advocacy, clinical training, dispute resolution, environmental law, health care law, intellectual property law, international law, tax law, trial advocacy

Fall 2009 faculty profile
Total teaching faculty: **54**. Full-time: 50%; 67% men, 33% women, 19% minorities. Part-time: 50%; 70% men, 30% women, 4% minorities
Student-to-faculty ratio: **19.1**

SPECIAL PROGRAMS *(as provided by law school):*
Marquette students have the opportunity to develop legal skills in one of the school's clinical programs. Students participate in internships with a variety of governmental and legal services agencies, as well as in internships with trial and appellate judges. Students may focus their studies in specific doctrinal

areas including dispute resolution, intellectual property, and sports law.

STUDENT BODY

Fall 2009 full-time enrollment: 563

Men: 59%	Women: 41%
African-American: 5.20%	American Indian: 0.70%
Asian-American: 2.80%	Mexican-American: 1.40%
Puerto Rican: 1.10%	Other Hisp-Amer: 3.70%
White: 84.70%	International: 0.00%
Unknown: 0.40%	

Fall 2009 part-time enrollment: 180

Men: 48%	Women: 52%
African-American: 2.80%	American Indian: 1.70%
Asian-American: 6.10%	Mexican-American: 1.10%
Puerto Rican: 0.00%	Other Hisp-Amer: 2.20%
White: 86.10%	International: 0.00%
Unknown: 0.00%	

Attrition rates for 2008-2009 full-time students
Percent of students discontinuing law school:

Men: 3%	Women: 3%
First-year students: 9%	Second-year students: 0%
Third-year students: N/A	Fourth-year students: N/A

LIBRARY RESOURCES
Total titles: 196,669
Total volumes: 368,627
Total seats available for library users: 406

INFORMATION TECHNOLOGY
Number of wired network connections available to students: 102 total (in the law library, excluding computer labs: 32; in classrooms: 45; in computer labs: 6; elsewhere in the law school: 19)
Law school has a wireless network.
Students are not required to own a computer.

EMPLOYMENT AND SALARIES
Proportion of 2008 graduates employed at graduation: 61%
Employed 9 months later, as of February 15, 2009: 93%
Salaries in the private sector (law firms, business, industry): $48,000 –$107,000 (25th-75th percentile)
Median salary in the private sector: $56,325
Percentage in the private sector who reported salary information: 76%
Median salary in public service (government, judicial clerkships, academic posts, non-profits): $49,000

Percentage of 2008 graduates in:

Law firms: 64%	Government: 10%
Bus./industry: 14%	Judicial clerkship: 4%
Public interest: 5%	Unknown: 0%
Academia : 3%	

2008 graduates employed in-state: 74%
2008 graduates employed in foreign countries: 1%
Number of states where graduates are employed: 16
Percentage of 2008 graduates working in: New England: 0%, Middle Atlantic: 1%, East North Central: 80%, West North Central: 2%, South Atlantic: 11%, East South Central: 0%, West South Central: 2%, Mountain: 1%, Pacific: 2%, Unknown: 0%

BAR PASSAGE RATES
Based on 2008 graduates taking Summer 2008 or Winter 2009 exams. Most of the school's first-time test takers took the bar in Wisconsin.

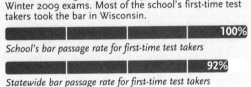

School's bar passage rate for first-time test takers

Statewide bar passage rate for first-time test takers

Mercer University

- 1021 Georgia Avenue, Macon, GA, 31207-0001
- http://www.law.mercer.edu
- Private
- Year founded: 1873
- 2009-2010 tuition: full-time: $34,330; part-time: N/A
- Enrollment 2009-10 academic year: full-time: 431
- U.S. News 2010 law specialty ranking: N/A

3.13-3.67 GPA, 25TH-75TH PERCENTILE

153-158 LSAT, 25TH-75TH PERCENTILE

38% ACCEPTANCE RATE

Tier 3 2011 U.S. NEWS LAW SCHOOL RANKING

ADMISSIONS

Admissions phone number: **(478) 301-2605**
Admissions email address: **martin_sv@law.mercer.edu**
Application website:
   http://www.law.mercer.edu/admissions/apply.cfm
Application deadline for Fall 2011 admission: **15-Mar**

Admissions statistics:
Number of applicants for Fall 2009: **1,571**
Number of acceptances: **600**
Number enrolled: **157**
Acceptance rate: **38%**
GPA, 25th-75th percentile, entering class Fall 2009: **3.13-3.67**
LSAT, 25th-75th percentile, entering class Fall 2009: **153-158**

FINANCIAL AID

Financial aid phone number: **(478) 301-2064**
Financial aid application deadline: **1-Apr**
Tuition 2009-2010 academic year: **full-time: $34,330**; part-time: **N/A**
Room and board: **$9,630** ; books: **$1,380** ; miscellaneous expenses: **$4,990**
Total of room/board/books/miscellaneous expenses: **$16,000**
University offers graduate student housing for which law students are eligible.

Financial aid profile
Percent of students that received grants for the 2008-2009 academic year: full-time: **31%**
Median grant amount: full-time: **$20,000**
The average law-school debt of those in the Class of 2009 who borrowed: **$99,038** . Proportion who borrowed: **92%**

ACADEMIC PROGRAMS

Calendar: **semester**
Joint degrees awarded: **J.D./M.B.A.**
Typical first-year section size: Full-time: **73**
Is there typically a "small section" of the first year class, other than Legal Writing, taught by full-time faculty?:
   Full-time: **yes**
Number of course titles, beyond the first year curriculum, offered last year: **112**
Percentages of upper division course sections, excluding seminars, with an enrollment of:
   Under 25: **75%**   25 to 49: **15%**
   50 to 74: **8%**   75 to 99: **2%**
   100+: **0%**
Areas of specialization: appellate advocacy, clinical training, dispute resolution, environmental law, health care law, intellectual property law, international law, tax law, trial advocacy

Fall 2009 faculty profile
Total teaching faculty: **46**. Full-time: **63%**; **66%** men, **34%** women, **10%** minorities. Part-time: **37%**; **76%** men, **24%** women, **6%** minorities
Student-to-faculty ratio: **13**

SPECIAL PROGRAMS *(as provided by law school):*
Mercer, home of the Legal Writing Institute, is the only school that offers a Legal Writing Certificate. The School also hosts the Mercer Center for Legal Ethics and Professionalism and a Law and Public Service Program that provides clinic and practicum courses as well as pro bono opportunities.

STUDENT BODY
Fall 2009 full-time enrollment: **431**
Men: **53%**   Women: **47%**
African-American: **9.00%**   American Indian: **0.70%**
Asian-American: **5.10%**   Mexican-American: **0.00%**
Puerto Rican: **0.50%**   Other Hisp-Amer: **1.20%**
White: **75.40%**   International: **0.00%**
Unknown: **8.10%**

Attrition rates for 2008-2009 full-time students
Percent of students discontinuing law school:
Men: **6%**   Women: **3%**
First-year students: **14%**   Second-year students: **N/A**
Third-year students: **N/A**   Fourth-year students: **N/A**

LIBRARY RESOURCES
Total titles: 77,783
Total volumes: 350,650
Total seats available for library users: 390

INFORMATION TECHNOLOGY
Number of wired network connections available to students: 748 total (in the law library, excluding computer labs: 100; in classrooms: 604; in computer labs: 36; elsewhere in the law school: 8)
Law school has a wireless network.
Students are required to own a computer.

EMPLOYMENT AND SALARIES
Proportion of 2008 graduates employed at graduation: N/A
Employed 9 months later, as of February 15, 2009: 92%
Salaries in the private sector (law firms, business, industry): $50,000 –$125,000 (25th-75th percentile)
Median salary in the private sector: $60,000
Percentage in the private sector who reported salary information: 80%
Median salary in public service (government, judicial clerkships, academic posts, non-profits): $48,000

Percentage of 2008 graduates in:

Law firms: 66%	Government: 18%
Bus./industry: 5%	Judicial clerkship: 8%
Public interest: 3%	Unknown: 0%
Academia : 0%	

2008 graduates employed in-state: 81%
2008 graduates employed in foreign countries: 0%
Number of states where graduates are employed: 12
Percentage of 2008 graduates working in: New England: 1%, Middle Atlantic: 0%, East North Central: 2%, West North Central: 0%, South Atlantic: 92%, East South Central: 2%, West South Central: 0%, Mountain: 1%, Pacific: 0%, Unknown: 3%

BAR PASSAGE RATES
Based on 2008 graduates taking Summer 2008 or Winter 2009 exams. Most of the school's first-time test takers took the bar in Georgia.

96%
School's bar passage rate for first-time test takers

89%
Statewide bar passage rate for first-time test takers

Michigan State University

- 368 Law College Building, East Lansing, MI, 48824-1300
- http://www.law.msu.edu
- Private
- Year founded: 1891
- 2009-2010 tuition: full-time: $32,828; part-time: $27,168
- Enrollment 2009-10 academic year: full-time: 892; part-time: 65
- U.S. News 2010 law specialty ranking: N/A

3.09-3.61 GPA, 25TH-75TH PERCENTILE

153-159 LSAT, 25TH-75TH PERCENTILE

48% ACCEPTANCE RATE

Tier 3 2011 U.S. NEWS LAW SCHOOL RANKING

ADMISSIONS

Admissions phone number: **(517) 432-0222**
Admissions email address: **law@msu.edu**
Application website:
   http://www.law.msu.edu/admissions/apply.html
Application deadline for Fall 2011 admission: **30-Apr**

Admissions statistics:

Number of applicants for Fall 2009: **2,547**
Number of acceptances: **1,214**
Number enrolled: **264**
Acceptance rate: **48%**
GPA, 25th-75th percentile, entering class Fall 2009: **3.09-3.61**
LSAT, 25th-75th percentile, entering class Fall 2009: **153-159**

Part-time program:

Number of applicants for Fall 2009: **189**
Number of acceptances: **52**
Number enrolled: **24**
Acceptance rate: **28%**
GPA, 25th-75th percentile, entering class Fall 2009: **2.67-3.53**
LSAT, 25th-75th percentile, entering class Fall 2009: **144-153**

FINANCIAL AID

Financial aid phone number: **(517) 432-6810**
Financial aid application deadline: **1-May**
Tuition 2009-2010 academic year: **full-time: $32,828; part-time: $27,168**
Room and board: **$10,886** ; books: **$1,368** ; miscellaneous expenses: **$1,736**
Total of room/board/books/miscellaneous expenses: **$13,990**
University offers graduate student housing for which law students are eligible.

Financial aid profile

Percent of students that received grants for the 2008-2009 academic year: full-time: **31%**; part-time **37%**
Median grant amount: full-time: **$23,814** ; part-time: **$15,912**
The average law-school debt of those in the Class of 2009 who borrowed: **$65,292** . Proportion who borrowed: **83%**

ACADEMIC PROGRAMS

Calendar: **semester**
Joint degrees awarded: **J.D./M.B.A. (Eli Broad C.O.B.); J.D./M.A. English; J.D./M.A. Interdisciplinary Studies; J.D./M.A. Labor Relations/Human Resources; J.D./M.A. Forestry; J.D./M.S. Fisheries and Wildlife; J.D./M.URP.; J.D./LL.B. (University of Ottawa); J.D./M.S.T. (Grand Valley State Univ.)**
Typical first-year section size: Full-time: **74**; Part-time: **80**
Is there typically a "small section" of the first year class, other than Legal Writing, taught by full-time faculty?: Full-time: **no**; Part-time: **no**
Number of course titles, beyond the first year curriculum, offered last year: **175**
Percentages of upper division course sections, excluding seminars, with an enrollment of:
   Under 25: **63%**   25 to 49: **23%**
   50 to 74: **8%**   75 to 99: **1%**
   100+: **5%**
Areas of specialization: appellate advocacy, clinical training, dispute resolution, environmental law, health care law, intellectual property law, international law, tax law, trial advocacy

Fall 2009 faculty profile

Total teaching faculty: **86.** Full-time: **37%**; **69%** men, **31%** women, **13%** minorities. Part-time: **63%**; **72%** men, **28%** women, **17%** minorities
Student-to-faculty ratio: **16.6**

SPECIAL PROGRAMS (as provided by law school):

MSU Law offers 10 concentrations including a nationally recognized Intellectual Property program. Students sharpen skills & build credentials through 5 legal clinics, 3 certificates, & many externships. Dual-degree programs, including the JD/LLB with the Univ. of Ottawa, provide cost-efficient interdisciplinary study. The Fieger Trial Practice Program trains students in a high-tech court setting.

STUDENT BODY

Fall 2009 full-time enrollment: 892

Men: 62%	Women: 38%
African-American: 4.80%	American Indian: 1.30%
Asian-American: 3.70%	Mexican-American: 0.30%
Puerto Rican: 0.00%	Other Hisp-Amer: 2.00%
White: 74.60%	International: 6.20%
Unknown: 7.10%	

Fall 2009 part-time enrollment: 65

Men: 49%	Women: 51%
African-American: 12.30%	American Indian: 3.10%
Asian-American: 4.60%	Mexican-American: 0.00%
Puerto Rican: 0.00%	Other Hisp-Amer: 7.70%
White: 41.50%	International: 29.20%
Unknown: 1.50%	

Attrition rates for 2008-2009 full-time students
Percent of students discontinuing law school:

Men: 5%	Women: 4%
First-year students: 15%	Second-year students: 1%
Third-year students: N/A	Fourth-year students: N/A

LIBRARY RESOURCES
Total titles: 179,455
Total volumes: 313,133
Total seats available for library users: 455

INFORMATION TECHNOLOGY
Number of wired network connections available to students: 1209 total (in the law library, excluding computer labs: 339; in classrooms: 800; in computer labs: 10; elsewhere in the law school: 60)
Law school has a wireless network.
Students are required to own a computer.

EMPLOYMENT AND SALARIES
Proportion of 2008 graduates employed at graduation: N/A
Employed 9 months later, as of February 15, 2009: 92%
Salaries in the private sector (law firms, business, industry): $45,000 –$100,000 (25th-75th percentile)
Median salary in the private sector: $70,000
Percentage in the private sector who reported salary information: 24%
Median salary in public service (government, judicial clerkships, academic posts, non-profits): $43,750

Percentage of 2008 graduates in:

Law firms: 48%	Government: 10%
Bus./industry: 23%	Judicial clerkship: 9%
Public interest: 3%	Unknown: 1%
Academia : 6%	

2008 graduates employed in-state: 55%
2008 graduates employed in foreign countries: 4%
Number of states where graduates are employed: 32
Percentage of 2008 graduates working in: New England: 2%, Middle Atlantic: 6%, East North Central: 63%, West North Central: 2%, South Atlantic: 9%, East South Central: 1%, West South Central: 1%, Mountain: 5%, Pacific: 4%, Unknown: 4%

BAR PASSAGE RATES
Based on 2008 graduates taking Summer 2008 or Winter 2009 exams. Most of the school's first-time test takers took the bar in Michigan.

84%
School's bar passage rate for first-time test takers

82%
Statewide bar passage rate for first-time test takers

Mississippi College

- 151 E. Griffith Street, Jackson, MS, 39201
- http://www.law.mc.edu
- Private
- **Year founded:** 1975
- **2009-2010 tuition:** full-time: $26,300; part-time: $834/credit hour
- **Enrollment 2009-10 academic year:** full-time: 521; part-time: 15
- **U.S. News 2010 law specialty ranking:** N/A

3.01-3.53 GPA, 25TH-75TH PERCENTILE

148-153 LSAT, 25TH-75TH PERCENTILE

57% ACCEPTANCE RATE

Tier 4 2011 U.S. NEWS LAW SCHOOL RANKING

ADMISSIONS

Admissions phone number: **(601) 925-7151**
Admissions email address: **hweaver@mc.edu**
Application website:
  http://www.law.mc.edu/admissions/apply_options.htm
Application deadline for Fall 2011 admission: **6-Jan**

Admissions statistics:

Number of applicants for Fall 2009: **1,315**
Number of acceptances: **744**
Number enrolled: **193**
Acceptance rate: **57%**
GPA, 25th-75th percentile, entering class Fall 2009: **3.01-3.53**
LSAT, 25th-75th percentile, entering class Fall 2009: **148-153**

Part-time program:

Number of applicants for Fall 2009: **1**
Number of acceptances: **1**
Number enrolled: **1**
Acceptance rate: **100%**
GPA, 25th-75th percentile, entering class Fall 2009: **4.00-4.00**
LSAT, 25th-75th percentile, entering class Fall 2009: **153-153**

FINANCIAL AID

Financial aid phone number: **(601) 925-7110**
Financial aid application deadline: **6-Jan**
Tuition 2009-2010 academic year: **full-time: $26,300; part-time: $834/credit hour**
Room and board: **$12,000** ; books: **$1,200** ; miscellaneous expenses: **$7,650**
Total of room/board/books/miscellaneous expenses: **$20,850**
University does not offer graduate student housing for which law students are eligible.

Financial aid profile

Percent of students that received grants for the 2008-2009 academic year: full-time: **35%**
Median grant amount: full-time: **$5,000** ; part-time: **$0**
The average law-school debt of those in the Class of 2009 who borrowed: **$89,906** . Proportion who borrowed: **82%**

ACADEMIC PROGRAMS

Calendar: **semester**
Joint degrees awarded: **J.D./M.B.A.**
Typical first-year section size: Full-time: **87**
Is there typically a "small section" of the first year class, other than Legal Writing, taught by full-time faculty?: Full-time: **yes**
Number of course titles, beyond the first year curriculum, offered last year: **84**
Percentages of upper division course sections, excluding seminars, with an enrollment of:

Under 25: **63%**	25 to 49: **18%**
50 to 74: **15%**	75 to 99: **3%**
100+: **1%**	

Areas of specialization: appellate advocacy, clinical training, dispute resolution, environmental law, health care law, intellectual property law, international law, tax law, trial advocacy

Fall 2009 faculty profile

Total teaching faculty: **109**. Full-time: **23%**; **44%** men, **56%** women, **20%** minorities. Part-time: **77%**; **57%** men, **43%** women, **11%** minorities
Student-to-faculty ratio: **18.2**

SPECIAL PROGRAMS (as provided by law school):

Child Advocacy students represent a child, interview, make court appearances. Legal Aid Office provides opportunity to assist the underserved, acquire basic consumer expertise, experience client interviewing. Externships provide practical experience with judges/govt agencies. Foreign study: Korea/Mexico. Legal Ctrs: Family, Bus/Tax, Bioethics/Health, Public Svc, Intl Law, Lit/Dispute Resolution.

STUDENT BODY

Fall 2009 full-time enrollment: 521

Men: **58%**	Women: **42%**
African-American: **9.20%**	American Indian: **0.40%**
Asian-American: **1.30%**	Mexican-American: **0.00%**
Puerto Rican: **0.00%**	Other Hisp-Amer: **0.80%**
White: **85.80%**	International: **0.20%**
Unknown: **2.30%**	

Fall 2009 part-time enrollment: 15

Men: **60%**	Women: **40%**
African-American: **13.30%**	American Indian: **0.00%**
Asian-American: **0.00%**	Mexican-American: **0.00%**
Puerto Rican: **0.00%**	Other Hisp-Amer: **0.00%**
White: **86.70%**	International: **0.00%**
Unknown: **0.00%**	

Attrition rates for 2008-2009 full-time students
Percent of students discontinuing law school:

Men: **7%**	Women: **4%**
First-year students: **15%**	Second-year students: **2%**
Third-year students: **N/A**	Fourth-year students: **N/A**

LIBRARY RESOURCES

Total titles: **207,477**
Total volumes: **361,979**
Total seats available for library users: **394**

INFORMATION TECHNOLOGY

Number of wired network connections available to students: **0** total (in the law library, excluding computer labs: **0**; in classrooms: **0**; in computer labs: **0**; elsewhere in the law school: **0**)
Law school has a wireless network.
Students are not required to own a computer.

EMPLOYMENT AND SALARIES

Proportion of 2008 graduates employed at graduation:
N/A
Employed 9 months later, as of February 15, 2009: **94%**
Salaries in the private sector (law firms, business, industry): **$48,000 –$90,000** (25th-75th percentile)
Median salary in the private sector: **$75,000**
Percentage in the private sector who reported salary information: **72%**
Median salary in public service (government, judicial clerkships, academic posts, non-profits): **$51,500**

Percentage of 2008 graduates in:

Law firms: **52%**	Government: **15%**
Bus./industry: **20%**	Judicial clerkship: **12%**
Public interest: **0%**	Unknown: **0%**
Academia : **1%**	

2008 graduates employed in-state: **66%**
2008 graduates employed in foreign countries: **1%**
Number of states where graduates are employed: **17**
Percentage of 2008 graduates working in: New England: **0%**, Middle Atlantic: **0%**, East North Central: **1%**, West North Central: **1%**, South Atlantic: **8%**, East South Central: **71%**, West South Central: **16%**, Mountain: **1%**, Pacific: **1%**, Unknown: **0%**

BAR PASSAGE RATES

Based on 2008 graduates taking Summer 2008 or Winter 2009 exams. Most of the school's first-time test takers took the bar in Mississippi.

94%

School's bar passage rate for first-time test takers

88%

Statewide bar passage rate for first-time test takers

New England School of Law

- 154 Stuart Street, Boston, MA, 2116
- http://www.nesl.edu
- Private
- **Year founded:** 1908
- **2009-2010 tuition:** full-time: $38,580; part-time: $28,960
- **Enrollment 2009-10 academic year:** full-time: 737; part-time: 359
- **U.S. News 2010 law specialty ranking:** N/A

3.00-3.45 GPA, 25TH-75TH PERCENTILE

151-154 LSAT, 25TH-75TH PERCENTILE

60% ACCEPTANCE RATE

Tier 4 2011 U.S. NEWS LAW SCHOOL RANKING

ADMISSIONS

Admissions phone number: **(617) 422-7210**
Admissions email address: **admit@nesl.edu**
Application website: **N/A**
Application deadline for Fall 2011 admission: **15-Mar**

Admissions statistics:
Number of applicants for Fall 2009: **2,678**
Number of acceptances: **1,599**
Number enrolled: **296**
Acceptance rate: **60%**
GPA, 25th-75th percentile, entering class Fall 2009: **3.00-3.45**
LSAT, 25th-75th percentile, entering class Fall 2009: **151-154**

Part-time program:
Number of applicants for Fall 2009: **765**
Number of acceptances: **391**
Number enrolled: **107**
Acceptance rate: **51%**
GPA, 25th-75th percentile, entering class Fall 2009: **2.80-3.40**
LSAT, 25th-75th percentile, entering class Fall 2009: **149-155**

FINANCIAL AID

Financial aid phone number: **(617) 422-7298**
Financial aid application deadline: **8-Apr**
Tuition 2009-2010 academic year: **full-time: $38,580; part-time: $28,960**
Room and board: **$11,950** ; books: **$1,250** ; miscellaneous expenses: **$4,925**
Total of room/board/books/miscellaneous expenses: **$18,125**
University does not offer graduate student housing for which law students are eligible.

Financial aid profile
Percent of students that received grants for the 2008-2009 academic year: full-time: **52%**; part-time **27%**

Median grant amount: full-time: **$5,000** ; part-time: **$5,000**
The average law-school debt of those in the Class of 2009 who borrowed: **$106,632** . Proportion who borrowed: **85%**

ACADEMIC PROGRAMS

Calendar: **semester**
Joint degrees awarded: **N/A**
Typical first-year section size: Full-time: **110**; Part-time: **105**
Is there typically a "small section" of the first year class, other than Legal Writing, taught by full-time faculty?: Full-time: **no**; Part-time: **no**
Number of course titles, beyond the first year curriculum, offered last year: **121**
Percentages of upper division course sections, excluding seminars, with an enrollment of:

Under 25: **55%**	25 to 49: **29%**
50 to 74: **8%**	75 to 99: **6%**
100+: **2%**	

Areas of specialization: appellate advocacy, clinical training, dispute resolution, environmental law, health care law, intellectual property law, international law, tax law, trial advocacy

Fall 2009 faculty profile
Total teaching faculty: **103**. Full-time: **34%**; **66%** men, **34%** women, **9%** minorities. Part-time: **66%**; **60%** men, **40%** women, **16%** minorities
Student-to-faculty ratio: **23.1**

SPECIAL PROGRAMS *(as provided by law school)*:
Clinics in 16 subject areas and in-house Clinical Law Office; academic centers - international law, law & social responsibility, business law - sponsoring conferences and research projects; three required semesters of legal research & writing; judicial clerkship opportunities; summer programs in Ireland, London/Edinburgh, Malta, Prague, Chile; semester programs in The Netherlands, Denmark, Paris

STUDENT BODY

Fall 2009 full-time enrollment: 737

Men: 41%	Women: 59%
African-American: 2.30%	American Indian: 0.30%
Asian-American: 6.50%	Mexican-American: 0.80%
Puerto Rican: 0.50%	Other Hisp-Amer: 1.80%
White: 73.30%	International: 0.00%
Unknown: 14.50%	

Fall 2009 part-time enrollment: 359

Men: 51%	Women: 49%
African-American: 1.10%	American Indian: 0.00%
Asian-American: 3.10%	Mexican-American: 0.60%
Puerto Rican: 0.00%	Other Hisp-Amer: 0.60%
White: 77.40%	International: 0.00%
Unknown: 17.30%	

Attrition rates for 2008-2009 full-time students
Percent of students discontinuing law school:

Men: 11%	Women: 8%
First-year students: 20%	Second-year students: 5%
Third-year students: 1%	Fourth-year students: 3%

LIBRARY RESOURCES

Total titles: 91,047
Total volumes: 320,682
Total seats available for library users: 473

INFORMATION TECHNOLOGY

Number of wired network connections available to students: **176** total (in the law library, excluding computer labs: **30**; in classrooms: **100**; in computer labs: **40**; elsewhere in the law school: **6**)
Law school has a wireless network.
Students are not required to own a computer.

EMPLOYMENT AND SALARIES

Proportion of 2008 graduates employed at graduation:
N/A
Employed 9 months later, as of February 15, 2009: **81%**
Salaries in the private sector (law firms, business, industry): **$50,625 –$95,000** (25th-75th percentile)
Median salary in the private sector: **$61,750**
Percentage in the private sector who reported salary information: **16%**
Median salary in public service (government, judicial clerkships, academic posts, non-profits): **$46,983**

Percentage of 2008 graduates in:

Law firms: 39%	Government: 15%
Bus./industry: 27%	Judicial clerkship: 13%
Public interest: 4%	Unknown: 0%
Academia : 2%	

2008 graduates employed in-state: **63%**
2008 graduates employed in foreign countries: **0%**
Number of states where graduates are employed: **28**
Percentage of 2008 graduates working in: New England: **68%**, Middle Atlantic: **12%**, East North Central: **2%**, West North Central: **1%**, South Atlantic: **9%**, East South Central: **2%**, West South Central: **2%**, Mountain: **1%**, Pacific: **3%**, Unknown: **0%**

BAR PASSAGE RATES

Based on 2008 graduates taking Summer 2008 or Winter 2009 exams. Most of the school's first-time test takers took the bar in Massachusetts.

91%
School's bar passage rate for first-time test takers

89%
Statewide bar passage rate for first-time test takers

New York Law School

- 185 W. Broadway, New York, NY, 10013-2960
- http://www.nyls.edu
- Private
- Year founded: 1891
- 2009-2010 tuition: full-time: $44,800; part-time: $34,500
- Enrollment 2009-10 academic year: full-time: 1,408; part-time: 448
- U.S. News 2010 law specialty ranking: N/A

3.02-3.48 GPA, 25TH-75TH PERCENTILE

152-157 LSAT, 25TH-75TH PERCENTILE

57% ACCEPTANCE RATE

Tier 3 2011 U.S. NEWS LAW SCHOOL RANKING

ADMISSIONS

Admissions phone number: **(212) 431-2888**
Admissions email address: **admissions@nyls.edu**
Application website: **N/A**
Application deadline for Fall 2011 admission: **1-Apr**

Admissions statistics:
Number of applicants for Fall 2009: **3,403**
Number of acceptances: **1,936**
Number enrolled: **569**
Acceptance rate: **57%**
GPA, 25th-75th percentile, entering class Fall 2009: **3.02-3.48**
LSAT, 25th-75th percentile, entering class Fall 2009: **152-157**

Part-time program:
Number of applicants for Fall 2009: **785**
Number of acceptances: **310**
Number enrolled: **167**
Acceptance rate: **39%**
GPA, 25th-75th percentile, entering class Fall 2009: **2.79-3.46**
LSAT, 25th-75th percentile, entering class Fall 2009: **149-155**

FINANCIAL AID

Financial aid phone number: **(212) 431-2828**
Financial aid application deadline: **1-Apr**
Tuition 2009-2010 academic year: **full-time: $44,800; part-time: $34,500**
Room and board: **$16,840** ; books: **$1,300** ; miscellaneous expenses: **$4,215**
Total of room/board/books/miscellaneous expenses: **$22,355**
University offers graduate student housing for which law students are eligible.

Financial aid profile
Percent of students that received grants for the 2008-2009 academic year: full-time: **31%**; part-time **21%**

Median grant amount: full-time: **$10,000** ; part-time: **$5,000**
The average law-school debt of those in the Class of 2009 who borrowed: **$129,410** . Proportion who borrowed: **87%**

ACADEMIC PROGRAMS

Calendar: **semester**
Joint degrees awarded: **J.D./M.B.A.**
Typical first-year section size: Full-time: **114**; Part-time: **80**
Is there typically a "small section" of the first year class, other than Legal Writing, taught by full-time faculty?: Full-time: **yes**; Part-time: **yes**
Number of course titles, beyond the first year curriculum, offered last year: **245**
Percentages of upper division course sections, excluding seminars, with an enrollment of:

Under 25: **48%**	25 to 49: **23%**
50 to 74: **10%**	75 to 99: **4%**
100+: **15%**	

Areas of specialization: appellate advocacy, clinical training, dispute resolution, environmental law, health care law, intellectual property law, international law, tax law, trial advocacy

Fall 2009 faculty profile
Total teaching faculty: **178**. Full-time: **31%**; **71%** men, **29%** women, **15%** minorities. Part-time: **69%**; **62%** men, **38%** women, **11%** minorities
Student-to-faculty ratio: **23.6**

SPECIAL PROGRAMS *(as provided by law school)*:
Liaison program linking students to administrators; faculty advising system; John Marshall Harlan Scholars; Lawyering Skills Center; Law & Journalism Program; Patent Law Program; Academic Centers: Business Law & Policy; Children & Families; Financial Services Law; Information Law & Policy; International Law; Justice Action Center; New York City Law; Professional Values & Practice; Real Estate.

STUDENT BODY

Fall 2009 full-time enrollment: 1,408

Men: 48%	Women: 52%
African-American: 5.30%	American Indian: 0.10%
Asian-American: 5.30%	Mexican-American: 0.60%
Puerto Rican: 1.10%	Other Hisp-Amer: 5.70%
White: 63.00%	International: 0.00%
Unknown: 18.90%	

Fall 2009 part-time enrollment: 448

Men: 54%	Women: 46%
African-American: 8.70%	American Indian: 0.40%
Asian-American: 4.00%	Mexican-American: 1.10%
Puerto Rican: 3.30%	Other Hisp-Amer: 7.80%
White: 58.00%	International: 0.00%
Unknown: 16.50%	

Attrition rates for 2008-2009 full-time students
Percent of students discontinuing law school:

Men: 5%	Women: 4%
First-year students: 11%	Second-year students: 0%
Third-year students: 0%	Fourth-year students: N/A

LIBRARY RESOURCES

Total titles: 488,794
Total volumes: 534,789
Total seats available for library users: 700

INFORMATION TECHNOLOGY

Number of wired network connections available to students: 95 total (in the law library, excluding computer labs: 25; in classrooms: 0; in computer labs: 70; elsewhere in the law school: 0)
Law school has a wireless network.
Students are not required to own a computer.

EMPLOYMENT AND SALARIES

Proportion of 2008 graduates employed at graduation: N/A
Employed 9 months later, as of February 15, 2009: 93%
Salaries in the private sector (law firms, business, industry): $71,250 –$160,000 (25th-75th percentile)
Median salary in the private sector: $160,000
Percentage in the private sector who reported salary information: 27%
Median salary in public service (government, judicial clerkships, academic posts, non-profits): $53,500

Percentage of 2008 graduates in:

Law firms: 43%	Government: 14%
Bus./industry: 23%	Judicial clerkship: 4%
Public interest: 6%	Unknown: 6%
Academia : 4%	

2008 graduates employed in-state: 71%
2008 graduates employed in foreign countries: 1%
Number of states where graduates are employed: 14
Percentage of 2008 graduates working in: New England: 0%, Middle Atlantic: 78%, East North Central: 1%, West North Central: 0%, South Atlantic: 6%, East South Central: 0%, West South Central: 1%, Mountain: 0%, Pacific: 2%, Unknown: 12%

BAR PASSAGE RATES

Based on 2008 graduates taking Summer 2008 or Winter 2009 exams. Most of the school's first-time test takers took the bar in New York.

91%
School's bar passage rate for first-time test takers

81%
Statewide bar passage rate for first-time test takers

New York University

- 40 Washington Square S, New York, NY, 10012
- http://www.law.nyu.edu
- Private
- Year founded: 1835
- 2009-2010 tuition: full-time: $44,820; part-time: N/A
- Enrollment 2009-10 academic year: full-time: 1,427
- U.S. News 2010 law specialty ranking: clinical training: 4, environmental law: 10, intellectual property law: 5, international law: 1, tax law: 1

3.57-3.86 GPA, 25TH-75TH PERCENTILE

169-173 LSAT, 25TH-75TH PERCENTILE

23% ACCEPTANCE RATE

6 2011 U.S. NEWS LAW SCHOOL RANKING

ADMISSIONS

Admissions phone number: **(212) 998-6060**
Admissions email address: **law.moreinfo@nyu.edu**
Application website:
   http://www.law.nyu.edu/admissions/jdadmissions/applicants/applications/index.htm
Application deadline for Fall 2011 admission: **1-Feb**

Admissions statistics:

Number of applicants for Fall 2009: **7,272**
Number of acceptances: **1,644**
Number enrolled: **450**
Acceptance rate: **23%**
GPA, 25th-75th percentile, entering class Fall 2009: **3.57-3.86**
LSAT, 25th-75th percentile, entering class Fall 2009: **169-173**

FINANCIAL AID

Financial aid phone number: **(212) 998-6050**
Financial aid application deadline: **15-Apr**
Tuition 2009-2010 academic year: **full-time: $44,820; part-time: N/A**
Room and board: **$20,914** ; books: **$1,370** ; miscellaneous expenses: **$2,946**
Total of room/board/books/miscellaneous expenses: **$25,230**
University does not offer graduate student housing for which law students are eligible.

Financial aid profile

Percent of students that received grants for the 2008-2009 academic year: full-time: **35%**
Median grant amount: full-time: **$20,000**
The average law-school debt of those in the Class of 2009 who borrowed: **$125,504** . Proportion who borrowed: **81%**

ACADEMIC PROGRAMS

Calendar: **semester**
Joint degrees awarded: **J.D./M.A.; J.D./M.B.A.; J.D./M.P.A. ; J.D./M.U.P.; J.D./M.S.W.; J.D./Ph.D.; J.D./M.P.A.** (Harvard); **J.D./M.P.A.** (Princeton); **J.D./LL.B.** (Osgoode); **J.D./M.P.P.**
Typical first-year section size: Full-time: **89**
Is there typically a "small section" of the first year class, other than Legal Writing, taught by full-time faculty?: Full-time: **no**
Number of course titles, beyond the first year curriculum, offered last year: **326**
Percentages of upper division course sections, excluding seminars, with an enrollment of:
   Under 25: **47%**   25 to 49: **28%**
   50 to 74: **13%**   75 to 99: **7%**
   100+: **6%**
Areas of specialization: appellate advocacy, clinical training, dispute resolution, environmental law, health care law, intellectual property law, international law, tax law, trial advocacy

Fall 2009 faculty profile

Total teaching faculty: **195**. Full-time: **64%**; **71%** men, **29%** women, **17%** minorities. Part-time: **36%**; **67%** men, **33%** women, **34%** minorities
Student-to-faculty ratio: **9.4**

SPECIAL PROGRAMS *(as provided by law school):*

NYU School of Law's curriculum is distinguished by its strength in traditional areas of legal study, interdisciplinary study, and clinical education, and has long been committed to educating lawyers who will use their degrees to serve the public. Students enjoy the intellectual and pedagogical diversity of NYU by mixing traditional courses with colloquia, research, clinics, and more.

STUDENT BODY

Fall 2009 full-time enrollment: 1,427

Men: **56%**	Women: **44%**
African-American: **6.20%**	American Indian: **0.20%**
Asian-American: **10.50%**	Mexican-American: **1.10%**
Puerto Rican: **0.80%**	Other Hisp-Amer: **4.40%**
White: **48.10%**	International: **3.10%**
Unknown: **25.60%**	

Attrition rates for 2008-2009 full-time students
Percent of students discontinuing law school:

Men: **1%**	Women: **1%**
First-year students: **1%**	Second-year students: **1%**
Third-year students: **N/A**	Fourth-year students: **N/A**

LIBRARY RESOURCES

Total titles: **694,671**
Total volumes: **1,098,972**
Total seats available for library users: **850**

INFORMATION TECHNOLOGY

Number of wired network connections available to students: **775** total (in the law library, excluding computer labs: **35**; in classrooms: **700**; in computer labs: **25**; elsewhere in the law school: **15**)
Law school has a wireless network.
Students are required to own a computer.

EMPLOYMENT AND SALARIES

Proportion of 2008 graduates employed at graduation: **99%**
Employed 9 months later, as of February 15, 2009: **99%**
Salaries in the private sector (law firms, business, industry): **$160,000 –$160,000** (25th-75th percentile)
Median salary in the private sector: **$160,000**
Percentage in the private sector who reported salary information: **96%**

Median salary in public service (government, judicial clerkships, academic posts, non-profits): **$57,354**

Percentage of 2008 graduates in:

Law firms: **75%**	Government: **2%**
Bus./industry: **2%**	Judicial clerkship: **11%**
Public interest: **9%**	Unknown: **0%**
Academia : **1%**	

2008 graduates employed in-state: **69%**
2008 graduates employed in foreign countries: **3%**
Number of states where graduates are employed: **28**
Percentage of 2008 graduates working in: New England: **2%**, Middle Atlantic: **71%**, East North Central: **1%**, West North Central: **1%**, South Atlantic: **9%**, East South Central: **2%**, West South Central: **1%**, Mountain: **1%**, Pacific: **9%**, Unknown: **0%**

BAR PASSAGE RATES

Based on 2008 graduates taking Summer 2008 or Winter 2009 exams. Most of the school's first-time test takers took the bar in New York.

97%

School's bar passage rate for first-time test takers

81%

Statewide bar passage rate for first-time test takers

North Carolina Central University

- 640 Nelson Street, Durham, NC, 27707
- http://www.nccu.edu/law
- Public
- Year founded: 1939
- 2009-2010 tuition: full-time: $8,097; part-time: $8,097
- Enrollment 2009-10 academic year: full-time: 480; part-time: 121
- U.S. News 2010 law specialty ranking: N/A

2.99-3.43 GPA, 25TH-75TH PERCENTILE

142-148 LSAT, 25TH-75TH PERCENTILE

18% ACCEPTANCE RATE

Tier 4 2011 U.S. NEWS LAW SCHOOL RANKING

ADMISSIONS

Admissions phone number: (919) 530-5243
Admissions email address: law_admissions@nccu.edu
Application website: N/A
Application deadline for Fall 2011 admission: 31-Mar

Admissions statistics:
Number of applicants for Fall 2009: 2,013
Number of acceptances: 353
Number enrolled: 169
Acceptance rate: 18%
GPA, 25th-75th percentile, entering class Fall 2009: 2.99-3.43
LSAT, 25th-75th percentile, entering class Fall 2009: 142-148

Part-time program:
Number of applicants for Fall 2009: 806
Number of acceptances: 127
Number enrolled: 35
Acceptance rate: 16%
GPA, 25th-75th percentile, entering class Fall 2009: 3.16-3.67
LSAT, 25th-75th percentile, entering class Fall 2009: 148-155

FINANCIAL AID

Financial aid phone number: (919) 530-7173
Financial aid application deadline: 1-Jul
Tuition 2009-2010 academic year: full-time: $8,097; part-time: $8,097
Room and board: $17,095 ; books: $2,100 ; miscellaneous expenses: $600
Total of room/board/books/miscellaneous expenses: $19,795
University offers graduate student housing for which law students are eligible.

Financial aid profile
Percent of students that received grants for the 2008-2009 academic year: full-time: 61%

Median grant amount: full-time: $4,536
The average law-school debt of those in the Class of 2009 who borrowed: $66,394 . Proportion who borrowed: 77%

ACADEMIC PROGRAMS

Calendar: semester
Joint degrees awarded: J.D./M.B.A.; J.D./M.L.S.
Typical first-year section size: Full-time: 65; Part-time: 65
Is there typically a "small section" of the first year class, other than Legal Writing, taught by full-time faculty?: Full-time: no; Part-time: no
Number of course titles, beyond the first year curriculum, offered last year: 77
Percentages of upper division course sections, excluding seminars, with an enrollment of:

Under 25: 50%	25 to 49: 32%
50 to 74: 10%	75 to 99: 5%
100+: 3%	

Areas of specialization: appellate advocacy, clinical training, dispute resolution, environmental law, health care law, intellectual property law, international law, tax law, trial advocacy

Fall 2009 faculty profile
Total teaching faculty: 41. Full-time: 51%; 38% men, 62% women, 67% minorities. Part-time: 49%; 55% men, 45% women, 40% minorities
Student-to-faculty ratio: 16.5

SPECIAL PROGRAMS *(as provided by law school):*
NCCU School of Law offers top notch clinics and externships, joint master's degree programs with the Business and Library schools, and certificates to J.D. graduates who complete related coursework in the school's Biotechnology and Pharmaceutical Law and Dispute Resolution Institutes.

STUDENT BODY

Fall 2009 full-time enrollment: 480

Men: 37%	Women: 63%
African-American: 55.80%	American Indian: 0.80%
Asian-American: 2.90%	Mexican-American: 0.00%

Puerto Rican: **0.00%** Other Hisp-Amer: **2.70%**
White: **34.00%** International: **3.10%**
Unknown: **0.60%**

Fall 2009 part-time enrollment: 121
Men: **48%** Women: **52%**
African-American: **20.70%** American Indian: **0.00%**
Asian-American: **5.00%** Mexican-American: **0.00%**
Puerto Rican: **0.00%** Other Hisp-Amer: **4.10%**
White: **65.30%** International: **4.10%**
Unknown: **0.80%**

Attrition rates for 2008-2009 full-time students
Percent of students discontinuing law school:
Men: **6%** Women: **4%**
First-year students: **14%** Second-year students: **1%**
Third-year students: **N/A** Fourth-year students: **N/A**

LIBRARY RESOURCES
Total titles: **437,861**
Total volumes: **388,660**
Total seats available for library users: **370**

INFORMATION TECHNOLOGY
Number of wired network connections available to students: **78** total (in the law library, excluding computer labs: **12**; in classrooms: **4**; in computer labs: **30**; elsewhere in the law school: **32**)
Law school has a wireless network.
Students are not required to own a computer.

EMPLOYMENT AND SALARIES
Proportion of 2008 graduates employed at graduation: **N/A**

Employed 9 months later, as of February 15, 2009: **81%**
Salaries in the private sector (law firms, business, industry): **N/A–N/A** (25th-75th percentile)
Median salary in the private sector: **N/A**
Percentage in the private sector who reported salary information: **N/A**
Median salary in public service (government, judicial clerkships, academic posts, non-profits): **N/A**

Percentage of 2008 graduates in:
Law firms: **53%** Government: **22%**
Bus./industry: **6%** Judicial clerkship: **6%**
Public interest: **7%** Unknown: **5%**
Academia : **1%**

2008 graduates employed in-state: **68%**
2008 graduates employed in foreign countries: **0%**
Number of states where graduates are employed: **11**
Percentage of 2008 graduates working in: New England: **0%**, Middle Atlantic: **3%**, East North Central: **0%**, West North Central: **0%**, South Atlantic: **87%**, East South Central: **1%**, West South Central: **0%**, Mountain: **2%**, Pacific: **2%**, Unknown: **5%**

BAR PASSAGE RATES
Based on 2008 graduates taking Summer 2008 or Winter 2009 exams. Most of the school's first-time test takers took the bar in North Carolina.

	81%

School's bar passage rate for first-time test takers

	83%

Statewide bar passage rate for first-time test takers

Northeastern University

- 400 Huntington Avenue, Boston, MA, 2115
- http://northeastern.edu/law
- Private
- Year founded: 1898
- 2009-2010 tuition: full-time: $39,866; part-time: N/A
- Enrollment 2009-10 academic year: full-time: 602
- U.S. News 2010 law specialty ranking: clinical training: 28

3.20-3.63 GPA, 25TH-75TH PERCENTILE

155-163 LSAT, 25TH-75TH PERCENTILE

34% ACCEPTANCE RATE

86 2011 U.S. NEWS LAW SCHOOL RANKING

ADMISSIONS

Admissions phone number: **(617) 373-2395**
Admissions email address: **lawadmissions@neu.edu**
Application website: **http://northeastern.edu/law/apply**
Application deadline for Fall 2011 admission: **1-Mar**

Admissions statistics:
Number of applicants for Fall 2009: **3,798**
Number of acceptances: **1,280**
Number enrolled: **214**
Acceptance rate: **34%**
GPA, 25th-75th percentile, entering class Fall 2009: **3.20-3.63**
LSAT, 25th-75th percentile, entering class Fall 2009: **155-163**

FINANCIAL AID

Financial aid phone number: **(617) 373-4620**
Financial aid application deadline: **15-Feb**
Tuition 2009-2010 academic year: **full-time: $39,866; part-time: N/A**
Room and board: **$15,414** ; books: **$1,500** ; miscellaneous expenses: **$2,875**
Total of room/board/books/miscellaneous expenses: **$19,789**
University offers graduate student housing for which law students are eligible.

Financial aid profile
Percent of students that received grants for the 2008-2009 academic year: full-time: **79%**
Median grant amount: full-time: **$9,200**
The average law-school debt of those in the Class of 2009 who borrowed: **$103,311** . Proportion who borrowed: **82%**

ACADEMIC PROGRAMS

Calendar: **quarter**
Joint degrees awarded: **J.D./M.P.H.; J.D./M.B.A.; J.D./M.S./M.B.A. Professional Accounting; JD./M.S. or Ph.D. Law, Policy & Society; J.D./Masters Environmental Law & Policy; J.D./M.A. Sustainable International Dev.**

Typical first-year section size: Full-time: **70**
Is there typically a "small section" of the first year class, other than Legal Writing, taught by full-time faculty?: Full-time: **yes**
Number of course titles, beyond the first year curriculum, offered last year: **93**
Percentages of upper division course sections, excluding seminars, with an enrollment of:
Under 25: **47%**   25 to 49: **37%**
50 to 74: **10%**   75 to 99: **4%**
100+: **1%**
Areas of specialization: appellate advocacy, clinical training, dispute resolution, environmental law, health care law, intellectual property law, international law, tax law, trial advocacy

Fall 2009 faculty profile
Total teaching faculty: **79**. Full-time: **43%**; **47%** men, **53%** women, **24%** minorities. Part-time: **57%**; **60%** men, **40%** women, **16%** minorities
Student-to-faculty ratio: **15.4**

SPECIAL PROGRAMS *(as provided by law school):*
Our program is unique in its integration of classroom rigor and real-world experience. Every first year student undertakes a team social justice project through our Legal Skills in Social Context course. Each student graduates with a full year of legal experience through our co-op externship program with four 11-week full-time jobs in 54 countries and the US. 45% also complete at least one clinic.

STUDENT BODY
Fall 2009 full-time enrollment: 602
Men: **41%**   Women: **59%**
African-American: **10.30%**   American Indian: **1.30%**
Asian-American: **8.60%**   Mexican-American: **0.00%**
Puerto Rican: **0.00%**   Other Hisp-Amer: **11.30%**
White: **53.20%**   International: **0.00%**
Unknown: **15.30%**

Attrition rates for 2008-2009 full-time students
Percent of students discontinuing law school:
Men: **3%**   Women: **1%**
First-year students: **2%**   Second-year students: **6%**
Third-year students: **N/A**   Fourth-year students: **N/A**

LIBRARY RESOURCES
Total titles: **141,107**
Total volumes: **329,771**
Total seats available for library users: **333**

INFORMATION TECHNOLOGY
Number of wired network connections available to students: **364** total (in the law library, excluding computer labs: **35**; in classrooms: **316**; in computer labs: **3**; elsewhere in the law school: **10**)
Law school has a wireless network.
Students are not required to own a computer.

EMPLOYMENT AND SALARIES
Proportion of 2008 graduates employed at graduation: **N/A**
Employed 9 months later, as of February 15, 2009: **94%**
Salaries in the private sector (law firms, business, industry): **$55,000 –$160,000** (25th-75th percentile)
Median salary in the private sector: **$85,000**
Percentage in the private sector who reported salary information: **60%**

Median salary in public service (government, judicial clerkships, academic posts, non-profits): **$47,000**

Percentage of 2008 graduates in:
Law firms: **34%**   Government: **8%**
Bus./industry: **26%**   Judicial clerkship: **13%**
Public interest: **16%**   Unknown: **0%**
Academia : **3%**

2008 graduates employed in-state: **69%**
2008 graduates employed in foreign countries: **2%**
Number of states where graduates are employed: **21**
Percentage of 2008 graduates working in: New England: **76%**, Middle Atlantic: **4%**, East North Central: **1%**, West North Central: **2%**, South Atlantic: **6%**, East South Central: **0%**, West South Central: **3%**, Mountain: **1%**, Pacific: **6%**, Unknown: **N/A**

BAR PASSAGE RATES
Based on 2008 graduates taking Summer 2008 or Winter 2009 exams. Most of the school's first-time test takers took the bar in Massachusetts.

94%
School's bar passage rate for first-time test takers

89%
Statewide bar passage rate for first-time test takers

Northern Illinois University

- Swen Parson Hall, Room 276, De Kalb, IL, 60115
- http://law.niu.edu
- Public
- Year founded: 1975
- 2009-2010 tuition: full-time: $14,847; part-time: $598/credit hour
- Enrollment 2009-10 academic year: full-time: 1,169; part-time: 14
- U.S. News 2010 law specialty ranking: N/A

2.93-3.51 GPA, 25TH-75TH PERCENTILE

153-156 LSAT, 25TH-75TH PERCENTILE

40% ACCEPTANCE RATE

Tier 4 2011 U.S. NEWS LAW SCHOOL RANKING

ADMISSIONS
Admissions phone number: **(815) 753-8595**
Admissions email address: **lawadm@niu.edu**
Application website: **http://law.niu.edu**
Application deadline for Fall 2011 admission: **15-May**

Admissions statistics:
Number of applicants for Fall 2009: **1,169**
Number of acceptances: **472**
Number enrolled: **105**
Acceptance rate: **40%**
GPA, 25th-75th percentile, entering class Fall 2009: **2.93-3.51**
LSAT, 25th-75th percentile, entering class Fall 2009: **153-156**

Part-time program:
Number of applicants for Fall 2009: **14**
Number of acceptances: **5**
Number enrolled: **3**
Acceptance rate: **36%**
GPA, 25th-75th percentile, entering class Fall 2009: **3.57-3.74**
LSAT, 25th-75th percentile, entering class Fall 2009: **150-153**

FINANCIAL AID
Financial aid phone number: **(815) 753-8595**
Financial aid application deadline: **1-Mar**
Tuition 2009-2010 academic year: **full-time: $14,847**; part-time: **$598/credit hour**
Room and board: **$10,032** ; books: **$1,500** ; miscellaneous expenses: **$4,080**
Total of room/board/books/miscellaneous expenses: **$15,612**
University offers graduate student housing for which law students are eligible.

Financial aid profile
Percent of students that received grants for the 2008-2009 academic year: full-time: **12%**; part-time **29%**

Median grant amount: full-time: **$5,846** ; part-time: **$9,105**
The average law-school debt of those in the Class of 2009 who borrowed: **$50,880** . Proportion who borrowed: **86%**

ACADEMIC PROGRAMS
Calendar: **semester**
Joint degrees awarded: **J.D./M.B.A.; J.D./M.P.A.**
Typical first-year section size: Full-time: **49**
Is there typically a "small section" of the first year class, other than Legal Writing, taught by full-time faculty?: Full-time: **no**
Number of course titles, beyond the first year curriculum, offered last year: **59**
Percentages of upper division course sections, excluding seminars, with an enrollment of:
Under 25: **62%**   25 to 49: **18%**
50 to 74: **15%**   75 to 99: **6%**
100+: **0%**
Areas of specialization: appellate advocacy, clinical training, dispute resolution, environmental law, health care law, intellectual property law, international law, tax law, trial advocacy

Fall 2009 faculty profile
Total teaching faculty: **20**. Full-time: **65%**; **62%** men, **38%** women, **38%** minorities. Part-time: **35%**; **57%** men, **43%** women, **14%** minorities
Student-to-faculty ratio: **18.7**

SPECIAL PROGRAMS *(as provided by law school):*
Students who have been exposed to the fundamentals of legal practice in the simulation courses have the opportunity in the Clinical Experiences to refine their practice skills and begin the transition from classroom to practice. The College of Law offers one international program – located in Agen, France – as well as a selection of upper-level courses during the summer.

STUDENT BODY
Fall 2009 full-time enrollment: **1,169**
Men: **63%**   Women: **37%**
African-American: **12.60%**   American Indian: **0.60%**

Asian-American: **9.40%** Mexican-American: **2.40%**
Puerto Rican: **0.10%** Other Hisp-Amer: **3.80%**
White: **61.80%** International: **0.00%**
Unknown: **9.30%**

Fall 2009 part-time enrollment: **14**
Men: **57%** Women: **43%**
African-American: **14.30%** American Indian: **0.00%**
Asian-American: **7.10%** Mexican-American: **0.00%**
Puerto Rican: **0.00%** Other Hisp-Amer: **0.00%**
White: **64.30%** International: **0.00%**
Unknown: **14.30%**

Attrition rates for 2008-2009 full-time students
Percent of students discontinuing law school:
Men: **3%** Women: **3%**
First-year students: **5%** Second-year students: **1%**
Third-year students: **2%** Fourth-year students: **N/A**

LIBRARY RESOURCES
Total titles: **43,084**
Total volumes: **262,244**
Total seats available for library users: **213**

INFORMATION TECHNOLOGY
Number of wired network connections available to students: **14** total (in the law library, excluding computer
   labs: **14**; in classrooms: **0**; in computer labs: **0**; elsewhere
   in the law school: **0**)
Law school has a wireless network.
Students are not required to own a computer.

EMPLOYMENT AND SALARIES
Proportion of 2008 graduates employed at graduation:
   N/A

Employed 9 months later, as of February 15, 2009: **89%**
Salaries in the private sector (law firms, business, indus-
   try): **$42,000 –$52,000** (25th-75th percentile)
Median salary in the private sector: **$45,250**
Percentage in the private sector who reported salary
   information: **71%**
Median salary in public service (government, judicial clerk-
   ships, academic posts, non-profits): **$44,435**

Percentage of 2008 graduates in:
Law firms: **58%** Government: **19%**
Bus./industry: **13%** Judicial clerkship: **2%**
Public interest: **5%** Unknown: **0%**
Academia : **2%**

2008 graduates employed in-state: **81%**
2008 graduates employed in foreign countries: **2%**
Number of states where graduates are employed: **11**
Percentage of 2008 graduates working in: New England:
   N/A, Middle Atlantic: **N/A**, East North Central: **86%**,
   West North Central: **2%**, South Atlantic: **3%**, East South
   Central: **N/A**, West South Central: **1%**, Mountain: **1%**,
   Pacific: **N/A**, Unknown: **4%**

BAR PASSAGE RATES
Based on 2008 graduates taking Summer 2008 or
Winter 2009 exams. Most of the school's first-time test
takers took the bar in Illinois.

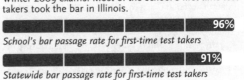

School's bar passage rate for first-time test takers

Statewide bar passage rate for first-time test takers

Northern Kentucky University (Chase)

- Nunn Hall, Highland Heights, KY, 41099-6031
- http://chaselaw.nku.edu
- Public
- Year founded: 1893
- 2009-2010 tuition: full-time: $14,812; part-time: $10,276
- Enrollment 2009-10 academic year: full-time: 374; part-time: 235
- U.S. News 2010 law specialty ranking: N/A

3.16-3.64 GPA, 25TH-75TH PERCENTILE

152-157 LSAT, 25TH-75TH PERCENTILE

43% ACCEPTANCE RATE

Tier 4 2011 U.S. NEWS LAW SCHOOL RANKING

ADMISSIONS

Admissions phone number: (859) 572-5841
Admissions email address: chaseadmissions@nku.edu
Application website:
  http://www4.lsac.org/lsacd_on_the_web/login/open.asp
  x?ID=KE931709A1489MO
Application deadline for Fall 2011 admission: 4-Jan

Admissions statistics:

Number of applicants for Fall 2009: 1,029
Number of acceptances: 439
Number enrolled: 135
Acceptance rate: 43%
GPA, 25th-75th percentile, entering class Fall 2009: 3.16-3.64
LSAT, 25th-75th percentile, entering class Fall 2009: 152-157

Part-time program:

Number of applicants for Fall 2009: 196
Number of acceptances: 87
Number enrolled: 59
Acceptance rate: 44%
GPA, 25th-75th percentile, entering class Fall 2009: 3.07-3.41
LSAT, 25th-75th percentile, entering class Fall 2009: 150-154

FINANCIAL AID

Financial aid phone number: (859) 572-6437
Financial aid application deadline: 3-Jan
Tuition 2009-2010 academic year: full-time: $14,812; part-time: $10,276
Room and board: $9,956 ; books: $1,000 ; miscellaneous expenses: $0
Total of room/board/books/miscellaneous expenses: $10,956
University offers graduate student housing for which law students are eligible.

Financial aid profile

Percent of students that received grants for the 2008-2009 academic year: full-time: 35%; part-time 10%
Median grant amount: full-time: $12,000 ; part-time: $10,000
The average law-school debt of those in the Class of 2009 who borrowed: $72,376 . Proportion who borrowed: 75%

ACADEMIC PROGRAMS

Calendar: semester
Joint degrees awarded: J.D./M.B.A.
Typical first-year section size: Full-time: 70; Part-time: 65
Is there typically a "small section" of the first year class, other than Legal Writing, taught by full-time faculty?: Full-time: no; Part-time: no
Number of course titles, beyond the first year curriculum, offered last year: 50
Percentages of upper division course sections, excluding seminars, with an enrollment of:

Under 25: 51%	25 to 49: 26%	
50 to 74: 20%	75 to 99: 3%	
100+: 0%		

Areas of specialization: appellate advocacy, clinical training, dispute resolution, environmental law, health care law, intellectual property law, international law, tax law, trial advocacy

Fall 2009 faculty profile

Total teaching faculty: 38. Full-time: 63%; 75% men, 25% women, 13% minorities. Part-time: 37%; 71% men, 29% women, 0% minorities
Student-to-faculty ratio: 15.1

SPECIAL PROGRAMS (as provided by law school):

Exceptional practical training is offered via clinical and externship opportunities. The Center for Excellence in Advocacy and Transactional Law Practice Center offer programs that enable students to acquire specialized knowledge. Students may also receive certificates in Advocacy or Transactional Law. The Pro Bono Service Program provides students with diverse public service opportunities.

STUDENT BODY

Fall 2009 full-time enrollment: 374

Men: 54%   Women: 46%
African-American: 5.90%   American Indian: 0.30%
Asian-American: 2.90%   Mexican-American: 0.00%
Puerto Rican: 0.00%   Other Hisp-Amer: 1.90%
White: 81.80%   International: 0.00%
Unknown: 7.20%

Fall 2009 part-time enrollment: 235

Men: 53%   Women: 47%
African-American: 4.70%   American Indian: 0.40%
Asian-American: 1.70%   Mexican-American: 0.00%
Puerto Rican: 0.00%   Other Hisp-Amer: 0.90%
White: 86.80%   International: 0.00%
Unknown: 5.50%

Attrition rates for 2008-2009 full-time students
Percent of students discontinuing law school:
Men: 8%   Women: 6%
First-year students: 9%   Second-year students: 10%
Third-year students: 2%   Fourth-year students: N/A

LIBRARY RESOURCES
Total titles: 79,436
Total volumes: 335,312
Total seats available for library users: 260

INFORMATION TECHNOLOGY
Number of wired network connections available to students: 31 total (in the law library, excluding computer labs: 27; in classrooms: 0; in computer labs: 0; elsewhere in the law school: 4)
Law school has a wireless network.
Students are not required to own a computer.

EMPLOYMENT AND SALARIES
Proportion of 2008 graduates employed at graduation:
   N/A
Employed 9 months later, as of February 15, 2009: 93%
Salaries in the private sector (law firms, business, industry): $40,000 –$80,000 (25th-75th percentile)
Median salary in the private sector: $55,000
Percentage in the private sector who reported salary information: 73%
Median salary in public service (government, judicial clerkships, academic posts, non-profits): $40,000

Percentage of 2008 graduates in:

Law firms: 52%   Government: 10%
Bus./industry: 21%   Judicial clerkship: 8%
Public interest: 7%   Unknown: 1%
Academia : 1%

2008 graduates employed in-state: 44%
2008 graduates employed in foreign countries: 0%
Number of states where graduates are employed: 9
Percentage of 2008 graduates working in: New England: 0%, Middle Atlantic: 2%, East North Central: 52%, West North Central: 0%, South Atlantic: 1%, East South Central: 45%, West South Central: 1%, Mountain: 0%, Pacific: 1%, Unknown: 0%

BAR PASSAGE RATES
Based on 2008 graduates taking Summer 2008 or Winter 2009 exams. Most of the school's first-time test takers took the bar in Ohio.

86%
School's bar passage rate for first-time test takers

88%
Statewide bar passage rate for first-time test takers

Northwestern University

- 375 E. Chicago Avenue, Chicago, IL, 60611
- http://www.law.northwestern.edu
- Private
- Year founded: 1859
- 2009-2010 tuition: full-time: $47,472; part-time: N/A
- Enrollment 2009-10 academic year: full-time: 814
- U.S. News 2010 law specialty ranking: clinical training: 12, dispute resolution: 12, international law: 15, tax law: 4, trial advocacy: 7

3.40-3.81 GPA, 25TH-75TH PERCENTILE

166-172 LSAT, 25TH-75TH PERCENTILE

18% ACCEPTANCE RATE

11 2011 U.S. NEWS LAW SCHOOL RANKING

ADMISSIONS

Admissions phone number: (312) 503-8465
Admissions email address: admissions@law.northwestern.edu
Application website:
http://www.law.northwestern.edu/admissions/applying/
Application deadline for Fall 2011 admission: 15-Feb

Admissions statistics:

Number of applicants for Fall 2009: 5,205
Number of acceptances: 952
Number enrolled: 271
Acceptance rate: 18%
GPA, 25th-75th percentile, entering class Fall 2009: 3.40-3.81
LSAT, 25th-75th percentile, entering class Fall 2009: 166-172

FINANCIAL AID

Financial aid phone number: (312) 503-8465
Financial aid application deadline: 15-Feb
Tuition 2009-2010 academic year: **full-time: $47,472; part-time: N/A**
Room and board: $12,376 ; books: $1,418 ; miscellaneous expenses: $6,555
Total of room/board/books/miscellaneous expenses: $20,349
University offers graduate student housing for which law students are eligible.

Financial aid profile

Percent of students that received grants for the 2008-2009 academic year: full-time: 34%
Median grant amount: full-time: $20,000
The average law-school debt of those in the Class of 2009 who borrowed: $127,242 . Proportion who borrowed: 80%

ACADEMIC PROGRAMS

Calendar: semester
Joint degrees awarded: **J.D./M.B.A.; J.D./Ph.D.; M.S.**

Law/M.S. Journalism; J.D./LL.M Tax; LL.M-Certificate in Management
Typical first-year section size: Full-time: 65
Is there typically a "small section" of the first year class, other than Legal Writing, taught by full-time faculty?: Full-time: no
Number of course titles, beyond the first year curriculum, offered last year: 217
Percentages of upper division course sections, excluding seminars, with an enrollment of:

Under 25: 61%   25 to 49: 28%
50 to 74: 10%   75 to 99: 1%
100+: 0%

Areas of specialization: appellate advocacy, clinical training, dispute resolution, environmental law, health care law, intellectual property law, international law, tax law, trial advocacy

Fall 2009 faculty profile

Total teaching faculty: 150. Full-time: 57%; 50% men, 50% women, 9% minorities. Part-time: 43%; 83% men, 17% women, 9% minorities
Student-to-faculty ratio: 8.8

SPECIAL PROGRAMS (as provided by law school):

We offer a three-year J.D. and a two-year Accelerated J.D. Both provide traditional core courses and emphasize communication and teamwork. Students can focus on theory and research in our academic training programs, work on cases in the Bluhm Legal Clinic, explore different legal systems through International Team Projects, or cross-train in business in classes at the Kellogg School of Management.

STUDENT BODY

Fall 2009 full-time enrollment: 814

Men: 54%	Women: 46%
African-American: 8.40%	American Indian: 1.10%
Asian-American: 17.30%	Mexican-American: 3.40%
Puerto Rican: 0.60%	Other Hisp-Amer: 4.70%
White: 57.00%	International: 7.50%
Unknown: 0.00%	

Attrition rates for 2008-2009 full-time students
Percent of students discontinuing law school:
Men: 1%   Women: 1%
First-year students: 2%   Second-year students: N/A
Third-year students: N/A   Fourth-year students: N/A

LIBRARY RESOURCES
Total titles: 367,579
Total volumes: 779,880
Total seats available for library users: 630

INFORMATION TECHNOLOGY
Number of wired network connections available to students: 236 total (in the law library, excluding computer labs: 75; in classrooms: 94; in computer labs: 2; elsewhere in the law school: 65)
Law school has a wireless network.
Students are required to own a computer.

EMPLOYMENT AND SALARIES
Proportion of 2008 graduates employed at graduation: 98%
Employed 9 months later, as of February 15, 2009: 100%
Salaries in the private sector (law firms, business, industry): $160,000 –$160,000 (25th-75th percentile)
Median salary in the private sector: $160,000
Percentage in the private sector who reported salary information: 74%

Median salary in public service (government, judicial clerkships, academic posts, non-profits): $46,500

Percentage of 2008 graduates in:
Law firms: 74%   Government: 2%
Bus./industry: 5%   Judicial clerkship: 12%
Public interest: 5%   Unknown: 0%
Academia : 2%

2008 graduates employed in-state: 41%
2008 graduates employed in foreign countries: 1%
Number of states where graduates are employed: 25
Percentage of 2008 graduates working in: New England: 3%, Middle Atlantic: 23%, East North Central: 48%, West North Central: 2%, South Atlantic: 7%, East South Central: 0%, West South Central: 3%, Mountain: 2%, Pacific: 10%, Unknown: 1%

BAR PASSAGE RATES
Based on 2008 graduates taking Summer 2008 or Winter 2009 exams. Most of the school's first-time test takers took the bar in Illinois.

98%

School's bar passage rate for first-time test takers

91%

Statewide bar passage rate for first-time test takers

Nova Southeastern University (Broad)

- 3305 College Avenue, Fort Lauderdale, FL, 33314-7721
- http://www.nsulaw.nova.edu/
- Private
- Year founded: 1974
- 2009-2010 tuition: full-time: $31,172; part-time: $23,378
- Enrollment 2009-10 academic year: full-time: 903; part-time: 189
- U.S. News 2010 law specialty ranking: N/A

3.02-3.47 GPA, 25TH-75TH PERCENTILE

147-152 LSAT, 25TH-75TH PERCENTILE

46% ACCEPTANCE RATE

Tier 4 2011 U.S. NEWS LAW SCHOOL RANKING

ADMISSIONS

Admissions phone number: **(954) 262-6117**
Admissions email address: **admission@nsu.law.nova.edu**
Application website:
http://www.nsulaw.nova.edu/admissions/index.cfm
Application deadline for Fall 2011 admission: **1-Apr**

Admissions statistics:
Number of applicants for Fall 2009: **2,122**
Number of acceptances: **969**
Number enrolled: **374**
Acceptance rate: **46%**
GPA, 25th-75th percentile, entering class Fall 2009: **3.02-3.47**
LSAT, 25th-75th percentile, entering class Fall 2009: **147-152**

Part-time program:
Number of applicants for Fall 2009: **421**
Number of acceptances: **126**
Number enrolled: **56**
Acceptance rate: **30%**
GPA, 25th-75th percentile, entering class Fall 2009: **2.94-3.45**
LSAT, 25th-75th percentile, entering class Fall 2009: **145-151**

FINANCIAL AID

Financial aid phone number: **(954) 262-7412**
Financial aid application deadline: **15-Apr**
Tuition 2009-2010 academic year: **full-time: $31,172; part-time: $23,378**
Room and board: **$16,281** ; books: **$2,626** ; miscellaneous expenses: **$6,318**
Total of room/board/books/miscellaneous expenses: **$25,225**
University offers graduate student housing for which law students are eligible.

Financial aid profile
Percent of students that received grants for the 2008-2009 academic year: full-time: **11%**; part-time **15%**
Median grant amount: full-time: **$14,000** ; part-time: **$9,000**
The average law-school debt of those in the Class of 2009 who borrowed: **$109,575** . Proportion who borrowed: **85%**

ACADEMIC PROGRAMS

Calendar: **semester**
Joint degrees awarded: **J.D./M.B.A.; J.D./M.S. Computers; J.D./M.S. Psychology; J.D./M.S. Dispute Resolution; J.D./M.URP.**
Typical first-year section size: Full-time: **63**; Part-time: **51**
Is there typically a "small section" of the first year class, other than Legal Writing, taught by full-time faculty?: Full-time: **no**; Part-time: **no**
Number of course titles, beyond the first year curriculum, offered last year: **119**
Percentages of upper division course sections, excluding seminars, with an enrollment of:

Under 25: **63%**		25 to 49: **18%**	
50 to 74: **17%**		75 to 99: **2%**	
100+: **0%**			

Areas of specialization: appellate advocacy, clinical training, dispute resolution, environmental law, health care law, intellectual property law, international law, tax law, trial advocacy

Fall 2009 faculty profile
Total teaching faculty: **99**. Full-time: **49%**; **55%** men, **45%** women, **24%** minorities. Part-time: **51%**; **74%** men, **26%** women, **12%** minorities
Student-to-faculty ratio: **16.7**

SPECIAL PROGRAMS *(as provided by law school)*:
Every student is guaranteed an opportunity to participate in an in-house clinic or an externship. Opportunities include ADR, Business, Children, Criminal, International, and Personal Injury. Students who are fluent in Spanish can participate in a dual degree opportunity offered with the University of Barcelona. Other semester-abroad opportunities are available in Prague and Venice.

STUDENT BODY

Fall 2009 full-time enrollment: 903

Men: 47%   Women: 53%
African-American: 4.30%   American Indian: 0.30%
Asian-American: 5.60%   Mexican-American: 0.70%
Puerto Rican: 1.00%   Other Hisp-Amer: 15.40%
White: 63.90%   International: 1.70%
Unknown: 7.10%

Fall 2009 part-time enrollment: 189

Men: 42%   Women: 58%
African-American: 10.10%   American Indian: 0.50%
Asian-American: 2.60%   Mexican-American: 1.10%
Puerto Rican: 1.60%   Other Hisp-Amer: 28.60%
White: 45.50%   International: 0.00%
Unknown: 10.10%

Attrition rates for 2008-2009 full-time students
Percent of students discontinuing law school:
Men: 4%   Women: 6%
First-year students: 12%   Second-year students: 2%
Third-year students: N/A   Fourth-year students: N/A

LIBRARY RESOURCES

Total titles: N/A
Total volumes: N/A
Total seats available for library users: 532

INFORMATION TECHNOLOGY

Number of wired network connections available to students: 4 total (in the law library, excluding computer labs: 4; in classrooms: 0; in computer labs: 0; elsewhere in the law school: 0)
Law school has a wireless network.
Students are required to own a computer.

EMPLOYMENT AND SALARIES

Proportion of 2008 graduates employed at graduation:
N/A
Employed 9 months later, as of February 15, 2009: 86%
Salaries in the private sector (law firms, business, industry): $45,000 –$75,000 (25th-75th percentile)
Median salary in the private sector: $60,000
Percentage in the private sector who reported salary information: 62%
Median salary in public service (government, judicial clerkships, academic posts, non-profits): $42,000

Percentage of 2008 graduates in:

Law firms: 68%   Government: 10%
Bus./industry: 10%   Judicial clerkship: 3%
Public interest: 7%   Unknown: 0%
Academia : 1%

2008 graduates employed in-state: 88%
2008 graduates employed in foreign countries: 1%
Number of states where graduates are employed: 14
Percentage of 2008 graduates working in: New England: 0%, Middle Atlantic: 2%, East North Central: 0%, West North Central: 0%, South Atlantic: 92%, East South Central: 1%, West South Central: 1%, Mountain: 2%, Pacific: 2%, Unknown: 0%

BAR PASSAGE RATES

Based on 2008 graduates taking Summer 2008 or Winter 2009 exams. Most of the school's first-time test takers took the bar in Florida.

84%

School's bar passage rate for first-time test takers

81%

Statewide bar passage rate for first-time test takers

Ohio Northern University (Pettit)

- 525 S. Main Street, Ada, OH, 45810-1599
- http://www.law.onu.edu
- Private
- Year founded: 1885
- 2009-2010 tuition: full-time: $28,600; part-time: N/A
- Enrollment 2009-10 academic year: full-time: 307
- U.S. News 2010 law specialty ranking: N/A

2.96-3.65 GPA, 25TH-75TH PERCENTILE

149-157 LSAT, 25TH-75TH PERCENTILE

36% ACCEPTANCE RATE

Tier 3 2011 U.S. NEWS LAW SCHOOL RANKING

ADMISSIONS

Admissions phone number: **(877) 452-9668**
Admissions email address: **law-admissions@onu.edu**
Application website: **N/A**
Application deadline for Fall 2011 admission: **rolling**

Admissions statistics:

Number of applicants for Fall 2009: **1,286**
Number of acceptances: **464**
Number enrolled: **113**
Acceptance rate: **36%**
GPA, 25th-75th percentile, entering class Fall 2009: **2.96-3.65**
LSAT, 25th-75th percentile, entering class Fall 2009: **149-157**

FINANCIAL AID

Financial aid phone number: **(419) 772-2272**
Financial aid application deadline: **1-Jun**
Tuition 2009-2010 academic year: **full-time: $28,600; part-time: N/A**
Room and board: **$9,880** ; books: **$1,200** ; miscellaneous expenses: **$2,500**
Total of room/board/books/miscellaneous expenses: **$13,580**
University offers graduate student housing for which law students are eligible.

Financial aid profile

Percent of students that received grants for the 2008-2009 academic year: full-time: **54%**
Median grant amount: full-time: **$20,000**
The average law-school debt of those in the Class of 2009 who borrowed: **$87,230** . Proportion who borrowed: **93%**

ACADEMIC PROGRAMS

Calendar: **semester**
Joint degrees awarded: **J.D./LL.M. Democratic Gov./Rule of Law**
Typical first-year section size: Full-time: **60**
Is there typically a "small section" of the first year class, other than Legal Writing, taught by full-time faculty?: Full-time: **no**
Number of course titles, beyond the first year curriculum, offered last year: **78**
Percentages of upper division course sections, excluding seminars, with an enrollment of:
  Under 25: **62%**   25 to 49: **32%**
  50 to 74: **6%**   75 to 99: **0%**
  100+: **0%**
Areas of specialization: appellate advocacy, clinical training, dispute resolution, environmental law, intellectual property law, international law, tax law, trial advocacy

Fall 2009 faculty profile

Total teaching faculty: **29**. Full-time: **72%**; **62%** men, **38%** women, **14%** minorities. Part-time: **28%**; **75%** men, **25%** women, **0%** minorities
Student-to-faculty ratio: **12.7**

SPECIAL PROGRAMS *(as provided by law school):*

The ONU Legal Clinic offers a number of programs which provide students with practical and educational experience. A detailed listing of clinical offerings can be seen at http://www.law.onu.edu.

STUDENT BODY

Fall 2009 full-time enrollment: 307

Men: **58%**	Women: **42%**
African-American: **7.20%**	American Indian: **0.70%**
Asian-American: **3.60%**	Mexican-American: **0.00%**
Puerto Rican: **0.00%**	Other Hisp-Amer: **2.00%**
White: **80.50%**	International: **0.00%**
Unknown: **6.20%**	

Attrition rates for 2008-2009 full-time students

Percent of students discontinuing law school:

Men: **8%**	Women: **6%**
First-year students: **19%**	Second-year students: **N/A**
Third-year students: **N/A**	Fourth-year students: **N/A**

LIBRARY RESOURCES

Total titles: 239,158
Total volumes: 423,180
Total seats available for library users: 303

INFORMATION TECHNOLOGY

Number of wired network connections available to students: 286 total (in the law library, excluding computer labs: 211; in classrooms: 68; in computer labs: 0; elsewhere in the law school: 7)
Law school has a wireless network.
Students are not required to own a computer.

EMPLOYMENT AND SALARIES

Proportion of 2008 graduates employed at graduation: N/A
Employed 9 months later, as of February 15, 2009: 93%
Salaries in the private sector (law firms, business, industry): $47,500 –$87,500 (25th-75th percentile)
Median salary in the private sector: $60,000
Percentage in the private sector who reported salary information: 22%
Median salary in public service (government, judicial clerkships, academic posts, non-profits): $42,500

Percentage of 2008 graduates in:

Law firms: 50%   Government: 27%
Bus./industry: 5%   Judicial clerkship: 3%
Public interest: 2%   Unknown: 9%
Academia : 4%

2008 graduates employed in-state: 38%
2008 graduates employed in foreign countries: 0%
Number of states where graduates are employed: 18
Percentage of 2008 graduates working in: New England: 1%, Middle Atlantic: 15%, East North Central: 47%, West North Central: 1%, South Atlantic: 22%, East South Central: 7%, West South Central: 1%, Mountain: 4%, Pacific: 1%, Unknown: 0%

BAR PASSAGE RATES

Based on 2008 graduates taking Summer 2008 or Winter 2009 exams. Most of the school's first-time test takers took the bar in Ohio.

94%

School's bar passage rate for first-time test takers

88%

Statewide bar passage rate for first-time test takers

Ohio State University (Moritz)

- 55 W. 12th Avenue, Columbus, OH, 43210
- http://www.moritzlaw.osu.edu
- Public
- Year founded: 1891
- 2009-2010 tuition: full-time: $22,433; part-time: N/A
- Enrollment 2009-10 academic year: full-time: 669
- U.S. News 2010 law specialty ranking: dispute resolution: 5

3.49-3.81 GPA, 25TH-75TH PERCENTILE

158-164 LSAT, 25TH-75TH PERCENTILE

34% ACCEPTANCE RATE

34 2011 U.S. NEWS LAW SCHOOL RANKING

ADMISSIONS

Admissions phone number: **(614) 292-8810**
Admissions email address: **lawadmit@osu.edu**
Application website: **N/A**
Application deadline for Fall 2011 admission: **15-Mar**

Admissions statistics:

Number of applicants for Fall 2009: **2,521**
Number of acceptances: **857**
Number enrolled: **225**
Acceptance rate: **34%**
GPA, 25th-75th percentile, entering class Fall 2009: **3.49-3.81**
LSAT, 25th-75th percentile, entering class Fall 2009: **158-164**

FINANCIAL AID

Financial aid phone number: **(614) 292-8807**
Financial aid application deadline: **1-Mar**
Tuition 2009-2010 academic year: **full-time: $22,433; part-time: N/A**
Room and board: **$8,172** ; books: **$3,860** ; miscellaneous expenses: **$6,080**
Total of room/board/books/miscellaneous expenses: **$18,112**
University offers graduate student housing for which law students are eligible.

Financial aid profile

Percent of students that received grants for the 2008-2009 academic year: full-time: **84%**
Median grant amount: full-time: **$5,500**
The average law-school debt of those in the Class of 2009 who borrowed: **$79,855** . Proportion who borrowed: **84%**

ACADEMIC PROGRAMS

Calendar: **semester**
Joint degrees awarded: **J.D./M.B.A.; J.D./M.A. Public Policy & Management; J.D./M.H.A.; J.D./M.A. City and Regional Planning; J.D./M.A. Education, Policy & Leadership; J.D./M.D.; J.D./M.P.H.; J.D./M.A.**

Typical first-year section size: Full-time: **75**
Is there typically a "small section" of the first year class, other than Legal Writing, taught by full-time faculty?: Full-time: **yes**
Number of course titles, beyond the first year curriculum, offered last year: **123**
Percentages of upper division course sections, excluding seminars, with an enrollment of:
Under 25: **56%**   25 to 49: **26%**
50 to 74: **18%**   75 to 99: **1%**
100+: **0%**
Areas of specialization: appellate advocacy, clinical training, dispute resolution, environmental law, health care law, intellectual property law, international law, tax law, trial advocacy

Fall 2009 faculty profile

Total teaching faculty: **57**. Full-time: **70%**; **63%** men, **38%** women, **15%** minorities. Part-time: **30%**; **88%** men, **12%** women, **6%** minorities
Student-to-faculty ratio: **13.3**

SPECIAL PROGRAMS (as provided by law school):

Moritz offers clinics in civil, criminal, juvenile, mediation, and legislation; certificates in ADR, Children's Justice, and Int'l Business/Trade; study abroad programs in Oxford, England; numerous joint degree opportunities including the JD/MBA, JD/MPA and the JD/MHA. Internship credit offered in our Judicial Extern and Washington, D.C. Summer Programs (government and nonprofit organizations).

STUDENT BODY

Fall 2009 full-time enrollment: 669

Men: **57%**	Women: **43%**
African-American: **8.10%**	American Indian: **0.30%**
Asian-American: **7.80%**	Mexican-American: **0.90%**
Puerto Rican: **0.60%**	Other Hisp-Amer: **3.70%**
White: **77.90%**	International: **0.70%**
Unknown: **0.00%**	

Attrition rates for 2008-2009 full-time students
Percent of students discontinuing law school:
Men: 1%   Women: 1%
First-year students: 2%   Second-year students: 1%
Third-year students: 0%   Fourth-year students: N/A

LIBRARY RESOURCES
Total titles: 218,600
Total volumes: 823,292
Total seats available for library users: 675

INFORMATION TECHNOLOGY
Number of wired network connections available to students: 0 total (in the law library, excluding computer labs: 0; in classrooms: 0; in computer labs: 0; elsewhere in the law school: 0)
Law school has a wireless network.
Students are not required to own a computer.

EMPLOYMENT AND SALARIES
Proportion of 2008 graduates employed at graduation: 88%
Employed 9 months later, as of February 15, 2009: 98%
Salaries in the private sector (law firms, business, industry): $75,000 –$120,000 (25th-75th percentile)
Median salary in the private sector: $100,000
Percentage in the private sector who reported salary information: 68%

Median salary in public service (government, judicial clerkships, academic posts, non-profits): $46,500

Percentage of 2008 graduates in:
Law firms: 54%   Government: 18%
Bus./industry: 14%   Judicial clerkship: 6%
Public interest: 3%   Unknown: 0%
Academia : 5%

2008 graduates employed in-state: 63%
2008 graduates employed in foreign countries: 1%
Number of states where graduates are employed: 24
Percentage of 2008 graduates working in: New England: 1%, Middle Atlantic: 7%, East North Central: 71%, West North Central: 1%, South Atlantic: 11%, East South Central: 1%, West South Central: 2%, Mountain: 1%, Pacific: 4%, Unknown: 0%

BAR PASSAGE RATES
Based on 2008 graduates taking Summer 2008 or Winter 2009 exams. Most of the school's first-time test takers took the bar in Ohio.

| 90% |
School's bar passage rate for first-time test takers

| 88% |
Statewide bar passage rate for first-time test takers

Oklahoma City University

■ 2501 N. Blackwelder Avenue, Oklahoma City, OK, 73106-1493
■ http://www.okcu.edu/law
■ Private
■ Year founded: 1907
■ 2009-2010 tuition: full-time: $995/credit hour; part-time: $995/credit hour
■ Enrollment 2009-10 academic year: full-time: 533; part-time: 90
■ U.S. News 2010 law specialty ranking: N/A

2.90-3.47 GPA, 25TH-75TH PERCENTILE

148-152 LSAT, 25TH-75TH PERCENTILE

56% ACCEPTANCE RATE

Tier 4 2011 U.S. NEWS LAW SCHOOL RANKING

ADMISSIONS
Admissions phone number: **(866) 529-6281**
Admissions email address: **lawquestions@okcu.edu**
Application website: **http://www.okcu.edu/law/applynow**
Application deadline for Fall 2011 admission: **1-Aug**

Admissions statistics:
Number of applicants for Fall 2009: **1,214**
Number of acceptances: **675**
Number enrolled: **200**
Acceptance rate: **56%**
GPA, 25th-75th percentile, entering class Fall 2009: **2.90-3.47**
LSAT, 25th-75th percentile, entering class Fall 2009: **148-152**

Part-time program:
Number of applicants for Fall 2009: **120**
Number of acceptances: **46**
Number enrolled: **24**
Acceptance rate: **38%**
GPA, 25th-75th percentile, entering class Fall 2009: **2.87-3.30**
LSAT, 25th-75th percentile, entering class Fall 2009: **148-153**

FINANCIAL AID
Financial aid phone number: **(800) 633-7242**
Financial aid application deadline: **5-Mar**
Tuition 2009-2010 academic year: **full-time: $995/credit hour; part-time: $995/credit hour**
Room and board: **$8,350** ; books: **$1,800** ; miscellaneous expenses: **$6,400**
Total of room/board/books/miscellaneous expenses: **$16,550**
University offers graduate student housing for which law students are eligible.

Financial aid profile
Percent of students that received grants for the 2008-2009 academic year: full-time: **38%**; part-time **16%**

Median grant amount: full-time: **$13,000** ; part-time: **$5,300**
The average law-school debt of those in the Class of 2009 who borrowed: **$102,125** . Proportion who borrowed: **85%**

ACADEMIC PROGRAMS
Calendar: **semester**
Joint degrees awarded: **J.D./M.B.A.**
Typical first-year section size: Full-time: **70**; Part-time: **72**
Is there typically a "small section" of the first year class, other than Legal Writing, taught by full-time faculty?: Full-time: **no**; Part-time: **no**
Number of course titles, beyond the first year curriculum, offered last year: **128**
Percentages of upper division course sections, excluding seminars, with an enrollment of:

Under 25: **71%**	25 to 49: **12%**
50 to 74: **15%**	75 to 99: **2%**
100+: **0%**	

Areas of specialization: appellate advocacy, clinical training, dispute resolution, environmental law, health care law, intellectual property law, international law, tax law, trial advocacy

Fall 2009 faculty profile
Total teaching faculty: **48**. Full-time: **56%**; **59%** men, **41%** women, **11%** minorities. Part-time: **44%**; **62%** men, **38%** women, **5%** minorities
Student-to-faculty ratio: **17.6**

SPECIAL PROGRAMS *(as provided by law school)*:
Five international programs. Externships: corporate counsel, judicial, governmental, Native American, and litigation. Licensed student internships. Certificates in Business Law, ADR, Health Law, and Public Law. Joint JD/MBA. Centers: Native American, ADR, and State Constitutional Law. Public interest fellowships.

STUDENT BODY
Fall 2009 full-time enrollment: **533**
Men: **60%**   Women: **40%**

African-American: 3.20%   American Indian: 3.90%
Asian-American: 3.40%   Mexican-American: 0.20%
Puerto Rican: 0.20%   Other Hisp-Amer: 4.10%
White: 82.20%   International: 0.90%
Unknown: 1.90%

Fall 2009 part-time enrollment: 90
Men: 53%   Women: 47%
African-American: 4.40%   American Indian: 13.30%
Asian-American: 1.10%   Mexican-American: 0.00%
Puerto Rican: 1.10%   Other Hisp-Amer: 4.40%
White: 70.00%   International: 1.10%
Unknown: 4.40%

Attrition rates for 2008-2009 full-time students
Percent of students discontinuing law school:
Men: 9%   Women: 8%
First-year students: 18%   Second-year students: 6%
Third-year students: N/A   Fourth-year students: N/A

LIBRARY RESOURCES
Total titles: 127,744
Total volumes: 322,061
Total seats available for library users: 384

INFORMATION TECHNOLOGY
Number of wired network connections available to students: 147 total (in the law library, excluding computer labs: 104; in classrooms: 26; in computer labs: 4; elsewhere in the law school: 13)
Law school has a wireless network.
Students are not required to own a computer.

EMPLOYMENT AND SALARIES
Proportion of 2008 graduates employed at graduation: N/A

Employed 9 months later, as of February 15, 2009: 92%
Salaries in the private sector (law firms, business, industry): $46,000 –$65,000 (25th-75th percentile)
Median salary in the private sector: $52,000
Percentage in the private sector who reported salary information: 77%
Median salary in public service (government, judicial clerkships, academic posts, non-profits): $42,000

Percentage of 2008 graduates in:
Law firms: 62%   Government: 15%
Bus./industry: 14%   Judicial clerkship: 0%
Public interest: 6%   Unknown: 0%
Academia : 3%

2008 graduates employed in-state: 66%
2008 graduates employed in foreign countries: 1%
Number of states where graduates are employed: 17
Percentage of 2008 graduates working in: New England: 0%, Middle Atlantic: 1%, East North Central: 2%, West North Central: 4%, South Atlantic: 2%, East South Central: 1%, West South Central: 80%, Mountain: 9%, Pacific: 0%, Unknown: 0%

BAR PASSAGE RATES
Based on 2008 graduates taking Summer 2008 or Winter 2009 exams. Most of the school's first-time test takers took the bar in Oklahoma.

	90%

School's bar passage rate for first-time test takers

	93%

Statewide bar passage rate for first-time test takers

Pace University

- 78 N. Broadway, White Plains, NY, 10603
- http://www.law.pace.edu
- Private
- Year founded: 1976
- 2009-2010 tuition: full-time: $39,794; part-time: $29,858
- Enrollment 2009-10 academic year: full-time: 562; part-time: 185
- U.S. News 2010 law specialty ranking: environmental law: 4

3.20-3.61 GPA, 25TH-75TH PERCENTILE

152-157 LSAT, 25TH-75TH PERCENTILE

41% ACCEPTANCE RATE

Tier 3 2011 U.S. NEWS LAW SCHOOL RANKING

ADMISSIONS

Admissions phone number: **(914) 422-4210**
Admissions email address: **admissions@law.pace.edu**
Application website:
   http://appserv.pace.edu/execute/page.cfm?doc_id=23688.
Application deadline for Fall 2011 admission: **1-Mar**

Admissions statistics:
Number of applicants for Fall 2009: **2,527**
Number of acceptances: **1,035**
Number enrolled: **204**
Acceptance rate: **41%**
GPA, 25th-75th percentile, entering class Fall 2009: **3.20-3.61**
LSAT, 25th-75th percentile, entering class Fall 2009: **152-157**

Part-time program:
Number of applicants for Fall 2009: **489**
Number of acceptances: **138**
Number enrolled: **58**
Acceptance rate: **28%**
GPA, 25th-75th percentile, entering class Fall 2009: **3.08-3.43**
LSAT, 25th-75th percentile, entering class Fall 2009: **149-155**

FINANCIAL AID

Financial aid phone number: **(914) 422-4050**
Financial aid application deadline: **1-Feb**
Tuition 2009-2010 academic year: **full-time: $39,794; part-time: $29,858**
Room and board: **$15,720** ; books: **$1,800** ; miscellaneous expenses: **$2,154**
Total of room/board/books/miscellaneous expenses: **$19,674**
University offers graduate student housing for which law students are eligible.

Financial aid profile
Percent of students that received grants for the 2008-2009 academic year: full-time: **69%**; part-time **68%**
Median grant amount: full-time: **$8,000** ; part-time: **$7,000**
The average law-school debt of those in the Class of 2009 who borrowed: **$83,515** . Proportion who borrowed: **87%**

ACADEMIC PROGRAMS
Calendar: **semester**
Joint degrees awarded: **J.D./M.B.A.; J.D./M.P.A.; J.D./M.E.M. (Environmental Management); J.D./M.S.; J.D./M.A.**
Typical first-year section size: Full-time: **52**; Part-time: **63**
Is there typically a "small section" of the first year class, other than Legal Writing, taught by full-time faculty?: Full-time: **yes**; Part-time: **yes**
Number of course titles, beyond the first year curriculum, offered last year: **148**
Percentages of upper division course sections, excluding seminars, with an enrollment of:
   Under 25: **71%**   25 to 49: **18%**
   50 to 74: **10%**   75 to 99: **2%**
   100+: **0%**
Areas of specialization: appellate advocacy, clinical training, dispute resolution, environmental law, health care law, intellectual property law, international law, tax law, trial advocacy

Fall 2009 faculty profile
Total teaching faculty: **82.** Full-time: **56%**; **61%** men, **39%** women, **9%** minorities. Part-time: **44%**; **67%** men, **33%** women, **6%** minorities
Student-to-faculty ratio: **12.7**

SPECIAL PROGRAMS *(as provided by law school)*:
Pace offers a wide variety of special programs through The Pace Women's Justice Center, The Land Use Law Center, the Federal Judicial Extern Honors Program and its many direct representation clinics and externships. There are also opportunities for a semester in London, as well as summer work for foreign law firms and at international war crimes tribunals.

STUDENT BODY

Fall 2009 full-time enrollment: 562

Men: 44%	Women: 56%
African-American: 4.10%	American Indian: 0.20%
Asian-American: 6.90%	Mexican-American: 0.20%
Puerto Rican: 0.20%	Other Hisp-Amer: 5.30%
White: 67.60%	International: 1.40%
Unknown: 14.10%	

Fall 2009 part-time enrollment: 185

Men: 35%	Women: 65%
African-American: 4.30%	American Indian: 0.00%
Asian-American: 6.50%	Mexican-American: 0.00%
Puerto Rican: 0.00%	Other Hisp-Amer: 8.60%
White: 67.60%	International: 0.00%
Unknown: 13.00%	

Attrition rates for 2008-2009 full-time students
Percent of students discontinuing law school:

Men: 7%	Women: 4%
First-year students: 13%	Second-year students: 2%
Third-year students: 1%	Fourth-year students: N/A

LIBRARY RESOURCES

Total titles: 137,495
Total volumes: 398,458
Total seats available for library users: 553

INFORMATION TECHNOLOGY

Number of wired network connections available to students: 320 total (in the law library, excluding computer labs: 78; in classrooms: 206; in computer labs: 0; elsewhere in the law school: 36)
Law school has a wireless network.
Students are not required to own a computer.

EMPLOYMENT AND SALARIES

Proportion of 2008 graduates employed at graduation: N/A
Employed 9 months later, as of February 15, 2009: 92%
Salaries in the private sector (law firms, business, industry): $65,000 –$160,000 (25th-75th percentile)
Median salary in the private sector: $100,000
Percentage in the private sector who reported salary information: 62%
Median salary in public service (government, judicial clerkships, academic posts, non-profits): $53,500

Percentage of 2008 graduates in:

Law firms: 44%	Government: 17%
Bus./industry: 17%	Judicial clerkship: 5%
Public interest: 7%	Unknown: 2%
Academia : 7%	

2008 graduates employed in-state: 62%
2008 graduates employed in foreign countries: 0%
Number of states where graduates are employed: 11
Percentage of 2008 graduates working in: New England: 7%, Middle Atlantic: 69%, East North Central: 0%, West North Central: 0%, South Atlantic: 1%, East South Central: 0%, West South Central: 0%, Mountain: 2%, Pacific: 1%, Unknown: 20%

BAR PASSAGE RATES

Based on 2008 graduates taking Summer 2008 or Winter 2009 exams. Most of the school's first-time test takers took the bar in New York.

83%
School's bar passage rate for first-time test takers

81%
Statewide bar passage rate for first-time test takers

Penn. State University (Dickinson)

■ Lewis Katz Building, University Park, PA, 16802
■ http://www.law.psu.edu
■ Public
■ Year founded: 1834
■ 2009-2010 tuition: full-time: $34,462; part-time: N/A
■ Enrollment 2009-10 academic year: full-time: 586; part-time: 11
■ U.S. News 2010 law specialty ranking: dispute resolution: 11

3.28-3.68 GPA, 25TH-75TH PERCENTILE

157-160 LSAT, 25TH-75TH PERCENTILE

29% ACCEPTANCE RATE

72 2011 U.S. NEWS LAW SCHOOL RANKING

ADMISSIONS

Admissions phone number: (800) 840-1122
Admissions email address: psulaw_admit@law.psu.edu
Application website:
   http://os.lsac.org/Release/Logon/Access.aspx
Application deadline for Fall 2011 admission: 15-Feb

Admissions statistics:

Number of applicants for Fall 2009: 4,047
Number of acceptances: 1,157
Number enrolled: 206
Acceptance rate: 29%
GPA, 25th-75th percentile, entering class Fall 2009: 3.28-3.68
LSAT, 25th-75th percentile, entering class Fall 2009: 157-160

FINANCIAL AID

Financial aid phone number: (800) 840-1122
Financial aid application deadline: 1-Mar
Tuition 2009-2010 academic year: **full-time: $34,462; part-time: N/A**
Room and board: $10,674 ; books: $1,360 ; miscellaneous expenses: $8,892
Total of room/board/books/miscellaneous expenses: $20,926
University offers graduate student housing for which law students are eligible.

Financial aid profile

Percent of students that received grants for the 2008-2009 academic year: full-time: 53%
Median grant amount: full-time: $6,500
The average law-school debt of those in the Class of 2009 who borrowed: $108,383 . Proportion who borrowed: 84%

ACADEMIC PROGRAMS

Calendar: semester
Joint degrees awarded: J.D./M.P.A.; J.D./M.B.A.; J.D./M.S.I.S.; J.D./M.S. Forest Resources; J.D./M.Agr.;

J.D./Ph.D. Forest Resources; J.D./M.A. Educational Theory & Policy; J.D./Ph.D. Educational Theory & Policy; J.D./M.Ed. College Student Affairs; J.D./M.Ed. Educational Leadership; J.D./M.S. Educational Leadership; J.D./D.Ed. Educational Leadership; J.D./Ph.D. Educational Leadership; J.D./Ph.D. Higher Education; J.D./D.Ed. Higher Education; J.D./M.Ed. Higher Education; J.D./M.S. Human Resources ; J.D./M.S. Env. Pol. Control; J.D//M.I.A. Master of Intl Affairs
Typical first-year section size: Full-time: 50
Is there typically a "small section" of the first year class, other than Legal Writing, taught by full-time faculty?: Full-time: **no**; Part-time: **no**
Number of course titles, beyond the first year curriculum, offered last year: 124
Percentages of upper division course sections, excluding seminars, with an enrollment of:
   Under 25: **79%**   25 to 49: **16%**
   50 to 74: **4%**   75 to 99: **1%**
   100+: **0%**
Areas of specialization: appellate advocacy, clinical training, dispute resolution, environmental law, health care law, intellectual property law, international law, tax law, trial advocacy

Fall 2009 faculty profile

Total teaching faculty: 68. Full-time: 79%; 56% men, 44% women, 13% minorities. Part-time: 21%; 57% men, 43% women, 7% minorities
Student-to-faculty ratio: 9.4

SPECIAL PROGRAMS *(as provided by law school):*

Students participate in Institutes: Arbitration Law & Practice; Miller Center for Public Interest Advocacy; Sports Law, Policy & Research; Vinogradoff (Russian/CIS legal systems); and Ag Law. Students represent clients in Immigration Policy, Appellate Civil Rights, Child Advocacy, Disability Law, Elder Law & Consumer Protection, and Family Law Clinics and serve in government externships.

STUDENT BODY

Fall 2009 full-time enrollment: 586

Men: 60%
African-American: 5.50%
Asian-American: 8.20%
Puerto Rican: 0.00%
White: 73.40%
Unknown: 6.50%

Women: 40%
American Indian: 0.30%
Mexican-American: 0.00%
Other Hisp-Amer: 6.10%
International: 0.00%

Fall 2009 part-time enrollment: 11

Men: 55%
African-American: 9.10%
Asian-American: 18.20%
Puerto Rican: 0.00%
White: 45.50%
Unknown: 18.20%

Women: 45%
American Indian: 0.00%
Mexican-American: 0.00%
Other Hisp-Amer: 9.10%
International: 0.00%

Attrition rates for 2008-2009 full-time students

Percent of students discontinuing law school:

Men: 5%
First-year students: 12%
Third-year students: 1%

Women: 5%
Second-year students: 2%
Fourth-year students: N/A

LIBRARY RESOURCES

Total titles: 159,848
Total volumes: 542,499
Total seats available for library users: 443

INFORMATION TECHNOLOGY

Number of wired network connections available to students: 24 total (in the law library, excluding computer labs: 0; in classrooms: 18; in computer labs: 0; elsewhere in the law school: 6)
Law school has a wireless network.
Students are not required to own a computer.

EMPLOYMENT AND SALARIES

Proportion of 2008 graduates employed at graduation: N/A
Employed 9 months later, as of February 15, 2009: 91%
Salaries in the private sector (law firms, business, industry): $50,000 –$115,000 (25th-75th percentile)
Median salary in the private sector: $71,000
Percentage in the private sector who reported salary information: 50%
Median salary in public service (government, judicial clerkships, academic posts, non-profits): $48,000

Percentage of 2008 graduates in:

Law firms: 39%
Bus./industry: 11%
Public interest: 3%
Academia : 3%

Government: 22%
Judicial clerkship: 20%
Unknown: 3%

2008 graduates employed in-state: 46%
2008 graduates employed in foreign countries: 1%
Number of states where graduates are employed: 24
Percentage of 2008 graduates working in: New England: 3%, Middle Atlantic: 56%, East North Central: 1%, West North Central: 0%, South Atlantic: 25%, East South Central: 1%, West South Central: 2%, Mountain: 3%, Pacific: 1%, Unknown: 6%

BAR PASSAGE RATES

Based on 2008 graduates taking Summer 2008 or Winter 2009 exams. Most of the school's first-time test takers took the bar in Pennsylvania.

85%
School's bar passage rate for first-time test takers

87%
Statewide bar passage rate for first-time test takers

Pepperdine University

- 24255 Pacific Coast Highway, Malibu, CA, 90263
- http://law.pepperdine.edu
- Private
- **Year founded:** 1969
- **2009-2010 tuition:** full-time: $39,340; part-time: N/A
- **Enrollment 2009-10 academic year:** full-time: 667
- **U.S. News 2010 law specialty ranking:** dispute resolution: 1

3.43-3.79 GPA, 25TH-75TH PERCENTILE

160-163 LSAT, 25TH-75TH PERCENTILE

27% ACCEPTANCE RATE

52 2011 U.S. NEWS LAW SCHOOL RANKING

ADMISSIONS

Admissions phone number: (310) 506-4631
Admissions email address: soladmis@pepperdine.edu
Application website:
  http://law.pepperdine.edu/admissions/apply
Application deadline for Fall 2011 admission: **1-Apr**

Admissions statistics:
Number of applicants for Fall 2009: **3,244**
Number of acceptances: **872**
Number enrolled: **230**
Acceptance rate: **27%**
GPA, 25th-75th percentile, entering class Fall 2009: **3.43-3.79**
LSAT, 25th-75th percentile, entering class Fall 2009: **160-163**

FINANCIAL AID

Financial aid phone number: (310) 506-4633
Financial aid application deadline: **1-Apr**
Tuition 2009-2010 academic year: **full-time: $39,340; part-time: N/A**
Room and board: **$16,366** ; books: **$980** ; miscellaneous expenses: **$5,100**
Total of room/board/books/miscellaneous expenses: **$22,446**
University offers graduate student housing for which law students are eligible.

Financial aid profile
Percent of students that received grants for the 2008-2009 academic year: full-time: **80%**
Median grant amount: full-time: **$4,300**
The average law-school debt of those in the Class of 2009 who borrowed: **$120,148** . Proportion who borrowed: **87%**

ACADEMIC PROGRAMS

Calendar: **semester**
Joint degrees awarded: **J.D./M.B.A.; J.D./M.D.R.; J.D./M.P.P.; J.D./M.DIV.**

Typical first-year section size: Full-time: **75**
Is there typically a "small section" of the first year class, other than Legal Writing, taught by full-time faculty?: Full-time: **no**
Number of course titles, beyond the first year curriculum, offered last year: **125**
Percentages of upper division course sections, excluding seminars, with an enrollment of:
  Under 25: **67%**   25 to 49: **21%**
  50 to 74: **6%**   75 to 99: **3%**
  100+: **3%**
Areas of specialization: appellate advocacy, clinical training, dispute resolution, environmental law, health care law, intellectual property law, international law, tax law, trial advocacy

Fall 2009 faculty profile
Total teaching faculty: **160**. Full-time: **41%**; 70% men, 30% women, 11% minorities. Part-time: **59%**; 30% men, 70% women, 4% minorities
Student-to-faculty ratio: **16**

SPECIAL PROGRAMS *(as provided by law school):*
We operate a summer/fall London program; a legal aid clinic at the Union Rescue Mission in L.A.; the Nootbaar Institute on Law, Religion, and Ethics; a Special Ed. Clinic; an Asylum and Refugee Law Clinic; Global Justice Prog; the Palmer Center for Entrepreneurship and the Law; and the Straus Institute for Dispute Resolution. We also have exchange programs: Universities of Augsburg and Copenhagen.

STUDENT BODY
Fall 2009 full-time enrollment: **667**
Men: **50%**   Women: **50%**
African-American: **3.60%**   American Indian: **0.40%**
Asian-American: **8.40%**   Mexican-American: **2.40%**
Puerto Rican: **0.30%**   Other Hisp-Amer: **1.20%**
White: **59.10%**   International: **0.00%**
Unknown: **24.60%**

Attrition rates for 2008-2009 full-time students
Percent of students discontinuing law school:
Men: **4%**   Women: **3%**
First-year students: **9%**   Second-year students: **N/A**
Third-year students: **N/A**   Fourth-year students: **N/A**

LIBRARY RESOURCES
Total titles: **138,624**
Total volumes: **397,290**
Total seats available for library users: **431**

INFORMATION TECHNOLOGY
Number of wired network connections available to students: **80** total (in the law library, excluding computer labs: **67**; in classrooms: **13**; in computer labs: **0**; elsewhere in the law school: **0**)
Law school has a wireless network.
Students are not required to own a computer.

EMPLOYMENT AND SALARIES
Proportion of 2008 graduates employed at graduation: **76%**
Employed 9 months later, as of February 15, 2009: **97%**
Salaries in the private sector (law firms, business, industry): **$72,000 –$150,000** (25th-75th percentile)
Median salary in the private sector: **$90,000**
Percentage in the private sector who reported salary information: **51%**

Median salary in public service (government, judicial clerkships, academic posts, non-profits): **$60,000**

Percentage of 2008 graduates in:
Law firms: **66%**   Government: **6%**
Bus./industry: **17%**   Judicial clerkship: **5%**
Public interest: **4%**   Unknown: **0%**
Academia : **3%**

2008 graduates employed in-state: **81%**
2008 graduates employed in foreign countries: **1%**
Number of states where graduates are employed: **21**
Percentage of 2008 graduates working in: New England: **0%**, Middle Atlantic: **2%**, East North Central: **1%**, West North Central: **1%**, South Atlantic: **2%**, East South Central: **1%**, West South Central: **2%**, Mountain: **7%**, Pacific: **83%**, Unknown: **0%**

BAR PASSAGE RATES
Based on 2008 graduates taking Summer 2008 or Winter 2009 exams. Most of the school's first-time test takers took the bar in California.

87%

School's bar passage rate for first-time test takers

71%

Statewide bar passage rate for first-time test takers

Quinnipiac University

- 275 Mount Carmel Avenue, Hamden, CT, 6518
- http://law.quinnipiac.edu
- Private
- Year founded: 1977
- 2009-2010 tuition: full-time: $40,780; part-time: $28,780
- Enrollment 2009-10 academic year: full-time: 291; part-time: 124
- U.S. News 2010 law specialty ranking: N/A

3.10-3.63 GPA, 25TH-75TH PERCENTILE

156-160 LSAT, 25TH-75TH PERCENTILE

41% ACCEPTANCE RATE

Tier 3 2011 U.S. NEWS LAW SCHOOL RANKING

ADMISSIONS

Admissions phone number: **(203) 582-3400**
Admissions email address: **ladm@quinnipiac.edu**
Application website: **http://law.quinnipiac.edu/x53.xml**
Application deadline for Fall 2011 admission: **1-Mar**

Admissions statistics:
Number of applicants for Fall 2009: **2,686**
Number of acceptances: **1,093**
Number enrolled: **113**
Acceptance rate: **41%**
GPA, 25th-75th percentile, entering class Fall 2009: **3.10-3.63**
LSAT, 25th-75th percentile, entering class Fall 2009: **156-160**

Part-time program:
Number of applicants for Fall 2009: **679**
Number of acceptances: **85**
Number enrolled: **47**
Acceptance rate: **13%**
GPA, 25th-75th percentile, entering class Fall 2009: **3.01-3.51**
LSAT, 25th-75th percentile, entering class Fall 2009: **151-154**

FINANCIAL AID

Financial aid phone number: **(203) 582-3405**
Financial aid application deadline: **15-Apr**
Tuition 2009-2010 academic year: full-time: **$40,780**; part-time: **$28,780**
Room and board: **$8,949** ; books: **$1,200** ; miscellaneous expenses: **$9,315**
Total of room/board/books/miscellaneous expenses: **$19,464**
University does not offer graduate student housing for which law students are eligible.

Financial aid profile
Percent of students that received grants for the 2008-2009 academic year: full-time: **71%**; part-time **48%**

Median grant amount: full-time: **$20,000** ; part-time: **$6,000**
The average law-school debt of those in the Class of 2009 who borrowed: **$95,691** . Proportion who borrowed: **85%**

ACADEMIC PROGRAMS

Calendar: **semester**
Joint degrees awarded: **J.D./M.B.A.; J.D./M.H.A.**
Typical first-year section size: Full-time: **75**; Part-time: **58**
Is there typically a "small section" of the first year class, other than Legal Writing, taught by full-time faculty?: Full-time: **yes**; Part-time: **yes**
Number of course titles, beyond the first year curriculum, offered last year: **106**
Percentages of upper division course sections, excluding seminars, with an enrollment of:
Under 25: **86%**   25 to 49: **11%**
50 to 74: **3%**   75 to 99: **1%**
100+: **0%**
Areas of specialization: appellate advocacy, clinical training, dispute resolution, environmental law, health care law, intellectual property law, international law, tax law, trial advocacy

Fall 2009 faculty profile
Total teaching faculty: **60**. Full-time: **45%**; **56%** men, **44%** women, **7%** minorities. Part-time: **55%**; **79%** men, **21%** women, **3%** minorities
Student-to-faculty ratio: **11.2**

SPECIAL PROGRAMS *(as provided by law school):*
Please see: http://law.quinnipiac.edu/x101.xml (for clinics and externships); http://law.quinnipiac.edu/x139.xml (for Ireland summer study); http://law.quinnipiac.edu/x88.xml (for concentration programs); http://law.quinnipiac.edu/x77.xml (for J.D./M.B.A.); http://law.quinnipiac.edu/x119.xml (for Centers)

STUDENT BODY
Fall 2009 full-time enrollment: **291**
Men: **47%**   Women: **53%**
African-American: **3.40%**   American Indian: **0.30%**

Asian-American: 5.20%   Mexican-American: 0.00%
Puerto Rican: 0.00%   Other Hisp-Amer: 3.10%
White: 79.40%   International: 2.40%
Unknown: 6.20%

Fall 2009 part-time enrollment: 124
Men: 53%   Women: 47%
African-American: 2.40% American Indian: 1.60%
Asian-American: 4.80%   Mexican-American: 0.00%
Puerto Rican: 0.00%   Other Hisp-Amer: 5.60%
White: 78.20%   International: 3.20%
Unknown: 4.00%

Attrition rates for 2008-2009 full-time students
Percent of students discontinuing law school:
Men: 5%   Women: 4%
First-year students: 10% Second-year students: 1%
Third-year students: 1% Fourth-year students: 4%

LIBRARY RESOURCES
Total titles: 175,817
Total volumes: 441,490
Total seats available for library users: 350

INFORMATION TECHNOLOGY
Number of wired network connections available to students: 264 total (in the law library, excluding computer labs: 189; in classrooms: 13; in computer labs: 0; elsewhere in the law school: 62)
Law school has a wireless network.
Students are not required to own a computer.

EMPLOYMENT AND SALARIES
Proportion of 2008 graduates employed at graduation: N/A

Employed 9 months later, as of February 15, 2009: 96%
Salaries in the private sector (law firms, business, industry): $60,000 –$95,000 (25th-75th percentile)
Median salary in the private sector: $75,000
Percentage in the private sector who reported salary information: 73%
Median salary in public service (government, judicial clerkships, academic posts, non-profits): $40,789

Percentage of 2008 graduates in:
Law firms: 30%   Government: 21%
Bus./industry: 25%   Judicial clerkship: 10%
Public interest: 2%   Unknown: 11%
Academia : 1%

2008 graduates employed in-state: 63%
2008 graduates employed in foreign countries: 0%
Number of states where graduates are employed: 13
Percentage of 2008 graduates working in: New England: 69%, Middle Atlantic: 12%, East North Central: 2%, West North Central: 0%, South Atlantic: 4%, East South Central: 0%, West South Central: 1%, Mountain: 2%, Pacific: 1%, Unknown: 11%

BAR PASSAGE RATES
Based on 2008 graduates taking Summer 2008 or Winter 2009 exams. Most of the school's first-time test takers took the bar in Connecticut.

93%

School's bar passage rate for first-time test takers

87%

Statewide bar passage rate for first-time test takers

Regent University

- 1000 Regent University Drive, Virginia Beach, VA, 23464-9880
- http://www.regent.edu/law/admissions
- Private
- Year founded: 1986
- 2009-2010 tuition: full-time: $975/credit hour; part-time: $975/credit hour
- Enrollment 2009-10 academic year: full-time: 394; part-time: 23
- U.S. News 2010 law specialty ranking: N/A

3.00-3.71 GPA, 25TH-75TH PERCENTILE

150-157 LSAT, 25TH-75TH PERCENTILE

45% ACCEPTANCE RATE

Tier 4 2011 U.S. NEWS LAW SCHOOL RANKING

ADMISSIONS

Admissions phone number: **(757) 226-4584**
Admissions email address: **lawschool@regent.edu**
Application website:
   http://www.regent.edu/acad/schlaw/admissions/apply.cfm
Application deadline for Fall 2011 admission: **rolling**

Admissions statistics:

Number of applicants for Fall 2009: **786**
Number of acceptances: **351**
Number enrolled: **152**
Acceptance rate: **45%**
GPA, 25th-75th percentile, entering class Fall 2009: **3.00-3.71**
LSAT, 25th-75th percentile, entering class Fall 2009: **150-157**

Part-time program:

Number of applicants for Fall 2009: **37**
Number of acceptances: **17**
Number enrolled: **10**
Acceptance rate: **46%**
GPA, 25th-75th percentile, entering class Fall 2009: **2.96-3.67**
LSAT, 25th-75th percentile, entering class Fall 2009: **148-153**

FINANCIAL AID

Financial aid phone number: **(757) 226-4559**
Financial aid application deadline:
Tuition 2009-2010 academic year: **full-time: $975/credit hour; part-time: $975/credit hour**
Room and board: **$9,450** ; books: **$1,620** ; miscellaneous expenses: **$9,152**
Total of room/board/books/miscellaneous expenses: **$20,222**
University offers graduate student housing for which law students are eligible.

Financial aid profile

Percent of students that received grants for the 2008-2009 academic year: full-time: **80%**; part-time **61%**
Median grant amount: full-time: **$6,000** ; part-time: **$2,000**
The average law-school debt of those in the Class of 2009 who borrowed: **$109,025** . Proportion who borrowed: **81%**

ACADEMIC PROGRAMS

Calendar: **semester**
Joint degrees awarded: **J.D./ M.A. Communications; J.D./ M.A. Management; J.D./ M.A. Journalism; J.D./ M.A. Counseling; J.D./M.B.A.; J.D./M.Div.; J.D. /M.A. Government; J.D./M.A. Public Policy; J.D./M.A. Div.**
Typical first-year section size: Full-time: **72**; Part-time: **72**
Is there typically a "small section" of the first year class, other than Legal Writing, taught by full-time faculty?: Full-time: **yes**; Part-time: **yes**
Number of course titles, beyond the first year curriculum, offered last year: **88**
Percentages of upper division course sections, excluding seminars, with an enrollment of:

Under 25: **74%**	25 to 49: **13%**
50 to 74: **6%**	75 to 99: **7%**
100+: **0%**	

Areas of specialization: appellate advocacy, clinical training, dispute resolution, environmental law, health care law, intellectual property law, international law, tax law, trial advocacy

Fall 2009 faculty profile

Total teaching faculty: **50**. Full-time: **50%**; **68%** men, **32%** women, **20%** minorities. Part-time: **50%**; **84%** men, **16%** women, **4%** minorities
Student-to-faculty ratio: **16.2**

SPECIAL PROGRAMS (as provided by law school):

Special programs include a summer program in Strasbourg, France focusing on international law and human rights; student-client contact through litigation and family mediation clinics; public interest opportunities involving the defense of religious liberties; the American Center for Law and Justice (ACLJ) D.C. Spring Semester Program; and exchange programs with law schools in Korea and Spain.

STUDENT BODY

Fall 2009 full-time enrollment: 394

Men: 51%	Women: 49%
African-American: 6.30%	American Indian: 1.50%
Asian-American: 5.10%	Mexican-American: 0.30%
Puerto Rican: 0.00%	Other Hisp-Amer: 2.00%
White: 80.20%	International: 1.00%
Unknown: 3.60%	

Fall 2009 part-time enrollment: 23

Men: 61%	Women: 39%
African-American: 13.00%	American Indian: 0.00%
Asian-American: 0.00%	Mexican-American: 0.00%
Puerto Rican: 0.00%	Other Hisp-Amer: 0.00%
White: 82.60%	International: 0.00%
Unknown: 4.30%	

Attrition rates for 2008-2009 full-time students

Percent of students discontinuing law school:

Men: 7%	Women: 4%
First-year students: 14%	Second-year students: 2%
Third-year students: N/A	Fourth-year students: N/A

LIBRARY RESOURCES

Total titles: 90,076
Total volumes: 401,284
Total seats available for library users: 324

INFORMATION TECHNOLOGY

Number of wired network connections available to students: 241 total (in the law library, excluding computer labs: 214; in classrooms: 10; in computer labs: 4; elsewhere in the law school: 13)

Law school has a wireless network.
Students are not required to own a computer.

EMPLOYMENT AND SALARIES

Proportion of 2008 graduates employed at graduation: 68%
Employed 9 months later, as of February 15, 2009: 94%
Salaries in the private sector (law firms, business, industry): $40,000 –$53,500 (25th-75th percentile)
Median salary in the private sector: $45,000
Percentage in the private sector who reported salary information: 54%
Median salary in public service (government, judicial clerkships, academic posts, non-profits): $48,000

Percentage of 2008 graduates in:

Law firms: 43%	Government: 19%
Bus./industry: 11%	Judicial clerkship: 11%
Public interest: 9%	Unknown: 1%
Academia : 5%	

2008 graduates employed in-state: 44%
2008 graduates employed in foreign countries: 1%
Number of states where graduates are employed: 25
Percentage of 2008 graduates working in: New England: 1%, Middle Atlantic: 4%, East North Central: 6%, West North Central: 2%, South Atlantic: 58%, East South Central: 3%, West South Central: 1%, Mountain: 4%, Pacific: 1%, Unknown: 19%

BAR PASSAGE RATES

Based on 2008 graduates taking Summer 2008 or Winter 2009 exams. Most of the school's first-time test takers took the bar in Virginia.

73%
School's bar passage rate for first-time test takers

82%
Statewide bar passage rate for first-time test takers

Roger Williams University

- 10 Metacom Avenue, Bristol, RI, 02809-5171
- http://law.rwu.edu
- Private
- **Year founded:** 1992
- **2009-2010 tuition:** full-time: $1,165/credit hour; part-time: N/A
- **Enrollment 2009-10 academic year:** full-time: 550
- **U.S. News 2010 law specialty ranking:** N/A

3.00-3.50 GPA, 25TH-75TH PERCENTILE

150-157 LSAT, 25TH-75TH PERCENTILE

58% ACCEPTANCE RATE

Tier 4 2011 U.S. NEWS LAW SCHOOL RANKING

ADMISSIONS
Admissions phone number: **(401) 254-4555**
Admissions email address: **Admissions@rwu.edu**
Application website: **http://law.rwu.edu/apply**
Application deadline for Fall 2011 admission: **15-Mar**

Admissions statistics:
Number of applicants for Fall 2009: **1,489**
Number of acceptances: **871**
Number enrolled: **210**
Acceptance rate: **58%**
GPA, 25th-75th percentile, entering class Fall 2009: **3.00-3.50**
LSAT, 25th-75th percentile, entering class Fall 2009: **150-157**

FINANCIAL AID
Financial aid phone number: **(401) 254-4641**
Financial aid application deadline: **15-Mar**
Tuition 2009-2010 academic year: **full-time: $1,165/credit hour; part-time: N/A**
Room and board: **N/A**; books: **N/A**; miscellaneous expenses: **N/A**
Total of room/board/books/miscellaneous expenses: **$22,072**
University offers graduate student housing for which law students are eligible.

Financial aid profile
Percent of students that received grants for the 2008-2009 academic year: full-time: **39%**
Median grant amount: full-time: **$12,500**
The average law-school debt of those in the Class of 2009 who borrowed: **$119,558** . Proportion who borrowed: **91%**

ACADEMIC PROGRAMS
Calendar: **semester**
Joint degrees awarded: **J.D./M.M.A.; J.D./M.L.R.H.R.; J.D./M.S.C.J.**
Typical first-year section size: Full-time: **60**
Is there typically a "small section" of the first year class,

other than Legal Writing, taught by full-time faculty?:
Full-time: **no**
Number of course titles, beyond the first year curriculum, offered last year: **110**
Percentages of upper division course sections, excluding seminars, with an enrollment of:
Under 25: **59%**   25 to 49: **17%**
50 to 74: **16%**   75 to 99: **7%**
100+: **1%**
Areas of specialization: appellate advocacy, clinical training, dispute resolution, environmental law, health care law, intellectual property law, international law, tax law, trial advocacy

Fall 2009 faculty profile
Total teaching faculty: **54**. Full-time: **50%**; **59%** men, **41%** women, **15%** minorities. Part-time: **50%**; **81%** men, **19%** women, **4%** minorities
Student-to-faculty ratio: **16.7**

SPECIAL PROGRAMS *(as provided by law school):*
The Marine Affairs Institute explores issues raised by the development of the ocean and coastal zone. Courses include admiralty law, environmental regulation, coastal zoning, fisheries, and international law of the sea. The Feinstein Institute is the public interest center of the law school, offering externships, summer stipends, scholarships, speaker series, and unique community partnerships.

STUDENT BODY
Fall 2009 full-time enrollment: 550
Men: **49%**   Women: **51%**
African-American: **2.40%**   American Indian: **0.50%**
Asian-American: **2.40%**   Mexican-American: **0.50%**
Puerto Rican: **0.40%**   Other Hisp-Amer: **4.20%**
White: **77.60%**   International: **0.90%**
Unknown: **11.10%**

Attrition rates for 2008-2009 full-time students
Percent of students discontinuing law school:
Men: **5%**   Women: **5%**

First-year students: **14%** Second-year students: **2%**
Third-year students: **N/A** Fourth-year students: **N/A**

LIBRARY RESOURCES
Total titles: **166,031**
Total volumes: **309,881**
Total seats available for library users: **403**

INFORMATION TECHNOLOGY
Number of wired network connections available to students: **196** total (in the law library, excluding computer labs: **120**; in classrooms: **0**; in computer labs: **44**; elsewhere in the law school: **32**)
Law school has a wireless network.
Students are not required to own a computer.

EMPLOYMENT AND SALARIES
Proportion of 2008 graduates employed at graduation: **N/A**
Employed 9 months later, as of February 15, 2009: **88%**
Salaries in the private sector (law firms, business, industry): **$43,500 –$65,000** (25th-75th percentile)
Median salary in the private sector: **$51,000**
Percentage in the private sector who reported salary information: **65%**
Median salary in public service (government, judicial clerkships, academic posts, non-profits): **$45,000**

Percentage of 2008 graduates in:
Law firms: **44%** Government: **13%**
Bus./industry: **21%** Judicial clerkship: **13%**
Public interest: **8%** Unknown: **0%**
Academia : **1%**

2008 graduates employed in-state: **43%**
2008 graduates employed in foreign countries: **1%**
Number of states where graduates are employed: **23**
Percentage of 2008 graduates working in: New England: **67%**, Middle Atlantic: **14%**, East North Central: **2%**, West North Central: **0%**, South Atlantic: **7%**, East South Central: **0%**, West South Central: **1%**, Mountain: **2%**, Pacific: **2%**, Unknown: **4%**

BAR PASSAGE RATES
Based on 2008 graduates taking Summer 2008 or Winter 2009 exams. Most of the school's first-time test takers took the bar in Massachusetts.

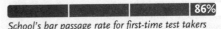

| 86% |
School's bar passage rate for first-time test takers

| 89% |
Statewide bar passage rate for first-time test takers

Rutgers–Camden

- 217 N. Fifth Street, Camden, NJ, 08102-1203
- http://www.camlaw.rutgers.edu
- Public
- Year founded: 1926
- 2009-2010 tuition: full-time: $23,860; part-time: $19,198
- Enrollment 2009-10 academic year: full-time: 619; part-time: 191
- U.S. News 2010 law specialty ranking: N/A

3.21-3.70 GPA, 25TH-75TH PERCENTILE

159-162 LSAT, 25TH-75TH PERCENTILE

26% ACCEPTANCE RATE

80 2011 U.S. NEWS LAW SCHOOL RANKING

ADMISSIONS

Admissions phone number: (800) 466-7561
Admissions email address: **admissions@camlaw.rutgers.edu**
Application website: **http://www-camlaw.rutgers.edu/admissions/**
Application deadline for Fall 2011 admission: **1-Apr**

Admissions statistics:

Number of applicants for Fall 2009: **2,005**
Number of acceptances: **519**
Number enrolled: **227**
Acceptance rate: **26%**
GPA, 25th-75th percentile, entering class Fall 2009: **3.21-3.70**
LSAT, 25th-75th percentile, entering class Fall 2009: **159-162**

Part-time program:

Number of applicants for Fall 2009: **440**
Number of acceptances: **100**
Number enrolled: **41**
Acceptance rate: **23%**
GPA, 25th-75th percentile, entering class Fall 2009: **3.05-3.70**
LSAT, 25th-75th percentile, entering class Fall 2009: **157-161**

FINANCIAL AID

Financial aid phone number: (856) 225-6039
Financial aid application deadline: 15-Jul
Tuition 2009-2010 academic year: **full-time: $23,860; part-time: $19,198**
Room and board: **$11,465** ; books: **$1,313** ; miscellaneous expenses: **$2,383**
Total of room/board/books/miscellaneous expenses: **$15,161**
University offers graduate student housing for which law students are eligible.

Financial aid profile

Percent of students that received grants for the 2008-2009 academic year: full-time: **30%**; part-time **8%**
Median grant amount: full-time: **$5,000** ; part-time: **$2,250**
The average law-school debt of those in the Class of 2009 who borrowed: **$28,767** . Proportion who borrowed: **84%**

ACADEMIC PROGRAMS

Calendar: **semester**
Joint degrees awarded: **J.D./M.B.A.; J.D./M.P.A.P.; J.D./M.S.W.; J.D./D.O.; J.D./M.D.; J.D./M.C.R.P.; J.D./M.P.A.**
Typical first-year section size: Full-time: **56**; Part-time: **40**
Is there typically a "small section" of the first year class, other than Legal Writing, taught by full-time faculty?: Full-time: **no**; Part-time: **no**
Number of course titles, beyond the first year curriculum, offered last year: **139**
Percentages of upper division course sections, excluding seminars, with an enrollment of:

Under 25: **69%**	25 to 49: **22%**
50 to 74: **7%**	75 to 99: **2%**
100+: **0%**	

Areas of specialization: appellate advocacy, clinical training, dispute resolution, environmental law, health care law, intellectual property law, international law, tax law, trial advocacy

Fall 2009 faculty profile

Total teaching faculty: **99**. Full-time: **42%**; **67%** men, **33%** women, **10%** minorities. Part-time: **58%**; **60%** men, **40%** women, **7%** minorities
Student-to-faculty ratio: **11.8**

SPECIAL PROGRAMS (as provided by law school):

Rutgers-Camden has special programs including business concentrations, outstanding externships, pro bono activities, and joint degree programs. The legal writing program provides excellent communications skills. The Law School's clinical program enables students to learn lawyering skills in a variety of areas. The School has one of the highest percentages students obtaining judicial clerkships.

STUDENT BODY

Fall 2009 full-time enrollment: 619

Men: **60%**	Women: **40%**
African-American: **5.80%**	American Indian: **0.20%**
Asian-American: **9.00%**	Mexican-American: **0.50%**
Puerto Rican: **1.50%**	Other Hisp-Amer: **3.70%**
White: **78.80%**	International: **0.50%**
Unknown: **0.00%**	

Fall 2009 part-time enrollment: 191

Men: **57%**	Women: **43%**
African-American: **4.70%**	American Indian: **0.00%**
Asian-American: **6.30%**	Mexican-American: **0.00%**
Puerto Rican: **1.00%**	Other Hisp-Amer: **1.00%**
White: **86.90%**	International: **0.00%**
Unknown: **0.00%**	

Attrition rates for 2008-2009 full-time students
Percent of students discontinuing law school:

Men: **4%**	Women: **3%**
First-year students: **10%**	Second-year students: **2%**
Third-year students: **N/A**	Fourth-year students: **N/A**

LIBRARY RESOURCES

Total titles: **109,723**
Total volumes: **455,141**
Total seats available for library users: **396**

INFORMATION TECHNOLOGY

Number of wired network connections available to students: **170** total (in the law library, excluding computer labs: **60**; in classrooms: **10**; in computer labs: **50**; elsewhere in the law school: **50**)
Law school has a wireless network.
Students are required to own a computer.

EMPLOYMENT AND SALARIES

Proportion of 2008 graduates employed at graduation: **75%**
Employed 9 months later, as of February 15, 2009: **90%**
Salaries in the private sector (law firms, business, industry): **$75,000 –$145,000** (25th-75th percentile)
Median salary in the private sector: **$125,000**
Percentage in the private sector who reported salary information: **50%**
Median salary in public service (government, judicial clerkships, academic posts, non-profits): **$40,746**

Percentage of 2008 graduates in:

Law firms: **41%**	Government: **7%**
Bus./industry: **9%**	Judicial clerkship: **40%**
Public interest: **2%**	Unknown: **1%**
Academia : **0%**	

2008 graduates employed in-state: **55%**
2008 graduates employed in foreign countries: **0%**
Number of states where graduates are employed: **18**
Percentage of 2008 graduates working in: New England: **0%**, Middle Atlantic: **81%**, East North Central: **1%**, West North Central: **0%**, South Atlantic: **8%**, East South Central: **1%**, West South Central: **1%**, Mountain: **0%**, Pacific: **3%**, Unknown: **3%**

BAR PASSAGE RATES

Based on 2008 graduates taking Summer 2008 or Winter 2009 exams. Most of the school's first-time test takers took the bar in New Jersey.

85%

School's bar passage rate for first-time test takers

85%

Statewide bar passage rate for first-time test takers

Rutgers–Newark

- 123 Washington Street, Newark, NJ, 7102
- http://law.newark.rutgers.edu
- Public
- Year founded: 1908
- 2009-2010 tuition: full-time: $23,676; part-time: $15,470
- Enrollment 2009-10 academic year: full-time: 593; part-time: 242
- U.S. News 2010 law specialty ranking: clinical training: 25

3.13-3.60 GPA, 25ᵀᴴ-75ᵀᴴ PERCENTILE

155-161 LSAT, 25ᵀᴴ-75ᵀᴴ PERCENTILE

30% ACCEPTANCE RATE

80 2011 U.S. NEWS LAW SCHOOL RANKING

ADMISSIONS

Admissions phone number: **(973) 353-5554**
Admissions email address: law-info@andromeda.rutgers.edu
Application website:
http://law.newark.rutgers.edu/files/u/Rev2010ApplicationForm.pdf
Application deadline for Fall 2011 admission: **15-Mar**

Admissions statistics:

Number of applicants for Fall 2009: **2,761**
Number of acceptances: **821**
Number enrolled: **191**
Acceptance rate: **30%**
GPA, 25th-75th percentile, entering class Fall 2009: **3.13-3.60**
LSAT, 25th-75th percentile, entering class Fall 2009: **155-161**

Part-time program:

Number of applicants for Fall 2009: **702**
Number of acceptances: **127**
Number enrolled: **69**
Acceptance rate: **18%**
GPA, 25th-75th percentile, entering class Fall 2009: **2.95-3.60**
LSAT, 25th-75th percentile, entering class Fall 2009: **154-159**

FINANCIAL AID

Financial aid phone number: **(973) 353-1702**
Financial aid application deadline: **15-Mar**
Tuition 2009-2010 academic year: **full-time: $23,676; part-time: $15,470**
Room and board: **$11,465** ; books: **$1,313** ; miscellaneous expenses: **$3,286**
Total of room/board/books/miscellaneous expenses: **$16,064**
University offers graduate student housing for which law students are eligible.

Financial aid profile

Percent of students that received grants for the 2008-2009 academic year: full-time: **41%**; part-time **15%**
Median grant amount: full-time: **$6,000** ; part-time: **$5,000**
The average law-school debt of those in the Class of 2009 who borrowed: **$73,244** . Proportion who borrowed: **90%**

ACADEMIC PROGRAMS

Calendar: **semester**
Joint degrees awarded: **J.D./M.A.; J.D./M.C.R.P.; J.D./M.D.; J.D./Ph.D.; J.D./M.B.A.; J.D./M.S.W.**
Typical first-year section size: Full-time: **60**; Part-time: **65**
Is there typically a "small section" of the first year class, other than Legal Writing, taught by full-time faculty?: Full-time: **yes**; Part-time: **yes**
Number of course titles, beyond the first year curriculum, offered last year: **109**
Percentages of upper division course sections, excluding seminars, with an enrollment of:
Under 25: **49%**   25 to 49: **38%**
50 to 74: **6%**   75 to 99: **4%**
100+: **4%**
Areas of specialization: appellate advocacy, clinical training, dispute resolution, environmental law, health care law, intellectual property law, international law, tax law, trial advocacy

Fall 2009 faculty profile

Total teaching faculty: **87**. Full-time: **52%; 60%** men, **40%** women, **36%** minorities. Part-time: **48%; 69%** men, **31%** women, **2%** minorities
Student-to-faculty ratio: **17.6**

SPECIAL PROGRAMS (as provided by law school):

MSP - post-admissions program for students who, regardless of race or ethnicity, demonstrate educational, cultural, or socioeconomic disadvantage; Clinical Prog. since 1970 offering faculty-supervised experience representing real clients; Global Legal Studies; Eric Neisser Public Interest Prog. fellowships, summer placement; LRAP; Externships - judicial, IP, immigration, labor law.

STUDENT BODY

Fall 2009 full-time enrollment: 593

Men: 56%	Women: 44%
African-American: 14.00%	American Indian: 0.20%
Asian-American: 10.10%	Mexican-American: 1.30%
Puerto Rican: 2.90%	Other Hisp-Amer: 6.90%
White: 63.10%	International: 1.50%
Unknown: 0.00%	

Fall 2009 part-time enrollment: 242

Men: 60%	Women: 40%
African-American: 17.80%	American Indian: 0.40%
Asian-American: 11.20%	Mexican-American: 0.80%
Puerto Rican: 2.10%	Other Hisp-Amer: 7.90%
White: 57.40%	International: 2.50%
Unknown: 0.00%	

Attrition rates for 2008-2009 full-time students
Percent of students discontinuing law school:

Men: 3%	Women: 4%
First-year students: 7%	Second-year students: 3%
Third-year students: 0%	Fourth-year students: N/A

LIBRARY RESOURCES

Total titles: 241,300
Total volumes: 572,750
Total seats available for library users: 522

INFORMATION TECHNOLOGY

Number of wired network connections available to students: 570 total (in the law library, excluding computer labs: 160; in classrooms: 350; in computer labs: 0; elsewhere in the law school: 60)
Law school has a wireless network.
Students are not required to own a computer.

EMPLOYMENT AND SALARIES

Proportion of 2008 graduates employed at graduation: 84%
Employed 9 months later, as of February 15, 2009: 96%
Salaries in the private sector (law firms, business, industry): $95,000 –$160,000 (25th-75th percentile)
Median salary in the private sector: $120,000
Percentage in the private sector who reported salary information: 71%
Median salary in public service (government, judicial clerkships, academic posts, non-profits): $41,000

Percentage of 2008 graduates in:

Law firms: 46%	Government: 11%
Bus./industry: 16%	Judicial clerkship: 21%
Public interest: 5%	Unknown: 0%
Academia : 1%	

2008 graduates employed in-state: 62%
2008 graduates employed in foreign countries: 1%
Number of states where graduates are employed: 15
Percentage of 2008 graduates working in: New England: 2%, Middle Atlantic: 92%, East North Central: 1%, West North Central: N/A, South Atlantic: 2%, East South Central: 0%, West South Central: 1%, Mountain: 0%, Pacific: 1%, Unknown: 0%

BAR PASSAGE RATES

Based on 2008 graduates taking Summer 2008 or Winter 2009 exams. Most of the school's first-time test takers took the bar in New Jersey.

87%
School's bar passage rate for first-time test takers

85%
Statewide bar passage rate for first-time test takers

Samford University (Cumberland)

- 800 Lakeshore Drive, Birmingham, AL, 35229
- http://cumberland.samford.edu
- Private
- Year founded: 1847
- 2009-2010 tuition: full-time: $31,733; part-time: $18,849
- Enrollment 2009-10 academic year: full-time: 493
- U.S. News 2010 law specialty ranking: N/A

3.01-3.59 GPA, 25TH-75TH PERCENTILE

153-157 LSAT, 25TH-75TH PERCENTILE

52% ACCEPTANCE RATE

Tier 3 2011 U.S. NEWS LAW SCHOOL RANKING

ADMISSIONS

Admissions phone number: (205) 726-2702
Admissions email address: law.admissions@samford.edu
Application website:
http://cumberland.samford.edu/application
Application deadline for Fall 2011 admission: **28-Feb**

Admissions statistics:

Number of applicants for Fall 2009: **980**
Number of acceptances: **506**
Number enrolled: **178**
Acceptance rate: **52%**
GPA, 25th-75th percentile, entering class Fall 2009: **3.01-3.59**
LSAT, 25th-75th percentile, entering class Fall 2009: **153-157**

FINANCIAL AID

Financial aid phone number: **(205) 726-2905**
Financial aid application deadline: **1-Mar**
Tuition 2009-2010 academic year: **full-time: $31,733; part-time: $18,849**
Room and board: **$13,500** ; books: **$2,000** ; miscellaneous expenses: **$6,720**
Total of room/board/books/miscellaneous expenses: **$22,220**
University does not offer graduate student housing for which law students are eligible.

Financial aid profile

Percent of students that received grants for the 2008-2009 academic year: full-time: **34%**
Median grant amount: full-time: **$20,000**
The average law-school debt of those in the Class of 2009 who borrowed: **$102,106** . Proportion who borrowed: **80%**

ACADEMIC PROGRAMS

Calendar: **semester**
Joint degrees awarded: **J.D./M.P.H.; J.D./M.B.A.; J.D./M.Acc.; J.D./M.Div; J.D./M.S. Environmental**

Management; **J.D./M.P.A.; J.D./M.T.S.**
Typical first-year section size: Full-time: **55**
Is there typically a "small section" of the first year class, other than Legal Writing, taught by full-time faculty?: Full-time: **no**
Number of course titles, beyond the first year curriculum, offered last year: **105**
Percentages of upper division course sections, excluding seminars, with an enrollment of:
Under 25: **56%**   25 to 49: **30%**
50 to 74: **14%**   75 to 99: **1%**
100+: **0%**
Areas of specialization: appellate advocacy, clinical training, dispute resolution, environmental law, health care law, intellectual property law, international law, tax law, trial advocacy

Fall 2009 faculty profile

Total teaching faculty: **43**. Full-time: **51%**; **68%** men, **32%** women, **18%** minorities. Part-time: **49%**; **67%** men, **33%** women, **5%** minorities
Student-to-faculty ratio: **18**

SPECIAL PROGRAMS (as provided by law school):

Semester-long and summer externships; Judicial Externships; Trial Advocacy and Advanced Trial Advocacy program; The Center for Biotechnology, Law and Ethics; Cumberland Community Mediation Center; Summer study abroad program in Sidney-Sussex College in Cambridge, England.

STUDENT BODY

Fall 2009 full-time enrollment: 493

Men: **55%**   Women: **45%**
African-American: **5.30%**   American Indian: **1.00%**
Asian-American: **0.80%**   Mexican-American: **0.00%**
Puerto Rican: **0.20%**   Other Hisp-Amer: **0.60%**
White: **75.70%**   International: **0.60%**
Unknown: **15.80%**

Attrition rates for 2008-2009 full-time students

Percent of students discontinuing law school:

Men: **5%**   Women: **2%**
First-year students: **9%**   Second-year students: **2%**
Third-year students: **N/A**   Fourth-year students: **N/A**

LIBRARY RESOURCES

Total titles: **39,205**
Total volumes: **326,005**
Total seats available for library users: **474**

INFORMATION TECHNOLOGY

Number of wired network connections available to students: **200** total (in the law library, excluding computer labs: **200**; in classrooms: **0**; in computer labs: **0**; elsewhere in the law school: **0**)
Law school has a wireless network.
Students are not required to own a computer.

EMPLOYMENT AND SALARIES

Proportion of 2008 graduates employed at graduation: **N/A**
Employed 9 months later, as of February 15, 2009: **94%**
Salaries in the private sector (law firms, business, industry): **$55,000 –$95,000** (25th-75th percentile)
Median salary in the private sector: **$65,000**
Percentage in the private sector who reported salary information: **58%**

Median salary in public service (government, judicial clerkships, academic posts, non-profits): **$46,000**

Percentage of 2008 graduates in:

Law firms: **73%**   Government: **11%**
Bus./industry: **11%**   Judicial clerkship: **3%**
Public interest: **0%**   Unknown: **0%**
Academia : **2%**

2008 graduates employed in-state: **58%**
2008 graduates employed in foreign countries: **1%**
Number of states where graduates are employed: **17**
Percentage of 2008 graduates working in: New England: **0%**, Middle Atlantic: **2%**, East North Central: **2%**, West North Central: **0%**, South Atlantic: **24%**, East South Central: **66%**, West South Central: **2%**, Mountain: **2%**, Pacific: **1%**, Unknown: **0%**

BAR PASSAGE RATES

Based on 2008 graduates taking Summer 2008 or Winter 2009 exams. Most of the school's first-time test takers took the bar in Alabama.

96%

School's bar passage rate for first-time test takers

79%

Statewide bar passage rate for first-time test takers

Santa Clara University

■ 500 El Camino Real, Santa Clara, CA, 95053-0421
■ http://www.scu.edu/law
■ Private
■ Year founded: 1851
■ 2009-2010 tuition: full-time: $1,268/credit hour; part-time: $1,268/credit hour
■ Enrollment 2009-10 academic year: full-time: 749; part-time: 252
■ U.S. News 2010 law specialty ranking: intellectual property law: 11

3.11-3.61 GPA, 25ᵀᴴ-75ᵀᴴ PERCENTILE

157-161 LSAT, 25ᵀᴴ-75ᵀᴴ PERCENTILE

45% ACCEPTANCE RATE

93 2011 U.S. NEWS LAW SCHOOL RANKING

ADMISSIONS
Admissions phone number: **(408) 554-4800**
Admissions email address: **lawadmissions@scu.edu**
Application website:
   http://os.lsac.org/Release/Logon/Access.aspx
Application deadline for Fall 2011 admission: **1-Jul**

Admissions statistics:
Number of applicants for Fall 2009: **4,099**
Number of acceptances: **1,826**
Number enrolled: **235**
Acceptance rate: **45%**
GPA, 25th-75th percentile, entering class Fall 2009: **3.11-3.61**
LSAT, 25th-75th percentile, entering class Fall 2009: **157-161**

Part-time program:
Number of applicants for Fall 2009: **481**
Number of acceptances: **129**
Number enrolled: **76**
Acceptance rate: **27%**
GPA, 25th-75th percentile, entering class Fall 2009: **2.88-3.43**
LSAT, 25th-75th percentile, entering class Fall 2009: **156-159**

FINANCIAL AID
Financial aid phone number: **(408) 554-4447**
Financial aid application deadline: **1-Jul**
Tuition 2009-2010 academic year: **full-time: $1,268/credit hour; part-time: $1,268/credit hour**
Room and board: **$13,906** ; books: **$1,200** ; miscellaneous expenses: **$6,688**
Total of room/board/books/miscellaneous expenses: **$21,794**
University offers graduate student housing for which law students are eligible.

Financial aid profile
Percent of students that received grants for the 2008-2009

academic year: full-time: **33%**; part-time **33%**
Median grant amount: full-time: **$12,500** ; part-time: **$10,000**
The average law-school debt of those in the Class of 2009 who borrowed: **$104,546** . Proportion who borrowed: **88%**

ACADEMIC PROGRAMS
Calendar: **semester**
Joint degrees awarded: **J.D./M.B.A.**
Typical first-year section size: Full-time: **73**; Part-time: **72**
Is there typically a "small section" of the first year class, other than Legal Writing, taught by full-time faculty?: Full-time: **yes**; Part-time: **yes**
Number of course titles, beyond the first year curriculum, offered last year: **179**
Percentages of upper division course sections, excluding seminars, with an enrollment of:
   Under 25: **66%**   25 to 49: **18%**
   50 to 74: **9%**   75 to 99: **6%**
   100+: **0%**
Areas of specialization: appellate advocacy, clinical training, dispute resolution, environmental law, health care law, intellectual property law, international law, tax law, trial advocacy

Fall 2009 faculty profile
Total teaching faculty: **77**. Full-time: **55%**; **52%** men, **48%** women, **24%** minorities. Part-time: **45%**; **57%** men, **43%** women, **17%** minorities
Student-to-faculty ratio: **17.8**

SPECIAL PROGRAMS (as provided by law school):
The Center for Social Justice and Public Interest, the Northern California Innocence Project, and the Alexander Community Law Center offer innovative courses and clinics under the supervision of experienced attorneys. The High Tech Law curriculum is one of the richest in the nation. The Center for Global Law and Policy offers 13 summer study abroad programs, most of which include field placement.

STUDENT BODY

Fall 2009 full-time enrollment: 749

Men: 54% | Women: 46%
African-American: 2.80% | American Indian: 1.50%
Asian-American: 28.20% | Mexican-American: 0.00%
Puerto Rican: 0.00% | Other Hisp-Amer: 9.10%
White: 58.30% | International: 0.00%
Unknown: 0.10%

Fall 2009 part-time enrollment: 252

Men: 58% | Women: 42%
African-American: 3.20% | American Indian: 2.00%
Asian-American: 35.30% | Mexican-American: 0.00%
Puerto Rican: 0.00% | Other Hisp-Amer: 7.10%
White: 52.40% | International: 0.00%
Unknown: 0.00%

Attrition rates for 2008-2009 full-time students
Percent of students discontinuing law school:

Men: 2% | Women: 2%
First-year students: 6% | Second-year students: N/A
Third-year students: N/A | Fourth-year students: 4%

LIBRARY RESOURCES

Total titles: 155,471
Total volumes: 385,193
Total seats available for library users: 452

INFORMATION TECHNOLOGY

Number of wired network connections available to students: 870 total (in the law library, excluding computer labs: 240; in classrooms: 605; in computer labs: 0; elsewhere in the law school: 25)
Law school has a wireless network.
Students are not required to own a computer.

EMPLOYMENT AND SALARIES

Proportion of 2008 graduates employed at graduation: 79%
Employed 9 months later, as of February 15, 2009: 93%
Salaries in the private sector (law firms, business, industry): $80,000 –$160,000 (25th-75th percentile)
Median salary in the private sector: $145,000
Percentage in the private sector who reported salary information: 59%
Median salary in public service (government, judicial clerkships, academic posts, non-profits): $56,000

Percentage of 2008 graduates in:

Law firms: 57% | Government: 9%
Bus./industry: 26% | Judicial clerkship: 2%
Public interest: 4% | Unknown: 1%
Academia : 1%

2008 graduates employed in-state: 90%
2008 graduates employed in foreign countries: 0%
Number of states where graduates are employed: 13
Percentage of 2008 graduates working in: New England: 0%, Middle Atlantic: 3%, East North Central: 1%, West North Central: 0%, South Atlantic: 3%, East South Central: 0%, West South Central: 0%, Mountain: 2%, Pacific: 91%, Unknown: 0%

BAR PASSAGE RATES

Based on 2008 graduates taking Summer 2008 or Winter 2009 exams. Most of the school's first-time test takers took the bar in California.

79%

School's bar passage rate for first-time test takers

71%

Statewide bar passage rate for first-time test takers

Seattle University

- 901 12th Avenue, Seattle, WA, 98122-1090
- http://www.law.seattleu.edu
- Private
- Year founded: 1972
- 2009-2010 tuition: full-time: $35,406; part-time: $29,494
- Enrollment 2009-10 academic year: full-time: 808; part-time: 228
- U.S. News 2010 law specialty ranking: clinical training: 14

3.16-3.63 GPA, 25TH-75TH PERCENTILE

155-160 LSAT, 25TH-75TH PERCENTILE

38% ACCEPTANCE RATE

86 2011 U.S. NEWS LAW SCHOOL RANKING

ADMISSIONS
Admissions phone number: (206) 398-4200
Admissions email address: **lawadmin@seattleu.edu**
Application website:
   http://www.law.seattleu.edu/admission/admissionapp.asp
Application deadline for Fall 2011 admission: **1-Mar**

Admissions statistics:
Number of applicants for Fall 2009: **2,374**
Number of acceptances: **895**
Number enrolled: **268**
Acceptance rate: **38%**
GPA, 25th-75th percentile, entering class Fall 2009: **3.16-3.63**
LSAT, 25th-75th percentile, entering class Fall 2009: **155-160**

Part-time program:
Number of applicants for Fall 2009: **252**
Number of acceptances: **103**
Number enrolled: **64**
Acceptance rate: **41%**
GPA, 25th-75th percentile, entering class Fall 2009: **2.99-3.55**
LSAT, 25th-75th percentile, entering class Fall 2009: **153-159**

FINANCIAL AID
Financial aid phone number: (206) 398-4250
Financial aid application deadline:
Tuition 2009-2010 academic year: **full-time: $35,406; part-time: $29,494**
Room and board: **$11,448** ; books: **$1,258** ; miscellaneous expenses: **$5,137**
Total of room/board/books/miscellaneous expenses: **$17,843**
University does not offer graduate student housing for which law students are eligible.

Financial aid profile
Percent of students that received grants for the 2008-2009 academic year: full-time: **53%**; part-time **37%**
Median grant amount: full-time: **$9,000** ; part-time: **$7,000**
The average law-school debt of those in the Class of 2009 who borrowed: **$95,572** . Proportion who borrowed: **91%**

ACADEMIC PROGRAMS
Calendar: **semester**
Joint degrees awarded: **J.D./M.B.A.; J.D./M.I.B.; J.D./M.S.F.; J.D./M.Acc.; J.D./M.P.A.; J.D./M.S.A.L.**
Typical first-year section size: Full-time: **85**; Part-time: **60**
Is there typically a "small section" of the first year class, other than Legal Writing, taught by full-time faculty?:
   Full-time: **no**; Part-time: **no**
Number of course titles, beyond the first year curriculum, offered last year: **160**
Percentages of upper division course sections, excluding seminars, with an enrollment of:

Under 25: **62%**	25 to 49: **25%**
50 to 74: **8%**	75 to 99: **6%**
100+: **0%**	

Areas of specialization: appellate advocacy, clinical training, dispute resolution, environmental law, health care law, intellectual property law, international law, tax law, trial advocacy

Fall 2009 faculty profile
Total teaching faculty: **106**. Full-time: **59%**; **59%** men, **41%** women, **29%** minorities. Part-time: **41%**; **63%** men, **37%** women, **5%** minorities
Student-to-faculty ratio: **12.3**

SPECIAL PROGRAMS *(as provided by law school):*
Clinics: Administrative; Arts; Bankruptcy; Community Development; Domestic Violence; Immigration; Human Rights; Mediation; Mental Health; Predatory Lending; Trusts and Estates; Youth Advocacy. Externships: numerous. Centers/Institutes: Academic Resource; Access to Justice; Corporations, Law & Society; Global Justice; Indian Estate Planning; Summer Study Abroad: Brazil; Ireland, South Africa.

STUDENT BODY

Fall 2009 full-time enrollment: 808

Men: **49%**   Women: **51%**
African-American: **4.20%**   American Indian: **1.10%**
Asian-American: **15.10%**   Mexican-American: **3.20%**
Puerto Rican: **0.20%**   Other Hisp-Amer: **2.00%**
White: **69.40%**   International: **1.00%**
Unknown: **3.70%**

Fall 2009 part-time enrollment: 228

Men: **51%**   Women: **49%**
African-American: **4.80%**   American Indian: **0.90%**
Asian-American: **12.70%**   Mexican-American: **0.90%**
Puerto Rican: **0.90%**   Other Hisp-Amer: **2.60%**
White: **72.40%**   International: **0.00%**
Unknown: **4.80%**

Attrition rates for 2008-2009 full-time students
Percent of students discontinuing law school:
Men: **2%**   Women: **3%**
First-year students: **7%**   Second-year students: **1%**
Third-year students: **0%**   Fourth-year students: **N/A**

LIBRARY RESOURCES

Total titles: **186,378**
Total volumes: **388,860**
Total seats available for library users: **429**

INFORMATION TECHNOLOGY

Number of wired network connections available to students: **2116** total (in the law library, excluding computer labs: **367**; in classrooms: **665**; in computer labs: **0**; elsewhere in the law school: **1,084**)
Law school has a wireless network.
Students are required to own a computer.

EMPLOYMENT AND SALARIES

Proportion of 2008 graduates employed at graduation: **59%**
Employed 9 months later, as of February 15, 2009: **97%**
Salaries in the private sector (law firms, business, industry): **$59,742 –$100,000** (25th-75th percentile)
Median salary in the private sector: **$75,000**
Percentage in the private sector who reported salary information: **32%**
Median salary in public service (government, judicial clerkships, academic posts, non-profits): **$48,925**

Percentage of 2008 graduates in:

Law firms: **45%**   Government: **12%**
Bus./industry: **30%**   Judicial clerkship: **7%**
Public interest: **5%**   Unknown: **0%**
Academia : **1%**

2008 graduates employed in-state: **84%**
2008 graduates employed in foreign countries: **1%**
Number of states where graduates are employed: **20**
Percentage of 2008 graduates working in: New England: **0%**, Middle Atlantic: **1%**, East North Central: **1%**, West North Central: **0%**, South Atlantic: **2%**, East South Central: **0%**, West South Central: **1%**, Mountain: **3%**, Pacific: **92%**, Unknown: **0%**

BAR PASSAGE RATES

Based on 2008 graduates taking Summer 2008 or Winter 2009 exams. Most of the school's first-time test takers took the bar in Washington.

79%

School's bar passage rate for first-time test takers

74%

Statewide bar passage rate for first-time test takers

Seton Hall University

- 1 Newark Center, Newark, NJ, 07102-5210
- http://law.shu.edu
- Private
- Year founded: 1951
- 2009-2010 tuition: full-time: $42,980; part-time: $32,430
- Enrollment 2009-10 academic year: full-time: 723; part-time: 367
- U.S. News 2010 law specialty ranking: healthcare law: 8

3.21-3.68 GPA, 25TH-75TH PERCENTILE

158-161 LSAT, 25TH-75TH PERCENTILE

52% ACCEPTANCE RATE

72 2011 U.S. NEWS LAW SCHOOL RANKING

ADMISSIONS

Admissions phone number: (888) 415-7271
Admissions email address: **admitme@shu.edu**
Application website:
  http://law.shu.edu/ProspectiveStudents/prospective_jd_students/jd_admission.cfm
Application deadline for Fall 2011 admission: **1-Apr**

Admissions statistics:

Number of applicants for Fall 2009: **2,804**
Number of acceptances: **1,453**
Number enrolled: **240**
Acceptance rate: **52%**
GPA, 25th-75th percentile, entering class Fall 2009: **3.21-3.68**
LSAT, 25th-75th percentile, entering class Fall 2009: **158-161**

Part-time program:

Number of applicants for Fall 2009: **588**
Number of acceptances: **226**
Number enrolled: **117**
Acceptance rate: **38%**
GPA, 25th-75th percentile, entering class Fall 2009: **3.00-3.47**
LSAT, 25th-75th percentile, entering class Fall 2009: **150-156**

FINANCIAL AID

Financial aid phone number: **(973) 642-8850**
Financial aid application deadline: **1-Apr**
Tuition 2009-2010 academic year: **full-time: $42,980; part-time: $32,430**
Room and board: **$13,050** ; books: **$1,200** ; miscellaneous expenses: **$5,355**
Total of room/board/books/miscellaneous expenses: **$19,605**
University does not offer graduate student housing for which law students are eligible.

Financial aid profile

Percent of students that received grants for the 2008-2009 academic year: full-time: **50%**; part-time **15%**
Median grant amount: full-time: **$20,000** ; part-time: **$5,425**
The average law-school debt of those in the Class of 2009 who borrowed: **$100,371** . Proportion who borrowed: **86%**

ACADEMIC PROGRAMS

Calendar: **semester**
Joint degrees awarded: **J.D./M.B.A.; J.D./M.D.; M.S.J./M.D.; J.D./M.A.D.I.R.**
Typical first-year section size: Full-time: **70**; Part-time: **75**
Is there typically a "small section" of the first year class, other than Legal Writing, taught by full-time faculty?: Full-time: **no**; Part-time: **no**
Number of course titles, beyond the first year curriculum, offered last year: **138**
Percentages of upper division course sections, excluding seminars, with an enrollment of:

Under 25: **71%**   25 to 49: **16%**
50 to 74: **10%**   75 to 99: **3%**
100+: **0%**

Areas of specialization: appellate advocacy, clinical training, dispute resolution, environmental law, health care law, intellectual property law, international law, tax law, trial advocacy

Fall 2009 faculty profile

Total teaching faculty: **135**. Full-time: **38%**; 55% men, 45% women, 18% minorities. Part-time: **62%**; 57% men, 43% women, 7% minorities
Student-to-faculty ratio: **15.4**

SPECIAL PROGRAMS (as provided by law school):

Our Center for Social Justice represents disadvantaged clients in diverse legal matters. We offer a JD concentration and LLM in Health Law through our Health Law & Policy Program. Students may pursue a JD concentration in Intellectual Property through our Institute of Law, Science & Technology.

Students participate in for-credit internships in state, federal and international courts and agencies.

STUDENT BODY

Fall 2009 full-time enrollment: 723

Men: 55%	Women: 45%
African-American: 2.10%	American Indian: 0.00%
Asian-American: 5.80%	Mexican-American: 0.00%
Puerto Rican: 1.00%	Other Hisp-Amer: 2.80%
White: 87.30%	International: 0.70%
Unknown: 0.40%	

Fall 2009 part-time enrollment: 367

Men: 54%	Women: 46%
African-American: 5.70%	American Indian: 0.30%
Asian-American: 10.10%	Mexican-American: 0.00%
Puerto Rican: 2.70%	Other Hisp-Amer: 4.40%
White: 73.30%	International: 1.90%
Unknown: 1.60%	

Attrition rates for 2008-2009 full-time students

Percent of students discontinuing law school:

Men: 5%	Women: 5%
First-year students: 8%	Second-year students: 7%
Third-year students: 0%	Fourth-year students: N/A

LIBRARY RESOURCES

Total titles: 308,989
Total volumes: 467,898
Total seats available for library users: 533

INFORMATION TECHNOLOGY

Number of wired network connections available to students: 54 total (in the law library, excluding computer labs: 10; in classrooms: 18; in computer labs: 8; elsewhere in the law school: 18)
Law school has a wireless network.
Students are required to own a computer.

EMPLOYMENT AND SALARIES

Proportion of 2008 graduates employed at graduation: 81%
Employed 9 months later, as of February 15, 2009: 97%
Salaries in the private sector (law firms, business, industry): $92,500 –$145,000 (25th-75th percentile)
Median salary in the private sector: $125,000
Percentage in the private sector who reported salary information: 52%
Median salary in public service (government, judicial clerkships, academic posts, non-profits): $39,179

Percentage of 2008 graduates in:

Law firms: 40%	Government: 6%
Bus./industry: 13%	Judicial clerkship: 39%
Public interest: 1%	Unknown: 1%
Academia : 1%	

2008 graduates employed in-state: 70%
2008 graduates employed in foreign countries: 0%
Number of states where graduates are employed: 13
Percentage of 2008 graduates working in: New England: 1%, Middle Atlantic: 90%, East North Central: 0%, West North Central: N/A, South Atlantic: 1%, East South Central: N/A, West South Central: 0%, Mountain: 1%, Pacific: 2%, Unknown: 5%

BAR PASSAGE RATES

Based on 2008 graduates taking Summer 2008 or Winter 2009 exams. Most of the school's first-time test takers took the bar in New Jersey.

89%

School's bar passage rate for first-time test takers

85%

Statewide bar passage rate for first-time test takers

South Texas College of Law

- 1303 San Jacinto Street, Houston, TX, 77002-7000
- http://www.stcl.edu
- Private
- Year founded: 1923
- 2009-2010 tuition: full-time: $25,710; part-time: $17,340
- Enrollment 2009-10 academic year: full-time: 973; part-time: 305
- U.S. News 2010 law specialty ranking: dispute resolution: 15, trial advocacy: 3

3.04-3.56 GPA, 25TH-75TH PERCENTILE

151-156 LSAT, 25TH-75TH PERCENTILE

48% ACCEPTANCE RATE

Tier 4 2011 U.S. NEWS LAW SCHOOL RANKING

ADMISSIONS
Admissions phone number: **(713) 646-1810**
Admissions email address: **admissions@stcl.edu**
Application website: **http://www.stcl.edu**
Application deadline for Fall 2011 admission: **15-Feb**

Admissions statistics:
Number of applicants for Fall 2009: **2,076**
Number of acceptances: **989**
Number enrolled: **350**
Acceptance rate: **48%**
GPA, 25th-75th percentile, entering class Fall 2009: **3.04-3.56**
LSAT, 25th-75th percentile, entering class Fall 2009: **151-156**

Part-time program:
Number of applicants for Fall 2009: **301**
Number of acceptances: **129**
Number enrolled: **84**
Acceptance rate: **43%**
GPA, 25th-75th percentile, entering class Fall 2009: **2.70-3.26**
LSAT, 25th-75th percentile, entering class Fall 2009: **150-155**

FINANCIAL AID
Financial aid phone number: **(713) 646-1820**
Financial aid application deadline: **1-May**
Tuition 2009-2010 academic year: **full-time: $25,710; part-time: $17,340**
Room and board: **$9,500** ; books: **$2,000** ; miscellaneous expenses: **$7,200**
Total of room/board/books/miscellaneous expenses: **$18,700**
University does not offer graduate student housing for which law students are eligible.

Financial aid profile
Percent of students that received grants for the 2008-2009 academic year: full-time: **37%**; part-time **24%**

Median grant amount: full-time: **$3,400** ; part-time: **$1,900**
The average law-school debt of those in the Class of 2009 who borrowed: **$93,494** . Proportion who borrowed: **87%**

ACADEMIC PROGRAMS
Calendar: **semester**
Joint degrees awarded: **J.D./M.B.A.**
Typical first-year section size: Full-time: **95**; Part-time: **70**
Is there typically a "small section" of the first year class, other than Legal Writing, taught by full-time faculty?: Full-time: **no**; Part-time: **no**
Number of course titles, beyond the first year curriculum, offered last year: **163**
Percentages of upper division course sections, excluding seminars, with an enrollment of:
Under 25: **64%**   25 to 49: **19%**
50 to 74: **9%**   75 to 99: **8%**
100+: **0%**
Areas of specialization: appellate advocacy, clinical training, dispute resolution, environmental law, health care law, intellectual property law, international law, tax law, trial advocacy

Fall 2009 faculty profile
Total teaching faculty: **91**. Full-time: **54%**; **65%** men, **35%** women, **10%** minorities. Part-time: **46%**; **64%** men, **36%** women, **17%** minorities
Student-to-faculty ratio: **20**

SPECIAL PROGRAMS *(as provided by law school):*
Development of strong legal skills is important at South Texas, as evidenced by its nationally recognized Advocacy Program, and its other three Centers of Excellence. South Texas offers numerous off-site clinics, placing students in the real world of lawyering. For students interested in the increased globalization of law, South Texas offers a wide variety of foreign programs throughout the year.

STUDENT BODY
Fall 2009 full-time enrollment: 973
Men: **51%**   Women: **49%**

African-American: 2.30%   American Indian: 0.90%
Asian-American: 9.60%   Mexican-American: 6.20%
Puerto Rican: 0.20%   Other Hisp-Amer: 4.10%
White: 76.50%   International: 0.30%
Unknown: 0.00%

Fall 2009 part-time enrollment: 305
Men: 55%   Women: 45%
African-American: 8.90%   American Indian: 2.00%
Asian-American: 11.80%   Mexican-American: 7.90%
Puerto Rican: 0.00%   Other Hisp-Amer: 4.30%
White: 65.20%   International: 0.00%
Unknown: 0.00%

Attrition rates for 2008-2009 full-time students
Percent of students discontinuing law school:
Men: 3%   Women: 3%
First-year students: 5%   Second-year students: 2%
Third-year students: 0%   Fourth-year students: N/A

LIBRARY RESOURCES
Total titles: 180,139
Total volumes: 527,825
Total seats available for library users: 877

INFORMATION TECHNOLOGY
Number of wired network connections available to students: 1150 total (in the law library, excluding computer labs: 1,150; in classrooms: 0; in computer labs: 0; elsewhere in the law school: 0)
Law school has a wireless network.
Students are not required to own a computer.

EMPLOYMENT AND SALARIES
Proportion of 2008 graduates employed at graduation: N/A

Employed 9 months later, as of February 15, 2009: 85%
Salaries in the private sector (law firms, business, industry): $55,000 –$120,000 (25th-75th percentile)
Median salary in the private sector: $71,000
Percentage in the private sector who reported salary information: 38%
Median salary in public service (government, judicial clerkships, academic posts, non-profits): $52,000

Percentage of 2008 graduates in:
Law firms: 62%   Government: 13%
Bus./industry: 17%   Judicial clerkship: 5%
Public interest: 3%   Unknown: 0%
Academia : 1%

2008 graduates employed in-state: 93%
2008 graduates employed in foreign countries: 0%
Number of states where graduates are employed: 8
Percentage of 2008 graduates working in: New England: 0%, Middle Atlantic: 0%, East North Central: 0%, West North Central: 0%, South Atlantic: 3%, East South Central: 0%, West South Central: 93%, Mountain: 0%, Pacific: 1%, Unknown: 2%

BAR PASSAGE RATES
Based on 2008 graduates taking Summer 2008 or Winter 2009 exams. Most of the school's first-time test takers took the bar in Texas.

89%
School's bar passage rate for first-time test takers

84%
Statewide bar passage rate for first-time test takers

Southern Illinois Univ.—Carbondale

- Lesar Law Building, Carbondale, IL, 62901
- http://www.law.siu.edu
- Public
- Year founded: 1973
- 2009-2010 tuition: full-time: $14,137; part-time: N/A
- Enrollment 2009-10 academic year: full-time: 382; part-time: 1
- U.S. News 2010 law specialty ranking: N/A

3.01-3.52 GPA, 25TH-75TH PERCENTILE

151-157 LSAT, 25TH-75TH PERCENTILE

48% ACCEPTANCE RATE

Tier 4 2011 U.S. NEWS LAW SCHOOL RANKING

ADMISSIONS

Admissions phone number: (800) 739-9187
Admissions email address: lawadmit@siu.edu
Application website: http://www.law.siu.edu
Application deadline for Fall 2011 admission: 10-Mar

Admissions statistics:
Number of applicants for Fall 2009: 753
Number of acceptances: 362
Number enrolled: 137
Acceptance rate: 48%
GPA, 25th-75th percentile, entering class Fall 2009: 3.01-3.52
LSAT, 25th-75th percentile, entering class Fall 2009: 151-157

FINANCIAL AID

Financial aid phone number: (618) 453-4334
Financial aid application deadline: 1-Apr
Tuition 2009-2010 academic year: **full-time: $14,137; part-time: N/A**
Room and board: $10,458 ; books: $1,150 ; miscellaneous expenses: $2,520
Total of room/board/books/miscellaneous expenses: $14,128
University offers graduate student housing for which law students are eligible.

Financial aid profile
Percent of students that received grants for the 2008-2009 academic year: full-time: 46%
Median grant amount: full-time: $5,000
The average law-school debt of those in the Class of 2009 who borrowed: $63,223 . Proportion who borrowed: 90%

ACADEMIC PROGRAMS

Calendar: semester
Joint degrees awarded: J.D./M.B.A.; J.D./M.Acc; J.D./M.P.A.; J.D./M.D.; J.D./Ph.D; J.D./M.S.W.; J.D./MS.Ed.; J.D./MS E CE
Typical first-year section size: Full-time: 56

Is there typically a "small section" of the first year class, other than Legal Writing, taught by full-time faculty?: Full-time: **no**
Number of course titles, beyond the first year curriculum, offered last year: **70**
Percentages of upper division course sections, excluding seminars, with an enrollment of:
Under 25: **70%**   25 to 49: **18%**
50 to 74: **11%**   75 to 99: **2%**
100+: **N/A**
Areas of specialization: appellate advocacy, clinical training, dispute resolution, environmental law, health care law, intellectual property law, international law, tax law, trial advocacy

Fall 2009 faculty profile
Total teaching faculty: 37. Full-time: 73%; 52% men, 48% women, 7% minorities. Part-time: 27%; 70% men, 30% women, 10% minorities
Student-to-faculty ratio: 11.7

SPECIAL PROGRAMS (as provided by law school):

Two in-house clinics: civil practice/elder law, and domestic violence. Externships in public interest and judicial offices (legal services, prosecutors, public defenders, judges, local and state agencies). Summer Study Abroad Program in Ireland. Semester-away programs in Springfield, IL and southeast MO. Other programs: Center for Health Law and Policy, and the Self Help Legal Center.

STUDENT BODY

Fall 2009 full-time enrollment: 382
Men: 62%   Women: 38%
African-American: 3.40%   American Indian: 0.50%
Asian-American: 2.40%   Mexican-American: 0.80%
Puerto Rican: 0.00%   Other Hisp-Amer: 1.00%
White: 83.20%   International: 0.30%
Unknown: 8.40%

Fall 2009 part-time enrollment: 1

Men: **100%**	Women: **N/A**
African-American: **0.00%**	American Indian: **0.00%**
Asian-American: **0.00%**	Mexican-American: **0.00%**
Puerto Rican: **0.00%**	Other Hisp-Amer: **100.00%**
White: **0.00%**	International: **0.00%**
Unknown: **0.00%**	

Attrition rates for 2008-2009 full-time students
Percent of students discontinuing law school:

Men: **4%**	Women: **7%**
First-year students: **13%**	Second-year students: **3%**
Third-year students: **N/A**	Fourth-year students: **N/A**

LIBRARY RESOURCES
Total titles: **79,450**
Total volumes: **421,497**
Total seats available for library users: **349**

INFORMATION TECHNOLOGY
Number of wired network connections available to students: **12** total (in the law library, excluding computer labs: **5**; in classrooms: **0**; in computer labs: **0**; elsewhere in the law school: **7**)
Law school has a wireless network.
Students are not required to own a computer.

EMPLOYMENT AND SALARIES
Proportion of 2008 graduates employed at graduation: **N/A**
Employed 9 months later, as of February 15, 2009: **85%**

Salaries in the private sector (law firms, business, industry): **$40,000 –$60,000** (25th-75th percentile)
Median salary in the private sector: **$50,000**
Percentage in the private sector who reported salary information: **61%**
Median salary in public service (government, judicial clerkships, academic posts, non-profits): **$42,000**

Percentage of 2008 graduates in:

Law firms: **47%**	Government: **27%**
Bus./industry: **14%**	Judicial clerkship: **2%**
Public interest: **7%**	Unknown: **0%**
Academia : **4%**	

2008 graduates employed in-state: **67%**
2008 graduates employed in foreign countries: **0%**
Number of states where graduates are employed: **14**
Percentage of 2008 graduates working in: New England: **0%**, Middle Atlantic: **1%**, East North Central: **72%**, West North Central: **11%**, South Atlantic: **7%**, East South Central: **1%**, West South Central: **0%**, Mountain: **5%**, Pacific: **1%**, Unknown: **2%**

BAR PASSAGE RATES
Based on 2008 graduates taking Summer 2008 or Winter 2009 exams. Most of the school's first-time test takers took the bar in Illinois.

95%
School's bar passage rate for first-time test takers

91%
Statewide bar passage rate for first-time test takers

Southern Methodist University

■ PO Box 750116, Dallas, TX, 75275-0116
■ http://www.law.smu.edu
■ Private
■ Year founded: 1911
■ 2009-2010 tuition: full-time: $38,406; part-time: $28,805
■ Enrollment 2009-10 academic year: full-time: 524; part-time: 379
■ U.S. News 2010 law specialty ranking: tax law: 14

3.30-3.87 GPA, 25TH-75TH PERCENTILE

158-165 LSAT, 25TH-75TH PERCENTILE

23% ACCEPTANCE RATE

48 2011 U.S. NEWS LAW SCHOOL RANKING

ADMISSIONS
Admissions phone number: **(214) 768-2550**
Admissions email address: **lawadmit@mail.smu.edu**
Application website: **N/A**
Application deadline for Fall 2011 admission: **1-Apr**

Admissions statistics:
Number of applicants for Fall 2009: **2,056**
Number of acceptances: **465**
Number enrolled: **178**
Acceptance rate: **23%**
GPA, 25th-75th percentile, entering class Fall 2009: **3.30-3.87**
LSAT, 25th-75th percentile, entering class Fall 2009: **158-165**

Part-time program:
Number of applicants for Fall 2009: **699**
Number of acceptances: **143**
Number enrolled: **78**
Acceptance rate: **20%**
GPA, 25th-75th percentile, entering class Fall 2009: **3.17-3.76**
LSAT, 25th-75th percentile, entering class Fall 2009: **153-160**

FINANCIAL AID
Financial aid phone number: **(214) 768-4119**
Financial aid application deadline: **15-Feb**
Tuition 2009-2010 academic year: **full-time: $38,406; part-time: $28,805**
Room and board: **$14,000** ; books: **$1,800** ; miscellaneous expenses: **$2,600**
Total of room/board/books/miscellaneous expenses: **$18,400**
University offers graduate student housing for which law students are eligible.

Financial aid profile
Percent of students that received grants for the 2008-2009 academic year: full-time: **96%**; part-time **70%**

Median grant amount: full-time: **$18,000** ; part-time: **$6,031**
The average law-school debt of those in the Class of 2009 who borrowed: **$91,210** . Proportion who borrowed: **84%**

ACADEMIC PROGRAMS
Calendar: **semester**
Joint degrees awarded: **J.D./M.B.A.**
Typical first-year section size: Full-time: **82**; Part-time: **96**
Is there typically a "small section" of the first year class, other than Legal Writing, taught by full-time faculty?: Full-time: **no**; Part-time: **no**
Number of course titles, beyond the first year curriculum, offered last year: **134**
Percentages of upper division course sections, excluding seminars, with an enrollment of:
Under 25: **48%**   25 to 49: **25%**
50 to 74: **16%**   75 to 99: **9%**
100+: **2%**
Areas of specialization: appellate advocacy, clinical training, dispute resolution, environmental law, health care law, intellectual property law, international law, tax law, trial advocacy

Fall 2009 faculty profile
Total teaching faculty: **51**. Full-time: **47%**; **71%** men, **29%** women, **21%** minorities. Part-time: **53%**; **81%** men, **19%** women, **4%** minorities
Student-to-faculty ratio: **14.9**

SPECIAL PROGRAMS *(as provided by law school):*
Criminal, Consumer Law, Civil, Child Advocacy, Taxpayers Clinics. Criminal Clinic is joint with the Dallas County DA to provide legal service to indigent individuals. Students choose faculty-approved externship in state and federal courts; local, state, and federal agencies; and various legal departments. There is a 7-week summer session and the Summer Program in Oxford.

STUDENT BODY

Fall 2009 full-time enrollment: 524

Men: 53%	Women: 47%
African-American: 4.20%	American Indian: 1.10%
Asian-American: 7.30%	Mexican-American: 0.20%
Puerto Rican: 0.00%	Other Hisp-Amer: 9.20%
White: 71.60%	International: 0.60%
Unknown: 5.90%	

Fall 2009 part-time enrollment: 379

Men: 54%	Women: 46%
African-American: 6.30%	American Indian: 1.80%
Asian-American: 8.20%	Mexican-American: 0.50%
Puerto Rican: 0.30%	Other Hisp-Amer: 9.20%
White: 66.80%	International: 0.30%
Unknown: 6.60%	

Attrition rates for 2008-2009 full-time students
Percent of students discontinuing law school:

Men: 3%	Women: 2%
First-year students: N/A	Second-year students: 4%
Third-year students: 3%	Fourth-year students: 3%

LIBRARY RESOURCES

Total titles: 305,722
Total volumes: 639,959
Total seats available for library users: 724

INFORMATION TECHNOLOGY

Number of wired network connections available to students: 0 total (in the law library, excluding computer labs: 0; in classrooms: 0; in computer labs: 0; elsewhere in the law school: 0)
Law school has a wireless network.
Students are not required to own a computer.

EMPLOYMENT AND SALARIES

Proportion of 2008 graduates employed at graduation: 76%
Employed 9 months later, as of February 15, 2009: 99%
Salaries in the private sector (law firms, business, industry): $70,000 –$160,000 (25th-75th percentile)
Median salary in the private sector: $85,000
Percentage in the private sector who reported salary information: 89%
Median salary in public service (government, judicial clerkships, academic posts, non-profits): $51,334

Percentage of 2008 graduates in:

Law firms: 66%	Government: 5%
Bus./industry: 23%	Judicial clerkship: 2%
Public interest: 1%	Unknown: 0%
Academia : 3%	

2008 graduates employed in-state: 94%
2008 graduates employed in foreign countries: N/A
Number of states where graduates are employed: 12
Percentage of 2008 graduates working in: New England: 0%, Middle Atlantic: N/A, East North Central: N/A, West North Central: N/A, South Atlantic: 2%, East South Central: N/A, West South Central: 95%, Mountain: 2%, Pacific: 1%, Unknown: N/A

BAR PASSAGE RATES

Based on 2008 graduates taking Summer 2008 or Winter 2009 exams. Most of the school's first-time test takers took the bar in Texas.

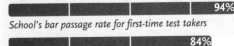

94%
School's bar passage rate for first-time test takers

84%
Statewide bar passage rate for first-time test takers

Southwestern Law School

- 3050 Wilshire Boulevard, Los Angeles, CA, 90010-1106
- http://www.swlaw.edu
- Private
- Year founded: 1911
- 2009-2010 tuition: full-time: $36,950; part-time: $22,250
- Enrollment 2009-10 academic year: full-time: 729; part-time: 323
- U.S. News 2010 law specialty ranking: N/A

3.10-3.56 GPA, 25TH-75TH PERCENTILE

153-157 LSAT, 25TH-75TH PERCENTILE

31% ACCEPTANCE RATE

Tier 3 2011 U.S. NEWS LAW SCHOOL RANKING

ADMISSIONS

Admissions phone number: (213) 738-6717
Admissions email address: admissions@swlaw.edu
Application website: http://www.swlaw.edu/applyonline
Application deadline for Fall 2011 admission: 1-Apr

Admissions statistics:

Number of applicants for Fall 2009: 2,994
Number of acceptances: 926
Number enrolled: 284
Acceptance rate: 31%
GPA, 25th-75th percentile, entering class Fall 2009: 3.10-3.56
LSAT, 25th-75th percentile, entering class Fall 2009: 153-157

Part-time program:

Number of applicants for Fall 2009: 500
Number of acceptances: 179
Number enrolled: 111
Acceptance rate: 36%
GPA, 25th-75th percentile, entering class Fall 2009: 2.89-3.41
LSAT, 25th-75th percentile, entering class Fall 2009: 151-155

FINANCIAL AID

Financial aid phone number: (213) 738-6719
Financial aid application deadline: 1-Jun
Tuition 2009-2010 academic year: **full-time: $36,950; part-time: $22,250**
Room and board: $19,620 ; books: $1,250 ; miscellaneous expenses: $5,949
Total of room/board/books/miscellaneous expenses: $26,819
University does not offer graduate student housing for which law students are eligible.

Financial aid profile

Percent of students that received grants for the 2008-2009 academic year: full-time: 35%; part-time 22%

Median grant amount: full-time: $15,000 ; part-time: $8,000
The average law-school debt of those in the Class of 2009 who borrowed: $107,383 . Proportion who borrowed: 83%

ACADEMIC PROGRAMS

Calendar: semester
Joint degrees awarded: JD/MBA; JD/EMBA; JD/MA in Management; JD/MA in Dispute Resolution
Typical first-year section size: Full-time: 76; Part-time: 79
Is there typically a "small section" of the first year class, other than Legal Writing, taught by full-time faculty?:
  Full-time: no; Part-time: no
Number of course titles, beyond the first year curriculum, offered last year: 151
Percentages of upper division course sections, excluding seminars, with an enrollment of:

Under 25: **62%**	25 to 49: **20%**
50 to 74: **15%**	75 to 99: **4%**
100+: **0%**	

Areas of specialization: appellate advocacy, clinical training, dispute resolution, environmental law, health care law, intellectual property law, international law, tax law, trial advocacy

Fall 2009 faculty profile

Total teaching faculty: 77. Full-time: 69%; 60% men, 40% women, 21% minorities. Part-time: 31%; 75% men, 25% women, 21% minorities
Student-to-faculty ratio: 14.3

SPECIAL PROGRAMS (as provided by law school):

4 J.D. programs: FT & PT day, PT evening, and 2-year FT alternative. J.D./M.B.A. programs with Drucker School of Mgmt of Claremont Graduate University. Entertainment Law Institute offering 40+ ent/sports law courses, 50 entertainment externships and law firm practicum. Clinics for children's rights, immigration law, and Street Law. Summer programs in Vancouver, Buenos Aires, London, Guanajuato.

STUDENT BODY

Fall 2009 full-time enrollment: 729

Men: 44%	Women: 56%
African-American: 5.50%	American Indian: 0.80%
Asian-American: 15.50%	Mexican-American: 6.30%
Puerto Rican: 0.40%	Other Hisp-Amer: 6.90%
White: 45.80%	International: 0.30%
Unknown: 18.50%	

Fall 2009 part-time enrollment: 323

Men: 50%	Women: 50%
African-American: 9.60%	American Indian: 0.30%
Asian-American: 14.20%	Mexican-American: 7.70%
Puerto Rican: 0.00%	Other Hisp-Amer: 5.30%
White: 45.80%	International: 0.00%
Unknown: 17.00%	

Attrition rates for 2008-2009 full-time students
Percent of students discontinuing law school:

Men: 7%	Women: 3%
First-year students: 6%	Second-year students: 10%
Third-year students: 1%	Fourth-year students: N/A

LIBRARY RESOURCES

Total titles: 164,809
Total volumes: 497,479
Total seats available for library users: 610

INFORMATION TECHNOLOGY

Number of wired network connections available to students: 326 total (in the law library, excluding computer labs: 326; in classrooms: 0; in computer labs: 0; elsewhere in the law school: 0)
Law school has a wireless network.
Students are not required to own a computer.

EMPLOYMENT AND SALARIES

Proportion of 2008 graduates employed at graduation: 85%
Employed 9 months later, as of February 15, 2009: 96%
Salaries in the private sector (law firms, business, industry): $66,000 –$87,500 (25th-75th percentile)
Median salary in the private sector: $77,000
Percentage in the private sector who reported salary information: 29%
Median salary in public service (government, judicial clerkships, academic posts, non-profits): $61,000

Percentage of 2008 graduates in:

Law firms: 60%	Government: 9%
Bus./industry: 19%	Judicial clerkship: 2%
Public interest: 4%	Unknown: 3%
Academia : 3%	

2008 graduates employed in-state: 91%
2008 graduates employed in foreign countries: 0%
Number of states where graduates are employed: 8
Percentage of 2008 graduates working in: New England: 1%, Middle Atlantic: 1%, East North Central: 0%, West North Central: 0%, South Atlantic: 1%, East South Central: 1%, West South Central: 0%, Mountain: 2%, Pacific: 92%, Unknown: 4%

BAR PASSAGE RATES

Based on 2008 graduates taking Summer 2008 or Winter 2009 exams. Most of the school's first-time test takers took the bar in California.

70%
School's bar passage rate for first-time test takers

71%
Statewide bar passage rate for first-time test takers

St. John's University

■ 8000 Utopia Parkway, Jamaica, NY, 11439
■ http://www.law.stjohns.edu/
■ Private
■ Year founded: 1925
■ 2009-2010 tuition: full-time: $42,200; part-time: $31,650
■ Enrollment 2009-10 academic year: full-time: 737; part-time: 178
■ U.S. News 2010 law specialty ranking: N/A

3.16-3.70 GPA, 25TH-75TH PERCENTILE

156-163 LSAT, 25TH-75TH PERCENTILE

39% ACCEPTANCE RATE

72 2011 U.S. NEWS LAW SCHOOL RANKING

ADMISSIONS
Admissions phone number: **(718) 990-6474**
Admissions email address: **lawinfo@stjohns.edu**
Application website: **http://www.law.stjohns.edu/**
Application deadline for Fall 2011 admission: **1-Apr**

Admissions statistics:
Number of applicants for Fall 2009: **3,232**
Number of acceptances: **1,260**
Number enrolled: **231**
Acceptance rate: **39%**
GPA, 25th-75th percentile, entering class Fall 2009: **3.16-3.70**
LSAT, 25th-75th percentile, entering class Fall 2009: **156-163**

Part-time program:
Number of applicants for Fall 2009: **804**
Number of acceptances: **219**
Number enrolled: **84**
Acceptance rate: **27%**
GPA, 25th-75th percentile, entering class Fall 2009: **3.12-3.77**
LSAT, 25th-75th percentile, entering class Fall 2009: **147-155**

FINANCIAL AID
Financial aid phone number: **(718) 990-1485**
Financial aid application deadline: **1-Apr**
Tuition 2009-2010 academic year: **full-time: $42,200; part-time: $31,650**
Room and board: **$16,677** ; books: **$1,400** ; miscellaneous expenses: **$4,140**
Total of room/board/books/miscellaneous expenses: **$22,217**
University offers graduate student housing for which law students are eligible.

Financial aid profile
Percent of students that received grants for the 2008-2009 academic year: full-time: **43%**; part-time **11%**

Median grant amount: full-time: **$22,500** ; part-time: **$7,500**
The average law-school debt of those in the Class of 2009 who borrowed: **$107,137** . Proportion who borrowed: **85%**

ACADEMIC PROGRAMS
Calendar: **semester**
Joint degrees awarded: **J.D./ M.A.; J.D./M.B.A.; J.D./LL.M.**
Typical first-year section size: Full-time: **85**; Part-time: **65**
Is there typically a "small section" of the first year class, other than Legal Writing, taught by full-time faculty?: Full-time: **no**; Part-time: **no**
Number of course titles, beyond the first year curriculum, offered last year: **184**
Percentages of upper division course sections, excluding seminars, with an enrollment of:
Under 25: **65%**   25 to 49: **18%**
50 to 74: **10%**   75 to 99: **5%**
100+: **1%**
Areas of specialization: appellate advocacy, clinical training, dispute resolution, environmental law, health care law, intellectual property law, international law, tax law, trial advocacy

Fall 2009 faculty profile
Total teaching faculty: **113**. Full-time: **44%**; **52%** men, **48%** women, **22%** minorities. Part-time: **56%**; **79%** men, **21%** women, **2%** minorities
Student-to-faculty ratio: **14.6**

SPECIAL PROGRAMS *(as provided by law school):*
We offer a summer Rome program & will begin a program in Barcelona Summer 2010. Our Centers include the Ronald H. Brown Center for Civil Rights and Economic Development; the Hugh L. Carey Center for Dispute Resolution; the Center for Professional Skills; the Writing Center;and the Center for Bankruptcy Studies. Eight clinics and hundreds of externships are available to students.

STUDENT BODY

Fall 2009 full-time enrollment: 737

Men: 55%	Women: 45%
African-American: 5.30%	American Indian: 0.00%
Asian-American: 8.80%	Mexican-American: 0.00%
Puerto Rican: 1.90%	Other Hisp-Amer: 5.60%
White: 65.30%	International: 1.40%
Unknown: 11.80%	

Fall 2009 part-time enrollment: 178

Men: 45%	Women: 55%
African-American: 10.70%	American Indian: 0.00%
Asian-American: 10.70%	Mexican-American: 0.60%
Puerto Rican: 1.10%	Other Hisp-Amer: 11.20%
White: 51.70%	International: 1.10%
Unknown: 12.90%	

Attrition rates for 2008-2009 full-time students
Percent of students discontinuing law school:

Men: 3%	Women: 3%
First-year students: 2%	Second-year students: 5%
Third-year students: 1%	Fourth-year students: N/A

LIBRARY RESOURCES

Total titles: 212,653
Total volumes: 443,675
Total seats available for library users: 564

INFORMATION TECHNOLOGY

Number of wired network connections available to students: 0 total (in the law library, excluding computer labs: 0; in classrooms: 0; in computer labs: 0; elsewhere in the law school: 0)
Law school has a wireless network.
Students are not required to own a computer.

EMPLOYMENT AND SALARIES

Proportion of 2008 graduates employed at graduation: 78%
Employed 9 months later, as of February 15, 2009: 96%
Salaries in the private sector (law firms, business, industry): $70,000 –$160,000 (25th-75th percentile)
Median salary in the private sector: $130,000
Percentage in the private sector who reported salary information: 63%
Median salary in public service (government, judicial clerkships, academic posts, non-profits): $53,000

Percentage of 2008 graduates in:

Law firms: 58%	Government: 17%
Bus./industry: 15%	Judicial clerkship: 4%
Public interest: 3%	Unknown: 0%
Academia : 3%	

2008 graduates employed in-state: 90%
2008 graduates employed in foreign countries: 0%
Number of states where graduates are employed: 11
Percentage of 2008 graduates working in: New England: 2%, Middle Atlantic: 93%, East North Central: 0%, West North Central: 0%, South Atlantic: 2%, East South Central: 0%, West South Central: 0%, Mountain: 0%, Pacific: 0%, Unknown: 1%

BAR PASSAGE RATES

Based on 2008 graduates taking Summer 2008 or Winter 2009 exams. Most of the school's first-time test takers took the bar in New York.

91%
School's bar passage rate for first-time test takers

81%
Statewide bar passage rate for first-time test takers

St. Louis University

- 3700 Lindell Boulevard, St. Louis, MO, 63108
- http://law.slu.edu
- Private
- Year founded: 1843
- 2009-2010 tuition: full-time: $34,362; part-time: $25,047
- Enrollment 2009-10 academic year: full-time: 771; part-time: 196
- U.S. News 2010 law specialty ranking: healthcare law: 1

3.21-3.64 GPA, 25TH-75TH PERCENTILE

154-160 LSAT, 25TH-75TH PERCENTILE

48% ACCEPTANCE RATE

Tier 3 2011 U.S. NEWS LAW SCHOOL RANKING

ADMISSIONS

Admissions phone number: **(314) 977-2800**
Admissions email address: **admissions@law.slu.edu**
Application website:
http://law.slu.edu/admissions/index.html
Application deadline for Fall 2011 admission: **1-Mar**

Admissions statistics:
Number of applicants for Fall 2009: **2,140**
Number of acceptances: **1,024**
Number enrolled: **243**
Acceptance rate: **48%**
GPA, 25th-75th percentile, entering class Fall 2009: **3.21-3.64**
LSAT, 25th-75th percentile, entering class Fall 2009: **154-160**

Part-time program:
Number of applicants for Fall 2009: **480**
Number of acceptances: **171**
Number enrolled: **88**
Acceptance rate: **36%**
GPA, 25th-75th percentile, entering class Fall 2009: **3.02-3.45**
LSAT, 25th-75th percentile, entering class Fall 2009: **152-155**

FINANCIAL AID

Financial aid phone number: **(314) 977-3369**
Financial aid application deadline: **1-Mar**
Tuition 2009-2010 academic year: **full-time: $34,362; part-time: $25,047**
Room and board: **$11,988** ; books: **$1,660** ; miscellaneous expenses: **$5,764**
Total of room/board/books/miscellaneous expenses: **$19,412**
University does not offer graduate student housing for which law students are eligible.

Financial aid profile
Percent of students that received grants for the 2008-2009

academic year: full-time: **47%**; part-time **27%**
Median grant amount: full-time: **$17,740** ; part-time: **$10,750**
The average law-school debt of those in the Class of 2009 who borrowed: **$99,000** . Proportion who borrowed: **80%**

ACADEMIC PROGRAMS

Calendar: **semester**
Joint degrees awarded: **J.D./M.H.A.; J.D./M.B.A.; J.D./M.A. Urban Affairs; J.D./M.P.A.; J.D./M.P.H.; J.D./Ph.D.; J.D./M.P.H. Health Policy; J.D./ M.S.W.**
Typical first-year section size: Full-time: **75**; Part-time: **88**
Is there typically a "small section" of the first year class, other than Legal Writing, taught by full-time faculty?:
Full-time: **yes**; Part-time: **no**
Number of course titles, beyond the first year curriculum, offered last year: **150**
Percentages of upper division course sections, excluding seminars, with an enrollment of:

Under 25: **70%**	25 to 49: **14%**	
50 to 74: **8%**	75 to 99: **5%**	
100+: **4%**		

Areas of specialization: appellate advocacy, clinical training, dispute resolution, environmental law, health care law, intellectual property law, international law, tax law, trial advocacy

Fall 2009 faculty profile
Total teaching faculty: **90**. Full-time: **54%**; **57%** men, **43%** women, **12%** minorities. Part-time: **46%**; **71%** men, **29%** women, **22%** minorities
Student-to-faculty ratio: **17**

SPECIAL PROGRAMS (as provided by law school):
The Saint Louis University School of Law provides a broad array of opportunities for students to practice law through clinical programs; it has three centers of excellence: Health Law, Employment Law and International and Comparative Law; it offers summer programs in St. Louis and two programs abroad: Madrid and Berlin; and it offers eight joint degree programs

STUDENT BODY

Fall 2009 full-time enrollment: 771

Men: 51%	Women: 49%
African-American: 7.00%	American Indian: 0.60%
Asian-American: 5.30%	Mexican-American: 1.30%
Puerto Rican: 0.10%	Other Hisp-Amer: 1.90%
White: 77.80%	International: 0.30%
Unknown: 5.60%	

Fall 2009 part-time enrollment: 196

Men: 61%	Women: 39%
African-American: 6.60%	American Indian: 0.50%
Asian-American: 4.60%	Mexican-American: 0.50%
Puerto Rican: 0.00%	Other Hisp-Amer: 1.00%
White: 76.50%	International: 0.50%
Unknown: 9.70%	

Attrition rates for 2008-2009 full-time students
Percent of students discontinuing law school:

Men: 0%	Women: 1%
First-year students: 2%	Second-year students: 0%
Third-year students: N/A	Fourth-year students: N/A

LIBRARY RESOURCES

Total titles: 607,322
Total volumes: 656,878
Total seats available for library users: 505

INFORMATION TECHNOLOGY

Number of wired network connections available to students: 594 total (in the law library, excluding computer labs: 166; in classrooms: 375; in computer labs: 5; elsewhere in the law school: 48)
Law school has a wireless network.
Students are not required to own a computer.

EMPLOYMENT AND SALARIES

Proportion of 2008 graduates employed at graduation: 70%
Employed 9 months later, as of February 15, 2009: 93%
Salaries in the private sector (law firms, business, industry): $50,000 –$80,500 (25th-75th percentile)
Median salary in the private sector: $59,500
Percentage in the private sector who reported salary information: 78%
Median salary in public service (government, judicial clerkships, academic posts, non-profits): $39,000

Percentage of 2008 graduates in:

Law firms: 62%	Government: 7%
Bus./industry: 17%	Judicial clerkship: 3%
Public interest: 11%	Unknown: 0%
Academia : 0%	

2008 graduates employed in-state: 62%
2008 graduates employed in foreign countries: 0%
Number of states where graduates are employed: 23
Percentage of 2008 graduates working in: New England: 0%, Middle Atlantic: 0%, East North Central: 20%, West North Central: 70%, South Atlantic: 9%, East South Central: 0%, West South Central: 0%, Mountain: 0%, Pacific: 0%, Unknown: 0%

BAR PASSAGE RATES

Based on 2008 graduates taking Summer 2008 or Winter 2009 exams. Most of the school's first-time test takers took the bar in Missouri.

94%
School's bar passage rate for first-time test takers

91%
Statewide bar passage rate for first-time test takers

St. Mary's University

■ 1 Camino Santa Maria, San Antonio, TX, 78228-8602
■ http://www.stmarytx.edu/law
■ Private
■ Year founded: 1927
■ 2009-2010 tuition: full-time: $27,404; part-time: $18,564
■ Enrollment 2009-10 academic year: full-time: 681; part-time: 182
■ U.S. News 2010 law specialty ranking: N/A

2.88-3.50 GPA, 25ᵀᴴ-75ᵀᴴ PERCENTILE

151-156 LSAT, 25ᵀᴴ-75ᵀᴴ PERCENTILE

43% ACCEPTANCE RATE

Tier 4 2011 U.S. NEWS LAW SCHOOL RANKING

ADMISSIONS

Admissions phone number: **(210) 436-3523**
Admissions email address: **lawadmissions@stmarytx.edu**
Application website: **N/A**
Application deadline for Fall 2011 admission: **1-Mar**

Admissions statistics:
Number of applicants for Fall 2009: **1,647**
Number of acceptances: **712**
Number enrolled: **231**
Acceptance rate: **43%**
GPA, 25th-75th percentile, entering class Fall 2009: **2.88-3.50**
LSAT, 25th-75th percentile, entering class Fall 2009: **151-156**

Part-time program:
Number of applicants for Fall 2009: **253**
Number of acceptances: **94**
Number enrolled: **61**
Acceptance rate: **37%**
GPA, 25th-75th percentile, entering class Fall 2009: **2.67-3.44**
LSAT, 25th-75th percentile, entering class Fall 2009: **150-155**

FINANCIAL AID

Financial aid phone number: **(210) 431-6743**
Financial aid application deadline: **31-Mar**
Tuition 2009-2010 academic year: **full-time: $27,404; part-time: $18,564**
Room and board: **$8,225** ; books: **$1,385** ; miscellaneous expenses: **$5,834**
Total of room/board/books/miscellaneous expenses: **$15,444**
University offers graduate student housing for which law students are eligible.

Financial aid profile
Percent of students that received grants for the 2008-2009 academic year: full-time: **37%**

Median grant amount: full-time: **$1,824**
The average law-school debt of those in the Class of 2009 who borrowed: **$91,518** . Proportion who borrowed: **85%**

ACADEMIC PROGRAMS

Calendar: **semester**
Joint degrees awarded: **J.D./M.B.A.; J.D./M.A International Relations ; J.D./M.P.A.; J.D./M.A. Engineering**
Typical first-year section size: Full-time: **80**; Part-time: **62**
Is there typically a "small section" of the first year class, other than Legal Writing, taught by full-time faculty?: Full-time: **no**; Part-time: **no**
Number of course titles, beyond the first year curriculum, offered last year: **115**
Percentages of upper division course sections, excluding seminars, with an enrollment of:

Under 25: **51%**	25 to 49: **23%**
50 to 74: **11%**	75 to 99: **15%**
100+: **0%**	

Areas of specialization: appellate advocacy, clinical training, dispute resolution, environmental law, health care law, intellectual property law, international law, tax law, trial advocacy

Fall 2009 faculty profile
Total teaching faculty: **79**. Full-time: **41%**; **63%** men, **38%** women, **19%** minorities. Part-time: **59%**; **60%** men, **40%** women, **13%** minorities
Student-to-faculty ratio: **20.9**

SPECIAL PROGRAMS *(as provided by law school):*
See the School of Law's website at
ww.stmarytx.edu/law/index.php?site=centerForLegalAndSocialJustice for Clinic information;
www.stmarytx.edu/law/index.php?site=innsBruckProgram for our Summer Study; and
www.stmarytx.edu/law/index.php?site=judicialInternships for Internship opportunites.

STUDENT BODY

Fall 2009 full-time enrollment: 681

Men: 56%	Women: 44%
African-American: 3.40%	American Indian: 0.70%
Asian-American: 4.40%	Mexican-American: 10.60%
Puerto Rican: 0.30%	Other Hisp-Amer: 12.30%
White: 68.10%	International: 0.10%
Unknown: 0.00%	

Fall 2009 part-time enrollment: 182

Men: 61%	Women: 39%
African-American: 4.40%	American Indian: 1.60%
Asian-American: 5.50%	Mexican-American: 14.30%
Puerto Rican: 1.10%	Other Hisp-Amer: 17.60%
White: 55.50%	International: 0.00%
Unknown: 0.00%	

Attrition rates for 2008-2009 full-time students
Percent of students discontinuing law school:

Men: 1%	Women: 3%
First-year students: 4%	Second-year students: N/A
Third-year students: N/A	Fourth-year students: N/A

LIBRARY RESOURCES

Total titles: 83,264
Total volumes: 421,407
Total seats available for library users: 390

INFORMATION TECHNOLOGY

Number of wired network connections available to students: 604 total (in the law library, excluding computer labs: 145; in classrooms: 420; in computer labs: 0; elsewhere in the law school: 39)
Law school has a wireless network.
Students are not required to own a computer.

EMPLOYMENT AND SALARIES

Proportion of 2008 graduates employed at graduation: 86%
Employed 9 months later, as of February 15, 2009: 91%
Salaries in the private sector (law firms, business, industry): $40,000 –$70,872 (25th-75th percentile)
Median salary in the private sector: $55,000
Percentage in the private sector who reported salary information: 61%
Median salary in public service (government, judicial clerkships, academic posts, non-profits): $54,250

Percentage of 2008 graduates in:

Law firms: 62%	Government: 18%
Bus./industry: 11%	Judicial clerkship: 5%
Public interest: 2%	Unknown: 0%
Academia : 2%	

2008 graduates employed in-state: 89%
2008 graduates employed in foreign countries: 0%
Number of states where graduates are employed: 10
Percentage of 2008 graduates working in: New England: 0%, Middle Atlantic: 1%, East North Central: 0%, West North Central: 1%, South Atlantic: 2%, East South Central: 0%, West South Central: 90%, Mountain: 3%, Pacific: 1%, Unknown: 2%

BAR PASSAGE RATES

Based on 2008 graduates taking Summer 2008 or Winter 2009 exams. Most of the school's first-time test takers took the bar in Texas.

87%
School's bar passage rate for first-time test takers

84%
Statewide bar passage rate for first-time test takers

Stanford University

- Crown Quadrangle, 559 Nathan Abbott Way, Stanford, CA, 94305-8610
- http://www.law.stanford.edu/
- Private
- Year founded: 1893
- 2009-2010 tuition: full-time: $44,121; part-time: N/A
- Enrollment 2009-10 academic year: full-time: 557
- U.S. News 2010 law specialty ranking: clinical training: 11, environmental law: 8, intellectual property law: 2, international law: 11, tax law: 13

3.77-3.97 GPA, 25ᵀᴴ-75ᵀᴴ PERCENTILE

167-172 LSAT, 25ᵀᴴ-75ᵀᴴ PERCENTILE

9% ACCEPTANCE RATE

3 2011 U.S. NEWS LAW SCHOOL RANKING

ADMISSIONS

Admissions phone number: **(650) 723-4985**
Admissions email address: **admissions@law.stanford.edu**
Application website:
http://www.law.stanford.edu/prospective/
Application deadline for Fall 2011 admission: **1-Feb**

Admissions statistics:

Number of applicants for Fall 2009: **4,082**
Number of acceptances: **373**
Number enrolled: **180**
Acceptance rate: **9%**
GPA, 25th-75th percentile, entering class Fall 2009: **3.77-3.97**
LSAT, 25th-75th percentile, entering class Fall 2009: **167-172**

FINANCIAL AID

Financial aid phone number: **(650) 723-9247**
Financial aid application deadline: **15-Mar**
Tuition 2009-2010 academic year: **full-time: $44,121; part-time: N/A**
Room and board: **$18,603** ; books: **$1,815** ; miscellaneous expenses: **$3,321**
Total of room/board/books/miscellaneous expenses: **$23,739**
University offers graduate student housing for which law students are eligible.

Financial aid profile

Percent of students that received grants for the 2008-2009 academic year: full-time: **48%**
Median grant amount: full-time: **$22,178**
The average law-school debt of those in the Class of 2009 who borrowed: **$96,533** . Proportion who borrowed: **81%**

ACADEMIC PROGRAMS

Calendar: **semester**
Joint degrees awarded: **J.D./M.B.A.; J.D./Ph.D.; J.D./M.D.; J.D./M.P.A.; J.D./M.A.; J.D./M.S.; J.D./M.P.P.; J.D./M.A.L.D.**

Typical first-year section size: Full-time: **60**
Is there typically a "small section" of the first year class, other than Legal Writing, taught by full-time faculty?: Full-time: **yes**
Number of course titles, beyond the first year curriculum, offered last year: **160**
Percentages of upper division course sections, excluding seminars, with an enrollment of:
Under 25: **81%**   25 to 49: **14%**
50 to 74: **4%**   75 to 99: **1%**
100+: **1%**
Areas of specialization: appellate advocacy, clinical training, dispute resolution, environmental law, health care law, intellectual property law, international law, tax law, trial advocacy

Fall 2009 faculty profile

Total teaching faculty: **87**. Full-time: **67%**; 67% men, 33% women, **17%** minorities. Part-time: **33%**; 52% men, 48% women, **10%** minorities
Student-to-faculty ratio: **8**

SPECIAL PROGRAMS *(as provided by law school):*

A leader in interdisciplinary education, SLS offers 25 joint degrees and virtually limitless opportunities to customize. With 10 clinics, SLS enables students to take on the roles and responsibilities of practicing lawyers. Students can engage in research and policy-oriented study through our 20 programs and centers. Learn more about these opportunities at http://www.law.stanford.edu/program

STUDENT BODY

Fall 2009 full-time enrollment: 557

Men: **53%**   Women: **47%**
African-American: **10.80%**   American Indian: **2.20%**
Asian-American: **12.60%**   Mexican-American: **8.60%**
Puerto Rican: **0.90%**   Other Hisp-Amer: **0.70%**
White: **56.20%**   International: **2.00%**
Unknown: **6.10%**

Attrition rates for 2008-2009 full-time students
Percent of students discontinuing law school:
Men: **1%**   Women: **N/A**
First-year students: **N/A**   Second-year students: **2%**
Third-year students: **1%**   Fourth-year students: **N/A**

LIBRARY RESOURCES
Total titles: **309,350**
Total volumes: **490,073**
Total seats available for library users: **508**

INFORMATION TECHNOLOGY
Number of wired network connections available to students: **250** total (in the law library, excluding computer labs: **10**; in classrooms: **160**; in computer labs: **40**; elsewhere in the law school: **40**)
Law school has a wireless network.
Students are required to own a computer.

EMPLOYMENT AND SALARIES
Proportion of 2008 graduates employed at graduation: **98%**
Employed 9 months later, as of February 15, 2009: **98%**
Salaries in the private sector (law firms, business, industry): **$160,000** –**$160,000** (25th-75th percentile)
Median salary in the private sector: **$160,000**
Percentage in the private sector who reported salary information: **61%**

Median salary in public service (government, judicial clerkships, academic posts, non-profits): **$57,845**

Percentage of 2008 graduates in:
Law firms: **61%**   Government: **4%**
Bus./industry: **5%**   Judicial clerkship: **23%**
Public interest: **6%**   Unknown: **0%**
Academia : **1%**

2008 graduates employed in-state: **44%**
2008 graduates employed in foreign countries: **2%**
Number of states where graduates are employed: **22**
Percentage of 2008 graduates working in: New England: **2%**, Middle Atlantic: **20%**, East North Central: **3%**, West North Central: **0%**, South Atlantic: **19%**, East South Central: **1%**, West South Central: **4%**, Mountain: **3%**, Pacific: **46%**, Unknown: **0%**

BAR PASSAGE RATES
Based on 2008 graduates taking Summer 2008 or Winter 2009 exams. Most of the school's first-time test takers took the bar in California.

96%

School's bar passage rate for first-time test takers

71%

Statewide bar passage rate for first-time test takers

Stetson University

- 1401 61st Street S, Gulfport, FL, 33707
- http://www.law.stetson.edu
- Private
- Year founded: 1900
- 2009-2010 tuition: full-time: $31,420; part-time: $21,700
- Enrollment 2009-10 academic year: full-time: 876; part-time: 208
- U.S. News 2010 law specialty ranking: trial advocacy: 1

3.21-3.65 GPA, 25TH-75TH PERCENTILE

153-158 LSAT, 25TH-75TH PERCENTILE

39% ACCEPTANCE RATE

Tier 3 2011 U.S. NEWS LAW SCHOOL RANKING

ADMISSIONS

Admissions phone number: **(727) 562-7802**
Admissions email address: **lawadmit@law.stetson.edu**
Application website:
  http://www.law.stetson.edu/admissions/
Application deadline for Fall 2011 admission: **rolling**

Admissions statistics:
Number of applicants for Fall 2009: **2,845**
Number of acceptances: **1,099**
Number enrolled: **335**
Acceptance rate: **39%**
GPA, 25th-75th percentile, entering class Fall 2009: **3.21-3.65**
LSAT, 25th-75th percentile, entering class Fall 2009: **153-158**

Part-time program:
Number of applicants for Fall 2009: **621**
Number of acceptances: **134**
Number enrolled: **60**
Acceptance rate: **22%**
GPA, 25th-75th percentile, entering class Fall 2009: **3.12-3.59**
LSAT, 25th-75th percentile, entering class Fall 2009: **151-156**

FINANCIAL AID

Financial aid phone number: **(727) 562-7813**
Financial aid application deadline:
Tuition 2009-2010 academic year: **full-time: $31,420; part-time: $21,700**
Room and board: **$10,248** ; books: **$1,800** ; miscellaneous expenses: **$8,774**
Total of room/board/books/miscellaneous expenses: **$20,822**
University does not offer graduate student housing for which law students are eligible.

Financial aid profile
Percent of students that received grants for the 2008-2009

academic year: full-time: **20%**; part-time **14%**
Median grant amount: full-time: **$15,250** ; part-time: **$5,000**
The average law-school debt of those in the Class of 2009 who borrowed: **$116,184** . Proportion who borrowed: **78%**

ACADEMIC PROGRAMS

Calendar: **semester**
Joint degrees awarded: **J.D./M.B.A.; J.D./M.P.H; J.D./M.D.**
Typical first-year section size: Full-time: **68**; Part-time: **60**
Is there typically a "small section" of the first year class, other than Legal Writing, taught by full-time faculty?:
  Full-time: **no**; Part-time: **no**
Number of course titles, beyond the first year curriculum, offered last year: **172**
Percentages of upper division course sections, excluding seminars, with an enrollment of:

Under 25: **75%**	25 to 49: **14%**
50 to 74: **9%**	75 to 99: **2%**
100+: **0%**	

Areas of specialization: appellate advocacy, clinical training, dispute resolution, environmental law, health care law, intellectual property law, international law, tax law, trial advocacy

Fall 2009 faculty profile
Total teaching faculty: **106**. Full-time: **46%**; **53%** men, **47%** women, **14%** minorities. Part-time: **54%**; **68%** men, **32%** women, **7%** minorities
Student-to-faculty ratio: **15.8**

SPECIAL PROGRAMS *(as provided by law school):*
Advocacy, elder law, higher education law and international law centers. Natl. Clearinghouse Science, Technology & Law. Internships & clinics. Part-time and J.D./M.B.A., J.D./M.P.H. and J.D./M.D. programs. Honors program. Summer abroad Spain, Argentina, Switzerland, Netherlands and China. January program in Cayman Islands. Spring Break abroad program. Summer internship program Washington, DC. Semester abroad London.

STUDENT BODY

Fall 2009 full-time enrollment: 876

Men: 48% Women: 52%
African-American: 7.20% American Indian: 0.70%
Asian-American: 3.40% Mexican-American: 0.50%
Puerto Rican: 1.70% Other Hisp-Amer: 6.80%
White: 69.30% International: 0.60%
Unknown: 9.80%

Fall 2009 part-time enrollment: 208

Men: 45% Women: 55%
African-American: 5.30% American Indian: 1.40%
Asian-American: 2.90% Mexican-American: 0.00%
Puerto Rican: 0.50% Other Hisp-Amer: 6.70%
White: 77.40% International: 0.00%
Unknown: 5.80%

Attrition rates for 2008-2009 full-time students
Percent of students discontinuing law school:
Men: 3% Women: 2%
First-year students: 5% Second-year students: 2%
Third-year students: N/A Fourth-year students: N/A

LIBRARY RESOURCES

Total titles: 732,148
Total volumes: 389,229
Total seats available for library users: 680

INFORMATION TECHNOLOGY

Number of wired network connections available to students: 1595 total (in the law library, excluding computer labs: 396; in classrooms: 1,005; in computer labs: 54; elsewhere in the law school: 140)
Law school has a wireless network.
Students are required to own a computer.

EMPLOYMENT AND SALARIES

Proportion of 2008 graduates employed at graduation: N/A
Employed 9 months later, as of February 15, 2009: 95%
Salaries in the private sector (law firms, business, industry): $65,000 –$95,000 (25th-75th percentile)
Median salary in the private sector: $84,442
Percentage in the private sector who reported salary information: 72%
Median salary in public service (government, judicial clerkships, academic posts, non-profits): $45,545

Percentage of 2008 graduates in:
Law firms: 61% Government: 11%
Bus./industry: 11% Judicial clerkship: 3%
Public interest: 7% Unknown: 4%
Academia : 3%

2008 graduates employed in-state: 81%
2008 graduates employed in foreign countries: 2%
Number of states where graduates are employed: 19
Percentage of 2008 graduates working in: New England: 0%, Middle Atlantic: 2%, East North Central: 2%, West North Central: 0%, South Atlantic: 91%, East South Central: 1%, West South Central: 0%, Mountain: 0%, Pacific: 1%, Unknown: 0%

BAR PASSAGE RATES

Based on 2008 graduates taking Summer 2008 or Winter 2009 exams. Most of the school's first-time test takers took the bar in Florida.

82%
School's bar passage rate for first-time test takers

81%
Statewide bar passage rate for first-time test takers

Suffolk University

- 120 Tremont Street, Boston, MA, 2108
- http://www.law.suffolk.edu/
- Private
- Year founded: 1906
- 2009-2010 tuition: full-time: $39,670; part-time: $29,754
- Enrollment 2009-10 academic year: full-time: 1,079; part-time: 603
- U.S. News 2010 law specialty ranking: clinical training: 22

3.30-3.50 GPA, 25TH-75TH PERCENTILE

154-159 LSAT, 25TH-75TH PERCENTILE

51% ACCEPTANCE RATE

Tier 3 2011 U.S. NEWS LAW SCHOOL RANKING

ADMISSIONS

Admissions phone number: **(617) 573-8144**
Admissions email address: **lawadm@admin.suffolk.edu**
Application website:
 http://www.law.suffolk.edu/admissions/how2Apply/
Application deadline for Fall 2011 admission: **3-Jan**

Admissions statistics:

Number of applicants for Fall 2009: **2,630**
Number of acceptances: **1,333**
Number enrolled: **339**
Acceptance rate: **51%**
GPA, 25th-75th percentile, entering class Fall 2009: **3.30-3.50**
LSAT, 25th-75th percentile, entering class Fall 2009: **154-159**

Part-time program:

Number of applicants for Fall 2009: **631**
Number of acceptances: **363**
Number enrolled: **192**
Acceptance rate: **58%**
GPA, 25th-75th percentile, entering class Fall 2009: **2.90-3.50**
LSAT, 25th-75th percentile, entering class Fall 2009: **151-156**

FINANCIAL AID

Financial aid phone number: **(617) 573-8147**
Financial aid application deadline: **3-Jan**
Tuition 2009-2010 academic year: **full-time: $39,670; part-time: $29,754**
Room and board: **$8,950**; books: **$900**; miscellaneous expenses: **$5,844**
Total of room/board/books/miscellaneous expenses: **$15,694**
University does not offer graduate student housing for which law students are eligible.

Financial aid profile

Percent of students that received grants for the 2008-2009

academic year: full-time: **51%**; part-time **21%**
Median grant amount: full-time: **$10,000**; part-time: **$5,550**
The average law-school debt of those in the Class of 2009 who borrowed: **$108,557**. Proportion who borrowed: **87%**

ACADEMIC PROGRAMS

Calendar: **semester**
Joint degrees awarded: **J.D./M.B.A.; J.D./M.P.A.; J.D./M.S.F.; J.D./M.S.I.E.; J.D./M.S.C.J.**
Typical first-year section size: Full-time: **89**; Part-time: **98**
Is there typically a "small section" of the first year class, other than Legal Writing, taught by full-time faculty?: Full-time: **yes**; Part-time: **no**
Number of course titles, beyond the first year curriculum, offered last year: **281**
Percentages of upper division course sections, excluding seminars, with an enrollment of:
 Under 25: **51%**   25 to 49: **23%**
 50 to 74: **12%**   75 to 99: **8%**
 100+: **6%**
Areas of specialization: appellate advocacy, clinical training, dispute resolution, environmental law, health care law, intellectual property law, international law, tax law, trial advocacy

Fall 2009 faculty profile

Total teaching faculty: **140**. Full-time: **56%**; **60%** men, **40%** women, **15%** minorities. Part-time: **44%**; **77%** men, **23%** women, **5%** minorities
Student-to-faculty ratio: **16.5**

SPECIAL PROGRAMS (as provided by law school):

Law students may take courses in Intellectual Property, Civil Litigation, Health and Biomedical Law, International Law, and Business and Financial Services. They may enroll in a broad array of clinical and internship programs, including international internships at law firms worldwide. The Rappaport Center for Law and Public Service offers opportunities in public policy and public service work.

STUDENT BODY

Fall 2009 full-time enrollment: 1,079

Men: 52%   Women: 48%
African-American: 2.70%   American Indian: 0.40%
Asian-American: 8.20%   Mexican-American: 0.00%
Puerto Rican: 0.00%   Other Hisp-Amer: 4.40%
White: 74.00%   International: 1.60%
Unknown: 8.80%

Fall 2009 part-time enrollment: 603

Men: 53%   Women: 47%
African-American: 2.20%   American Indian: 0.50%
Asian-American: 5.10%   Mexican-American: 0.00%
Puerto Rican: 0.00%   Other Hisp-Amer: 3.50%
White: 76.60%   International: 2.30%
Unknown: 9.80%

Attrition rates for 2008-2009 full-time students
Percent of students discontinuing law school:
Men: 2%   Women: 4%
First-year students: 6%   Second-year students: 3%
Third-year students: 0%   Fourth-year students: N/A

LIBRARY RESOURCES

Total titles: 170,490
Total volumes: 303,568
Total seats available for library users: 880

INFORMATION TECHNOLOGY

Number of wired network connections available to students: 3700 total (in the law library, excluding computer labs: 2,000; in classrooms: 1,400; in computer labs: 100; elsewhere in the law school: 200)
Law school has a wireless network.
Students are not required to own a computer.

EMPLOYMENT AND SALARIES

Proportion of 2008 graduates employed at graduation: N/A
Employed 9 months later, as of February 15, 2009: 90%
Salaries in the private sector (law firms, business, industry): $57,500 –$130,000 (25th-75th percentile)
Median salary in the private sector: $79,000
Percentage in the private sector who reported salary information: 67%
Median salary in public service (government, judicial clerkships, academic posts, non-profits): $47,800

Percentage of 2008 graduates in:

Law firms: 40%   Government: 13%
Bus./industry: 28%   Judicial clerkship: 11%
Public interest: 3%   Unknown: 2%
Academia : 3%

2008 graduates employed in-state: 81%
2008 graduates employed in foreign countries: 0%
Number of states where graduates are employed: 22
Percentage of 2008 graduates working in: New England: 88%, Middle Atlantic: 4%, East North Central: 2%, West North Central: 0%, South Atlantic: 3%, East South Central: 1%, West South Central: 0%, Mountain: 1%, Pacific: 1%, Unknown: 0%

BAR PASSAGE RATES

Based on 2008 graduates taking Summer 2008 or Winter 2009 exams. Most of the school's first-time test takers took the bar in Massachusetts.

93%

School's bar passage rate for first-time test takers

89%

Statewide bar passage rate for first-time test takers

Syracuse University

- Suite 440, Syracuse, NY, 13244-1030
- http://www.law.syr.edu
- Private
- Year founded: 1895
- 2009-2010 tuition: full-time: $44,856; part-time: $1,899/credit hour
- Enrollment 2009-10 academic year: full-time: 598; part-time: 5
- U.S. News 2010 law specialty ranking: N/A

3.13-3.51 GPA, 25TH-75TH PERCENTILE

153-157 LSAT, 25TH-75TH PERCENTILE

38% ACCEPTANCE RATE

86 2011 U.S. NEWS LAW SCHOOL RANKING

ADMISSIONS

Admissions phone number: (315) 443-1962
Admissions email address: admissions@law.syr.edu
Application website: N/A
Application deadline for Fall 2011 admission: 1-Apr

Admissions statistics:

Number of applicants for Fall 2009: 2,518
Number of acceptances: 960
Number enrolled: 225
Acceptance rate: 38%
GPA, 25th-75th percentile, entering class Fall 2009: 3.13-3.51
LSAT, 25th-75th percentile, entering class Fall 2009: 153-157

FINANCIAL AID

Financial aid phone number: (315) 443-1963
Financial aid application deadline: 15-Feb
Tuition 2009-2010 academic year: **full-time: $44,856; part-time: $1,899/credit hour**
Room and board: **$11,830** ; books: **$1,300** ; miscellaneous expenses: **$5,394**
Total of room/board/books/miscellaneous expenses: **$18,524**
University offers graduate student housing for which law students are eligible.

Financial aid profile

Percent of students that received grants for the 2008-2009 academic year: full-time: **78%**; part-time **140%**
Median grant amount: full-time: **$6,500** ; part-time: **$5,250**
The average law-school debt of those in the Class of 2009 who borrowed: **$119,076** . Proportion who borrowed: **84%**

ACADEMIC PROGRAMS

Calendar: **semester**
Joint degrees awarded: J.D./M.B.A.; J.D./M.A. Economics; J.D./M.A. International Relations; J.D./M.P.A.; J.D./M.S. Information Management; J.D./M.A. TV, Radio and Film; J.D./M.A. History; J.D./M.A. Political Science; J.D/M.A. Journalism; J.D./M.S. Cultural Foundations of Edu.; J.D./M.S. Bioengineering; J.D./M.S. Media Management; J.D./M.S. Electrical Engineering; J.D./M.A. Advertising; J.D./M.S. Computer Science; J.D./M.S. Education, Disability Studies; J.D./M.S.W.; J.D./M.S/Forestry and Natural Resources ; J.D/M.A./Philosophy
Typical first-year section size: Full-time: **68**
Is there typically a "small section" of the first year class, other than Legal Writing, taught by full-time faculty?: Full-time: **yes**
Number of course titles, beyond the first year curriculum, offered last year: **129**
Percentages of upper division course sections, excluding seminars, with an enrollment of:

Under 25: **73%**   25 to 49: **15%**
50 to 74: **9%**   75 to 99: **3%**
100+: **0%**

Areas of specialization: appellate advocacy, clinical training, dispute resolution, environmental law, health care law, intellectual property law, international law, tax law, trial advocacy

Fall 2009 faculty profile

Total teaching faculty: **63**. Full-time: **73%**; **63%** men, **37%** women, **24%** minorities. Part-time: **27%**; **76%** men, **24%** women, **18%** minorities
Student-to-faculty ratio: **10.9**

SPECIAL PROGRAMS (as provided by law school):

As part of a leading research university, the law curriculum combines a commitment to scholarship, teaching, and research. We offer innovative interdisciplinary programs, with 7 Centers and 2 Institutes; a clinical program with 7 in-house clinics and externship program; a highly competitive advocacy skills training program with award-winning student teams; and 10 joint-degree programs.

STUDENT BODY

Fall 2009 full-time enrollment: 598

Men: 59%	Women: 41%
African-American: 3.70%	American Indian: 0.50%
Asian-American: 11.90%	Mexican-American: 1.20%
Puerto Rican: 0.50%	Other Hisp-Amer: 3.20%
White: 54.20%	International: 4.20%
Unknown: 20.70%	

Fall 2009 part-time enrollment: 5

Men: 0%	Women: 100%
African-American: 0.00%	American Indian: 0.00%
Asian-American: 20.00%	Mexican-American: 0.00%
Puerto Rican: 0.00%	Other Hisp-Amer: 0.00%
White: 60.00%	International: 20.00%
Unknown: 0.00%	

Attrition rates for 2008-2009 full-time students

Percent of students discontinuing law school:

Men: 6%	Women: 8%
First-year students: 14%	Second-year students: 8%
Third-year students: N/A	Fourth-year students: N/A

LIBRARY RESOURCES

Total titles: 98,644
Total volumes: 491,149
Total seats available for library users: 402

INFORMATION TECHNOLOGY

Number of wired network connections available to students: **19** total (in the law library, excluding computer labs: **14**; in classrooms: **0**; in computer labs: **0**; elsewhere in the law school: **5**)
Law school has a wireless network.
Students are required to own a computer.

EMPLOYMENT AND SALARIES

Proportion of 2008 graduates employed at graduation: **N/A**
Employed 9 months later, as of February 15, 2009: **95%**
Salaries in the private sector (law firms, business, industry): **$55,000 –$110,000** (25th-75th percentile)
Median salary in the private sector: **$80,000**
Percentage in the private sector who reported salary information: **71%**
Median salary in public service (government, judicial clerkships, academic posts, non-profits): **$49,500**

Percentage of 2008 graduates in:

Law firms: 46%	Government: 14%
Bus./industry: 24%	Judicial clerkship: 9%
Public interest: 6%	Unknown: 0%
Academia : 1%	

2008 graduates employed in-state: **40%**
2008 graduates employed in foreign countries: **1%**
Number of states where graduates are employed: **26**
Percentage of 2008 graduates working in: New England: **9%**, Middle Atlantic: **55%**, East North Central: **4%**, West North Central: **1%**, South Atlantic: **15%**, East South Central: **1%**, West South Central: **1%**, Mountain: **3%**, Pacific: **9%**, Unknown: **1%**

BAR PASSAGE RATES

Based on 2008 graduates taking Summer 2008 or Winter 2009 exams. Most of the school's first-time test takers took the bar in New York.

84%
School's bar passage rate for first-time test takers

81%
Statewide bar passage rate for first-time test takers

Temple University (Beasley)

- 1719 N. Broad Street, Philadelphia, PA, 19122
- http://www.law.temple.edu
- Public
- Year founded: 1895
- 2009-2010 tuition: full-time: $17,226; part-time: $13,908
- Enrollment 2009-10 academic year: full-time: 784; part-time: 192
- U.S. News 2010 law specialty ranking: international law: 12, trial advocacy: 2

3.14-3.60 GPA, 25TH-75TH PERCENTILE

160-163 LSAT, 25TH-75TH PERCENTILE

41% ACCEPTANCE RATE

72 2011 U.S. NEWS LAW SCHOOL RANKING

ADMISSIONS

Admissions phone number: **(800) 560-1428**
Admissions email address: **lawadmis@temple.edu**
Application website:
  http://www.law.temple.edu/admissions
Application deadline for Fall 2011 admission: **1-Mar**

Admissions statistics:

Number of applicants for Fall 2009: **4,194**
Number of acceptances: **1,737**
Number enrolled: **239**
Acceptance rate: **41%**
GPA, 25th-75th percentile, entering class Fall 2009: **3.14-3.60**
LSAT, 25th-75th percentile, entering class Fall 2009: **160-163**

Part-time program:

Number of applicants for Fall 2009: **457**
Number of acceptances: **132**
Number enrolled: **64**
Acceptance rate: **29%**
GPA, 25th-75th percentile, entering class Fall 2009: **2.89-3.65**
LSAT, 25th-75th percentile, entering class Fall 2009: **156-161**

FINANCIAL AID

Financial aid phone number: **(800) 560-1428**
Financial aid application deadline: **1-Mar**
Tuition 2009-2010 academic year: **full-time: $17,226; part-time: $13,908**
Room and board: **$11,416** ; books: **$1,500** ; miscellaneous expenses: **$7,138**
Total of room/board/books/miscellaneous expenses: **$20,054**
University offers graduate student housing for which law students are eligible.

Financial aid profile

Percent of students that received grants for the 2008-2009 academic year: full-time: **53%**; part-time **18%**
Median grant amount: full-time: **$7,500** ; part-time: **$3,750**
The average law-school debt of those in the Class of 2009 who borrowed: **$78,502** . Proportion who borrowed: **84%**

ACADEMIC PROGRAMS

Calendar: **semester**
Joint degrees awarded: **J.D./M.B.A.**
Typical first-year section size: Full-time: **60**; Part-time: **60**
Is there typically a "small section" of the first year class, other than Legal Writing, taught by full-time faculty?:
  Full-time: **no**; Part-time: **no**
Number of course titles, beyond the first year curriculum, offered last year: **185**
Percentages of upper division course sections, excluding seminars, with an enrollment of:
  Under 25: **70%**   25 to 49: **19%**
  50 to 74: **7%**   75 to 99: **3%**
  100+: **1%**
Areas of specialization: appellate advocacy, clinical training, dispute resolution, environmental law, health care law, intellectual property law, international law, tax law, trial advocacy

Fall 2009 faculty profile

Total teaching faculty: **147**. Full-time: **38%**; **59%** men, **41%** women, **23%** minorities. Part-time: **62%**; **56%** men, **44%** women, **15%** minorities
Student-to-faculty ratio: **13**

SPECIAL PROGRAMS *(as provided by law school)*:

Temple's curriculum integrates both critical thinking and practical legal skills. Temple boasts a prize-winning trial advocacy program, an extensive clinical program, business and transactional skills courses, unique opportunities to study international law at home and abroad, traditional IP law and the law of emerging technologies, and a longstanding tradition of public service to the community.

STUDENT BODY

Fall 2009 full-time enrollment: **784**

Men: **53%**	Women: **47%**
African-American: **7.50%**	American Indian: **1.00%**
Asian-American: **9.40%**	Mexican-American: **0.60%**
Puerto Rican: **1.00%**	Other Hisp-Amer: **3.60%**
White: **74.20%**	International: **0.90%**
Unknown: **1.70%**	

Fall 2009 part-time enrollment: **192**

Men: **58%**	Women: **42%**
African-American: **5.20%**	American Indian: **0.50%**
Asian-American: **10.40%**	Mexican-American: **0.00%**
Puerto Rican: **1.00%**	Other Hisp-Amer: **3.10%**
White: **77.60%**	International: **0.50%**
Unknown: **1.60%**	

Attrition rates for 2008-2009 full-time students
Percent of students discontinuing law school:

Men: **2%**	Women: **2%**
First-year students: **2%**	Second-year students: **4%**
Third-year students: **1%**	Fourth-year students: **N/A**

LIBRARY RESOURCES

Total titles: **150,164**
Total volumes: **616,905**
Total seats available for library users: **664**

INFORMATION TECHNOLOGY

Number of wired network connections available to students: **425** total (in the law library, excluding computer labs: **160**; in classrooms: **143**; in computer labs: **56**; elsewhere in the law school: **66**)
Law school has a wireless network.
Students are not required to own a computer.

EMPLOYMENT AND SALARIES

Proportion of 2008 graduates employed at graduation: **66%**
Employed 9 months later, as of February 15, 2009: **91%**
Salaries in the private sector (law firms, business, industry): **$69,000 –$145,000** (25th-75th percentile)
Median salary in the private sector: **$125,000**
Percentage in the private sector who reported salary information: **60%**
Median salary in public service (government, judicial clerkships, academic posts, non-profits): **$45,000**

Percentage of 2008 graduates in:

Law firms: **46%**	Government: **14%**
Bus./industry: **15%**	Judicial clerkship: **16%**
Public interest: **7%**	Unknown: **0%**
Academia : **3%**	

2008 graduates employed in-state: **69%**
2008 graduates employed in foreign countries: **1%**
Number of states where graduates are employed: **20**
Percentage of 2008 graduates working in: New England: **1%**, Middle Atlantic: **84%**, East North Central: **0%**, West North Central: **0%**, South Atlantic: **8%**, East South Central: **0%**, West South Central: **1%**, Mountain: **2%**, Pacific: **2%**, Unknown: **0%**

BAR PASSAGE RATES

Based on 2008 graduates taking Summer 2008 or Winter 2009 exams. Most of the school's first-time test takers took the bar in Pennsylvania.

89%
School's bar passage rate for first-time test takers

87%
Statewide bar passage rate for first-time test takers

Texas Southern University (Marshall)

- 3100 Cleburne Street, Houston, TX, 77004
- http://www.tsulaw.edu
- Public
- Year founded: 1947
- 2009-2010 tuition: full-time: $13,235; part-time: N/A
- Enrollment 2009-10 academic year: full-time: 542
- U.S. News 2010 law specialty ranking: N/A

2.66-3.21 GPA, 25TH-75TH PERCENTILE

144-148 LSAT, 25TH-75TH PERCENTILE

34% ACCEPTANCE RATE

Tier 4 2011 U.S. NEWS LAW SCHOOL RANKING

ADMISSIONS

Admissions phone number: **(713) 313-7114**
Admissions email address: **lawadmit@tsulaw.edu**
Application website:
  **http://www.tsulaw.edu/admissions/overview/application
  .asp**
Application deadline for Fall 2011 admission: **1-Apr**

Admissions statistics:

Number of applicants for Fall 2009: **2,003**
Number of acceptances: **684**
Number enrolled: **219**
Acceptance rate: **34%**
GPA, 25th-75th percentile, entering class Fall 2009: **2.66-3.21**
LSAT, 25th-75th percentile, entering class Fall 2009: **144-148**

FINANCIAL AID

Financial aid phone number: **(713) 313-7243**
Financial aid application deadline: **1-Apr**
Tuition 2009-2010 academic year: **full-time: $13,235; part-time: N/A**
Room and board: **$12,380** ; books: **$1,918** ; miscellaneous expenses: **$4,394**
Total of room/board/books/miscellaneous expenses: **$18,692**
University does not offer graduate student housing for which law students are eligible.

Financial aid profile

Percent of students that received grants for the 2008-2009 academic year: full-time: **43%**
Median grant amount: full-time: **$3,000**
The average law-school debt of those in the Class of 2009 who borrowed: **$20,429** . Proportion who borrowed: **100%**

ACADEMIC PROGRAMS

Calendar: **semester**
Joint degrees awarded: **M.P.A.; M.B.A.**

Typical first-year section size: Full-time: **60**
Is there typically a "small section" of the first year class, other than Legal Writing, taught by full-time faculty?: Full-time: **no**
Number of course titles, beyond the first year curriculum, offered last year: **74**
Percentages of upper division course sections, excluding seminars, with an enrollment of:
  Under 25: **65%**   25 to 49: **23%**
  50 to 74: **10%**   75 to 99: **1%**
  100+: **1%**
Areas of specialization: appellate advocacy, clinical training, dispute resolution, environmental law, health care law, intellectual property law, international law, tax law, trial advocacy

Fall 2009 faculty profile

Total teaching faculty: **46**. Full-time: **74%**; **41%** men, **59%** women, **79%** minorities. Part-time: **26%**; **50%** men, **50%** women, **75%** minorities
Student-to-faculty ratio: **12.8**

SPECIAL PROGRAMS *(as provided by law school):*

The law school is proud of its wide array of special programs offered to the student body. The school offers criminal and civil clinics, and awards mediation certification. The Institute for International and Immigration Law, The Earl Carl Institute for Legal and Social Policy, and the Center for Government Law provide certifications and several internship and externship programs.

STUDENT BODY

Fall 2009 full-time enrollment: 542

Men: **48%**	Women: **52%**
African-American: **50.20%**	American Indian: **0.40%**
Asian-American: **6.50%**	Mexican-American: **23.80%**
Puerto Rican: **0.00%**	Other Hisp-Amer: **0.00%**
White: **16.60%**	International: **2.40%**
Unknown: **0.20%**	

Attrition rates for 2008-2009 full-time students
Percent of students discontinuing law school:
Men: **6%**   Women: **7%**
First-year students: **16%**   Second-year students: **1%**
Third-year students: **1%**   Fourth-year students: **N/A**

LIBRARY RESOURCES
Total titles: **194,719**
Total volumes: **696,747**
Total seats available for library users: **378**

INFORMATION TECHNOLOGY
Number of wired network connections available to students: **955** total (in the law library, excluding computer labs: **300**; in classrooms: **560**; in computer labs: **65**; elsewhere in the law school: **30**)
Law school has a wireless network.
Students are not required to own a computer.

EMPLOYMENT AND SALARIES
Proportion of 2008 graduates employed at graduation: **N/A**
Employed 9 months later, as of February 15, 2009: **83%**
Salaries in the private sector (law firms, business, industry): **$47,250 –$70,000** (25th-75th percentile)
Median salary in the private sector: **$55,000**
Percentage in the private sector who reported salary information: **42%**

Median salary in public service (government, judicial clerkships, academic posts, non-profits): **$55,000**

Percentage of 2008 graduates in:
Law firms: **57%**   Government: **10%**
Bus./industry: **24%**   Judicial clerkship: **1%**
Public interest: **1%**   Unknown: **4%**
Academia : **3%**

2008 graduates employed in-state: **64%**
2008 graduates employed in foreign countries: **1%**
Number of states where graduates are employed: **15**
Percentage of 2008 graduates working in: New England: **0%**, Middle Atlantic: **5%**, East North Central: **3%**, West North Central: **1%**, South Atlantic: **9%**, East South Central: **3%**, West South Central: **61%**, Mountain: **2%**, Pacific: **0%**, Unknown: **16%**

BAR PASSAGE RATES
Based on 2008 graduates taking Summer 2008 or Winter 2009 exams. Most of the school's first-time test takers took the bar in Texas.

60%
School's bar passage rate for first-time test takers

84%
Statewide bar passage rate for first-time test takers

Texas Tech University

- 1802 Hartford Avenue, Lubbock, TX, 79409-0004
- http://www.law.ttu.edu
- Public
- Year founded: 1967
- 2009-2010 tuition: full-time: $16,200; part-time: N/A
- Enrollment 2009-10 academic year: full-time: 637
- U.S. News 2010 law specialty ranking: N/A

3.13-3.62 GPA, 25TH-75TH PERCENTILE

153-158 LSAT, 25TH-75TH PERCENTILE

37% ACCEPTANCE RATE

Tier 3 2011 U.S. NEWS LAW SCHOOL RANKING

ADMISSIONS

Admissions phone number: **(806) 742-3990**
Admissions email address: **donna.williams@ttu.edu**
Application website: **N/A**
Application deadline for Fall 2011 admission: **1-Feb**

Admissions statistics:

Number of applicants for Fall 2009: **1,768**
Number of acceptances: **652**
Number enrolled: **213**
Acceptance rate: **37%**
GPA, 25th-75th percentile, entering class Fall 2009: **3.13-3.62**
LSAT, 25th-75th percentile, entering class Fall 2009: **153-158**

FINANCIAL AID

Financial aid phone number: **(806) 742-3990**
Financial aid application deadline: **15-Apr**
Tuition 2009-2010 academic year: **full-time: $16,200; part-time: N/A**
Room and board: **$8,110** ; books: **$1,000** ; miscellaneous expenses: **$4,366**
Total of room/board/books/miscellaneous expenses: **$13,476**
University offers graduate student housing for which law students are eligible.

Financial aid profile

Percent of students that received grants for the 2008-2009 academic year: full-time: **54%**
Median grant amount: full-time: **$7,000**
The average law-school debt of those in the Class of 2009 who borrowed: **$54,373** . Proportion who borrowed: **86%**

ACADEMIC PROGRAMS

Calendar: **semester**
Joint degrees awarded: **J.D./M.B.A.; J.D./M.P.A.; J.D./M.S. Taxation; J.D./M.S. Agr. & Applied Economics; J.D./M.S. Environmental Toxicology; J.D./M.S. Personal Financial Planning; J.D./M.S. Biotechnology; J.D./M.S.**

C.S./H./S.S./E.
Typical first-year section size: Full-time: **51**
Is there typically a "small section" of the first year class, other than Legal Writing, taught by full-time faculty?: Full-time: **no**
Number of course titles, beyond the first year curriculum, offered last year: **95**
Percentages of upper division course sections, excluding seminars, with an enrollment of:

Under 25: **60%**	25 to 49: **15%**
50 to 74: **14%**	75 to 99: **5%**
100+: **5%**	

Areas of specialization: appellate advocacy, clinical training, dispute resolution, environmental law, health care law, intellectual property law, international law, tax law, trial advocacy

Fall 2009 faculty profile

Total teaching faculty: **63**. Full-time: **60%**; **61%** men, **39%** women, **21%** minorities. Part-time: **40%**; **80%** men, **20%** women, **16%** minorities
Student-to-faculty ratio: **15.3**

SPECIAL PROGRAMS (as provided by law school):

Clinical Programs: To represent clients in real cases through clinical courses. Summer Law Institute: Guanajuato, Mexico. Semester Abroad: University of Lyon, Lyon, France; Universidad Pablo de Olavide, Sevilla, Spain; La Trobe Univ., Australia. Ctr. for Military Law and Policy; Ctr. for Biodefense Law and Public Policy; Ctr. for Water Law and Policy. Please see: http://www.law.ttu.edu

STUDENT BODY

Fall 2009 full-time enrollment: 637

Men: **58%**	Women: **42%**
African-American: **3.80%**	American Indian: **0.90%**
Asian-American: **4.40%**	Mexican-American: **15.40%**
Puerto Rican: **0.30%**	Other Hisp-Amer: **0.20%**
White: **75.00%**	International: **0.00%**
Unknown: **0.00%**	

Percent of students discontinuing law school:

Men: **0%**	Women: **1%**
First-year students: **0%**	Second-year students: **1%**
Third-year students: **N/A**	Fourth-year students: **N/A**

LIBRARY RESOURCES

Total titles: **109,211**
Total volumes: **331,191**
Total seats available for library users: **578**

INFORMATION TECHNOLOGY

Number of wired network connections available to students: **1118** total (in the law library, excluding computer labs: **473**; in classrooms: **606**; in computer labs: **5**; elsewhere in the law school: **34**)
Law school has a wireless network.
Students are not required to own a computer.

EMPLOYMENT AND SALARIES

Proportion of 2008 graduates employed at graduation: **N/A**
Employed 9 months later, as of February 15, 2009: **88%**
Salaries in the private sector (law firms, business, industry): **$50,000 –$72,500** (25th-75th percentile)
Median salary in the private sector: **$55,000**
Percentage in the private sector who reported salary information: **85%**

Median salary in public service (government, judicial clerkships, academic posts, non-profits): **$50,000**

Percentage of 2008 graduates in:

Law firms: **55%**	Government: **21%**
Bus./industry: **17%**	Judicial clerkship: **5%**
Public interest: **3%**	Unknown: **0%**
Academia : **1%**	

2008 graduates employed in-state: **85%**
2008 graduates employed in foreign countries: **1%**
Number of states where graduates are employed: **14**
Percentage of 2008 graduates working in: New England: **0%**, Middle Atlantic: **1%**, East North Central: **0%**, West North Central: **2%**, South Atlantic: **6%**, East South Central: **0%**, West South Central: **83%**, Mountain: **5%**, Pacific: **1%**, Unknown: **3%**

BAR PASSAGE RATES

Based on 2008 graduates taking Summer 2008 or Winter 2009 exams. Most of the school's first-time test takers took the bar in Texas.

87%
School's bar passage rate for first-time test takers

84%
Statewide bar passage rate for first-time test takers

Texas Wesleyan University

- 1515 Commerce Street, Fort Worth, TX, 76102
- http://www.law.txwes.edu/
- Private
- Year founded: 1992
- 2009-2010 tuition: full-time: $26,000; part-time: $18,650
- Enrollment 2009-10 academic year: full-time: 522; part-time: 271
- U.S. News 2010 law specialty ranking: N/A

2.93-3.46 GPA, 25TH-75TH PERCENTILE

151-156 LSAT, 25TH-75TH PERCENTILE

47% ACCEPTANCE RATE

Tier 4 2011 U.S. NEWS LAW SCHOOL RANKING

ADMISSIONS
Admissions phone number: **(817) 212-4040**
Admissions email address: lawadmissions@law.txwes.edu
Application website:
  http://www.law.txwes.edu/ProspectiveStudents/Admissions/Apply/tabid/156/Default.aspx
Application deadline for Fall 2011 admission: **31-Mar**

Admissions statistics:
Number of applicants for Fall 2009: **1,606**
Number of acceptances: **757**
Number enrolled: **170**
Acceptance rate: **47%**
GPA, 25th-75th percentile, entering class Fall 2009: **2.93-3.46**
LSAT, 25th-75th percentile, entering class Fall 2009: **151-156**

Part-time program:
Number of applicants for Fall 2009: **371**
Number of acceptances: **115**
Number enrolled: **63**
Acceptance rate: **31%**
GPA, 25th-75th percentile, entering class Fall 2009: **2.73-3.33**
LSAT, 25th-75th percentile, entering class Fall 2009: **151-154**

FINANCIAL AID
Financial aid phone number: **(817) 212-4090**
Financial aid application deadline: **31-Aug**
Tuition 2009-2010 academic year: **full-time: $26,000; part-time: $18,650**
Room and board: **$10,521** ; books: **$1,740** ; miscellaneous expenses: **$2,114**
Total of room/board/books/miscellaneous expenses: **$14,375**
University offers graduate student housing for which law students are eligible.

Financial aid profile
Percent of students that received grants for the 2008-2009 academic year: full-time: **47%**; part-time **43%**
Median grant amount: full-time: **$7,500** ; part-time: **$5,000**
The average law-school debt of those in the Class of 2009 who borrowed: **$82,913** . Proportion who borrowed: **65%**

ACADEMIC PROGRAMS
Calendar: **semester**
Joint degrees awarded: **N/A**
Typical first-year section size: Full-time: **95**; Part-time: **65**
Is there typically a "small section" of the first year class, other than Legal Writing, taught by full-time faculty?: Full-time: **no**; Part-time: **no**
Number of course titles, beyond the first year curriculum, offered last year: **94**
Percentages of upper division course sections, excluding seminars, with an enrollment of:
  Under 25: **61%**   25 to 49: **18%**
  50 to 74: **11%**   75 to 99: **8%**
  100+: **2%**
Areas of specialization: appellate advocacy, clinical training, dispute resolution, environmental law, health care law, intellectual property law, international law, tax law, trial advocacy

Fall 2009 faculty profile
Total teaching faculty: **47**. Full-time: **66%**; **65%** men, **35%** women, **10%** minorities. Part-time: **34%**; **69%** men, **31%** women, **13%** minorities
Student-to-faculty ratio: **21**

SPECIAL PROGRAMS *(as provided by law school)*:
In clinics, students represent clients in social security & family law cases. As externs, students work with practicing attorneys. In practicums, students learn practical skills such as drafting & mediation. A summer Art Law program is taught in Santa Fe, NM. Students participate in the Innocence Project, investigate claims of actual innocence by prisoners resulting in several exonerations.

STUDENT BODY

Fall 2009 full-time enrollment: 522

Men: 49%	Women: 51%
African-American: 5.20%	American Indian: 1.50%
Asian-American: 5.90%	Mexican-American: 0.00%
Puerto Rican: 0.00%	Other Hisp-Amer: 8.60%
White: 75.70%	International: 0.00%
Unknown: 3.10%	

Fall 2009 part-time enrollment: 271

Men: 50%	Women: 50%
African-American: 8.50%	American Indian: 1.50%
Asian-American: 8.90%	Mexican-American: 0.00%
Puerto Rican: 0.00%	Other Hisp-Amer: 12.50%
White: 66.40%	International: 0.00%
Unknown: 2.20%	

Attrition rates for 2008-2009 full-time students
Percent of students discontinuing law school:

Men: 5%	Women: 3%
First-year students: 7%	Second-year students: N/A
Third-year students: N/A	Fourth-year students: N/A

LIBRARY RESOURCES

Total titles: 193,131
Total volumes: 271,805
Total seats available for library users: 383

INFORMATION TECHNOLOGY

Number of wired network connections available to students: 0 total (in the law library, excluding computer labs: 0; in classrooms: 0; in computer labs: 0; elsewhere in the law school: 0)
Law school has a wireless network.
Students are not required to own a computer.

EMPLOYMENT AND SALARIES

Proportion of 2008 graduates employed at graduation: 57%
Employed 9 months later, as of February 15, 2009: 76%
Salaries in the private sector (law firms, business, industry): $50,000 –$90,000 (25th-75th percentile)
Median salary in the private sector: $61,000
Percentage in the private sector who reported salary information: 87%
Median salary in public service (government, judicial clerkships, academic posts, non-profits): $50,000

Percentage of 2008 graduates in:

Law firms: 58%	Government: 10%
Bus./industry: 29%	Judicial clerkship: 2%
Public interest: 1%	Unknown: 0%
Academia : 0%	

2008 graduates employed in-state: 89%
2008 graduates employed in foreign countries: 0%
Number of states where graduates are employed: 9
Percentage of 2008 graduates working in: New England: 0%, Middle Atlantic: 0%, East North Central: 0%, West North Central: 2%, South Atlantic: 4%, East South Central: 0%, West South Central: 93%, Mountain: 1%, Pacific: 0%, Unknown: 0%

BAR PASSAGE RATES

Based on 2008 graduates taking Summer 2008 or Winter 2009 exams. Most of the school's first-time test takers took the bar in Texas.

78%
School's bar passage rate for first-time test takers

84%
Statewide bar passage rate for first-time test takers

Thomas Jefferson School of Law

- 2121 San Diego Avenue, San Diego, CA, 92110
- http://www.tjsl.edu
- Private
- Year founded: 1969
- 2009-2010 tuition: full-time: $36,300; part-time: $24,000
- Enrollment 2009-10 academic year: full-time: 648; part-time: 241
- U.S. News 2010 law specialty ranking: N/A

2.71-3.22 GPA, 25TH-75TH PERCENTILE

149-153 LSAT, 25TH-75TH PERCENTILE

52% ACCEPTANCE RATE

Tier 4 2011 U.S. NEWS LAW SCHOOL RANKING

ADMISSIONS

Admissions phone number: **(619) 297-9700**
Admissions email address: **info@tjsl.edu**
Application website: **N/A**
Application deadline for Fall 2011 admission: **rolling**

Admissions statistics:

Number of applicants for Fall 2009: **2,587**
Number of acceptances: **1,339**
Number enrolled: **305**
Acceptance rate: **52%**
GPA, 25th-75th percentile, entering class Fall 2009: **2.71-3.22**
LSAT, 25th-75th percentile, entering class Fall 2009: **149-153**

Part-time program:

Number of applicants for Fall 2009: **395**
Number of acceptances: **194**
Number enrolled: **90**
Acceptance rate: **49%**
GPA, 25th-75th percentile, entering class Fall 2009: **2.63-3.10**
LSAT, 25th-75th percentile, entering class Fall 2009: **147-152**

FINANCIAL AID

Financial aid phone number: **(619) 297-9700**
Financial aid application deadline:
Tuition 2009-2010 academic year: **full-time: $36,300; part-time: $24,000**
Room and board: **N/A**; books: **N/A**; miscellaneous expenses: **N/A**
Total of room/board/books/miscellaneous expenses: **$28,860**
University does not offer graduate student housing for which law students are eligible.

Financial aid profile

Percent of students that received grants for the 2008-2009 academic year: full-time: **42%**; part-time **31%**

Median grant amount: full-time: **$12,500** ; part-time: **$8,000**
The average law-school debt of those in the Class of 2009 who borrowed: **$131,800** . Proportion who borrowed: **95%**

ACADEMIC PROGRAMS

Calendar: **semester**
Joint degrees awarded: **J.D./M.B.A.**
Typical first-year section size: Full-time: **85**; Part-time: **50**
Is there typically a "small section" of the first year class, other than Legal Writing, taught by full-time faculty?: Full-time: **no**; Part-time: **no**
Number of course titles, beyond the first year curriculum, offered last year: **95**
Percentages of upper division course sections, excluding seminars, with an enrollment of:
    Under 25: **70%**   25 to 49: **16%**
    50 to 74: **5%**   75 to 99: **7%**
    100+: **1%**
Areas of specialization: appellate advocacy, clinical training, dispute resolution, environmental law, health care law, intellectual property law, international law, tax law, trial advocacy

Fall 2009 faculty profile

Total teaching faculty: **93**. Full-time: **42%**; **46%** men, **54%** women, **23%** minorities. Part-time: **58%**; **78%** men, **22%** women, **6%** minorities
Student-to-faculty ratio: **17.9**

SPECIAL PROGRAMS *(as provided by law school):*

To provide an institutional framework for the study of technological change and globalization, the law school has established three academic centers: The Centers for Law Technology and Communications, Global Legal studies, and Law and Social Justice. Each center combines the scholarship of the faculty with special programs that attract leading legal experts from throughout the world.

STUDENT BODY

Fall 2009 full-time enrollment: 648

Men: 55%	Women: 45%
African-American: 6.90%	American Indian: 0.80%
Asian-American: 11.00%	Mexican-American: 7.60%
Puerto Rican: 0.30%	Other Hisp-Amer: 5.20%
White: 67.10%	International: 1.10%
Unknown: 0.00%	

Fall 2009 part-time enrollment: 241

Men: 53%	Women: 47%
African-American: 6.20%	American Indian: 1.70%
Asian-American: 12.90%	Mexican-American: 9.10%
Puerto Rican: 1.20%	Other Hisp-Amer: 5.00%
White: 63.90%	International: 0.00%
Unknown: 0.00%	

Attrition rates for 2008-2009 full-time students
Percent of students discontinuing law school:

Men: 4%	Women: 4%
First-year students: 10%	Second-year students: 2%
Third-year students: N/A	Fourth-year students: N/A

LIBRARY RESOURCES

Total titles: 192,050
Total volumes: 262,199
Total seats available for library users: 266

INFORMATION TECHNOLOGY

Number of wired network connections available to students: 12 total (in the law library, excluding computer labs: 0; in classrooms: 0; in computer labs: 12; elsewhere in the law school: 0)
Law school has a wireless network.
Students are required to own a computer.

EMPLOYMENT AND SALARIES

Proportion of 2008 graduates employed at graduation: N/A
Employed 9 months later, as of February 15, 2009: 92%
Salaries in the private sector (law firms, business, industry): $50,000 –$80,000 (25th-75th percentile)
Median salary in the private sector: $65,000
Percentage in the private sector who reported salary information: 33%
Median salary in public service (government, judicial clerkships, academic posts, non-profits): $60,000

Percentage of 2008 graduates in:

Law firms: 47%	Government: 9%
Bus./industry: 22%	Judicial clerkship: 6%
Public interest: 3%	Unknown: 10%
Academia : 3%	

2008 graduates employed in-state: 71%
2008 graduates employed in foreign countries: 1%
Number of states where graduates are employed: 18
Percentage of 2008 graduates working in: New England: 0%, Middle Atlantic: 2%, East North Central: 3%, West North Central: 1%, South Atlantic: 2%, East South Central: 0%, West South Central: 2%, Mountain: 9%, Pacific: 72%, Unknown: 8%

BAR PASSAGE RATES

Based on 2008 graduates taking Summer 2008 or Winter 2009 exams. Most of the school's first-time test takers took the bar in California.

70%
School's bar passage rate for first-time test takers

71%
Statewide bar passage rate for first-time test takers

Touro College (Fuchsberg)

- 225 Eastview Drive, Central Islip, NY, 11722
- http://www.tourolaw.edu
- Private
- Year founded: 1980
- 2009-2010 tuition: full-time: $39,130; part-time: $29,330
- Enrollment 2009-10 academic year: full-time: 553; part-time: 233
- U.S. News 2010 law specialty ranking: N/A

2.88-3.41 GPA, 25TH-75TH PERCENTILE

149-153 LSAT, 25TH-75TH PERCENTILE

49% ACCEPTANCE RATE

Tier 4 2011 U.S. NEWS LAW SCHOOL RANKING

ADMISSIONS

Admissions phone number: **(631) 761-7010**
Admissions email address: **admissions@tourolaw.edu**
Application website:
   http://www.tourolaw.edu/admissions/app.asp
Application deadline for Fall 2011 admission: **rolling**

Admissions statistics:

Number of applicants for Fall 2009: **1,610**
Number of acceptances: **793**
Number enrolled: **234**
Acceptance rate: **49%**
GPA, 25th-75th percentile, entering class Fall 2009: **2.88-3.41**
LSAT, 25th-75th percentile, entering class Fall 2009: **149-153**

Part-time program:

Number of applicants for Fall 2009: **485**
Number of acceptances: **169**
Number enrolled: **81**
Acceptance rate: **35%**
GPA, 25th-75th percentile, entering class Fall 2009: **2.81-3.33**
LSAT, 25th-75th percentile, entering class Fall 2009: **149-152**

FINANCIAL AID

Financial aid phone number: **(631) 761-7020**
Financial aid application deadline: **15-Apr**
Tuition 2009-2010 academic year: **full-time: $39,130; part-time: $29,330**
Room and board: **$18,691** ; books: **$1,500** ; miscellaneous expenses: **$3,369**
Total of room/board/books/miscellaneous expenses: **$23,560**
University does not offer graduate student housing for which law students are eligible.

Financial aid profile

Percent of students that received grants for the 2008-2009 academic year: full-time: **63%**; part-time **57%**
Median grant amount: full-time: **$4,000** ; part-time: **$2,420**
The average law-school debt of those in the Class of 2009 who borrowed: **$94,680** . Proportion who borrowed: **92%**

ACADEMIC PROGRAMS

Calendar: **semester**
Joint degrees awarded: **J.D./M.P.A.; J.D./M.B.A. (C.W. Post); J.D./M.S.W.; J.D./M.B.A. (Dowling)**
Typical first-year section size: Full-time: **70**; Part-time: **61**
Is there typically a "small section" of the first year class, other than Legal Writing, taught by full-time faculty?: Full-time: **no**; Part-time: **no**
Number of course titles, beyond the first year curriculum, offered last year: **91**
Percentages of upper division course sections, excluding seminars, with an enrollment of:

Under 25: **63%**	25 to 49: **25%**
50 to 74: **8%**	75 to 99: **3%**
100+: **1%**	

Areas of specialization: appellate advocacy, clinical training, dispute resolution, environmental law, health care law, intellectual property law, international law, tax law, trial advocacy

Fall 2009 faculty profile

Total teaching faculty: **61**. Full-time: **59%; 56% men, 44% women, 11% minorities**. Part-time: **41%; 72% men, 28% women, 16% minorities**
Student-to-faculty ratio: **15.9**

SPECIAL PROGRAMS (as provided by law school):

Touro Law students benefit from our location across from the federal and state courthouses and our unique Court Observation Program. We offer clinics and externship opportunities as well as five summer study abroad programs and several institutes and centers. We also offer a Court Collaboration Program for upper-division students. Students must complete a pro-bono requirement.

STUDENT BODY

Fall 2009 full-time enrollment: 553

Men: 53%	Women: 47%
African-American: 6.90%	American Indian: 0.40%
Asian-American: 6.90%	Mexican-American: 0.50%
Puerto Rican: 0.70%	Other Hisp-Amer: 4.20%
White: 73.80%	International: 2.50%
Unknown: 4.20%	

Fall 2009 part-time enrollment: 233

Men: 50%	Women: 50%
African-American: 13.70%	American Indian: 0.00%
Asian-American: 4.70%	Mexican-American: 0.40%
Puerto Rican: 2.10%	Other Hisp-Amer: 5.60%
White: 67.80%	International: 0.00%
Unknown: 5.60%	

Attrition rates for 2008-2009 full-time students

Percent of students discontinuing law school:

Men: 3%	Women: 4%
First-year students: 7%	Second-year students: 2%
Third-year students: N/A	Fourth-year students: N/A

LIBRARY RESOURCES

Total titles: 99,244
Total volumes: 455,553
Total seats available for library users: 476

INFORMATION TECHNOLOGY

Number of wired network connections available to students: 0 total (in the law library, excluding computer labs: 0; in classrooms: 0; in computer labs: 0; elsewhere in the law school: 0)
Law school has a wireless network.
Students are not required to own a computer.

EMPLOYMENT AND SALARIES

Proportion of 2008 graduates employed at graduation: N/A
Employed 9 months later, as of February 15, 2009: 72%
Salaries in the private sector (law firms, business, industry): $51,250 –$66,500 (25th-75th percentile)
Median salary in the private sector: $57,500
Percentage in the private sector who reported salary information: 15%
Median salary in public service (government, judicial clerkships, academic posts, non-profits): $47,500

Percentage of 2008 graduates in:

Law firms: 58%	Government: 19%
Bus./industry: 14%	Judicial clerkship: 5%
Public interest: 3%	Unknown: 0%
Academia : 1%	

2008 graduates employed in-state: 90%
2008 graduates employed in foreign countries: 0%
Number of states where graduates are employed: 5
Percentage of 2008 graduates working in: New England: 0%, Middle Atlantic: 96%, East North Central: 1%, West North Central: 0%, South Atlantic: 2%, East South Central: 0%, West South Central: 0%, Mountain: 0%, Pacific: 1%, Unknown: 0%

BAR PASSAGE RATES

Based on 2008 graduates taking Summer 2008 or Winter 2009 exams. Most of the school's first-time test takers took the bar in New York.

79%
School's bar passage rate for first-time test takers

81%
Statewide bar passage rate for first-time test takers

Tulane University

- 6329 Freret Street, John Giffen Weinmann Hall, New Orleans, LA, 70118-6231
- http://www.law.tulane.edu
- Private
- Year founded: 1847
- 2009-2010 tuition: full-time: $40,644; part-time: N/A
- Enrollment 2009-10 academic year: full-time: 771; part-time: 3
- U.S. News 2010 law specialty ranking: environmental law: 12

3.34-3.75 GPA, 25TH-75TH PERCENTILE

160-164 LSAT, 25TH-75TH PERCENTILE

30% ACCEPTANCE RATE

48 2011 U.S. NEWS LAW SCHOOL RANKING

ADMISSIONS

Admissions phone number: **(504) 865-5930**
Admissions email address: **admissions@law.tulane.edu**
Application website:
https://www.law.tulane.edu/tlsadmissions/index.aspx
Application deadline for Fall 2011 admission: **15-Mar**

Admissions statistics:

Number of applicants for Fall 2009: **2,990**
Number of acceptances: **894**
Number enrolled: **284**
Acceptance rate: **30%**
GPA, 25th-75th percentile, entering class Fall 2009: **3.34-3.75**
LSAT, 25th-75th percentile, entering class Fall 2009: **160-164**

FINANCIAL AID

Financial aid phone number: **(504) 865-5931**
Financial aid application deadline: **15-Feb**
Tuition 2009-2010 academic year: **full-time: $40,644; part-time: N/A**
Room and board: **$12,100** ; books: **$1,500** ; miscellaneous expenses: **$5,770**
Total of room/board/books/miscellaneous expenses: **$19,370**
University offers graduate student housing for which law students are eligible.

Financial aid profile

Percent of students that received grants for the 2008-2009 academic year: full-time: **60%**
Median grant amount: full-time: **$15,000**
The average law-school debt of those in the Class of 2009 who borrowed: **$114,266** . Proportion who borrowed: **85%**

ACADEMIC PROGRAMS

Calendar: **semester**
Joint degrees awarded: **J.D./M.B.A.; J.D./M.P.H.; J.D./M.A. Political Science/Intl Affairs; J.D./M.A. Classical Studies; J.D./M.S. International Development; J.D./B.S.; J.D./B.A.; J.D./M.H.A.; J.D./M.S.W.; J.D./M.A. Latin American Studies; J.D./M.Acc.; J.D./Ph.D.**
Typical first-year section size: Full-time: **83**
Is there typically a "small section" of the first year class, other than Legal Writing, taught by full-time faculty?: Full-time: **no**; Part-time: **no**
Number of course titles, beyond the first year curriculum, offered last year: **193**
Percentages of upper division course sections, excluding seminars, with an enrollment of:

Under 25: **57%**	25 to 49: **31%**
50 to 74: **6%**	75 to 99: **3%**
100+: **3%**	

Areas of specialization: appellate advocacy, clinical training, dispute resolution, environmental law, health care law, intellectual property law, international law, tax law, trial advocacy

Fall 2009 faculty profile

Total teaching faculty: **73**. Full-time: **62%**; **67%** men, **33%** women, **11%** minorities. Part-time: **38%**; **89%** men, **11%** women, **7%** minorities
Student-to-faculty ratio: **14.1**

SPECIAL PROGRAMS *(as provided by law school):*

Clinics-criminal, civil, environmental, juvenile, domestic violence, legislative, mediation. Centers/Institutes-maritime, comparative, water law, IP. Summer abroad in 6 countries; semester abroad in 11. Externships-fed'l & state judges, NLRB, public interest. Certificates-environmental law, admiralty, sports law, European legal studies, civil law, int'l/comparative law. Mandatory pro bono program.

STUDENT BODY

Fall 2009 full-time enrollment: **771**

Men: **59%**	Women: **41%**
African-American: **7.30%**	American Indian: **1.40%**
Asian-American: **2.50%**	Mexican-American: **0.10%**
Puerto Rican: **0.90%**	Other Hisp-Amer: **4.20%**
White: **75.00%**	International: **1.90%**
Unknown: **6.70%**	

Fall 2009 part-time enrollment: 3

Men: **67%**	Women: **33%**
African-American: **0.00%**	American Indian: **0.00%**
Asian-American: **0.00%**	Mexican-American: **0.00%**
Puerto Rican: **0.00%**	Other Hisp-Amer: **0.00%**
White: **33.30%**	International: **66.70%**
Unknown: **0.00%**	

Attrition rates for 2008-2009 full-time students
Percent of students discontinuing law school:

Men: **1%**	Women: **0%**
First-year students: **0%**	Second-year students: **1%**
Third-year students: **1%**	Fourth-year students: **N/A**

LIBRARY RESOURCES

Total titles: **390,280**
Total volumes: **653,600**
Total seats available for library users: **553**

INFORMATION TECHNOLOGY

Number of wired network connections available to students: **293** total (in the law library, excluding computer labs: **293**; in classrooms: **0**; in computer labs: **0**; elsewhere in the law school: **0**)
Law school has a wireless network.
Students are not required to own a computer.

EMPLOYMENT AND SALARIES

Proportion of 2008 graduates employed at graduation: **71%**
Employed 9 months later, as of February 15, 2009: **91%**
Salaries in the private sector (law firms, business, industry): **$70,000 –$145,000** (25th-75th percentile)

Median salary in the private sector: **$90,000**
Percentage in the private sector who reported salary information: **72%**
Median salary in public service (government, judicial clerkships, academic posts, non-profits): **$38,000**

Percentage of 2008 graduates in:

Law firms: **57%**	Government: **10%**
Bus./industry: **10%**	Judicial clerkship: **12%**
Public interest: **9%**	Unknown: **0%**
Academia : **2%**	

2008 graduates employed in-state: **38%**
2008 graduates employed in foreign countries: **2%**
Number of states where graduates are employed: **32**
Percentage of 2008 graduates working in: New England: **2%**, Middle Atlantic: **12%**, East North Central: **3%**, West North Central: **3%**, South Atlantic: **16%**, East South Central: **3%**, West South Central: **47%**, Mountain: **3%**, Pacific: **8%**, Unknown: **1%**

BAR PASSAGE RATES

Based on 2008 graduates taking Summer 2008 or Winter 2009 exams. Most of the school's first-time test takers took the bar in Louisiana.

76%
School's bar passage rate for first-time test takers

66%
Statewide bar passage rate for first-time test takers

University at Buffalo–SUNY

■ John Lord O'Brian Hall, Buffalo, NY, 14260
■ http://www.law.buffalo.edu
■ Public
■ Year founded: 1887
■ 2009-2010 tuition: full-time: $16,010; part-time: N/A
■ Enrollment 2009-10 academic year: full-time: 718; part-time: 8
■ U.S. News 2010 law specialty ranking: N/A

3.19-3.73 GPA, 25TH-75TH PERCENTILE

153-159 LSAT, 25TH-75TH PERCENTILE

32% ACCEPTANCE RATE

Tier 3 2011 U.S. NEWS LAW SCHOOL RANKING

ADMISSIONS

Admissions phone number: **(716) 645-2907**
Admissions email address: **law-admissions@buffalo.edu**
Application website:
  http://www.law.buffalo.edu/admissions
Application deadline for Fall 2011 admission: **15-Mar**

Admissions statistics:

Number of applicants for Fall 2009: **2,104**
Number of acceptances: **678**
Number enrolled: **208**
Acceptance rate: **32%**
GPA, 25th-75th percentile, entering class Fall 2009: **3.19-3.73**
LSAT, 25th-75th percentile, entering class Fall 2009: **153-159**

FINANCIAL AID

Financial aid phone number: **(716) 645-7324**
Financial aid application deadline: **15-Mar**
Tuition 2009-2010 academic year: **full-time: $16,010; part-time: N/A**
Room and board: **$10,980** ; books: **$1,627** ; miscellaneous expenses: **$3,381**
Total of room/board/books/miscellaneous expenses: **$15,988**
University offers graduate student housing for which law students are eligible.

Financial aid profile

Percent of students that received grants for the 2008-2009 academic year: full-time: **78%**
Median grant amount: full-time: **$550**
The average law-school debt of those in the Class of 2009 who borrowed: **$56,880** . Proportion who borrowed: **100%**

ACADEMIC PROGRAMS

Calendar: **semester**
Joint degrees awarded: N/A
Typical first-year section size: Full-time: **65**

Is there typically a "small section" of the first year class, other than Legal Writing, taught by full-time faculty?:
  Full-time: **no**
Number of course titles, beyond the first year curriculum, offered last year: **220**
Percentages of upper division course sections, excluding seminars, with an enrollment of:
  Under 25: **71%**   25 to 49: **20%**
  50 to 74: **4%**   75 to 99: **4%**
  100+: **0%**
Areas of specialization: appellate advocacy, clinical training, dispute resolution, environmental law, health care law, intellectual property law, international law, tax law, trial advocacy

Fall 2009 faculty profile

Total teaching faculty: **88**. Full-time: **47%**; **71%** men, **29%** women, **15%** minorities. Part-time: **53%**; **70%** men, **30%** women, **11%** minorities
Student-to-faculty ratio: **15.3**

SPECIAL PROGRAMS (as provided by law school):

10 concentrations (civil litigation, finance transactions, intellectual property, etc.); 7 nationally renowned clinics (including affordable housing and family violence); numerous joint degrees (JD/MBA, JD/PharmD, JD/MPH,...); a New York City-based semester studying finance (includes projects with international banking, investment and law firms); and international bridge (winter-break) courses.

STUDENT BODY

Fall 2009 full-time enrollment: 718

Men: **54%**	Women: **46%**
African-American: **4.60%**	American Indian: **0.60%**
Asian-American: **5.70%**	Mexican-American: **0.40%**
Puerto Rican: **1.30%**	Other Hisp-Amer: **2.40%**
White: **72.60%**	International: **0.00%**
Unknown: **12.50%**	

Fall 2009 part-time enrollment: 8

Men: **50%**	Women: **50%**

African-American: 12.50% American Indian: 0.00%
Asian-American: 0.00% Mexican-American: 0.00%
Puerto Rican: 0.00% Other Hisp-Amer: 0.00%
White: 87.50% International: 0.00%
Unknown: 0.00%

Attrition rates for 2008-2009 full-time students
Percent of students discontinuing law school:
Men: 3% Women: 3%
First-year students: 2% Second-year students: 5%
Third-year students: 0% Fourth-year students: N/A

LIBRARY RESOURCES
Total titles: 123,208
Total volumes: 582,475
Total seats available for library users: 590

INFORMATION TECHNOLOGY
Number of wired network connections available to students: 74 total (in the law library, excluding computer labs: 44; in classrooms: 18; in computer labs: 12; elsewhere in the law school: 0)
Law school has a wireless network.
Students are not required to own a computer.

EMPLOYMENT AND SALARIES
Proportion of 2008 graduates employed at graduation: 76%
Employed 9 months later, as of February 15, 2009: 91%
Salaries in the private sector (law firms, business, industry): $55,000 –$160,000 (25th-75th percentile)
Median salary in the private sector: $75,000

Percentage in the private sector who reported salary information: 46%
Median salary in public service (government, judicial clerkships, academic posts, non-profits): $55,000

Percentage of 2008 graduates in:
Law firms: 61% Government: 11%
Bus./industry: 11% Judicial clerkship: 5%
Public interest: 7% Unknown: 2%
Academia : 4%

2008 graduates employed in-state: 82%
2008 graduates employed in foreign countries: 1%
Number of states where graduates are employed: 20
Percentage of 2008 graduates working in: New England: 2%, Middle Atlantic: 83%, East North Central: 1%, West North Central: 1%, South Atlantic: 5%, East South Central: 0%, West South Central: 1%, Mountain: 1%, Pacific: 3%, Unknown: 4%

BAR PASSAGE RATES
Based on 2008 graduates taking Summer 2008 or Winter 2009 exams. Most of the school's first-time test takers took the bar in New York.

81%
School's bar passage rate for first-time test takers

81%
Statewide bar passage rate for first-time test takers

University of Akron

- C. Blake McDowell Law Center, Akron, OH, 44325-2901
- http://www.uakron.edu/law
- Public
- Year founded: 1921
- 2009-2010 tuition: full-time: $19,570; part-time: $15,958
- Enrollment 2009-10 academic year: full-time: 279; part-time: 238
- U.S. News 2010 law specialty ranking: trial advocacy: 7

3.16-3.70 GPA, 25TH-75TH PERCENTILE

152-159 LSAT, 25TH-75TH PERCENTILE

38% ACCEPTANCE RATE

Tier 3 2011 U.S. NEWS LAW SCHOOL RANKING

ADMISSIONS

Admissions phone number: (800) 425-7668
Admissions email address: **lawadmissions@uakron.edu**
Application website:
  http://www.uakron.edu/law/lawadmissions/application.
  php
Application deadline for Fall 2011 admission: **1-Mar**

Admissions statistics:
Number of applicants for Fall 2009: **1,541**
Number of acceptances: **585**
Number enrolled: **117**
Acceptance rate: **38%**
GPA, 25th-75th percentile, entering class Fall 2009: **3.16-3.70**
LSAT, 25th-75th percentile, entering class Fall 2009: **152-159**

Part-time program:
Number of applicants for Fall 2009: **335**
Number of acceptances: **162**
Number enrolled: **85**
Acceptance rate: **48%**
GPA, 25th-75th percentile, entering class Fall 2009: **3.05-3.60**
LSAT, 25th-75th percentile, entering class Fall 2009: **148-153**

FINANCIAL AID

Financial aid phone number: (800) 621-3847
Financial aid application deadline: **1-Mar**
Tuition 2009-2010 academic year: **full-time: $19,570**; **part-time: $15,958**
Room and board: **$14,247** ; books: **$1,157** ; miscellaneous expenses: N/A
Total of room/board/books/miscellaneous expenses: **$15,404**
University offers graduate student housing for which law students are eligible.

Financial aid profile
Percent of students that received grants for the 2008-2009 academic year: full-time: **42%**; part-time **29%**
Median grant amount: full-time: **$14,006** ; part-time: **$10,000**
The average law-school debt of those in the Class of 2009 who borrowed: **$71,836** . Proportion who borrowed **93%**

ACADEMIC PROGRAMS

Calendar: **semester**
Joint degrees awarded: **J.D./M.B.A.; J.D./M.Tax; J.D./M.P.A.; J.D./M.B.A. Human Resources; J.D./M.A.P.**
Typical first-year section size: Full-time: **41**; Part-time: **49**
Is there typically a "small section" of the first year class, other than Legal Writing, taught by full-time faculty?: Full-time: **yes**; Part-time: **yes**
Number of course titles, beyond the first year curriculum, offered last year: **92**
Percentages of upper division course sections, excluding seminars, with an enrollment of:

Under 25: **57%**	25 to 49: **29%**
50 to 74: **13%**	75 to 99: **1%**
100+: **1%**	

Areas of specialization: appellate advocacy, clinical training, dispute resolution, environmental law, health care law, intellectual property law, international law, tax law, trial advocacy

Fall 2009 faculty profile
Total teaching faculty: 52. Full-time: **63%**; 58% men, **42%** women, 12% minorities. Part-time: **37%**; 79% men, **21%** women, 5% minorities
Student-to-faculty ratio: 11.2

SPECIAL PROGRAMS *(as provided by law school):*
Clinical Programs: Appellate Review; Jail Inmate Assistance Program; New Business Legal Clinic; Civil Litigation; Trial Litigation. Certificate Programs: Intellectual Property; Litigation. Joint degree programs: JD/MBA, JD/MS, JD/MBA HR; JD/MPA; JD/MTax; JD/MAP. Centers: Intellectual Property; Constitutional Law; Institute for Professional Responsibility. Summer study-abroad: Geneva, Switzerland.

STUDENT BODY

Fall 2009 full-time enrollment: 279

Men: 59%	Women: 41%
African-American: 3.90%	American Indian: 0.40%
Asian-American: 5.00%	Mexican-American: 0.00%
Puerto Rican: 0.00%	Other Hisp-Amer: 3.90%
White: 75.60%	International: 0.00%
Unknown: 11.10%	

Fall 2009 part-time enrollment: 238

Men: 49%	Women: 51%
African-American: 10.50%	American Indian: 0.80%
Asian-American: 1.70%	Mexican-American: 0.00%
Puerto Rican: 0.00%	Other Hisp-Amer: 2.90%
White: 76.50%	International: 0.00%
Unknown: 7.60%	

Attrition rates for 2008-2009 full-time students
Percent of students discontinuing law school:

Men: 9%	Women: 7%
First-year students: 20%	Second-year students: 4%
Third-year students: N/A	Fourth-year students: N/A

LIBRARY RESOURCES

Total titles: 77,876
Total volumes: 288,330
Total seats available for library users: 287

INFORMATION TECHNOLOGY

Number of wired network connections available to students: 16 total (in the law library, excluding computer labs: 0; in classrooms: 0; in computer labs: 16; elsewhere in the law school: 0)
Law school has a wireless network.
Students are not required to own a computer.

EMPLOYMENT AND SALARIES

Proportion of 2008 graduates employed at graduation: 74%
Employed 9 months later, as of February 15, 2009: 88%
Salaries in the private sector (law firms, business, industry): $49,500 –$81,250 (25th-75th percentile)
Median salary in the private sector: $63,000
Percentage in the private sector who reported salary information: 100%
Median salary in public service (government, judicial clerkships, academic posts, non-profits): $49,210

Percentage of 2008 graduates in:

Law firms: 48%	Government: 19%
Bus./industry: 23%	Judicial clerkship: 4%
Public interest: 5%	Unknown: 0%
Academia : 1%	

2008 graduates employed in-state: 80%
2008 graduates employed in foreign countries: 0%
Number of states where graduates are employed: 15
Percentage of 2008 graduates working in: New England: 2%, Middle Atlantic: 2%, East North Central: 82%, West North Central: 0%, South Atlantic: 9%, East South Central: 0%, West South Central: 1%, Mountain: 3%, Pacific: 2%, Unknown: 0%

BAR PASSAGE RATES

Based on 2008 graduates taking Summer 2008 or Winter 2009 exams. Most of the school's first-time test takers took the bar in Ohio.

90%
School's bar passage rate for first-time test takers

88%
Statewide bar passage rate for first-time test takers

University of Alabama

- Box 870382, Tuscaloosa, AL, 35487
- http://www.law.ua.edu
- Public
- Year founded: 1872
- 2009-2010 tuition: full-time: $14,450; part-time: N/A
- Enrollment 2009-10 academic year: full-time: 527; part-time: 20
- U.S. News 2010 law specialty ranking: N/A

3.42-3.91 GPA, 25ᵀᴴ-75ᵀᴴ PERCENTILE

160-166 LSAT, 25ᵀᴴ-75ᵀᴴ PERCENTILE

31% ACCEPTANCE RATE

38 2011 U.S. NEWS LAW SCHOOL RANKING

ADMISSIONS

Admissions phone number: (205) 348-5440
Admissions email address: **admissions@law.ua.edu**
Application website:
   http://www.law.ua.edu/admissions/info.php?re=onlinea
   pp
Application deadline for Fall 2011 admission: **rolling**

Admissions statistics:

Number of applicants for Fall 2009: **1,403**
Number of acceptances: **433**
Number enrolled: **164**
Acceptance rate: **31%**
GPA, 25th-75th percentile, entering class Fall 2009: **3.42-3.91**
LSAT, 25th-75th percentile, entering class Fall 2009: **160-166**

Part-time program:

Number of applicants for Fall 2009: **N/A**
Number of acceptances: **26**
Number enrolled: **20**
Acceptance rate: **N/A**
GPA, 25th-75th percentile, entering class Fall 2009: **3.02-3.75**
LSAT, 25th-75th percentile, entering class Fall 2009: **153-165**

FINANCIAL AID

Financial aid phone number: (205) 348-6756
Financial aid application deadline:
Tuition 2009-2010 academic year: **full-time: $14,450; part-time: N/A**
Room and board: **$10,400** ; books: **$1,400** ; miscellaneous expenses: **$4,667**
Total of room/board/books/miscellaneous expenses: **$16,467**
University offers graduate student housing for which law students are eligible.

Financial aid profile

Percent of students that received grants for the 2008-2009 academic year: full-time: **43%**; part-time **45%**
Median grant amount: full-time: **$12,564** ; part-time: **$2,540**
The average law-school debt of those in the Class of 2009 who borrowed: **$56,643** . Proportion who borrowed: **76%**

ACADEMIC PROGRAMS

Calendar: **semester**
Joint degrees awarded: **J.D./M.B.A.**
Typical first-year section size: Full-time: **63**
Is there typically a "small section" of the first year class, other than Legal Writing, taught by full-time faculty?: Full-time: **no**; Part-time: **no**
Number of course titles, beyond the first year curriculum, offered last year: **149**
Percentages of upper division course sections, excluding seminars, with an enrollment of:

Under 25: **65%**	25 to 49: **27%**
50 to 74: **4%**	75 to 99: **2%**
100+: **1%**	

Areas of specialization: appellate advocacy, clinical training, dispute resolution, environmental law, health care law, intellectual property law, international law, tax law, trial advocacy

Fall 2009 faculty profile

Total teaching faculty: **66**. Full-time: **62%**; **66%** men, **34%** women, **12%** minorities. Part-time: **38%**; **92%** men, **8%** women, **12%** minorities
Student-to-faculty ratio: **10.2**

SPECIAL PROGRAMS *(as provided by law school):*

Clinics: Civil, Elder, Domestic Violence, Community Development, Capital Representation, Criminal Defense Mediation; Summer and Academic Year Externships; Summer Abroad in Canberra, Australia; Summer Abroad in Fribourg, Switzerland; Public Interest Institute; courses in other parts of the University; J.D./M.B.A.; Dual Enrollment in other departments; Certificate Program in Public Interest

STUDENT BODY

Fall 2009 full-time enrollment: 527

Men: 58%
African-American: 8.30%
Asian-American: 2.80%
Puerto Rican: 0.00%
White: 86.30%
Unknown: 0.00%

Women: 42%
American Indian: 0.80%
Mexican-American: 0.00%
Other Hisp-Amer: 1.70%
International: 0.00%

Fall 2009 part-time enrollment: 20

Men: 45%
African-American: 30.00%
Asian-American: 0.00%
Puerto Rican: 0.00%
White: 65.00%
Unknown: 0.00%

Women: 55%
American Indian: 0.00%
Mexican-American: 0.00%
Other Hisp-Amer: 5.00%
International: 0.00%

Attrition rates for 2008-2009 full-time students
Percent of students discontinuing law school:

Men: 2%
First-year students: 6%
Third-year students: **N/A**

Women: 2%
Second-year students: **N/A**
Fourth-year students: **N/A**

LIBRARY RESOURCES

Total titles: 188,116
Total volumes: 611,041
Total seats available for library users: 506

INFORMATION TECHNOLOGY

Number of wired network connections available to students: **73** total (in the law library, excluding computer labs: **10**; in classrooms: **18**; in computer labs: **10**; elsewhere in the law school: **35**)
Law school has a wireless network.
Students are not required to own a computer.

EMPLOYMENT AND SALARIES

Proportion of 2008 graduates employed at graduation:
N/A
Employed 9 months later, as of February 15, 2009: **97%**
Salaries in the private sector (law firms, business, industry): **$63,000 –$102,000** (25th-75th percentile)
Median salary in the private sector: **$90,000**
Percentage in the private sector who reported salary information: **70%**
Median salary in public service (government, judicial clerkships, academic posts, non-profits): **$43,750**

Percentage of 2008 graduates in:

Law firms: **54%**
Bus./industry: **13%**
Public interest: **4%**
Academia : **1%**

Government: **15%**
Judicial clerkship: **12%**
Unknown: **1%**

2008 graduates employed in-state: **61%**
2008 graduates employed in foreign countries: **2%**
Number of states where graduates are employed: **18**
Percentage of 2008 graduates working in: New England: **0%**, Middle Atlantic: **2%**, East North Central: **1%**, West North Central: **1%**, South Atlantic: **20%**, East South Central: **66%**, West South Central: **4%**, Mountain: **2%**, Pacific: **2%**, Unknown: **0%**

BAR PASSAGE RATES

Based on 2008 graduates taking Summer 2008 or Winter 2009 exams. Most of the school's first-time test takers took the bar in Alabama.

97%

School's bar passage rate for first-time test takers

79%

Statewide bar passage rate for first-time test takers

University of Arizona (Rogers)

- PO Box 210176, Tucson, AZ, 85721-0176
- http://www.law.arizona.edu
- Public
- Year founded: 1915
- 2009-2010 tuition: full-time: $20,895; part-time: N/A
- Enrollment 2009-10 academic year: full-time: 475
- U.S. News 2010 law specialty ranking: N/A

3.34-3.71 GPA, 25TH-75TH PERCENTILE

159-163 LSAT, 25TH-75TH PERCENTILE

33% ACCEPTANCE RATE

42 2011 U.S. NEWS LAW SCHOOL RANKING

ADMISSIONS

Admissions phone number: (520) 621-3477
Admissions email address: admissions@law.arizona.edu
Application website:
  http://www.law.arizona.edu/Admissions/
Application deadline for Fall 2011 admission: 1-Mar

Admissions statistics:

Number of applicants for Fall 2009: 2,241
Number of acceptances: 738
Number enrolled: 153
Acceptance rate: 33%
GPA, 25th-75th percentile, entering class Fall 2009: 3.34-3.71
LSAT, 25th-75th percentile, entering class Fall 2009: 159-163

FINANCIAL AID

Financial aid phone number: (520) 626-8101
Financial aid application deadline: 15-Mar
Tuition 2009-2010 academic year: full-time: $20,895; part-time: N/A
Room and board: $11,840 ; books: $816 ; miscellaneous expenses: $8,094
Total of room/board/books/miscellaneous expenses: $20,750
University offers graduate student housing for which law students are eligible.

Financial aid profile

Percent of students that received grants for the 2008-2009 academic year: full-time: 68%
Median grant amount: full-time: $10,000
The average law-school debt of those in the Class of 2009 who borrowed: $74,678 . Proportion who borrowed: 88%

ACADEMIC PROGRAMS

Calendar: semester
Joint degrees awarded: J.D./Ph.D. Economics; J.D./Ph.D. Philosophy; J.D./Ph.D. Psychology; J.D./M.B.A.; J.D./M.P.A.; J.D./M.A. American Indian Studies;
J.D./M.A. Economics; J.D./M.A. Latin American Studies; J.D./M.A. Women's Studies; J.D./M.M.F. Finance
Typical first-year section size: Full-time: 77
Is there typically a "small section" of the first year class, other than Legal Writing, taught by full-time faculty?: Full-time: yes
Number of course titles, beyond the first year curriculum, offered last year: 120
Percentages of upper division course sections, excluding seminars, with an enrollment of:
  Under 25: 81%   25 to 49: 12%
  50 to 74: 5%   75 to 99: 0%
  100+: 2%
Areas of specialization: appellate advocacy, clinical training, dispute resolution, environmental law, health care law, intellectual property law, international law, tax law, trial advocacy

Fall 2009 faculty profile

Total teaching faculty: 64. Full-time: 55%; 54% men, 46% women, 20% minorities. Part-time: 45%; 62% men, 38% women, 7% minorities
Student-to-faculty ratio: 10.6

SPECIAL PROGRAMS (as provided by law school):

Economics, Law and Environment; Indigenous Peoples Law and Policy; Intellectual Property; Criminal Law and Policy; International Trade and Business; Trial Advocacy; Rehnquist Center on Constitutional Structures of Government; 1L Small Section Program. Clinics in Child Advocacy; Domestic Violence; Immigration; Indigenous Peoples; 9th Circuit Pro Bono; Bankruptcy. 10 Masters/PhD dual degree programs.

STUDENT BODY

Fall 2009 full-time enrollment: 475

Men: 53%	Women: 47%
African-American: 3.20%	American Indian: 6.30%
Asian-American: 8.60%	Mexican-American: 2.10%
Puerto Rican: 0.00%	Other Hisp-Amer: 6.50%
White: 69.30%	International: 1.10%
Unknown: 2.90%	

Attrition rates for 2008-2009 full-time students
Percent of students discontinuing law school:

Men: **0%**	Women: **N/A**
First-year students: **1%**	Second-year students: **N/A**
Third-year students: **N/A**	Fourth-year students: **N/A**

LIBRARY RESOURCES

Total titles: **126,625**
Total volumes: **404,616**
Total seats available for library users: **379**

INFORMATION TECHNOLOGY

Number of wired network connections available to students: **0** total (in the law library, excluding computer labs: **0**; in classrooms: **0**; in computer labs: **0**; elsewhere in the law school: **0**)
Law school has a wireless network.
Students are not required to own a computer.

EMPLOYMENT AND SALARIES

Proportion of 2008 graduates employed at graduation: **77%**
Employed 9 months later, as of February 15, 2009: **97%**
Salaries in the private sector (law firms, business, industry): **$80,000 –$125,000** (25th-75th percentile)
Median salary in the private sector: **$115,000**
Percentage in the private sector who reported salary information: **55%**

Median salary in public service (government, judicial clerkships, academic posts, non-profits): **$52,000**

Percentage of 2008 graduates in:

Law firms: **48%**	Government: **21%**
Bus./industry: **9%**	Judicial clerkship: **18%**
Public interest: **2%**	Unknown: **0%**
Academia : **2%**	

2008 graduates employed in-state: **65%**
2008 graduates employed in foreign countries: **1%**
Number of states where graduates are employed: **15**
Percentage of 2008 graduates working in: New England: **1%**, Middle Atlantic: **2%**, East North Central: **2%**, West North Central: **2%**, South Atlantic: **5%**, East South Central: **1%**, West South Central: **0%**, Mountain: **69%**, Pacific: **19%**, Unknown: **1%**

BAR PASSAGE RATES

Based on 2008 graduates taking Summer 2008 or Winter 2009 exams. Most of the school's first-time test takers took the bar in Arizona.

92%
School's bar passage rate for first-time test takers

84%
Statewide bar passage rate for first-time test takers

University of Arkansas–Fayetteville

■ Robert A. Leflar Law Center, Fayetteville, AR, 72701
■ http://law.uark.edu/
■ Public
■ Year founded: 1928
■ 2009-2010 tuition: full-time: $359/credit hour; part-time: N/A
■ Enrollment 2009-10 academic year: full-time: 398
■ U.S. News 2010 law specialty ranking: N/A

3.16-3.74 GPA, 25TH-75TH PERCENTILE

153-158 LSAT, 25TH-75TH PERCENTILE

34% ACCEPTANCE RATE

86 2011 U.S. NEWS LAW SCHOOL RANKING

ADMISSIONS

Admissions phone number: **(479) 575-3102**
Admissions email address: jkmiller@uark.edu
Application website: **N/A**
Application deadline for Fall 2011 admission: **1-Apr**

Admissions statistics:
Number of applicants for Fall 2009: **1,167**
Number of acceptances: **395**
Number enrolled: **139**
Acceptance rate: **34%**
GPA, 25th-75th percentile, entering class Fall 2009: **3.16-3.74**
LSAT, 25th-75th percentile, entering class Fall 2009: **153-158**

FINANCIAL AID

Financial aid phone number: **(479) 575-3806**
Financial aid application deadline:
Tuition 2009-2010 academic year: **full-time: $359/credit hour; part-time: N/A**
Room and board: **$9,910** ; books: **$1,082** ; miscellaneous expenses: **$2,968**
Total of room/board/books/miscellaneous expenses: **$13,960**
University does not offer graduate student housing for which law students are eligible.

Financial aid profile
Percent of students that received grants for the 2008-2009 academic year: full-time: **40%**
Median grant amount: full-time: **$6,000**
The average law-school debt of those in the Class of 2009 who borrowed: **$55,305** . Proportion who borrowed: **90%**

ACADEMIC PROGRAMS

Calendar: **semester**
Joint degrees awarded: **J.D./M.P.A.; J.D./M.B.A.; J.D./M.A.**
Typical first-year section size: Full-time: **70**
Is there typically a "small section" of the first year class, other than Legal Writing, taught by full-time faculty?:

Full-time: **no**
Number of course titles, beyond the first year curriculum, offered last year: **88**
Percentages of upper division course sections, excluding seminars, with an enrollment of:
Under 25: **75%**   25 to 49: **18%**
50 to 74: **5%**   75 to 99: **2%**
100+: **0%**
Areas of specialization: appellate advocacy, clinical training, dispute resolution, environmental law, health care law, intellectual property law, international law, tax law, trial advocacy

Fall 2009 faculty profile
Total teaching faculty: **46**. Full-time: **59%**; **56%** men, **44%** women, **11%** minorities. Part-time: **41%**; **74%** men, **26%** women, **5%** minorities
Student-to-faculty ratio: **12.2**

SPECIAL PROGRAMS *(as provided by law school):*
Nine clinics are available. Students must earn at least 3 credits in certified skills courses from a variety of available offerings designed specifically for this purpose. We have an extensive summer curriculum and offer foreign programs in England and Russia. Judicial, Legislative, Public Service, Corporate, Juvenile Justice, and Federal Public Defender externships are available.

STUDENT BODY
Fall 2009 full-time enrollment: 398
Men: **59%**   Women: **41%**
African-American: **9.30%**   American Indian: **2.80%**
Asian-American: **2.50%**   Mexican-American: **0.50%**
Puerto Rican: **0.00%**   Other Hisp-Amer: **2.30%**
White: **82.20%**   International: **0.30%**
Unknown: **0.30%**

Attrition rates for 2008-2009 full-time students
Percent of students discontinuing law school:
Men: **1%**   Women: **1%**
First-year students: **3%**   Second-year students: **N/A**
Third-year students: **N/A**   Fourth-year students: **N/A**

LIBRARY RESOURCES

Total titles: **195,071**
Total volumes: **361,758**
Total seats available for library users: **413**

INFORMATION TECHNOLOGY

Number of wired network connections available to students: **73** total (in the law library, excluding computer labs: **55**; in classrooms: **0**; in computer labs: **0**; elsewhere in the law school: **18**)
Law school has a wireless network.
Students are not required to own a computer.

EMPLOYMENT AND SALARIES

Proportion of 2008 graduates employed at graduation: **N/A**
Employed 9 months later, as of February 15, 2009: **96%**
Salaries in the private sector (law firms, business, industry): **$42,500 –$70,000** (25th-75th percentile)
Median salary in the private sector: **$52,000**
Percentage in the private sector who reported salary information: **98%**
Median salary in public service (government, judicial clerkships, academic posts, non-profits): **$42,000**

Percentage of 2008 graduates in:

Law firms: **62%**	Government: **11%**
Bus./industry: **17%**	Judicial clerkship: **3%**
Public interest: **5%**	Unknown: **0%**
Academia : **2%**	

2008 graduates employed in-state: **64%**
2008 graduates employed in foreign countries: **0%**
Number of states where graduates are employed: **14**
Percentage of 2008 graduates working in: New England: **0%**, Middle Atlantic: **N/A**, East North Central: **3%**, West North Central: **4%**, South Atlantic: **5%**, East South Central: **5%**, West South Central: **80%**, Mountain: **N/A**, Pacific: **3%**, Unknown: **0%**

BAR PASSAGE RATES

Based on 2008 graduates taking Summer 2008 or Winter 2009 exams. Most of the school's first-time test takers took the bar in Arkansas.

82%

School's bar passage rate for first-time test takers

83%

Statewide bar passage rate for first-time test takers

University of Arkansas–Little Rock

■ 1201 McMath Avenue, Little Rock, AR, 72202-5142
■ http://www.law.ualr.edu/
■ Public
■ Year founded: 1969
■ 2009-2010 tuition: full-time: $11,456; part-time: $7,557
■ Enrollment 2009-10 academic year: full-time: 316; part-time: 155
■ U.S. News 2010 law specialty ranking: N/A

2.92-3.70 GPA, 25TH-75TH PERCENTILE

150-158 LSAT, 25TH-75TH PERCENTILE

24% ACCEPTANCE RATE

Tier 3 2011 U.S. NEWS LAW SCHOOL RANKING

ADMISSIONS

Admissions phone number: (501) 324-9439
Admissions email address: lawadm@ualr.edu
Application website:
  http://www.law.ualr.edu/admissions.html
Application deadline for Fall 2011 admission: 15-Apr

Admissions statistics:

Number of applicants for Fall 2009: 1,372
Number of acceptances: 334
Number enrolled: 99
Acceptance rate: 24%
GPA, 25th-75th percentile, entering class Fall 2009: 2.92-3.70
LSAT, 25th-75th percentile, entering class Fall 2009: 150-158

Part-time program:

Number of applicants for Fall 2009: 198
Number of acceptances: 68
Number enrolled: 62
Acceptance rate: 34%
GPA, 25th-75th percentile, entering class Fall 2009: 2.86-3.61
LSAT, 25th-75th percentile, entering class Fall 2009: 148-156

FINANCIAL AID

Financial aid phone number: (501) 569-3035
Financial aid application deadline: 1-Mar
Tuition 2009-2010 academic year: full-time: $11,456; part-time: $7,557
Room and board: $7,726 ; books: $1,250 ; miscellaneous expenses: $4,160
Total of room/board/books/miscellaneous expenses: $13,136
University does not offer graduate student housing for which law students are eligible.

Financial aid profile

Percent of students that received grants for the 2008-2009 academic year: full-time: 40%; part-time 24%
Median grant amount: full-time: $2,750 ; part-time: $1,250
The average law-school debt of those in the Class of 2009 who borrowed: $56,585 . Proportion who borrowed: 76%

ACADEMIC PROGRAMS

Calendar: semester
Joint degrees awarded: J.D./M.B.A.; J.D./M.P.A.; J.D./M.P.H.; J.D./M.D.; J.D./M.P.S.
Typical first-year section size: Full-time: 93; Part-time: 61
Is there typically a "small section" of the first year class, other than Legal Writing, taught by full-time faculty?: Full-time: no; Part-time: no
Number of course titles, beyond the first year curriculum, offered last year: 83
Percentages of upper division course sections, excluding seminars, with an enrollment of:

Under 25: 60%	25 to 49: 18%
50 to 74: 5%	75 to 99: 16%
100+: 1%	

Areas of specialization: appellate advocacy, clinical training, dispute resolution, environmental law, health care law, intellectual property law, international law, tax law, trial advocacy

Fall 2009 faculty profile

Total teaching faculty: 102. Full-time: 21%; 57% men, 43% women, 29% minorities. Part-time: 79%; 68% men, 32% women, 6% minorities
Student-to-faculty ratio: 16.2

SPECIAL PROGRAMS (as provided by law school):

We offer five joint degrees: J.D./M.B.A., J.D./M.P.A., J.D./M.P.H., J.D./M.P.S. and J.D./MD. The J.D./M.P.S., with the University of Arkansas Clinton School of Public Service, is the only one of its kind in the United States. We have three clinics: Litigation, Tax, and Mediation. We have a Public Service Externship Program and a Pro Bono Opportunities Program.

STUDENT BODY

Fall 2009 full-time enrollment: 316

Men: 54%	Women: 46%
African-American: 12.00%	American Indian: 1.60%
Asian-American: 2.20%	Mexican-American: 1.90%
Puerto Rican: 0.00%	Other Hisp-Amer: 1.30%
White: 75.60%	International: 1.90%
Unknown: 3.50%	

Fall 2009 part-time enrollment: 155

Men: 48%	Women: 52%
African-American: 12.30%	American Indian: 0.00%
Asian-American: 3.20%	Mexican-American: 1.30%
Puerto Rican: 0.00%	Other Hisp-Amer: 5.20%
White: 74.20%	International: 2.60%
Unknown: 1.30%	

Attrition rates for 2008-2009 full-time students
Percent of students discontinuing law school:

Men: 5%	Women: 4%
First-year students: 4%	Second-year students: 9%
Third-year students: N/A	Fourth-year students: N/A

LIBRARY RESOURCES

Total titles: 139,520
Total volumes: 317,304
Total seats available for library users: 347

INFORMATION TECHNOLOGY

Number of wired network connections available to students: 1 total (in the law library, excluding computer labs: 0; in classrooms: 0; in computer labs: 1; elsewhere in the law school: 0)
Law school has a wireless network.
Students are not required to own a computer.

EMPLOYMENT AND SALARIES

Proportion of 2008 graduates employed at graduation: 38%
Employed 9 months later, as of February 15, 2009: 96%
Salaries in the private sector (law firms, business, industry): $42,000 –$70,000 (25th-75th percentile)
Median salary in the private sector: $55,000
Percentage in the private sector who reported salary information: 66%
Median salary in public service (government, judicial clerkships, academic posts, non-profits): $47,635

Percentage of 2008 graduates in:

Law firms: 51%	Government: 13%
Bus./industry: 14%	Judicial clerkship: 13%
Public interest: 4%	Unknown: 1%
Academia : 5%	

2008 graduates employed in-state: 85%
2008 graduates employed in foreign countries: 0%
Number of states where graduates are employed: 12
Percentage of 2008 graduates working in: New England: 0%, Middle Atlantic: 0%, East North Central: 1%, West North Central: 1%, South Atlantic: 6%, East South Central: 2%, West South Central: 89%, Mountain: 1%, Pacific: 0%, Unknown: 0%

BAR PASSAGE RATES

Based on 2008 graduates taking Summer 2008 or Winter 2009 exams. Most of the school's first-time test takers took the bar in Arkansas.

81%
School's bar passage rate for first-time test takers

83%
Statewide bar passage rate for first-time test takers

University of Baltimore

- 1420 N. Charles Street, Baltimore, MD, 21201-5779
- http://law.ubalt.edu
- Public
- Year founded: 1925
- 2009-2010 tuition: full-time: $23,992; part-time: $17,916
- Enrollment 2009-10 academic year: full-time: 672; part-time: 431
- U.S. News 2010 law specialty ranking: clinical training: 24

3.03-3.67 GPA, 25TH-75TH PERCENTILE

153-158 LSAT, 25TH-75TH PERCENTILE

40% ACCEPTANCE RATE

Tier 3 2011 U.S. NEWS LAW SCHOOL RANKING

ADMISSIONS
Admissions phone number: (410) 837-4459
Admissions email address: lwadmiss@ubalt.edu
Application website: http://law.ubalt.edu/admissions
Application deadline for Fall 2011 admission: 15-Jul

Admissions statistics:
Number of applicants for Fall 2009: 1,990
Number of acceptances: 803
Number enrolled: 245
Acceptance rate: 40%
GPA, 25th-75th percentile, entering class Fall 2009: 3.03-3.67
LSAT, 25th-75th percentile, entering class Fall 2009: 153-158

Part-time program:
Number of applicants for Fall 2009: 758
Number of acceptances: 322
Number enrolled: 134
Acceptance rate: 42%
GPA, 25th-75th percentile, entering class Fall 2009: 2.80-3.40
LSAT, 25th-75th percentile, entering class Fall 2009: 150-154

FINANCIAL AID
Financial aid phone number: (410) 837-4763
Financial aid application deadline: 1-Mar
Tuition 2009-2010 academic year: **full-time: $23,992; part-time: $17,916**
Room and board: $13,100 ; books: $1,600 ; miscellaneous expenses: $6,380
Total of room/board/books/miscellaneous expenses: $21,080
University does not offer graduate student housing for which law students are eligible.

Financial aid profile
Percent of students that received grants for the 2008-2009 academic year: full-time: 20%; part-time 7%

Median grant amount: full-time: $14,000 ; part-time: $10,147
The average law-school debt of those in the Class of 2009 who borrowed: $86,133 . Proportion who borrowed: 84%

ACADEMIC PROGRAMS
Calendar: semester
Joint degrees awarded: J.D./M.B.A.; J.D./M.P.A.; J.D./M.S. Negotiation
Typical first-year section size: Full-time: 58; Part-time: 43
Is there typically a "small section" of the first year class, other than Legal Writing, taught by full-time faculty?: Full-time: no; Part-time: no
Number of course titles, beyond the first year curriculum, offered last year: 150
Percentages of upper division course sections, excluding seminars, with an enrollment of:

Under 25: 73%	25 to 49: 16%
50 to 74: 8%	75 to 99: 3%
100+: N/A	

Areas of specialization: appellate advocacy, clinical training, dispute resolution, environmental law, health care law, intellectual property law, international law, tax law, trial advocacy

Fall 2009 faculty profile
Total teaching faculty: 119. Full-time: 41%; 61% men, 39% women, 16% minorities. Part-time: 59%; 66% men, 34% women, 13% minorities
Student-to-faculty ratio: 15.8

SPECIAL PROGRAMS (as provided by law school):
At the University of Baltimore School of Law, students learn doctrine, perspective and skills through traditional study and through clinical and lawyering courses. Their education is enriched by work on journals, membership in student organizations and government, and by centers focused on local, national and global issues.

STUDENT BODY

Fall 2009 full-time enrollment: 672

Men: 48%	Women: 52%
African-American: 4.00%	American Indian: 0.30%
Asian-American: 6.30%	Mexican-American: 0.00%
Puerto Rican: 0.00%	Other Hisp-Amer: 1.90%
White: 72.60%	International: 0.40%
Unknown: 14.40%	

Fall 2009 part-time enrollment: 431

Men: 49%	Women: 51%
African-American: 9.50%	American Indian: 0.20%
Asian-American: 4.60%	Mexican-American: 0.00%
Puerto Rican: 0.00%	Other Hisp-Amer: 2.80%
White: 67.30%	International: 0.90%
Unknown: 14.60%	

Attrition rates for 2008-2009 full-time students
Percent of students discontinuing law school:

Men: 5%	Women: 4%
First-year students: 11%	Second-year students: 1%
Third-year students: N/A	Fourth-year students: N/A

LIBRARY RESOURCES

Total titles: 69,158
Total volumes: 372,444
Total seats available for library users: 317

INFORMATION TECHNOLOGY

Number of wired network connections available to students: 30 total (in the law library, excluding computer labs: 1; in classrooms: 0; in computer labs: 28; elsewhere in the law school: 1)
Law school has a wireless network.
Students are not required to own a computer.

EMPLOYMENT AND SALARIES

Proportion of 2008 graduates employed at graduation: 93%
Employed 9 months later, as of February 15, 2009: 96%
Salaries in the private sector (law firms, business, industry): $55,000 –$83,000 (25th-75th percentile)
Median salary in the private sector: $65,000
Percentage in the private sector who reported salary information: 45%
Median salary in public service (government, judicial clerkships, academic posts, non-profits): $43,000

Percentage of 2008 graduates in:

Law firms: 31%	Government: 20%
Bus./industry: 18%	Judicial clerkship: 21%
Public interest: 7%	Unknown: 0%
Academia : 3%	

2008 graduates employed in-state: 83%
2008 graduates employed in foreign countries: 0%
Number of states where graduates are employed: 11
Percentage of 2008 graduates working in: New England: 0%, Middle Atlantic: 3%, East North Central: 0%, West North Central: 0%, South Atlantic: 96%, East South Central: 0%, West South Central: 0%, Mountain: 0%, Pacific: 0%, Unknown: 0%

BAR PASSAGE RATES

Based on 2008 graduates taking Summer 2008 or Winter 2009 exams. Most of the school's first-time test takers took the bar in Maryland.

85%

School's bar passage rate for first-time test takers

85%

Statewide bar passage rate for first-time test takers

University of California (Hastings)

- 200 McAllister Street, San Francisco, CA, 94102
- http://www.uchastings.edu
- Public
- Year founded: 1878
- 2009-2010 tuition: full-time: $32,468; part-time: N/A
- Enrollment 2009-10 academic year: full-time: 1,292
- U.S. News 2010 law specialty ranking: clinical training: 20, dispute resolution: 12, tax law: 18

3.39-3.71 GPA, 25TH-75TH PERCENTILE

161-165 LSAT, 25TH-75TH PERCENTILE

24% ACCEPTANCE RATE

42 2011 U.S. NEWS LAW SCHOOL RANKING

ADMISSIONS

Admissions phone number: **(415) 565-4623**
Admissions email address: **admiss@uchastings.edu**
Application website:
  http://www.uchastings.edu/prospective-students/
Application deadline for Fall 2011 admission: **1-Mar**

Admissions statistics:
Number of applicants for Fall 2009: **6,150**
Number of acceptances: **1,454**
Number enrolled: **469**
Acceptance rate: **24%**
GPA, 25th-75th percentile, entering class Fall 2009: **3.39-3.71**
LSAT, 25th-75th percentile, entering class Fall 2009: **161-165**

FINANCIAL AID

Financial aid phone number: **(415) 565-4624**
Financial aid application deadline: **1-Mar**
Tuition 2009-2010 academic year: **full-time: $32,468; part-time: N/A**
Room and board: **$14,040** ; books: **$1,150** ; miscellaneous expenses: **$4,708**
Total of room/board/books/miscellaneous expenses: **$19,898**
University does not offer graduate student housing for which law students are eligible.

Financial aid profile
Percent of students that received grants for the 2008-2009 academic year: full-time: **72%**
Median grant amount: full-time: **$7,500**
The average law-school debt of those in the Class of 2009 who borrowed: **$92,327** . Proportion who borrowed: **87%**

ACADEMIC PROGRAMS

Calendar: **semester**
Joint degrees awarded: **N/A**
Typical first-year section size: Full-time: **95**
Is there typically a "small section" of the first year class,
other than Legal Writing, taught by full-time faculty?:
  Full-time: **no**
Number of course titles, beyond the first year curriculum, offered last year: **161**
Percentages of upper division course sections, excluding seminars, with an enrollment of:
  Under 25: **61%**   25 to 49: **20%**
  50 to 74: **10%**   75 to 99: **8%**
  100+: **1%**
Areas of specialization: appellate advocacy, clinical training, dispute resolution, environmental law, health care law, intellectual property law, international law, tax law, trial advocacy

Fall 2009 faculty profile
Total teaching faculty: **129**. Full-time: **51%**; **61%** men, **39%** women, **21%** minorities. Part-time: **49%**; **63%** men, **37%** women, **16%** minorities
Student-to-faculty ratio: **16.5**

SPECIAL PROGRAMS (as provided by law school):

Hastings' strengths include civil, criminal, and transactional clinical programs and cutting-edge research and advocacy centers. We offer formal study abroad programs in Argentina, Australia, China, Denmark, England, Germany, Hungary, Italy, and the Netherlands. We offer joint degrees and concentrations in civil litigation, family law, international law, tax, criminal law, public interest law.

STUDENT BODY
Fall 2009 full-time enrollment: 1,292
Men: **49%**   Women: **51%**
African-American: **2.60%**   American Indian: **0.90%**
Asian-American: **20.50%**   Mexican-American: **4.60%**
Puerto Rican: **0.30%**   Other Hisp-Amer: **3.30%**
White: **49.40%**   International: **1.80%**
Unknown: **16.60%**

Attrition rates for 2008-2009 full-time students
Percent of students discontinuing law school:
Men: **1%**   Women: **0%**

First-year students: **1%**   Second-year students: **0%**
Third-year students: **N/A**   Fourth-year students: **N/A**

LIBRARY RESOURCES

Total titles: **311,962**
Total volumes: **721,858**
Total seats available for library users: **796**

INFORMATION TECHNOLOGY

Number of wired network connections available to students: total (in the law library, excluding computer labs: **220**; in classrooms: **182**; in computer labs: **N/A**; elsewhere in the law school: **88**)
Law school has a wireless network.
Students are not required to own a computer.

EMPLOYMENT AND SALARIES

Proportion of 2008 graduates employed at graduation: **70%**
Employed 9 months later, as of February 15, 2009: **93%**
Salaries in the private sector (law firms, business, industry): **$85,000 –$160,000** (25th-75th percentile)
Median salary in the private sector: **$160,000**
Percentage in the private sector who reported salary information: **72%**
Median salary in public service (government, judicial clerkships, academic posts, non-profits): **$56**

Percentage of 2008 graduates in:
Law firms: **63%**   Government: **9%**
Bus./industry: **8%**   Judicial clerkship: **6%**
Public interest: **6%**   Unknown: **0%**
Academia : **8%**

2008 graduates employed in-state: **87%**
2008 graduates employed in foreign countries: **0%**
Number of states where graduates are employed: **19**
Percentage of 2008 graduates working in: New England: **0%**, Middle Atlantic: **2%**, East North Central: **1%**, West North Central: **0%**, South Atlantic: **2%**, East South Central: **0%**, West South Central: **1%**, Mountain: **3%**, Pacific: **89%**, Unknown: **2%**

BAR PASSAGE RATES

Based on 2008 graduates taking Summer 2008 or Winter 2009 exams. Most of the school's first-time test takers took the bar in California.

| 80% |

School's bar passage rate for first-time test takers

| 71% |

Statewide bar passage rate for first-time test takers

University of California–Berkeley

- Boalt Hall, Berkeley, CA, 94720-7200
- http://www.law.berkeley.edu
- Public
- Year founded: 1894
- 2009-2010 tuition: full-time: $35,907; part-time: N/A
- Enrollment 2009-10 academic year: full-time: 892
- U.S. News 2010 law specialty ranking: clinical training: 14, environmental law: 3, intellectual property law: 1, international law: 12

3.68-3.95 GPA, 25TH-75TH PERCENTILE

165-170 LSAT, 25TH-75TH PERCENTILE

10% ACCEPTANCE RATE

7 2011 U.S. NEWS LAW SCHOOL RANKING

ADMISSIONS

Admissions phone number: (510) 642-2274
Admissions email address: **admissions@law.berkeley.edu**
Application website:
 http://www.law.berkeley.edu/prospectives/admissions/
Application deadline for Fall 2011 admission: **1-Feb**

Admissions statistics:

Number of applicants for Fall 2009: **7,960**
Number of acceptances: **803**
Number enrolled: **292**
Acceptance rate: **10%**
GPA, 25th-75th percentile, entering class Fall 2009: **3.68-3.95**
LSAT, 25th-75th percentile, entering class Fall 2009: **165-170**

FINANCIAL AID

Financial aid phone number: (510) 642-1563
Financial aid application deadline:
Tuition 2009-2010 academic year: **full-time: $35,907; part-time: N/A**
Room and board: **$15,485** ; books: **$1,495** ; miscellaneous expenses: **$4,741**
Total of room/board/books/miscellaneous expenses: **$21,721**
University offers graduate student housing for which law students are eligible.

Financial aid profile

Percent of students that received grants for the 2008-2009 academic year: full-time: **46%**
Median grant amount: full-time: **$14,349**
The average law-school debt of those in the Class of 2009 who borrowed: **$90,164** . Proportion who borrowed: **88%**

ACADEMIC PROGRAMS

Calendar: **semester**
Joint degrees awarded: **J.D./Ph.D. Jurisprudence & Social Policy; J.D./M.P.P.; J.D./M.A. Asian Studies; J.D./M.A./Ph.D. Economics; J.D./M.B.A.; J.D./M.C.P.;**
J.D./M.J.; J.D./M.S.W.
Typical first-year section size: Full-time: **90**
Is there typically a "small section" of the first year class, other than Legal Writing, taught by full-time faculty?: Full-time: **yes**
Number of course titles, beyond the first year curriculum, offered last year: **252**
Percentages of upper division course sections, excluding seminars, with an enrollment of:

Under 25: **31%**	25 to 49: **42%**
50 to 74: **9%**	75 to 99: **2%**
100+: **16%**	

Areas of specialization: appellate advocacy, clinical training, dispute resolution, environmental law, health care law, intellectual property law, international law, tax law, trial advocacy

Fall 2009 faculty profile

Total teaching faculty: **116**. Full-time: **55%; 63%** men, **38%** women, **11%** minorities. Part-time: **45%; 73%** men, **27%** women, **6%** minorities
Student-to-faculty ratio: **11.4**

SPECIAL PROGRAMS (as provided by law school):

Boalt offers a wide array of special programs for J.D. students, including guaranteed funding for summer public interest fellowships, an array of employment opportunities at our cutting edge research centers, and our clinical education program. Our financial aid programs, including our Loan Repayment Assistance Program, are among the best in the nation.

STUDENT BODY

Fall 2009 full-time enrollment: 892

Men: **48%**	Women: **52%**
African-American: **4.80%**	American Indian: **1.70%**
Asian-American: **17.50%**	Mexican-American: **5.30%**
Puerto Rican: **0.00%**	Other Hisp-Amer: **5.40%**
White: **46.30%**	International: **0.00%**
Unknown: **19.10%**	

Attrition rates for 2008-2009 full-time students
Percent of students discontinuing law school:
Men: **1%**   Women: **1%**
First-year students: **3%**   Second-year students: **N/A**
Third-year students: **N/A**   Fourth-year students: **N/A**

LIBRARY RESOURCES
Total titles: **338,405**
Total volumes: **907,409**
Total seats available for library users: **307**

INFORMATION TECHNOLOGY
Number of wired network connections available to students: **213** total (in the law library, excluding computer labs: **32**; in classrooms: **0**; in computer labs: **6**; elsewhere in the law school: **175**)
Law school has a wireless network.
Students are not required to own a computer.

EMPLOYMENT AND SALARIES
Proportion of 2008 graduates employed at graduation: **97%**
Employed 9 months later, as of February 15, 2009: **99%**
Salaries in the private sector (law firms, business, industry): **$160,000 –$160,000** (25th-75th percentile)
Median salary in the private sector: **$160,000**
Percentage in the private sector who reported salary information: **94%**

Median salary in public service (government, judicial clerkships, academic posts, non-profits): **$51,000**

Percentage of 2008 graduates in:
Law firms: **72%**   Government: **5%**
Bus./industry: **4%**   Judicial clerkship: **9%**
Public interest: **10%**   Unknown: **0%**
Academia : **0%**

2008 graduates employed in-state: **69%**
2008 graduates employed in foreign countries: **2%**
Number of states where graduates are employed: **23**
Percentage of 2008 graduates working in: New England: **3%**, Middle Atlantic: **11%**, East North Central: **3%**, West North Central: **0%**, South Atlantic: **7%**, East South Central: **0%**, West South Central: **1%**, Mountain: **2%**, Pacific: **72%**, Unknown: **0%**

BAR PASSAGE RATES
Based on 2008 graduates taking Summer 2008 or Winter 2009 exams. Most of the school's first-time test takers took the bar in California.

88%

School's bar passage rate for first-time test takers

71%

Statewide bar passage rate for first-time test takers

University of California–Davis

- 400 Mrak Hall Drive, Davis, CA, 95616-5201
- http://www.law.ucdavis.edu
- Public
- Year founded: 1965
- 2009-2010 tuition: full-time: $33,949; part-time: N/A
- Enrollment 2009-10 academic year: full-time: 606
- U.S. News 2010 law specialty ranking: N/A

3.23-3.72 GPA, 25TH-75TH PERCENTILE

160-165 LSAT, 25TH-75TH PERCENTILE

32% ACCEPTANCE RATE

28 2011 U.S. NEWS LAW SCHOOL RANKING

ADMISSIONS

Admissions phone number: **(530) 752-6477**
Admissions email address: **admissions@law.ucdavis.edu**
Application website:
  https://www4.lsac.org/lsacd_on_the_web/login/openfirst.aspx?ID=KE934834A1489MO
Application deadline for Fall 2011 admission: **1-Feb**

Admissions statistics:
Number of applicants for Fall 2009: **3,189**
Number of acceptances: **1,026**
Number enrolled: **213**
Acceptance rate: **32%**
GPA, 25th-75th percentile, entering class Fall 2009: **3.23-3.72**
LSAT, 25th-75th percentile, entering class Fall 2009: **160-165**

FINANCIAL AID

Financial aid phone number: **(530) 752-6573**
Financial aid application deadline: **2-Mar**
Tuition 2009-2010 academic year: **full-time: $33,949; part-time: N/A**
Room and board: **$11,584** ; books: **$1,014** ; miscellaneous expenses: **$3,734**
Total of room/board/books/miscellaneous expenses: **$16,332**
University offers graduate student housing for which law students are eligible.

Financial aid profile
Percent of students that received grants for the 2008-2009 academic year: full-time: **60%**
Median grant amount: full-time: **$11,991**
The average law-school debt of those in the Class of 2009 who borrowed: **$72,959** . Proportion who borrowed: **72%**

ACADEMIC PROGRAMS

Calendar: **semester**
Joint degrees awarded: **J.D./M.B.A.; J.D./M.S.; J.D./M.A.; J.D./M.C.P.**

Typical first-year section size: Full-time: **72**
Is there typically a "small section" of the first year class, other than Legal Writing, taught by full-time faculty?: Full-time: **yes**
Number of course titles, beyond the first year curriculum, offered last year: **75**
Percentages of upper division course sections, excluding seminars, with an enrollment of:
  Under 25: **52%**   25 to 49: **25%**
  50 to 74: **8%**   75 to 99: **11%**
  100+: **4%**
Areas of specialization: appellate advocacy, clinical training, dispute resolution, environmental law, health care law, intellectual property law, international law, tax law, trial advocacy

Fall 2009 faculty profile
Total teaching faculty: **61**. Full-time: **77%**; **55%** men, **45%** women, **36%** minorities. Part-time: **23%**; **50%** men, **50%** women, **43%** minorities
Student-to-faculty ratio: **11.6**

SPECIAL PROGRAMS *(as provided by law school):*

Nationally renowned faculty; talented, diverse students; 70 student 1L sections, 30-35 student small sections; immigration, civil rights, prison and family law clinics; externships: employment, tax, criminal, govt., judicial; Litigation and nonlitigation skills courses; Public Service Law program, certificate, externship; Environmental Law certificate, externship. See http://www.law.ucdavis.edu

STUDENT BODY

Fall 2009 full-time enrollment: 606
Men: **47%**   Women: **53%**
African-American: **1.70%**   American Indian: **0.30%**
Asian-American: **26.70%**   Mexican-American: **5.10%**
Puerto Rican: **0.20%**   Other Hisp-Amer: **1.80%**
White: **48.00%**   International: **1.70%**
Unknown: **14.50%**

Attrition rates for 2008-2009 full-time students
Percent of students discontinuing law school:
Men: 3%   Women: 4%
First-year students: 8%   Second-year students: 1%
Third-year students: 2%   Fourth-year students: N/A

LIBRARY RESOURCES

Total titles: 108,445
Total volumes: 457,868
Total seats available for library users: 311

INFORMATION TECHNOLOGY

Number of wired network connections available to students: 0 total (in the law library, excluding computer labs: 0; in classrooms: 0; in computer labs: 0; elsewhere in the law school: 0)
Law school has a wireless network.
Students are not required to own a computer.

EMPLOYMENT AND SALARIES

Proportion of 2008 graduates employed at graduation: 97%
Employed 9 months later, as of February 15, 2009: 98%
Salaries in the private sector (law firms, business, industry): $85,000 –$160,000 (25th-75th percentile)
Median salary in the private sector: $152,500
Percentage in the private sector who reported salary information: 52%

Median salary in public service (government, judicial clerkships, academic posts, non-profits): $54,494

Percentage of 2008 graduates in:
Law firms: 53%   Government: 11%
Bus./industry: 7%   Judicial clerkship: 7%
Public interest: 12%   Unknown: 7%
Academia : 3%

2008 graduates employed in-state: 87%
2008 graduates employed in foreign countries: 0%
Number of states where graduates are employed: 12
Percentage of 2008 graduates working in: New England: 1%, Middle Atlantic: 0%, East North Central: 1%, West North Central: 0%, South Atlantic: 3%, East South Central: 0%, West South Central: 1%, Mountain: 3%, Pacific: 89%, Unknown: 2%

BAR PASSAGE RATES

Based on 2008 graduates taking Summer 2008 or Winter 2009 exams. Most of the school's first-time test takers took the bar in California.

80%
School's bar passage rate for first-time test takers

71%
Statewide bar passage rate for first-time test takers

University of California–Los Angeles

- 71 Dodd Hall, PO Box 951445, Los Angeles, CA, 90095-1445
- http://www.law.ucla.edu
- Public
- Year founded: 1949
- 2009-2010 tuition: full-time: $35,327; part-time: N/A
- Enrollment 2009-10 academic year: full-time: 1,011
- U.S. News 2010 law specialty ranking: environmental law: 16, intellectual property law: 16, tax law: 11

3.57-3.88	GPA, 25TH-75TH PERCENTILE
164-169	LSAT, 25TH-75TH PERCENTILE
17%	ACCEPTANCE RATE
15	2011 U.S. NEWS LAW SCHOOL RANKING

ADMISSIONS

Admissions phone number: (310) 825-2260
Admissions email address: admissions@law.ucla.edu
Application website:
  http://www1.law.ucla.edu/~admissions/
Application deadline for Fall 2011 admission: 1-Feb

Admissions statistics:

Number of applicants for Fall 2009: 8,225
Number of acceptances: 1,383
Number enrolled: 320
Acceptance rate: 17%
GPA, 25th-75th percentile, entering class Fall 2009: 3.57-3.88
LSAT, 25th-75th percentile, entering class Fall 2009: 164-169

FINANCIAL AID

Financial aid phone number: (310) 825-2459
Financial aid application deadline: 2-Mar
Tuition 2009-2010 academic year: **full-time: $35,327; part-time: N/A**
Room and board: $13,968 ; books: $1,941 ; miscellaneous expenses: $5,160
Total of room/board/books/miscellaneous expenses: $21,069
University offers graduate student housing for which law students are eligible.

Financial aid profile

Percent of students that received grants for the 2008-2009 academic year: full-time: 61%
Median grant amount: full-time: $9,557
The average law-school debt of those in the Class of 2009 who borrowed: $97,140 . Proportion who borrowed: 80%

ACADEMIC PROGRAMS

Calendar: semester
Joint degrees awarded: J.D./M.B.A.; J.D./M.A. Urban Planning; J.D./M.A. American Indian Studies; J.D./M.S.W.; J.D./M.P.P.; J.D./M.A. African American Studies; J.D./M.P.H.

Typical first-year section size: Full-time: 80
Is there typically a "small section" of the first year class, other than Legal Writing, taught by full-time faculty?: Full-time: **yes**
Number of course titles, beyond the first year curriculum, offered last year: **188**
Percentages of upper division course sections, excluding seminars, with an enrollment of:

Under 25: **49%**   25 to 49: **26%**
50 to 74: **11%**   75 to 99: **8%**
100+: **6%**

Areas of specialization: appellate advocacy, clinical training, dispute resolution, environmental law, health care law, intellectual property law, international law, tax law, trial advocacy

Fall 2009 faculty profile

Total teaching faculty: **90**. Full-time: **79%**; **69%** men, **31%** women, **14%** minorities. Part-time: **21%**; **84%** men, **16%** women, **5%** minorities
Student-to-faculty ratio: **11.3**

SPECIAL PROGRAMS (as provided by law school):

Students participate in supervised educational experiences in our clinical program; choose academic specializations in business, critical race studies, entertainment, law and philosophy, and public interest; participate in academic centers in human rights, real estate, environmental/climate law, law and econ, public policy, international law, Indian law, sexual orientation law; pursue foreign legal study

STUDENT BODY

Fall 2009 full-time enrollment: 1,011

Men: **52%**	Women: **48%**
African-American: **4.50%**	American Indian: **1.20%**
Asian-American: **18.00%**	Mexican-American: **5.60%**
Puerto Rican: **0.20%**	Other Hisp-Amer: **3.00%**
White: **43.30%**	International: **2.00%**
Unknown: **22.20%**	

Attrition rates for 2008-2009 full-time students
Percent of students discontinuing law school:
Men: 2%   Women: 2%
First-year students: 5%   Second-year students: 1%
Third-year students: 1%   Fourth-year students: N/A

LIBRARY RESOURCES
Total titles: 273,029
Total volumes: 669,881
Total seats available for library users: 774

INFORMATION TECHNOLOGY
Number of wired network connections available to students: 1820 total (in the law library, excluding computer labs: 450; in classrooms: 1,200; in computer labs: 48; elsewhere in the law school: 122)
Law school has a wireless network.
Students are not required to own a computer.

EMPLOYMENT AND SALARIES
Proportion of 2008 graduates employed at graduation: 97%
Employed 9 months later, as of February 15, 2009: 99%
Salaries in the private sector (law firms, business, industry): $145,000 –$160,000 (25th-75th percentile)
Median salary in the private sector: $160,000
Percentage in the private sector who reported salary information: 71%

Median salary in public service (government, judicial clerkships, academic posts, non-profits): $59,800

Percentage of 2008 graduates in:
Law firms: 64%   Government: 8%
Bus./industry: 7%   Judicial clerkship: 11%
Public interest: 9%   Unknown: 1%
Academia : 2%

2008 graduates employed in-state: 87%
2008 graduates employed in foreign countries: 0%
Number of states where graduates are employed: 16
Percentage of 2008 graduates working in: New England: 0%, Middle Atlantic: 4%, East North Central: 2%, West North Central: 0%, South Atlantic: 3%, East South Central: 0%, West South Central: 0%, Mountain: 1%, Pacific: 90%, Unknown: 0%

BAR PASSAGE RATES
Based on 2008 graduates taking Summer 2008 or Winter 2009 exams. Most of the school's first-time test takers took the bar in California.

89%

School's bar passage rate for first-time test takers

71%

Statewide bar passage rate for first-time test takers

University of Chicago

- 1111 E. 6oth Street, Chicago, IL, 60637
- http://www.law.uchicago.edu
- Private
- Year founded: 1902
- 2009-2010 tuition: full-time: $44,757; part-time: N/A
- Enrollment 2009-10 academic year: full-time: 590
- U.S. News 2010 law specialty ranking: clinical training: 18, tax law: 21

3.63-3.84 GPA, 25TH-75TH PERCENTILE

169-173 LSAT, 25TH-75TH PERCENTILE

18% ACCEPTANCE RATE

5 2011 U.S. NEWS LAW SCHOOL RANKING

ADMISSIONS

Admissions phone number: **(773) 702-9484**
Admissions email address: **admissions@law.uchicago.edu**
Application website: **https://grad-application.uchicago.edu/intro/law/intro1.cfm**
Application deadline for Fall 2011 admission: **1-Feb**

Admissions statistics:

Number of applicants for Fall 2009: **5,403**
Number of acceptances: **982**
Number enrolled: **191**
Acceptance rate: **18%**
GPA, 25th-75th percentile, entering class Fall 2009: **3.63-3.84**
LSAT, 25th-75th percentile, entering class Fall 2009: **169-173**

FINANCIAL AID

Financial aid phone number: **(773) 702-9484**
Financial aid application deadline:
Tuition 2009-2010 academic year: **full-time: $44,757; part-time: N/A**
Room and board: **$13,455** ; books: **$1,650** ; miscellaneous expenses: **$7,194**
Total of room/board/books/miscellaneous expenses: **$22,299**
University offers graduate student housing for which law students are eligible.

Financial aid profile

Percent of students that received grants for the 2008-2009 academic year: full-time: **56%**
Median grant amount: full-time: **$10,800**
The average law-school debt of those in the Class of 2009 who borrowed: **$123,904** . Proportion who borrowed: **88%**

ACADEMIC PROGRAMS

Calendar: **quarter**
Joint degrees awarded: **J.D./M.B.A.; J.D./M.P.P.; J.D./A.M. International Relations; J.D./Ph.D.**

Typical first-year section size: Full-time: **93**
Is there typically a "small section" of the first year class, other than Legal Writing, taught by full-time faculty?: Full-time: **no**
Number of course titles, beyond the first year curriculum, offered last year: **193**
Percentages of upper division course sections, excluding seminars, with an enrollment of:

Under 25: **41%**   25 to 49: **36%**
50 to 74: **12%**   75 to 99: **8%**
100+: **3%**

Areas of specialization: appellate advocacy, clinical training, dispute resolution, environmental law, health care law, intellectual property law, international law, tax law, trial advocacy

Fall 2009 faculty profile

Total teaching faculty: **83**. Full-time: **63%**; **67%** men, **33%** women, **13%** minorities. Part-time: **37%**; **77%** men, **23%** women, **6%** minorities
Student-to-faculty ratio: **9.5**

SPECIAL PROGRAMS (as provided by law school):

The Chicago Policy Initiatives encourage faculty and students to explore social problems and propose solutions. Most recent initiatives include a published protocol for foster care and the creation of a wiki on climate change. Centers include Comparative Constitutionalism and the Olin Program in Law and Economics. The Mandel Legal Aid Clinic provides assistance to people in Chicago.

STUDENT BODY

Fall 2009 full-time enrollment: 590

Men: **55%**   Women: **45%**
African-American: **6.30%**   American Indian: **0.30%**
Asian-American: **11.50%**   Mexican-American: **3.60%**
Puerto Rican: **1.00%**   Other Hisp-Amer: **5.60%**
White: **58.60%**   International: **2.40%**
Unknown: **10.70%**

Attrition rates for 2008-2009 full-time students
Percent of students discontinuing law school:
Men: **2%**   Women: **2%**
First-year students: **1%**   Second-year students: **4%**
Third-year students: **1%**   Fourth-year students: **N/A**

LIBRARY RESOURCES

Total titles: **316,019**
Total volumes: **656,779**
Total seats available for library users: **483**

INFORMATION TECHNOLOGY

Number of wired network connections available to students: **1115** total (in the law library, excluding computer labs: **307**; in classrooms: **800**; in computer labs: **0**; elsewhere in the law school: **8**)
Law school has a wireless network.
Students are required to own a computer.

EMPLOYMENT AND SALARIES

Proportion of 2008 graduates employed at graduation: **97%**
Employed 9 months later, as of February 15, 2009: **99%**
Salaries in the private sector (law firms, business, industry): **$160,000 –$160,000** (25th-75th percentile)
Median salary in the private sector: **$160,000**
Percentage in the private sector who reported salary information: **99%**

Median salary in public service (government, judicial clerkships, academic posts, non-profits): **$50,000**

Percentage of 2008 graduates in:
Law firms: **82%**   Government: **2%**
Bus./industry: **3%**   Judicial clerkship: **13%**
Public interest: **1%**   Unknown: **0%**
Academia : **0%**

2008 graduates employed in-state: **35%**
2008 graduates employed in foreign countries: **1%**
Number of states where graduates are employed: **22**
Percentage of 2008 graduates working in: New England: **1%**, Middle Atlantic: **19%**, East North Central: **36%**, West North Central: **3%**, South Atlantic: **11%**, East South Central: **2%**, West South Central: **6%**, Mountain: **3%**, Pacific: **19%**, Unknown: **0%**

BAR PASSAGE RATES

Based on 2008 graduates taking Summer 2008 or Winter 2009 exams. Most of the school's first-time test takers took the bar in Illinois.

95%
School's bar passage rate for first-time test takers

91%
Statewide bar passage rate for first-time test takers

University of Cincinnati

- PO Box 210040, Cincinnati, OH, 45221-0040
- http://www.law.uc.edu
- Public
- Year founded: 1833
- 2009-2010 tuition: full-time: $19,942; part-time: N/A
- Enrollment 2009-10 academic year: full-time: 391
- U.S. News 2010 law specialty ranking: N/A

3.29-3.79 GPA, 25TH-75TH PERCENTILE

156-161 LSAT, 25TH-75TH PERCENTILE

50% ACCEPTANCE RATE

56 2011 U.S. NEWS LAW SCHOOL RANKING

ADMISSIONS

Admissions phone number: **(513) 556-6805**
Admissions email address: **admissions@law.uc.edu**
Application website: **http://www.law.uc.edu/admissions**
Application deadline for Fall 2011 admission: **1-Mar**

Admissions statistics:

Number of applicants for Fall 2009: **1,322**
Number of acceptances: **666**
Number enrolled: **138**
Acceptance rate: **50%**
GPA, 25th-75th percentile, entering class Fall 2009: **3.29-3.79**
LSAT, 25th-75th percentile, entering class Fall 2009: **156-161**

FINANCIAL AID

Financial aid phone number: **(513) 556-0078**
Financial aid application deadline: **1-Mar**
Tuition 2009-2010 academic year: **full-time: $19,942; part-time: N/A**
Room and board: **$10,596** ; books: **$1,275** ; miscellaneous expenses: **$4,575**
Total of room/board/books/miscellaneous expenses: **$16,446**
University offers graduate student housing for which law students are eligible.

Financial aid profile

Percent of students that received grants for the 2008-2009 academic year: full-time: **66%**
Median grant amount: full-time: **$7,000**
The average law-school debt of those in the Class of 2009 who borrowed: **$58,376** . Proportion who borrowed: **86%**

ACADEMIC PROGRAMS

Calendar: **semester**
Joint degrees awarded: **J.D./M.B.A.; J.D./M.C.P.; J.D./M.A. Women's Studies; J.D./M.S. Political Science; J.D./Ph.D Political Science; J.D./M.S. Economics; J.D./M.S.W.**
Typical first-year section size: Full-time: **54**

Is there typically a "small section" of the first year class, other than Legal Writing, taught by full-time faculty?: Full-time: **yes**
Number of course titles, beyond the first year curriculum, offered last year: **103**
Percentages of upper division course sections, excluding seminars, with an enrollment of:
Under 25: **57%**   25 to 49: **29%**
50 to 74: **12%**   75 to 99: **1%**
100+: **1%**
Areas of specialization: appellate advocacy, clinical training, dispute resolution, environmental law, health care law, intellectual property law, international law, tax law, trial advocacy

Fall 2009 faculty profile

Total teaching faculty: **65**. Full-time: **48%**; **48%** men, **52%** women, **16%** minorities. Part-time: **52%**; **71%** men, **29%** women, **6%** minorities
Student-to-faculty ratio: **9.9**

SPECIAL PROGRAMS *(as provided by law school)*:

Institutes/Centers: Center for Corporate Law, Center for Practice, Glenn M. Weaver Institute of Law and Psychiatry, Lois & Richard Rosenthal Institute for Justice/Ohio Innocence Project, Urban Morgan Institute for Human Rights. Clinics: Sixth Circuit Appellate Practice Clinic, Domestic Relations & Civil Protection Order. Joint degrees: MBA, MCP, MSW, Women's Studies & Political Science.

STUDENT BODY

Fall 2009 full-time enrollment: 391

Men: **58%**	Women: **42%**
African-American: **5.90%**	American Indian: **0.30%**
Asian-American: **7.70%**	Mexican-American: **0.00%**
Puerto Rican: **0.00%**	Other Hisp-Amer: **2.30%**
White: **83.90%**	International: **0.00%**
Unknown: **0.00%**	

Attrition rates for 2008-2009 full-time students

Percent of students discontinuing law school:

Men: **4%** Women: **3%**
First-year students: **10%** Second-year students: **1%**
Third-year students: **N/A** Fourth-year students: **N/A**

LIBRARY RESOURCES
Total titles: **237,352**
Total volumes: **437,356**
Total seats available for library users: **336**

INFORMATION TECHNOLOGY
Number of wired network connections available to students: **6** total (in the law library, excluding computer labs: **6**; in classrooms: **0**; in computer labs: **0**; elsewhere in the law school: **0**)
Law school has a wireless network.
Students are not required to own a computer.

EMPLOYMENT AND SALARIES
Proportion of 2008 graduates employed at graduation: **74%**
Employed 9 months later, as of February 15, 2009: **96%**
Salaries in the private sector (law firms, business, industry): **$56,250 –$115,000** (25th-75th percentile)
Median salary in the private sector: **$80,000**
Percentage in the private sector who reported salary information: **51%**

Median salary in public service (government, judicial clerkships, academic posts, non-profits): **$47,436**

Percentage of 2008 graduates in:
Law firms: **50%** Government: **12%**
Bus./industry: **13%** Judicial clerkship: **6%**
Public interest: **13%** Unknown: **1%**
Academia : **5%**

2008 graduates employed in-state: **68%**
2008 graduates employed in foreign countries: **0%**
Number of states where graduates are employed: **17**
Percentage of 2008 graduates working in: New England: **0%**, Middle Atlantic: **5%**, East North Central: **74%**, West North Central: **0%**, South Atlantic: **8%**, East South Central: **4%**, West South Central: **0%**, Mountain: **6%**, Pacific: **1%**, Unknown: **3%**

BAR PASSAGE RATES
Based on 2008 graduates taking Summer 2008 or Winter 2009 exams. Most of the school's first-time test takers took the bar in Ohio.

| 82% |
School's bar passage rate for first-time test takers

| 88% |
Statewide bar passage rate for first-time test takers

University of Colorado–Boulder

■ Box 401, Boulder, CO, 80309-0401
■ http://www.colorado.edu/law/
■ Public
■ Year founded: 1892
■ 2009-2010 tuition: full-time: $25,399; part-time: N/A
■ Enrollment 2009-10 academic year: full-time: 547
■ U.S. News 2010 law specialty ranking: environmental law: 6

3.42-3.78 GPA, 25ᵀᴴ-75ᵀᴴ PERCENTILE

160-165 LSAT, 25ᵀᴴ-75ᵀᴴ PERCENTILE

23% ACCEPTANCE RATE

38 2011 U.S. NEWS LAW SCHOOL RANKING

ADMISSIONS

Admissions phone number: **(303) 492-7203**
Admissions email address: **lawadmin@colorado.edu**
Application website:
   http://www.colorado.edu/law/admissions/catalog/2009J DApplication.pdf
Application deadline for Fall 2011 admission: **15-Mar**

Admissions statistics:

Number of applicants for Fall 2009: **3,059**
Number of acceptances: **709**
Number enrolled: **166**
Acceptance rate: **23%**
GPA, 25th-75th percentile, entering class Fall 2009: **3.42-3.78**
LSAT, 25th-75th percentile, entering class Fall 2009: **160-165**

FINANCIAL AID

Financial aid phone number: **(303) 492-8223**
Financial aid application deadline: **1-Apr**
Tuition 2009-2010 academic year: **full-time: $25,399; part-time: N/A**
Room and board: **$8,478** ; books: **$1,749** ; miscellaneous expenses: **$5,570**
Total of room/board/books/miscellaneous expenses: **$15,797**
University offers graduate student housing for which law students are eligible.

Financial aid profile

Percent of students that received grants for the 2008-2009 academic year: full-time: **66%**
Median grant amount: full-time: **$9,838**
The average law-school debt of those in the Class of 2009 who borrowed: **$74,916** . Proportion who borrowed: **84%**

ACADEMIC PROGRAMS

Calendar: **semester**
Joint degrees awarded: **J.D./M.B.A; J.D./M.P.A.; J.D./M.A. International Affairs; J.D./M.S. Environmental Studies;** J.D./M.D.; J.D./M.URP.; J.D./Ph.D. Environmental Studies; J.D./M.S.T.
Typical first-year section size: Full-time: **84**
Is there typically a "small section" of the first year class, other than Legal Writing, taught by full-time faculty?: Full-time: **yes**
Number of course titles, beyond the first year curriculum, offered last year: **105**
Percentages of upper division course sections, excluding seminars, with an enrollment of:

Under 25: **63%**   25 to 49: **23%**
50 to 74: **10%**   75 to 99: **5%**
100+: **0%**

Areas of specialization: appellate advocacy, clinical training, dispute resolution, environmental law, health care law, intellectual property law, international law, tax law, trial advocacy

Fall 2009 faculty profile

Total teaching faculty: **62**. Full-time: **66%**; **59%** men, **41%** women, **22%** minorities. Part-time: **34%**; **81%** men, **19%** women, **5%** minorities
Student-to-faculty ratio: **11.5**

SPECIAL PROGRAMS *(as provided by law school):*

Colorado Law offers 8 dual degrees, 4 certificates, 4 research centers, and a formal Experiential Learning Program that includes 9 clinics, externship and public service programs, and appellate and trial coaching and competitions. Areas of academic excellence include environmental, natural resources, energy, technology, entrepreneurial, American Indian, and juvenile and family law.

STUDENT BODY

Fall 2009 full-time enrollment: 547

Men: **50%**   Women: **50%**
African-American: **2.70%**   American Indian: **3.10%**
Asian-American: **7.10%**   Mexican-American: **1.80%**
Puerto Rican: **0.90%**   Other Hisp-Amer: **4.60%**
White: **79.20%**   International: **0.50%**
Unknown: **0.00%**

Attrition rates for 2008-2009 full-time students
Percent of students discontinuing law school:

Men: **0%** — Women: **N/A**
First-year students: **N/A** — Second-year students: **1%**
Third-year students: **N/A** — Fourth-year students: **N/A**

LIBRARY RESOURCES

Total titles: **217,637**
Total volumes: **741,484**
Total seats available for library users: **444**

INFORMATION TECHNOLOGY

Number of wired network connections available to students: **81** total (in the law library, excluding computer labs: **0**; in classrooms: **16**; in computer labs: **54**; elsewhere in the law school: **11**)
Law school has a wireless network.
Students are not required to own a computer.

EMPLOYMENT AND SALARIES

Proportion of 2008 graduates employed at graduation: **80%**
Employed 9 months later, as of February 15, 2009: **96%**
Salaries in the private sector (law firms, business, industry): **$60,000 –$120,000** (25th-75th percentile)
Median salary in the private sector: **$82,500**
Percentage in the private sector who reported salary information: **81%**

Median salary in public service (government, judicial clerkships, academic posts, non-profits): **$47,000**

Percentage of 2008 graduates in:

Law firms: **43%** — Government: **14%**
Bus./industry: **6%** — Judicial clerkship: **25%**
Public interest: **7%** — Unknown: **1%**
Academia : **4%**

2008 graduates employed in-state: **80%**
2008 graduates employed in foreign countries: **2%**
Number of states where graduates are employed: **8**
Percentage of 2008 graduates working in: New England: **1%**, Middle Atlantic: **2%**, East North Central: **1%**, West North Central: **1%**, South Atlantic: **3%**, East South Central: **1%**, West South Central: **1%**, Mountain: **80%**, Pacific: **5%**, Unknown: **2%**

BAR PASSAGE RATES

Based on 2008 graduates taking Summer 2008 or Winter 2009 exams. Most of the school's first-time test takers took the bar in Colorado.

93%
School's bar passage rate for first-time test takers

83%
Statewide bar passage rate for first-time test takers

University of Connecticut

- 55 Elizabeth Street, Hartford, CT, 06105-2296
- http://www.law.uconn.edu
- Public
- **Year founded:** 1921
- **2009-2010 tuition:** full-time: $20,374; part-time: $14,246
- **Enrollment 2009-10 academic year:** full-time: 450; part-time: 191
- **U.S. News 2010 law specialty ranking:** N/A

3.22-3.59	GPA, 25TH-75TH PERCENTILE
160-163	LSAT, 25TH-75TH PERCENTILE
26%	ACCEPTANCE RATE
54	2011 U.S. NEWS LAW SCHOOL RANKING

ADMISSIONS

Admissions phone number: **(860) 570-5100**
Admissions email address: **admit@law.uconn.edu**
Application website:
   http://os.lsac.org/Release/Logon/Access.aspx
Application deadline for Fall 2011 admission: **1-Mar**

Admissions statistics:

Number of applicants for Fall 2009: **2,268**
Number of acceptances: **582**
Number enrolled: **120**
Acceptance rate: **26%**
GPA, 25th-75th percentile, entering class Fall 2009: **3.22-3.59**
LSAT, 25th-75th percentile, entering class Fall 2009: **160-163**

Part-time program:

Number of applicants for Fall 2009: **992**
Number of acceptances: **255**
Number enrolled: **62**
Acceptance rate: **26%**
GPA, 25th-75th percentile, entering class Fall 2009: **3.06-3.59**
LSAT, 25th-75th percentile, entering class Fall 2009: **156-160**

FINANCIAL AID

Financial aid phone number: **(860) 570-5147**
Financial aid application deadline: **1-Mar**
Tuition 2009-2010 academic year: **full-time: $20,374; part-time: $14,246**
Room and board: **$11,800** ; books: **$1,200** ; miscellaneous expenses: **$4,300**
Total of room/board/books/miscellaneous expenses: **$17,300**
University does not offer graduate student housing for which law students are eligible.

Financial aid profile

Percent of students that received grants for the 2008-2009 academic year: full-time: **74%**; part-time **24%**
Median grant amount: full-time: **$10,000** ; part-time: **$5,000**
The average law-school debt of those in the Class of 2009 who borrowed: **$65,224** . Proportion who borrowed: **81%**

ACADEMIC PROGRAMS

Calendar: **semester**
Joint degrees awarded: **J.D./M.S.W.; J.D./M.B.A.; J.D./M.P.A.; J.D./M.P.H.; J.D./LL.M Insurance Law; J.D./M.L.S.**
Typical first-year section size: Full-time: **62**; Part-time: **69**
Is there typically a "small section" of the first year class, other than Legal Writing, taught by full-time faculty?: Full-time: **yes**; Part-time: **yes**
Number of course titles, beyond the first year curriculum, offered last year: **147**
Percentages of upper division course sections, excluding seminars, with an enrollment of:

Under 25: **68%**	25 to 49: **20%**
50 to 74: **11%**	75 to 99: **0%**
100+: **0%**	

Areas of specialization: appellate advocacy, clinical training, dispute resolution, environmental law, health care law, intellectual property law, international law, tax law, trial advocacy

Fall 2009 faculty profile

Total teaching faculty: **88**. Full-time: **50%; 66%** men, **34%** women, **16%** minorities. Part-time: **50%; 82%** men, **18%** women, **9%** minorities
Student-to-faculty ratio: **11.4**

SPECIAL PROGRAMS (as provided by law school):

In-house clinics represent low-income taxpayers, political asylum seekers, entrepreneurs, and criminal defendants. Other clinics focus on mediation, children's advocacy, urban revitalization, environmental law, women's rights, GLBTQ rights, and criminal prosecution. Certificate programs in tax, IP, law and public policy, and human rights, plus foreign study and dual degree programs, are available.

STUDENT BODY

Fall 2009 full-time enrollment: 450

Men: 53%	Women: 47%
African-American: 6.00%	American Indian: 0.40%
Asian-American: 8.70%	Mexican-American: 0.40%
Puerto Rican: 0.70%	Other Hisp-Amer: 4.00%
White: 69.60%	International: 1.30%
Unknown: 8.90%	

Fall 2009 part-time enrollment: 191

Men: 59%	Women: 41%
African-American: 5.20%	American Indian: 1.00%
Asian-American: 6.30%	Mexican-American: 0.50%
Puerto Rican: 1.60%	Other Hisp-Amer: 6.80%
White: 69.10%	International: 1.00%
Unknown: 8.40%	

Attrition rates for 2008-2009 full-time students
Percent of students discontinuing law school:

Men: N/A	Women: N/A
First-year students: N/A	Second-year students: N/A
Third-year students: N/A	Fourth-year students: N/A

LIBRARY RESOURCES

Total titles: 207,022
Total volumes: 562,885
Total seats available for library users: 810

INFORMATION TECHNOLOGY

Number of wired network connections available to students: 778 total (in the law library, excluding computer labs: 388; in classrooms: 370; in computer labs: 0; elsewhere in the law school: 20)
Law school has a wireless network.
Students are not required to own a computer.

EMPLOYMENT AND SALARIES

Proportion of 2008 graduates employed at graduation: 72%
Employed 9 months later, as of February 15, 2009: 94%
Salaries in the private sector (law firms, business, industry): $95,000 –$160,000 (25th-75th percentile)
Median salary in the private sector: $120,000
Percentage in the private sector who reported salary information: 64%
Median salary in public service (government, judicial clerkships, academic posts, non-profits): $52,125

Percentage of 2008 graduates in:

Law firms: 58%	Government: 10%
Bus./industry: 14%	Judicial clerkship: 13%
Public interest: 2%	Unknown: 0%
Academia : 2%	

2008 graduates employed in-state: 66%
2008 graduates employed in foreign countries: 1%
Number of states where graduates are employed: 14
Percentage of 2008 graduates working in: New England: 78%, Middle Atlantic: 15%, East North Central: 2%, West North Central: 0%, South Atlantic: 3%, East South Central: 0%, West South Central: 1%, Mountain: 0%, Pacific: 1%, Unknown: 0%

BAR PASSAGE RATES

Based on 2008 graduates taking Summer 2008 or Winter 2009 exams. Most of the school's first-time test takers took the bar in Connecticut.

92%
School's bar passage rate for first-time test takers

87%
Statewide bar passage rate for first-time test takers

University of Dayton

- 300 College Park, Dayton, OH, 45469-2772
- http://law.udayton.edu
- Private
- Year founded: 1974
- 2009-2010 tuition: full-time: $32,684; part-time: N/A
- Enrollment 2009-10 academic year: full-time: 500
- U.S. News 2010 law specialty ranking: N/A

2.87-3.40 GPA, 25TH-75TH PERCENTILE

148-153 LSAT, 25TH-75TH PERCENTILE

58% ACCEPTANCE RATE

Tier 4 2011 U.S. NEWS LAW SCHOOL RANKING

ADMISSIONS
Admissions phone number: **(937) 229-3555**
Admissions email address: **lawinfo@notes.udayton.edu**
Application website:
    http://www4.lsac.org/LSACD_Forms/1834/2010_1834A3
    /2010_1834A3.PDF
Application deadline for Fall 2011 admission: **1-May**

Admissions statistics:
Number of applicants for Fall 2009: **2,097**
Number of acceptances: **1,214**
Number enrolled: **202**
Acceptance rate: **58%**
GPA, 25th-75th percentile, entering class Fall 2009: **2.87-3.40**
LSAT, 25th-75th percentile, entering class Fall 2009: **148-153**

FINANCIAL AID
Financial aid phone number: **(937) 229-3555**
Financial aid application deadline: **1-May**
Tuition 2009-2010 academic year: **full-time: $32,684; part-time: N/A**
Room and board: **$13,000** ; books: **$1,500** ; miscellaneous expenses: **$0**
Total of room/board/books/miscellaneous expenses: **$14,500**
University offers graduate student housing for which law students are eligible.

Financial aid profile
Percent of students that received grants for the 2008-2009 academic year: full-time: **45%**
Median grant amount: full-time: **$10,000**
The average law-school debt of those in the Class of 2009 who borrowed: **$71,525** . Proportion who borrowed: **91%**

ACADEMIC PROGRAMS
Calendar: **semester**
Joint degrees awarded: **J.D./M.B.A.; J.D./M.S. Education**
Typical first-year section size: Full-time: **90**

Is there typically a "small section" of the first year class, other than Legal Writing, taught by full-time faculty?: Full-time: **no**
Number of course titles, beyond the first year curriculum, offered last year: **70**
Percentages of upper division course sections, excluding seminars, with an enrollment of:
    Under 25: **58%**   25 to 49: **20%**
    50 to 74: **14%**   75 to 99: **6%**
    100+: **1%**
Areas of specialization: appellate advocacy, clinical training, dispute resolution, environmental law, health care law, intellectual property law, international law, tax law, trial advocacy

Fall 2009 faculty profile
Total teaching faculty: **56.** Full-time: **45%**; **56%** men, **44%** women, **16%** minorities. Part-time: **55%**; **71%** men, **29%** women, **3%** minorities
Student-to-faculty ratio: **16.7**

SPECIAL PROGRAMS *(as provided by law school)*:
Clinic, Summer Study, Externships.

STUDENT BODY
Fall 2009 full-time enrollment: 500
Men: **58%**   Women: **42%**
African-American: **7.40%**   American Indian: **0.60%**
Asian-American: **2.60%**   Mexican-American: **0.60%**
Puerto Rican: **0.40%**   Other Hisp-Amer: **2.40%**
White: **85.00%**   International: **1.00%**
Unknown: **0.00%**

Attrition rates for 2008-2009 full-time students
Percent of students discontinuing law school:
Men: **1%**   Women: **3%**
First-year students: **3%**   Second-year students: **3%**
Third-year students: **N/A**   Fourth-year students: **N/A**

LIBRARY RESOURCES
Total titles: 43,724
Total volumes: 333,162
Total seats available for library users: 489

INFORMATION TECHNOLOGY
Number of wired network connections available to students: 43 total (in the law library, excluding computer labs: 6; in classrooms: 0; in computer labs: 30; elsewhere in the law school: 7)
Law school has a wireless network.
Students are not required to own a computer.

EMPLOYMENT AND SALARIES
Proportion of 2008 graduates employed at graduation: N/A
Employed 9 months later, as of February 15, 2009: 92%
Salaries in the private sector (law firms, business, industry): $47,500 – $65,000 (25th-75th percentile)
Median salary in the private sector: $58,900
Percentage in the private sector who reported salary information: 81%
Median salary in public service (government, judicial clerkships, academic posts, non-profits): $45,000

Percentage of 2008 graduates in:

Law firms: 58%   Government: 13%
Bus./industry: 13%   Judicial clerkship: 9%
Public interest: 4%   Unknown: 0%
Academia : 3%

2008 graduates employed in-state: 62%
2008 graduates employed in foreign countries: 0%
Number of states where graduates are employed: 22
Percentage of 2008 graduates working in: New England: 1%, Middle Atlantic: 2%, East North Central: 73%, West North Central: 2%, South Atlantic: 11%, East South Central: 3%, West South Central: 2%, Mountain: 2%, Pacific: 4%, Unknown: 0%

BAR PASSAGE RATES
Based on 2008 graduates taking Summer 2008 or Winter 2009 exams. Most of the school's first-time test takers took the bar in Ohio.

92%

School's bar passage rate for first-time test takers

88%

Statewide bar passage rate for first-time test takers

University of Denver (Sturm)

- 2255 E. Evans Avenue, Denver, CO, 80208
- http://www.law.du.edu
- Private
- **Year founded:** 1864
- **2009-2010 tuition:** full-time: $35,700; part-time: $26,244
- **Enrollment 2009-10 academic year:** full-time: 786; part-time: 232
- **U.S. News 2010 law specialty ranking:** clinical training: 25, environmental law: 14, tax law: 12

3.27-3.69 GPA, 25TH-75TH PERCENTILE

156-161 LSAT, 25TH-75TH PERCENTILE

33% ACCEPTANCE RATE

80 2011 U.S. NEWS LAW SCHOOL RANKING

ADMISSIONS

Admissions phone number: (303) 871-6135
Admissions email address: **admissions@law.du.edu**
Application website:
  http://www.law.du.edu/index.php/admissions/apply-online
Application deadline for Fall 2011 admission: **rolling**

Admissions statistics:

Number of applicants for Fall 2009: **2,587**
Number of acceptances: **862**
Number enrolled: **237**
Acceptance rate: **33%**
GPA, 25th-75th percentile, entering class Fall 2009: **3.27-3.69**
LSAT, 25th-75th percentile, entering class Fall 2009: **156-161**

Part-time program:

Number of applicants for Fall 2009: **338**
Number of acceptances: **99**
Number enrolled: **63**
Acceptance rate: **29%**
GPA, 25th-75th percentile, entering class Fall 2009: **3.15-3.67**
LSAT, 25th-75th percentile, entering class Fall 2009: **154-158**

FINANCIAL AID

Financial aid phone number: (303) 871-6136
Financial aid application deadline:
Tuition 2009-2010 academic year: **full-time: $35,700; part-time: $26,244**
Room and board: **$9,963** ; books: **$1,749** ; miscellaneous expenses: **$4,825**
Total of room/board/books/miscellaneous expenses: **$16,537**
University offers graduate student housing for which law students are eligible.

Financial aid profile

Percent of students that received grants for the 2008-2009 academic year: full-time: **37%**; part-time **18%**
Median grant amount: full-time: **$17,600** ; part-time: **$10,630**
The average law-school debt of those in the Class of 2009 who borrowed: **$104,926** . Proportion who borrowed: **84%**

ACADEMIC PROGRAMS

Calendar: **semester**
Joint degrees awarded: **J.D./M.B.A.; J.D./M.A. International Studies; J.D./M.S.W.; J.D./M.A. Philosophy; J.D./M.A. Economics; J.D./M.I.M.; J.D./M.S.L.A.; J.D./PSY; J.D./L.L.M. TAX; J.D./M.P.P.; J.D./M.A. Mass Communications; J.D./M.S. Computer Science; J.D./R.E.C.M.; JD/G.S.I.S.**
Typical first-year section size: Full-time: **80**; Part-time: **60**
Is there typically a "small section" of the first year class, other than Legal Writing, taught by full-time faculty?: Full-time: **yes**; Part-time: **yes**
Number of course titles, beyond the first year curriculum, offered last year: **171**
Percentages of upper division course sections, excluding seminars, with an enrollment of:

Under 25: **66%**	25 to 49: **22%**
50 to 74: **8%**	75 to 99: **3%**
100+: **0%**	

Areas of specialization: appellate advocacy, clinical training, dispute resolution, environmental law, health care law, intellectual property law, international law, tax law, trial advocacy

Fall 2009 faculty profile

Total teaching faculty: 95. Full-time: **41%; 56% men, 44% women, 18% minorities.** Part-time: **59%; 80% men, 20% women, N/A minorities**
Student-to-faculty ratio: **15.5**

SPECIAL PROGRAMS *(as provided by law school):*

DU offers students an extensive externship program including over 400 placements a year and summer international externships particularly in Latin America; J.D. specializations in International Law, Work Law, Lawyering in Spanish and Environmental and Natural Resources Law, including an LL.M. in Environmental and Natural Resources; and extensive clinical programs.

STUDENT BODY

Fall 2009 full-time enrollment: 786

Men: 52%	Women: 48%
African-American: 2.00%	American Indian: 1.70%
Asian-American: 6.10%	Mexican-American: 0.00%
Puerto Rican: 0.00%	Other Hisp-Amer: 7.30%
White: 77.60%	International: 0.00%
Unknown: 5.30%	

Fall 2009 part-time enrollment: 232

Men: 55%	Women: 45%
African-American: 4.70%	American Indian: 3.00%
Asian-American: 4.30%	Mexican-American: 0.00%
Puerto Rican: 0.00%	Other Hisp-Amer: 7.80%
White: 75.90%	International: 0.00%
Unknown: 4.30%	

Attrition rates for 2008-2009 full-time students

Percent of students discontinuing law school:

Men: 2%	Women: 3%
First-year students: 7%	Second-year students: 2%
Third-year students: 0%	Fourth-year students: N/A

LIBRARY RESOURCES

Total titles: 236,612
Total volumes: 412,187
Total seats available for library users: 333

INFORMATION TECHNOLOGY

Number of wired network connections available to students: 1567 total (in the law library, excluding computer labs: 167; in classrooms: 878; in computer labs: 32; elsewhere in the law school: 490)

Law school has a wireless network.
Students are required to own a computer.

EMPLOYMENT AND SALARIES

Proportion of 2008 graduates employed at graduation: 71%
Employed 9 months later, as of February 15, 2009: 94%
Salaries in the private sector (law firms, business, industry): $51,000 –$105,000 (25th-75th percentile)
Median salary in the private sector: $70,000
Percentage in the private sector who reported salary information: 58%
Median salary in public service (government, judicial clerkships, academic posts, non-profits): $49,400

Percentage of 2008 graduates in:

Law firms: 52%	Government: 14%
Bus./industry: 17%	Judicial clerkship: 10%
Public interest: 4%	Unknown: 2%
Academia : 1%	

2008 graduates employed in-state: 77%
2008 graduates employed in foreign countries: 1%
Number of states where graduates are employed: 23
Percentage of 2008 graduates working in: New England: 1%, Middle Atlantic: 1%, East North Central: 2%, West North Central: 2%, South Atlantic: 5%, East South Central: 0%, West South Central: 1%, Mountain: 83%, Pacific: 3%, Unknown: 2%

BAR PASSAGE RATES

Based on 2008 graduates taking Summer 2008 or Winter 2009 exams. Most of the school's first-time test takers took the bar in Colorado.

80%
School's bar passage rate for first-time test takers

83%
Statewide bar passage rate for first-time test takers

University of Detroit Mercy

- 651 E. Jefferson Avenue, Detroit, MI, 48226
- http://www.law.udmercy.edu
- Private
- Year founded: 1912
- 2009-2010 tuition: full-time: $32,090; part-time: $25,688
- Enrollment 2009-10 academic year: full-time: 586; part-time: 144
- U.S. News 2010 law specialty ranking: N/A

2.93-3.38 GPA, 25TH-75TH PERCENTILE

147-154 LSAT, 25TH-75TH PERCENTILE

45% ACCEPTANCE RATE

Tier 4 2011 U.S. NEWS LAW SCHOOL RANKING

ADMISSIONS

Admissions phone number: (313) 596-0264
Admissions email address: **udmlawao@udmercy.edu**
Application website:
http://www.law.udmercy.edu/prospective/admission/Fall2010Application.pdf
Application deadline for Fall 2011 admission: **15-Apr**

Admissions statistics:

Number of applicants for Fall 2009: **1,707**
Number of acceptances: **772**
Number enrolled: **243**
Acceptance rate: **45%**
GPA, 25th-75th percentile, entering class Fall 2009: **2.93-3.38**
LSAT, 25th-75th percentile, entering class Fall 2009: **147-154**

Part-time program:

Number of applicants for Fall 2009: **219**
Number of acceptances: **87**
Number enrolled: **39**
Acceptance rate: **40%**
GPA, 25th-75th percentile, entering class Fall 2009: **2.91-3.31**
LSAT, 25th-75th percentile, entering class Fall 2009: **144-149**

FINANCIAL AID

Financial aid phone number: (313) 596-0214
Financial aid application deadline: **1-Apr**
Tuition 2009-2010 academic year: **full-time: $32,090; part-time: $25,688**
Room and board: **$11,340** ; books: **$1,920** ; miscellaneous expenses: **$7,496**
Total of room/board/books/miscellaneous expenses: **$20,756**
University offers graduate student housing for which law students are eligible.

Financial aid profile

Percent of students that received grants for the 2008-2009 academic year: full-time: **25%**; part-time **18%**
Median grant amount: full-time: **$5,500** ; part-time: **$3,011**
The average law-school debt of those in the Class of 2009 who borrowed: **$107,139** . Proportion who borrowed: **81%**

ACADEMIC PROGRAMS

Calendar: **semester**
Joint degrees awarded: **J.D./M.B.A.; J.D./LL.B.**
Typical first-year section size: Full-time: **58**; Part-time: **32**
Is there typically a "small section" of the first year class, other than Legal Writing, taught by full-time faculty?:
Full-time: **no**; Part-time: **no**
Number of course titles, beyond the first year curriculum, offered last year: **96**
Percentages of upper division course sections, excluding seminars, with an enrollment of:

Under 25: **65%**	25 to 49: **26%**
50 to 74: **9%**	75 to 99: **0%**
100+: **0%**	

Areas of specialization: appellate advocacy, clinical training, dispute resolution, environmental law, health care law, intellectual property law, international law, tax law, trial advocacy

Fall 2009 faculty profile

Total teaching faculty: **74**. Full-time: **53%**; **54%** men, **46%** women, **8%** minorities. Part-time: **47%**; **71%** men, **29%** women, **3%** minorities
Student-to-faculty ratio: **14.1**

SPECIAL PROGRAMS *(as provided by law school):*

Law Firm Program; JD/LED Courses (Joint American/Mexican Degree Program Courses);Veterans Clinic; Consumer Debt Clinic; Environmental Law Clinic; Mediation Training and Clinic; Asylum Clinic; Immigration Law Clinic; Mobile Law Office; Appellate Advocacy Clinic; Urban Law Clinic; NITA Intersession; American Inns of Court; Public Service Fellowships; Teaching Law in High School.

STUDENT BODY

Fall 2009 full-time enrollment: 586

Men: 55%	Women: 45%
African-American: 6.50%	American Indian: 0.70%
Asian-American: 4.40%	Mexican-American: 0.00%
Puerto Rican: 0.00%	Other Hisp-Amer: 2.00%
White: 61.60%	International: 24.70%
Unknown: 0.00%	

Fall 2009 part-time enrollment: 144

Men: 51%	Women: 49%
African-American: 27.80%	American Indian: 0.00%
Asian-American: 2.10%	Mexican-American: 0.00%
Puerto Rican: 0.00%	Other Hisp-Amer: 4.20%
White: 63.90%	International: 2.10%
Unknown: 0.00%	

Attrition rates for 2008-2009 full-time students
Percent of students discontinuing law school:

Men: 8%	Women: 11%
First-year students: 26%	Second-year students: N/A
Third-year students: 1%	Fourth-year students: 4%

LIBRARY RESOURCES

Total titles: 190,670
Total volumes: 395,124
Total seats available for library users: 323

INFORMATION TECHNOLOGY

Number of wired network connections available to students: 0 total (in the law library, excluding computer labs: 0; in classrooms: 0; in computer labs: 0; elsewhere in the law school: 0)
Law school has a wireless network.
Students are not required to own a computer.

EMPLOYMENT AND SALARIES

Proportion of 2008 graduates employed at graduation: N/A
Employed 9 months later, as of February 15, 2009: 78%
Salaries in the private sector (law firms, business, industry): $42,500 –$80,000 (25th-75th percentile)
Median salary in the private sector: $50,500
Percentage in the private sector who reported salary information: 34%
Median salary in public service (government, judicial clerkships, academic posts, non-profits): $48,500

Percentage of 2008 graduates in:

Law firms: 57%	Government: 5%
Bus./industry: 22%	Judicial clerkship: 6%
Public interest: 5%	Unknown: 0%
Academia : 5%	

2008 graduates employed in-state: 58%
2008 graduates employed in foreign countries: 17%
Number of states where graduates are employed: 19
Percentage of 2008 graduates working in: New England: 0%, Middle Atlantic: 6%, East North Central: 67%, West North Central: 1%, South Atlantic: 4%, East South Central: 0%, West South Central: 3%, Mountain: 3%, Pacific: 1%, Unknown: 0%

BAR PASSAGE RATES

Based on 2008 graduates taking Summer 2008 or Winter 2009 exams. Most of the school's first-time test takers took the bar in Michigan.

71%
School's bar passage rate for first-time test takers

82%
Statewide bar passage rate for first-time test takers

University of Florida (Levin)

- PO Box 117620, Gainesville, FL, 32611-7620
- http://www.law.ufl.edu
- Public
- Year founded: 1909
- 2009-2010 tuition: full-time: $14,228; part-time: N/A
- Enrollment 2009-10 academic year: full-time: 1,106
- U.S. News 2010 law specialty ranking: environmental law: 16, tax law: 3

3.42-3.85 GPA, 25TH-75TH PERCENTILE

158-163 LSAT, 25TH-75TH PERCENTILE

25% ACCEPTANCE RATE

47 2011 U.S. NEWS LAW SCHOOL RANKING

ADMISSIONS

Admissions phone number: (352) 273-0890
Admissions email address: admissions@law.ufl.edu
Application website: http://www.law.ufl.edu/admissions
Application deadline for Fall 2011 admission: 15-Jan

Admissions statistics:

Number of applicants for Fall 2009: 3,170
Number of acceptances: 780
Number enrolled: 307
Acceptance rate: 25%
GPA, 25th-75th percentile, entering class Fall 2009: 3.42-3.85
LSAT, 25th-75th percentile, entering class Fall 2009: 158-163

FINANCIAL AID

Financial aid phone number: (352) 273-0628
Financial aid application deadline: 7-Apr
Tuition 2009-2010 academic year: **full-time: $14,228; part-time: N/A**
Room and board: **$8,170** ; books: **$990** ; miscellaneous expenses: **$3,940**
Total of room/board/books/miscellaneous expenses: **$13,100**
University offers graduate student housing for which law students are eligible.

Financial aid profile

Percent of students that received grants for the 2008-2009 academic year: full-time: **31%**
Median grant amount: full-time: **$3,000**
The average law-school debt of those in the Class of 2009 who borrowed: **$63,509** . Proportion who borrowed: **80%**

ACADEMIC PROGRAMS

Calendar: semester
Joint degrees awarded: J.D./M.S. Accounting; J.D./M.B.A.; J.D./M.S. or Ph.D. Political Science; J.D./M.D.; J.D./M.S. or Ph.D. Sociology; J.D./M.A. or Ph.D. Mass Communication; J.D./M.A. or Ph.D. History; J.D./Ph.D. Education Leadership; J.D./M.S. Urban Planning; J.D./Ph.D. Psychology; J.D./M.A. Real Estate; J.D./M.B.A. Finance; J.D./M.S. Sports Management; J.D./M.S. Forest Conservation; J.D./M.A. Women's Studies; J.D./M.A. or Ph.D. Anthropology; J.D./M.S. Environmental Engineering; J.D./M.A. Latin American Studies; J.D./M.A. or Ph.D. Medical Science; J.D./M.A. Public Administration; J.D./D.V.M.; J.D./M.S. Family, Youth & Comm. Services; J.D./M.S. Electrical & Computer Engineer; J.D./M.S. Public Health; J.D./M.A. International Relations; J.D./M.S. or Ph.D. Building Construction; J.D./M.S. Exercise and Sport Sciences; J.D./M.A. or Ph.D. History; J.D./M.S. Natural Resources; J.D./M.B.A. International Business
Typical first-year section size: Full-time: **105**
Is there typically a "small section" of the first year class, other than Legal Writing, taught by full-time faculty?: Full-time: **no**
Number of course titles, beyond the first year curriculum, offered last year: **166**
Percentages of upper division course sections, excluding seminars, with an enrollment of:

Under 25: **49%**	25 to 49: **24%**
50 to 74: **16%**	75 to 99: **6%**
100+: **5%**	

Areas of specialization: appellate advocacy, clinical training, dispute resolution, environmental law, health care law, intellectual property law, international law, tax law, trial advocacy

Fall 2009 faculty profile

Total teaching faculty: 88. Full-time: **67%**; 51% men, **49%** women, 19% minorities. Part-time: **33%**; 66% men, **34%** women, 7% minorities
Student-to-faculty ratio: **15.4**

SPECIAL PROGRAMS *(as provided by law school):*

The college offers both civil and criminal clinics, as well as numerous simulation courses. It also offers certificates in Children and Family Law, International Law, Estates and Trusts Practice, Intellectual Property Law, and Environmental and

Land Use Law. The college also has a number of academic year exchange and summer abroad programs.

STUDENT BODY

Fall 2009 full-time enrollment: 1,106

Men: 52%	Women: 48%
African-American: 6.20%	American Indian: 0.70%
Asian-American: 6.80%	Mexican-American: 0.00%
Puerto Rican: 0.00%	Other Hisp-Amer: 9.70%
White: 72.70%	International: 1.80%
Unknown: 2.10%	

Attrition rates for 2008-2009 full-time students

Percent of students discontinuing law school:

Men: N/A	Women: 0%
First-year students: 0%	Second-year students: N/A
Third-year students: N/A	Fourth-year students: N/A

LIBRARY RESOURCES

Total titles: 208,639

Total volumes: 643,282

Total seats available for library users: 765

INFORMATION TECHNOLOGY

Number of wired network connections available to students: 0 total (in the law library, excluding computer labs: 0; in classrooms: 0; in computer labs: 0; elsewhere in the law school: 0)

Law school has a wireless network.

Students are required to own a computer.

EMPLOYMENT AND SALARIES

Proportion of 2008 graduates employed at graduation: 76%

Employed 9 months later, as of February 15, 2009: 97%

Salaries in the private sector (law firms, business, industry): $70,000 –$130,000 (25th-75th percentile)

Median salary in the private sector: $85,000

Percentage in the private sector who reported salary information: 73%

Median salary in public service (government, judicial clerkships, academic posts, non-profits): $44,500

Percentage of 2008 graduates in:

Law firms: 65%	Government: 13%
Bus./industry: 8%	Judicial clerkship: 5%
Public interest: 5%	Unknown: 1%
Academia : 3%	

2008 graduates employed in-state: 75%

2008 graduates employed in foreign countries: 1%

Number of states where graduates are employed: 23

Percentage of 2008 graduates working in: New England: 1%, Middle Atlantic: 3%, East North Central: 2%, West North Central: 0%, South Atlantic: 87%, East South Central: 1%, West South Central: 1%, Mountain: 0%, Pacific: 2%, Unknown: 2%

BAR PASSAGE RATES

Based on 2008 graduates taking Summer 2008 or Winter 2009 exams. Most of the school's first-time test takers took the bar in Florida.

89%

School's bar passage rate for first-time test takers

81%

Statewide bar passage rate for first-time test takers

University of Georgia

- Herty Drive, Athens, GA, 30602
- http://www.law.uga.edu
- Public
- Year founded: 1859
- 2009-2010 tuition: full-time: $14,448; part-time: N/A
- Enrollment 2009-10 academic year: full-time: 694
- U.S. News 2010 law specialty ranking: N/A

3.40-3.80 GPA, 25TH-75TH PERCENTILE

161-165 LSAT, 25TH-75TH PERCENTILE

28% ACCEPTANCE RATE

28 2011 U.S. NEWS LAW SCHOOL RANKING

ADMISSIONS

Admissions phone number: **(706) 542-7060**
Admissions email address: **ugajd@uga.edu**
Application website: **http://www.law.uga.edu/how-apply**
Application deadline for Fall 2011 admission: **1-Mar**

Admissions statistics:
Number of applicants for Fall 2009: **3,076**
Number of acceptances: **857**
Number enrolled: **241**
Acceptance rate: **28%**
GPA, 25th-75th percentile, entering class Fall 2009: **3.40-3.80**
LSAT, 25th-75th percentile, entering class Fall 2009: **161-165**

FINANCIAL AID

Financial aid phone number: **(706) 542-6147**
Financial aid application deadline: **1-Mar**
Tuition 2009-2010 academic year: **full-time: $14,448; part-time: N/A**
Room and board: **$10,600** ; books: **$1,400** ; miscellaneous expenses: **$3,320**
Total of room/board/books/miscellaneous expenses: **$15,320**
University offers graduate student housing for which law students are eligible.

Financial aid profile
Percent of students that received grants for the 2008-2009 academic year: full-time: **61%**
Median grant amount: full-time: **$5,000**
The average law-school debt of those in the Class of 2009 who borrowed: **$65,047** . Proportion who borrowed: **78%**

ACADEMIC PROGRAMS

Calendar: **semester**
Joint degrees awarded: **J.D./M.B.A.; J.D./M.A. Historical Preservation; J.D./M.P.A.; J.D./M.A. Sports Management; J.D./M.S.W.**
Typical first-year section size: Full-time: **80**

Is there typically a "small section" of the first year class, other than Legal Writing, taught by full-time faculty?: Full-time: **no**
Number of course titles, beyond the first year curriculum, offered last year: **124**
Percentages of upper division course sections, excluding seminars, with an enrollment of:
Under 25: **61%**   25 to 49: **22%**
50 to 74: **12%**   75 to 99: **6%**
100+: **N/A**
Areas of specialization: appellate advocacy, clinical training, dispute resolution, environmental law, health care law, intellectual property law, international law, tax law, trial advocacy

Fall 2009 faculty profile
Total teaching faculty: **56**. Full-time: **80%**; **64%** men, **36%** women, **11%** minorities. Part-time: **20%**; **82%** men, **18%** women, **0%** minorities
Student-to-faculty ratio: **12.2**

SPECIAL PROGRAMS (as provided by law school):
Georgia Law operates 9 clinics. Georgia is part of a spring term overseas (a joint program with Ohio State at Oxford University, England). Summer programs are held in China and Brussels, Belgium. Overseas internships in law firms and government agencies also provide a chance for international experience.

STUDENT BODY
Fall 2009 full-time enrollment: 694
Men: **53%**   Women: **47%**
African-American: **12.00%**   American Indian: **0.10%**
Asian-American: **4.50%**   Mexican-American: **0.00%**
Puerto Rican: **0.00%**   Other Hisp-Amer: **1.30%**
White: **66.70%**   International: **0.30%**
Unknown: **15.10%**

Attrition rates for 2008-2009 full-time students
Percent of students discontinuing law school:
Men: **N/A**   Women: **0%**
First-year students: **0%**   Second-year students: **N/A**
Third-year students: **N/A**   Fourth-year students: **N/A**

LIBRARY RESOURCES

Total titles: **409,123**
Total volumes: **537,274**
Total seats available for library users: **433**

INFORMATION TECHNOLOGY

Number of wired network connections available to students: **o** total (in the law library, excluding computer labs: **o**; in classrooms: **o**; in computer labs: **o**; elsewhere in the law school: **o**)
Law school has a wireless network.
Students are not required to own a computer.

EMPLOYMENT AND SALARIES

Proportion of 2008 graduates employed at graduation: **90%**
Employed 9 months later, as of February 15, 2009: **98%**
Salaries in the private sector (law firms, business, industry): **$80,000 –$145,000** (25th-75th percentile)
Median salary in the private sector: **$130,000**
Percentage in the private sector who reported salary information: **65%**
Median salary in public service (government, judicial clerkships, academic posts, non-profits): **$55,000**

Percentage of 2008 graduates in:

Law firms: **58%**	Government: **11%**
Bus./industry: **7%**	Judicial clerkship: **17%**
Public interest: **6%**	Unknown: **0%**
Academia : **1%**	

2008 graduates employed in-state: **77%**
2008 graduates employed in foreign countries: **1%**
Number of states where graduates are employed: **18**
Percentage of 2008 graduates working in: New England: **0%**, Middle Atlantic: **1%**, East North Central: **0%**, West North Central: **0%**, South Atlantic: **89%**, East South Central: **5%**, West South Central: **3%**, Mountain: **2%**, Pacific: **1%**, Unknown: **0%**

BAR PASSAGE RATES

Based on 2008 graduates taking Summer 2008 or Winter 2009 exams. Most of the school's first-time test takers took the bar in Georgia.

99%

School's bar passage rate for first-time test takers

89%

Statewide bar passage rate for first-time test takers

University of Hawaii (Richardson)

- 2515 Dole Street, Honolulu, HI, 96822-2328
- http://www.law.hawaii.edu/
- Public
- **Year founded:** 1973
- **2009-2010 tuition:** full-time: $15,581; part-time: $633/credit hour
- **Enrollment 2009-10 academic year:** full-time: 285; part-time: 41
- **U.S. News 2010 law specialty ranking:** N/A

3.21-3.68 GPA, 25TH-75TH PERCENTILE

155-160 LSAT, 25TH-75TH PERCENTILE

20% ACCEPTANCE RATE

72 2011 U.S. NEWS LAW SCHOOL RANKING

ADMISSIONS

Admissions phone number: **(808) 956-7966**
Admissions email address: **lawadm@hawaii.edu**
Application website:
    http://www.law.hawaii.edu/admissions
Application deadline for Fall 2011 admission: **1-Mar**

Admissions statistics:
Number of applicants for Fall 2009: **1,098**
Number of acceptances: **224**
Number enrolled: **87**
Acceptance rate: **20%**
GPA, 25th-75th percentile, entering class Fall 2009: **3.21-3.68**
LSAT, 25th-75th percentile, entering class Fall 2009: **155-160**

Part-time program:
Number of applicants for Fall 2009: **318**
Number of acceptances: **45**
Number enrolled: **37**
Acceptance rate: **14%**
GPA, 25th-75th percentile, entering class Fall 2009: **3.02-3.61**
LSAT, 25th-75th percentile, entering class Fall 2009: **147-154**

FINANCIAL AID

Financial aid phone number: **(808) 956-7966**
Financial aid application deadline: **1-Mar**
Tuition 2009-2010 academic year: **full-time: $15,581; part-time: $633/credit hour**
Room and board: **$12,802** ; books: **$1,123** ; miscellaneous expenses: **$1,674**
Total of room/board/books/miscellaneous expenses: **$15,599**
University offers graduate student housing for which law students are eligible.

Financial aid profile
Percent of students that received grants for the 2008-2009 academic year: full-time: **33%**; part-time **5%**
Median grant amount: full-time: **$5,223** ; part-time: **$5,223**
The average law-school debt of those in the Class of 2009 who borrowed: **$53,569** . Proportion who borrowed: **74%**

ACADEMIC PROGRAMS
Calendar: **semester**
Joint degrees awarded: **J.D./M.B.A.; J.D./M.A.; J.D./M.S.W.**
Typical first-year section size: Full-time: **97**; Part-time: **24**
Is there typically a "small section" of the first year class, other than Legal Writing, taught by full-time faculty?: Full-time: **no**; Part-time: **no**
Number of course titles, beyond the first year curriculum, offered last year: **87**
Percentages of upper division course sections, excluding seminars, with an enrollment of:

Under 25: **79%**	25 to 49: **14%**
50 to 74: **4%**	75 to 99: **3%**
100+: **0%**	

Areas of specialization: appellate advocacy, clinical training, dispute resolution, environmental law, health care law, intellectual property law, international law, tax law, trial advocacy

Fall 2009 faculty profile
Total teaching faculty: **47**. Full-time: **68%**; **47%** men, **53%** women, **38%** minorities. Part-time: **32%**; **60%** men, **40%** women, **60%** minorities
Student-to-faculty ratio: **7.8**

SPECIAL PROGRAMS (as provided by law school):
Students have many opportunities to engage in real life learning through clinics in criminal law, Family Law, Immigration Law, and Small Business. Richardson also offers certificate programs in Environmental Law, Native Hawaiian Law, and Pacific Asian Legal Studies. Students engage in exciting legal issues through the Center for Excellence in Native Hawaiian Law and the Elder Law Program.

STUDENT BODY

Fall 2009 full-time enrollment: 285

Men: 42%	Women: 58%
African-American: 1.80%	American Indian: 0.70%
Asian-American: 57.90%	Mexican-American: 0.40%
Puerto Rican: 0.40%	Other Hisp-Amer: 1.10%
White: 17.90%	International: 2.10%
Unknown: 17.90%	

Fall 2009 part-time enrollment: 41

Men: 41%	Women: 59%
African-American: 2.40%	American Indian: 0.00%
Asian-American: 48.80%	Mexican-American: 0.00%
Puerto Rican: 0.00%	Other Hisp-Amer: 2.40%
White: 24.40%	International: 0.00%
Unknown: 22.00%	

Attrition rates for 2008-2009 full-time students
Percent of students discontinuing law school:

Men: 2%	Women: 3%
First-year students: 5%	Second-year students: 2%
Third-year students: N/A	Fourth-year students: N/A

LIBRARY RESOURCES

Total titles: 48,901
Total volumes: 356,649
Total seats available for library users: 380

INFORMATION TECHNOLOGY

Number of wired network connections available to students: 280 total (in the law library, excluding computer labs: 254; in classrooms: 11; in computer labs: 5; elsewhere in the law school: 10)
Law school has a wireless network.
Students are required to own a computer.

EMPLOYMENT AND SALARIES

Proportion of 2008 graduates employed at graduation: 71%
Employed 9 months later, as of February 15, 2009: 100%
Salaries in the private sector (law firms, business, industry): $55,000 –$80,000 (25th-75th percentile)
Median salary in the private sector: $71,000
Percentage in the private sector who reported salary information: 75%
Median salary in public service (government, judicial clerkships, academic posts, non-profits): $55,200

Percentage of 2008 graduates in:

Law firms: 37%	Government: 19%
Bus./industry: 9%	Judicial clerkship: 24%
Public interest: 4%	Unknown: 0%
Academia : 7%	

2008 graduates employed in-state: 85%
2008 graduates employed in foreign countries: 3%
Number of states where graduates are employed: 8
Percentage of 2008 graduates working in: New England: 2%, Middle Atlantic: 1%, East North Central: 0%, West North Central: 1%, South Atlantic: 0%, East South Central: 0%, West South Central: 1%, Mountain: 1%, Pacific: 91%, Unknown: 0%

BAR PASSAGE RATES

Based on 2008 graduates taking Summer 2008 or Winter 2009 exams. Most of the school's first-time test takers took the bar in Hawaii.

87%
School's bar passage rate for first-time test takers

88%
Statewide bar passage rate for first-time test takers

University of Houston

- 100 Law Center, Houston, TX, 77204-6060
- http://www.law.uh.edu
- Public
- Year founded: 1947
- 2009-2010 tuition: full-time: $21,029; part-time: $15,125
- Enrollment 2009-10 academic year: full-time: 715; part-time: 183
- U.S. News 2010 law specialty ranking: healthcare law: 4, intellectual property law: 8

3.08-3.63	GPA, 25TH-75TH PERCENTILE
160-164	LSAT, 25TH-75TH PERCENTILE
27%	ACCEPTANCE RATE
60	2011 U.S. NEWS LAW SCHOOL RANKING

ADMISSIONS
Admissions phone number: **(713) 743-2280**
Admissions email address: **lawadmissions@uh.edu**
Application website: **http://www.law.uh.edu/admissions/**
Application deadline for Fall 2011 admission: **15-Feb**

Admissions statistics:
Number of applicants for Fall 2009: **3,021**
Number of acceptances: **817**
Number enrolled: **205**
Acceptance rate: **27%**
GPA, 25th-75th percentile, entering class Fall 2009: **3.08-3.63**
LSAT, 25th-75th percentile, entering class Fall 2009: **160-164**

Part-time program:
Number of applicants for Fall 2009: **631**
Number of acceptances: **86**
Number enrolled: **51**
Acceptance rate: **14%**
GPA, 25th-75th percentile, entering class Fall 2009: **3.02-3.54**
LSAT, 25th-75th percentile, entering class Fall 2009: **156-161**

FINANCIAL AID
Financial aid phone number: **(713) 743-2269**
Financial aid application deadline: **1-Apr**
Tuition 2009-2010 academic year: **full-time: $21,029; part-time: $15,125**
Room and board: **$9,234** ; books: **$1,100** ; miscellaneous expenses: **$5,122**
Total of room/board/books/miscellaneous expenses: **$15,456**
University offers graduate student housing for which law students are eligible.

Financial aid profile
Percent of students that received grants for the 2008-2009 academic year: full-time: **65%**

Median grant amount: full-time: **$5,000**
The average law-school debt of those in the Class of 2009 who borrowed: **$70,575** . Proportion who borrowed: **79%**

ACADEMIC PROGRAMS
Calendar: **semester**
Joint degrees awarded: **J.D./M.B.A.; J.D./M.P.H.; J.D./Ph.D. Criminal Justice; J.D./M.A. History; J.D./M.S.W.; J.D./Ph.D. Medical Humanities; J.D./M.D.**
Typical first-year section size: Full-time: **70**; Part-time: **50**
Is there typically a "small section" of the first year class, other than Legal Writing, taught by full-time faculty?: Full-time: **yes**; Part-time: **yes**
Number of course titles, beyond the first year curriculum, offered last year: **196**
Percentages of upper division course sections, excluding seminars, with an enrollment of:

Under 25: **65%**	25 to 49: **20%**
50 to 74: **9%**	75 to 99: **5%**
100+: **2%**	

Areas of specialization: appellate advocacy, clinical training, dispute resolution, environmental law, health care law, intellectual property law, international law, tax law, trial advocacy

Fall 2009 faculty profile
Total teaching faculty: **268**. Full-time: **44%**; **70%** men, **30%** women, **15%** minorities. Part-time: **56%**; **72%** men, **28%** women, **17%** minorities
Student-to-faculty ratio: **11.8**

SPECIAL PROGRAMS *(as provided by law school):*
Nationally ranked programs include our Health Law & Policy Institute and the nation's largest and most comprehensive health law curriculum; and Institute for Intellectual Property & Information Law. Other top programs include the Blakely Advocacy Institute (15 mock trial and moot court titles since 2004) and the Center for Consumer Law, which administers the Texas Consumer Complaint Center.

STUDENT BODY

Fall 2009 full-time enrollment: 715

Men: 55%	Women: 45%
African-American: 7.30%	American Indian: 0.30%
Asian-American: 10.10%	Mexican-American: 5.50%
Puerto Rican: 0.10%	Other Hisp-Amer: 4.60%
White: 69.70%	International: 1.70%
Unknown: 0.80%	

Fall 2009 part-time enrollment: 183

Men: 60%	Women: 40%
African-American: 10.90%	American Indian: 1.10%
Asian-American: 10.90%	Mexican-American: 4.90%
Puerto Rican: 0.50%	Other Hisp-Amer: 2.70%
White: 67.80%	International: 0.50%
Unknown: 0.50%	

Attrition rates for 2008-2009 full-time students
Percent of students discontinuing law school:

Men: 1%	Women: 3%
First-year students: 1%	Second-year students: 3%
Third-year students: 1%	Fourth-year students: 2%

LIBRARY RESOURCES

Total titles: 119,869
Total volumes: 542,164
Total seats available for library users: 546

INFORMATION TECHNOLOGY

Number of wired network connections available to students: 12 total (in the law library, excluding computer labs: 7; in classrooms: 0; in computer labs: 5; elsewhere in the law school: 0)
Law school has a wireless network.
Students are not required to own a computer.

EMPLOYMENT AND SALARIES

Proportion of 2008 graduates employed at graduation: 76%
Employed 9 months later, as of February 15, 2009: 97%
Salaries in the private sector (law firms, business, industry): $60,000 –$160,000 (25th-75th percentile)
Median salary in the private sector: $95,000
Percentage in the private sector who reported salary information: 78%
Median salary in public service (government, judicial clerkships, academic posts, non-profits): $47,400

Percentage of 2008 graduates in:

Law firms: 58%	Government: 10%
Bus./industry: 21%	Judicial clerkship: 4%
Public interest: 4%	Unknown: 1%
Academia : 2%	

2008 graduates employed in-state: 90%
2008 graduates employed in foreign countries: 1%
Number of states where graduates are employed: 15
Percentage of 2008 graduates working in: New England: 0%, Middle Atlantic: 1%, East North Central: 1%, West North Central: 0%, South Atlantic: 2%, East South Central: 0%, West South Central: 91%, Mountain: 2%, Pacific: 1%, Unknown: 1%

BAR PASSAGE RATES

Based on 2008 graduates taking Summer 2008 or Winter 2009 exams. Most of the school's first-time test takers took the bar in Texas.

91%
School's bar passage rate for first-time test takers

84%
Statewide bar passage rate for first-time test takers

University of Idaho

- PO Box 442321, Moscow, ID, 83844-2321
- http://www.law.uidaho.edu
- Public
- **Year founded:** 1909
- **2009-2010 tuition:** full-time: $11,776; part-time: N/A
- **Enrollment 2009-10 academic year:** full-time: 114
- **U.S. News 2010 law specialty ranking:** N/A

2.85-3.58 GPA, 25ᵀᴴ-75ᵀᴴ PERCENTILE

152-157 LSAT, 25ᵀᴴ-75ᵀᴴ PERCENTILE

48% ACCEPTANCE RATE

Tier 3 2011 U.S. NEWS LAW SCHOOL RANKING

ADMISSIONS

Admissions phone number: **(208) 885-2300**
Admissions email address: **lawadmit@uidaho.edu**
Application website:
  http://www.law.uidaho.edu/admissions/applynow
Application deadline for Fall 2011 admission: **15-Feb**

Admissions statistics:
Number of applicants for Fall 2009: **743**
Number of acceptances: **355**
Number enrolled: **114**
Acceptance rate: **48%**
GPA, 25th-75th percentile, entering class Fall 2009: **2.85-3.58**
LSAT, 25th-75th percentile, entering class Fall 2009: **152-157**

FINANCIAL AID

Financial aid phone number: **(208) 885-6312**
Financial aid application deadline: **15-Feb**
Tuition 2009-2010 academic year: **full-time: $11,776; part-time: N/A**
Room and board: **$9,292** ; books: **$1,474** ; miscellaneous expenses: **$4,038**
Total of room/board/books/miscellaneous expenses: **$14,804**
University offers graduate student housing for which law students are eligible.

Financial aid profile
Percent of students that received grants for the 2008-2009 academic year: full-time: **N/A**
Median grant amount: full-time: **N/A**
The average law-school debt of those in the Class of 2009 who borrowed: **$25,268** . Proportion who borrowed: **94%**

ACADEMIC PROGRAMS

Calendar: **semester**
Joint degrees awarded: **N/A**
Typical first-year section size: Full-time: **53**
Is there typically a "small section" of the first year class, other than Legal Writing, taught by full-time faculty?: Full-time: **no**
Number of course titles, beyond the first year curriculum, offered last year: **96**
Percentages of upper division course sections, excluding seminars, with an enrollment of:
  Under 25: **74%**   25 to 49: **16%**
  50 to 74: **4%**   75 to 99: **5%**
  100+: **1%**
Areas of specialization: appellate advocacy, clinical training, dispute resolution, environmental law, health care law, intellectual property law, international law, tax law, trial advocacy

Fall 2009 faculty profile
Total teaching faculty: **38**. Full-time: **63%**; **46%** men, **54%** women, **8%** minorities. Part-time: **37%**; **71%** men, **29%** women, **0%** minorities
Student-to-faculty ratio: **16.5**

SPECIAL PROGRAMS *(as provided by law school):*
Students may focus on natural resources law, entrepreneurism, or advocacy/dispute resolution. There is also a concentration in Native American law and classes in international law. Students must also perform at least 40 hours of pro bono legal work in order to graduate, the only such program in the Northwest. The College of Law is home to the renowned Northwest Institute for Dispute Resolution.

STUDENT BODY
Fall 2009 full-time enrollment: **114**
Men: **67%**   Women: **33%**
African-American: **0.90%**   American Indian: **2.60%**
Asian-American: **0.90%**   Mexican-American: **0.90%**
Puerto Rican: **0.00%**   Other Hisp-Amer: **7.00%**
White: **81.60%**   International: **0.90%**
Unknown: **5.30%**

Attrition rates for 2008-2009 full-time students
Percent of students discontinuing law school:
Men: **3%**   Women: **2%**

First-year students: **7%**   Second-year students: **1%**
Third-year students: **N/A**   Fourth-year students: **N/A**

LIBRARY RESOURCES
Total titles: **68,896**
Total volumes: **270,391**
Total seats available for library users: **330**

INFORMATION TECHNOLOGY
Number of wired network connections available to students: **306** total (in the law library, excluding computer labs: **143**; in classrooms: **106**; in computer labs: **0**; elsewhere in the law school: **57**)
Law school has a wireless network.
Students are not required to own a computer.

EMPLOYMENT AND SALARIES
Proportion of 2008 graduates employed at graduation: **N/A**
Employed 9 months later, as of February 15, 2009: **88%**
Salaries in the private sector (law firms, business, industry): **$42,500 –$60,000** (25th-75th percentile)
Median salary in the private sector: **$52,500**
Percentage in the private sector who reported salary information: **50%**
Median salary in public service (government, judicial clerkships, academic posts, non-profits): **$45,000**

Percentage of 2008 graduates in:
Law firms: **37%**   Government: **21%**
Bus./industry: **6%**   Judicial clerkship: **24%**
Public interest: **8%**   Unknown: **1%**
Academia : **2%**

2008 graduates employed in-state: **64%**
2008 graduates employed in foreign countries: **0%**
Number of states where graduates are employed: **13**
Percentage of 2008 graduates working in: New England: **0%**, Middle Atlantic: **1%**, East North Central: **1%**, West North Central: **0%**, South Atlantic: **8%**, East South Central: **0%**, West South Central: **1%**, Mountain: **79%**, Pacific: **10%**, Unknown: **0%**

BAR PASSAGE RATES
Based on 2008 graduates taking Summer 2008 or Winter 2009 exams. Most of the school's first-time test takers took the bar in Idaho.

81%
School's bar passage rate for first-time test takers

80%
Statewide bar passage rate for first-time test takers

Univ. of Illinois–Urbana-Champaign

- 504 E. Pennsylvania Avenue, Champaign, IL, 61820
- http://www.law.illinois.edu
- Public
- Year founded: 1897
- 2009-2010 tuition: full-time: $36,420; part-time: N/A
- Enrollment 2009-10 academic year: full-time: 617
- U.S. News 2010 law specialty ranking: N/A

3.20-3.90 GPA, 25TH-75TH PERCENTILE

160-167 LSAT, 25TH-75TH PERCENTILE

29% ACCEPTANCE RATE

21 2011 U.S. NEWS LAW SCHOOL RANKING

ADMISSIONS

Admissions phone number: (217) 244-6415
Admissions email address: **admissions@law.illinois.edu**
Application website:
  http://www.law.illinois.edu/prospective-students/apply-now.asp
Application deadline for Fall 2011 admission: **15-Mar**

Admissions statistics:
Number of applicants for Fall 2009: **3,516**
Number of acceptances: **1,031**
Number enrolled: **232**
Acceptance rate: **29%**
GPA, 25th-75th percentile, entering class Fall 2009: **3.20-3.90**
LSAT, 25th-75th percentile, entering class Fall 2009: **160-167**

FINANCIAL AID

Financial aid phone number: (217) 244-6415
Financial aid application deadline: **15-Mar**
Tuition 2009-2010 academic year: **full-time: $36,420; part-time: N/A**
Room and board: **$10,964** ; books: **$1,750** ; miscellaneous expenses: **$2,760**
Total of room/board/books/miscellaneous expenses: **$15,474**
University offers graduate student housing for which law students are eligible.

Financial aid profile
Percent of students that received grants for the 2008-2009 academic year: full-time: **85%**
Median grant amount: full-time: **$11,500**
The average law-school debt of those in the Class of 2009 who borrowed: **$87,194** . Proportion who borrowed: **97%**

ACADEMIC PROGRAMS

Calendar: **semester**
Joint degrees awarded: **J.D./M.Business Administration; J.D./M.Human Resources & Industrial Rltn; J.D./M.** Education; J.D./Doctorate in Education; J.D./Doctorate of Medicine; J.D./M. Urban Planning; J.D./Doctorate of Veterinary Medicine; J.D./M.Computer Science; J.D./M.S. Journalism; J.D./M.S. Natural Resources & Envir Sci; J.D./M.S. Chemistry; J.D./Doctorate of Political Science; J.D./Doctorate of Philosophy; J.D./Interdisciplinary
Typical first-year section size: Full-time: **63**
Is there typically a "small section" of the first year class, other than Legal Writing, taught by full-time faculty?: Full-time: **yes**
Number of course titles, beyond the first year curriculum, offered last year: **128**
Percentages of upper division course sections, excluding seminars, with an enrollment of:
  Under 25: **55%** 25 to 49: **31%**
  50 to 74: **8%** 75 to 99: **6%**
  100+: **0%**
Areas of specialization: appellate advocacy, clinical training, dispute resolution, environmental law, health care law, intellectual property law, international law, tax law, trial advocacy

Fall 2009 faculty profile
Total teaching faculty: **72**. Full-time: **53%; 71%** men, **29%** women, **21%** minorities. Part-time: **47%; 71%** men, **29%** women, **9%** minorities
Student-to-faculty ratio: **13.1**

SPECIAL PROGRAMS *(as provided by law school):*
The College of Law offers multiple courses in topics ranging from traditional to practical with clinics and very robust externship, trial advocacy and experiential programs. Around 70 of the upper-level courses had an enrollment of less than 25 students. There are also study abroad options. Finally, students may pursue multidisciplinary study with cross-listed courses and joint degree programs.

STUDENT BODY
Fall 2009 full-time enrollment: **617**
Men: **58%** Women: **42%**

African-American: **7.60%**   American Indian: **0.80%**
Asian-American: **8.90%**   Mexican-American: **0.00%**
Puerto Rican: **0.00%**   Other Hisp-Amer: **5.20%**
White: **62.70%**   International: **5.20%**
Unknown: **9.60%**

Attrition rates for 2008-2009 full-time students
Percent of students discontinuing law school:
Men: **2%**   Women: **2%**
First-year students: **5%**   Second-year students: **1%**
Third-year students: **N/A**   Fourth-year students: **N/A**

LIBRARY RESOURCES

Total titles: **304,120**
Total volumes: **780,230**
Total seats available for library users: **313**

INFORMATION TECHNOLOGY

Number of wired network connections available to students: **802** total (in the law library, excluding computer labs: **80**; in classrooms: **574**; in computer labs: **48**; elsewhere in the law school: **100**)
Law school has a wireless network.
Students are required to own a computer.

EMPLOYMENT AND SALARIES

Proportion of 2008 graduates employed at graduation: **85%**
Employed 9 months later, as of February 15, 2009: **97%**
Salaries in the private sector (law firms, business, industry): **$70,000 –$160,000** (25th-75th percentile)
Median salary in the private sector: **$145,000**

Percentage in the private sector who reported salary information: **82%**
Median salary in public service (government, judicial clerkships, academic posts, non-profits): **$52,000**

Percentage of 2008 graduates in:
Law firms: **60%**   Government: **14%**
Bus./industry: **14%**   Judicial clerkship: **7%**
Public interest: **3%**   Unknown: **0%**
Academia : **3%**

2008 graduates employed in-state: **64%**
2008 graduates employed in foreign countries: **1%**
Number of states where graduates are employed: **22**
Percentage of 2008 graduates working in: New England: **0%**, Middle Atlantic: **4%**, East North Central: **68%**, West North Central: **4%**, South Atlantic: **13%**, East South Central: **1%**, West South Central: **2%**, Mountain: **3%**, Pacific: **5%**, Unknown: **0%**

BAR PASSAGE RATES

Based on 2008 graduates taking Summer 2008 or Winter 2009 exams. Most of the school's first-time test takers took the bar in Illinois.

91%
School's bar passage rate for first-time test takers

91%
Statewide bar passage rate for first-time test takers

University of Iowa

- 320 Melrose Avenue, Iowa City, IA, 52242
- http://www.law.uiowa.edu
- Public
- Year founded: 1865
- 2009-2010 tuition: full-time: $21,432; part-time: N/A
- Enrollment 2009-10 academic year: full-time: 590
- U.S. News 2010 law specialty ranking: N/A

3.43-3.81 GPA, 25TH-75TH PERCENTILE

158-164 LSAT, 25TH-75TH PERCENTILE

44% ACCEPTANCE RATE

26 2011 U.S. NEWS LAW SCHOOL RANKING

ADMISSIONS
Admissions phone number: (319) 335-9095
Admissions email address: law-admissions@uiowa.edu
Application website:
   http://www.uiowa.edu/admissions/graduate/programs/
   program-details/jd-main.html
Application deadline for Fall 2011 admission: 1-Mar

Admissions statistics:
Number of applicants for Fall 2009: 1,291
Number of acceptances: 566
Number enrolled: 195
Acceptance rate: 44%
GPA, 25th-75th percentile, entering class Fall 2009: 3.43-3.81
LSAT, 25th-75th percentile, entering class Fall 2009: 158-164

FINANCIAL AID
Financial aid phone number: (319) 335-9142
Financial aid application deadline: 1-Jan
Tuition 2009-2010 academic year: **full-time: $21,432; part-time: N/A**
Room and board: $9,900 ; books: $2,300 ; miscellaneous expenses: $4,530
Total of room/board/books/miscellaneous expenses: $16,730
University does not offer graduate student housing for which law students are eligible.

Financial aid profile
Percent of students that received grants for the 2008-2009 academic year: full-time: 34%
Median grant amount: full-time: $16,758
The average law-school debt of those in the Class of 2009 who borrowed: $81,735 . Proportion who borrowed: 84%

ACADEMIC PROGRAMS
Calendar: semester
Joint degrees awarded: J.D./M.B.A.; J.D./M.A. Sociology; J.D./M.A. Philosophy; J.D./M.A. Journalism; J.D./M.A.

Higher Ed; J.D./M.Acc; J.D./M.P.H.; J.D./M. Psych & Quantitative Foundations; J.D./M.D.; J.D./M.A. Religious Studies; J.D./M.URP.; J.D./M.S.W.
Typical first-year section size: Full-time: 75
Is there typically a "small section" of the first year class, other than Legal Writing, taught by full-time faculty?: Full-time: yes
Number of course titles, beyond the first year curriculum, offered last year: 65
Percentages of upper division course sections, excluding seminars, with an enrollment of:

Under 25: 54%	25 to 49: 28%
50 to 74: 9%	75 to 99: 9%
100+: 0%	

Areas of specialization: appellate advocacy, clinical training, dispute resolution, environmental law, health care law, intellectual property law, international law, tax law, trial advocacy

Fall 2009 faculty profile
Total teaching faculty: 39. Full-time: 77%; 73% men, 27% women, 13% minorities. Part-time: 23%; 56% men, 44% women, 0% minorities
Student-to-faculty ratio: 15.5

SPECIAL PROGRAMS *(as provided by law school):*
The University of Iowa College of Law offers the following special programs to students: Innovation, Business and Law Program; International and Comparative Law Program; Writing Resource Center; Clinical Law Program; The Iowa/Bordeaux Summer Program; London Law Consortium; and the Summer Entrant Program. For more information please see, http://www.law.uiowa.edu

STUDENT BODY
Fall 2009 full-time enrollment: 590

Men: 56%	Women: 44%
African-American: 3.60%	American Indian: 1.00%
Asian-American: 6.10%	Mexican-American: 4.70%
Puerto Rican: 0.00%	Other Hisp-Amer: 0.00%
White: 81.40%	International: 3.20%
Unknown: 0.00%	

Attrition rates for 2008-2009 full-time students
Percent of students discontinuing law school:

Men: **3%**   Women: **1%**
First-year students: **4%**   Second-year students: **2%**
Third-year students: **N/A**   Fourth-year students: **N/A**

LIBRARY RESOURCES
Total titles: **948,593**
Total volumes: **1,260,524**
Total seats available for library users: **705**

INFORMATION TECHNOLOGY
Number of wired network connections available to students: **488** total (in the law library, excluding computer labs: **424**; in classrooms: **20**; in computer labs: **24**; elsewhere in the law school: **20**)
Law school has a wireless network.
Students are not required to own a computer.

EMPLOYMENT AND SALARIES
Proportion of 2008 graduates employed at graduation: **85%**
Employed 9 months later, as of February 15, 2009: **100%**
Salaries in the private sector (law firms, business, industry): **$65,000 –$145,000** (25th-75th percentile)
Median salary in the private sector: **$92,500**
Percentage in the private sector who reported salary information: **65%**

Median salary in public service (government, judicial clerkships, academic posts, non-profits): **$47,750**

Percentage of 2008 graduates in:
Law firms: **52%**   Government: **16%**
Bus./industry: **14%**   Judicial clerkship: **12%**
Public interest: **3%**   Unknown: **0%**
Academia : **3%**

2008 graduates employed in-state: **34%**
2008 graduates employed in foreign countries: **0%**
Number of states where graduates are employed: **30**
Percentage of 2008 graduates working in: New England: **2%**, Middle Atlantic: **3%**, East North Central: **22%**, West North Central: **48%**, South Atlantic: **9%**, East South Central: **0%**, West South Central: **3%**, Mountain: **7%**, Pacific: **7%**, Unknown: **0%**

BAR PASSAGE RATES
Based on 2008 graduates taking Summer 2008 or Winter 2009 exams. Most of the school's first-time test takers took the bar in Iowa.

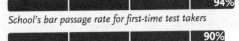

School's bar passage rate for first-time test takers

Statewide bar passage rate for first-time test takers

University of Kansas

■ Green Hall, 1535 W. 15th Street, Lawrence, KS, 66045-7608
■ http://www.law.ku.edu
■ Public
■ Year founded: 1878
■ 2009-2010 tuition: full-time: $14,478; part-time: N/A
■ Enrollment 2009-10 academic year: full-time: 499
■ U.S. News 2010 law specialty ranking: N/A

3.25-3.71 GPA, 25TH-75TH PERCENTILE

155-160 LSAT, 25TH-75TH PERCENTILE

35% ACCEPTANCE RATE

67 2011 U.S. NEWS LAW SCHOOL RANKING

ADMISSIONS

Admissions phone number: (866) 220-3654
Admissions email address: **admitlaw@ku.edu**
Application website:
  http://www.law.ku.edu/prospective/admissions/howtoapply/
Application deadline for Fall 2011 admission: **15-Mar**

Admissions statistics:

Number of applicants for Fall 2009: **1,098**
Number of acceptances: **387**
Number enrolled: **163**
Acceptance rate: **35%**
GPA, 25th-75th percentile, entering class Fall 2009: **3.25-3.71**
LSAT, 25th-75th percentile, entering class Fall 2009: **155-160**

FINANCIAL AID

Financial aid phone number: **(785) 864-4700**
Financial aid application deadline: **1-Mar**
Tuition 2009-2010 academic year: **full-time: $14,478; part-time: N/A**
Room and board: **$10,002** ; books: **$900** ; miscellaneous expenses: **$5,284**
Total of room/board/books/miscellaneous expenses: **$16,186**
University offers graduate student housing for which law students are eligible.

Financial aid profile

Percent of students that received grants for the 2008-2009 academic year: full-time: **79%**
Median grant amount: full-time: **$3,450**
The average law-school debt of those in the Class of 2009 who borrowed: **$39,099** . Proportion who borrowed: **82%**

ACADEMIC PROGRAMS

Calendar: **semester**
Joint degrees awarded: **J.D./M.B.A.; J.D./M.A. Economics; J.D./M.H.S.A.; J.D./M.A. Philosophy; J.D./M.P.A.;** J.D./M.S.W.; J.D./M.U.P.; J.D./M.S. Journalism; J.D./M.A. Global Indigenous Nations Stud; J.D./M.A. East Asian Languages & Culture; J.D./M.A. Political Science

Typical first-year section size: Full-time: **67**
Is there typically a "small section" of the first year class, other than Legal Writing, taught by full-time faculty?: Full-time: **yes**
Number of course titles, beyond the first year curriculum, offered last year: **93**
Percentages of upper division course sections, excluding seminars, with an enrollment of:

Under 25: **68%**   25 to 49: **24%**
50 to 74: **4%**   75 to 99: **4%**
100+: **0%**

Areas of specialization: appellate advocacy, clinical training, dispute resolution, environmental law, health care law, intellectual property law, international law, tax law, trial advocacy

Fall 2009 faculty profile

Total teaching faculty: **46.** Full-time: **70%**; 59% men, 41% women, 16% minorities. Part-time: **30%**; 64% men, 36% women, 0% minorities
Student-to-faculty ratio: **12.4**

SPECIAL PROGRAMS *(as provided by law school):*

The School offers eight certificate programs including elder law, environmental law, international trade law and tax law; eleven clinics and externships, including prosecution, legal aid, media, and tribal law; eleven joint degrees including business, health services, social welfare, and urban planning; two summer abroad programs in Ireland and Turkey; and a semester abroad program in London.

STUDENT BODY

Fall 2009 full-time enrollment: 499
Men: **60%**   Women: **40%**
African-American: **3.00%**   American Indian: **3.80%**
Asian-American: **5.40%**   Mexican-American: **0.80%**
Puerto Rican: **0.00%**   Other Hisp-Amer: **3.40%**

White: **73.10%**   International: **4.40%**
Unknown: **6.00%**

Attrition rates for 2008-2009 full-time students
Percent of students discontinuing law school:
Men: **1%**   Women: **3%**
First-year students: **1%**   Second-year students: **3%**
Third-year students: **1%**   Fourth-year students: **N/A**

LIBRARY RESOURCES
Total titles: **171,881**
Total volumes: **360,139**
Total seats available for library users: **481**

INFORMATION TECHNOLOGY
Number of wired network connections available to students: **0** total (in the law library, excluding computer labs: **0**; in classrooms: **0**; in computer labs: **0**; elsewhere in the law school: **0**)
Law school has a wireless network.
Students are not required to own a computer.

EMPLOYMENT AND SALARIES
Proportion of 2008 graduates employed at graduation: **69%**
Employed 9 months later, as of February 15, 2009: **94%**
Salaries in the private sector (law firms, business, industry): **$50,000 –$105,000** (25th-75th percentile)
Median salary in the private sector: **$62,500**
Percentage in the private sector who reported salary information: **71%**

Median salary in public service (government, judicial clerkships, academic posts, non-profits): **$46,000**

Percentage of 2008 graduates in:
Law firms: **56%**   Government: **18%**
Bus./industry: **15%**   Judicial clerkship: **7%**
Public interest: **4%**   Unknown: **0%**
Academia : **1%**

2008 graduates employed in-state: **45%**
2008 graduates employed in foreign countries: **2%**
Number of states where graduates are employed: **21**
Percentage of 2008 graduates working in: New England: **2%**, Middle Atlantic: **2%**, East North Central: **2%**, West North Central: **68%**, South Atlantic: **5%**, East South Central: **0%**, West South Central: **5%**, Mountain: **9%**, Pacific: **4%**, Unknown: **1%**

BAR PASSAGE RATES
Based on 2008 graduates taking Summer 2008 or Winter 2009 exams. Most of the school's first-time test takers took the bar in Kansas.

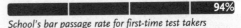

94%
School's bar passage rate for first-time test takers

89%
Statewide bar passage rate for first-time test takers

University of Kentucky

- 209 Law Building, Lexington, KY, 40506-0048
- http://www.law.uky.edu
- Public
- **Year founded:** 1908
- **2009-2010 tuition:** full-time: $16,020; part-time: N/A
- **Enrollment 2009-10 academic year:** full-time: 406
- **U.S. News 2010 law specialty ranking:** N/A

3.33-3.82 GPA, 25TH-75TH PERCENTILE

156-161 LSAT, 25TH-75TH PERCENTILE

38% ACCEPTANCE RATE

64 2011 U.S. NEWS LAW SCHOOL RANKING

ADMISSIONS
Admissions phone number: **(859) 257-6770**
Admissions email address: **lawadmissions@email.uky.edu**
Application website:
http://www.law.uky.edu/index.php?pid=108
Application deadline for Fall 2011 admission: **15-Mar**

Admissions statistics:
Number of applicants for Fall 2009: **1,080**
Number of acceptances: **414**
Number enrolled: **152**
Acceptance rate: **38%**
GPA, 25th-75th percentile, entering class Fall 2009: **3.33-3.82**
LSAT, 25th-75th percentile, entering class Fall 2009: **156-161**

FINANCIAL AID
Financial aid phone number: **(859) 257-3172**
Financial aid application deadline: **4-Jan**
Tuition 2009-2010 academic year: **full-time: $16,020; part-time: N/A**
Room and board: **$11,050** ; books: **$900** ; miscellaneous expenses: **$3,192**
Total of room/board/books/miscellaneous expenses: **$15,142**
University offers graduate student housing for which law students are eligible.

Financial aid profile
Percent of students that received grants for the 2008-2009 academic year: full-time: **63%**
Median grant amount: full-time: **$4,000**
The average law-school debt of those in the Class of 2009 who borrowed: **$55,870** . Proportion who borrowed: **81%**

ACADEMIC PROGRAMS
Calendar: **semester**
Joint degrees awarded: **J.D./M.B.A.; J.D./M.P.A.; J.D./M.A.**
Typical first-year section size: Full-time: **56**
Is there typically a "small section" of the first year class, other than Legal Writing, taught by full-time faculty?: Full-time: **yes**
Number of course titles, beyond the first year curriculum, offered last year: **72**
Percentages of upper division course sections, excluding seminars, with an enrollment of:
Under 25: **49%**   25 to 49: **37%**
50 to 74: **13%**   75 to 99: **0%**
100+: **0%**
Areas of specialization: appellate advocacy, clinical training, dispute resolution, environmental law, health care law, intellectual property law, international law, tax law, trial advocacy

Fall 2009 faculty profile
Total teaching faculty: **45**. Full-time: **51%**; **70%** men, **30%** women, **17%** minorities. Part-time: **49%**; **82%** men, **18%** women, **0%** minorities
Student-to-faculty ratio: **16.8**

SPECIAL PROGRAMS *(as provided by law school):*
Student lawyers in the UK Law Clinic represent needy clients on a variety of matters. UK Law offers 8 externship programs with: the Children's Law Center; the Department of Public Advocacy; the Innocence Project; state and federal judges; the Federal Correctional Institute; the Fayette County Prosecutor; the UK HealthCare Risk Management Office; and the U.S. Attorney's Office Appellate Section.

STUDENT BODY
Fall 2009 full-time enrollment: **406**
Men: **56%**   Women: **44%**
African-American: **8.90%**   American Indian: **0.70%**
Asian-American: **2.20%**   Mexican-American: **0.50%**
Puerto Rican: **0.20%**   Other Hisp-Amer: **1.20%**
White: **84.50%**   International: **0.20%**
Unknown: **1.50%**

Attrition rates for 2008-2009 full-time students
Percent of students discontinuing law school:
Men: **0%**   Women: **N/A**

First-year students: **1%**   Second-year students: **N/A**
Third-year students: **N/A**   Fourth-year students: **N/A**

LIBRARY RESOURCES

Total titles: 80,047
Total volumes: 492,579
Total seats available for library users: 354

INFORMATION TECHNOLOGY

Number of wired network connections available to students: 103 total (in the law library, excluding computer labs: 56; in classrooms: 7; in computer labs: 25; elsewhere in the law school: 15)
Law school has a wireless network.
Students are not required to own a computer.

EMPLOYMENT AND SALARIES

Proportion of 2008 graduates employed at graduation: 76%
Employed 9 months later, as of February 15, 2009: **98%**
Salaries in the private sector (law firms, business, industry): **$45,000 –$92,000** (25th-75th percentile)
Median salary in the private sector: **$60,000**
Percentage in the private sector who reported salary information: **69%**
Median salary in public service (government, judicial clerkships, academic posts, non-profits): **$35,000**

Percentage of 2008 graduates in:
Law firms: **58%**   Government: **9%**
Bus./industry: **7%**   Judicial clerkship: **19%**
Public interest: **5%**   Unknown: **0%**
Academia : **1%**

2008 graduates employed in-state: **69%**
2008 graduates employed in foreign countries: **0%**
Number of states where graduates are employed: **24**
Percentage of 2008 graduates working in: New England: 0%, Middle Atlantic: 4%, East North Central: 5%, West North Central: 1%, South Atlantic: 12%, East South Central: 72%, West South Central: 1%, Mountain: 1%, Pacific: 4%, Unknown: 0%

BAR PASSAGE RATES

Based on 2008 graduates taking Summer 2008 or Winter 2009 exams. Most of the school's first-time test takers took the bar in Kentucky.

94%
School's bar passage rate for first-time test takers

83%
Statewide bar passage rate for first-time test takers

University of Louisville (Brandeis)

■ 2301 S. Third Street, Louisville, KY, 40292
■ http://www.law.louisville.edu
■ Public
■ Year founded: 1846
■ 2009-2010 tuition: full-time: $14,632; part-time: $7,412
■ Enrollment 2009-10 academic year: full-time: 368; part-time: 67
■ U.S. News 2010 law specialty ranking: N/A

3.15-3.75 GPA, 25TH-75TH PERCENTILE

154-159 LSAT, 25TH-75TH PERCENTILE

37% ACCEPTANCE RATE

Tier 3 2011 U.S. NEWS LAW SCHOOL RANKING

ADMISSIONS

Admissions phone number: **(502) 852-6365**
Admissions email address: **lawadmissions@louisville.edu**
Application website:
http://www.law.louisville.edu/admissions/apply-now
Application deadline for Fall 2011 admission: **1-May**

Admissions statistics:
Number of applicants for Fall 2009: **1,162**
Number of acceptances: **432**
Number enrolled: **118**
Acceptance rate: **37%**
GPA, 25th-75th percentile, entering class Fall 2009: **3.15-3.75**
LSAT, 25th-75th percentile, entering class Fall 2009: **154-159**

Part-time program:
Number of applicants for Fall 2009: **93**
Number of acceptances: **33**
Number enrolled: **23**
Acceptance rate: **35%**
GPA, 25th-75th percentile, entering class Fall 2009: **3.04-3.67**
LSAT, 25th-75th percentile, entering class Fall 2009: **151-155**

FINANCIAL AID

Financial aid phone number: **(502) 852-6391**
Financial aid application deadline: **15-Mar**
Tuition 2009-2010 academic year: **full-time: $14,632; part-time: $7,412**
Room and board: **$8,490** ; books: **$1,000** ; miscellaneous expenses: **$7,240**
Total of room/board/books/miscellaneous expenses: **$16,730**
University offers graduate student housing for which law students are eligible.

Financial aid profile
Percent of students that received grants for the 2008-2009

academic year: full-time: **44%**; part-time **30%**
Median grant amount: full-time: **$4,000** ; part-time: **$4,000**
The average law-school debt of those in the Class of 2009 who borrowed: **$26,177** . Proportion who borrowed: **87%**

ACADEMIC PROGRAMS

Calendar: **semester**
Joint degrees awarded: **J.D./M.B.A.; J.D./M.A. Political Science**
Typical first-year section size: Full-time: **62**; Part-time: **62**
Is there typically a "small section" of the first year class, other than Legal Writing, taught by full-time faculty?: Full-time: **no**; Part-time: **no**
Number of course titles, beyond the first year curriculum, offered last year: **67**
Percentages of upper division course sections, excluding seminars, with an enrollment of:

Under 25: **52%**	25 to 49: **29%**
50 to 74: **18%**	75 to 99: **0%**
100+: **0%**	

Areas of specialization: appellate advocacy, clinical training, dispute resolution, environmental law, health care law, intellectual property law, international law, tax law, trial advocacy

Fall 2009 faculty profile
Total teaching faculty: **36**. Full-time: **67%; 54%** men, **46%** women, **8%** minorities. Part-time: **33%; 67%** men, **33%** women, **8%** minorities
Student-to-faculty ratio: **15.4**

SPECIAL PROGRAMS *(as provided by law school):*
All students take part in a public service program. We offer faculty-supervised externships (judicial, legal aid, public defender, technology, tax, and domestic violence). We opened a clinic in January 2009. The clinic represents individuals in family court and housing court. We hope to an innovation clinic, focusing on intellectual property and entrepreneurship, during 2010.

STUDENT BODY

Fall 2009 full-time enrollment: 368

Men: 53%	Women: 47%
African-American: 4.60%	American Indian: 0.00%
Asian-American: 2.70%	Mexican-American: 2.40%
Puerto Rican: 0.00%	Other Hisp-Amer: 0.00%
White: 85.90%	International: 1.60%
Unknown: 2.70%	

Fall 2009 part-time enrollment: 67

Men: 64%	Women: 36%
African-American: 0.00%	American Indian: 0.00%
Asian-American: 0.00%	Mexican-American: 0.00%
Puerto Rican: 0.00%	Other Hisp-Amer: 0.00%
White: 98.50%	International: 0.00%
Unknown: 1.50%	

Attrition rates for 2008-2009 full-time students

Percent of students discontinuing law school:

Men: 2%	Women: 3%
First-year students: 6%	Second-year students: 1%
Third-year students: N/A	Fourth-year students: N/A

LIBRARY RESOURCES

Total titles: 83,481

Total volumes: 425,681

Total seats available for library users: 357

INFORMATION TECHNOLOGY

Number of wired network connections available to students: 5 total (in the law library, excluding computer labs: 5; in classrooms: 0; in computer labs: 0; elsewhere in the law school: 0)

Law school has a wireless network.

Students are not required to own a computer.

EMPLOYMENT AND SALARIES

Proportion of 2008 graduates employed at graduation: 65%

Employed 9 months later, as of February 15, 2009: 95%

Salaries in the private sector (law firms, business, industry): $45,000 –$90,000 (25th-75th percentile)

Median salary in the private sector: $55,000

Percentage in the private sector who reported salary information: 56%

Median salary in public service (government, judicial clerkships, academic posts, non-profits): $44,000

Percentage of 2008 graduates in:

Law firms: 57%	Government: 11%
Bus./industry: 16%	Judicial clerkship: 5%
Public interest: 8%	Unknown: 0%
Academia : 3%	

2008 graduates employed in-state: 79%

2008 graduates employed in foreign countries: 3%

Number of states where graduates are employed: 15

Percentage of 2008 graduates working in: New England: 0%, Middle Atlantic: 2%, East North Central: 5%, West North Central: 1%, South Atlantic: 5%, East South Central: 81%, West South Central: 1%, Mountain: 1%, Pacific: 2%, Unknown: 0%

BAR PASSAGE RATES

Based on 2008 graduates taking Summer 2008 or Winter 2009 exams. Most of the school's first-time test takers took the bar in Kentucky.

88%

School's bar passage rate for first-time test takers

83%

Statewide bar passage rate for first-time test takers

University of Maine

- 246 Deering Avenue, Portland, ME, 4102
- http://mainelaw.maine.edu/
- Public
- Year founded: 1961
- 2009-2010 tuition: full-time: $20,702; part-time: N/A
- Enrollment 2009-10 academic year: full-time: 264
- U.S. News 2010 law specialty ranking: N/A

3.06-3.61 GPA, 25TH-75TH PERCENTILE

152-158 LSAT, 25TH-75TH PERCENTILE

48% ACCEPTANCE RATE

Tier 3 2011 U.S. NEWS LAW SCHOOL RANKING

ADMISSIONS

Admissions phone number: **(207) 780-4341**
Admissions email address: **mainelaw@usm.maine.edu**
Application website:
  http://mainelaw.maine.edu/admissions/pdf/application.pdf
Application deadline for Fall 2011 admission: **1-Mar**

Admissions statistics:
Number of applicants for Fall 2009: **705**
Number of acceptances: **341**
Number enrolled: **90**
Acceptance rate: **48%**
GPA, 25th-75th percentile, entering class Fall 2009: **3.06-3.61**
LSAT, 25th-75th percentile, entering class Fall 2009: **152-158**

FINANCIAL AID

Financial aid phone number: **(207) 780-5250**
Financial aid application deadline: **15-Feb**
Tuition 2009-2010 academic year: **full-time: $20,702**; part-time: N/A
Room and board: **$10,444** ; books: **$1,400** ; miscellaneous expenses: **$3,628**
Total of room/board/books/miscellaneous expenses: **$15,472**
University offers graduate student housing for which law students are eligible.

Financial aid profile
Percent of students that received grants for the 2008-2009 academic year: full-time: **30%**
Median grant amount: full-time: **$3,133**
The average law-school debt of those in the Class of 2009 who borrowed: **$72,627** . Proportion who borrowed: **90%**

ACADEMIC PROGRAMS

Calendar: **semester**
Joint degrees awarded: **J.D./M.B.A.; J.D./M.A. Public Policy & Mgmt; J.D/M.C.P.; J.D./M.S. Health Policy**

Typical first-year section size: Full-time: **91**
Is there typically a "small section" of the first year class, other than Legal Writing, taught by full-time faculty?: Full-time: **yes**
Number of course titles, beyond the first year curriculum, offered last year: **73**
Percentages of upper division course sections, excluding seminars, with an enrollment of:

Under 25: **70%**	25 to 49: **19%**
50 to 74: **10%**	75 to 99: **2%**
100+: **0%**	

Areas of specialization: appellate advocacy, clinical training, dispute resolution, environmental law, health care law, intellectual property law, international law, tax law, trial advocacy

Fall 2009 faculty profile
Total teaching faculty: **29**. Full-time: **55%**; **69%** men, **31%** women, **0%** minorities. Part-time: **45%**; **77%** men, **23%** women, **0%** minorities
Student-to-faculty ratio: **14.2**

SPECIAL PROGRAMS *(as provided by law school):*

Clinic students represent clients in civil, criminal, juvenile, domestic violence, family law, & patent law matters. The Marine Law Institute & Maine Patent Program provide service & research opportunities for students. Maine Law's coastal location enhances study in environmental, ocean, & coastal law. Externships, bridge courses, & fellowships link theory & practice. www.mainelaw.maine.edu

STUDENT BODY

Fall 2009 full-time enrollment: 264

Men: **58%**	Women: **42%**
African-American: **1.90%**	American Indian: **1.50%**
Asian-American: **2.70%**	Mexican-American: **0.40%**
Puerto Rican: **0.80%**	Other Hisp-Amer: **1.10%**
White: **90.50%**	International: **1.10%**
Unknown: **0.00%**	

Percent of students discontinuing law school:

Men: 3%	Women: 3%
First-year students: 10%	Second-year students: N/A
Third-year students: N/A	Fourth-year students: N/A

LIBRARY RESOURCES

Total titles: 123,866
Total volumes: 318,077
Total seats available for library users: 218

INFORMATION TECHNOLOGY

Number of wired network connections available to students: 0 total (in the law library, excluding computer labs: 0; in classrooms: 0; in computer labs: 0; elsewhere in the law school: 0)
Law school has a wireless network.
Students are not required to own a computer.

EMPLOYMENT AND SALARIES

Proportion of 2008 graduates employed at graduation: N/A
Employed 9 months later, as of February 15, 2009: **92%**
Salaries in the private sector (law firms, business, industry): **$45,000 –$68,000** (25th-75th percentile)
Median salary in the private sector: **$60,000**
Percentage in the private sector who reported salary information: **58%**

Median salary in public service (government, judicial clerkships, academic posts, non-profits): **$41,000**

Percentage of 2008 graduates in:

Law firms: 55%	Government: 11%
Bus./industry: 11%	Judicial clerkship: 16%
Public interest: 7%	Unknown: N/A
Academia : N/A	

2008 graduates employed in-state: **70%**
2008 graduates employed in foreign countries: **2%**
Number of states where graduates are employed: **9**
Percentage of 2008 graduates working in: New England: **81%**, Middle Atlantic: **3%**, East North Central: **2%**, West North Central: **0%**, South Atlantic: **10%**, East South Central: **0%**, West South Central: **0%**, Mountain: **0%**, Pacific: **2%**, Unknown: **0%**

BAR PASSAGE RATES

Based on 2008 graduates taking Summer 2008 or Winter 2009 exams. Most of the school's first-time test takers took the bar in Maine.

92%

School's bar passage rate for first-time test takers

91%

Statewide bar passage rate for first-time test takers

University of Maryland

- 500 W. Baltimore Street, Baltimore, MD, 21201-1786
- http://www.law.umaryland.edu
- Public
- Year founded: 1870
- 2009-2010 tuition: full-time: $23,762; part-time: $18,053
- Enrollment 2009-10 academic year: full-time: 723; part-time: 230
- U.S. News 2010 law specialty ranking: clinical training: 9, environmental law: 10, healthcare law: 2

3.29-3.67 GPA, 25TH-75TH PERCENTILE

161-167 LSAT, 25TH-75TH PERCENTILE

19% ACCEPTANCE RATE

48 2011 U.S. NEWS LAW SCHOOL RANKING

ADMISSIONS
Admissions phone number: (410) 706-3492
Admissions email address: **admissions@law.umaryland.edu**
Application website:
  http://www.law.umaryland.edu/prospective/applying/index.html
Application deadline for Fall 2011 admission: **15-Mar**

Admissions statistics:
Number of applicants for Fall 2009: **3,073**
Number of acceptances: **588**
Number enrolled: **226**
Acceptance rate: **19%**
GPA, 25th-75th percentile, entering class Fall 2009: **3.29-3.67**
LSAT, 25th-75th percentile, entering class Fall 2009: **161-167**

Part-time program:
Number of applicants for Fall 2009: **535**
Number of acceptances: **111**
Number enrolled: **72**
Acceptance rate: **21%**
GPA, 25th-75th percentile, entering class Fall 2009: **3.12-3.61**
LSAT, 25th-75th percentile, entering class Fall 2009: **154-161**

FINANCIAL AID
Financial aid phone number: (410) 706-0873
Financial aid application deadline: **1-Mar**
Tuition 2009-2010 academic year: **full-time: $23,762; part-time: $18,053**
Room and board: **$19,350** ; books: **$1,725** ; miscellaneous expenses: **$7,484**
Total of room/board/books/miscellaneous expenses: **$28,559**
University offers graduate student housing for which law students are eligible.

Financial aid profile
Percent of students that received grants for the 2008-2009 academic year: full-time: **57%**; part-time **20%**
Median grant amount: full-time: **$3,571** ; part-time: **$3,000**
The average law-school debt of those in the Class of 2009 who borrowed: **$81,872** . Proportion who borrowed: **88%**

ACADEMIC PROGRAMS
Calendar: **semester**
Joint degrees awarded: **J.D./Ph.D. Public Policy; J.D./M.A. Public Policy; J.D./M.P.H.; J.D./M.B.A.; J.D./M.A. Criminal Justice; J.D./M.A. Liberal Arts; J.D./M.A. Public Management; J.D./M.S.W.; J.D./Pharm.D.; J.D./M.A. Community Planning; J.D./M.S.N.; J.D./ M.A. Government**
Typical first-year section size: Full-time: **78**; Part-time: **74**
Is there typically a "small section" of the first year class, other than Legal Writing, taught by full-time faculty?: Full-time: **yes**; Part-time: **yes**
Number of course titles, beyond the first year curriculum, offered last year: **223**
Percentages of upper division course sections, excluding seminars, with an enrollment of:
  Under 25: **79%**   25 to 49: **12%**
  50 to 74: **6%**   75 to 99: **1%**
  100+: **1%**
Areas of specialization: appellate advocacy, clinical training, dispute resolution, environmental law, health care law, intellectual property law, international law, tax law, trial advocacy

Fall 2009 faculty profile
Total teaching faculty: **114**. Full-time: **56%**; **44%** men, **56%** women, **19%** minorities. Part-time: **44%**; **70%** men, **30%** women, **10%** minorities
Student-to-faculty ratio: **11.7**

SPECIAL PROGRAMS (as provided by law school):
The law school offers specialty programs in: Business Law; Clinical Law; Environmental Law; Intellectual Property Law; Law & Health Care; Women, Leadership & Equality. It houses

interdisciplinary centers for: Health and Homeland Security; Dispute Resolution; Tobacco Regulation, Litigation & Advocacy; Intellectual Property. The school offers a wide range of domestic and international externships.

STUDENT BODY

Fall 2009 full-time enrollment: 723
Men: 49%	Women: 51%
African-American: 12.00%	American Indian: 0.40%
Asian-American: 11.20%	Mexican-American: 0.10%
Puerto Rican: 0.00%	Other Hisp-Amer: 8.00%
White: 63.50%	International: 1.40%
Unknown: 3.30%	

Fall 2009 part-time enrollment: 230
Men: 54%	Women: 46%
African-American: 14.30%	American Indian: 0.40%
Asian-American: 9.60%	Mexican-American: 0.00%
Puerto Rican: 0.00%	Other Hisp-Amer: 6.10%
White: 67.80%	International: 0.90%
Unknown: 0.90%	

Attrition rates for 2008-2009 full-time students
Percent of students discontinuing law school:
Men: 2%	Women: 1%
First-year students: 4%	Second-year students: 1%
Third-year students: N/A	Fourth-year students: N/A

LIBRARY RESOURCES
Total titles: 159,566
Total volumes: 514,356
Total seats available for library users: 490

INFORMATION TECHNOLOGY
Number of wired network connections available to students: total (in the law library, excluding computer labs: 385; in classrooms: 718; in computer labs: N/A; elsewhere in the law school: 106)
Law school has a wireless network.
Students are required to own a computer.

EMPLOYMENT AND SALARIES
Proportion of 2008 graduates employed at graduation: 89%
Employed 9 months later, as of February 15, 2009: 95%
Salaries in the private sector (law firms, business, industry): $65,000 –$150,000 (25th-75th percentile)
Median salary in the private sector: $109,999
Percentage in the private sector who reported salary information: 52%
Median salary in public service (government, judicial clerkships, academic posts, non-profits): $45,000

Percentage of 2008 graduates in:
Law firms: 40%	Government: 15%
Bus./industry: 15%	Judicial clerkship: 18%
Public interest: 6%	Unknown: 0%
Academia : 6%	

2008 graduates employed in-state: 58%
2008 graduates employed in foreign countries: 0%
Number of states where graduates are employed: 27
Percentage of 2008 graduates working in: New England: 1%, Middle Atlantic: 12%, East North Central: 1%, West North Central: 0%, South Atlantic: 83%, East South Central: 0%, West South Central: 1%, Mountain: 1%, Pacific: 1%, Unknown: 0%

BAR PASSAGE RATES
Based on 2008 graduates taking Summer 2008 or Winter 2009 exams. Most of the school's first-time test takers took the bar in Maryland.

90%

School's bar passage rate for first-time test takers

85%

Statewide bar passage rate for first-time test takers

University of Memphis (Humphreys)

- 1 North Front Street, Memphis, TN, 38103-2189
- http://www.memphis.edu/law
- Public
- Year founded: 1962
- 2009-2010 tuition: full-time: $13,710; part-time: $11,999
- Enrollment 2009-10 academic year: full-time: 392; part-time: 28
- U.S. News 2010 law specialty ranking: N/A

3.17-3.68 GPA, 25TH-75TH PERCENTILE

153-158 LSAT, 25TH-75TH PERCENTILE

32% ACCEPTANCE RATE

Tier 3 2011 U.S. NEWS LAW SCHOOL RANKING

ADMISSIONS

Admissions phone number: (901) 678-5403
Admissions email address: lawadmissions@memphis.edu
Application website:
  http://www.memphis.edu/lawadmissions
Application deadline for Fall 2011 admission: 1-Mar

Admissions statistics:
Number of applicants for Fall 2009: 905
Number of acceptances: 293
Number enrolled: 136
Acceptance rate: 32%
GPA, 25th-75th percentile, entering class Fall 2009: 3.17-3.68
LSAT, 25th-75th percentile, entering class Fall 2009: 153-158

Part-time program:
Number of applicants for Fall 2009: 46
Number of acceptances: 10
Number enrolled: 7
Acceptance rate: 22%
GPA, 25th-75th percentile, entering class Fall 2009: 3.22-3.69
LSAT, 25th-75th percentile, entering class Fall 2009: 150-156

FINANCIAL AID

Financial aid phone number: (901) 678-3737
Financial aid application deadline: 1-Mar
Tuition 2009-2010 academic year: **full-time: $13,710**; part-time: $11,999
Room and board: $8,731 ; books: $1,700 ; miscellaneous expenses: $4,401
Total of room/board/books/miscellaneous expenses: $14,832
University offers graduate student housing for which law students are eligible.

Financial aid profile
Percent of students that received grants for the 2008-2009 academic year: full-time: 29%; part-time 50%
Median grant amount: full-time: $8,891 ; part-time: $4,633
The average law-school debt of those in the Class of 2009 who borrowed: $49,737 . Proportion who borrowed: 80%

ACADEMIC PROGRAMS
Calendar: **semester**
Joint degrees awarded: **J.D./M.B.A.; J.D./M.A.**
Typical first-year section size: Full-time: **75**
Is there typically a "small section" of the first year class, other than Legal Writing, taught by full-time faculty?:
  Full-time: **no**; Part-time: **no**
Number of course titles, beyond the first year curriculum, offered last year: **62**
Percentages of upper division course sections, excluding seminars, with an enrollment of:
  Under 25: **41%** 25 to 49: **34%**
  50 to 74: **14%** 75 to 99: **10%**
  100+: **1%**
Areas of specialization: appellate advocacy, clinical training, dispute resolution, environmental law, health care law, intellectual property law, international law, tax law, trial advocacy

Fall 2009 faculty profile
Total teaching faculty: **44**. Full-time: **41%**; **61%** men, **39%** women, **11%** minorities. Part-time: **59%**; **69%** men, **31%** women, **12%** minorities
Student-to-faculty ratio: **17.7**

SPECIAL PROGRAMS *(as provided by law school)*:
The TIP Program is a 5-week admission by performance summer program for TN residents and MS & AR residents which provides access to law school for underrepresented populations. Child and Family Advocacy, Civil Litigation, Elder Law and Small Business Clinics provide students with client contact and legal skills training. Externships are available at federal and state governmental agencies.

STUDENT BODY

Fall 2009 full-time enrollment: 392

Men: **59%**	Women: **41%**
African-American: **5.90%**	American Indian: **0.30%**
Asian-American: **1.80%**	Mexican-American: **0.00%**
Puerto Rican: **0.00%**	Other Hisp-Amer: **1.50%**
White: **87.20%**	International: **0.30%**
Unknown: **3.10%**	

Fall 2009 part-time enrollment: 28

Men: **39%**	Women: **61%**
African-American: **60.70%**	American Indian: **7.10%**
Asian-American: **7.10%**	Mexican-American: **0.00%**
Puerto Rican: **0.00%**	Other Hisp-Amer: **3.60%**
White: **21.40%**	International: **0.00%**
Unknown: **0.00%**	

Attrition rates for 2008-2009 full-time students
Percent of students discontinuing law school:

Men: **0%**	Women: **3%**
First-year students: **2%**	Second-year students: **2%**
Third-year students: **N/A**	Fourth-year students: **N/A**

LIBRARY RESOURCES

Total titles: **50,777**
Total volumes: **274,325**
Total seats available for library users: **203**

INFORMATION TECHNOLOGY

Number of wired network connections available to students: **71** total (in the law library, excluding computer labs: **71**; in classrooms: **0**; in computer labs: **0**; elsewhere in the law school: **0**)
Law school has a wireless network.
Students are not required to own a computer.

EMPLOYMENT AND SALARIES

Proportion of 2008 graduates employed at graduation: **41%**
Employed 9 months later, as of February 15, 2009: **93%**
Salaries in the private sector (law firms, business, industry): **$50,000 –$80,000** (25th-75th percentile)
Median salary in the private sector: **$59,281**
Percentage in the private sector who reported salary information: **42%**
Median salary in public service (government, judicial clerkships, academic posts, non-profits): **$47,000**

Percentage of 2008 graduates in:

Law firms: **70%**	Government: **9%**
Bus./industry: **11%**	Judicial clerkship: **5%**
Public interest: **4%**	Unknown: **0%**
Academia : **2%**	

2008 graduates employed in-state: **88%**
2008 graduates employed in foreign countries: **0%**
Number of states where graduates are employed: **12**
Percentage of 2008 graduates working in: New England: **0%**, Middle Atlantic: **2%**, East North Central: **2%**, West North Central: **1%**, South Atlantic: **2%**, East South Central: **89%**, West South Central: **2%**, Mountain: **3%**, Pacific: **0%**, Unknown: **0%**

BAR PASSAGE RATES

Based on 2008 graduates taking Summer 2008 or Winter 2009 exams. Most of the school's first-time test takers took the bar in Tennessee.

93%
School's bar passage rate for first-time test takers

83%
Statewide bar passage rate for first-time test takers

University of Miami

- PO Box 248087, Coral Gables, FL, 33124-8087
- http://www.law.miami.edu
- Private
- Year founded: 1926
- **2009-2010 tuition:** full-time: $38,012; part-time: $1,633/credit hour
- **Enrollment 2009-10 academic year:** full-time: 1,351; part-time: 33
- **U.S. News 2010 law specialty ranking:** tax law: 5

3.25-3.66 GPA, 25TH-75TH PERCENTILE

155-159 LSAT, 25TH-75TH PERCENTILE

52% ACCEPTANCE RATE

60 2011 U.S. NEWS LAW SCHOOL RANKING

ADMISSIONS
Admissions phone number: **(305) 284-2795**
Admissions email address: **admissions@law.miami.edu**
Application website:
  http://www.law.miami.edu/admissions/forms
Application deadline for Fall 2011 admission: **31-Jul**

Admissions statistics:
Number of applicants for Fall 2009: **4,605**
Number of acceptances: **2,409**
Number enrolled: **530**
Acceptance rate: **52%**
GPA, 25th-75th percentile, entering class Fall 2009: **3.25-3.66**
LSAT, 25th-75th percentile, entering class Fall 2009: **155-159**

FINANCIAL AID
Financial aid phone number: **(305) 284-3115**
Financial aid application deadline: **1-Mar**
Tuition 2009-2010 academic year: **full-time: $38,012; part-time: $1,633/credit hour**
Room and board: **$13,302** ; books: **$1,200** ; miscellaneous expenses: **$7,161**
Total of room/board/books/miscellaneous expenses: **$21,663**
University does not offer graduate student housing for which law students are eligible.

Financial aid profile
Percent of students that received grants for the 2008-2009 academic year: full-time: **31%**
Median grant amount: full-time: **$20,000** ; part-time: **$0**
The average law-school debt of those in the Class of 2009 who borrowed: **$87,272** . Proportion who borrowed: **77%**

ACADEMIC PROGRAMS
Calendar: **semester**
Joint degrees awarded: **J.D./M.B.A.; J.D./M.A.; J.D./LL.M. TAX**
Typical first-year section size: Full-time: **100**

Is there typically a "small section" of the first year class, other than Legal Writing, taught by full-time faculty?:
  Full-time: **yes**; Part-time: **no**
Number of course titles, beyond the first year curriculum, offered last year: **82**
Percentages of upper division course sections, excluding seminars, with an enrollment of:
  Under 25: **30%**   25 to 49: **36%**
  50 to 74: **15%**   75 to 99: **7%**
  100+: **13%**
Areas of specialization: appellate advocacy, clinical training, dispute resolution, environmental law, health care law, intellectual property law, international law, tax law, trial advocacy

Fall 2009 faculty profile
Total teaching faculty: **169.** Full-time: **38%**; **63%** men, **37%** women, **18%** minorities. Part-time: **62%**; **72%** men, **28%** women, **20%** minorities
Student-to-faculty ratio: **16.5**

SPECIAL PROGRAMS *(as provided by law school):*
A small sample of the many programs that enrich UM's first-rate education: skills training, integrating trial, pre-trial, and clinical; joint degree and LL.M. programs; multiple clinics on immigration, children, elderly, healthcare and impact litigation; summer programs abroad; mock trial and negotiations competitions including international. For detailed information visit www.law.miami.edu

STUDENT BODY
Fall 2009 full-time enrollment: 1,351
Men: **57%**   Women: **43%**
African-American: **6.90%**   American Indian: **0.30%**
Asian-American: **4.40%**   Mexican-American: **0.00%**
Puerto Rican: **0.00%**   Other Hisp-Amer: **11.80%**
White: **65.30%**   International: **4.00%**
Unknown: **7.30%**

Fall 2009 part-time enrollment: 33
Men: **70%**   Women: **30%**

African-American: **3.00%**
American Indian: **0.00%**
Asian-American: **3.00%**
Mexican-American: **0.00%**
Puerto Rican: **0.00%**
Other Hisp-Amer: **6.10%**
White: **66.70%**
International: **15.20%**
Unknown: **6.10%**

Attrition rates for 2008-2009 full-time students
Percent of students discontinuing law school:
Men: **2%**
Women: **3%**
First-year students: **8%**
Second-year students: **N/A**
Third-year students: **N/A**
Fourth-year students: **N/A**

LIBRARY RESOURCES
Total titles: **129,371**
Total volumes: **649,661**
Total seats available for library users: **698**

INFORMATION TECHNOLOGY
Number of wired network connections available to students: **28** total (in the law library, excluding computer labs: **10**; in classrooms: **18**; in computer labs: **0**; elsewhere in the law school: **0**)
Law school has a wireless network.
Students are not required to own a computer.

EMPLOYMENT AND SALARIES
Proportion of 2008 graduates employed at graduation: **78%**
Employed 9 months later, as of February 15, 2009: **96%**
Salaries in the private sector (law firms, business, industry): **$70,000 –$135,000** (25th-75th percentile)
Median salary in the private sector: **$102,000**

Percentage in the private sector who reported salary information: **30%**
Median salary in public service (government, judicial clerkships, academic posts, non-profits): **$44,000**

Percentage of 2008 graduates in:
Law firms: **66%**
Government: **10%**
Bus./industry: **10%**
Judicial clerkship: **5%**
Public interest: **3%**
Unknown: **4%**
Academia : **1%**

2008 graduates employed in-state: **66%**
2008 graduates employed in foreign countries: **1%**
Number of states where graduates are employed: **26**
Percentage of 2008 graduates working in: New England: **1%**, Middle Atlantic: **7%**, East North Central: **3%**, West North Central: **1%**, South Atlantic: **76%**, East South Central: **1%**, West South Central: **1%**, Mountain: **2%**, Pacific: **1%**, Unknown: **6%**

BAR PASSAGE RATES
Based on 2008 graduates taking Summer 2008 or Winter 2009 exams. Most of the school's first-time test takers took the bar in Florida.

91%
School's bar passage rate for first-time test takers

81%
Statewide bar passage rate for first-time test takers

University of Michigan–Ann Arbor

- 625 S. State Street, Ann Arbor, MI, 48109-1215
- http://www.law.umich.edu/
- Public
- Year founded: 1859
- 2009-2010 tuition: full-time: $43,250; part-time: N/A
- Enrollment 2009-10 academic year: full-time: 1,117
- U.S. News 2010 law specialty ranking: clinical training: 7, intellectual property law: 7, international law: 6, tax law: 16

3.55-3.84 GPA, 25TH-75TH PERCENTILE

167-170 LSAT, 25TH-75TH PERCENTILE

22% ACCEPTANCE RATE

9 2011 U.S. NEWS LAW SCHOOL RANKING

ADMISSIONS

Admissions phone number: **(734) 764-0537**
Admissions email address: **law.jd.admissions@umich.edu**
Application website:
  https://apply.embark.com/law/umich/jd/78/
Application deadline for Fall 2011 admission: **15-Feb**

Admissions statistics:

Number of applicants for Fall 2009: **5,414**
Number of acceptances: **1,178**
Number enrolled: **371**
Acceptance rate: **22%**
GPA, 25th-75th percentile, entering class Fall 2009: **3.55-3.84**
LSAT, 25th-75th percentile, entering class Fall 2009: **167-170**

FINANCIAL AID

Financial aid phone number: **(734) 764-5289**
Financial aid application deadline:
Tuition 2009-2010 academic year: **full-time: $43,250; part-time: N/A**
Room and board: **$11,386** ; books: **$1,050** ; miscellaneous expenses: **$5,064**
Total of room/board/books/miscellaneous expenses: **$17,500**
University offers graduate student housing for which law students are eligible.

Financial aid profile

Percent of students that received grants for the 2008-2009 academic year: full-time: **60%**
Median grant amount: full-time: **$11,300**
The average law-school debt of those in the Class of 2009 who borrowed: **$103,251** . Proportion who borrowed: **85%**

ACADEMIC PROGRAMS

Calendar: **semester**
Joint degrees awarded: **J.D./Ph.D. Economics; J.D./M.S. Information; J.D./M.S. Natural Resources; J.D./M.P.H.; J.D./M.P.P.; J.D./M.S.W.; J.D./M.U.P.; J.D./M.B.A.;** J.D./M.A. Kinesiology; J.D./M.A. South Asian Studies; J.D./M.A. South East Asian Studies; J.D./M.A. Japanese Studies; J.D./M.A. Russian/E. European Studies; J.D./M.A. Political Science; J.D./M.A. Chinese Studies; J.D./M.A. Modern Mid East/N African Stud; J.D./M.A. World Politics; J.D./M.H.S.A. Masters of Hlth Serv Admin
Typical first-year section size: Full-time: **91**
Is there typically a "small section" of the first year class, other than Legal Writing, taught by full-time faculty?: Full-time: **yes**
Number of course titles, beyond the first year curriculum, offered last year: **191**
Percentages of upper division course sections, excluding seminars, with an enrollment of:

Under 25: **51%**	25 to 49: **26%**
50 to 74: **10%**	75 to 99: **8%**
100+: **5%**	

Areas of specialization: appellate advocacy, clinical training, dispute resolution, environmental law, health care law, intellectual property law, international law, tax law, trial advocacy

Fall 2009 faculty profile

Total teaching faculty: **114**. Full-time: **71%**; 70% men, 30% women, **10%** minorities. Part-time: **29%**; 67% men, 33% women, **3%** minorities
Student-to-faculty ratio: **11.3**

SPECIAL PROGRAMS (as provided by law school):

Michigan Law offers extensive clinical, research, scholarly, and practice opportunities – including 13 clinics, study abroad in one of 8 established programs, domestic and international externships and internships, 14 dual degree programs, 6 international centers and programs, and prestigious clerkships in the U.S., the European Court of Justice and International Court of Justice.

STUDENT BODY

Fall 2009 full-time enrollment: 1,117
Men: **56%**   Women: **44%**

African-American: 5.10%   American Indian: 1.50%
Asian-American: 12.10%   Mexican-American: 0.00%
Puerto Rican: 0.00%   Other Hisp-Amer: 4.20%
White: 62.20%   International: 3.40%
Unknown: 11.50%

Attrition rates for 2008-2009 full-time students
Percent of students discontinuing law school:
Men: 1%   Women: 1%
First-year students: 0%   Second-year students: 1%
Third-year students: 1%   Fourth-year students: N/A

LIBRARY RESOURCES
Total titles: 362,247
Total volumes: 1,002,273
Total seats available for library users: 854

INFORMATION TECHNOLOGY
Number of wired network connections available to students: 332 total (in the law library, excluding computer labs: 8; in classrooms: 280; in computer labs: 24; elsewhere in the law school: 20)
Law school has a wireless network.
Students are not required to own a computer.

EMPLOYMENT AND SALARIES
Proportion of 2008 graduates employed at graduation: 98%
Employed 9 months later, as of February 15, 2009: 100%
Salaries in the private sector (law firms, business, industry): $160,000 –$160,000 (25th-75th percentile)
Median salary in the private sector: $160,000

Percentage in the private sector who reported salary information: 88%
Median salary in public service (government, judicial clerkships, academic posts, non-profits): $56,386

Percentage of 2008 graduates in:
Law firms: 73%   Government: 3%
Bus./industry: 5%   Judicial clerkship: 14%
Public interest: 5%   Unknown: 0%
Academia : 1%

2008 graduates employed in-state: 10%
2008 graduates employed in foreign countries: 2%
Number of states where graduates are employed: 31
Percentage of 2008 graduates working in: New England: 4%, Middle Atlantic: 28%, East North Central: 28%, West North Central: 2%, South Atlantic: 12%, East South Central: 1%, West South Central: 3%, Mountain: 4%, Pacific: 17%, Unknown: 1%

BAR PASSAGE RATES
Based on 2008 graduates taking Summer 2008 or Winter 2009 exams. Most of the school's first-time test takers took the bar in New York.

91%
School's bar passage rate for first-time test takers

81%
Statewide bar passage rate for first-time test takers

University of Minnesota–Twin Cities

- 229 19th Avenue S, Minneapolis, MN, 55455
- http://www.law.umn.edu
- Public
- Year founded: 1888
- 2009-2010 tuition: full-time: $28,203; part-time: N/A
- Enrollment 2009-10 academic year: full-time: 766
- U.S. News 2010 law specialty ranking: healthcare law: 10

3.30-3.85 GPA, 25TH-75TH PERCENTILE

160-168 LSAT, 25TH-75TH PERCENTILE

25% ACCEPTANCE RATE

22 2011 U.S. NEWS LAW SCHOOL RANKING

ADMISSIONS

Admissions phone number: **(612) 625-3487**
Admissions email address: **umnlsadm@umn.edu**
Application website:
   http://www.law.umn.edu/prospective/online_app.html
Application deadline for Fall 2011 admission: **1-Apr**

Admissions statistics:
Number of applicants for Fall 2009: **3,594**
Number of acceptances: **911**
Number enrolled: **213**
Acceptance rate: **25%**
GPA, 25th-75th percentile, entering class Fall 2009: **3.30-3.85**
LSAT, 25th-75th percentile, entering class Fall 2009: **160-168**

FINANCIAL AID

Financial aid phone number: **(612) 625-3487**
Financial aid application deadline: **1-Apr**
Tuition 2009-2010 academic year: **full-time: $28,203; part-time: N/A**
Room and board: **$1,666** ; books: **$9,612** ; miscellaneous expenses: **$2,750**
Total of room/board/books/miscellaneous expenses: **$14,028**
University does not offer graduate student housing for which law students are eligible.

Financial aid profile
Percent of students that received grants for the 2008-2009 academic year: full-time: **65%**
Median grant amount: full-time: **$8,150**
The average law-school debt of those in the Class of 2009 who borrowed: **$94,087** . Proportion who borrowed: **85%**

ACADEMIC PROGRAMS

Calendar: **semester**
Joint degrees awarded: J.D./M.U.R.P.; J.D./M.P.H.; J.D./Ph.D.; J.D./M.D.; J.D./M.B.A.; J.D./M.S.; J.D./M.A.; J.D./M.P.P.; J.D./M.H.A

Typical first-year section size: Full-time: **96**
Is there typically a "small section" of the first year class, other than Legal Writing, taught by full-time faculty?: Full-time: **yes**
Number of course titles, beyond the first year curriculum, offered last year: **178**
Percentages of upper division course sections, excluding seminars, with an enrollment of:
   Under 25: **55%**   25 to 49: **24%**
   50 to 74: **10%**   75 to 99: **9%**
   100+: **2%**
Areas of specialization: appellate advocacy, clinical training, dispute resolution, environmental law, health care law, intellectual property law, international law, tax law, trial advocacy

Fall 2009 faculty profile
Total teaching faculty: **242**. Full-time: **26%**; **63%** men, **38%** women, **8%** minorities. Part-time: **74%**; **55%** men, **45%** women, **4%** minorities
Student-to-faculty ratio: **11.9**

SPECIAL PROGRAMS (as provided by law school):

17 clinics including Civil Practice Clinic, Tax Clinic. 10 institutes including Human Rights Center, Institute on Race and Poverty. 9 foreign semester exchange programs.' Public Service Program encourages 50 pro bono hours per student. Judicial externship program with federal and state courts. 12 joint degree programs.

STUDENT BODY

Fall 2009 full-time enrollment: **766**
Men: **58%**   Women: **42%**
African-American: **2.90%**   American Indian: **1.40%**
Asian-American: **8.20%**   Mexican-American: **0.00%**
Puerto Rican: **0.00%**   Other Hisp-Amer: **3.40%**
White: **75.10%**   International: **2.70%**
Unknown: **6.30%**

Attrition rates for 2008-2009 full-time students
Percent of students discontinuing law school:

Men: **3%**
First-year students: **6%**
Third-year students: **N/A**

Women: **2%**
Second-year students: **3%**
Fourth-year students: **N/A**

LIBRARY RESOURCES

Total titles: **336,912**
Total volumes: **1,083,918**
Total seats available for library users: **775**

INFORMATION TECHNOLOGY

Number of wired network connections available to students: **0** total (in the law library, excluding computer labs: **0**; in classrooms: **0**; in computer labs: **0**; elsewhere in the law school: **0**)
Law school has a wireless network.
Students are required to own a computer.

EMPLOYMENT AND SALARIES

Proportion of 2008 graduates employed at graduation: **84%**
Employed 9 months later, as of February 15, 2009: **97%**
Salaries in the private sector (law firms, business, industry): **$80,000 –$140,000** (25th-75th percentile)
Median salary in the private sector: **$120,000**
Percentage in the private sector who reported salary information: **60%**

Median salary in public service (government, judicial clerkships, academic posts, non-profits): **$50,000**

Percentage of 2008 graduates in:
Law firms: **60%**
Bus./industry: **8%**
Public interest: **4%**
Academia : **0%**

Government: **11%**
Judicial clerkship: **17%**
Unknown: **0%**

2008 graduates employed in-state: **52%**
2008 graduates employed in foreign countries: **1%**
Number of states where graduates are employed: **28**
Percentage of 2008 graduates working in: New England: **1%**, Middle Atlantic: **5%**, East North Central: **11%**, West North Central: **54%**, South Atlantic: **11%**, East South Central: **1%**, West South Central: **4%**, Mountain: **4%**, Pacific: **7%**, Unknown: **2%**

BAR PASSAGE RATES

Based on 2008 graduates taking Summer 2008 or Winter 2009 exams. Most of the school's first-time test takers took the bar in Minnesota.

97%

School's bar passage rate for first-time test takers

91%

Statewide bar passage rate for first-time test takers

University of Mississippi

■ PO Box 1848, University, MS, 38677
■ http://law.olemiss.edu
■ Public
■ Year founded: 1854
■ 2009-2010 tuition: full-time: $9,350; part-time: N/A
■ Enrollment 2009-10 academic year: full-time: 495
■ U.S. News 2010 law specialty ranking: N/A

3.27-3.71 GPA, 25TH-75TH PERCENTILE

151-157 LSAT, 25TH-75TH PERCENTILE

41% ACCEPTANCE RATE

Tier 3 2011 U.S. NEWS LAW SCHOOL RANKING

ADMISSIONS

Admissions phone number: (662) 915-6910
Admissions email address: lawmiss@olemiss.edu
Application website: http://www.lsac.org
Application deadline for Fall 2011 admission: 1-Mar

Admissions statistics:

Number of applicants for Fall 2009: 1,164
Number of acceptances: 472
Number enrolled: 173
Acceptance rate: 41%
GPA, 25th-75th percentile, entering class Fall 2009: 3.27-3.71
LSAT, 25th-75th percentile, entering class Fall 2009: 151-157

FINANCIAL AID

Financial aid phone number: (800) 891-4569
Financial aid application deadline: 1-Mar
Tuition 2009-2010 academic year: **full-time: $9,350**; part-time: N/A
Room and board: $12,800 ; books: $1,300 ; miscellaneous expenses: $4,660
Total of room/board/books/miscellaneous expenses: $18,760
University offers graduate student housing for which law students are eligible.

Financial aid profile

Percent of students that received grants for the 2008-2009 academic year: full-time: 29%
Median grant amount: full-time: $1,000
The average law-school debt of those in the Class of 2009 who borrowed: $60,121 . Proportion who borrowed: 73%

ACADEMIC PROGRAMS

Calendar: **semester**
Joint degrees awarded: **N/A**
Typical first-year section size: Full-time: 57
Is there typically a "small section" of the first year class, other than Legal Writing, taught by full-time faculty?:

Full-time: **no**
Number of course titles, beyond the first year curriculum, offered last year: **89**
Percentages of upper division course sections, excluding seminars, with an enrollment of:

Under 25: 55%	25 to 49: 27%
50 to 74: 8%	75 to 99: 9%
100+: 1%	

Areas of specialization: appellate advocacy, clinical training, dispute resolution, environmental law, health care law, intellectual property law, international law, tax law, trial advocacy

Fall 2009 faculty profile

Total teaching faculty: 34. Full-time: 65%; 77% men, 23% women, 14% minorities. Part-time: 35%; 50% men, 50% women, 17% minorities
Student-to-faculty ratio: 18.2

SPECIAL PROGRAMS *(as provided by law school):*

Public Service Externship, Prosecutorial Externship, Criminal Appeals Clinic, Civil Law Clinic, Mississippi Innocence Project, Business Regulation Externship, Summer session in Cambridge, England, Appellate Judicial Externship, Concentration in Criminal Law, and Concentration in Remote Sensing Air and Space Law

STUDENT BODY

Fall 2009 full-time enrollment: 495

Men: 57%	Women: 43%
African-American: 12.10%	American Indian: 0.80%
Asian-American: 0.80%	Mexican-American: 0.00%
Puerto Rican: 0.00%	Other Hisp-Amer: 0.80%
White: 85.30%	International: 0.00%
Unknown: 0.20%	

Attrition rates for 2008-2009 full-time students

Percent of students discontinuing law school:

Men: 2%	Women: 3%
First-year students: 7%	Second-year students: 1%
Third-year students: N/A	Fourth-year students: N/A

LIBRARY RESOURCES

Total titles: 110,840
Total volumes: 331,549
Total seats available for library users: 305

INFORMATION TECHNOLOGY

Number of wired network connections available to students: 737 total (in the law library, excluding computer labs: 121; in classrooms: 458; in computer labs: 4; elsewhere in the law school: 154)
Law school has a wireless network.
Students are not required to own a computer.

EMPLOYMENT AND SALARIES

Proportion of 2008 graduates employed at graduation: 54%
Employed 9 months later, as of February 15, 2009: 90%
Salaries in the private sector (law firms, business, industry): $56,250 –$100,000 (25th-75th percentile)
Median salary in the private sector: $81,500
Percentage in the private sector who reported salary information: 63%
Median salary in public service (government, judicial clerkships, academic posts, non-profits): $52,000

Percentage of 2008 graduates in:

Law firms: 50%   Government: 14%
Bus./industry: 11%   Judicial clerkship: 17%
Public interest: 5%   Unknown: 0%
Academia : 3%

2008 graduates employed in-state: 60%
2008 graduates employed in foreign countries: 0%
Number of states where graduates are employed: 17
Percentage of 2008 graduates working in: New England: 1%, Middle Atlantic: 4%, East North Central: 2%, West North Central: 0%, South Atlantic: 13%, East South Central: 75%, West South Central: 5%, Mountain: 1%, Pacific: 0%, Unknown: 0%

BAR PASSAGE RATES

Based on 2008 graduates taking Summer 2008 or Winter 2009 exams. Most of the school's first-time test takers took the bar in Mississippi.

90%
School's bar passage rate for first-time test takers

88%
Statewide bar passage rate for first-time test takers

University of Missouri–Columbia

■ 203 Hulston Hall, Columbia, MO, 65211-4300
■ http://www.law.missouri.edu
■ Public
■ Year founded: 1872
■ 2009-2010 tuition: full-time: $16,017; part-time: N/A
■ Enrollment 2009-10 academic year: full-time: 441; part-time: 4
■ U.S. News 2010 law specialty ranking: dispute resolution: 2

3.24-3.70 GPA, 25ᵀᴴ-75ᵀᴴ PERCENTILE

156-161 LSAT, 25ᵀᴴ-75ᵀᴴ PERCENTILE

44% ACCEPTANCE RATE

93 2011 U.S. NEWS LAW SCHOOL RANKING

ADMISSIONS

Admissions phone number: **(573) 882-6042**
Admissions email address: **umclawadmissions@missouri.edu**
Application website:
http://www.law.missouri.edu/admissions/pdf/applicatio nF10all.pdf
Application deadline for Fall 2011 admission: **1-Mar**

Admissions statistics:

Number of applicants for Fall 2009: **914**
Number of acceptances: **400**
Number enrolled: **147**
Acceptance rate: **44%**
GPA, 25th-75th percentile, entering class Fall 2009: **3.24-3.70**
LSAT, 25th-75th percentile, entering class Fall 2009: **156-161**

FINANCIAL AID

Financial aid phone number: **(573) 882-6643**
Financial aid application deadline: **1-Mar**
Tuition 2009-2010 academic year: **full-time: $16,017; part-time: N/A**
Room and board: **$8,590** ; books: **$1,550** ; miscellaneous expenses: **$6,884**
Total of room/board/books/miscellaneous expenses: **$17,024**
University does not offer graduate student housing for which law students are eligible.

Financial aid profile

Percent of students that received grants for the 2008-2009 academic year: full-time: **59%**
Median grant amount: full-time: **$4,025**
The average law-school debt of those in the Class of 2009 who borrowed: **$54,896** . Proportion who borrowed: **99%**

ACADEMIC PROGRAMS

Calendar: **semester**
Joint degrees awarded: **J.D./M.B.A.; J.D./M.P.A.; JD/ MA Biology**

Typical first-year section size: Full-time: **73**
Is there typically a "small section" of the first year class, other than Legal Writing, taught by full-time faculty?: Full-time: **yes**; Part-time: **no**
Number of course titles, beyond the first year curriculum, offered last year: **119**
Percentages of upper division course sections, excluding seminars, with an enrollment of:

Under 25: **66%**   25 to 49: **22%**
50 to 74: **10%**   75 to 99: **2%**
100+: **0%**

Areas of specialization: appellate advocacy, clinical training, dispute resolution, environmental law, health care law, intellectual property law, international law, tax law, trial advocacy

Fall 2009 faculty profile

Total teaching faculty: 26. Full-time: **85%**; **73%** men, **27%** women, **14%** minorities. Part-time: **15%**; **75%** men, **25%** women, **0%** minorities
Student-to-faculty ratio: **16.8**

SPECIAL PROGRAMS *(as provided by law school):*

The Center for the Study of Dispute Resolution attracts students worldwide. Law students can extern in the MO Supreme Court, MO & US Attorney's Offices, and the Compliance Office of MU Athletics, study abroad in S. Africa or London, and gain representation and mediation experience in the Criminal Prosecution, Family Violence, Child Protection, Mediation Clinics, and the MO Innocence Project.

STUDENT BODY

Fall 2009 full-time enrollment: 441

Men: **62%**   Women: **38%**
African-American: **6.30%**   American Indian: **0.70%**
Asian-American: **3.40%**   Mexican-American: **0.90%**
Puerto Rican: **0.00%**   Other Hisp-Amer: **2.00%**
White: **84.40%**   International: **0.20%**
Unknown: **2.00%**

Fall 2009 part-time enrollment: 4

Men: 25%	Women: 75%
African-American: 25.00%	American Indian: 0.00%
Asian-American: 25.00%	Mexican-American: 0.00%
Puerto Rican: 0.00%	Other Hisp-Amer: 0.00%
White: 50.00%	International: 0.00%
Unknown: 0.00%	

Attrition rates for 2008-2009 full-time students
Percent of students discontinuing law school:

Men: 4%	Women: 3%
First-year students: 9%	Second-year students: 1%
Third-year students: 1%	Fourth-year students: N/A

LIBRARY RESOURCES

Total titles: 234,137
Total volumes: 401,578
Total seats available for library users: 472

INFORMATION TECHNOLOGY

Number of wired network connections available to students: 6 total (in the law library, excluding computer labs: 0; in classrooms: 0; in computer labs: 6; elsewhere in the law school: 0)
Law school has a wireless network.
Students are not required to own a computer.

EMPLOYMENT AND SALARIES

Proportion of 2008 graduates employed at graduation: 51%
Employed 9 months later, as of February 15, 2009: 90%
Salaries in the private sector (law firms, business, industry): $52,500 –$92,000 (25th-75th percentile)

Median salary in the private sector: $60,000
Percentage in the private sector who reported salary information: 42%
Median salary in public service (government, judicial clerkships, academic posts, non-profits): $44,000

Percentage of 2008 graduates in:

Law firms: 54%	Government: 14%
Bus./industry: 11%	Judicial clerkship: 13%
Public interest: 5%	Unknown: 2%
Academia : 2%	

2008 graduates employed in-state: 80%
2008 graduates employed in foreign countries: 1%
Number of states where graduates are employed: 13
Percentage of 2008 graduates working in: New England: 1%, Middle Atlantic: 3%, East North Central: 5%, West North Central: 83%, South Atlantic: 1%, East South Central: 0%, West South Central: 2%, Mountain: 1%, Pacific: 3%, Unknown: 0%

BAR PASSAGE RATES

Based on 2008 graduates taking Summer 2008 or Winter 2009 exams. Most of the school's first-time test takers took the bar in Missouri.

92%

School's bar passage rate for first-time test takers

91%

Statewide bar passage rate for first-time test takers

University of Missouri–Kansas City

- 5100 Rockhill Road, Kansas City, MO, 64110
- http://www.law.umkc.edu
- Public
- Year founded: 1895
- 2009-2010 tuition: full-time: $14,242; part-time: $10,248
- Enrollment 2009-10 academic year: full-time: 489; part-time: 26
- U.S. News 2010 law specialty ranking: N/A

3.03-3.58 GPA, 25TH-75TH PERCENTILE

152-156 LSAT, 25TH-75TH PERCENTILE

48% ACCEPTANCE RATE

Tier 3 2011 U.S. NEWS LAW SCHOOL RANKING

ADMISSIONS

Admissions phone number: (816) 235-1644
Admissions email address: law@umkc.edu
Application website:
   http://www1.law.umkc.edu/admissions/
Application deadline for Fall 2011 admission: rolling

Admissions statistics:

Number of applicants for Fall 2009: 914
Number of acceptances: 437
Number enrolled: 155
Acceptance rate: 48%
GPA, 25th-75th percentile, entering class Fall 2009: 3.03-3.58
LSAT, 25th-75th percentile, entering class Fall 2009: 152-156

Part-time program:

Number of applicants for Fall 2009: 36
Number of acceptances: 14
Number enrolled: 9
Acceptance rate: 39%
GPA, 25th-75th percentile, entering class Fall 2009: 2.70-3.54
LSAT, 25th-75th percentile, entering class Fall 2009: 148-161

FINANCIAL AID

Financial aid phone number: (816) 235-1154
Financial aid application deadline:
Tuition 2009-2010 academic year: full-time: $14,242; part-time: $10,248
Room and board: $8,970 ; books: $4,470 ; miscellaneous expenses: $7,350
Total of room/board/books/miscellaneous expenses: $20,790
University offers graduate student housing for which law students are eligible.

Financial aid profile

Percent of students that received grants for the 2008-2009 academic year: full-time: 36%; part-time 23%
Median grant amount: full-time: $6,023 ; part-time: $6,000
The average law-school debt of those in the Class of 2009 who borrowed: $75,093 . Proportion who borrowed: 85%

ACADEMIC PROGRAMS

Calendar: semester
Joint degrees awarded: JD/MBA; JD/MPA; JD/LLM Taxation
Typical first-year section size: Full-time: 56
Is there typically a "small section" of the first year class, other than Legal Writing, taught by full-time faculty?: Full-time: no; Part-time: no
Number of course titles, beyond the first year curriculum, offered last year: 114
Percentages of upper division course sections, excluding seminars, with an enrollment of:

Under 25: 67%	25 to 49: 15%
50 to 74: 9%	75 to 99: 9%
100+: 0%	

Areas of specialization: appellate advocacy, clinical training, dispute resolution, environmental law, intellectual property law, international law, tax law, trial advocacy

Fall 2009 faculty profile

Total teaching faculty: 46. Full-time: 70%; 59% men, 41% women, 13% minorities. Part-time: 30%; 79% men, 21% women, 0% minorities
Student-to-faculty ratio: 14.1

SPECIAL PROGRAMS (as provided by law school):

The school's location in a metropolitan area provides many opportunities for students to engage in real-life representation of clients in clinical programs that include UMKC's Child and Family Services Clinic, Guardian Ad Litem Workshop, Tax Clinic, Entrepreneurial Law and Practice Clinic, and the school's Innocence Project. Summer abroad programs in Ireland, China and Wales.

STUDENT BODY

Fall 2009 full-time enrollment: 489

Men: 60%	Women: 40%
African-American: 4.70%	American Indian: 0.80%
Asian-American: 2.50%	Mexican-American: 0.00%
Puerto Rican: 0.00%	Other Hisp-Amer: 3.30%
White: 75.90%	International: 1.20%
Unknown: 11.70%	

Fall 2009 part-time enrollment: 26

Men: 58%	Women: 42%
African-American: 30.80%	American Indian: 0.00%
Asian-American: 3.80%	Mexican-American: 0.00%
Puerto Rican: 0.00%	Other Hisp-Amer: 3.80%
White: 53.80%	International: 3.80%
Unknown: 3.80%	

Attrition rates for 2008-2009 full-time students
Percent of students discontinuing law school:

Men: 5%	Women: 4%
First-year students: 13%	Second-year students: 1%
Third-year students: N/A	Fourth-year students: N/A

LIBRARY RESOURCES

Total titles: 147,421
Total volumes: 348,358
Total seats available for library users: 377

INFORMATION TECHNOLOGY

Number of wired network connections available to students: 46 total (in the law library, excluding computer labs: 14; in classrooms: 0; in computer labs: 8; elsewhere in the law school: 24)
Law school has a wireless network.
Students are not required to own a computer.

EMPLOYMENT AND SALARIES

Proportion of 2008 graduates employed at graduation:
N/A
Employed 9 months later, as of February 15, 2009: 96%
Salaries in the private sector (law firms, business, industry): $50,000 –$100,000 (25th-75th percentile)
Median salary in the private sector: $62,500
Percentage in the private sector who reported salary information: 66%
Median salary in public service (government, judicial clerkships, academic posts, non-profits): $43,800

Percentage of 2008 graduates in:

Law firms: 58%	Government: 17%
Bus./industry: 8%	Judicial clerkship: 11%
Public interest: 5%	Unknown: 1%
Academia : 1%	

2008 graduates employed in-state: 76%
2008 graduates employed in foreign countries: 1%
Number of states where graduates are employed: 15
Percentage of 2008 graduates working in: New England: 0%, Middle Atlantic: 0%, East North Central: 2%, West North Central: 88%, South Atlantic: 3%, East South Central: 1%, West South Central: 1%, Mountain: 2%, Pacific: 2%, Unknown: 0%

BAR PASSAGE RATES

Based on 2008 graduates taking Summer 2008 or Winter 2009 exams. Most of the school's first-time test takers took the bar in Missouri.

98%

School's bar passage rate for first-time test takers

91%

Statewide bar passage rate for first-time test takers

University of Montana

- 32 Campus Drive, Missoula, MT, 59812
- http://www.umt.edu/law
- Public
- Year founded: 1911
- 2009-2010 tuition: full-time: $10,620; part-time: N/A
- Enrollment 2009-10 academic year: full-time: 252
- U.S. News 2010 law specialty ranking: N/A

3.26-3.69 GPA, 25TH-75TH PERCENTILE

151-157 LSAT, 25TH-75TH PERCENTILE

50% ACCEPTANCE RATE

Tier 3 2011 U.S. NEWS LAW SCHOOL RANKING

ADMISSIONS

Admissions phone number: (406) 243-2698
Admissions email address: heidi.fanslow@umontana.edu
Application website:
　http://www.umt.edu/law/admissions/default.htm
Application deadline for Fall 2011 admission: 12-Mar

Admissions statistics:
Number of applicants for Fall 2009: 396
Number of acceptances: 199
Number enrolled: 84
Acceptance rate: 50%
GPA, 25th-75th percentile, entering class Fall 2009: 3.26-3.69
LSAT, 25th-75th percentile, entering class Fall 2009: 151-157

FINANCIAL AID

Financial aid phone number: (406) 243-5524
Financial aid application deadline: 1-Mar
Tuition 2009-2010 academic year: full-time: $10,620; part-time: N/A
Room and board: $12,000 ; books: $1,200 ; miscellaneous expenses: $486
Total of room/board/books/miscellaneous expenses: $13,686
University offers graduate student housing for which law students are eligible.

Financial aid profile
Percent of students that received grants for the 2008-2009 academic year: full-time: N/A
Median grant amount: full-time: $2,200
The average law-school debt of those in the Class of 2009 who borrowed: $58,962 . Proportion who borrowed: 96%

ACADEMIC PROGRAMS

Calendar: semester
Joint degrees awarded: N/A
Typical first-year section size: Full-time: 42
Is there typically a "small section" of the first year class, other than Legal Writing, taught by full-time faculty?:
　Full-time: no
Number of course titles, beyond the first year curriculum, offered last year: N/A
Percentages of upper division course sections, excluding seminars, with an enrollment of:
　Under 25: 67%　　　25 to 49: 11%
　50 to 74: 6%　　　　75 to 99: 14%
　100+: 3%
Areas of specialization: appellate advocacy, clinical training, dispute resolution, environmental law, health care law, intellectual property law, international law, tax law, trial advocacy

Fall 2009 faculty profile
Total teaching faculty: 26. Full-time: 62%; 56% men, 44% women, 25% minorities. Part-time: 38%; 80% men, 20% women, 0% minorities
Student-to-faculty ratio: 12.3

SPECIAL PROGRAMS (as provided by law school):

All third-year students practice in a public interest setting, either in an in-house clinic at the law school or under the supervision of an attorney in the community. Students apply the skills and knowledge from their first two years of law school to a practice setting where they are challenged to identify and resolve legal, ethical and professionalism issues like those faced in practice.

STUDENT BODY

Fall 2009 full-time enrollment: 252

Men: N/A	Women: N/A
African-American: N/A	American Indian: N/A
Asian-American: N/A	Mexican-American: N/A
Puerto Rican: N/A	Other Hisp-Amer: N/A
White: N/A	International: N/A
Unknown: N/A	

Attrition rates for 2008-2009 full-time students
Percent of students discontinuing law school:

Men: N/A	Women: N/A

First-year students: **N/A**   Second-year students: **N/A**
Third-year students: **N/A**   Fourth-year students: **N/A**

LIBRARY RESOURCES
Total titles: **26,640**
Total volumes: **132,140**
Total seats available for library users: **364**

INFORMATION TECHNOLOGY
Number of wired network connections available to students: **214** total (in the law library, excluding computer labs: **48**; in classrooms: **51**; in computer labs: **7**; elsewhere in the law school: **108**)
Law school has a wireless network.
Students are not required to own a computer.

EMPLOYMENT AND SALARIES
Proportion of 2008 graduates employed at graduation: **N/A**
Employed 9 months later, as of February 15, 2009: **92%**
Salaries in the private sector (law firms, business, industry): **$43,500 –$60,000** (25th-75th percentile)
Median salary in the private sector: **$53,500**
Percentage in the private sector who reported salary information: **85%**
Median salary in public service (government, judicial clerkships, academic posts, non-profits): **$45,000**

Percentage of 2008 graduates in:
Law firms: **46%**   Government: **10%**
Bus./industry: **4%**   Judicial clerkship: **25%**
Public interest: **10%**   Unknown: **5%**
Academia : **0%**

2008 graduates employed in-state: **72%**
2008 graduates employed in foreign countries: **0%**
Number of states where graduates are employed: **9**
Percentage of 2008 graduates working in: New England: **0%**, Middle Atlantic: **0%**, East North Central: **N/A**, West North Central: **0%**, South Atlantic: **0%**, East South Central: **0%**, West South Central: **0%**, Mountain: **N/A**, Pacific: **N/A**, Unknown: **5%**

BAR PASSAGE RATES
Based on 2008 graduates taking Summer 2008 or Winter 2009 exams. Most of the school's first-time test takers took the bar in Montana.

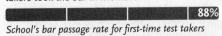

88%
School's bar passage rate for first-time test takers

93%
Statewide bar passage rate for first-time test takers

University of Nebraska–Lincoln

■ PO Box 830902, Lincoln, NE, 68583-0902
■ http://law.unl.edu
■ Public
■ Year founded: 1891
■ 2009-2010 tuition: full-time: $12,154; part-time: N/A
■ Enrollment 2009-10 academic year: full-time: 394
■ U.S. News 2010 law specialty ranking: N/A

3.29-3.82 GPA, 25ᵀᴴ-75ᵀᴴ PERCENTILE

154-158 LSAT, 25ᵀᴴ-75ᵀᴴ PERCENTILE

52% ACCEPTANCE RATE

93 2011 U.S. NEWS LAW SCHOOL RANKING

ADMISSIONS
Admissions phone number: **(402) 472-2161**
Admissions email address: **lawadm@unl.edu**
Application website: **http://law.unl.edu**
Application deadline for Fall 2011 admission: **1-Mar**

Admissions statistics:
Number of applicants for Fall 2009: **712**
Number of acceptances: **369**
Number enrolled: **137**
Acceptance rate: **52%**
GPA, 25th-75th percentile, entering class Fall 2009: **3.29-3.82**
LSAT, 25th-75th percentile, entering class Fall 2009: **154-158**

FINANCIAL AID
Financial aid phone number: **(402) 472-2161**
Financial aid application deadline: **1-May**
Tuition 2009-2010 academic year: **full-time: $12,154; part-time: N/A**
Room and board: **$7,900** ; books: **$1,340** ; miscellaneous expenses: **$3,538**
Total of room/board/books/miscellaneous expenses: **$12,778**
University offers graduate student housing for which law students are eligible.

Financial aid profile
Percent of students that received grants for the 2008-2009 academic year: full-time: **41%**
Median grant amount: full-time: **$10,000**
The average law-school debt of those in the Class of 2009 who borrowed: **$49,946** . Proportion who borrowed: **82%**

ACADEMIC PROGRAMS
Calendar: **semester**
Joint degrees awarded: **J.D./M.A. Economics; J.D./M.P.A.; J.D./M.A. Psychology; J.D./M.B.A.; J.D./Ph.D. Education; J.D./Ph.D. Psychology; J.D./M.A. Political Science; J.D./M.C.R.P.; J.D./M.A. International Affairs**

Typical first-year section size: Full-time: **70**
Is there typically a "small section" of the first year class, other than Legal Writing, taught by full-time faculty?: Full-time: **yes**
Number of course titles, beyond the first year curriculum, offered last year: **91**
Percentages of upper division course sections, excluding seminars, with an enrollment of:
Under 25: **64%**   25 to 49: **26%**
50 to 74: **9%**   75 to 99: **1%**
100+: **0%**
Areas of specialization: appellate advocacy, clinical training, dispute resolution, environmental law, health care law, intellectual property law, international law, tax law, trial advocacy

Fall 2009 faculty profile
Total teaching faculty: **47**. Full-time: **51%; 83%** men, **17%** women, **4%** minorities. Part-time: **49%; 61%** men, **39%** women, **0%** minorities
Student-to-faculty ratio: **13.6**

SPECIAL PROGRAMS *(as provided by law school):*
Strong interdisciplinary programs, including the renowned Law & Psychology program. LL.M program in Space & Telecommunications Law with all courses open to JD students. Concentrations in litigation, business transactions and most substantive areas. Practice-oriented experiences in civil, criminal & immigration clinics, externships & pro bono activities. Summer program at Cambridge University.

STUDENT BODY
Fall 2009 full-time enrollment: **394**
Men: **60%**   Women: **40%**
African-American: **2.80%**   American Indian: **0.50%**
Asian-American: **1.80%**   Mexican-American: **1.00%**
Puerto Rican: **0.00%**   Other Hisp-Amer: **1.30%**
White: **92.10%**   International: **0.50%**
Unknown: **0.00%**

Attrition rates for 2008-2009 full-time students
Percent of students discontinuing law school:

Men: **5%**   Women: **4%**
First-year students: **9%**   Second-year students: **3%**
Third-year students: **N/A**   Fourth-year students: **N/A**

LIBRARY RESOURCES

Total titles: **117,160**
Total volumes: **419,532**
Total seats available for library users: **372**

INFORMATION TECHNOLOGY

Number of wired network connections available to students: **16** total (in the law library, excluding computer labs: **0**; in classrooms: **0**; in computer labs: **16**; elsewhere in the law school: **0**)
Law school has a wireless network.
Students are not required to own a computer.

EMPLOYMENT AND SALARIES

Proportion of 2008 graduates employed at graduation: **64%**
Employed 9 months later, as of February 15, 2009: **94%**
Salaries in the private sector (law firms, business, industry): **$48,000 –$75,000** (25th-75th percentile)
Median salary in the private sector: **$55,000**
Percentage in the private sector who reported salary information: **56%**

Median salary in public service (government, judicial clerkships, academic posts, non-profits): **$44,100**

Percentage of 2008 graduates in:
Law firms: **41%**   Government: **26%**
Bus./industry: **15%**   Judicial clerkship: **11%**
Public interest: **4%**   Unknown: **0%**
Academia : **4%**

2008 graduates employed in-state: **66%**
2008 graduates employed in foreign countries: **0%**
Number of states where graduates are employed: **15**
Percentage of 2008 graduates working in: New England: **0%**, Middle Atlantic: **2%**, East North Central: **3%**, West North Central: **71%**, South Atlantic: **11%**, East South Central: **0%**, West South Central: **1%**, Mountain: **10%**, Pacific: **2%**, Unknown: **0%**

BAR PASSAGE RATES

Based on 2008 graduates taking Summer 2008 or Winter 2009 exams. Most of the school's first-time test takers took the bar in Nebraska.

91%
School's bar passage rate for first-time test takers

89%
Statewide bar passage rate for first-time test takers

Univ. of Nevada–Las Vegas (Boyd)

■ 4505 S. Maryland Parkway, PO Box 451003, Las Vegas, NV, 89154-1003
■ http://www.law.unlv.edu/
■ Public
■ Year founded: 1997
■ 2009-2010 tuition: full-time: $18,838; part-time: $12,328
■ Enrollment 2009-10 academic year: full-time: 366; part-time: 118
■ U.S. News 2010 law specialty ranking: clinical training: 28, dispute resolution: 10

3.19-3.67 GPA, 25TH-75TH PERCENTILE

156-160 LSAT, 25TH-75TH PERCENTILE

22% ACCEPTANCE RATE

78 2011 U.S. NEWS LAW SCHOOL RANKING

ADMISSIONS

Admissions phone number: (702) 895-2440
Admissions email address: request@law.unlv.edu
Application website:
  http://www.law.unlv.edu/application.html
Application deadline for Fall 2011 admission: 15-Mar

Admissions statistics:
Number of applicants for Fall 2009: 1,511
Number of acceptances: 333
Number enrolled: 122
Acceptance rate: 22%
GPA, 25th-75th percentile, entering class Fall 2009: 3.19-3.67
LSAT, 25th-75th percentile, entering class Fall 2009: 156-160

Part-time program:
Number of applicants for Fall 2009: 226
Number of acceptances: 48
Number enrolled: 36
Acceptance rate: 21%
GPA, 25th-75th percentile, entering class Fall 2009: 3.13-3.64
LSAT, 25th-75th percentile, entering class Fall 2009: 152-158

FINANCIAL AID

Financial aid phone number: (702) 895-0630
Financial aid application deadline: 1-Feb
Tuition 2009-2010 academic year: **full-time: $18,838; part-time: $12,328**
Room and board: $15,925 ; books: $1,700 ; miscellaneous expenses: $250
Total of room/board/books/miscellaneous expenses: $17,875
University does not offer graduate student housing for which law students are eligible.

Financial aid profile
Percent of students that received grants for the 2008-2009 academic year: full-time: 38%; part-time 8%
Median grant amount: full-time: $7,000 ; part-time: $3,500
The average law-school debt of those in the Class of 2009 who borrowed: $55,944 . Proportion who borrowed: 86%

ACADEMIC PROGRAMS

Calendar: **semester**
Joint degrees awarded: **J.D./M.B.A. ; J.D./M.S.W. ; J.D./Ph.D.**
Typical first-year section size: Full-time: **65**; Part-time: **34**
Is there typically a "small section" of the first year class, other than Legal Writing, taught by full-time faculty?: Full-time: **no**; Part-time: **no**
Number of course titles, beyond the first year curriculum, offered last year: **79**
Percentages of upper division course sections, excluding seminars, with an enrollment of:
  Under 25: **73%**   25 to 49: **16%**
  50 to 74: **9%**   75 to 99: **2%**
  100+: **0%**
Areas of specialization: appellate advocacy, clinical training, dispute resolution, environmental law, intellectual property law, international law, tax law, trial advocacy

Fall 2009 faculty profile
Total teaching faculty: 34. Full-time: 62%; 43% men, 57% women, 19% minorities. Part-time: 38%; 77% men, 23% women, 0% minorities
Student-to-faculty ratio: 16.8

SPECIAL PROGRAMS *(as provided by law school):*
Students have a variety of opportunities for learning by doing. Through clinical programs, externships, the Saltman Center for Conflict Resolution and service learning courses, all students are ensured to have at least one service learning experience. For information about these programs and the Saltman Center see the law school website at: http://www.law.unlv.edu

STUDENT BODY

Fall 2009 full-time enrollment: 366

Men: 54%	Women: 46%
African-American: 4.10%	American Indian: 2.70%
Asian-American: 12.30%	Mexican-American: 0.00%
Puerto Rican: 0.00%	Other Hisp-Amer: 10.40%
White: 62.60%	International: 0.30%
Unknown: 7.70%	

Fall 2009 part-time enrollment: 118

Men: 53%	Women: 47%
African-American: 10.20%	American Indian: 0.80%
Asian-American: 7.60%	Mexican-American: 1.70%
Puerto Rican: 0.80%	Other Hisp-Amer: 5.90%
White: 66.10%	International: 0.80%
Unknown: 5.90%	

Attrition rates for 2008-2009 full-time students
Percent of students discontinuing law school:

Men: 5%	Women: 3%
First-year students: 9%	Second-year students: 3%
Third-year students: N/A	Fourth-year students: N/A

LIBRARY RESOURCES

Total titles: 198,953
Total volumes: 330,808
Total seats available for library users: 313

INFORMATION TECHNOLOGY

Number of wired network connections available to students: 1215 total (in the law library, excluding computer labs: 395; in classrooms: 629; in computer labs: 46; elsewhere in the law school: 145)
Law school has a wireless network.
Students are not required to own a computer.

EMPLOYMENT AND SALARIES

Proportion of 2008 graduates employed at graduation: 87%
Employed 9 months later, as of February 15, 2009: 98%
Salaries in the private sector (law firms, business, industry): $62,000 –$105,000 (25th-75th percentile)
Median salary in the private sector: $78,000
Percentage in the private sector who reported salary information: 67%
Median salary in public service (government, judicial clerkships, academic posts, non-profits): $56,000

Percentage of 2008 graduates in:

Law firms: 55%	Government: 10%
Bus./industry: 12%	Judicial clerkship: 16%
Public interest: 4%	Unknown: 1%
Academia : 2%	

2008 graduates employed in-state: 83%
2008 graduates employed in foreign countries: 1%
Number of states where graduates are employed: 11
Percentage of 2008 graduates working in: New England: 0%, Middle Atlantic: 0%, East North Central: 2%, West North Central: 0%, South Atlantic: 4%, East South Central: 0%, West South Central: 1%, Mountain: 88%, Pacific: 5%, Unknown: 0%

BAR PASSAGE RATES

Based on 2008 graduates taking Summer 2008 or Winter 2009 exams. Most of the school's first-time test takers took the bar in Nevada.

82%
School's bar passage rate for first-time test takers

77%
Statewide bar passage rate for first-time test takers

University of New Mexico

- 1117 Stanford Drive NE, MSC11 6070, Albuquerque, NM, 87131-0001
- http://lawschool.unm.edu
- Public
- Year founded: 1947
- 2009-2010 tuition: full-time: $12,620; part-time: N/A
- Enrollment 2009-10 academic year: full-time: 351
- U.S. News 2010 law specialty ranking: clinical training: 6

3.12-3.67 GPA, 25TH-75TH PERCENTILE

152-158 LSAT, 25TH-75TH PERCENTILE

24% ACCEPTANCE RATE

67 2011 U.S. NEWS LAW SCHOOL RANKING

ADMISSIONS

Admissions phone number: **(505) 277-0958**
Admissions email address: **admissions@law.unm.edu**
Application website: **http://lawschool.unm.edu**
Application deadline for Fall 2011 admission: **15-Feb**

Admissions statistics:

Number of applicants for Fall 2009: **1,039**
Number of acceptances: **254**
Number enrolled: **117**
Acceptance rate: **24%**
GPA, 25th-75th percentile, entering class Fall 2009: **3.12-3.67**
LSAT, 25th-75th percentile, entering class Fall 2009: **152-158**

FINANCIAL AID

Financial aid phone number: **(505) 277-0572**
Financial aid application deadline: **15-Feb**
Tuition 2009-2010 academic year: **full-time: $12,620; part-time: N/A**
Room and board: **$8,180** ; books: **$1,082** ; miscellaneous expenses: **$4,884**
Total of room/board/books/miscellaneous expenses: **$14,146**
University does not offer graduate student housing for which law students are eligible.

Financial aid profile

Percent of students that received grants for the 2008-2009 academic year: full-time: **23%**
Median grant amount: full-time: **$6,498**
The average law-school debt of those in the Class of 2009 who borrowed: **$51,685** . Proportion who borrowed: **94%**

ACADEMIC PROGRAMS

Calendar: **semester**
Joint degrees awarded: **J.D./M.B.A.; J.D./M.P.A.; J.D./M.L.A.S.; J.D./MED**
Typical first-year section size: Full-time: **56**
Is there typically a "small section" of the first year class,
other than Legal Writing, taught by full-time faculty?:
Full-time: **yes**
Number of course titles, beyond the first year curriculum, offered last year: **81**
Percentages of upper division course sections, excluding seminars, with an enrollment of:
Under 25: **66%**   25 to 49: **23%**
50 to 74: **11%**   75 to 99: **0%**
100+: **0%**
Areas of specialization: appellate advocacy, clinical training, dispute resolution, environmental law, health care law, intellectual property law, international law, tax law, trial advocacy

Fall 2009 faculty profile

Total teaching faculty: **47.** Full-time: **57%**; **41%** men, **59%** women, **48%** minorities. Part-time: **43%**; **60%** men, **40%** women, **20%** minorities
Student-to-faculty ratio: **11.3**

SPECIAL PROGRAMS (as provided by law school):

UNM Law School's curriculum stands out for its clinical, Indian, international, and natural resources law programs. The Clinical Program is nationally recognized as one of the best in the U.S.; the Indian law program offers the Indian law certificate; UNM offers summer law study in Guanajuato, Mexico; and the school is known for its faculty strength in natural resources and environmental law.

STUDENT BODY

Fall 2009 full-time enrollment: 351

Men: **46%**   Women: **54%**
African-American: **3.70%**   American Indian: **10.00%**
Asian-American: **2.80%**   Mexican-American: **28.20%**
Puerto Rican: **0.00%**   Other Hisp-Amer: **0.00%**
White: **45.00%**   International: **0.00%**
Unknown: **10.30%**

Attrition rates for 2008-2009 full-time students

Percent of students discontinuing law school:
Men: **2%**   Women: **N/A**

First-year students: **3%**   Second-year students: **N/A**
Third-year students: **N/A**   Fourth-year students: **N/A**

LIBRARY RESOURCES
Total titles: **135,794**
Total volumes: **429,385**
Total seats available for library users: **275**

INFORMATION TECHNOLOGY
Number of wired network connections available to students: **331** total (in the law library, excluding computer labs: **143**; in classrooms: **156**; in computer labs: **12**; elsewhere in the law school: **20**)
Law school has a wireless network.
Students are required to own a computer.

EMPLOYMENT AND SALARIES
Proportion of 2008 graduates employed at graduation: **82%**
Employed 9 months later, as of February 15, 2009: **96%**
Salaries in the private sector (law firms, business, industry): **$52,000 –$70,000** (25th-75th percentile)
Median salary in the private sector: **$61,000**
Percentage in the private sector who reported salary information: **82%**
Median salary in public service (government, judicial clerkships, academic posts, non-profits): **$44,000**

Percentage of 2008 graduates in:
Law firms: **35%**   Government: **17%**
Bus./industry: **14%**   Judicial clerkship: **13%**
Public interest: **16%**   Unknown: **1%**
Academia : **3%**

2008 graduates employed in-state: **79%**
2008 graduates employed in foreign countries: **1%**
Number of states where graduates are employed: **11**
Percentage of 2008 graduates working in: New England: **0%**, Middle Atlantic: **2%**, East North Central: **0%**, West North Central: **1%**, South Atlantic: **0%**, East South Central: **0%**, West South Central: **2%**, Mountain: **89%**, Pacific: **4%**, Unknown: **1%**

BAR PASSAGE RATES
Based on 2008 graduates taking Summer 2008 or Winter 2009 exams. Most of the school's first-time test takers took the bar in New Mexico.

92%
School's bar passage rate for first-time test takers

92%
Statewide bar passage rate for first-time test takers

Univ. of North Carolina–Chapel Hill

- Van Hecke-Wettach Hall, CB No. 3380, Chapel Hill, NC, 27599-3380
- http://www.law.unc.edu
- Public
- Year founded: 1843
- 2009-2010 tuition: full-time: $16,014; part-time: N/A
- Enrollment 2009-10 academic year: full-time: 765
- U.S. News 2010 law specialty ranking: N/A

3.43-3.73 GPA, 25TH-75TH PERCENTILE

157-164 LSAT, 25TH-75TH PERCENTILE

15% ACCEPTANCE RATE

28 2011 U.S. NEWS LAW SCHOOL RANKING

ADMISSIONS

Admissions phone number: **(919) 962-5109**
Admissions email address: **law_admission@unc.edu**
Application website:
 http://www.law.unc.edu/PDFs/lawapplicationfinal.pdf
Application deadline for Fall 2011 admission: **11-Mar**

Admissions statistics:

Number of applicants for Fall 2009: **2,905**
Number of acceptances: **426**
Number enrolled: **262**
Acceptance rate: **15%**
GPA, 25th-75th percentile, entering class Fall 2009: **3.43-3.73**
LSAT, 25th-75th percentile, entering class Fall 2009: **157-164**

FINANCIAL AID

Financial aid phone number: **(919) 962-8396**
Financial aid application deadline: **1-Mar**
Tuition 2009-2010 academic year: **full-time: $16,014; part-time: N/A**
Room and board: **$12,920** ; books: **$1,000** ; miscellaneous expenses: **$4,012**
Total of room/board/books/miscellaneous expenses: **$17,932**
University offers graduate student housing for which law students are eligible.

Financial aid profile

Percent of students that received grants for the 2008-2009 academic year: full-time: **80%**
Median grant amount: full-time: **$3,900**
The average law-school debt of those in the Class of 2009 who borrowed: **$63,621** . Proportion who borrowed: **84%**

ACADEMIC PROGRAMS

Calendar: **semester**
Joint degrees awarded: **J.D./M.B.A.; J.D./M.P.A.; J.D./M.P.P.; J.D./M.P.H.; J.D./M.R.P.; J.D./M.S.W.; J.D./M.L.S.; J.D./M.I.S.; J.D./M.S.A.; J.D./M.M.C.**

Typical first-year section size: Full-time: **85**
Is there typically a "small section" of the first year class, other than Legal Writing, taught by full-time faculty?: Full-time: **yes**
Number of course titles, beyond the first year curriculum, offered last year: **117**
Percentages of upper division course sections, excluding seminars, with an enrollment of:
 Under 25: **53%**   25 to 49: **28%**
 50 to 74: **8%**   75 to 99: **7%**
 100+: **4%**
Areas of specialization: appellate advocacy, clinical training, dispute resolution, environmental law, health care law, intellectual property law, international law, tax law, trial advocacy

Fall 2009 faculty profile

Total teaching faculty: **105**. Full-time: **48%**; **60%** men, **40%** women, **12%** minorities. Part-time: **52%**; **69%** men, **31%** women, **13%** minorities
Student-to-faculty ratio: **15.4**

SPECIAL PROGRAMS (as provided by law school):

UNC offers externship placement to over 120 students. It sponsors 4 clinical programs: Civil Litigation; Community Development Law; Immigration/Human Rights Policy; Juvenile Justice; and 5 centers:Banking & Finance; Civil Rights; Law & Government; Poverty, Work & Opportunity; Law, Environment, Adaptation & Resources, plus a summer program in Sydney and exchanges with 4 European law schools.

STUDENT BODY

Fall 2009 full-time enrollment: 765

Men: **47%**	Women: **53%**
African-American: **7.60%**	American Indian: **2.50%**
Asian-American: **6.80%**	Mexican-American: **0.70%**
Puerto Rican: **0.00%**	Other Hisp-Amer: **6.40%**
White: **55.80%**	International: **0.10%**
Unknown: **20.10%**	

Attrition rates for 2008-2009 full-time students
Percent of students discontinuing law school:
Men: 2%   Women: 1%
First-year students: 4%   Second-year students: 0%
Third-year students: 0%   Fourth-year students: N/A

LIBRARY RESOURCES
Total titles: 153,579
Total volumes: 547,598
Total seats available for library users: 530

INFORMATION TECHNOLOGY
Number of wired network connections available to students: 560 total (in the law library, excluding computer labs: 175; in classrooms: 157; in computer labs: 0; elsewhere in the law school: 228)
Law school has a wireless network.
Students are not required to own a computer.

EMPLOYMENT AND SALARIES
Proportion of 2008 graduates employed at graduation: 75%
Employed 9 months later, as of February 15, 2009: 95%
Salaries in the private sector (law firms, business, industry): $90,000 –$160,000 (25th-75th percentile)
Median salary in the private sector: $130,000
Percentage in the private sector who reported salary information: 67%

Median salary in public service (government, judicial clerkships, academic posts, non-profits): $46,000

Percentage of 2008 graduates in:
Law firms: 63%   Government: 7%
Bus./industry: 9%   Judicial clerkship: 10%
Public interest: 9%   Unknown: 1%
Academia : 1%

2008 graduates employed in-state: 55%
2008 graduates employed in foreign countries: 0%
Number of states where graduates are employed: 22
Percentage of 2008 graduates working in: New England: 2%, Middle Atlantic: 6%, East North Central: 5%, West North Central: 1%, South Atlantic: 80%, East South Central: 1%, West South Central: 2%, Mountain: 1%, Pacific: 1%, Unknown: 1%

BAR PASSAGE RATES
Based on 2008 graduates taking Summer 2008 or Winter 2009 exams. Most of the school's first-time test takers took the bar in North Carolina.

90%

School's bar passage rate for first-time test takers

83%

Statewide bar passage rate for first-time test takers

University of North Dakota

- 215 Centennial Drive, Stop 9003, Grand Forks, ND, 58202
- http://www.law.und.nodak.edu
- Public
- Year founded: 1899
- 2009-2010 tuition: full-time: $9,461; part-time: N/A
- Enrollment 2009-10 academic year: full-time: 247
- U.S. News 2010 law specialty ranking: N/A

3.30-3.73 GPA, 25TH-75TH PERCENTILE

149-155 LSAT, 25TH-75TH PERCENTILE

35% ACCEPTANCE RATE

Tier 4 2011 U.S. NEWS LAW SCHOOL RANKING

ADMISSIONS

Admissions phone number: **(701) 777-2260**
Admissions email address: **hoffman@law.und.edu**
Application website:
   http://www.law.und.nodak.edu/FutureStudents/web_ass ets/pdf/UNDLawApp.pdf
Application deadline for Fall 2011 admission: **rolling**

Admissions statistics:
Number of applicants for Fall 2009: **534**
Number of acceptances: **187**
Number enrolled: **86**
Acceptance rate: **35%**
GPA, 25th-75th percentile, entering class Fall 2009: **3.30-3.73**
LSAT, 25th-75th percentile, entering class Fall 2009: **149-155**

FINANCIAL AID

Financial aid phone number: **(701) 777-3121**
Financial aid application deadline: **15-Apr**
Tuition 2009-2010 academic year: **full-time: $9,461; part-time: N/A**
Room and board: **$8,750** ; books: **$1,100** ; miscellaneous expenses: **$4,950**
Total of room/board/books/miscellaneous expenses: **$14,800**
University offers graduate student housing for which law students are eligible.

Financial aid profile
Percent of students that received grants for the 2008-2009 academic year: full-time: **33%**
Median grant amount: full-time: **$4,000**
The average law-school debt of those in the Class of 2009 who borrowed: **$67,236** . Proportion who borrowed: **83%**

ACADEMIC PROGRAMS

Calendar: **semester**
Joint degrees awarded: **J.D./M.P.A.; J.D./M.B.A.**
Typical first-year section size: Full-time: **85**

Is there typically a "small section" of the first year class, other than Legal Writing, taught by full-time faculty?:
   Full-time: **no**
Number of course titles, beyond the first year curriculum, offered last year: **53**
Percentages of upper division course sections, excluding seminars, with an enrollment of:

Under 25: **55%**	25 to 49: **29%**
50 to 74: **14%**	75 to 99: **2%**
100+: **N/A**	

Areas of specialization: appellate advocacy, clinical training, dispute resolution, environmental law, health care law, intellectual property law, international law, tax law, trial advocacy

Fall 2009 faculty profile
Total teaching faculty: **21**. Full-time: **67%**; **57%** men, **43%** women, **14%** minorities. Part-time: **33%**; **57%** men, **43%** women, **0%** minorities
Student-to-faculty ratio: **16.8**

SPECIAL PROGRAMS *(as provided by law school)*:
Law School Clinic; Externship Program; Summer Federal Externships; Legislative Internships; Summer Classes; Summer Program with Norway; Tribal Judicial Institute; Tribal Gaming Institute; Tribal Environmental Law Project; Northern Plains Indian Law Center; Tribal Advocacy Training Program.

STUDENT BODY

Fall 2009 full-time enrollment: 247

Men: **55%**	Women: **45%**
African-American: **2.40%**	American Indian: **3.60%**
Asian-American: **1.20%**	Mexican-American: **1.20%**
Puerto Rican: **0.00%**	Other Hisp-Amer: **1.60%**
White: **81.00%**	International: **7.30%**
Unknown: **1.60%**	

Attrition rates for 2008-2009 full-time students
Percent of students discontinuing law school:

Men: **N/A**	Women: **1%**
First-year students: **1%**	Second-year students: **N/A**
Third-year students: **N/A**	Fourth-year students: **N/A**

LIBRARY RESOURCES

Total titles: **155,880**
Total volumes: **334,454**
Total seats available for library users: **222**

INFORMATION TECHNOLOGY

Number of wired network connections available to students: **173** total (in the law library, excluding computer labs: **169**; in classrooms: **0**; in computer labs: **0**; elsewhere in the law school: **4**)
Law school has a wireless network.
Students are not required to own a computer.

EMPLOYMENT AND SALARIES

Proportion of 2008 graduates employed at graduation: **N/A**
Employed 9 months later, as of February 15, 2009: **90%**
Salaries in the private sector (law firms, business, industry): **$36,000 – $71,000** (25th-75th percentile)
Median salary in the private sector: **$48,000**
Percentage in the private sector who reported salary information: **30%**
Median salary in public service (government, judicial clerkships, academic posts, non-profits): **$47,100**

Percentage of 2008 graduates in:

Law firms: **44%**	Government: **10%**
Bus./industry: **17%**	Judicial clerkship: **22%**
Public interest: **6%**	Unknown: **0%**
Academia : **1%**	

2008 graduates employed in-state: **64%**
2008 graduates employed in foreign countries: **0%**
Number of states where graduates are employed: **14**
Percentage of 2008 graduates working in: New England: **1%**, Middle Atlantic: **0%**, East North Central: **3%**, West North Central: **77%**, South Atlantic: **3%**, East South Central: **3%**, West South Central: **4%**, Mountain: **9%**, Pacific: **0%**, Unknown: **0%**

BAR PASSAGE RATES

Based on 2008 graduates taking Summer 2008 or Winter 2009 exams. Most of the school's first-time test takers took the bar in North Dakota.

92%
School's bar passage rate for first-time test takers

86%
Statewide bar passage rate for first-time test takers

University of Notre Dame

- PO Box 780, Notre Dame, IN, 46556-0780
- http://law.nd.edu
- Private
- Year founded: 1869
- 2009-2010 tuition: full-time: $39,320; part-time: N/A
- Enrollment 2009-10 academic year: full-time: 548
- U.S. News 2010 law specialty ranking: N/A

3.36-3.74 GPA, 25TH-75TH PERCENTILE

163-167 LSAT, 25TH-75TH PERCENTILE

25% ACCEPTANCE RATE

22 2011 U.S. NEWS LAW SCHOOL RANKING

ADMISSIONS

Admissions phone number: **(574) 631-6626**
Admissions email address: **lawadmit@nd.edu**
Application website:
   https://os.lsac.org/release/startup.aspx?appl=1841A1
Application deadline for Fall 2011 admission: **15-Mar**

Admissions statistics:
Number of applicants for Fall 2009: **3,178**
Number of acceptances: **810**
Number enrolled: **186**
Acceptance rate: **25%**
GPA, 25th-75th percentile, entering class Fall 2009: **3.36-3.74**
LSAT, 25th-75th percentile, entering class Fall 2009: **163-167**

FINANCIAL AID

Financial aid phone number: **(574) 631-6626**
Financial aid application deadline: **15-Feb**
Tuition 2009-2010 academic year: **full-time: $39,320; part-time: N/A**
Room and board: **$8,500** ; books: **$1,400** ; miscellaneous expenses: **$6,500**
Total of room/board/books/miscellaneous expenses: **$16,400**
University offers graduate student housing for which law students are eligible.

Financial aid profile
Percent of students that received grants for the 2008-2009 academic year: full-time: **80%**
Median grant amount: full-time: **$13,000**
The average law-school debt of those in the Class of 2009 who borrowed: **$92,955** . Proportion who borrowed: **86%**

ACADEMIC PROGRAMS

Calendar: **semester**
Joint degrees awarded: **J.D./M.B.A.; J.D./M.A.; J.D./M.S.; J.D./Ph.D.**
Typical first-year section size: Full-time: **64**

Is there typically a "small section" of the first year class, other than Legal Writing, taught by full-time faculty?:
   Full-time: **no**
Number of course titles, beyond the first year curriculum, offered last year: **128**
Percentages of upper division course sections, excluding seminars, with an enrollment of:
   Under 25: **64%**   25 to 49: **20%**
   50 to 74: **10%**   75 to 99: **5%**
   100+: **1%**
Areas of specialization: appellate advocacy, clinical training, dispute resolution, environmental law, health care law, intellectual property law, international law, tax law, trial advocacy

Fall 2009 faculty profile
Total teaching faculty: **83**. Full-time: **48%**; **75%** men, **25%** women, **18%** minorities. Part-time: **52%**; **60%** men, **40%** women, **2%** minorities
Student-to-faculty ratio: **10.9**

SPECIAL PROGRAMS (as provided by law school):
Second year in London; Trial Advocacy; Center for Civil & Human Rights; Legal Aid Clinic; Summer London Program; Public Defender Externship; Group Alternative Live-In Legal Education; Asylum Externship; 7th Circuit Appellate Advocacy; Street Law.

STUDENT BODY
Fall 2009 full-time enrollment: 548
Men: **58%**	Women: **42%**
African-American: **5.10%**	American Indian: **1.30%**
Asian-American: **8.40%**	Mexican-American: **1.80%**
Puerto Rican: **0.20%**	Other Hisp-Amer: **6.60%**
White: **63.70%**	International: **0.70%**
Unknown: **12.20%**	

Attrition rates for 2008-2009 full-time students
Percent of students discontinuing law school:
Men: **1%**	Women: **2%**
First-year students: **1%**	Second-year students: **2%**
Third-year students: **1%**	Fourth-year students: **N/A**

LIBRARY RESOURCES

Total titles: 247,061
Total volumes: 672,384
Total seats available for library users: 0

INFORMATION TECHNOLOGY

Number of wired network connections available to students: 18 total (in the law library, excluding computer labs: 0; in classrooms: 8; in computer labs: 0; elsewhere in the law school: 10)
Law school has a wireless network.
Students are not required to own a computer.

EMPLOYMENT AND SALARIES

Proportion of 2008 graduates employed at graduation: 90%
Employed 9 months later, as of February 15, 2009: 99%
Salaries in the private sector (law firms, business, industry): $120,000 –$160,000 (25th-75th percentile)
Median salary in the private sector: $150,000
Percentage in the private sector who reported salary information: 68%
Median salary in public service (government, judicial clerkships, academic posts, non-profits): $52,500

Percentage of 2008 graduates in:

Law firms: 61%	Government: 12%
Bus./industry: 6%	Judicial clerkship: 14%
Public interest: 7%	Unknown: 0%
Academia : 1%	

2008 graduates employed in-state: 7%
2008 graduates employed in foreign countries: 0%
Number of states where graduates are employed: 34
Percentage of 2008 graduates working in: New England: 3%, Middle Atlantic: 13%, East North Central: 36%, West North Central: 3%, South Atlantic: 18%, East South Central: 1%, West South Central: 6%, Mountain: 6%, Pacific: 15%, Unknown: 0%

BAR PASSAGE RATES

Based on 2008 graduates taking Summer 2008 or Winter 2009 exams. Most of the school's first-time test takers took the bar in Illinois.

100%
School's bar passage rate for first-time test takers

91%
Statewide bar passage rate for first-time test takers

University of Oklahoma

- Andrew M. Coats Hall, 300 Timberdell Road, Norman, OK, 73019-5081
- http://www.law.ou.edu
- Public
- Year founded: 1909
- 2009-2010 tuition: full-time: $16,976; part-time: N/A
- Enrollment 2009-10 academic year: full-time: 550
- U.S. News 2010 law specialty ranking: N/A

3.29-3.72 GPA, 25TH-75TH PERCENTILE

155-161 LSAT, 25TH-75TH PERCENTILE

31% ACCEPTANCE RATE

72 2011 U.S. NEWS LAW SCHOOL RANKING

ADMISSIONS
Admissions phone number: **(405) 325-4728**
Admissions email address: **admissions@law.ou.edu**
Application website:
http://www.law.ou.edu/prospective/admissions
Application deadline for Fall 2011 admission: **15-Mar**

Admissions statistics:
Number of applicants for Fall 2009: **1,151**
Number of acceptances: **355**
Number enrolled: **199**
Acceptance rate: **31%**
GPA, 25th-75th percentile, entering class Fall 2009: **3.29-3.72**
LSAT, 25th-75th percentile, entering class Fall 2009: **155-161**

FINANCIAL AID
Financial aid phone number: **(405) 325-4521**
Financial aid application deadline: **1-Mar**
Tuition 2009-2010 academic year: **full-time: $16,976**; part-time: N/A
Room and board: **$11,781** ; books: **$1,235** ; miscellaneous expenses: **$3,658**
Total of room/board/books/miscellaneous expenses: **$16,674**
University offers graduate student housing for which law students are eligible.

Financial aid profile
Percent of students that received grants for the 2008-2009 academic year: full-time: **74%**
Median grant amount: full-time: **$3,000**
The average law-school debt of those in the Class of 2009 who borrowed: **$65,775** . Proportion who borrowed: **87%**

ACADEMIC PROGRAMS
Calendar: **semester**
Joint degrees awarded: **J.D./M.B.A.; J.D./M.P.H.**
Typical first-year section size: Full-time: **44**
Is there typically a "small section" of the first year class, other than Legal Writing, taught by full-time faculty?:
Full-time: **no**
Number of course titles, beyond the first year curriculum, offered last year: **108**
Percentages of upper division course sections, excluding seminars, with an enrollment of:
Under 25: **49%**   25 to 49: **24%**
50 to 74: **18%**   75 to 99: **9%**
100+: **0%**
Areas of specialization: appellate advocacy, clinical training, dispute resolution, environmental law, health care law, intellectual property law, international law, tax law, trial advocacy

Fall 2009 faculty profile
Total teaching faculty: **49**. Full-time: **63%**; **58%** men, **42%** women, **10%** minorities. Part-time: **37%**; **72%** men, **28%** women, **6%** minorities
Student-to-faculty ratio: **14.2**

SPECIAL PROGRAMS (as provided by law school):
The College of Law offers students the opportunity to participate in live-client civil and criminal clinics, judicial externships, and internships with the United States Department of Justice and the United States Department of the Interior in Washington, D.C. Also, the College offers a study abroad program with Brasenose College in Oxford, England.

STUDENT BODY
Fall 2009 full-time enrollment: 550
Men: **57%**   Women: **43%**
African-American: **4.20%**   American Indian: **8.50%**
Asian-American: **4.50%**   Mexican-American: **3.60%**
Puerto Rican: **0.00%**   Other Hisp-Amer: **0.00%**
White: **77.60%**   International: **0.40%**
Unknown: **1.10%**

Attrition rates for 2008-2009 full-time students
Percent of students discontinuing law school:
Men: **0%**   Women: **3%**
First-year students: **5%**   Second-year students: **N/A**
Third-year students: **N/A**   Fourth-year students: **N/A**

LIBRARY RESOURCES
Total titles: 174,314
Total volumes: 364,449
Total seats available for library users: 442

INFORMATION TECHNOLOGY
Number of wired network connections available to students: 105 total (in the law library, excluding computer labs: 92; in classrooms: 11; in computer labs: 0; elsewhere in the law school: 2)
Law school has a wireless network.
Students are not required to own a computer.

EMPLOYMENT AND SALARIES
Proportion of 2008 graduates employed at graduation: 61%
Employed 9 months later, as of February 15, 2009: 96%
Salaries in the private sector (law firms, business, industry): $45,500 –$80,000 (25th-75th percentile)
Median salary in the private sector: $52,250
Percentage in the private sector who reported salary information: 89%
Median salary in public service (government, judicial clerkships, academic posts, non-profits): $45,040

Percentage of 2008 graduates in:

Law firms: 57%   Government: 20%
Bus./industry: 15%   Judicial clerkship: 3%
Public interest: 2%   Unknown: 0%
Academia : 3%

2008 graduates employed in-state: 76%
2008 graduates employed in foreign countries: 0%
Number of states where graduates are employed: 11
Percentage of 2008 graduates working in: New England: 0%, Middle Atlantic: 0%, East North Central: 1%, West North Central: 1%, South Atlantic: 2%, East South Central: 1%, West South Central: 89%, Mountain: 3%, Pacific: 2%, Unknown: 0%

BAR PASSAGE RATES
Based on 2008 graduates taking Summer 2008 or Winter 2009 exams. Most of the school's first-time test takers took the bar in Oklahoma.

| 96% |
School's bar passage rate for first-time test takers

| 93% |
Statewide bar passage rate for first-time test takers

University of Oregon

- 1221 University of Oregon, Eugene, OR, 97403-1221
- http://www.law.uoregon.edu
- Public
- Year founded: 1884
- 2009-2010 tuition: full-time: $22,328; part-time: N/A
- Enrollment 2009-10 academic year: full-time: 544
- U.S. News 2010 law specialty ranking: dispute resolution: 7, environmental law: 8

3.12-3.56 GPA, 25TH-75TH PERCENTILE

157-161 LSAT, 25TH-75TH PERCENTILE

42% ACCEPTANCE RATE

80 2011 U.S. NEWS LAW SCHOOL RANKING

ADMISSIONS

Admissions phone number: (541) 346-3846
Admissions email address: admissions@law.uoregon.edu
Application website:
  http://www.law.uoregon.edu/admissions
Application deadline for Fall 2011 admission: 1-Mar

Admissions statistics:
Number of applicants for Fall 2009: **2,093**
Number of acceptances: **888**
Number enrolled: **182**
Acceptance rate: **42%**
GPA, 25th-75th percentile, entering class Fall 2009: **3.12-3.56**
LSAT, 25th-75th percentile, entering class Fall 2009: **157-161**

FINANCIAL AID

Financial aid phone number: (800) 760-6953
Financial aid application deadline: 1-Mar
Tuition 2009-2010 academic year: **full-time: $22,328; part-time: N/A**
Room and board: $10,260 ; books: $1,050 ; miscellaneous expenses: $2,556
Total of room/board/books/miscellaneous expenses: **$13,866**
University offers graduate student housing for which law students are eligible.

Financial aid profile
Percent of students that received grants for the 2008-2009 academic year: full-time: **49%**
Median grant amount: full-time: **$5,941**
The average law-school debt of those in the Class of 2009 who borrowed: **$77,571** . Proportion who borrowed: **89%**

ACADEMIC PROGRAMS

Calendar: **semester**
Joint degrees awarded: **J.D./M.B.A.; J.D./M.A./M.S. Environmental Studies; J.D./M.P.A.; J.D./M.A. International Studies; J.D./M.C.R.P.**

Typical first-year section size: Full-time: **61**
Is there typically a "small section" of the first year class, other than Legal Writing, taught by full-time faculty?: Full-time: **no**
Number of course titles, beyond the first year curriculum, offered last year: **103**
Percentages of upper division course sections, excluding seminars, with an enrollment of:
  Under 25: **66%**   25 to 49: **22%**
  50 to 74: **9%**   75 to 99: **3%**
  100+: **0%**
Areas of specialization: appellate advocacy, clinical training, dispute resolution, environmental law, health care law, intellectual property law, international law, tax law, trial advocacy

Fall 2009 faculty profile
Total teaching faculty: 52. Full-time: **52%**; 52% men, **48%** women, **26%** minorities. Part-time: **48%**; 44% men, 56% women, **24%** minorities
Student-to-faculty ratio: **16.4**

SPECIAL PROGRAMS *(as provided by law school):*
UO offers six centers and programs (Environment, ADR, Law and Entrepreneurship, Public Interest/Public Service, Law and Politics, and Portland Program), seven clinics (Civil, Crim. Defense, Crim. Prosecution, Domestic Violence, Environmental, Small Business, and Mediation), eleven certificate programs, numerous externships, multiple concurrent degree programs, and a Masters in Conflict Resolution.

STUDENT BODY
Fall 2009 full-time enrollment: 544
Men: **55%**   Women: **45%**
African-American: **2.90%** American Indian: **2.00%**
Asian-American: **9.60%**   Mexican-American: **1.10%**
Puerto Rican: **0.00%**   Other Hisp-Amer: **2.60%**
White: **71.10%**   International: **0.70%**
Unknown: **9.90%**

Percent of students discontinuing law school:

Men: **2%**   Women: **1%**

First-year students: **5%**   Second-year students: **N/A**

Third-year students: **N/A**   Fourth-year students: **N/A**

LIBRARY RESOURCES

Total titles: **84,563**

Total volumes: **390,744**

Total seats available for library users: **322**

INFORMATION TECHNOLOGY

Number of wired network connections available to students: **1354** total (in the law library, excluding computer labs: **288**; in classrooms: **632**; in computer labs: **0**; elsewhere in the law school: **434**)

Law school has a wireless network.

Students are required to own a computer.

EMPLOYMENT AND SALARIES

Proportion of 2008 graduates employed at graduation: **58%**

Employed 9 months later, as of February 15, 2009: **90%**

Salaries in the private sector (law firms, business, industry): **$48,000 –$97,000** (25th-75th percentile)

Median salary in the private sector: **$72,500**

Percentage in the private sector who reported salary information: **53%**

Median salary in public service (government, judicial clerkships, academic posts, non-profits): **$47,000**

Percentage of 2008 graduates in:

Law firms: **45%**   Government: **16%**

Bus./industry: **11%**   Judicial clerkship: **14%**

Public interest: **11%**   Unknown: **0%**

Academia : **4%**

2008 graduates employed in-state: **62%**

2008 graduates employed in foreign countries: **1%**

Number of states where graduates are employed: **17**

Percentage of 2008 graduates working in: New England: **0%**, Middle Atlantic: **1%**, East North Central: **1%**, West North Central: **0%**, South Atlantic: **4%**, East South Central: **0%**, West South Central: **1%**, Mountain: **11%**, Pacific: **81%**, Unknown: **0%**

BAR PASSAGE RATES

Based on 2008 graduates taking Summer 2008 or Winter 2009 exams. Most of the school's first-time test takers took the bar in Oregon.

85%

School's bar passage rate for first-time test takers

79%

Statewide bar passage rate for first-time test takers

University of Pennsylvania

- 3400 Chestnut Street, Philadelphia, PA, 19104-6204
- http://www.law.upenn.edu
- Private
- **Year founded:** 1790
- **2009-2010 tuition:** full-time: $46,514; part-time: N/A
- **Enrollment 2009-10 academic year:** full-time: 790
- **U.S. News 2010 law specialty ranking:** intellectual property law: 26

3.57-3.90 GPA, 25TH-75TH PERCENTILE

166-171 LSAT, 25TH-75TH PERCENTILE

14% ACCEPTANCE RATE

7 2011 U.S. NEWS LAW SCHOOL RANKING

ADMISSIONS

Admissions phone number: **(215) 898-7400**
Admissions email address: **admissions@law.upenn.edu**
Application website: **http://www.law.upenn.edu/apply**
Application deadline for Fall 2011 admission: **15-Feb**

Admissions statistics:

Number of applicants for Fall 2009: **6,205**
Number of acceptances: **895**
Number enrolled: **255**
Acceptance rate: **14%**
GPA, 25th-75th percentile, entering class Fall 2009: **3.57-3.90**
LSAT, 25th-75th percentile, entering class Fall 2009: **166-171**

FINANCIAL AID

Financial aid phone number: **(215) 898-7400**
Financial aid application deadline: **1-Mar**
Tuition 2009-2010 academic year: **full-time: $46,514; part-time: N/A**
Room and board: **$12,654** ; books: **$1,225** ; miscellaneous expenses: **$5,217**
Total of room/board/books/miscellaneous expenses: **$19,096**
University offers graduate student housing for which law students are eligible.

Financial aid profile

Percent of students that received grants for the 2008-2009 academic year: full-time: **40%**
Median grant amount: full-time: **$14,000**
The average law-school debt of those in the Class of 2009 who borrowed: **$108,601** . Proportion who borrowed: **84%**

ACADEMIC PROGRAMS

Calendar: **semester**
Joint degrees awarded: **J.D./M. Bioethics; J.D./M.B.A.; J.D./M.C.P. City Planning; J.D./M.A./M.S. Criminology; J.D./M.A./M.S.Ed.; J.D./M.E.S.; J.D./M.G.A.; J.D./A.M.** Islamic Studies; J.D./M.A. Philosophy; J.D./Ph.D. Communications; J.D./Ph.D. Economics; J.D./M.P.H.; J.D./M.S.W.; J.D./Ph.D. American Legal History; J.D./BSE Engineering; J.D./Ph.D. Philosophy; J.D./M.A. Global Business Law; J.D./M.D.; J.D./M.A. History; J.S./M.A. International Studies; J.D./B.A. or B.S.; J.D./Ph.D. NELC (ad hoc); J.D./Ph.D. Political Science (ad hoc)

Typical first-year section size: Full-time: **85**
Is there typically a "small section" of the first year class, other than Legal Writing, taught by full-time faculty?: Full-time: **yes**
Number of course titles, beyond the first year curriculum, offered last year: **172**
Percentages of upper division course sections, excluding seminars, with an enrollment of:

Under 25: **45%**	25 to 49: **28%**
50 to 74: **15%**	75 to 99: **8%**
100+: **4%**	

Areas of specialization: appellate advocacy, clinical training, dispute resolution, environmental law, health care law, intellectual property law, international law, tax law, trial advocacy

Fall 2009 faculty profile

Total teaching faculty: **99**. Full-time: **61%**; **73%** men, **27%** women, **15%** minorities. Part-time: **39%**; **64%** men, **36%** women, **10%** minorities
Student-to-faculty ratio: **10.7**

SPECIAL PROGRAMS (as provided by law school):

Special program: Cross-disciplinary study. Faculty: more than 70% hold non-law advanced degrees. Programs: joint degree and certificates with nation's finest array of grad. and professional schools (e.g. Wharton, Annenberg). Public Interest and Clinics; institutes & programs (economics, health, int'l, philosophy, con. law, criminal, IP/technology, legal hist., environment, tax, and regulation).

STUDENT BODY

Fall 2009 full-time enrollment: 790

Men: **53%**
Women: **47%**
African-American: **7.30%**
American Indian: **0.30%**
Asian-American: **13.90%**
Mexican-American: **0.90%**
Puerto Rican: **0.50%**
Other Hisp-Amer: **5.10%**
White: **64.80%**
International: **2.40%**
Unknown: **4.80%**

Attrition rates for 2008-2009 full-time students

Percent of students discontinuing law school:

Men: **N/A**
Women: **N/A**
First-year students: **N/A**
Second-year students: **N/A**
Third-year students: **N/A**
Fourth-year students: **N/A**

LIBRARY RESOURCES

Total titles: **849,434**
Total volumes: **1,040,919**
Total seats available for library users: **520**

INFORMATION TECHNOLOGY

Number of wired network connections available to students: **28** total (in the law library, excluding computer labs: **0**; in classrooms: **28**; in computer labs: **0**; elsewhere in the law school: **0**)

Law school has a wireless network.

Students are not required to own a computer.

EMPLOYMENT AND SALARIES

Proportion of 2008 graduates employed at graduation: **98%**

Employed 9 months later, as of February 15, 2009: **100%**

Salaries in the private sector (law firms, business, industry): **$160,000 –$160,000** (25th-75th percentile)

Median salary in the private sector: **$160,000**

Percentage in the private sector who reported salary information: **81%**

Median salary in public service (government, judicial clerkships, academic posts, non-profits): **$53,626**

Percentage of 2008 graduates in:

Law firms: **77%**
Government: **0%**
Bus./industry: **4%**
Judicial clerkship: **17%**
Public interest: **3%**
Unknown: **0%**
Academia : **0%**

2008 graduates employed in-state: **16%**
2008 graduates employed in foreign countries: **2%**
Number of states where graduates are employed: **22**
Percentage of 2008 graduates working in: New England: **3%**, Middle Atlantic: **61%**, East North Central: **4%**, West North Central: **0%**, South Atlantic: **15%**, East South Central: **0%**, West South Central: **2%**, Mountain: **2%**, Pacific: **12%**, Unknown: **0%**

BAR PASSAGE RATES

Based on 2008 graduates taking Summer 2008 or Winter 2009 exams. Most of the school's first-time test takers took the bar in New York.

98%

School's bar passage rate for first-time test takers

81%

Statewide bar passage rate for first-time test takers

University of Pittsburgh

■ 3900 Forbes Avenue, Pittsburgh, PA, 15260
■ http://www.law.pitt.edu
■ Public
■ Year founded: 1895
■ 2009-2010 tuition: full-time: $25,098; part-time: N/A
■ Enrollment 2009-10 academic year: full-time: 682
■ U.S. News 2010 law specialty ranking: healthcare law: 15

3.18-3.63 GPA, 25TH-75TH PERCENTILE

157-161 LSAT, 25TH-75TH PERCENTILE

37% ACCEPTANCE RATE

67 2011 U.S. NEWS LAW SCHOOL RANKING

ADMISSIONS

Admissions phone number: **(412) 648-1415**
Admissions email address: **admissions@law.pitt.edu**
Application website: **N/A**
Application deadline for Fall 2011 admission: **1-Mar**

Admissions statistics:
Number of applicants for Fall 2009: **2,177**
Number of acceptances: **811**
Number enrolled: **235**
Acceptance rate: **37%**
GPA, 25th-75th percentile, entering class Fall 2009: **3.18-3.63**
LSAT, 25th-75th percentile, entering class Fall 2009: **157-161**

FINANCIAL AID

Financial aid phone number: **(412) 648-1415**
Financial aid application deadline: **1-Apr**
Tuition 2009-2010 academic year: **full-time: $25,098; part-time: N/A**
Room and board: **$15,054** ; books: **$1,530** ; miscellaneous expenses: **$730**
Total of room/board/books/miscellaneous expenses: **$17,314**
University does not offer graduate student housing for which law students are eligible.

Financial aid profile
Percent of students that received grants for the 2008-2009 academic year: full-time: **58%**
Median grant amount: full-time: **$10,000**
The average law-school debt of those in the Class of 2009 who borrowed: **$83,826** . Proportion who borrowed: **88%**

ACADEMIC PROGRAMS

Calendar: **semester**
Joint degrees awarded: **J.D./M.B.A.; J.D./M.P.I.A.; J.D./M.P.H.; J.D./M.I.D.; J.D./M.A.; J.D./M.S. (CMU); J.D./M.P.A.; J.D./M.S.W; J.D./M.B.A. (CMU)**
Typical first-year section size: Full-time: **82**

Is there typically a "small section" of the first year class, other than Legal Writing, taught by full-time faculty?: Full-time: **no**
Number of course titles, beyond the first year curriculum, offered last year: **192**
Percentages of upper division course sections, excluding seminars, with an enrollment of:
Under 25: **70%**   25 to 49: **16%**
50 to 74: **9%**   75 to 99: **2%**
100+: **3%**
Areas of specialization: appellate advocacy, clinical training, dispute resolution, environmental law, health care law, intellectual property law, international law, tax law, trial advocacy

Fall 2009 faculty profile
Total teaching faculty: **88**. Full-time: **49%**; **63%** men, **37%** women, **7%** minorities. Part-time: **51%**; **69%** men, **31%** women, **13%** minorities
Student-to-faculty ratio: **12.9**

SPECIAL PROGRAMS (as provided by law school):

We have 5 Certificate Programs, 6 clinics, and an externship program that most students enroll in. The Innovation Practice Institute provides courses on advising entrepreneurs. We offer the unique Languages for Lawyers Program and JURIST, our student-edited, award-winning website. Our Mellon Program has been key to our success in graduating the students who matriculate here.

STUDENT BODY

Fall 2009 full-time enrollment: **682**
Men: **54%**   Women: **46%**
African-American: **6.70%**   American Indian: **0.10%**
Asian-American: **6.30%**   Mexican-American: **0.00%**
Puerto Rican: **0.10%**   Other Hisp-Amer: **2.50%**
White: **64.50%**   International: **0.00%**
Unknown: **19.60%**

Attrition rates for 2008-2009 full-time students
Percent of students discontinuing law school:

Men: **2%**   Women: **2%**
First-year students: **5%**   Second-year students: **0%**
Third-year students: **N/A**   Fourth-year students: **N/A**

LIBRARY RESOURCES
Total titles: **271,306**
Total volumes: **470,958**
Total seats available for library users: **438**

INFORMATION TECHNOLOGY
Number of wired network connections available to students: **282** total (in the law library, excluding computer labs: **55**; in classrooms: **196**; in computer labs: **31**; elsewhere in the law school: **0**)
Law school has a wireless network.
Students are not required to own a computer.

EMPLOYMENT AND SALARIES
Proportion of 2008 graduates employed at graduation: **72%**
Employed 9 months later, as of February 15, 2009: **94%**
Salaries in the private sector (law firms, business, industry): **$56,500 –$145,000** (25th-75th percentile)
Median salary in the private sector: **$102,500**
Percentage in the private sector who reported salary information: **64%**

Median salary in public service (government, judicial clerkships, academic posts, non-profits): **$47,000**

Percentage of 2008 graduates in:
Law firms: **62%**   Government: **10%**
Bus./industry: **17%**   Judicial clerkship: **7%**
Public interest: **4%**   Unknown: **0%**
Academia : **1%**

2008 graduates employed in-state: **63%**
2008 graduates employed in foreign countries: **1%**
Number of states where graduates are employed: **24**
Percentage of 2008 graduates working in: New England: **2%**, Middle Atlantic: **67%**, East North Central: **5%**, West North Central: **1%**, South Atlantic: **18%**, East South Central: **1%**, West South Central: **1%**, Mountain: **1%**, Pacific: **4%**, Unknown: **0%**

BAR PASSAGE RATES
Based on 2008 graduates taking Summer 2008 or Winter 2009 exams. Most of the school's first-time test takers took the bar in Pennsylvania.

91%
School's bar passage rate for first-time test takers

87%
Statewide bar passage rate for first-time test takers

University of Richmond (Williams)

- 28 Westhampton Way, Richmond, VA, 23173
- http://law.richmond.edu
- Private
- **Year founded:** 1870
- **2009-2010 tuition:** full-time: $32,450; part-time: $1,700/credit hour
- **Enrollment 2009-10 academic year:** full-time: 465
- **U.S. News 2010 law specialty ranking:** N/A

3.19-3.63 GPA, 25TH-75TH PERCENTILE

159-163 LSAT, 25TH-75TH PERCENTILE

29% ACCEPTANCE RATE

86 2011 U.S. NEWS LAW SCHOOL RANKING

ADMISSIONS

Admissions phone number: **(804) 289-8189**
Admissions email address: **mrahman@richmond.edu**
Application website:
  http://law.richmond.edu/admissions/apply.php
Application deadline for Fall 2011 admission: **15-Feb**

Admissions statistics:
Number of applicants for Fall 2009: **2,036**
Number of acceptances: **584**
Number enrolled: **149**
Acceptance rate: **29%**
GPA, 25th-75th percentile, entering class Fall 2009: **3.19-3.63**
LSAT, 25th-75th percentile, entering class Fall 2009: **159-163**

FINANCIAL AID

Financial aid phone number: **(804) 289-8438**
Financial aid application deadline: **1-Mar**
Tuition 2009-2010 academic year: **full-time: $32,450; part-time: $1,700/credit hour**
Room and board: **$10,530** ; books: **$1,300** ; miscellaneous expenses: **$3,440**
Total of room/board/books/miscellaneous expenses: **$15,270**
University offers graduate student housing for which law students are eligible.

Financial aid profile
Percent of students that received grants for the 2008-2009 academic year: full-time: **74%**
Median grant amount: full-time: **$7,500**
The average law-school debt of those in the Class of 2009 who borrowed: **$93,200** . Proportion who borrowed: **72%**

ACADEMIC PROGRAMS

Calendar: **semester**
Joint degrees awarded: **J.D./M.B.A.; J.D./M.S.W.; J.D./M.P.A.; J.D./M.H.A.; J.D./M.U.P.**
Typical first-year section size: Full-time: **55**

Is there typically a "small section" of the first year class, other than Legal Writing, taught by full-time faculty?: Full-time: **yes**
Number of course titles, beyond the first year curriculum, offered last year: **104**
Percentages of upper division course sections, excluding seminars, with an enrollment of:
  Under 25: **73%**   25 to 49: **18%**
  50 to 74: **6%**   75 to 99: **4%**
  100+: **0%**
Areas of specialization: appellate advocacy, clinical training, dispute resolution, environmental law, health care law, intellectual property law, international law, tax law, trial advocacy

Fall 2009 faculty profile
Total teaching faculty: **81.** Full-time: **35%**; **71%** men, **29%** women, **7%** minorities. Part-time: **65%**; **68%** men, **32%** women, **6%** minorities
Student-to-faculty ratio: **13.8**

SPECIAL PROGRAMS *(as provided by law school):*
Intellectual Property and Transactions Clinic, Family Law Clinic, Juvenile Delinquency Clinic, Disabilities Law Clinic, Juvenile Law & Policy Clinic, Wrongful Conviction Clinic, Clinical Placement Program, Merhige Environmental Law Center, Intellectual Property Center, National Family Law Center, Cambridge Summer Study Abroad, John Marshall Scholars Program

STUDENT BODY
Fall 2009 full-time enrollment: **465**
Men: **52%**   Women: **48%**
African-American: **9.00%**   American Indian: **0.90%**
Asian-American: **6.00%**   Mexican-American: **0.00%**
Puerto Rican: **0.00%**   Other Hisp-Amer: **0.60%**
White: **82.80%**   International: **0.60%**
Unknown: **0.00%**

Attrition rates for 2008-2009 full-time students
Percent of students discontinuing law school:
Men: **5%**   Women: **4%**
First-year students: **14%**   Second-year students: **N/A**
Third-year students: **N/A**   Fourth-year students: **N/A**

LIBRARY RESOURCES
Total titles: **207,374**
Total volumes: **407,871**
Total seats available for library users: **675**

INFORMATION TECHNOLOGY
Number of wired network connections available to students: **809** total (in the law library, excluding computer labs: **490**; in classrooms: **289**; in computer labs: **5**; elsewhere in the law school: **25**)
Law school has a wireless network.
Students are required to own a computer.

EMPLOYMENT AND SALARIES
Proportion of 2008 graduates employed at graduation: **61%**
Employed 9 months later, as of February 15, 2009: **91%**
Salaries in the private sector (law firms, business, industry): **$70,000 –$127,000** (25th-75th percentile)
Median salary in the private sector: **$90,000**
Percentage in the private sector who reported salary information: **28%**

Median salary in public service (government, judicial clerkships, academic posts, non-profits): **$48,000**

Percentage of 2008 graduates in:
Law firms: **53%**   Government: **12%**
Bus./industry: **8%**   Judicial clerkship: **17%**
Public interest: **2%**   Unknown: **8%**
Academia : **0%**

2008 graduates employed in-state: **72%**
2008 graduates employed in foreign countries: **0%**
Number of states where graduates are employed: **18**
Percentage of 2008 graduates working in: New England: **1%**, Middle Atlantic: **3%**, East North Central: **0%**, West North Central: **1%**, South Atlantic: **88%**, East South Central: **2%**, West South Central: **1%**, Mountain: **3%**, Pacific: **1%**, Unknown: **0%**

BAR PASSAGE RATES
Based on 2008 graduates taking Summer 2008 or Winter 2009 exams. Most of the school's first-time test takers took the bar in Virginia.

91%
School's bar passage rate for first-time test takers

82%
Statewide bar passage rate for first-time test takers

University of San Diego

- 5998 Alcala Park, San Diego, CA, 92110-2492
- http://www.law.sandiego.edu
- Private
- Year founded: 1954
- 2009-2010 tuition: full-time: $40,014; part-time: $28,904
- Enrollment 2009-10 academic year: full-time: 816; part-time: 184
- U.S. News 2010 law specialty ranking: tax law: 6

3.24-3.60 GPA, 25TH-75TH PERCENTILE

158-162 LSAT, 25TH-75TH PERCENTILE

35% ACCEPTANCE RATE

56 2011 U.S. NEWS LAW SCHOOL RANKING

ADMISSIONS

Admissions phone number: (619) 260-4528
Admissions email address: jdinfo@SanDiego.edu
Application website: http://www.law.sandiego.edu
Application deadline for Fall 2011 admission: 1-Feb

Admissions statistics:

Number of applicants for Fall 2009: **4,010**
Number of acceptances: **1,416**
Number enrolled: **281**
Acceptance rate: **35%**
GPA, 25th-75th percentile, entering class Fall 2009: **3.24-3.60**
LSAT, 25th-75th percentile, entering class Fall 2009: **158-162**

Part-time program:

Number of applicants for Fall 2009: **394**
Number of acceptances: **88**
Number enrolled: **40**
Acceptance rate: **22%**
GPA, 25th-75th percentile, entering class Fall 2009: **3.10-3.56**
LSAT, 25th-75th percentile, entering class Fall 2009: **156-160**

FINANCIAL AID

Financial aid phone number: (619) 260-4570
Financial aid application deadline: 1-Feb
Tuition 2009-2010 academic year: **full-time: $40,014; part-time: $28,904**
Room and board: **$12,080** ; books: **$1,129** ; miscellaneous expenses: **$7,391**
Total of room/board/books/miscellaneous expenses: **$20,600**
University offers graduate student housing for which law students are eligible.

Financial aid profile

Percent of students that received grants for the 2008-2009 academic year: full-time: **43%**; part-time **43%**

Median grant amount: full-time: **$21,000** ; part-time: **$15,000**
The average law-school debt of those in the Class of 2009 who borrowed: **$109,657** . Proportion who borrowed: **84%**

ACADEMIC PROGRAMS

Calendar: **semester**
Joint degrees awarded: **J.D./M.B.A.; J.D./International M.B.A.; J.D./M.A. International Relations**
Typical first-year section size: Full-time: **80**; Part-time: **80**
Is there typically a "small section" of the first year class, other than Legal Writing, taught by full-time faculty?: Full-time: **yes**; Part-time: **yes**
Number of course titles, beyond the first year curriculum, offered last year: **133**
Percentages of upper division course sections, excluding seminars, with an enrollment of:

Under 25: **76%**		25 to 49: **9%**	
50 to 74: **7%**		75 to 99: **9%**	
100+: **0%**			

Areas of specialization: appellate advocacy, clinical training, dispute resolution, environmental law, health care law, intellectual property law, international law, tax law, trial advocacy

Fall 2009 faculty profile

Total teaching faculty: **100**. Full-time: **51%**; **71%** men, **29%** women, **6%** minorities. Part-time: **49%**; **69%** men, **31%** women, **10%** minorities
Student-to-faculty ratio: **14.2**

SPECIAL PROGRAMS (as provided by law school):

Our Clinical program is among the most extensive and successful in the nation. Students interview, counsel, and represent clients under faculty supervision. The Center for Public Interest Law, the Children's Advocacy Institute, and the Energy Policy and Initiatives Center offer research and training opportunities. Summer sessions are offered in England, Ireland, France, Spain, Italy & Russia.

STUDENT BODY

Fall 2009 full-time enrollment: 816

Men: 53%	Women: 47%
African-American: 1.50%	American Indian: 1.00%
Asian-American: 16.70%	Mexican-American: 4.70%
Puerto Rican: 0.10%	Other Hisp-Amer: 2.70%
White: 72.40%	International: 0.50%
Unknown: 0.50%	

Fall 2009 part-time enrollment: 184

Men: 60%	Women: 40%
African-American: 1.60%	American Indian: 1.60%
Asian-American: 17.40%	Mexican-American: 4.30%
Puerto Rican: 0.50%	Other Hisp-Amer: 5.40%
White: 68.50%	International: 0.00%
Unknown: 0.50%	

Attrition rates for 2008-2009 full-time students

Percent of students discontinuing law school:

Men: 5%	Women: 4%
First-year students: 12%	Second-year students: 1%
Third-year students: 1%	Fourth-year students: N/A

LIBRARY RESOURCES

Total titles: 371,062

Total volumes: 538,289

Total seats available for library users: 590

INFORMATION TECHNOLOGY

Number of wired network connections available to students: 240 total (in the law library, excluding computer labs: 202; in classrooms: 17; in computer labs: 0; elsewhere in the law school: 21)

Law school has a wireless network.

Students are not required to own a computer.

EMPLOYMENT AND SALARIES

Proportion of 2008 graduates employed at graduation: N/A

Employed 9 months later, as of February 15, 2009: 98%

Salaries in the private sector (law firms, business, industry): $65,000 –$135,000 (25th-75th percentile)

Median salary in the private sector: $85,000

Percentage in the private sector who reported salary information: 68%

Median salary in public service (government, judicial clerkships, academic posts, non-profits): $60,000

Percentage of 2008 graduates in:

Law firms: 56%	Government: 13%
Bus./industry: 18%	Judicial clerkship: 4%
Public interest: 6%	Unknown: 1%
Academia : 2%	

2008 graduates employed in-state: 88%

2008 graduates employed in foreign countries: 1%

Number of states where graduates are employed: 17

Percentage of 2008 graduates working in: New England: 1%, Middle Atlantic: 0%, East North Central: 1%, West North Central: 0%, South Atlantic: 4%, East South Central: 0%, West South Central: 0%, Mountain: 2%, Pacific: 90%, Unknown: 1%

BAR PASSAGE RATES

Based on 2008 graduates taking Summer 2008 or Winter 2009 exams. Most of the school's first-time test takers took the bar in California.

79%

School's bar passage rate for first-time test takers

71%

Statewide bar passage rate for first-time test takers

University of San Francisco

- 2130 Fulton Street, San Francisco, CA, 94117-1080
- http://www.law.usfca.edu
- Private
- **Year founded:** 1912
- **2009-2010 tuition:** full-time: $37,310; part-time: $26,645
- **Enrollment 2009-10 academic year:** full-time: 574; part-time: 132
- **U.S. News 2010 law specialty ranking:** N/A

3.15-3.57 GPA, 25TH-75TH PERCENTILE

156-160 LSAT, 25TH-75TH PERCENTILE

37% ACCEPTANCE RATE

98 2011 U.S. NEWS LAW SCHOOL RANKING

ADMISSIONS
Admissions phone number: **(415) 422-6586**
Admissions email address: **lawadmissions@usfca.edu**
Application website: **http://www.law.usfca.edu**
Application deadline for Fall 2011 admission: **1-Feb**

Admissions statistics:
Number of applicants for Fall 2009: **3,391**
Number of acceptances: **1,247**
Number enrolled: **227**
Acceptance rate: **37%**
GPA, 25th-75th percentile, entering class Fall 2009: **3.15-3.57**
LSAT, 25th-75th percentile, entering class Fall 2009: **156-160**

Part-time program:
Number of applicants for Fall 2009: **485**
Number of acceptances: **104**
Number enrolled: **45**
Acceptance rate: **21%**
GPA, 25th-75th percentile, entering class Fall 2009: **2.96-3.61**
LSAT, 25th-75th percentile, entering class Fall 2009: **153-160**

FINANCIAL AID
Financial aid phone number: **(415) 422-6210**
Financial aid application deadline: **15-Feb**
Tuition 2009-2010 academic year: **full-time: $37,310; part-time: $26,645**
Room and board: **$13,500** ; books: **$1,500** ; miscellaneous expenses: **$5,660**
Total of room/board/books/miscellaneous expenses: **$20,660**
University offers graduate student housing for which law students are eligible.

Financial aid profile
Percent of students that received grants for the 2008-2009 academic year: full-time: **39%**; part-time **44%**

Median grant amount: full-time: **$18,000** ; part-time: **$6,500**
The average law-school debt of those in the Class of 2009 who borrowed: **$109,696** . Proportion who borrowed: **89%**

ACADEMIC PROGRAMS
Calendar: **semester**
Joint degrees awarded: **J.D./M.B.A.**
Typical first-year section size: Full-time: **97**; Part-time: **51**
Is there typically a "small section" of the first year class, other than Legal Writing, taught by full-time faculty?: Full-time: **no**; Part-time: **no**
Number of course titles, beyond the first year curriculum, offered last year: **101**
Percentages of upper division course sections, excluding seminars, with an enrollment of:

Under 25: **60%**	25 to 49: **28%**
50 to 74: **10%**	75 to 99: **1%**
100+: **0%**	

Areas of specialization: appellate advocacy, clinical training, dispute resolution, environmental law, health care law, intellectual property law, international law, tax law, trial advocacy

Fall 2009 faculty profile
Total teaching faculty: **75**. Full-time: **45%**; 50% men, 50% women, 35% minorities. Part-time: **55%**; 73% men, 27% women, 17% minorities
Student-to-faculty ratio: **15.2**

SPECIAL PROGRAMS *(as provided by law school):*
Law study is enriched by multiple in-house clinics, and numerous civil, criminal and judicial externship opportunities. CLGJ externships are offered in Cambodia, China, Dominican Republic, India, Spain & Vietnam. The McCarthy Institute promotes IP & Cyberlaw development, while focusing on the intersection of theory and practice. The Intensive Advocacy Program builds students' litigation skills.

STUDENT BODY

Fall 2009 full-time enrollment: 574

Men: 45%	Women: 55%
African-American: 5.60%	American Indian: 0.70%
Asian-American: 16.20%	Mexican-American: 5.20%
Puerto Rican: 0.20%	Other Hisp-Amer: 5.10%
White: 46.20%	International: 2.30%
Unknown: 18.60%	

Fall 2009 part-time enrollment: 132

Men: 48%	Women: 52%
African-American: 16.70%	American Indian: 2.30%
Asian-American: 16.70%	Mexican-American: 4.50%
Puerto Rican: 0.80%	Other Hisp-Amer: 3.80%
White: 41.70%	International: 0.80%
Unknown: 12.90%	

Attrition rates for 2008-2009 full-time students
Percent of students discontinuing law school:

Men: 6%	Women: 5%
First-year students: 13%	Second-year students: 2%
Third-year students: 1%	Fourth-year students: N/A

LIBRARY RESOURCES

Total titles: 197,097
Total volumes: 371,531
Total seats available for library users: 419

INFORMATION TECHNOLOGY

Number of wired network connections available to students: 300 total (in the law library, excluding computer labs: 192; in classrooms: 108; in computer labs: 0; elsewhere in the law school: 0)
Law school has a wireless network.
Students are not required to own a computer.

EMPLOYMENT AND SALARIES

Proportion of 2008 graduates employed at graduation: N/A
Employed 9 months later, as of February 15, 2009: 93%
Salaries in the private sector (law firms, business, industry): $61,000 –$128,000 (25th-75th percentile)
Median salary in the private sector: $83,000
Percentage in the private sector who reported salary information: 45%
Median salary in public service (government, judicial clerkships, academic posts, non-profits): $48,000

Percentage of 2008 graduates in:

Law firms: 49%	Government: 10%
Bus./industry: 24%	Judicial clerkship: 1%
Public interest: 10%	Unknown: 5%
Academia : 1%	

2008 graduates employed in-state: 85%
2008 graduates employed in foreign countries: 0%
Number of states where graduates are employed: 9
Percentage of 2008 graduates working in: New England: 0%, Middle Atlantic: 2%, East North Central: 0%, West North Central: 0%, South Atlantic: 0%, East South Central: 0%, West South Central: 0%, Mountain: 2%, Pacific: 90%, Unknown: 5%

BAR PASSAGE RATES

Based on 2008 graduates taking Summer 2008 or Winter 2009 exams. Most of the school's first-time test takers took the bar in California.

86%
School's bar passage rate for first-time test takers

71%
Statewide bar passage rate for first-time test takers

University of South Carolina

- 701 S. Main Street, Columbia, SC, 29208
- http://www.law.sc.edu/admissions
- Public
- **Year founded:** 1867
- **2009-2010 tuition:** full-time: $19,034; part-time: N/A
- **Enrollment 2009-10 academic year:** full-time: 685
- **U.S. News 2010 law specialty ranking:** N/A

3.14-3.70 GPA, 25TH-75TH PERCENTILE

156-160 LSAT, 25TH-75TH PERCENTILE

37% ACCEPTANCE RATE

Tier 3 2011 U.S. NEWS LAW SCHOOL RANKING

ADMISSIONS

Admissions phone number: **(803) 777-6605**
Admissions email address: **usclaw@law.sc.edu**
Application website: **http://www.lsac.org/**
Application deadline for Fall 2011 admission: **1-Mar**

Admissions statistics:

Number of applicants for Fall 2009: **1,973**
Number of acceptances: **730**
Number enrolled: **240**
Acceptance rate: **37%**
GPA, 25th-75th percentile, entering class Fall 2009: **3.14-3.70**
LSAT, 25th-75th percentile, entering class Fall 2009: **156-160**

FINANCIAL AID

Financial aid phone number: **(803) 777-6605**
Financial aid application deadline: **1-Mar**
Tuition 2009-2010 academic year: **full-time: $19,034; part-time: N/A**
Room and board: **$11,661** ; books: **$936** ; miscellaneous expenses: **$4,070**
Total of room/board/books/miscellaneous expenses: **$16,667**
University offers graduate student housing for which law students are eligible.

Financial aid profile

Percent of students that received grants for the 2008-2009 academic year: full-time: **50%**
Median grant amount: full-time: **$8,912**
The average law-school debt of those in the Class of 2009 who borrowed: **$41,612** . Proportion who borrowed: **87%**

ACADEMIC PROGRAMS

Calendar: **semester**
Joint degrees awarded: **J.D./I.M.B.A.; J.D./M.Acc.; J.D./M.C.J.; J.D./M.E.E.R.M.; J.D./M.H.A.; J.D./M.H.R.; J.D./M.P.A.; J.D./MSB; J.D./M.S.E.L.; J.D./M.S.W.**
Typical first-year section size: Full-time: **82**

Is there typically a "small section" of the first year class, other than Legal Writing, taught by full-time faculty?: Full-time: **no**
Number of course titles, beyond the first year curriculum, offered last year: **116**
Percentages of upper division course sections, excluding seminars, with an enrollment of:

Under 25: **51%**	25 to 49: **25%**
50 to 74: **18%**	75 to 99: **6%**
100+: **1%**	

Areas of specialization: appellate advocacy, clinical training, dispute resolution, environmental law, health care law, intellectual property law, international law, tax law, trial advocacy

Fall 2009 faculty profile

Total teaching faculty: **48**. Full-time: **79%**; **61%** men, **39%** women, **13%** minorities. Part-time: **21%**; **70%** men, **30%** women, **0%** minorities
Student-to-faculty ratio: **14.8**

SPECIAL PROGRAMS (as provided by law school):

Third-year students may represent clients in one of 6 clinics, developing practical lawyering skills such as trial advocacy, interviewing, counseling, negotiation, alternative dispute resolution, and legal drafting. Judicial internships place students with trial and appellate judges. The School of Law offers a summer abroad program on Transnational Dispute Resolution at Gray's Inn in London.

STUDENT BODY

Fall 2009 full-time enrollment: 685

Men: **58%**	Women: **42%**
African-American: **8.50%**	American Indian: **0.10%**
Asian-American: **1.90%**	Mexican-American: **0.00%**
Puerto Rican: **0.00%**	Other Hisp-Amer: **1.30%**
White: **78.80%**	International: **0.00%**
Unknown: **9.30%**	

Attrition rates for 2008-2009 full-time students

Percent of students discontinuing law school:

Men: **1%**   Women: **0%**
First-year students: **1%**   Second-year students: **N/A**
Third-year students: **1%**   Fourth-year students: **N/A**

LIBRARY RESOURCES
Total titles: **84,163**
Total volumes: **544,921**
Total seats available for library users: **504**

INFORMATION TECHNOLOGY
Number of wired network connections available to students: **42** total (in the law library, excluding computer labs: **12**; in classrooms: **0**; in computer labs: **30**; elsewhere in the law school: **0**)
Law school has a wireless network.
Students are required to own a computer.

EMPLOYMENT AND SALARIES
Proportion of 2008 graduates employed at graduation: **56%**
Employed 9 months later, as of February 15, 2009: **91%**
Salaries in the private sector (law firms, business, industry): **$51,000 –$107,500** (25th-75th percentile)
Median salary in the private sector: **$75,000**
Percentage in the private sector who reported salary information: **61%**
Median salary in public service (government, judicial clerkships, academic posts, non-profits): **$39,000**

Percentage of 2008 graduates in:
Law firms: **51%**   Government: **15%**
Bus./industry: **9%**   Judicial clerkship: **19%**
Public interest: **4%**   Unknown: **0%**
Academia : **1%**

2008 graduates employed in-state: **73%**
2008 graduates employed in foreign countries: **1%**
Number of states where graduates are employed: **13**
Percentage of 2008 graduates working in: New England: **0%**, Middle Atlantic: **3%**, East North Central: **1%**, West North Central: **1%**, South Atlantic: **95%**, East South Central: **0%**, West South Central: **1%**, Mountain: **0%**, Pacific: **0%**, Unknown: **0%**

BAR PASSAGE RATES
Based on 2008 graduates taking Summer 2008 or Winter 2009 exams. Most of the school's first-time test takers took the bar in South Carolina.

91%
School's bar passage rate for first-time test takers

82%
Statewide bar passage rate for first-time test takers

University of South Dakota

- 414 E. Clark Street, Vermillion, SD, 57069-2390
- http://www.usd.edu/law/
- Public
- Year founded: 1901
- 2009-2010 tuition: full-time: $10,695; part-time: $5,508
- Enrollment 2009-10 academic year: full-time: 202
- U.S. News 2010 law specialty ranking: N/A

3.13-3.65 GPA, 25TH-75TH PERCENTILE

149-155 LSAT, 25TH-75TH PERCENTILE

57% ACCEPTANCE RATE

Tier 3 2011 U.S. NEWS LAW SCHOOL RANKING

ADMISSIONS

Admissions phone number: **(605) 677-5443**
Admissions email address: **lawreq@usd.edu**
Application website: **http://www.usd.edu/law/apply.cfm**
Application deadline for Fall 2011 admission: **rolling**

Admissions statistics:

Number of applicants for Fall 2009: **382**
Number of acceptances: **217**
Number enrolled: **78**
Acceptance rate: **57%**
GPA, 25th-75th percentile, entering class Fall 2009: **3.13-3.65**
LSAT, 25th-75th percentile, entering class Fall 2009: **149-155**

FINANCIAL AID

Financial aid phone number: **(605) 677-5446**
Financial aid application deadline: **1-Mar**
Tuition 2009-2010 academic year: **full-time: $10,695; part-time: $5,508**
Room and board: **$6,970** ; books: **$1,400** ; miscellaneous expenses: **$4,838**
Total of room/board/books/miscellaneous expenses: **$13,208**
University offers graduate student housing for which law students are eligible.

Financial aid profile

Percent of students that received grants for the 2008-2009 academic year: full-time: **42%**
Median grant amount: full-time: **$1,305**
The average law-school debt of those in the Class of 2009 who borrowed: **$56,112** . Proportion who borrowed: **90%**

ACADEMIC PROGRAMS

Calendar: **semester**
Joint degrees awarded: **J.D./M.B.A.; J.D./MPA**
Typical first-year section size: Full-time: **61**
Is there typically a "small section" of the first year class, other than Legal Writing, taught by full-time faculty?:

Full-time: **yes**
Number of course titles, beyond the first year curriculum, offered last year: **52**
Percentages of upper division course sections, excluding seminars, with an enrollment of:

Under 25: **67%**	25 to 49: **22%**
50 to 74: **9%**	75 to 99: **2%**
100+: **N/A**	

Areas of specialization: appellate advocacy, dispute resolution, environmental law, health care law, intellectual property law, international law, tax law, trial advocacy

Fall 2009 faculty profile

Total teaching faculty: **16**. Full-time: **81%**; **69%** men, **31%** women, **N/A** minorities. Part-time: **19%**; **67%** men, **33%** women, **N/A** minorities
Student-to-faculty ratio: **12.3**

SPECIAL PROGRAMS *(as provided by law school):*

Joint-degree programs allow students to earn both JD and masters degree in one of nine disciplines in three years. Students may also broaden their education and earn up to six credit hours toward the JD through interdisciplinary study. The Extern Education Program offers students direct, personal experience working in a public or private law office while earning six credit hours in the summer.

STUDENT BODY

Fall 2009 full-time enrollment: 202

Men: **49%**	Women: **51%**
African-American: **1.50%**	American Indian: **4.00%**
Asian-American: **0.50%**	Mexican-American: **0.50%**
Puerto Rican: **0.00%**	Other Hisp-Amer: **1.00%**
White: **92.60%**	International: **0.00%**
Unknown: **0.00%**	

Attrition rates for 2008-2009 full-time students

Percent of students discontinuing law school:

Men: **4%**	Women: **N/A**
First-year students: **5%**	Second-year students: **2%**
Third-year students: **N/A**	Fourth-year students: **N/A**

LIBRARY RESOURCES

Total titles: N/A
Total volumes: N/A
Total seats available for library users: 227

INFORMATION TECHNOLOGY

Number of wired network connections available to students: 452 total (in the law library, excluding computer labs: 190; in classrooms: 250; in computer labs: 2; elsewhere in the law school: 10)
Law school has a wireless network.
Students are not required to own a computer.

EMPLOYMENT AND SALARIES

Proportion of 2008 graduates employed at graduation: 54%
Employed 9 months later, as of February 15, 2009: 94%
Salaries in the private sector (law firms, business, industry): $42,500 –$55,000 (25th-75th percentile)
Median salary in the private sector: $49,000
Percentage in the private sector who reported salary information: 46%
Median salary in public service (government, judicial clerkships, academic posts, non-profits): $42,422

Percentage of 2008 graduates in:

Law firms: 32%	Government: 22%
Bus./industry: 14%	Judicial clerkship: 18%
Public interest: 8%	Unknown: 2%
Academia : 4%	

2008 graduates employed in-state: 64%
2008 graduates employed in foreign countries: N/A
Number of states where graduates are employed: 13
Percentage of 2008 graduates working in: New England: 1%, Middle Atlantic: N/A, East North Central: N/A, West North Central: 84%, South Atlantic: 3%, East South Central: N/A, West South Central: 1%, Mountain: 10%, Pacific: N/A, Unknown: 1%

BAR PASSAGE RATES

Based on 2008 graduates taking Summer 2008 or Winter 2009 exams. Most of the school's first-time test takers took the bar in South Dakota.

95%
School's bar passage rate for first-time test takers

95%
Statewide bar passage rate for first-time test takers

Univ. of Southern California (Gould)

- 699 Exposition Boulevard, Los Angeles, CA, 90089-0071
- http://lawweb.usc.edu
- Private
- Year founded: 1900
- 2009-2010 tuition: full-time: $46,264; part-time: N/A
- Enrollment 2009-10 academic year: full-time: 618
- U.S. News 2010 law specialty ranking: tax law: 16

3.47-3.71 GPA, 25TH-75TH PERCENTILE

165-167 LSAT, 25TH-75TH PERCENTILE

22% ACCEPTANCE RATE

18 2011 U.S. NEWS LAW SCHOOL RANKING

ADMISSIONS
Admissions phone number: (213) 740-2523
Admissions email address: admissions@law.usc.edu
Application website: http://lawweb.usc.edu/how/
Application deadline for Fall 2011 admission: 2-Feb

Admissions statistics:
Number of applicants for Fall 2009: 6,024
Number of acceptances: 1,322
Number enrolled: 215
Acceptance rate: 22%
GPA, 25th-75th percentile, entering class Fall 2009: 3.47-3.71
LSAT, 25th-75th percentile, entering class Fall 2009: 165-167

FINANCIAL AID
Financial aid phone number: (213) 740-6314
Financial aid application deadline: 1-Mar
Tuition 2009-2010 academic year: **full-time: $46,264; part-time: N/A**
Room and board: **$15,842** ; books: **$1,664** ; miscellaneous expenses: **$4,148**
Total of room/board/books/miscellaneous expenses: **$21,654**
University offers graduate student housing for which law students are eligible.

Financial aid profile
Percent of students that received grants for the 2008-2009 academic year: full-time: **67%**
Median grant amount: full-time: **$12,000**
The average law-school debt of those in the Class of 2009 who borrowed: **$120,161** . Proportion who borrowed: **81%**

ACADEMIC PROGRAMS
Calendar: **semester**
Joint degrees awarded: **J.D./M.A. Economics; J.D./M.A. International Relations; J.D./M.P.A.; J.D./M.S.W.; J.D./M.B.A.; J.D./M.B.T.; J.D./M.A. Communications Management; J.D./M.R.E.D.; J.D./M.A. Philosophy;** J.D./M.S. Gerontology; J.D./M.P.P.; J.D./Ph.D.; J.D./Pharm.D.
Typical first-year section size: Full-time: **70**
Is there typically a "small section" of the first year class, other than Legal Writing, taught by full-time faculty?: Full-time: **no**
Number of course titles, beyond the first year curriculum, offered last year: **107**
Percentages of upper division course sections, excluding seminars, with an enrollment of:

Under 25: **67%**	25 to 49: **21%**
50 to 74: **7%**	75 to 99: **3%**
100+: **3%**	

Areas of specialization: appellate advocacy, clinical training, dispute resolution, environmental law, health care law, intellectual property law, international law, tax law, trial advocacy

Fall 2009 faculty profile
Total teaching faculty: **93**. Full-time: **43%**; **65%** men, **35%** women, **15%** minorities. Part-time: **57%**; **62%** men, **38%** women, **26%** minorities
Student-to-faculty ratio: **12.4**

SPECIAL PROGRAMS *(as provided by law school):*
Clinics in: IP; immigration; employment; nonprofit business; children's issues; post-conviction matters. Research centers in law and: economics; philosophy; politics; humanities; health; communication; and direct democracy. Broad internship/externship program with entertainment law, public interest and other placements. Joint degree programs with USC schools, Caltech, London School of Economics.

STUDENT BODY
Fall 2009 full-time enrollment: 618

Men: **50%**	Women: **50%**
African-American: **7.10%**	American Indian: **0.60%**
Asian-American: **20.60%**	Mexican-American: **6.10%**
Puerto Rican: **0.50%**	Other Hisp-Amer: **4.40%**
White: **44.20%**	International: **1.80%**
Unknown: **14.70%**	

Attrition rates for 2008-2009 full-time students
Percent of students discontinuing law school:

Men: 2%	Women: 1%
First-year students: 3%	Second-year students: 1%
Third-year students: N/A	Fourth-year students: N/A

LIBRARY RESOURCES
Total titles: 198,289
Total volumes: 442,932
Total seats available for library users: 230

INFORMATION TECHNOLOGY
Number of wired network connections available to students: 42 total (in the law library, excluding computer labs: 30; in classrooms: 12; in computer labs: 0; elsewhere in the law school: 0)
Law school has a wireless network.
Students are not required to own a computer.

EMPLOYMENT AND SALARIES
Proportion of 2008 graduates employed at graduation: 92%
Employed 9 months later, as of February 15, 2009: 97%
Salaries in the private sector (law firms, business, industry): $145,000 –$160,000 (25th-75th percentile)
Median salary in the private sector: $160,000
Percentage in the private sector who reported salary information: 82%

Median salary in public service (government, judicial clerkships, academic posts, non-profits): $45,000

Percentage of 2008 graduates in:

Law firms: 76%	Government: 4%
Bus./industry: 7%	Judicial clerkship: 5%
Public interest: 6%	Unknown: 0%
Academia : 3%	

2008 graduates employed in-state: 86%
2008 graduates employed in foreign countries: 0%
Number of states where graduates are employed: 13
Percentage of 2008 graduates working in: New England: 1%, Middle Atlantic: 7%, East North Central: 0%, West North Central: 0%, South Atlantic: 2%, East South Central: 0%, West South Central: 3%, Mountain: 3%, Pacific: 86%, Unknown: 0%

BAR PASSAGE RATES
Based on 2008 graduates taking Summer 2008 or Winter 2009 exams. Most of the school's first-time test takers took the bar in California.

90%
School's bar passage rate for first-time test takers

71%
Statewide bar passage rate for first-time test takers

University of St. Thomas

- MSL 411, 1000 LaSalle Avenue, Minneapolis, MN, 55403-2015
- http://www.stthomas.edu/law
- Private
- Year founded: 2001
- 2009-2010 tuition: full-time: $34,756; part-time: N/A
- Enrollment 2009-10 academic year: full-time: 457
- U.S. News 2010 law specialty ranking: N/A

3.07-3.59 GPA, 25TH-75TH PERCENTILE

153-161 LSAT, 25TH-75TH PERCENTILE

51% ACCEPTANCE RATE

Tier 3 2011 U.S. NEWS LAW SCHOOL RANKING

ADMISSIONS

Admissions phone number: **(651) 962-4895**
Admissions email address: **lawschool@stthomas.edu**
Application website:
   http://www.stthomas.edu/law/admissions/apply/default.html
Application deadline for Fall 2011 admission: **7-Jan**

Admissions statistics:

Number of applicants for Fall 2009: **1,551**
Number of acceptances: **785**
Number enrolled: **174**
Acceptance rate: **51%**
GPA, 25th-75th percentile, entering class Fall 2009: **3.07-3.59**
LSAT, 25th-75th percentile, entering class Fall 2009: **153-161**

FINANCIAL AID

Financial aid phone number: **(651) 962-4895**
Financial aid application deadline: **1-Jul**
Tuition 2009-2010 academic year: **full-time: $34,756; part-time: N/A**
Room and board: **N/A**; books: **N/A**; miscellaneous expenses: **N/A**
Total of room/board/books/miscellaneous expenses: **$18,187**
University does not offer graduate student housing for which law students are eligible.

Financial aid profile

Percent of students that received grants for the 2008-2009 academic year: full-time: **59%**
Median grant amount: full-time: **$20,000**
The average law-school debt of those in the Class of 2009 who borrowed: **$92,637** . Proportion who borrowed: **95%**

ACADEMIC PROGRAMS

Calendar: **semester**
Joint degrees awarded: **J.D./M.A. Catholic Studies; J.D./M.A. Educational Leadership; J.D./M.B.A.;**
J.D./M.S.W.; J.D./M.A. Professional Psychology
Typical first-year section size: Full-time: **75**
Is there typically a "small section" of the first year class, other than Legal Writing, taught by full-time faculty?: Full-time: **yes**
Number of course titles, beyond the first year curriculum, offered last year: **76**
Percentages of upper division course sections, excluding seminars, with an enrollment of:

Under 25: **77%**	25 to 49: **14%**
50 to 74: **6%**	75 to 99: **3%**
100+: **N/A**	

Areas of specialization: appellate advocacy, clinical training, dispute resolution, environmental law, health care law, intellectual property law, international law, tax law, trial advocacy

Fall 2009 faculty profile

Total teaching faculty: **82**. Full-time: **26%**; **62%** men, **38%** women, **19%** minorities. Part-time: **74%**; **66%** men, **34%** women, **13%** minorities
Student-to-faculty ratio: **17.7**

SPECIAL PROGRAMS *(as provided by law school)*:

UST Law students participate in a nationally-recognized, three-year Mentor Externship. In Elder Law, Immigration, and Community Justice Clinics, law students work with psychology and social work graduate students in an innovative Interprofessional Center for Counseling and Legal Services. UST Law offers five joint degrees, Judicial and Business Law Externships, and a summer program in Rome.

STUDENT BODY

Fall 2009 full-time enrollment: 457

Men: **54%**	Women: **46%**
African-American: **4.20%**	American Indian: **0.20%**
Asian-American: **6.30%**	Mexican-American: **0.70%**
Puerto Rican: **0.20%**	Other Hisp-Amer: **2.00%**
White: **75.30%**	International: **0.00%**
Unknown: **11.20%**	

Attrition rates for 2008-2009 full-time students
Percent of students discontinuing law school:

Men: **3%**   Women: **3%**
First-year students: **1%**   Second-year students: **9%**
Third-year students: **N/A**   Fourth-year students: **N/A**

LIBRARY RESOURCES

Total titles: **180,066**
Total volumes: **207,979**
Total seats available for library users: **379**

INFORMATION TECHNOLOGY

Number of wired network connections available to students: **595** total (in the law library, excluding computer labs: **335**; in classrooms: **165**; in computer labs: **0**; elsewhere in the law school: **95**)
Law school has a wireless network.
Students are not required to own a computer.

EMPLOYMENT AND SALARIES

Proportion of 2008 graduates employed at graduation: **N/A**
Employed 9 months later, as of February 15, 2009: **91%**
Salaries in the private sector (law firms, business, industry): **$50,000 –$120,000** (25th-75th percentile)
Median salary in the private sector: **$66,000**
Percentage in the private sector who reported salary information: **47%**

Median salary in public service (government, judicial clerkships, academic posts, non-profits): **$48,229**

Percentage of 2008 graduates in:

Law firms: **44%**   Government: **12%**
Bus./industry: **21%**   Judicial clerkship: **14%**
Public interest: **6%**   Unknown: **1%**
Academia : **2%**

2008 graduates employed in-state: **72%**
2008 graduates employed in foreign countries: **0%**
Number of states where graduates are employed: **17**
Percentage of 2008 graduates working in: New England: **0%**, Middle Atlantic: **3%**, East North Central: **10%**, West North Central: **72%**, South Atlantic: **4%**, East South Central: **0%**, West South Central: **0%**, Mountain: **3%**, Pacific: **5%**, Unknown: **3%**

BAR PASSAGE RATES

Based on 2008 graduates taking Summer 2008 or Winter 2009 exams. Most of the school's first-time test takers took the bar in Minnesota.

90%
School's bar passage rate for first-time test takers

91%
Statewide bar passage rate for first-time test takers

University of Tennessee–Knoxville

■ 1505 W. Cumberland Avenue, Knoxville, TN, 37996-1810
■ http://www.law.utk.edu
■ Public
■ Year founded: 1890
■ 2009-2010 tuition: full-time: $13,118; part-time: N/A
■ Enrollment 2009-10 academic year: full-time: 471
■ U.S. News 2010 law specialty ranking: clinical training: 18

3.28-3.77 GPA, 25TH-75TH PERCENTILE

157-161 LSAT, 25TH-75TH PERCENTILE

27% ACCEPTANCE RATE

60 2011 U.S. NEWS LAW SCHOOL RANKING

ADMISSIONS

Admissions phone number: **(865) 974-4131**
Admissions email address: **lawadmit@utk.edu**
Application website:
   http://www.law.utk.edu/departments/admiss/prospecstu home.htm
Application deadline for Fall 2011 admission: **15-Feb**

Admissions statistics:
Number of applicants for Fall 2009: **1,468**
Number of acceptances: **398**
Number enrolled: **158**
Acceptance rate: **27%**
GPA, 25th-75th percentile, entering class Fall 2009: **3.28-3.77**
LSAT, 25th-75th percentile, entering class Fall 2009: **157-161**

FINANCIAL AID

Financial aid phone number: **(865) 974-4131**
Financial aid application deadline: **1-Mar**
Tuition 2009-2010 academic year: **full-time: $13,118; part-time: N/A**
Room and board: **$10,060** ; books: **$1,606** ; miscellaneous expenses: **$3,676**
Total of room/board/books/miscellaneous expenses: **$15,342**
University offers graduate student housing for which law students are eligible.

Financial aid profile
Percent of students that received grants for the 2008-2009 academic year: full-time: **62%**
Median grant amount: full-time: **$4,000**
The average law-school debt of those in the Class of 2009 who borrowed: **$53,751** . Proportion who borrowed: **80%**

ACADEMIC PROGRAMS

Calendar: **semester**
Joint degrees awarded: **J.D./M.B.A.; J.D./M.P.A.**
Typical first-year section size: Full-time: **55**

Is there typically a "small section" of the first year class, other than Legal Writing, taught by full-time faculty?:
   Full-time: **no**
Number of course titles, beyond the first year curriculum, offered last year: **130**
Percentages of upper division course sections, excluding seminars, with an enrollment of:
   Under 25: **70%**   25 to 49: **20%**
   50 to 74: **8%**   75 to 99: **2%**
   100+: **0%**
Areas of specialization: appellate advocacy, clinical training, dispute resolution, environmental law, health care law, intellectual property law, international law, tax law, trial advocacy

Fall 2009 faculty profile
Total teaching faculty: **69**. Full-time: **41%**; **68%** men, **32%** women, **11%** minorities. Part-time: **59%**; **66%** men, **34%** women, **0%** minorities
Student-to-faculty ratio: **13.9**

SPECIAL PROGRAMS *(as provided by law school):*
Joint JD/MBA and JD/MPA programs and concentrations in Advocacy & Dispute Resolution and Business Transactions are offered. Clinical programs include Advocacy, Business, Mediation, Domestic Violence, Environmental Law and 3 externship programs, -judicial, prosecutorial and public defender. With other schools, we offer summer study programs in England and Brazil.

STUDENT BODY
Fall 2009 full-time enrollment: **471**
Men: **53%**   Women: **47%**
African-American: **11.90%**   American Indian: **0.80%**
Asian-American: **4.20%**   Mexican-American: **1.30%**
Puerto Rican: **0.40%**   Other Hisp-Amer: **1.70%**
White: **76.00%**   International: **0.80%**
Unknown: **2.80%**

Attrition rates for 2008-2009 full-time students
Percent of students discontinuing law school:

Men: 2% Women: 2%
First-year students: 1% Second-year students: 4%
Third-year students: 1% Fourth-year students: N/A

LIBRARY RESOURCES
Total titles: 154,862
Total volumes: 590,896
Total seats available for library users: 437

INFORMATION TECHNOLOGY
Number of wired network connections available to students: 77 total (in the law library, excluding computer labs: 13; in classrooms: 0; in computer labs: 29; elsewhere in the law school: 35)
Law school has a wireless network.
Students are not required to own a computer.

EMPLOYMENT AND SALARIES
Proportion of 2008 graduates employed at graduation: 72%
Employed 9 months later, as of February 15, 2009: 95%
Salaries in the private sector (law firms, business, industry): $66,250 –$88,750 (25th-75th percentile)
Median salary in the private sector: $76,250
Percentage in the private sector who reported salary information: 59%
Median salary in public service (government, judicial clerkships, academic posts, non-profits): $48,750

Percentage of 2008 graduates in:
Law firms: 59% Government: 16%
Bus./industry: 6% Judicial clerkship: 13%
Public interest: 4% Unknown: 0%
Academia : 2%

2008 graduates employed in-state: 68%
2008 graduates employed in foreign countries: 1%
Number of states where graduates are employed: 17
Percentage of 2008 graduates working in: New England: 0%, Middle Atlantic: 2%, East North Central: 0%, West North Central: 2%, South Atlantic: 22%, East South Central: 68%, West South Central: 2%, Mountain: 2%, Pacific: 1%, Unknown: 0%

BAR PASSAGE RATES
Based on 2008 graduates taking Summer 2008 or Winter 2009 exams. Most of the school's first-time test takers took the bar in Tennessee.

| 90% |
School's bar passage rate for first-time test takers

| 83% |
Statewide bar passage rate for first-time test takers

University of Texas–Austin

- 727 E. Dean Keeton Street, Austin, TX, 78705-3299
- http://www.utexas.edu/law
- Public
- Year founded: 1883
- 2009-2010 tuition: full-time: $27,177; part-time: N/A
- Enrollment 2009-10 academic year: full-time: 1,182
- U.S. News 2010 law specialty ranking: intellectual property law: 22, international law: 15, tax law: 18

3.54-3.87 GPA, 25TH-75TH PERCENTILE

164-168 LSAT, 25TH-75TH PERCENTILE

23% ACCEPTANCE RATE

15 2011 U.S. NEWS LAW SCHOOL RANKING

ADMISSIONS

Admissions phone number: **(512) 232-1200**
Admissions email address: **admissions@law.utexas.edu**
Application website:
  http://www.utexas.edu/law/depts/admissions/
Application deadline for Fall 2011 admission: **1-Feb**

Admissions statistics:

Number of applicants for Fall 2009: **5,275**
Number of acceptances: **1,224**
Number enrolled: **379**
Acceptance rate: **23%**
GPA, 25th-75th percentile, entering class Fall 2009: **3.54-3.87**
LSAT, 25th-75th percentile, entering class Fall 2009: **164-168**

FINANCIAL AID

Financial aid phone number: **(512) 232-1130**
Financial aid application deadline: **31-Mar**
Tuition 2009-2010 academic year: **full-time: $27,177**; part-time: N/A
Room and board: **$9,980** ; books: **$1,076** ; miscellaneous expenses: **$4,020**
Total of room/board/books/miscellaneous expenses: **$15,076**
University offers graduate student housing for which law students are eligible.

Financial aid profile

Percent of students that received grants for the 2008-2009 academic year: full-time: **80%**
Median grant amount: full-time: **$8,320**
The average law-school debt of those in the Class of 2009 who borrowed: **$80,322** . Proportion who borrowed: **73%**

ACADEMIC PROGRAMS

Calendar: **semester**
Joint degrees awarded: **J.D./M.B.A.; J.D./M.P.A.; J.D./M.A.; J.D./M.S.C.R.P.; J.D./M.G.P.S.; J.D./M.S.S.W.**
Typical first-year section size: Full-time: **99**

Is there typically a "small section" of the first year class, other than Legal Writing, taught by full-time faculty?:
Full-time: **yes**
Number of course titles, beyond the first year curriculum, offered last year: **158**
Percentages of upper division course sections, excluding seminars, with an enrollment of:

Under 25: **69%**   25 to 49: **20%**
50 to 74: **4%**   75 to 99: **2%**
100+: **5%**

Areas of specialization: appellate advocacy, clinical training, dispute resolution, environmental law, health care law, intellectual property law, international law, tax law, trial advocacy

Fall 2009 faculty profile

Total teaching faculty: **143**. Full-time: **62%**; **61%** men, **39%** women, **13%** minorities. Part-time: **38%**; **75%** men, **25%** women, **16%** minorities
Student-to-faculty ratio: **11.3**

SPECIAL PROGRAMS *(as provided by law school):*

UT Law provides an extensive clinical education program to help students incorporate law, theory, strategy, and skills in client settings. Internships let students obtain academic credit working with non-profits, the government, or the court. UT operates centers, institutes, and scholar programs and offers a summer academic program and study abroad programs.

STUDENT BODY

Fall 2009 full-time enrollment: **1,182**

Men: **55%**   Women: **45%**
African-American: **6.00%**   American Indian: **0.60%**
Asian-American: **6.80%**   Mexican-American: **14.20%**
Puerto Rican: **0.00%**   Other Hisp-Amer: **1.40%**
White: **57.40%**   International: **0.60%**
Unknown: **12.90%**

Attrition rates for 2008-2009 full-time students

Percent of students discontinuing law school:
Men: **1%**   Women: **2%**

First-year students: **1%**   Second-year students: **4%**
Third-year students: **0%**   Fourth-year students: **N/A**

LIBRARY RESOURCES

Total titles: **509,835**
Total volumes: **1,076,215**
Total seats available for library users: **1,039**

INFORMATION TECHNOLOGY

Number of wired network connections available to students: **310** total (in the law library, excluding computer labs: **24**; in classrooms: **98**; in computer labs: **38**; elsewhere in the law school: **150**)
Law school has a wireless network.
Students are not required to own a computer.

EMPLOYMENT AND SALARIES

Proportion of 2008 graduates employed at graduation: **97%**
Employed 9 months later, as of February 15, 2009: **98%**
Salaries in the private sector (law firms, business, industry): **$125,000 –$160,000** (25th-75th percentile)
Median salary in the private sector: **$160,000**
Percentage in the private sector who reported salary information: **80%**
Median salary in public service (government, judicial clerkships, academic posts, non-profits): **$51,617**

Percentage of 2008 graduates in:
Law firms: **63%**   Government: **10%**
Bus./industry: **10%**   Judicial clerkship: **13%**
Public interest: **3%**   Unknown: **0%**
Academia : **1%**

2008 graduates employed in-state: **67%**
2008 graduates employed in foreign countries: **1%**
Number of states where graduates are employed: **24**
Percentage of 2008 graduates working in: New England: **1%**, Middle Atlantic: **8%**, East North Central: **2%**, West North Central: **0%**, South Atlantic: **9%**, East South Central: **1%**, West South Central: **68%**, Mountain: **3%**, Pacific: **8%**, Unknown: **0%**

BAR PASSAGE RATES

Based on 2008 graduates taking Summer 2008 or Winter 2009 exams. Most of the school's first-time test takers took the bar in Texas.

89%
School's bar passage rate for first-time test takers

84%
Statewide bar passage rate for first-time test takers

Univ. of the Dist. of Columbia (Clarke)

■ 4200 Connecticut Avenue NW, Building 38 & 39, Washington, DC, 20008
■ http://www.law.udc.edu
■ Public
■ Year founded: 1988
■ 2009-2010 tuition: full-time: $7,350; part-time: $250/credit hour
■ Enrollment 2009-10 academic year: full-time: 266; part-time: 27
■ U.S. News 2010 law specialty ranking: clinical training: 10

2.83-3.28 GPA, 25TH-75TH PERCENTILE

149-153 LSAT, 25TH-75TH PERCENTILE

21% ACCEPTANCE RATE

Tier 4 2011 U.S. NEWS LAW SCHOOL RANKING

ADMISSIONS

Admissions phone number: **(202) 274-7341**
Admissions email address: **vcanty@udc.edu**
Application website:
  http://www.law.udc.edu/resource/resmgr/admissiondocs/application_only.pdf
Application deadline for Fall 2011 admission: **15-Mar**

Admissions statistics:
Number of applicants for Fall 2009: **1,601**
Number of acceptances: **336**
Number enrolled: **96**
Acceptance rate: **21%**
GPA, 25th-75th percentile, entering class Fall 2009: **2.83-3.28**
LSAT, 25th-75th percentile, entering class Fall 2009: **149-153**

Part-time program:
Number of applicants for Fall 2009: **40**
Number of acceptances: **30**
Number enrolled: **27**
Acceptance rate: **75%**
GPA, 25th-75th percentile, entering class Fall 2009: **2.60-3.21**
LSAT, 25th-75th percentile, entering class Fall 2009: **149-154**

FINANCIAL AID

Financial aid phone number: **(202) 274-7337**
Financial aid application deadline: **2-Mar**
Tuition 2009-2010 academic year: **full-time: $7,350; part-time: $250/credit hour**
Room and board: **N/A**; books: **N/A**; miscellaneous expenses: **N/A**
Total of room/board/books/miscellaneous expenses: **$30,440**
University does not offer graduate student housing for which law students are eligible.

Financial aid profile
Percent of students that received grants for the 2008-2009 academic year: full-time: **56%**
Median grant amount: full-time: **$3,800**
The average law-school debt of those in the Class of 2009 who borrowed: **$86,297** . Proportion who borrowed: **90%**

ACADEMIC PROGRAMS

Calendar: **semester**
Joint degrees awarded: **N/A**
Typical first-year section size: Full-time: **96**; Part-time: **27**
Is there typically a "small section" of the first year class, other than Legal Writing, taught by full-time faculty?:
  Full-time: **yes**; Part-time: **no**
Number of course titles, beyond the first year curriculum, offered last year: **44**
Percentages of upper division course sections, excluding seminars, with an enrollment of:
  Under 25: **60%**   25 to 49: **26%**
  50 to 74: **8%**   75 to 99: **6%**
  100+: **0%**
Areas of specialization: appellate advocacy, clinical training, dispute resolution, environmental law, international law, tax law, trial advocacy

Fall 2009 faculty profile
Total teaching faculty: **37**. Full-time: **54%**; **60%** men, **40%** women, **45%** minorities. Part-time: **46%**; **47%** men, **53%** women, **65%** minorities
Student-to-faculty ratio: **12.2**

SPECIAL PROGRAMS *(as provided by law school)*:

The School of Law trains attorneys who have the knowledge, skills and practical experience to practice law upon graduation. We occupy a unique niche in legal education as a publicly-funded urban land grant HBCU committed to public service and clinical legal education. Our graduates have a minimum of 700 hours of hands-on legal experience in the two required 7-credit clinics.

STUDENT BODY

Fall 2009 full-time enrollment: 266

Men: 40%	Women: 60%
African-American: 28.20%	American Indian: 1.10%
Asian-American: 7.50%	Mexican-American: 2.30%
Puerto Rican: 2.60%	Other Hisp-Amer: 7.50%
White: 47.40%	International: 0.00%
Unknown: 3.40%	

Fall 2009 part-time enrollment: 27

Men: 63%	Women: 37%
African-American: 40.70%	American Indian: 0.00%
Asian-American: 11.10%	Mexican-American: 0.00%
Puerto Rican: 0.00%	Other Hisp-Amer: 0.00%
White: 48.10%	International: 0.00%
Unknown: 0.00%	

Attrition rates for 2008-2009 full-time students
Percent of students discontinuing law school:

Men: 6%	Women: 5%
First-year students: 13%	Second-year students: 2%
Third-year students: N/A	Fourth-year students: N/A

LIBRARY RESOURCES

Total titles: 157,492
Total volumes: 262,868
Total seats available for library users: 230

INFORMATION TECHNOLOGY

Number of wired network connections available to students: 16 total (in the law library, excluding computer labs: 6; in classrooms: 0; in computer labs: 0; elsewhere in the law school: 10)
Law school has a wireless network.
Students are required to own a computer.

EMPLOYMENT AND SALARIES

Proportion of 2008 graduates employed at graduation: N/A
Employed 9 months later, as of February 15, 2009: 80%
Salaries in the private sector (law firms, business, industry): N/A–N/A (25th-75th percentile)
Median salary in the private sector: N/A
Percentage in the private sector who reported salary information: N/A
Median salary in public service (government, judicial clerkships, academic posts, non-profits): N/A

Percentage of 2008 graduates in:

Law firms: 27%	Government: 19%
Bus./industry: 17%	Judicial clerkship: 11%
Public interest: 19%	Unknown: 2%
Academia : 5%	

2008 graduates employed in-state: 55%
2008 graduates employed in foreign countries: 0%
Number of states where graduates are employed: 11
Percentage of 2008 graduates working in: New England: 0%, Middle Atlantic: 7%, East North Central: 2%, West North Central: 0%, South Atlantic: 83%, East South Central: 2%, West South Central: 2%, Mountain: 2%, Pacific: 0%, Unknown: 0%

BAR PASSAGE RATES

Based on 2008 graduates taking Summer 2008 or Winter 2009 exams. Most of the school's first-time test takers took the bar in Maryland.

92%
School's bar passage rate for first-time test takers

85%
Statewide bar passage rate for first-time test takers

University of the Pacific (McGeorge)

- 3200 Fifth Avenue, Sacramento, CA, 95817
- http://www.mcgeorge.edu
- Private
- Year founded: 1924
- 2009-2010 tuition: full-time: $38,629; part-time: $25,705
- Enrollment 2009-10 academic year: full-time: 660; part-time: 377
- U.S. News 2010 law specialty ranking: international law: 15, trial advocacy: 5

3.07-3.60 GPA, 25TH-75TH PERCENTILE

155-160 LSAT, 25TH-75TH PERCENTILE

43% ACCEPTANCE RATE

98 2011 U.S. NEWS LAW SCHOOL RANKING

ADMISSIONS

Admissions phone number: (916) 739-7105
Admissions email address: **admissionsmcge-orge@pacific.edu**
Application website:
http://www.mcgeorge.edu/admissions/apply/index.htm
Application deadline for Fall 2011 admission: **rolling**

Admissions statistics:

Number of applicants for Fall 2009: **2,657**
Number of acceptances: **1,138**
Number enrolled: **236**
Acceptance rate: **43%**
GPA, 25th-75th percentile, entering class Fall 2009: **3.07-3.60**
LSAT, 25th-75th percentile, entering class Fall 2009: **155-160**

Part-time program:

Number of applicants for Fall 2009: **378**
Number of acceptances: **149**
Number enrolled: **85**
Acceptance rate: **39%**
GPA, 25th-75th percentile, entering class Fall 2009: **3.05-3.51**
LSAT, 25th-75th percentile, entering class Fall 2009: **151-157**

FINANCIAL AID

Financial aid phone number: (916) 739-7158
Financial aid application deadline:
Tuition 2009-2010 academic year: **full-time: $38,629; part-time: $25,705**
Room and board: **$9,738** ; books: **$1,600** ; miscellaneous expenses: **$11,720**
Total of room/board/books/miscellaneous expenses: **$23,058**
University offers graduate student housing for which law students are eligible.

Financial aid profile

Percent of students that received grants for the 2008-2009 academic year: full-time: **58%**; part-time **42%**
Median grant amount: full-time: **$10,000** ; part-time: **$5,000**
The average law-school debt of those in the Class of 2009 who borrowed: **$124,488** . Proportion who borrowed: **90%**

ACADEMIC PROGRAMS

Calendar: **semester**
Joint degrees awarded: **J.D./M.B.A.; J.D./M.S. M.I.S.; J.D./M.P.P.A.; J.D./M.Acc.**
Typical first-year section size: Full-time: **79**; Part-time: **103**
Is there typically a "small section" of the first year class, other than Legal Writing, taught by full-time faculty?: Full-time: **yes**; Part-time: **yes**
Number of course titles, beyond the first year curriculum, offered last year: **176**
Percentages of upper division course sections, excluding seminars, with an enrollment of:

Under 25: **66%**	25 to 49: **16%**
50 to 74: **7%**	75 to 99: **8%**
100+: **3%**	

Areas of specialization: appellate advocacy, clinical training, dispute resolution, environmental law, health care law, intellectual property law, international law, tax law, trial advocacy

Fall 2009 faculty profile

Total teaching faculty: **75**. Full-time: **56%**; 60% men, 40% women, 19% minorities. Part-time: **44%**; 70% men, 30% women, 9% minorities
Student-to-faculty ratio: **14**

SPECIAL PROGRAMS (as provided by law school):

Students can concentrate in Advocacy, Criminal Justice, Governmental Law & Policy, Intellectual Property, International Law, or Taxation. Students can also create individualized programs from our extensive elective offerings, including clinical, internships, and study-abroad. Our unique LL.M. programs in international law attract foreign graduate students, giving our campus an international flavor.

STUDENT BODY

Fall 2009 full-time enrollment: 660

Men: 51%	Women: 49%
African-American: 2.00%	American Indian: 1.20%
Asian-American: 15.00%	Mexican-American: 5.20%
Puerto Rican: 1.10%	Other Hisp-Amer: 3.50%
White: 72.10%	International: 0.00%
Unknown: 0.00%	

Fall 2009 part-time enrollment: 377

Men: 48%	Women: 52%
African-American: 5.30%	American Indian: 0.80%
Asian-American: 14.60%	Mexican-American: 4.80%
Puerto Rican: 0.50%	Other Hisp-Amer: 2.40%
White: 71.60%	International: 0.00%
Unknown: 0.00%	

Attrition rates for 2008-2009 full-time students
Percent of students discontinuing law school:

Men: 8%	Women: 4%
First-year students: 8%	Second-year students: 11%
Third-year students: 1%	Fourth-year students: 1%

LIBRARY RESOURCES
Total titles: 128,113
Total volumes: 509,762
Total seats available for library users: 345

INFORMATION TECHNOLOGY
Number of wired network connections available to students: 271 total (in the law library, excluding computer labs: 265; in classrooms: 0; in computer labs: 6; elsewhere in the law school: 0)
Law school has a wireless network.
Students are not required to own a computer.

EMPLOYMENT AND SALARIES
Proportion of 2008 graduates employed at graduation: N/A
Employed 9 months later, as of February 15, 2009: **96%**
Salaries in the private sector (law firms, business, industry): **$60,000 –$90,000** (25th-75th percentile)
Median salary in the private sector: **$72,000**
Percentage in the private sector who reported salary information: **68%**
Median salary in public service (government, judicial clerkships, academic posts, non-profits): **$56,400**

Percentage of 2008 graduates in:

Law firms: 50%	Government: 25%
Bus./industry: 9%	Judicial clerkship: 3%
Public interest: 9%	Unknown: 1%
Academia : 3%	

2008 graduates employed in-state: **90%**
2008 graduates employed in foreign countries: **0%**
Number of states where graduates are employed: **14**
Percentage of 2008 graduates working in: New England: 0%, Middle Atlantic: 0%, East North Central: 0%, West North Central: 0%, South Atlantic: 2%, East South Central: 0%, West South Central: 0%, Mountain: 4%, Pacific: 90%, Unknown: 3%

BAR PASSAGE RATES
Based on 2008 graduates taking Summer 2008 or Winter 2009 exams. Most of the school's first-time test takers took the bar in California.

80%

School's bar passage rate for first-time test takers

71%

Statewide bar passage rate for first-time test takers

University of Toledo

■ 2801 W. Bancroft, Toledo, OH, 43606
■ http://www.utlaw.edu
■ Public
■ Year founded: 1906
■ 2009-2010 tuition: full-time: $19,137; part-time: $14,343
■ Enrollment 2009-10 academic year: full-time: 346; part-time: 147
■ U.S. News 2010 law specialty ranking: N/A

3.07-3.59 GPA, 25TH-75TH PERCENTILE

152-158 LSAT, 25TH-75TH PERCENTILE

57% ACCEPTANCE RATE

Tier 3 2011 U.S. NEWS LAW SCHOOL RANKING

ADMISSIONS
Admissions phone number: **(419) 530-4131**
Admissions email address: **law.admissions@utoledo.edu**
Application website: **http://www.utlaw.edu/admissions**
Application deadline for Fall 2011 admission: **1-Aug**

Admissions statistics:
Number of applicants for Fall 2009: **639**
Number of acceptances: **367**
Number enrolled: **99**
Acceptance rate: **57%**
GPA, 25th-75th percentile, entering class Fall 2009: **3.07-3.59**
LSAT, 25th-75th percentile, entering class Fall 2009: **152-158**

Part-time program:
Number of applicants for Fall 2009: **229**
Number of acceptances: **154**
Number enrolled: **82**
Acceptance rate: **67%**
GPA, 25th-75th percentile, entering class Fall 2009: **2.60-3.36**
LSAT, 25th-75th percentile, entering class Fall 2009: **149-152**

FINANCIAL AID
Financial aid phone number: **(419) 530-7929**
Financial aid application deadline: **1-Aug**
Tuition 2009-2010 academic year: **full-time: $19,137; part-time: $14,343**
Room and board: **$10,440** ; books: **$1,164** ; miscellaneous expenses: **$4,784**
Total of room/board/books/miscellaneous expenses: **$16,388**
University offers graduate student housing for which law students are eligible.

Financial aid profile
Percent of students that received grants for the 2008-2009 academic year: full-time: **63%**; part-time **7%**

Median grant amount: full-time: **$15,216** ; part-time: **$2,742**
The average law-school debt of those in the Class of 2009 who borrowed: **$74,167** . Proportion who borrowed: **88%**

ACADEMIC PROGRAMS
Calendar: **semester**
Joint degrees awarded: **J.D./M.B.A.; J.D./M.S.E.; J.D./M.P.A.; J.D./M.C.J.**
Typical first-year section size: Full-time: **55**; Part-time: **36**
Is there typically a "small section" of the first year class, other than Legal Writing, taught by full-time faculty?: Full-time: **no**; Part-time: **no**
Number of course titles, beyond the first year curriculum, offered last year: **88**
Percentages of upper division course sections, excluding seminars, with an enrollment of:

Under 25: **69%**	25 to 49: **19%**
50 to 74: **9%**	75 to 99: **3%**
100+: **0%**	

Areas of specialization: appellate advocacy, clinical training, dispute resolution, environmental law, health care law, intellectual property law, international law, tax law, trial advocacy

Fall 2009 faculty profile
Total teaching faculty: **46**. Full-time: **61%**; **57%** men, **43%** women, **7%** minorities. Part-time: **39%**; **72%** men, **28%** women, **11%** minorities
Student-to-faculty ratio: **13.4**

SPECIAL PROGRAMS *(as provided by law school):*
Students are offered actual legal experience with a practicing attorney through clinics and externships. Five certificate programs are offered: Environmental, International, Intellectual Property, Labor, and Homeland Security Law. Our lecture series greatly enriches the intellectual atmosphere of the College and provides students with timely discussion of legal and policy issues.

STUDENT BODY

Fall 2009 full-time enrollment: 346

Men: 61%	Women: 39%
African-American: 2.30%	American Indian: 0.00%
Asian-American: 2.60%	Mexican-American: 0.00%
Puerto Rican: 0.00%	Other Hisp-Amer: 2.60%
White: 63.90%	International: 2.60%
Unknown: 26.00%	

Fall 2009 part-time enrollment: 147

Men: 58%	Women: 42%
African-American: 7.50%	American Indian: 0.00%
Asian-American: 4.10%	Mexican-American: 0.00%
Puerto Rican: 0.00%	Other Hisp-Amer: 3.40%
White: 70.10%	International: 0.70%
Unknown: 14.30%	

Attrition rates for 2008-2009 full-time students
Percent of students discontinuing law school:

Men: 11%	Women: 3%
First-year students: 8%	Second-year students: 8%
Third-year students: 8%	Fourth-year students: N/A

LIBRARY RESOURCES

Total titles: 58,145
Total volumes: 360,833
Total seats available for library users: 449

INFORMATION TECHNOLOGY

Number of wired network connections available to students: 34 total (in the law library, excluding computer labs: 18; in classrooms: 0; in computer labs: 0; elsewhere in the law school: 16)
Law school has a wireless network.
Students are not required to own a computer.

EMPLOYMENT AND SALARIES

Proportion of 2008 graduates employed at graduation: 89%
Employed 9 months later, as of February 15, 2009: 96%
Salaries in the private sector (law firms, business, industry): $55,000 –$105,000 (25th-75th percentile)
Median salary in the private sector: $70,000
Percentage in the private sector who reported salary information: 63%
Median salary in public service (government, judicial clerkships, academic posts, non-profits): $42,500

Percentage of 2008 graduates in:

Law firms: 43%	Government: 25%
Bus./industry: 13%	Judicial clerkship: 4%
Public interest: 8%	Unknown: 2%
Academia : 5%	

2008 graduates employed in-state: 62%
2008 graduates employed in foreign countries: 1%
Number of states where graduates are employed: 19
Percentage of 2008 graduates working in: New England: 0%, Middle Atlantic: 3%, East North Central: 75%, West North Central: 1%, South Atlantic: 11%, East South Central: 0%, West South Central: 1%, Mountain: 5%, Pacific: 2%, Unknown: 2%

BAR PASSAGE RATES

Based on 2008 graduates taking Summer 2008 or Winter 2009 exams. Most of the school's first-time test takers took the bar in Ohio.

88%
School's bar passage rate for first-time test takers

88%
Statewide bar passage rate for first-time test takers

University of Tulsa

- 3120 E. Fourth Place, Tulsa, OK, 74104
- http://www.utulsa.edu/law
- Private
- Year founded: 1923
- 2009-2010 tuition: full-time: $29,040; part-time: N/A
- Enrollment 2009-10 academic year: full-time: 382; part-time: 40
- U.S. News 2010 law specialty ranking: N/A

2.83-3.55 GPA, 25TH-75TH PERCENTILE

152-157 LSAT, 25TH-75TH PERCENTILE

51% ACCEPTANCE RATE

Tier 3 2011 U.S. NEWS LAW SCHOOL RANKING

ADMISSIONS

Admissions phone number: (918) 631-2709
Admissions email address: lawadmissions@utulsa.edu
Application website:
   http://www.law.utulsa.edu/admissions
Application deadline for Fall 2011 admission: 30-Jul

Admissions statistics:

Number of applicants for Fall 2009: 1,304
Number of acceptances: 659
Number enrolled: 140
Acceptance rate: 51%
GPA, 25th-75th percentile, entering class Fall 2009: 2.83-3.55
LSAT, 25th-75th percentile, entering class Fall 2009: 152-157

FINANCIAL AID

Financial aid phone number: (918) 631-2526
Financial aid application deadline: 30-Jul
Tuition 2009-2010 academic year: **full-time: $29,040;**
   part-time: N/A
Room and board: $7,000 ; books: $1,500 ; miscellaneous
   expenses: $6,810
Total of room/board/books/miscellaneous expenses:
   $15,310
University offers graduate student housing for which law
   students are eligible.

Financial aid profile

Percent of students that received grants for the 2008-2009
   academic year: full-time: 50%; part-time 58%
Median grant amount: full-time: $12,000 ; part-time:
   $11,500
The average law-school debt of those in the Class of 2009
   who borrowed: $68,642 . Proportion who borrowed: 70%

ACADEMIC PROGRAMS

Calendar: semester
Joint degrees awarded: J.D./Anthropology;
   J.D./Accounting; J.D./Biology; J.D./English;
J.D./History; J.D./M.B.A.; J.D./Clinical Psychology;
J.D./Psychology & IO; J.D./Taxation; J.D./Geoscience;
J.D./M.S.F.
Typical first-year section size: Full-time: 45
Is there typically a "small section" of the first year class,
   other than Legal Writing, taught by full-time faculty?:
   Full-time: no; Part-time: no
Number of course titles, beyond the first year curriculum,
   offered last year: 132
Percentages of upper division course sections, excluding
   seminars, with an enrollment of:

Under 25: 73%	25 to 49: 20%
50 to 74: 7%	75 to 99: 0%
100+: 0%	

Areas of specialization: appellate advocacy, clinical training, dispute resolution, environmental law, health care
   law, intellectual property law, international law, tax law,
   trial advocacy

Fall 2009 faculty profile

Total teaching faculty: 53. Full-time: 55%; 52% men, 48%
   women, 17% minorities. Part-time: 45%; 67% men, 33%
   women, 8% minorities
Student-to-faculty ratio: 11.9

SPECIAL PROGRAMS (as provided by law school):

Programs include International Law, Native American Law,
Sustainability Energy & Resources Law Program, and Health
Law. Summer programs offered in Dublin, Geneva, Buenos
Aires, and Tianjin. Legal Clinics in Immigrant Rights and
Social Enterprise & Economic Development. Judicial and
licensed legal internships. Pro Bono program and services.

STUDENT BODY

Fall 2009 full-time enrollment: 382

Men: 61%	Women: 39%
African-American: 1.00%	American Indian: 8.90%
Asian-American: 2.60%	Mexican-American: 2.90%
Puerto Rican: 0.00%	Other Hisp-Amer: 0.00%
White: 70.70%	International: 0.30%
Unknown: 13.60%	

Fall 2009 part-time enrollment: 40

Men: 60%   Women: 40%
African-American: 0.00%   American Indian: 15.00%
Asian-American: 5.00%   Mexican-American: 2.50%
Puerto Rican: 0.00%   Other Hisp-Amer: 0.00%
White: 65.00%   International: 0.00%
Unknown: 12.50%

Attrition rates for 2008-2009 full-time students
Percent of students discontinuing law school:
Men: 4%   Women: 6%
First-year students: 7%   Second-year students: 9%
Third-year students: N/A   Fourth-year students: N/A

LIBRARY RESOURCES
Total titles: 223,464
Total volumes: 410,962
Total seats available for library users: 718

INFORMATION TECHNOLOGY
Number of wired network connections available to students: 376 total (in the law library, excluding computer labs: 276; in classrooms: 100; in computer labs: 0; elsewhere in the law school: 0)
Law school has a wireless network.
Students are not required to own a computer.

EMPLOYMENT AND SALARIES
Proportion of 2008 graduates employed at graduation: N/A
Employed 9 months later, as of February 15, 2009: 92%
Salaries in the private sector (law firms, business, industry): $55,000 –$95,000 (25th-75th percentile)

Median salary in the private sector: $70,000
Percentage in the private sector who reported salary information: 80%
Median salary in public service (government, judicial clerkships, academic posts, non-profits): $47,500

Percentage of 2008 graduates in:
Law firms: 59%   Government: 11%
Bus./industry: 21%   Judicial clerkship: 1%
Public interest: 5%   Unknown: 0%
Academia : 3%

2008 graduates employed in-state: 57%
2008 graduates employed in foreign countries: 1%
Number of states where graduates are employed: 21
Percentage of 2008 graduates working in: New England: 1%, Middle Atlantic: 0%, East North Central: 1%, West North Central: 10%, South Atlantic: 3%, East South Central: 1%, West South Central: 74%, Mountain: 8%, Pacific: 2%, Unknown: 0%

BAR PASSAGE RATES
Based on 2008 graduates taking Summer 2008 or Winter 2009 exams. Most of the school's first-time test takers took the bar in Oklahoma.

93%
School's bar passage rate for first-time test takers

93%
Statewide bar passage rate for first-time test takers

University of Utah (Quinney)

- 332 S. 1400 E, Room 101, Salt Lake City, UT, 84112
- http://www.law.utah.edu
- Public
- Year founded: 1913
- 2009-2010 tuition: full-time: $17,948; part-time: N/A
- Enrollment 2009-10 academic year: full-time: 381; part-time: 19
- U.S. News 2010 law specialty ranking: environmental law: 15

3.41-3.76 GPA, 25TH-75TH PERCENTILE

156-163 LSAT, 25TH-75TH PERCENTILE

29% ACCEPTANCE RATE

42 2011 U.S. NEWS LAW SCHOOL RANKING

ADMISSIONS
Admissions phone number: **(801) 581-7479**
Admissions email address: **admissions@law.utah.edu**
Application website:
 http://www.law.utah.edu/admissions/apply-now/
Application deadline for Fall 2011 admission: **15-Feb**

Admissions statistics:
Number of applicants for Fall 2009: **1,277**
Number of acceptances: **375**
Number enrolled: **129**
Acceptance rate: **29%**
GPA, 25th-75th percentile, entering class Fall 2009: **3.41-3.76**
LSAT, 25th-75th percentile, entering class Fall 2009: **156-163**

FINANCIAL AID
Financial aid phone number: **(801) 581-6211**
Financial aid application deadline: **15-Apr**
Tuition 2009-2010 academic year: **full-time: $17,948; part-time: N/A**
Room and board: **$9,360** ; books: **$2,784** ; miscellaneous expenses: **$4,950**
Total of room/board/books/miscellaneous expenses: **$17,094**
University offers graduate student housing for which law students are eligible.

Financial aid profile
Percent of students that received grants for the 2008-2009 academic year: full-time: **52%**
Median grant amount: full-time: **$5,406**
The average law-school debt of those in the Class of 2009 who borrowed: **$56,685** . Proportion who borrowed: **91%**

ACADEMIC PROGRAMS
Calendar: **semester**
Joint degrees awarded: **J.D./M.B.A.; J.D./M.P.A.; J.D./M.P.P.**
Typical first-year section size: Full-time: **39**

Is there typically a "small section" of the first year class, other than Legal Writing, taught by full-time faculty?:
 Full-time: **yes**; Part-time: **no**
Number of course titles, beyond the first year curriculum, offered last year: **120**
Percentages of upper division course sections, excluding seminars, with an enrollment of:
 Under 25: **78%** 25 to 49: **15%**
 50 to 74: **7%** 75 to 99: **1%**
 100+: **0%**
Areas of specialization: appellate advocacy, clinical training, dispute resolution, environmental law, health care law, intellectual property law, international law, tax law, trial advocacy

Fall 2009 faculty profile
Total teaching faculty: **62**. Full-time: **65%**; **73%** men, **28%** women, **15%** minorities. Part-time: **35%**; **59%** men, **41%** women, **0%** minorities
Student-to-faculty ratio: **8.1**

SPECIAL PROGRAMS (as provided by law school):
Please see: http://www.law.utah.edu/access-to-justice/clinic; http://www.law.utah.edu/stegner; http://www.law.utah.edu/prospective/summer-school; http://www.law.utah.edu/prospective/degree%2Dprograms

STUDENT BODY
Fall 2009 full-time enrollment: 381
Men: **59%**	Women: **41%**
African-American: **1.80%**	American Indian: **2.10%**
Asian-American: **3.70%**	Mexican-American: **0.80%**
Puerto Rican: **0.00%**	Other Hisp-Amer: **5.00%**
White: **74.80%**	International: **0.00%**
Unknown: **11.80%**	

Fall 2009 part-time enrollment: 19
Men: **53%**	Women: **47%**
African-American: **0.00%**	American Indian: **0.00%**
Asian-American: **0.00%**	Mexican-American: **0.00%**
Puerto Rican: **0.00%**	Other Hisp-Amer: **10.50%**

White: **84.20%**   International: **0.00%**
Unknown: **5.30%**

Attrition rates for 2008-2009 full-time students
Percent of students discontinuing law school:
Men: **3%**   Women: **2%**
First-year students: **7%**   Second-year students: **1%**
Third-year students: **N/A**   Fourth-year students: **N/A**

LIBRARY RESOURCES
Total titles: **139,945**
Total volumes: **357,118**
Total seats available for library users: **665**

INFORMATION TECHNOLOGY
Number of wired network connections available to students: **334** total (in the law library, excluding computer labs: **32**; in classrooms: **250**; in computer labs: **27**; elsewhere in the law school: **25**)
Law school has a wireless network.
Students are required to own a computer.

EMPLOYMENT AND SALARIES
Proportion of 2008 graduates employed at graduation: **92%**
Employed 9 months later, as of February 15, 2009: **100%**
Salaries in the private sector (law firms, business, industry): **$60,000 –$110,000** (25th-75th percentile)
Median salary in the private sector: **$80,000**

Percentage in the private sector who reported salary information: **71%**
Median salary in public service (government, judicial clerkships, academic posts, non-profits): **$53,961**

Percentage of 2008 graduates in:
Law firms: **60%**   Government: **15%**
Bus./industry: **7%**   Judicial clerkship: **10%**
Public interest: **5%**   Unknown: **0%**
Academia : **3%**

2008 graduates employed in-state: **78%**
2008 graduates employed in foreign countries: **1%**
Number of states where graduates are employed: **13**
Percentage of 2008 graduates working in: New England: **0%**, Middle Atlantic: **0%**, East North Central: **0%**, West North Central: **1%**, South Atlantic: **3%**, East South Central: **0%**, West South Central: **1%**, Mountain: **86%**, Pacific: **6%**, Unknown: **2%**

BAR PASSAGE RATES
Based on 2008 graduates taking Summer 2008 or Winter 2009 exams. Most of the school's first-time test takers took the bar in Utah.

87%

School's bar passage rate for first-time test takers

87%

Statewide bar passage rate for first-time test takers

University of Virginia

- 580 Massie Road, Charlottesville, VA, 22903-1738
- http://www.law.virginia.edu
- Public
- Year founded: 1819
- 2009-2010 tuition: full-time: $38,800; part-time: N/A
- Enrollment 2009-10 academic year: full-time: 1,122
- U.S. News 2010 law specialty ranking: intellectual property law: 19, international law: 9, tax law: 10

3.54-3.92 GPA, 25TH-75TH PERCENTILE

165-171 LSAT, 25TH-75TH PERCENTILE

15% ACCEPTANCE RATE

10 2011 U.S. NEWS LAW SCHOOL RANKING

ADMISSIONS

Admissions phone number: **(434) 924-7351**
Admissions email address: **lawadmit@virginia.edu**
Application website:
   http://www.law.virginia.edu/admissions
Application deadline for Fall 2011 admission: **1-Mar**

Admissions statistics:

Number of applicants for Fall 2009: **7,880**
Number of acceptances: **1,166**
Number enrolled: **368**
Acceptance rate: **15%**
GPA, 25th-75th percentile, entering class Fall 2009: **3.54-3.92**
LSAT, 25th-75th percentile, entering class Fall 2009: **165-171**

FINANCIAL AID

Financial aid phone number: **(434) 924-7805**
Financial aid application deadline: **1-Mar**
Tuition 2009-2010 academic year: **full-time: $38,800;** part-time: N/A
Room and board: **$14,050** ; books: **$1,800** ; miscellaneous expenses: **$3,350**
Total of room/board/books/miscellaneous expenses: **$19,200**
University offers graduate student housing for which law students are eligible.

Financial aid profile

Percent of students that received grants for the 2008-2009 academic year: full-time: **59%**
Median grant amount: full-time: **$15,000**
The average law-school debt of those in the Class of 2009 who borrowed: **$103,645** . Proportion who borrowed: **76%**

ACADEMIC PROGRAMS

Calendar: **semester**
Joint degrees awarded: **J.D./M.B.A.; J.D./M.A. History; J.D./M.P.H.; J.D./M.A. English; J.D./M.S. Accounting;** J.D./M.A. Economics; J.D./M.A. Government/Foreign Affairs; J.D./M.A. Philosophy; J.D./M.A. Sociology; J.D./MUEP Urban & Environmental Planning; J.D./M.A. Int'l Relations; J.D./M.A.L.D.; J.D./M.P.A.
Typical first-year section size: Full-time: **72**
Is there typically a "small section" of the first year class, other than Legal Writing, taught by full-time faculty?: Full-time: **yes**
Number of course titles, beyond the first year curriculum, offered last year: **233**
Percentages of upper division course sections, excluding seminars, with an enrollment of:
   Under 25: **58%**   25 to 49: **18%**
   50 to 74: **13%**   75 to 99: **8%**
   100+: **4%**
Areas of specialization: appellate advocacy, clinical training, dispute resolution, environmental law, health care law, intellectual property law, international law, tax law, trial advocacy

Fall 2009 faculty profile

Total teaching faculty: **164.** Full-time: **46%; 71%** men, **29%** women, **9%** minorities. Part-time: **54%; 82%** men, **18%** women, **6%** minorities
Student-to-faculty ratio: **12.6**

SPECIAL PROGRAMS *(as provided by law school)*:

Virginia offers special curricular programs in law and business, law and public service, international law, legal history, criminal justice, human rights, race and law, environmental law, intellectual property, health law, and law and humanities. Virginia faculty members run institutes and centers in law and psychiatry, law and economics, oceans law, national security law, and family law.

STUDENT BODY

Fall 2009 full-time enrollment: 1,122

Men: **56%**	Women: **44%**
African-American: **5.30%**	American Indian: **1.40%**
Asian-American: **8.40%**	Mexican-American: **0.00%**
Puerto Rican: **0.00%**	Other Hisp-Amer: **4.50%**

White: 59.50% International: 0.90%
Unknown: 19.90%

Attrition rates for 2008-2009 full-time students
Percent of students discontinuing law school:
Men: 1% Women: 1%
First-year students: 2% Second-year students: 1%
Third-year students: 0% Fourth-year students: N/A

LIBRARY RESOURCES
Total titles: 350,960
Total volumes: 876,458
Total seats available for library users: 798

INFORMATION TECHNOLOGY
Number of wired network connections available to students: 84 total (in the law library, excluding computer labs: 84; in classrooms: 0; in computer labs: 0; elsewhere in the law school: 0)
Law school has a wireless network.
Students are required to own a computer.

EMPLOYMENT AND SALARIES
Proportion of 2008 graduates employed at graduation: 96%
Employed 9 months later, as of February 15, 2009: 100%
Salaries in the private sector (law firms, business, industry): $160,000 – $160,000 (25th-75th percentile)
Median salary in the private sector: $160,000
Percentage in the private sector who reported salary information: 89%

Median salary in public service (government, judicial clerkships, academic posts, non-profits): $52,500

Percentage of 2008 graduates in:
Law firms: 77% Government: 5%
Bus./industry: 1% Judicial clerkship: 14%
Public interest: 4% Unknown: 0%
Academia : 0%

2008 graduates employed in-state: 11%
2008 graduates employed in foreign countries: 2%
Number of states where graduates are employed: 34
Percentage of 2008 graduates working in: New England: 4%, Middle Atlantic: 22%, East North Central: 5%, West North Central: 1%, South Atlantic: 46%, East South Central: 3%, West South Central: 7%, Mountain: 1%, Pacific: 9%, Unknown: 0%

BAR PASSAGE RATES
Based on 2008 graduates taking Summer 2008 or Winter 2009 exams. Most of the school's first-time test takers took the bar in New York.

98%
School's bar passage rate for first-time test takers

81%
Statewide bar passage rate for first-time test takers

University of Washington

- Campus Box 353020, Seattle, WA, 98195-3020
- http://www.law.washington.edu
- Public
- Year founded: 1899
- 2009-2010 tuition: full-time: $22,267; part-time: N/A
- Enrollment 2009-10 academic year: full-time: 530
- U.S. News 2010 law specialty ranking: clinical training: 28, intellectual property law: 19

3.47-3.80 GPA, 25TH-75TH PERCENTILE

160-166 LSAT, 25TH-75TH PERCENTILE

25% ACCEPTANCE RATE

34 2011 U.S. NEWS LAW SCHOOL RANKING

ADMISSIONS

Admissions phone number: **(206) 543-4078**
Admissions email address: **lawadm@u.washington.edu**
Application website:
  http://www.law.washington.edu/admissions
Application deadline for Fall 2011 admission: **1-Jan**

Admissions statistics:
Number of applicants for Fall 2009: **2,448**
Number of acceptances: **622**
Number enrolled: **181**
Acceptance rate: **25%**
GPA, 25th-75th percentile, entering class Fall 2009: **3.47-3.80**
LSAT, 25th-75th percentile, entering class Fall 2009: **160-166**

FINANCIAL AID

Financial aid phone number: **(206) 543-4552**
Financial aid application deadline: **28-Feb**
Tuition 2009-2010 academic year: **full-time: $22,267; part-time: N/A**
Room and board: **$12,876** ; books: **$1,206** ; miscellaneous expenses: **$3,789**
Total of room/board/books/miscellaneous expenses: **$17,871**
University offers graduate student housing for which law students are eligible.

Financial aid profile
Percent of students that received grants for the 2008-2009 academic year: full-time: **49%**
Median grant amount: full-time: **$6,000**
The average law-school debt of those in the Class of 2009 who borrowed: **$69,945** . Proportion who borrowed: **78%**

ACADEMIC PROGRAMS

Calendar: **quarter**
Joint degrees awarded: **J.D./M.A. International Studies; J.D./LL.M. Intellectual Property Law ; J.D./M.P.A.; J.D./M.P.H.; J.D./M.U.P.; J.D./M.B.A.**

Typical first-year section size: Full-time: **52**
Is there typically a "small section" of the first year class, other than Legal Writing, taught by full-time faculty?: Full-time: **yes**
Number of course titles, beyond the first year curriculum, offered last year: **126**
Percentages of upper division course sections, excluding seminars, with an enrollment of:
  Under 25: **49%**   25 to 49: **34%**
  50 to 74: **13%**   75 to 99: **3%**
  100+: **0%**
Areas of specialization: appellate advocacy, clinical training, dispute resolution, environmental law, health care law, intellectual property law, international law, tax law, trial advocacy

Fall 2009 faculty profile
Total teaching faculty: 92. Full-time: **50%**; 57% men, **43%** women, **15%** minorities. Part-time: **50%**; 67% men, **33%** women, **11%** minorities
Student-to-faculty ratio: **10**

SPECIAL PROGRAMS (as provided by law school):
Clinics: Innocence Project, Unemployment Compensation, Mediation, Immigration, Environmental, Child Advocacy, Tribal, Entrepreneurship, Tax. Centers: Asian Law; Law, Technology & Arts (IP); Native American; Rural Development Institute (international development); Global Health; Climate Change; Gates Public Service Law Program. Externships, Internships, and Summer Programs in Kenya and Italy.

STUDENT BODY
Fall 2009 full-time enrollment: 530
Men: **45%**	Women: **55%**
African-American: **2.10%**	American Indian: **2.60%**
Asian-American: **13.20%**	Mexican-American: **2.10%**
Puerto Rican: **0.00%**	Other Hisp-Amer: **2.10%**
White: **73.60%**	International: **3.00%**
Unknown: **1.30%**	

Attrition rates for 2008-2009 full-time students
Percent of students discontinuing law school:

Men: **0%**   Women: **1%**
First-year students: **2%**   Second-year students: **N/A**
Third-year students: **N/A**   Fourth-year students: **N/A**

LIBRARY RESOURCES

Total titles: **174,114**
Total volumes: **638,180**
Total seats available for library users: **391**

INFORMATION TECHNOLOGY

Number of wired network connections available to students: **0** total (in the law library, excluding computer labs: **0**; in classrooms: **0**; in computer labs: **0**; elsewhere in the law school: **0**)
Law school has a wireless network.
Students are not required to own a computer.

EMPLOYMENT AND SALARIES

Proportion of 2008 graduates employed at graduation: **91%**
Employed 9 months later, as of February 15, 2009: **98%**
Salaries in the private sector (law firms, business, industry): **$80,000 –$160,000** (25th-75th percentile)
Median salary in the private sector: **$125,000**
Percentage in the private sector who reported salary information: **61%**

Median salary in public service (government, judicial clerkships, academic posts, non-profits): **$49,000**

Percentage of 2008 graduates in:

Law firms: **54%**   Government: **14%**
Bus./industry: **7%**   Judicial clerkship: **16%**
Public interest: **8%**   Unknown: **0%**
Academia : **1%**

2008 graduates employed in-state: **62%**
2008 graduates employed in foreign countries: **2%**
Number of states where graduates are employed: **16**
Percentage of 2008 graduates working in: New England: **1%**, Middle Atlantic: **2%**, East North Central: **2%**, West North Central: **0%**, South Atlantic: **12%**, East South Central: **1%**, West South Central: **1%**, Mountain: **3%**, Pacific: **77%**, Unknown: **0%**

BAR PASSAGE RATES

Based on 2008 graduates taking Summer 2008 or Winter 2009 exams. Most of the school's first-time test takers took the bar in Washington.

85%
School's bar passage rate for first-time test takers

74%
Statewide bar passage rate for first-time test takers

University of Wisconsin–Madison

■ 975 Bascom Mall, Madison, WI, 53706-1399
■ http://www.law.wisc.edu
■ Public
■ Year founded: 1868
■ 2009-2010 tuition: full-time: $16,426; part-time: $1,372/credit hour
■ Enrollment 2009-10 academic year: full-time: 792; part-time: 33
■ U.S. News 2010 law specialty ranking: N/A

3.31-3.76 GPA, 25TH-75TH PERCENTILE

156-163 LSAT, 25TH-75TH PERCENTILE

24% ACCEPTANCE RATE

28 2011 U.S. NEWS LAW SCHOOL RANKING

ADMISSIONS

Admissions phone number: **(608) 262-5914**
Admissions email address: **admissions@law.wisc.edu**
Application website:
  http://law.wisc.edu/prospective/admissions/reqform.htm
Application deadline for Fall 2011 admission: **1-Mar**

Admissions statistics:

Number of applicants for Fall 2009: **2,936**
Number of acceptances: **697**
Number enrolled: **278**
Acceptance rate: **24%**
GPA, 25th-75th percentile, entering class Fall 2009: **3.31-3.76**
LSAT, 25th-75th percentile, entering class Fall 2009: **156-163**

FINANCIAL AID

Financial aid phone number: **(608) 262-5914**
Financial aid application deadline: **1-Mar**
Tuition 2009-2010 academic year: **full-time: $16,426; part-time: $1,372/credit hour**
Room and board: **$8,740** ; books: **$2,250** ; miscellaneous expenses: **$6,000**
Total of room/board/books/miscellaneous expenses: **$16,990**
University offers graduate student housing for which law students are eligible.

Financial aid profile

Percent of students that received grants for the 2008-2009 academic year: full-time: **28%**
Median grant amount: full-time: **$12,000**
The average law-school debt of those in the Class of 2009 who borrowed: **$67,655** . Proportion who borrowed: **87%**

ACADEMIC PROGRAMS

Calendar: **semester**
Joint degrees awarded: **J.D./M.B.A.; J.D./M.S. Environmental Studies; J.D./M.A. Library & Information** Sciences; J.D./M.A. Philosophy; J.D./M.A. Journalism/Mass Communications; J.D./M.A. Political Science; J.D./M.S.W.; JD/M.P.A. International Public Affairs; J.D./M.A. Latin Amer/Carribean/Iberian ; J.D./M.P.H.; J.D./M.P.A.; J.D./M.A. History; J.D./Master of Sociology & Rural Soc.; J.D./M.U.R.P.; J.D./M.A. Ed. Leadership/Policy Studies; J.D./M.A. English; J.D./M.S. Bacteriology
Typical first-year section size: Full-time: **71**
Is there typically a "small section" of the first year class, other than Legal Writing, taught by full-time faculty?: Full-time: **yes**
Number of course titles, beyond the first year curriculum, offered last year: **167**
Percentages of upper division course sections, excluding seminars, with an enrollment of:

Under 25: **62%**	25 to 49: **24%**
50 to 74: **8%**	75 to 99: **3%**
100+: **3%**	

Areas of specialization: appellate advocacy, clinical training, dispute resolution, environmental law, health care law, intellectual property law, international law, tax law, trial advocacy

Fall 2009 faculty profile

Total teaching faculty: **109**. Full-time: **46%**; **56%** men, **44%** women, **24%** minorities. Part-time: **54%**; **53%** men, **47%** women, **22%** minorities
Student-to-faculty ratio: **12.7**

SPECIAL PROGRAMS (as provided by law school):

Clinicals are encouraged. Majority of students participate; 25+ faculty, 10+ clinics provide opportunities. Dual degrees enhance interdisciplinary approach; students can combine JD and grad. degrees in 8 progs. with flexibility to create individualized progs. Many study abroad progs. are available; the East Asian Legal Studies Center offers additional experiences. Core courses offered in summer.

STUDENT BODY

Fall 2009 full-time enrollment: 792

Men: 54%   Women: 46%
African-American: 7.30%   American Indian: 2.50%
Asian-American: 7.10%   Mexican-American: 4.30%
Puerto Rican: 1.40%   Other Hisp-Amer: 1.50%
White: 67.20%   International: 2.80%
Unknown: 5.90%

Fall 2009 part-time enrollment: 33

Men: 55%   Women: 45%
African-American: 0.00%   American Indian: 0.00%
Asian-American: 15.20%   Mexican-American: 0.00%
Puerto Rican: 0.00%   Other Hisp-Amer: 0.00%
White: 81.80%   International: 0.00%
Unknown: 3.00%

Attrition rates for 2008-2009 full-time students
Percent of students discontinuing law school:
Men: 1%   Women: 2%
First-year students: 4%   Second-year students: 0%
Third-year students: N/A   Fourth-year students: N/A

LIBRARY RESOURCES

Total titles: 332,710
Total volumes: 583,080
Total seats available for library users: 613

INFORMATION TECHNOLOGY

Number of wired network connections available to students: 526 total (in the law library, excluding computer labs: 333; in classrooms: 184; in computer labs: 0; elsewhere in the law school: 9)
Law school has a wireless network.
Students are required to own a computer.

EMPLOYMENT AND SALARIES

Proportion of 2008 graduates employed at graduation: 81%
Employed 9 months later, as of February 15, 2009: 98%
Salaries in the private sector (law firms, business, industry): $67,625 –$160,000 (25th-75th percentile)
Median salary in the private sector: $125,000
Percentage in the private sector who reported salary information: 54%
Median salary in public service (government, judicial clerkships, academic posts, non-profits): $47,500

Percentage of 2008 graduates in:

Law firms: 58%   Government: 15%
Bus./industry: 12%   Judicial clerkship: 6%
Public interest: 7%   Unknown: 0%
Academia : 2%

2008 graduates employed in-state: 51%
2008 graduates employed in foreign countries: 3%
Number of states where graduates are employed: 26
Percentage of 2008 graduates working in: New England: 3%, Middle Atlantic: 4%, East North Central: 64%, West North Central: 6%, South Atlantic: 9%, East South Central: 0%, West South Central: 3%, Mountain: 2%, Pacific: 6%, Unknown: 0%

BAR PASSAGE RATES

Based on 2008 graduates taking Summer 2008 or Winter 2009 exams. Most of the school's first-time test takers took the bar in Wisconsin.

99%
School's bar passage rate for first-time test takers

92%
Statewide bar passage rate for first-time test takers

University of Wyoming

- Department 3035, 1000 E. University Avenue, Laramie, WY, 82071
- http://www.uwyo.edu/law
- Public
- Year founded: 1920
- 2009-2010 tuition: full-time: $9,966; part-time: N/A
- Enrollment 2009-10 academic year: full-time: 225
- U.S. News 2010 law specialty ranking: N/A

3.25-3.68 GPA, 25TH-75TH PERCENTILE

150-157 LSAT, 25TH-75TH PERCENTILE

34% ACCEPTANCE RATE

Tier 3 2011 U.S. NEWS LAW SCHOOL RANKING

ADMISSIONS

Admissions phone number: **(307) 766-6416**
Admissions email address: **lawadmis@uwyo.edu**
Application website: **N/A**
Application deadline for Fall 2011 admission: **1-Mar**

Admissions statistics:
Number of applicants for Fall 2009: **583**
Number of acceptances: **198**
Number enrolled: **83**
Acceptance rate: **34%**
GPA, 25th-75th percentile, entering class Fall 2009: **3.25-3.68**
LSAT, 25th-75th percentile, entering class Fall 2009: **150-157**

FINANCIAL AID

Financial aid phone number: **(307) 766-2116**
Financial aid application deadline: **1-Mar**
Tuition 2009-2010 academic year: **full-time: $9,966; part-time: N/A**
Room and board: **$10,919** ; books: **$1,200** ; miscellaneous expenses: **$2,200**
Total of room/board/books/miscellaneous expenses: **$14,319**
University offers graduate student housing for which law students are eligible.

Financial aid profile
Percent of students that received grants for the 2008-2009 academic year: full-time: **56%**
Median grant amount: full-time: **$2,000**
The average law-school debt of those in the Class of 2009 who borrowed: **$36,016** . Proportion who borrowed: **90%**

ACADEMIC PROGRAMS

Calendar: **semester**
Joint degrees awarded: **J.D./M.P.A.; J.D./MA Environment & Natural Resources; J.D./M.B.A**
Typical first-year section size: Full-time: **75**
Is there typically a "small section" of the first year class, other than Legal Writing, taught by full-time faculty?:
Full-time: **no**
Number of course titles, beyond the first year curriculum, offered last year: **61**
Percentages of upper division course sections, excluding seminars, with an enrollment of:
Under 25: **70%**   25 to 49: **16%**
50 to 74: **13%**   75 to 99: **0%**
100+: **0%**
Areas of specialization: appellate advocacy, clinical training, dispute resolution, environmental law, health care law, intellectual property law, international law, tax law, trial advocacy

Fall 2009 faculty profile
Total teaching faculty: **18**. Full-time: **72%**; **85%** men, **15%** women, **15%** minorities. Part-time: **28%**; **20%** men, **80%** women, **0%** minorities
Student-to-faculty ratio: **12.3**

SPECIAL PROGRAMS *(as provided by law school):*

UW Law offers practical experience for academic credit in four clinical programs: Defender Aid, Prosecution Assistance, Legal Services, and Domestic Violence. Students have a wide variety of externships from which to choose, including placement with the US Attorney; federal, state, and local judges; the Wyoming Attorney General, other governmental agencies, as well as non-profit groups.

STUDENT BODY

Fall 2009 full-time enrollment: 225
Men: **52%**   Women: **48%**
African-American: **0.90%**   American Indian: **0.90%**
Asian-American: **3.10%**   Mexican-American: **5.30%**
Puerto Rican: **0.00%**   Other Hisp-Amer: **0.00%**
White: **73.80%**   International: **0.40%**
Unknown: **15.60%**

Attrition rates for 2008-2009 full-time students
Percent of students discontinuing law school:
Men: **1%**   Women: **N/A**

First-year students: **1%**   Second-year students: **N/A**
Third-year students: **N/A**   Fourth-year students: **N/A**

LIBRARY RESOURCES
Total titles: **77,450**
Total volumes: **322,174**
Total seats available for library users: **282**

INFORMATION TECHNOLOGY
Number of wired network connections available to students: **326** total (in the law library, excluding computer labs: **98**; in classrooms: **178**; in computer labs: **20**; elsewhere in the law school: **30**)
Law school has a wireless network.
Students are not required to own a computer.

EMPLOYMENT AND SALARIES
Proportion of 2008 graduates employed at graduation: **59%**
Employed 9 months later, as of February 15, 2009: **89%**
Salaries in the private sector (law firms, business, industry): **$40,000 –$54,000** (25th-75th percentile)
Median salary in the private sector: **$48,000**
Percentage in the private sector who reported salary information: **57%**
Median salary in public service (government, judicial clerkships, academic posts, non-profits): **$46,000**

Percentage of 2008 graduates in:
Law firms: **41%**   Government: **16%**
Bus./industry: **16%**   Judicial clerkship: **14%**
Public interest: **7%**   Unknown: **5%**
Academia : **2%**

2008 graduates employed in-state: **57%**
2008 graduates employed in foreign countries: **2%**
Number of states where graduates are employed: **9**
Percentage of 2008 graduates working in: New England: **0%**, Middle Atlantic: **0%**, East North Central: **0%**, West North Central: **0%**, South Atlantic: **2%**, East South Central: **2%**, West South Central: **0%**, Mountain: **90%**, Pacific: **5%**, Unknown: **0%**

BAR PASSAGE RATES
Based on 2008 graduates taking Summer 2008 or Winter 2009 exams. Most of the school's first-time test takers took the bar in Wyoming.

76%
School's bar passage rate for first-time test takers

67%
Statewide bar passage rate for first-time test takers

Valparaiso University

- 656 S. Greenwich Street, Wesemann Hall, Valparaiso, IN, 46383
- http://www.valpo.edu/law
- Private
- Year founded: 1879
- 2009-2010 tuition: full-time: $35,230; part-time: $1,376/credit hour
- Enrollment 2009-10 academic year: full-time: 541; part-time: 41
- U.S. News 2010 law specialty ranking: N/A

3.08-3.59 GPA, 25TH-75TH PERCENTILE

148-152 LSAT, 25TH-75TH PERCENTILE

62% ACCEPTANCE RATE

Tier 4 2011 U.S. NEWS LAW SCHOOL RANKING

ADMISSIONS

Admissions phone number: **(888) 825-7652**
Admissions email address: **valpolaw@valpo.edu**
Application website:
  https://www.valpo.edu/law/admissions/apply.php
Application deadline for Fall 2011 admission: **1-Jun**

Admissions statistics:

Number of applicants for Fall 2009: **1,440**
Number of acceptances: **889**
Number enrolled: **191**
Acceptance rate: **62%**
GPA, 25th-75th percentile, entering class Fall 2009: **3.08-3.59**
LSAT, 25th-75th percentile, entering class Fall 2009: **148-152**

Part-time program:

Number of applicants for Fall 2009: **135**
Number of acceptances: **45**
Number enrolled: **12**
Acceptance rate: **33%**
GPA, 25th-75th percentile, entering class Fall 2009: **2.82-3.22**
LSAT, 25th-75th percentile, entering class Fall 2009: **147-151**

FINANCIAL AID

Financial aid phone number: **(219) 465-7818**
Financial aid application deadline: **1-Mar**
Tuition 2009-2010 academic year: **full-time: $35,230; part-time: $1,376/credit hour**
Room and board: **$8,800** ; books: **$1,200** ; miscellaneous expenses: **$2,760**
Total of room/board/books/miscellaneous expenses: **$12,760**
University offers graduate student housing for which law students are eligible.

Financial aid profile

Percent of students that received grants for the 2008-2009 academic year: full-time: **26%**; part-time **17%**
Median grant amount: full-time: **$16,250** ; part-time: **$0**
The average law-school debt of those in the Class of 2009 who borrowed: **$107,313** . Proportion who borrowed: **89%**

ACADEMIC PROGRAMS

Calendar: **semester**
Joint degrees awarded: **J.D./M.A. Psychology; J.D./M.A. C.M.H.C.; J.D./M.B.A.; J.D./M.A.L.S.; J.D./M.S.I.C.P.; J.D./M.S. Sports Administration; J.D./M.A. China Studies**
Typical first-year section size: Full-time: **72**
Is there typically a "small section" of the first year class, other than Legal Writing, taught by full-time faculty?:
  Full-time: **no**; Part-time: **no**
Number of course titles, beyond the first year curriculum, offered last year: **100**
Percentages of upper division course sections, excluding seminars, with an enrollment of:
  Under 25: **66%**   25 to 49: **22%**
  50 to 74: **7%**   75 to 99: **2%**
  100+: **3%**
Areas of specialization: appellate advocacy, clinical training, dispute resolution, environmental law, health care law, intellectual property law, international law, tax law, trial advocacy

Fall 2009 faculty profile

Total teaching faculty: **57**. Full-time: **53%**; **63%** men, **37%** women, **10%** minorities. Part-time: **47%**; **63%** men, **37%** women, **11%** minorities
Student-to-faculty ratio: **15.8**

SPECIAL PROGRAMS *(as provided by law school)*:

The law school is home to seven clinics (Criminal, Civil, Low Income Taxpayer, Mediation, Juvenile Justice, Guardianship ad Litem, and the nation's only Sports Law Clinic), has summer study programs in England and in Chile/Argentina, houses the Tabor Institute on Law and Ethics, and offers a wealth of judicial, governmental, law practice, non-profit, and business-related externships.

STUDENT BODY

Fall 2009 full-time enrollment: 541

Men: 52%	Women: 48%
African-American: 7.20%	American Indian: 0.70%
Asian-American: 2.60%	Mexican-American: 2.40%
Puerto Rican: 0.00%	Other Hisp-Amer: 3.50%
White: 76.20%	International: 1.10%
Unknown: 6.30%	

Fall 2009 part-time enrollment: 41

Men: 61%	Women: 39%
African-American: 9.80%	American Indian: 0.00%
Asian-American: 4.90%	Mexican-American: 0.00%
Puerto Rican: 0.00%	Other Hisp-Amer: 0.00%
White: 58.50%	International: 2.40%
Unknown: 24.40%	

Attrition rates for 2008-2009 full-time students

Percent of students discontinuing law school:

Men: 7%	Women: 3%
First-year students: 13%	Second-year students: N/A
Third-year students: 1%	Fourth-year students: N/A

LIBRARY RESOURCES

Total titles: 165,823
Total volumes: 342,938
Total seats available for library users: 386

INFORMATION TECHNOLOGY

Number of wired network connections available to students: 46 total (in the law library, excluding computer labs: 33; in classrooms: 3; in computer labs: 0; elsewhere in the law school: 10)
Law school has a wireless network.
Students are not required to own a computer.

EMPLOYMENT AND SALARIES

Proportion of 2008 graduates employed at graduation: N/A
Employed 9 months later, as of February 15, 2009: 89%
Salaries in the private sector (law firms, business, industry): $50,000 –$80,000 (25th-75th percentile)
Median salary in the private sector: $55,000
Percentage in the private sector who reported salary information: N/A
Median salary in public service (government, judicial clerkships, academic posts, non-profits): N/A

Percentage of 2008 graduates in:

Law firms: 60%	Government: 12%
Bus./industry: 13%	Judicial clerkship: 12%
Public interest: 0%	Unknown: 0%
Academia : 3%	

2008 graduates employed in-state: 45%
2008 graduates employed in foreign countries: 0%
Number of states where graduates are employed: 23
Percentage of 2008 graduates working in: New England: 1%, Middle Atlantic: 6%, East North Central: 65%, West North Central: 4%, South Atlantic: 14%, East South Central: 1%, West South Central: 0%, Mountain: 4%, Pacific: 2%, Unknown: 3%

BAR PASSAGE RATES

Based on 2008 graduates taking Summer 2008 or Winter 2009 exams. Most of the school's first-time test takers took the bar in Indiana.

83%
School's bar passage rate for first-time test takers

84%
Statewide bar passage rate for first-time test takers

Vanderbilt University

- 131 21st Avenue S, Nashville, TN, 37203-1181
- http://www.vanderbilt.edu/law/
- Private
- Year founded: 1874
- 2009-2010 tuition: full-time: $44,074; part-time: N/A
- Enrollment 2009-10 academic year: full-time: 594
- U.S. News 2010 law specialty ranking: N/A

3.50-3.86 GPA, 25TH-75TH PERCENTILE

164-169 LSAT, 25TH-75TH PERCENTILE

24% ACCEPTANCE RATE

17 2011 U.S. NEWS LAW SCHOOL RANKING

ADMISSIONS

Admissions phone number: **(615) 322-6452**
Admissions email address: **admissions@law.vanderbilt.edu**
Application website: **http://law.vanderbilt.edu/prospective-students/admissions/apply/index.aspx**
Application deadline for Fall 2011 admission: **15-Mar**

Admissions statistics:

Number of applicants for Fall 2009: **4,850**
Number of acceptances: **1,181**
Number enrolled: **195**
Acceptance rate: **24%**
GPA, 25th-75th percentile, entering class Fall 2009: **3.50-3.86**
LSAT, 25th-75th percentile, entering class Fall 2009: **164-169**

FINANCIAL AID

Financial aid phone number: **(615) 322-6452**
Financial aid application deadline: **15-Feb**
Tuition 2009-2010 academic year: **full-time: $44,074; part-time: N/A**
Room and board: **$12,900** ; books: **$1,720** ; miscellaneous expenses: **$7,328**
Total of room/board/books/miscellaneous expenses: **$21,948**
University offers graduate student housing for which law students are eligible.

Financial aid profile

Percent of students that received grants for the 2008-2009 academic year: full-time: **69%**
Median grant amount: full-time: **$15,000**
The average law-school debt of those in the Class of 2009 who borrowed: **$118,220** . Proportion who borrowed: **82%**

ACADEMIC PROGRAMS

Calendar: **semester**
Joint degrees awarded: **J.D./M.B.A.; J.D./M.T.S.;** J.D./M.Div; J.D./M.A.; J.D./Ph.D.; J.D./M.D.; J.D./M.P.P.

Typical first-year section size: Full-time: **97**
Is there typically a "small section" of the first year class, other than Legal Writing, taught by full-time faculty?: Full-time: **yes**
Number of course titles, beyond the first year curriculum, offered last year: **151**
Percentages of upper division course sections, excluding seminars, with an enrollment of:

Under 25: **64%**   25 to 49: **26%**
50 to 74: **5%**   75 to 99: **3%**
100+: **2%**

Areas of specialization: appellate advocacy, clinical training, dispute resolution, environmental law, health care law, intellectual property law, international law, tax law, trial advocacy

Fall 2009 faculty profile

Total teaching faculty: **66**. Full-time: **48%**; **59%** men, **41%** women, **13%** minorities. Part-time: **52%**; **59%** men, **41%** women, **12%** minorities
Student-to-faculty ratio: **14.4**

SPECIAL PROGRAMS *(as provided by law school)*:

Specialized programs are offered in Law & Business; Litigation & Dispute Resolution; Constitutional Law; Regulatory Law; Intellectual Property; International Law; Environmental Law; Social Justice; and Law & Human Behavior. Joint degree programs offered include a JD/PhD program in Law & Economics. Students participate in live-client clinics, externships, and other experiential learning courses.

STUDENT BODY

Fall 2009 full-time enrollment: 594

Men: **52%**	Women: **48%**
African-American: **9.10%**	American Indian: **0.50%**
Asian-American: **3.50%**	Mexican-American: **0.00%**
Puerto Rican: **0.00%**	Other Hisp-Amer: **3.90%**
White: **58.90%**	International: **2.90%**
Unknown: **21.20%**	

Attrition rates for 2008-2009 full-time students
Percent of students discontinuing law school:
Men: 1%   Women: 1%
First-year students: 2%   Second-year students: 0%
Third-year students: N/A   Fourth-year students: N/A

LIBRARY RESOURCES

Total titles: 224,223
Total volumes: 606,449
Total seats available for library users: 278

INFORMATION TECHNOLOGY

Number of wired network connections available to students: 270 total (in the law library, excluding computer labs: 100; in classrooms: 100; in computer labs: 20; elsewhere in the law school: 50)
Law school has a wireless network.
Students are not required to own a computer.

EMPLOYMENT AND SALARIES

Proportion of 2008 graduates employed at graduation: 97%
Employed 9 months later, as of February 15, 2009: 98%
Salaries in the private sector (law firms, business, industry): $112,500 –$160,000 (25th-75th percentile)
Median salary in the private sector: $145,000
Percentage in the private sector who reported salary information: 74%

Median salary in public service (government, judicial clerkships, academic posts, non-profits): $50,000

Percentage of 2008 graduates in:
Law firms: 74%   Government: 6%
Bus./industry: 3%   Judicial clerkship: 15%
Public interest: 2%   Unknown: 0%
Academia : 0%

2008 graduates employed in-state: 19%
2008 graduates employed in foreign countries: 2%
Number of states where graduates are employed: 32
Percentage of 2008 graduates working in: New England: 3%, Middle Atlantic: 13%, East North Central: 9%, West North Central: 4%, South Atlantic: 28%, East South Central: 23%, West South Central: 10%, Mountain: 3%, Pacific: 6%, Unknown: 0%

BAR PASSAGE RATES

Based on 2008 graduates taking Summer 2008 or Winter 2009 exams. Most of the school's first-time test takers took the bar in Tennessee.

96%

School's bar passage rate for first-time test takers

83%

Statewide bar passage rate for first-time test takers

Vermont Law School

- Chelsea Street, South Royalton, VT, 05068-0096
- http://www.vermontlaw.edu
- Private
- Year founded: 1972
- 2009-2010 tuition: full-time: $40,420; part-time: N/A
- Enrollment 2009-10 academic year: full-time: 567
- U.S. News 2010 law specialty ranking: clinical training: 28, environmental law: 1

3.05-3.57 GPA, 25TH-75TH PERCENTILE

152-158 LSAT, 25TH-75TH PERCENTILE

67% ACCEPTANCE RATE

Tier 3 2011 U.S. NEWS LAW SCHOOL RANKING

ADMISSIONS
Admissions phone number: (888) 277-5985
Admissions email address: admiss@vermontlaw.edu
Application website: N/A
Application deadline for Fall 2011 admission: 1-Mar

Admissions statistics:
Number of applicants for Fall 2009: 884
Number of acceptances: 590
Number enrolled: 233
Acceptance rate: 67%
GPA, 25th-75th percentile, entering class Fall 2009: 3.05-3.57
LSAT, 25th-75th percentile, entering class Fall 2009: 152-158

FINANCIAL AID
Financial aid phone number: (888) 277-5985
Financial aid application deadline: 1-Mar
Tuition 2009-2010 academic year: full-time: $40,420; part-time: N/A
Room and board: $10,080 ; books: $1,500 ; miscellaneous expenses: $9,480
Total of room/board/books/miscellaneous expenses: $21,060
University does not offer graduate student housing for which law students are eligible.

Financial aid profile
Percent of students that received grants for the 2008-2009 academic year: full-time: 65%
Median grant amount: full-time: $8,000
The average law-school debt of those in the Class of 2009 who borrowed: $122,475 . Proportion who borrowed: 89%

ACADEMIC PROGRAMS
Calendar: semester
Joint degrees awarded: J.D./M.E.L.P
Typical first-year section size: Full-time: 65
Is there typically a "small section" of the first year class, other than Legal Writing, taught by full-time faculty?: Full-time: yes
Number of course titles, beyond the first year curriculum, offered last year: 128
Percentages of upper division course sections, excluding seminars, with an enrollment of:
Under 25: 60%   25 to 49: 32%
50 to 74: 6%   75 to 99: 2%
100+: 0%
Areas of specialization: appellate advocacy, clinical training, dispute resolution, environmental law, intellectual property law, international law, tax law, trial advocacy

Fall 2009 faculty profile
Total teaching faculty: 48. Full-time: 71%; 62% men, 38% women, 12% minorities. Part-time: 29%; 57% men, 43% women, 7% minorities
Student-to-faculty ratio: 13.5

SPECIAL PROGRAMS *(as provided by law school):*
Clinics offered. Semester in Practice; Legislation Clinic; Environmental Semester in Washington, D.C.; Environmental and Natural Resources Law Clinic, South Royalton Legal Clinic, General Practice Program, Judicial Externships, Mediation Clinic, MELP and LLM Environmental Internships, JD Internships.

STUDENT BODY
Fall 2009 full-time enrollment: 567
Men: 50%	Women: 50%
African-American: 2.80%	American Indian: 0.40%
Asian-American: 2.80%	Mexican-American: 0.70%
Puerto Rican: 0.50%	Other Hisp-Amer: 1.40%
White: 79.90%	International: 1.10%
Unknown: 10.40%	

Attrition rates for 2008-2009 full-time students
Percent of students discontinuing law school:
Men: 2%	Women: 1%
First-year students: 4%	Second-year students: 1%
Third-year students: N/A	Fourth-year students: N/A

LIBRARY RESOURCES

Total titles: 99,520
Total volumes: 254,127
Total seats available for library users: 382

INFORMATION TECHNOLOGY

Number of wired network connections available to students: 110 total (in the law library, excluding computer labs: 54; in classrooms: 45; in computer labs: 1; elsewhere in the law school: 10)
Law school has a wireless network.
Students are not required to own a computer.

EMPLOYMENT AND SALARIES

Proportion of 2008 graduates employed at graduation: 60%
Employed 9 months later, as of February 15, 2009: 95%
Salaries in the private sector (law firms, business, industry): $50,000 –$80,000 (25th-75th percentile)
Median salary in the private sector: $65,000
Percentage in the private sector who reported salary information: 54%
Median salary in public service (government, judicial clerkships, academic posts, non-profits): $43,000

Percentage of 2008 graduates in:

Law firms: 35%
Bus./industry: 19%
Public interest: 15%
Academia : 1%

Government: 16%
Judicial clerkship: 15%
Unknown: 0%

2008 graduates employed in-state: 15%
2008 graduates employed in foreign countries: 1%
Number of states where graduates are employed: 29
Percentage of 2008 graduates working in: New England: 34%, Middle Atlantic: 17%, East North Central: 3%, West North Central: 1%, South Atlantic: 29%, East South Central: 1%, West South Central: 0%, Mountain: 5%, Pacific: 10%, Unknown: 0%

BAR PASSAGE RATES

Based on 2008 graduates taking Summer 2008 or Winter 2009 exams. Most of the school's first-time test takers took the bar in New York.

83%
School's bar passage rate for first-time test takers

81%
Statewide bar passage rate for first-time test takers

Villanova University

- 299 N. Spring Mill Road, Villanova, PA, 19085
- http://www.law.villanova.edu/
- Private
- Year founded: 1953
- 2009-2010 tuition: full-time: $35,250; part-time: N/A
- Enrollment 2009-10 academic year: full-time: 754
- U.S. News 2010 law specialty ranking: tax law: 21

3.17-3.63 GPA, 25TH-75TH PERCENTILE

160-163 LSAT, 25TH-75TH PERCENTILE

43% ACCEPTANCE RATE

67 2011 U.S. NEWS LAW SCHOOL RANKING

ADMISSIONS

Admissions phone number: (610) 519-7010
Admissions email address: **admissions@law.villanova.edu**
Application website: **N/A**
Application deadline for Fall 2011 admission: **rolling**

Admissions statistics:
Number of applicants for Fall 2009: **3,254**
Number of acceptances: **1,401**
Number enrolled: **255**
Acceptance rate: **43%**
GPA, 25th-75th percentile, entering class Fall 2009: **3.17-3.63**
LSAT, 25th-75th percentile, entering class Fall 2009: **160-163**

FINANCIAL AID

Financial aid phone number: (610) 519-7015
Financial aid application deadline:
Tuition 2009-2010 academic year: **full-time: $35,250; part-time: N/A**
Room and board: **$14,850** ; books: **$1,400** ; miscellaneous expenses: **$3,445**
Total of room/board/books/miscellaneous expenses: **$19,695**
University does not offer graduate student housing for which law students are eligible.

Financial aid profile
Percent of students that received grants for the 2008-2009 academic year: full-time: **21%**
Median grant amount: full-time: **$15,000**
The average law-school debt of those in the Class of 2009 who borrowed: **$116,878** . Proportion who borrowed: **89%**

ACADEMIC PROGRAMS

Calendar: **semester**
Joint degrees awarded: **J.D./Ph.D.; J.D./M.B.A.; J.D./LL.M.**
Typical first-year section size: Full-time: **85**
Is there typically a "small section" of the first year class, other than Legal Writing, taught by full-time faculty?:
Full-time: **yes**
Number of course titles, beyond the first year curriculum, offered last year: **117**
Percentages of upper division course sections, excluding seminars, with an enrollment of:
Under 25: **61%**   25 to 49: **20%**
50 to 74: **11%**   75 to 99: **7%**
100+: **1%**
Areas of specialization: appellate advocacy, clinical training, dispute resolution, environmental law, health care law, intellectual property law, international law, tax law, trial advocacy

Fall 2009 faculty profile
Total teaching faculty: **101**. Full-time: **36%**; **58%** men, **42%** women, **11%** minorities. Part-time: **64%**; **80%** men, **20%** women, **14%** minorities
Student-to-faculty ratio: **17**

SPECIAL PROGRAMS *(as provided by law school)*:

We offer five clinics supervised by full-time faculty, Capital Defense and Federal Defenders Practicums, and 25 externships overseen by full-time faculty. We host the PA Criminal Sentencing Institute and a Sentencing Workshop involving students, judges and lawyers. We have joint JD/MBA and JD/LLM degrees and summer study in Rome. Students participate in national moot court and trial competitions.

STUDENT BODY

Fall 2009 full-time enrollment: **754**
Men: **56%**   Women: **44%**
African-American: **2.00%**   American Indian: **0.40%**
Asian-American: **8.60%**   Mexican-American: **0.00%**
Puerto Rican: **0.00%**   Other Hisp-Amer: **6.20%**
White: **82.00%**   International: **0.80%**
Unknown: **0.00%**

Attrition rates for 2008-2009 full-time students
Percent of students discontinuing law school:
Men: **1%**   Women: **1%**

First-year students: **2%**   Second-year students: **N/A**
Third-year students: **0%**   Fourth-year students: **N/A**

LIBRARY RESOURCES
Total titles: **151,901**
Total volumes: **555,571**
Total seats available for library users: **445**

INFORMATION TECHNOLOGY
Number of wired network connections available to students: **329** total (in the law library, excluding computer labs: **106**; in classrooms: **60**; in computer labs: **148**; elsewhere in the law school: **15**)
Law school has a wireless network.
Students are not required to own a computer.

EMPLOYMENT AND SALARIES
Proportion of 2008 graduates employed at graduation: **65%**
Employed 9 months later, as of February 15, 2009: **94%**
Salaries in the private sector (law firms, business, industry): **$55,781 –$108,750** (25th-75th percentile)
Median salary in the private sector: **$101,250**
Percentage in the private sector who reported salary information: **72%**
Median salary in public service (government, judicial clerkships, academic posts, non-profits): **$49,000**

Percentage of 2008 graduates in:
Law firms: **56%**   Government: **6%**
Bus./industry: **17%**   Judicial clerkship: **15%**
Public interest: **6%**   Unknown: **0%**
Academia : **0%**

2008 graduates employed in-state: **60%**
2008 graduates employed in foreign countries: **1%**
Number of states where graduates are employed: **15**
Percentage of 2008 graduates working in: New England: **3%**, Middle Atlantic: **80%**, East North Central: **1%**, West North Central: **0%**, South Atlantic: **14%**, East South Central: **0%**, West South Central: **1%**, Mountain: **1%**, Pacific: **1%**, Unknown: **0%**

BAR PASSAGE RATES
Based on 2008 graduates taking Summer 2008 or Winter 2009 exams. Most of the school's first-time test takers took the bar in Pennsylvania.

| 92% |
School's bar passage rate for first-time test takers

| 87% |
Statewide bar passage rate for first-time test takers

Wake Forest University

- Reynolda Station, PO Box 7206, Winston-Salem, NC, 27109
- http://www.law.wfu.edu
- Private
- Year founded: 1894
- 2009-2010 tuition: full-time: $35,450; part-time: N/A
- Enrollment 2009-10 academic year: full-time: 463; part-time: 13
- U.S. News 2010 law specialty ranking: healthcare law: 17

3.20-3.70	GPA, 25TH-75TH PERCENTILE
160-164	LSAT, 25TH-75TH PERCENTILE
33%	ACCEPTANCE RATE
38	2011 U.S. NEWS LAW SCHOOL RANKING

ADMISSIONS

Admissions phone number: (336) 758-5437
Admissions email address: lawadmissions@wfu.edu
Application website: http://law.wfu.edu/admissions/apply/
Application deadline for Fall 2011 admission: 1-Mar

Admissions statistics:

Number of applicants for Fall 2009: 2,775
Number of acceptances: 905
Number enrolled: 154
Acceptance rate: 33%
GPA, 25th-75th percentile, entering class Fall 2009: 3.20-3.70
LSAT, 25th-75th percentile, entering class Fall 2009: 160-164

FINANCIAL AID

Financial aid phone number: (336) 758-5437
Financial aid application deadline: 1-Apr
Tuition 2009-2010 academic year: **full-time: $35,450**; part-time: N/A
Room and board: $8,810 ; books: $1,200 ; miscellaneous expenses: $6,600
Total of room/board/books/miscellaneous expenses: $16,610
University does not offer graduate student housing for which law students are eligible.

Financial aid profile

Percent of students that received grants for the 2008-2009 academic year: full-time: 52%
Median grant amount: full-time: $12,000
The average law-school debt of those in the Class of 2009 who borrowed: $83,700 . Proportion who borrowed: 97%

ACADEMIC PROGRAMS

Calendar: **semester**
Joint degrees awarded: **J.D./M.B.A.; J.D./MDiv; J.D./M.A./Religion; J.D./M.A./Bioethics**
Typical first-year section size: Full-time: 38
Is there typically a "small section" of the first year class, other than Legal Writing, taught by full-time faculty?: Full-time: **no**
Number of course titles, beyond the first year curriculum, offered last year: 108
Percentages of upper division course sections, excluding seminars, with an enrollment of:

Under 25: **55%**   25 to 49: **30%**
50 to 74: **14%**   75 to 99: **1%**
100+: **0%**

Areas of specialization: appellate advocacy, clinical training, dispute resolution, environmental law, health care law, intellectual property law, international law, tax law, trial advocacy

Fall 2009 faculty profile

Total teaching faculty: 57. Full-time: **68%**; 59% men, 41% women, 13% minorities. Part-time: **32%**; 83% men, 17% women, 0% minorities
Student-to-faculty ratio: 9.8

SPECIAL PROGRAMS (as provided by law school):

Clinics: Litigation, Elder Law, Appellate Advocacy, Community Law and Business (CLBC), and Innocence and Justice. The relatively new CLBC allows students to assist low-income entrepreneurs in a transactional/business setting. Wake also supports a Children's Law Externship and a Domestic Violence Advocacy Center. Summer abroad programs are held in England, Italy and Austria.

STUDENT BODY

Fall 2009 full-time enrollment: 463

Men: 58%	Women: 42%
African-American: 8.90%	American Indian: 0.90%
Asian-American: 3.50%	Mexican-American: 0.00%
Puerto Rican: 0.00%	Other Hisp-Amer: 4.10%
White: 74.30%	International: 0.20%
Unknown: 8.20%	

Fall 2009 part-time enrollment: 13

Men: 54%	Women: 46%
African-American: 7.70%	American Indian: 0.00%

Asian-American: **0.00%**   Mexican-American: **0.00%**
Puerto Rican: **0.00%**   Other Hisp-Amer: **0.00%**
White: **84.60%**   International: **0.00%**
Unknown: **7.70%**

Attrition rates for 2008-2009 full-time students
Percent of students discontinuing law school:
Men: **2%**   Women: **4%**
First-year students: **2%**   Second-year students: **4%**
Third-year students: **2%**   Fourth-year students: **N/A**

LIBRARY RESOURCES
Total titles: **634,010**
Total volumes: **419,496**
Total seats available for library users: **576**

INFORMATION TECHNOLOGY
Number of wired network connections available to students: **24** total (in the law library, excluding computer labs: **12**; in classrooms: **0**; in computer labs: **12**; elsewhere in the law school: **0**)
Law school has a wireless network.
Students are required to own a computer.

EMPLOYMENT AND SALARIES
Proportion of 2008 graduates employed at graduation: **75%**
Employed 9 months later, as of February 15, 2009: **96%**
Salaries in the private sector (law firms, business, industry): **$73,000 –$145,000** (25th-75th percentile)
Median salary in the private sector: **$120,000**

Percentage in the private sector who reported salary information: **76%**
Median salary in public service (government, judicial clerkships, academic posts, non-profits): **$45,742**

Percentage of 2008 graduates in:
Law firms: **70%**   Government: **9%**
Bus./industry: **6%**   Judicial clerkship: **9%**
Public interest: **N/A**   Unknown: **3%**
Academia : **3%**

2008 graduates employed in-state: **56%**
2008 graduates employed in foreign countries: **N/A**
Number of states where graduates are employed: **20**
Percentage of 2008 graduates working in: New England: **1%**, Middle Atlantic: **11%**, East North Central: **2%**, West North Central: **1%**, South Atlantic: **78%**, East South Central: **1%**, West South Central: **4%**, Mountain: **2%**, Pacific: **1%**, Unknown: **N/A**

BAR PASSAGE RATES
Based on 2008 graduates taking Summer 2008 or Winter 2009 exams. Most of the school's first-time test takers took the bar in North Carolina.

	96%

School's bar passage rate for first-time test takers

	83%

Statewide bar passage rate for first-time test takers

Washburn University

- 1700 S.W. College Avenue, Topeka, KS, 66621
- http://washburnlaw.edu
- Public
- Year founded: 1903
- 2009-2010 tuition: full-time: $536/credit hour; part-time: N/A
- Enrollment 2009-10 academic year: full-time: 441
- U.S. News 2010 law specialty ranking: N/A

2.95-3.68 GPA, 25TH-75TH PERCENTILE

152-157 LSAT, 25TH-75TH PERCENTILE

47% ACCEPTANCE RATE

Tier 3 2011 U.S. NEWS LAW SCHOOL RANKING

ADMISSIONS
Admissions phone number: **(785) 670-1185**
Admissions email address: **admissions@washburnlaw.edu**
Application website: **http://washburnlaw.edu/applyonline/**
Application deadline for Fall 2011 admission: **1-Apr**

Admissions statistics:
Number of applicants for Fall 2009: **957**
Number of acceptances: **453**
Number enrolled: **159**
Acceptance rate: **47%**
GPA, 25th-75th percentile, entering class Fall 2009: **2.95-3.68**
LSAT, 25th-75th percentile, entering class Fall 2009: **152-157**

FINANCIAL AID
Financial aid phone number: **(785) 670-1151**
Financial aid application deadline: **1-Jul**
Tuition 2009-2010 academic year: **full-time: $536/credit hour; part-time: N/A**
Room and board: **$8,942** ; books: **$2,005** ; miscellaneous expenses: **$5,044**
Total of room/board/books/miscellaneous expenses: **$15,991**
University offers graduate student housing for which law students are eligible.

Financial aid profile
Percent of students that received grants for the 2008-2009 academic year: full-time: **46%**
Median grant amount: full-time: **$7,500**
The average law-school debt of those in the Class of 2009 who borrowed: **$71,661** . Proportion who borrowed: **85%**

ACADEMIC PROGRAMS
Calendar: **semester**
Joint degrees awarded: **J.D./M.S.W.; J.D./M.B.A.**
Typical first-year section size: Full-time: **76**
Is there typically a "small section" of the first year class, other than Legal Writing, taught by full-time faculty?: Full-time: **yes**

Number of course titles, beyond the first year curriculum, offered last year: **97**
Percentages of upper division course sections, excluding seminars, with an enrollment of:
Under 25: **66%**   25 to 49: **19%**
50 to 74: **13%**   75 to 99: **2%**
100+: **0%**
Areas of specialization: appellate advocacy, clinical training, dispute resolution, environmental law, health care law, intellectual property law, international law, tax law, trial advocacy

Fall 2009 faculty profile
Total teaching faculty: **84**. Full-time: **39%**; **61%** men, **39%** women, **15%** minorities. Part-time: **61%**; **61%** men, **39%** women, **0%** minorities
Student-to-faculty ratio: **12.9**

SPECIAL PROGRAMS *(as provided by law school):*
Clinic (criminal defense, family law, civil law, Native American Law, appellate practice, transactional); Centers (Advocacy, Business & Transactional, Children & Family, Law & Government); Certificates (advocacy, business & transactional, estate planning, family law, natural resources, tax, and international & comparative); Study abroad (summer in Barbados, semester in Netherlands).

STUDENT BODY
Fall 2009 full-time enrollment: **441**
Men: **59%**   Women: **41%**
African-American: **4.10%**   American Indian: **1.40%**
Asian-American: **2.90%**   Mexican-American: **2.30%**
Puerto Rican: **0.50%**   Other Hisp-Amer: **1.80%**
White: **84.60%**   International: **0.50%**
Unknown: **2.00%**

Attrition rates for 2008-2009 full-time students
Percent of students discontinuing law school:
Men: **4%**   Women: **6%**
First-year students: **13%**   Second-year students: **1%**
Third-year students: **N/A**   Fourth-year students: **N/A**

LIBRARY RESOURCES

Total titles: 297,699
Total volumes: 395,673
Total seats available for library users: 384

INFORMATION TECHNOLOGY

Number of wired network connections available to students: 26 total (in the law library, excluding computer labs: 20; in classrooms: 0; in computer labs: 6; elsewhere in the law school: 0)
Law school has a wireless network.
Students are not required to own a computer.

EMPLOYMENT AND SALARIES

Proportion of 2008 graduates employed at graduation: N/A
Employed 9 months later, as of February 15, 2009: 94%
Salaries in the private sector (law firms, business, industry): $45,000 –$64,000 (25th-75th percentile)
Median salary in the private sector: $55,000
Percentage in the private sector who reported salary information: 44%
Median salary in public service (government, judicial clerkships, academic posts, non-profits): $45,600

Percentage of 2008 graduates in:

Law firms: 43%	Government: 24%
Bus./industry: 13%	Judicial clerkship: 9%
Public interest: 9%	Unknown: 1%
Academia : 1%	

2008 graduates employed in-state: 65%
2008 graduates employed in foreign countries: 0%
Number of states where graduates are employed: 15
Percentage of 2008 graduates working in: New England: 0%, Middle Atlantic: 1%, East North Central: 1%, West North Central: 79%, South Atlantic: 1%, East South Central: 1%, West South Central: 5%, Mountain: 7%, Pacific: 4%, Unknown: 1%

BAR PASSAGE RATES

Based on 2008 graduates taking Summer 2008 or Winter 2009 exams. Most of the school's first-time test takers took the bar in Kansas.

89%
School's bar passage rate for first-time test takers

89%
Statewide bar passage rate for first-time test takers

Washington and Lee University

- Sydney Lewis Hall, Lexington, VA, 24450-0303
- http://law.wlu.edu
- Private
- Year founded: 1849
- 2009-2010 tuition: full-time: $38,062; part-time: N/A
- Enrollment 2009-10 academic year: full-time: 390
- U.S. News 2010 law specialty ranking: N/A

3.28-3.78 GPA, 25TH-75TH PERCENTILE

160-167 LSAT, 25TH-75TH PERCENTILE

26% ACCEPTANCE RATE

34 2011 U.S. NEWS LAW SCHOOL RANKING

ADMISSIONS
Admissions phone number: **(540) 458-8504**
Admissions email address: **lawadm@wlu.edu**
Application website:
   http://law.wlu.edu/admissions/page.asp?pageid=305&op enpanel=2
Application deadline for Fall 2011 admission: **1-Mar**

Admissions statistics:
Number of applicants for Fall 2009: **3,416**
Number of acceptances: **873**
Number enrolled: **135**
Acceptance rate: **26%**
GPA, 25th-75th percentile, entering class Fall 2009: **3.28-3.78**
LSAT, 25th-75th percentile, entering class Fall 2009: **160-167**

FINANCIAL AID
Financial aid phone number: **(540) 458-8729**
Financial aid application deadline: **15-Mar**
Tuition 2009-2010 academic year: **full-time: $38,062; part-time: N/A**
Room and board: **$10,315** ; books: **$2,000** ; miscellaneous expenses: **$6,728**
Total of room/board/books/miscellaneous expenses: **$19,043**
University offers graduate student housing for which law students are eligible.

Financial aid profile
Percent of students that received grants for the 2008-2009 academic year: full-time: **63%**
Median grant amount: full-time: **$15,000**
The average law-school debt of those in the Class of 2009 who borrowed: **$100,670** . Proportion who borrowed: **91%**

ACADEMIC PROGRAMS
Calendar: **semester**
Joint degrees awarded: **J.D./M.H.A.**

Typical first-year section size: Full-time: **51**
Is there typically a "small section" of the first year class, other than Legal Writing, taught by full-time faculty?: Full-time: **yes**
Number of course titles, beyond the first year curriculum, offered last year: **81**
Percentages of upper division course sections, excluding seminars, with an enrollment of:

Under 25: **74%**	25 to 49: **18%**
50 to 74: **6%**	75 to 99: **2%**
100+: **1%**	

Areas of specialization: appellate advocacy, clinical training, dispute resolution, environmental law, health care law, intellectual property law, international law, tax law, trial advocacy

Fall 2009 faculty profile
Total teaching faculty: **56**. Full-time: **63%**; **71%** men, **29%** women, **17%** minorities. Part-time: **38%**; **100%** men, **N/A** women, **N/A** minorities
Student-to-faculty ratio: **9.4**

SPECIAL PROGRAMS *(as provided by law school):*
Community Legal Practice Center, Black Lung Benefits Program, VA Capital Case Clearinghouse, externships with public interest employers and judges, Shepherd Poverty Program. Exchange programs with law schools in Germany, Ireland, Denmark, and Canada. Transnational Law Institute, Criminal Justice Clinic, Tax Clinic

STUDENT BODY
Fall 2009 full-time enrollment: 390

Men: **57%**	Women: **43%**
African-American: **7.90%**	American Indian: **1.50%**
Asian-American: **5.40%**	Mexican-American: **0.30%**
Puerto Rican: **0.00%**	Other Hisp-Amer: **3.60%**
White: **78.50%**	International: **2.30%**
Unknown: **0.50%**	

Attrition rates for 2008-2009 full-time students
Percent of students discontinuing law school:

Men: **3%**   Women: **1%**
First-year students: **N/A**   Second-year students: **7%**
Third-year students: **N/A**   Fourth-year students: **N/A**

LIBRARY RESOURCES
Total titles: **193,666**
Total volumes: **444,532**
Total seats available for library users: **517**

INFORMATION TECHNOLOGY
Number of wired network connections available to students: **325** total (in the law library, excluding computer labs: **10**; in classrooms: **305**; in computer labs: **0**; elsewhere in the law school: **10**)
Law school has a wireless network.
Students are not required to own a computer.

EMPLOYMENT AND SALARIES
Proportion of 2008 graduates employed at graduation: **82%**
Employed 9 months later, as of February 15, 2009: **89%**
Salaries in the private sector (law firms, business, industry): **$80,000 –$160,000** (25th-75th percentile)
Median salary in the private sector: **$128,500**
Percentage in the private sector who reported salary information: **89%**
Median salary in public service (government, judicial clerkships, academic posts, non-profits): **$50,000**

Percentage of 2008 graduates in:
Law firms: **57%**   Government: **9%**
Bus./industry: **7%**   Judicial clerkship: **20%**
Public interest: **6%**   Unknown: **0%**
Academia : **1%**

2008 graduates employed in-state: **27%**
2008 graduates employed in foreign countries: **2%**
Number of states where graduates are employed: **27**
Percentage of 2008 graduates working in: New England: **3%**, Middle Atlantic: **19%**, East North Central: **5%**, West North Central: **0%**, South Atlantic: **52%**, East South Central: **4%**, West South Central: **4%**, Mountain: **4%**, Pacific: **6%**, Unknown: **1%**

BAR PASSAGE RATES
Based on 2008 graduates taking Summer 2008 or Winter 2009 exams. Most of the school's first-time test takers took the bar in Virginia.

84%

School's bar passage rate for first-time test takers

82%

Statewide bar passage rate for first-time test takers

Washington University in St. Louis

- 1 Brookings Drive, Box 1120, St. Louis, MO, 63130
- http://www.law.wustl.edu/
- Private
- Year founded: 1867
- 2009-2010 tuition: full-time: $42,330; part-time: N/A
- Enrollment 2009-10 academic year: full-time: 851; part-time: 5
- U.S. News 2010 law specialty ranking: clinical training: 5, international law: 14, trial advocacy: 7

3.30-3.80 GPA, 25TH-75TH PERCENTILE

161-168 LSAT, 25TH-75TH PERCENTILE

27% ACCEPTANCE RATE

19 2011 U.S. NEWS LAW SCHOOL RANKING

ADMISSIONS

Admissions phone number: **(314) 935-4525**
Admissions email address: **admiss@wulaw.wustl.edu**
Application website:
  http://law.wustl.edu/admissions/index.asp?id=92
Application deadline for Fall 2011 admission: **1-Mar**

Admissions statistics:
Number of applicants for Fall 2009: **3,690**
Number of acceptances: **987**
Number enrolled: **261**
Acceptance rate: **27%**
GPA, 25th-75th percentile, entering class Fall 2009: **3.30-3.80**
LSAT, 25th-75th percentile, entering class Fall 2009: **161-168**

FINANCIAL AID

Financial aid phone number: **(314) 935-4605**
Financial aid application deadline: **1-Mar**
Tuition 2009-2010 academic year: **full-time: $42,330; part-time: N/A**
Room and board: **$11,000** ; books: **$2,000** ; miscellaneous expenses: **$6,600**
Total of room/board/books/miscellaneous expenses: **$19,600**
University offers graduate student housing for which law students are eligible.

Financial aid profile
Percent of students that received grants for the 2008-2009 academic year: full-time: **61%**
Median grant amount: full-time: **$20,000**
The average law-school debt of those in the Class of 2009 who borrowed: **$106,614** . Proportion who borrowed: **71%**

ACADEMIC PROGRAMS

Calendar: **semester**
Joint degrees awarded: **J.D./M.B.A.; J.D./M.A. East Asian Studies; J.D./M.S.W.; J.D./M.A. European Studies;**
J.D./M.S. Biology; J.D./M.H.A.; J.D./M.S. Engineering and Policy; J.D./M.A. Political Economy; J.D./M.A. Islamic Studies; J.D./M.A. International Affairs; J.D./M.A. History; J.D./M.S. Environmental Engineering
Typical first-year section size: Full-time: **96**
Is there typically a "small section" of the first year class, other than Legal Writing, taught by full-time faculty?:
  Full-time: **yes**
Number of course titles, beyond the first year curriculum, offered last year: **154**
Percentages of upper division course sections, excluding seminars, with an enrollment of:
  Under 25: **60%**   25 to 49: **25%**
  50 to 74: **11%**   75 to 99: **3%**
  100+: **1%**
Areas of specialization: appellate advocacy, clinical training, dispute resolution, environmental law, health care law, intellectual property law, international law, tax law, trial advocacy

Fall 2009 faculty profile
Total teaching faculty: **143**. Full-time: **46%**; **44%** men, **56%** women, **8%** minorities. Part-time: **54%**; **82%** men, **18%** women, **10%** minorities
Student-to-faculty ratio: **10.7**

SPECIAL PROGRAMS *(as provided by law school):*
Clinical Courses and Externships:
http://law.wustl.edu/clinics_programs; Summer School Program: http://law.case.edu/summer-institute; Centers and Institutes: http://law.wustl.edu/centers_institutes/; Joint degrees: http://law.wustl.edu/academics/index.asp?id=59

STUDENT BODY
Fall 2009 full-time enrollment: **851**

Men: **58%**	Women: **42%**
African-American: **10.60%**	American Indian: **0.70%**
Asian-American: **10.60%**	Mexican-American: **0.50%**
Puerto Rican: **0.40%**	Other Hisp-Amer: **1.30%**
White: **49.60%**	International: **6.70%**
Unknown: **19.70%**	

Fall 2009 part-time enrollment: 5

Men: **40%**	Women: **60%**
African-American: **0.00%**	American Indian: **0.00%**
Asian-American: **60.00%**	Mexican-American: **0.00%**
Puerto Rican: **0.00%**	Other Hisp-Amer: **0.00%**
White: **40.00%**	International: **0.00%**
Unknown: **0.00%**	

Attrition rates for 2008-2009 full-time students

Percent of students discontinuing law school:

Men: **2%**	Women: **3%**
First-year students: **6%**	Second-year students: **2%**
Third-year students: **N/A**	Fourth-year students: **N/A**

LIBRARY RESOURCES

Total titles: **224,898**
Total volumes: **718,831**
Total seats available for library users: **486**

INFORMATION TECHNOLOGY

Number of wired network connections available to students: **814** total (in the law library, excluding computer labs: **415**; in classrooms: **300**; in computer labs: **14**; elsewhere in the law school: **85**)

Law school has a wireless network.

Students are not required to own a computer.

EMPLOYMENT AND SALARIES

Proportion of 2008 graduates employed at graduation: **89%**

Employed 9 months later, as of February 15, 2009: **95%**

Salaries in the private sector (law firms, business, industry): **$110,000 –$160,000** (25th-75th percentile)

Median salary in the private sector: **$152,500**

Percentage in the private sector who reported salary information: **65%**

Median salary in public service (government, judicial clerkships, academic posts, non-profits): **$39,750**

Percentage of 2008 graduates in:

Law firms: **62%**	Government: **11%**
Bus./industry: **10%**	Judicial clerkship: **11%**
Public interest: **2%**	Unknown: **3%**
Academia : **2%**	

2008 graduates employed in-state: **23%**

2008 graduates employed in foreign countries: **4%**

Number of states where graduates are employed: **30**

Percentage of 2008 graduates working in: New England: **2%**, Middle Atlantic: **14%**, East North Central: **16%**, West North Central: **24%**, South Atlantic: **17%**, East South Central: **3%**, West South Central: **6%**, Mountain: **4%**, Pacific: **7%**, Unknown: **4%**

BAR PASSAGE RATES

Based on 2008 graduates taking Summer 2008 or Winter 2009 exams. Most of the school's first-time test takers took the bar in Missouri.

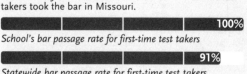

100%

School's bar passage rate for first-time test takers

91%

Statewide bar passage rate for first-time test takers

Wayne State University

- 471 W. Palmer Street, Detroit, MI, 48202
- http://www.law.wayne.edu
- Public
- **Year founded:** 1927
- **2009-2010 tuition:** full-time: $23,713; part-time: $12,815
- **Enrollment 2009-10 academic year:** full-time: 457; part-time: 112
- U.S. News 2010 law specialty ranking: N/A

3.25-3.69 GPA, 25TH-75TH PERCENTILE

153-159 LSAT, 25TH-75TH PERCENTILE

39% ACCEPTANCE RATE

Tier 3 2011 U.S. NEWS LAW SCHOOL RANKING

ADMISSIONS

Admissions phone number: (313) 577-3937
Admissions email address: lawinquire@wayne.edu
Application website: http://www.law.wayne.edu
Application deadline for Fall 2011 admission: 15-Mar

Admissions statistics:

Number of applicants for Fall 2009: 1,364
Number of acceptances: 537
Number enrolled: 163
Acceptance rate: 39%
GPA, 25th-75th percentile, entering class Fall 2009: **3.25-3.69**
LSAT, 25th-75th percentile, entering class Fall 2009: **153-159**

Part-time program:

Number of applicants for Fall 2009: **146**
Number of acceptances: **31**
Number enrolled: **22**
Acceptance rate: **21%**
GPA, 25th-75th percentile, entering class Fall 2009: **3.11-3.70**
LSAT, 25th-75th percentile, entering class Fall 2009: **154-160**

FINANCIAL AID

Financial aid phone number: (313) 577-5142
Financial aid application deadline: 1-Mar
Tuition 2009-2010 academic year: **full-time: $23,713; part-time: $12,815**
Room and board: $12,350 ; books: $1,240 ; miscellaneous expenses: $9,090
Total of room/board/books/miscellaneous expenses: $22,680
University offers graduate student housing for which law students are eligible.

Financial aid profile

Percent of students that received grants for the 2008-2009 academic year: full-time: **70%**; part-time **22%**

Median grant amount: full-time: **$4,000** ; part-time: **$5,200**
The average law-school debt of those in the Class of 2009 who borrowed: **$61,180** . Proportion who borrowed: **90%**

ACADEMIC PROGRAMS

Calendar: **semester**
Joint degrees awarded: **J.D./M.A. History; J.D./M.A. Political Science; J.D./M.B.A.; J.D./M.A. Dispute Resolution; J.D./M.A. Economics**
Typical first-year section size: Full-time: **90**; Part-time: **43**
Is there typically a "small section" of the first year class, other than Legal Writing, taught by full-time faculty?: Full-time: **yes**; Part-time: **no**
Number of course titles, beyond the first year curriculum, offered last year: **75**
Percentages of upper division course sections, excluding seminars, with an enrollment of:

Under 25: **66%**	25 to 49: **21%**
50 to 74: **11%**	75 to 99: **2%**
100+: **0%**	

Areas of specialization: appellate advocacy, clinical training, dispute resolution, environmental law, health care law, intellectual property law, international law, tax law, trial advocacy

Fall 2009 faculty profile

Total teaching faculty: **58**. Full-time: **59%**; **59%** men, **41%** women, **15%** minorities. Part-time: **41%**; **88%** men, **13%** women, **0%** minorities
Student-to-faculty ratio: **14.4**

SPECIAL PROGRAMS *(as provided by law school):*

Wayne State offers six clinics (Asylum/Immigration, Child Advocacy, Criminal Appeals, Disability, Environmental, and Small Business/Nonprofit). We place 90-120 students per year in internships with judges, prosecutors, public defenders, government agencies, public interest law offices, and nonprofit organizations. We have a summer term, and exchange programs with several foreign universities.

STUDENT BODY

Fall 2009 full-time enrollment: 457

Men: 50%	Women: 50%
African-American: 6.10%	American Indian: 1.10%
Asian-American: 4.40%	Mexican-American: 1.10%
Puerto Rican: 0.00%	Other Hisp-Amer: 1.30%
White: 82.70%	International: 3.30%
Unknown: 0.00%	

Fall 2009 part-time enrollment: 112

Men: 50%	Women: 50%
African-American: 14.30%	American Indian: 0.90%
Asian-American: 3.60%	Mexican-American: 0.00%
Puerto Rican: 0.00%	Other Hisp-Amer: 1.80%
White: 77.70%	International: 1.80%
Unknown: 0.00%	

Attrition rates for 2008-2009 full-time students
Percent of students discontinuing law school:

Men: 4%	Women: 2%
First-year students: 4%	Second-year students: 8%
Third-year students: N/A	Fourth-year students: N/A

LIBRARY RESOURCES

Total titles: 493,288
Total volumes: 627,452
Total seats available for library users: 400

INFORMATION TECHNOLOGY

Number of wired network connections available to students: 203 total (in the law library, excluding computer labs: 68; in classrooms: 46; in computer labs: 25; elsewhere in the law school: 64)
Law school has a wireless network.
Students are not required to own a computer.

EMPLOYMENT AND SALARIES

Proportion of 2008 graduates employed at graduation: N/A
Employed 9 months later, as of February 15, 2009: 88%
Salaries in the private sector (law firms, business, industry): $50,000 –$100,000 (25th-75th percentile)
Median salary in the private sector: $75,000
Percentage in the private sector who reported salary information: 86%
Median salary in public service (government, judicial clerkships, academic posts, non-profits): $48,000

Percentage of 2008 graduates in:

Law firms: 66%	Government: 12%
Bus./industry: 13%	Judicial clerkship: 2%
Public interest: 6%	Unknown: 0%
Academia : 2%	

2008 graduates employed in-state: 90%
2008 graduates employed in foreign countries: 0%
Number of states where graduates are employed: 10
Percentage of 2008 graduates working in: New England: 0%, Middle Atlantic: 1%, East North Central: 90%, West North Central: 0%, South Atlantic: 5%, East South Central: 0%, West South Central: 1%, Mountain: 0%, Pacific: 4%, Unknown: 0%

BAR PASSAGE RATES

Based on 2008 graduates taking Summer 2008 or Winter 2009 exams. Most of the school's first-time test takers took the bar in Michigan.

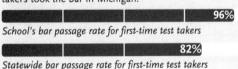

96%
School's bar passage rate for first-time test takers

82%
Statewide bar passage rate for first-time test takers

West Virginia University

- PO Box 6130, Morgantown, WV, 26506-6130
- http://law.wvu.edu/
- Public
- Year founded: 1878
- 2009-2010 tuition: full-time: $10,644; part-time: $595/credit hour
- Enrollment 2009-10 academic year: full-time: 412; part-time: 6
- U.S. News 2010 law specialty ranking: N/A

3.12-3.70 GPA, 25TH-75TH PERCENTILE

151-156 LSAT, 25TH-75TH PERCENTILE

50% ACCEPTANCE RATE

93 2011 U.S. NEWS LAW SCHOOL RANKING

ADMISSIONS

Admissions phone number: **(304) 293-5304**
Admissions email address: **wvu-law.admissions@mail.wvu.edu**
Application website: **https://law.wvu.edu/admissions**
Application deadline for Fall 2011 admission: **1-Mar**

Admissions statistics:
Number of applicants for Fall 2009: **648**
Number of acceptances: **327**
Number enrolled: **153**
Acceptance rate: **50%**
GPA, 25th-75th percentile, entering class Fall 2009: **3.12-3.70**
LSAT, 25th-75th percentile, entering class Fall 2009: **151-156**

FINANCIAL AID

Financial aid phone number: **(304) 293-5302**
Financial aid application deadline: **1-Mar**
Tuition 2009-2010 academic year: **full-time: $10,644; part-time: $595/credit hour**
Room and board: **$8,900** ; books: **$1,250** ; miscellaneous expenses: **$2,840**
Total of room/board/books/miscellaneous expenses: **$12,990**
University offers graduate student housing for which law students are eligible.

Financial aid profile
Percent of students that received grants for the 2008-2009 academic year: full-time: **50%**
Median grant amount: full-time: **$5,322**
The average law-school debt of those in the Class of 2009 who borrowed: **$65,602** . Proportion who borrowed: **84%**

ACADEMIC PROGRAMS

Calendar: **semester**
Joint degrees awarded: **J.D./M.B.A.; J.D./M.P.A.**
Typical first-year section size: Full-time: **70**; Part-time: **70**
Is there typically a "small section" of the first year class,

other than Legal Writing, taught by full-time faculty?:
Full-time: **no**; Part-time: **no**
Number of course titles, beyond the first year curriculum, offered last year: **79**
Percentages of upper division course sections, excluding seminars, with an enrollment of:
Under 25: **53%**   25 to 49: **34%**
50 to 74: **10%**   75 to 99: **3%**
100+: **0%**
Areas of specialization: appellate advocacy, clinical training, dispute resolution, environmental law, health care law, intellectual property law, international law, tax law, trial advocacy

Fall 2009 faculty profile
Total teaching faculty: **53**. Full-time: **53%**; **82%** men, **18%** women, **21%** minorities. Part-time: **47%**; **56%** men, **44%** women, **0%** minorities
Student-to-faculty ratio: **12.9**

SPECIAL PROGRAMS *(as provided by law school):*
Live client controversy clinical program (civil, tax, innocence project, immigration cases); Entrepreneurial clinic; Federal Judicial Externship Program; summer international study.

STUDENT BODY
Fall 2009 full-time enrollment: **412**

Men: **59%**	Women: **41%**
African-American: **5.60%**	American Indian: **0.20%**
Asian-American: **1.70%**	Mexican-American: **0.00%**
Puerto Rican: **0.00%**	Other Hisp-Amer: **0.20%**
White: **92.20%**	International: **0.00%**
Unknown: **0.00%**	

Fall 2009 part-time enrollment: **6**

Men: **83%**	Women: **17%**
African-American: **16.70%**	American Indian: **0.00%**
Asian-American: **0.00%**	Mexican-American: **0.00%**
Puerto Rican: **0.00%**	Other Hisp-Amer: **0.00%**
White: **83.30%**	International: **0.00%**
Unknown: **0.00%**	

Percent of students discontinuing law school:

Men: **4%**   Women: **2%**

First-year students: **8%**   Second-year students: **N/A**

Third-year students: **N/A**   Fourth-year students: **N/A**

LIBRARY RESOURCES

Total titles: **86,212**

Total volumes: **361,080**

Total seats available for library users: **383**

INFORMATION TECHNOLOGY

Number of wired network connections available to students: **140** total (in the law library, excluding computer labs: **130**; in classrooms: **0**; in computer labs: **0**; elsewhere in the law school: **10**)

Law school has a wireless network.

Students are not required to own a computer.

EMPLOYMENT AND SALARIES

Proportion of 2008 graduates employed at graduation: **70%**

Employed 9 months later, as of February 15, 2009: **98%**

Salaries in the private sector (law firms, business, industry): **$55,000 –$73,000** (25th-75th percentile)

Median salary in the private sector: **$66,000**

Percentage in the private sector who reported salary information: **58%**

Median salary in public service (government, judicial clerkships, academic posts, non-profits): **$42,612**

Percentage of 2008 graduates in:

Law firms: **45%**   Government: **8%**

Bus./industry: **23%**   Judicial clerkship: **16%**

Public interest: **5%**   Unknown: **0%**

Academia : **3%**

2008 graduates employed in-state: **73%**

2008 graduates employed in foreign countries: **0%**

Number of states where graduates are employed: **16**

Percentage of 2008 graduates working in: New England: **1%**, Middle Atlantic: **9%**, East North Central: **2%**, West North Central: **0%**, South Atlantic: **86%**, East South Central: **1%**, West South Central: **0%**, Mountain: **1%**, Pacific: **0%**, Unknown: **0%**

BAR PASSAGE RATES

Based on 2008 graduates taking Summer 2008 or Winter 2009 exams. Most of the school's first-time test takers took the bar in West Virginia.

76%

School's bar passage rate for first-time test takers

79%

Statewide bar passage rate for first-time test takers

Western New England College

- 1215 Wilbraham Road, Springfield, MA, 01119-2684
- http://www.law.wnec.edu
- Private
- Year founded: 1919
- 2009-2010 tuition: full-time: $35,612; part-time: $26,328
- Enrollment 2009-10 academic year: full-time: 389; part-time: 149
- U.S. News 2010 law specialty ranking: N/A

2.94-3.55 GPA, 25TH-75TH PERCENTILE

151-156 LSAT, 25TH-75TH PERCENTILE

54% ACCEPTANCE RATE

Tier 4 2011 U.S. NEWS LAW SCHOOL RANKING

ADMISSIONS

Admissions phone number: **(413) 782-1406**
Admissions email address: **admissions@law.wnec.edu**
Application website:
  http://assets.wnec.edu/21/LawApp_2010.pdf
Application deadline for Fall 2011 admission: **15-Mar**

Admissions statistics:

Number of applicants for Fall 2009: **1,423**
Number of acceptances: **769**
Number enrolled: **131**
Acceptance rate: **54%**
GPA, 25th-75th percentile, entering class Fall 2009: **2.94-3.55**
LSAT, 25th-75th percentile, entering class Fall 2009: **151-156**

Part-time program:

Number of applicants for Fall 2009: **273**
Number of acceptances: **132**
Number enrolled: **50**
Acceptance rate: **48%**
GPA, 25th-75th percentile, entering class Fall 2009: **3.09-3.40**
LSAT, 25th-75th percentile, entering class Fall 2009: **147-151**

FINANCIAL AID

Financial aid phone number: **(413) 796-2080**
Financial aid application deadline:
Tuition 2009-2010 academic year: **full-time: $35,612; part-time: $26,328**
Room and board: **$13,400** ; books: **$1,528** ; miscellaneous expenses: **$6,465**
Total of room/board/books/miscellaneous expenses: **$21,393**
University does not offer graduate student housing for which law students are eligible.

Financial aid profile

Percent of students that received grants for the 2008-2009 academic year: full-time: **67%**; part-time **39%**
Median grant amount: full-time: **$13,000** ; part-time: **$4,000**
The average law-school debt of those in the Class of 2009 who borrowed: **$94,496** . Proportion who borrowed: **62%**

ACADEMIC PROGRAMS

Calendar: **semester**
Joint degrees awarded: **J.D./M.S.W. ; J.D./M.R.P. ; J.D./M.B.A.**
Typical first-year section size: Full-time: **46**; Part-time: **40**
Is there typically a "small section" of the first year class, other than Legal Writing, taught by full-time faculty?:
  Full-time: **no**; Part-time: **no**
Number of course titles, beyond the first year curriculum, offered last year: **95**
Percentages of upper division course sections, excluding seminars, with an enrollment of:
  Under 25: **46%**   25 to 49: **38%**
  50 to 74: **13%**   75 to 99: **2%**
  100+: **0%**
Areas of specialization: appellate advocacy, clinical training, dispute resolution, environmental law, health care law, intellectual property law, international law, tax law, trial advocacy

Fall 2009 faculty profile

Total teaching faculty: **46**. Full-time: **63%**; **48%** men, **52%** women, **17%** minorities. Part-time: **37%**; **82%** men, **18%** women, **0%** minorities
Student-to-faculty ratio: **12.7**

SPECIAL PROGRAMS (as provided by law school):

1L classes: 50 students or less. Clinics: Criminal; Consumer Protection; Legal Services; Small Business; Real Estate. Externships: Judicial & Public Interest. Centers: Law & Business Advancing Entrepreneurship; Legislative & Governmental Affairs. Skills training simulation courses. Concentrations: Criminal; Business; Estate Planning; International & Comparative; Public Interest; Real Estate.

STUDENT BODY

Fall 2009 full-time enrollment: 389

Men: 48%	Women: 52%
African-American: 2.30%	American Indian: 0.50%
Asian-American: 5.40%	Mexican-American: 0.00%
Puerto Rican: 0.00%	Other Hisp-Amer: 3.60%
White: 74.30%	International: 0.80%
Unknown: 13.10%	

Fall 2009 part-time enrollment: 149

Men: 46%	Women: 54%
African-American: 5.40%	American Indian: 0.00%
Asian-American: 2.00%	Mexican-American: 0.00%
Puerto Rican: 0.00%	Other Hisp-Amer: 3.40%
White: 72.50%	International: 0.00%
Unknown: 16.80%	

Attrition rates for 2008-2009 full-time students
Percent of students discontinuing law school:

Men: 5%	Women: 4%
First-year students: 12%	Second-year students: 2%
Third-year students: N/A	Fourth-year students: N/A

LIBRARY RESOURCES

Total titles: 139,209
Total volumes: 357,451
Total seats available for library users: 482

INFORMATION TECHNOLOGY

Number of wired network connections available to students: 58 total (in the law library, excluding computer labs: 12; in classrooms: 8; in computer labs: 33; elsewhere in the law school: 5)
Law school has a wireless network.
Students are not required to own a computer.

EMPLOYMENT AND SALARIES

Proportion of 2008 graduates employed at graduation: N/A
Employed 9 months later, as of February 15, 2009: 81%
Salaries in the private sector (law firms, business, industry): $50,000 –$75,000 (25th-75th percentile)
Median salary in the private sector: $60,000
Percentage in the private sector who reported salary information: 33%
Median salary in public service (government, judicial clerkships, academic posts, non-profits): $47,000

Percentage of 2008 graduates in:

Law firms: 49%	Government: 10%
Bus./industry: 17%	Judicial clerkship: 16%
Public interest: 8%	Unknown: 0%
Academia : 2%	

2008 graduates employed in-state: 36%
2008 graduates employed in foreign countries: 1%
Number of states where graduates are employed: 16
Percentage of 2008 graduates working in: New England: 71%, Middle Atlantic: 18%, East North Central: 1%, West North Central: 1%, South Atlantic: 3%, East South Central: 1%, West South Central: 1%, Mountain: 2%, Pacific: 1%, Unknown: 0%

BAR PASSAGE RATES

Based on 2008 graduates taking Summer 2008 or Winter 2009 exams. Most of the school's first-time test takers took the bar in Connecticut.

77%
School's bar passage rate for first-time test takers

87%
Statewide bar passage rate for first-time test takers

Western State University

- 1111 N. State College Boulevard, Fullerton, CA, 92831
- http://www.wsulaw.edu
- Private
- Year founded: 1966
- 2009-2010 tuition: full-time: $32,870; part-time: $22,070
- Enrollment 2009-10 academic year: full-time: 276; part-time: 141
- U.S. News 2010 law specialty ranking: N/A

2.83-3.40 GPA, 25TH-75TH PERCENTILE

149-154 LSAT, 25TH-75TH PERCENTILE

52% ACCEPTANCE RATE

Tier 4 2011 U.S. NEWS LAW SCHOOL RANKING

ADMISSIONS
Admissions phone number: **(714) 459-1101**
Admissions email address: **adm@wsulaw.edu**
Application website:
https://www.applyweb.com/aw?wsulaw
Application deadline for Fall 2011 admission: **1-Jun**

Admissions statistics:
Number of applicants for Fall 2009: **1,266**
Number of acceptances: **663**
Number enrolled: **130**
Acceptance rate: **52%**
GPA, 25th-75th percentile, entering class Fall 2009: **2.83-3.40**
LSAT, 25th-75th percentile, entering class Fall 2009: **149-154**

Part-time program:
Number of applicants for Fall 2009: **374**
Number of acceptances: **131**
Number enrolled: **58**
Acceptance rate: **35%**
GPA, 25th-75th percentile, entering class Fall 2009: **2.81-3.36**
LSAT, 25th-75th percentile, entering class Fall 2009: **148-154**

FINANCIAL AID
Financial aid phone number: **(714) 459-1120**
Financial aid application deadline: **2-Mar**
Tuition 2009-2010 academic year: **full-time: $32,870; part-time: $22,070**
Room and board: **$14,018** ; books: **$1,500** ; miscellaneous expenses: **$7,299**
Total of room/board/books/miscellaneous expenses: **$22,817**
University does not offer graduate student housing for which law students are eligible.

Financial aid profile
Percent of students that received grants for the 2008-2009 academic year: full-time: **49%**; part-time **47%**
Median grant amount: full-time: **$12,000** ; part-time: **$6,475**
The average law-school debt of those in the Class of 2009 who borrowed: **$97,530** . Proportion who borrowed: **89%**

ACADEMIC PROGRAMS
Calendar: **semester**
Joint degrees awarded: **J.D./M.B.A.**
Typical first-year section size: Full-time: **52**; Part-time: **35**
Is there typically a "small section" of the first year class, other than Legal Writing, taught by full-time faculty?: Full-time: **no**; Part-time: **no**
Number of course titles, beyond the first year curriculum, offered last year: **48**
Percentages of upper division course sections, excluding seminars, with an enrollment of:
- Under 25: **74%**   25 to 49: **16%**
- 50 to 74: **10%**   75 to 99: **0%**
- 100+: **0%**

Areas of specialization: appellate advocacy, clinical training, dispute resolution, environmental law, health care law, intellectual property law, international law, tax law, trial advocacy

Fall 2009 faculty profile
Total teaching faculty: **34**. Full-time: **41%**; **71%** men, **29%** women, **14%** minorities. Part-time: **59%**; **65%** men, **35%** women, **35%** minorities
Student-to-faculty ratio: **22.6**

SPECIAL PROGRAMS (as provided by law school):
On Site Civil and Family Law Clinic; Business Law Center offers Certificate in Business Law; Criminal Law Practice Center offers Certificate in Criminal Law; Civil and Criminal Internships and Externships.

STUDENT BODY

Fall 2009 full-time enrollment: 276

Men: 50%
African-American: 2.50%
Asian-American: 16.70%
Puerto Rican: 0.00%
White: 56.50%
Unknown: 7.60%

Women: 50%
American Indian: 0.40%
Mexican-American: 7.20%
Other Hisp-Amer: 6.50%
International: 2.50%

Fall 2009 part-time enrollment: 141

Men: 50%
African-American: 6.40%
Asian-American: 17.70%
Puerto Rican: 0.00%
White: 56.70%
Unknown: 7.80%

Women: 50%
American Indian: 1.40%
Mexican-American: 4.30%
Other Hisp-Amer: 5.70%
International: 0.00%

Attrition rates for 2008-2009 full-time students
Percent of students discontinuing law school:

Men: 15%
First-year students: 33%
Third-year students: 2%

Women: 21%
Second-year students: 9%
Fourth-year students: N/A

LIBRARY RESOURCES

Total titles: 49,549
Total volumes: 203,832
Total seats available for library users: 336

INFORMATION TECHNOLOGY

Number of wired network connections available to students: 42 total (in the law library, excluding computer labs: 15; in classrooms: 9; in computer labs: 16; elsewhere in the law school: 2)
Law school has a wireless network.
Students are not required to own a computer.

EMPLOYMENT AND SALARIES

Proportion of 2008 graduates employed at graduation:
N/A
Employed 9 months later, as of February 15, 2009: 71%
Salaries in the private sector (law firms, business, industry): $39,250 –$90,000 (25th-75th percentile)
Median salary in the private sector: $55,640
Percentage in the private sector who reported salary information: 73%
Median salary in public service (government, judicial clerkships, academic posts, non-profits): $60,000

Percentage of 2008 graduates in:

Law firms: 76%
Bus./industry: 13%
Public interest: 1%
Academia : 4%

Government: 6%
Judicial clerkship: 0%
Unknown: 0%

2008 graduates employed in-state: 81%
2008 graduates employed in foreign countries: 0%
Number of states where graduates are employed: 12
Percentage of 2008 graduates working in: New England: 0%, Middle Atlantic: 1%, East North Central: 3%, West North Central: 0%, South Atlantic: 1%, East South Central: 1%, West South Central: 1%, Mountain: 9%, Pacific: 84%, Unknown: 0%

BAR PASSAGE RATES

Based on 2008 graduates taking Summer 2008 or Winter 2009 exams. Most of the school's first-time test takers took the bar in California.

65%
School's bar passage rate for first-time test takers

71%
Statewide bar passage rate for first-time test takers

Whittier College

- 3333 Harbor Boulevard, Costa Mesa, CA, 92626-1501
- http://www.law.whittier.edu
- Private
- Year founded: 1975
- 2009-2010 tuition: full-time: $37,060; part-time: $24,720
- Enrollment 2009-10 academic year: full-time: 450; part-time: 141
- U.S. News 2010 law specialty ranking: N/A

2.82-3.35 GPA, 25TH-75TH PERCENTILE

149-153 LSAT, 25TH-75TH PERCENTILE

47% ACCEPTANCE RATE

Tier 4 2011 U.S. NEWS LAW SCHOOL RANKING

ADMISSIONS

Admissions phone number: (800) 808-8188
Admissions email address: info@law.whittier.edu
Application website:
http://www.law.whittier.edu/pstudents/admissions/adm
issions_apply.html
Application deadline for Fall 2011 admission: 15-Jul

Admissions statistics:

Number of applicants for Fall 2009: 1,914
Number of acceptances: 906
Number enrolled: 235
Acceptance rate: 47%
GPA, 25th-75th percentile, entering class Fall 2009: 2.82-3.35
LSAT, 25th-75th percentile, entering class Fall 2009: 149-153

Part-time program:

Number of applicants for Fall 2009: 370
Number of acceptances: 134
Number enrolled: 61
Acceptance rate: 36%
GPA, 25th-75th percentile, entering class Fall 2009: 2.85-3.40
LSAT, 25th-75th percentile, entering class Fall 2009: 149-153

FINANCIAL AID

Financial aid phone number: (714) 444-4141
Financial aid application deadline: 1-May
Tuition 2009-2010 academic year: full-time: $37,060; part-time: $24,720
Room and board: $16,944 ; books: $1,740 ; miscellaneous expenses: $8,376
Total of room/board/books/miscellaneous expenses: $27,060
University does not offer graduate student housing for which law students are eligible.

Financial aid profile

Percent of students that received grants for the 2008-2009 academic year: full-time: 35%; part-time 36%
Median grant amount: full-time: $15,000 ; part-time: $8,000
The average law-school debt of those in the Class of 2009 who borrowed: $96,506 . Proportion who borrowed: 94%

ACADEMIC PROGRAMS

Calendar: semester
Joint degrees awarded: N/A
Typical first-year section size: Full-time: 85; Part-time: 55
Is there typically a "small section" of the first year class, other than Legal Writing, taught by full-time faculty?: Full-time: no; Part-time: no
Number of course titles, beyond the first year curriculum, offered last year: 112
Percentages of upper division course sections, excluding seminars, with an enrollment of:

Under 25: 80%	25 to 49: 16%
50 to 74: 3%	75 to 99: 1%
100+: 0%	

Areas of specialization: appellate advocacy, clinical training, dispute resolution, environmental law, health care law, intellectual property law, international law, tax law, trial advocacy

Fall 2009 faculty profile

Total teaching faculty: 35. Full-time: 66%; 70% men, 30% women, 13% minorities. Part-time: 34%; 50% men, 50% women, 33% minorities
Student-to-faculty ratio: 17.6

SPECIAL PROGRAMS (as provided by law school):

Center for Children's Rights; Center for Intellectual Property Law; Center for International and Comparative Law; Exchange Programs in France and Spain; five Summer Abroad Programs: Spain, France, Amsterdam, China, and Israel; Institute for Student and Graduate Academic Support; Institute for Legal Writing and Professional Skills; LL.M. Degree in U.S. Legal Studies for Foreign Lawyers.

STUDENT BODY

Fall 2009 full-time enrollment: 450
Men: 44%	Women: 56%
African-American: 2.40%	American Indian: 0.40%
Asian-American: 14.90%	Mexican-American: 4.90%
Puerto Rican: 0.00%	Other Hisp-Amer: 5.30%
White: 31.80%	International: 0.40%
Unknown: 39.80%	

Fall 2009 part-time enrollment: 141
Men: 50%	Women: 50%
African-American: 3.50%	American Indian: 0.00%
Asian-American: 9.20%	Mexican-American: 6.40%
Puerto Rican: 0.70%	Other Hisp-Amer: 6.40%
White: 43.30%	International: 0.00%
Unknown: 30.50%	

Attrition rates for 2008-2009 full-time students
Percent of students discontinuing law school:
Men: 5%	Women: 4%
First-year students: 10%	Second-year students: 4%
Third-year students: 1%	Fourth-year students: N/A

LIBRARY RESOURCES

Total titles: 209,433
Total volumes: 443,239
Total seats available for library users: 386

INFORMATION TECHNOLOGY

Number of wired network connections available to students: 223 total (in the law library, excluding computer labs: 110; in classrooms: 0; in computer labs: 48; elsewhere in the law school: 65)
Law school has a wireless network.
Students are not required to own a computer.

EMPLOYMENT AND SALARIES

Proportion of 2008 graduates employed at graduation: 51%
Employed 9 months later, as of February 15, 2009: 96%
Salaries in the private sector (law firms, business, industry): $60,000 –$80,000 (25th-75th percentile)
Median salary in the private sector: $70,000
Percentage in the private sector who reported salary information: 48%
Median salary in public service (government, judicial clerkships, academic posts, non-profits): $65,000

Percentage of 2008 graduates in:
Law firms: 62%	Government: 8%
Bus./industry: 22%	Judicial clerkship: 2%
Public interest: 3%	Unknown: 0%
Academia : 3%	

2008 graduates employed in-state: 86%
2008 graduates employed in foreign countries: 4%
Number of states where graduates are employed: 17
Percentage of 2008 graduates working in: New England: 0%, Middle Atlantic: 1%, East North Central: 3%, West North Central: 0%, South Atlantic: 3%, East South Central: 1%, West South Central: 0%, Mountain: 6%, Pacific: 83%, Unknown: 0%

BAR PASSAGE RATES

Based on 2008 graduates taking Summer 2008 or Winter 2009 exams. Most of the school's first-time test takers took the bar in California.

83%
School's bar passage rate for first-time test takers

71%
Statewide bar passage rate for first-time test takers

Widener University

- PO Box 7474, Wilmington, DE, 19803-0474
- http://www.law.widener.edu
- Private
- Year founded: 1971
- 2009-2010 tuition: full-time: $33,540; part-time: $24,620
- Enrollment 2009-10 academic year: full-time: 970; part-time: 466
- U.S. News 2010 law specialty ranking: healthcare law: 15

2.82-3.44	GPA, 25TH-75TH PERCENTILE
150-154	LSAT, 25TH-75TH PERCENTILE
57%	ACCEPTANCE RATE
Tier 4	2011 U.S. NEWS LAW SCHOOL RANKING

ADMISSIONS

Admissions phone number: (302) 477-2162
Admissions email address:
  law.admissions@law.widener.edu
Application website: http://www.law.widener.edu
Application deadline for Fall 2011 admission: 15-May

Admissions statistics:
Number of applicants for Fall 2009: 2,411
Number of acceptances: 1,368
Number enrolled: 392
Acceptance rate: 57%
GPA, 25th-75th percentile, entering class Fall 2009: 2.82-3.44
LSAT, 25th-75th percentile, entering class Fall 2009: 150-154

Part-time program:
Number of applicants for Fall 2009: 631
Number of acceptances: 281
Number enrolled: 174
Acceptance rate: 45%
GPA, 25th-75th percentile, entering class Fall 2009: 2.81-3.54
LSAT, 25th-75th percentile, entering class Fall 2009: 148-152

FINANCIAL AID

Financial aid phone number: (302) 477-2272
Financial aid application deadline: 1-Apr
Tuition 2009-2010 academic year: full-time: $33,540; part-time: $24,620
Room and board: $9,900 ; books: $1,200 ; miscellaneous expenses: $5,364
Total of room/board/books/miscellaneous expenses: $16,464
University offers graduate student housing for which law students are eligible.

Financial aid profile
Percent of students that received grants for the 2008-2009 academic year: full-time: 32%; part-time 18%
Median grant amount: full-time: $9,612 ; part-time: $7,028
The average law-school debt of those in the Class of 2009 who borrowed: $100,849 . Proportion who borrowed: 92%

ACADEMIC PROGRAMS

Calendar: semester
Joint degrees awarded: J.D./Psy.D; J.D./M.B.A.; J.D./M.S.L.S.; J.D./M.M.P.; J.D/M.P.H.; J.D./M.H.A.; M.J./M.H.A.
Typical first-year section size: Full-time: 69; Part-time: 45
Is there typically a "small section" of the first year class, other than Legal Writing, taught by full-time faculty?: Full-time: yes; Part-time: no
Number of course titles, beyond the first year curriculum, offered last year: 198
Percentages of upper division course sections, excluding seminars, with an enrollment of:

Under 25: 70%	25 to 49: 15%
50 to 74: 12%	75 to 99: 2%
100+: 1%	

Areas of specialization: appellate advocacy, clinical training, dispute resolution, environmental law, health care law, intellectual property law, international law, tax law, trial advocacy

Fall 2009 faculty profile
Total teaching faculty: 119. Full-time: 50%; 69% men, 31% women, 10% minorities. Part-time: 50%; 62% men, 38% women, 5% minorities
Student-to-faculty ratio: 19

SPECIAL PROGRAMS *(as provided by law school):*
Clinics: Env'l, CrimLaw, Veterans, 3 Civil Clinics. Pro bono opportunities. Judicial externships w/ fed/state courts in DE, PA, NJ, MD, VA, DC. Special institutes offer certificates in Health Law, Corp. Law, Tech & Trial Advoc., Law & Gov't. Health Law–LL.M., D.L., S.J.D., M.J.; Corp. Law/Finance–LL.M, M.J., D.L., S.J.D. Study Abroad: Chongqing, China; Summer Study: Sydney, Nairobi, Lausanne, Venice.

STUDENT BODY

Fall 2009 full-time enrollment: 970

Men: 57%   Women: 43%
African-American: 3.90%   American Indian: 0.20%
Asian-American: 4.80%   Mexican-American: 0.40%
Puerto Rican: 0.50%   Other Hisp-Amer: 2.40%
White: 74.10%   International: 0.10%
Unknown: 13.50%

Fall 2009 part-time enrollment: 466

Men: 50%   Women: 50%
African-American: 6.70%   American Indian: 1.10%
Asian-American: 3.90%   Mexican-American: 0.00%
Puerto Rican: 0.90%   Other Hisp-Amer: 0.90%
White: 72.10%   International: 0.00%
Unknown: 14.60%

Attrition rates for 2008-2009 full-time students

Percent of students discontinuing law school:
Men: 13%   Women: 11%
First-year students: 29%   Second-year students: 2%
Third-year students: N/A   Fourth-year students: N/A

LIBRARY RESOURCES

Total titles: 101,118
Total volumes: 590,752
Total seats available for library users: 670

INFORMATION TECHNOLOGY

Number of wired network connections available to students: 85 total (in the law library, excluding computer labs: 60; in classrooms: 25; in computer labs: 0; elsewhere in the law school: 0)
Law school has a wireless network.
Students are not required to own a computer.

EMPLOYMENT AND SALARIES

Proportion of 2008 graduates employed at graduation: 55%
Employed 9 months later, as of February 15, 2009: 84%
Salaries in the private sector (law firms, business, industry): $50,000 –$135,000 (25th-75th percentile)
Median salary in the private sector: $79,000
Percentage in the private sector who reported salary information: 35%
Median salary in public service (government, judicial clerkships, academic posts, non-profits): $42,000

Percentage of 2008 graduates in:

Law firms: 42%   Government: 12%
Bus./industry: 20%   Judicial clerkship: 20%
Public interest: 4%   Unknown: 0%
Academia : 2%

2008 graduates employed in-state: 16%
2008 graduates employed in foreign countries: 0%
Number of states where graduates are employed: 17
Percentage of 2008 graduates working in: New England: 0%, Middle Atlantic: 76%, East North Central: 0%, West North Central: 0%, South Atlantic: 22%, East South Central: 0%, West South Central: 0%, Mountain: 0%, Pacific: 1%, Unknown: 0%

BAR PASSAGE RATES

Based on 2008 graduates taking Summer 2008 or Winter 2009 exams. Most of the school's first-time test takers took the bar in Pennsylvania.

	88%

School's bar passage rate for first-time test takers

	87%

Statewide bar passage rate for first-time test takers

Willamette University (Collins)

■ 245 Winter Street SE, Salem, OR, 97301
■ http://www.willamette.edu/wucl
■ Private
■ Year founded: 1883
■ 2009-2010 tuition: full-time: $29,680; part-time: N/A
■ Enrollment 2009-10 academic year: full-time: 421; part-time: 5
■ U.S. News 2010 law specialty ranking: N/A

3.05-3.51 GPA, 25TH-75TH PERCENTILE

153-157 LSAT, 25TH-75TH PERCENTILE

39% ACCEPTANCE RATE

Tier 3 2011 U.S. NEWS LAW SCHOOL RANKING

ADMISSIONS

Admissions phone number: **(503) 370-6282**
Admissions email address: **law-admission@willamette.edu**
Application website:
   http://www.willamette.edu/wucl/admission/information
   /process.htm
Application deadline for Fall 2011 admission: **1-Mar**

Admissions statistics:
Number of applicants for Fall 2009: **1,532**
Number of acceptances: **598**
Number enrolled: **148**
Acceptance rate: **39%**
GPA, 25th-75th percentile, entering class Fall 2009: **3.05-3.51**
LSAT, 25th-75th percentile, entering class Fall 2009: **153-157**

FINANCIAL AID

Financial aid phone number: **(503) 370-6273**
Financial aid application deadline:
Tuition 2009-2010 academic year: **full-time: $29,680; part-time: N/A**
Room and board: **$14,510** ; books: **$1,460** ; miscellaneous expenses: **$80**
Total of room/board/books/miscellaneous expenses: **$16,050**
University offers graduate student housing for which law students are eligible.

Financial aid profile
Percent of students that received grants for the 2008-2009 academic year: full-time: **55%**
Median grant amount: full-time: **$12,000** ; part-time: **$0**
The average law-school debt of those in the Class of 2009 who borrowed: **$78,393** . Proportion who borrowed: **89%**

ACADEMIC PROGRAMS

Calendar: **semester**
Joint degrees awarded: **J.D./M.B.A.**
Typical first-year section size: Full-time: **80**

Is there typically a "small section" of the first year class, other than Legal Writing, taught by full-time faculty?:
   Full-time: **yes**; Part-time: **no**
Number of course titles, beyond the first year curriculum, offered last year: **N/A**
Percentages of upper division course sections, excluding seminars, with an enrollment of:
   Under 25: **67%**   25 to 49: **17%**
   50 to 74: **14%**   75 to 99: **0%**
   100+: **1%**
Areas of specialization: appellate advocacy, clinical training, dispute resolution, environmental law, health care law, intellectual property law, international law, tax law, trial advocacy

Fall 2009 faculty profile
Total teaching faculty: **35**. Full-time: **63%**; **64%** men, **36%** women, **18%** minorities. Part-time: **37%**; **77%** men, **23%** women, **8%** minorities
Student-to-faculty ratio: **15**

SPECIAL PROGRAMS *(as provided by law school):*
The law school offers certificate programs in business law, international and comparative law, sustainability, dispute resolution, and law and government. Students may also enroll in a joint degree program that offers an MBA in addition to the JD. The law school offers programs in foreign study enabling students to study in China, Ecuador and Germany and has an LLM program in Transnational Law.

STUDENT BODY
Fall 2009 full-time enrollment: **421**
Men: **57%**   Women: **43%**
African-American: **1.70%**   American Indian: **1.40%**
Asian-American: **7.60%**   Mexican-American: **2.40%**
Puerto Rican: **1.00%**   Other Hisp-Amer: **2.60%**
White: **74.30%**   International: **0.50%**
Unknown: **8.60%**

Fall 2009 part-time enrollment: 5
Men: **40%**   Women: **60%**

African-American: **0.00%** American Indian: **0.00%**
Asian-American: **0.00%** Mexican-American: **20.00%**
Puerto Rican: **0.00%** Other Hisp-Amer: **0.00%**
White: **60.00%** International: **0.00%**
Unknown: **20.00%**

Attrition rates for 2008-2009 full-time students
Percent of students discontinuing law school:
Men: **6%** Women: **8%**
First-year students: **11%** Second-year students: **9%**
Third-year students: **N/A** Fourth-year students: **N/A**

LIBRARY RESOURCES
Total titles: **40,195**
Total volumes: **299,123**
Total seats available for library users: **492**

INFORMATION TECHNOLOGY
Number of wired network connections available to students: **104** total (in the law library, excluding computer labs: **80**; in classrooms: **13**; in computer labs: **9**; elsewhere in the law school: **2**)
Law school has a wireless network.
Students are not required to own a computer.

EMPLOYMENT AND SALARIES
Proportion of 2008 graduates employed at graduation: **N/A**
Employed 9 months later, as of February 15, 2009: **91%**
Salaries in the private sector (law firms, business, industry): **$45,800 –$76,000** (25th-75th percentile)

Median salary in the private sector: **$59,625**
Percentage in the private sector who reported salary information: **65%**
Median salary in public service (government, judicial clerkships, academic posts, non-profits): **$45,000**

Percentage of 2008 graduates in:
Law firms: **49%** Government: **19%**
Bus./industry: **20%** Judicial clerkship: **6%**
Public interest: **5%** Unknown: **1%**
Academia : **1%**

2008 graduates employed in-state: **67%**
2008 graduates employed in foreign countries: **0%**
Number of states where graduates are employed: **14**
Percentage of 2008 graduates working in: New England: **0%**, Middle Atlantic: **0%**, East North Central: **1%**, West North Central: **0%**, South Atlantic: **6%**, East South Central: **2%**, West South Central: **0%**, Mountain: **11%**, Pacific: **80%**, Unknown: **0%**

BAR PASSAGE RATES
Based on 2008 graduates taking Summer 2008 or Winter 2009 exams. Most of the school's first-time test takers took the bar in Oregon.

84%
School's bar passage rate for first-time test takers

79%
Statewide bar passage rate for first-time test takers

William Mitchell College of Law

- 875 Summit Avenue, St. Paul, MN, 55105-3076
- http://www.wmitchell.edu
- Private
- Year founded: 1900
- 2009-2010 tuition: full-time: $32,340; part-time: $23,400
- Enrollment 2009-10 academic year: full-time: 603; part-time: 374
- U.S. News 2010 law specialty ranking: clinical training: 22

3.29-3.67 GPA, 25TH-75TH PERCENTILE

154-159 LSAT, 25TH-75TH PERCENTILE

47% ACCEPTANCE RATE

98 2011 U.S. NEWS LAW SCHOOL RANKING

ADMISSIONS

Admissions phone number: **(651) 290-6476**
Admissions email address: **admissions@wmitchell.edu**
Application website:
http://www.wmitchell.edu/admissions/applying/law-school-admission.html
Application deadline for Fall 2011 admission: **1-May**

Admissions statistics:

Number of applicants for Fall 2009: **1,268**
Number of acceptances: **602**
Number enrolled: **197**
Acceptance rate: **47%**
GPA, 25th-75th percentile, entering class Fall 2009: **3.29-3.67**
LSAT, 25th-75th percentile, entering class Fall 2009: **154-159**

Part-time program:

Number of applicants for Fall 2009: **424**
Number of acceptances: **190**
Number enrolled: **103**
Acceptance rate: **45%**
GPA, 25th-75th percentile, entering class Fall 2009: **2.95-3.48**
LSAT, 25th-75th percentile, entering class Fall 2009: **147-154**

FINANCIAL AID

Financial aid phone number: **(651) 290-6403**
Financial aid application deadline: **15-Mar**
Tuition 2009-2010 academic year: **full-time: $32,340; part-time: $23,400**
Room and board: **$14,500** ; books: **$1,550** ; miscellaneous expenses: **$800**
Total of room/board/books/miscellaneous expenses: **$16,850**
University does not offer graduate student housing for which law students are eligible.

Financial aid profile

Percent of students that received grants for the 2008-2009 academic year: full-time: **41%**; part-time **25%**
Median grant amount: full-time: **$19,923** ; part-time: **$9,143**
The average law-school debt of those in the Class of 2009 who borrowed: **$81,532** . Proportion who borrowed: **96%**

ACADEMIC PROGRAMS

Calendar: **semester**
Joint degrees awarded: **MS - Health; MA - Public Administration; MS - Women's Studies**
Typical first-year section size: Full-time: **80**; Part-time: **80**
Is there typically a "small section" of the first year class, other than Legal Writing, taught by full-time faculty?: Full-time: **yes**; Part-time: **yes**
Number of course titles, beyond the first year curriculum, offered last year: **149**
Percentages of upper division course sections, excluding seminars, with an enrollment of:

Under 25: **60%**	25 to 49: **26%**
50 to 74: **11%**	75 to 99: **2%**
100+: **0%**	

Areas of specialization: appellate advocacy, clinical training, dispute resolution, environmental law, health care law, intellectual property law, international law, tax law, trial advocacy

Fall 2009 faculty profile

Total teaching faculty: **265**. Full-time: **14%**; 50% men, 50% women, 14% minorities. Part-time: **86%**; 59% men, 41% women, 26% minorities
Student-to-faculty ratio: **20.4**

SPECIAL PROGRAMS (as provided by law school):

William Mitchell's distinctive educational approach develops practical wisdom in students by embracing both scholarship and practice. We offer over 100 intellectually rigorous courses, top-ranked clinical and legal writing programs, externships that put students to work as judicial clerks or researchers, study abroad programs, transactional simulations, and innovative new programming.

STUDENT BODY

Fall 2009 full-time enrollment: 603

Men: 50%	Women: 50%
African-American: 1.80%	American Indian: 1.00%
Asian-American: 3.30%	Mexican-American: 0.70%
Puerto Rican: 0.00%	Other Hisp-Amer: 0.80%
White: 73.60%	International: 0.20%
Unknown: 18.60%	

Fall 2009 part-time enrollment: 374

Men: 51%	Women: 49%
African-American: 2.90%	American Indian: 1.10%
Asian-American: 7.20%	Mexican-American: 0.30%
Puerto Rican: 0.30%	Other Hisp-Amer: 1.10%
White: 69.30%	International: 0.80%
Unknown: 17.10%	

Attrition rates for 2008-2009 full-time students
Percent of students discontinuing law school:

Men: 3%	Women: 3%
First-year students: 9%	Second-year students: 1%
Third-year students: N/A	Fourth-year students: N/A

LIBRARY RESOURCES

Total titles: 231,784
Total volumes: 356,269
Total seats available for library users: 671

INFORMATION TECHNOLOGY

Number of wired network connections available to students: 175 total (in the law library, excluding computer labs: 25; in classrooms: 70; in computer labs: 60; elsewhere in the law school: 20)
Law school has a wireless network.
Students are not required to own a computer.

EMPLOYMENT AND SALARIES

Proportion of 2008 graduates employed at graduation:
N/A
Employed 9 months later, as of February 15, 2009: 97%
Salaries in the private sector (law firms, business, industry): $47,500 –$85,000 (25th-75th percentile)
Median salary in the private sector: $60,000
Percentage in the private sector who reported salary information: 72%
Median salary in public service (government, judicial clerkships, academic posts, non-profits): $45,000

Percentage of 2008 graduates in:

Law firms: 52%	Government: 8%
Bus./industry: 26%	Judicial clerkship: 9%
Public interest: 3%	Unknown: 1%
Academia : 1%	

2008 graduates employed in-state: 84%
2008 graduates employed in foreign countries: 0%
Number of states where graduates are employed: 15
Percentage of 2008 graduates working in: New England: 0%, Middle Atlantic: 0%, East North Central: 2%, West North Central: 91%, South Atlantic: 0%, East South Central: 0%, West South Central: 0%, Mountain: 2%, Pacific: 1%, Unknown: 4%

BAR PASSAGE RATES

Based on 2008 graduates taking Summer 2008 or Winter 2009 exams. Most of the school's first-time test takers took the bar in Minnesota.

90%
School's bar passage rate for first-time test takers

91%
Statewide bar passage rate for first-time test takers

Yale University

- PO Box 208215, New Haven, CT, 06520-8215
- http://www.law.yale.edu
- Private
- Year founded: 1824
- 2009-2010 tuition: full-time: $48,340; part-time: $24,170
- Enrollment 2009-10 academic year: full-time: 613
- U.S. News 2010 law specialty ranking: clinical training: 8, international law: 5

3.82-3.96 GPA, 25TH-75TH PERCENTILE

170-176 LSAT, 25TH-75TH PERCENTILE

8% ACCEPTANCE RATE

1 2011 U.S. NEWS LAW SCHOOL RANKING

ADMISSIONS

Admissions phone number: **(203) 432-4995**
Admissions email address: **admissions.law@yale.edu**
Application website: **http://www.law.yale.edu/admissions**
Application deadline for Fall 2011 admission: **15-Feb**

Admissions statistics:
Number of applicants for Fall 2009: **3,363**
Number of acceptances: **270**
Number enrolled: **214**
Acceptance rate: **8%**
GPA, 25th-75th percentile, entering class Fall 2009: **3.82-3.96**
LSAT, 25th-75th percentile, entering class Fall 2009: **170-176**

FINANCIAL AID

Financial aid phone number: **(203) 432-1688**
Financial aid application deadline: **15-Mar**
Tuition 2009-2010 academic year: **full-time: $48,340; part-time: $24,170**
Room and board: **$16,000** ; books: **$1,100** ; miscellaneous expenses: **$1,800**
Total of room/board/books/miscellaneous expenses: **$18,900**
University offers graduate student housing for which law students are eligible.

Financial aid profile
Percent of students that received grants for the 2008-2009 academic year: full-time: **51%**
Median grant amount: full-time: **$21,410**
The average law-school debt of those in the Class of 2009 who borrowed: **$99,989** . Proportion who borrowed: **77%**

ACADEMIC PROGRAMS

Calendar: **semester**
Joint degrees awarded: **J.D./Ph.D. Philosophy; J.D./Ph.D. History; J.D./Ph.D. American Studies; J.D./Ph.D. Political Science; J.D./M.E.S. Forestry; J.D./M.A. Arts & Sciences; J.D./M.D. ; J.D./Ph.D. Sociology; J.D./M.A.**
International Relations; J.D./M.A.R. Ethics; J.D./Ph.D. Economics; J.D./M.F.S. Forestry; J.D./M.B.A.; J.D./M.A. East Asian Studies; J.D./M.P.H.; J.D./M.E.M. Forestry; J.D./M.P.P.; J.D./M.A. Economics; J.D./Ph.D. German Language/Literature; J.D./Ph.D. Anthropology; J.D./Ph.D. English; J.D./M.A. Political Science; J.D./M.P.A.; J.D./Ph.D. History of Art; J.D./Ph.D. Finance
Typical first-year section size: Full-time: **58**
Is there typically a "small section" of the first year class, other than Legal Writing, taught by full-time faculty?: Full-time: **yes**
Number of course titles, beyond the first year curriculum, offered last year: **163**
Percentages of upper division course sections, excluding seminars, with an enrollment of:

Under 25: **56%**	25 to 49: **24%**
50 to 74: **13%**	75 to 99: **4%**
100+: **3%**	

Areas of specialization: appellate advocacy, clinical training, dispute resolution, environmental law, health care law, intellectual property law, international law, tax law, trial advocacy

Fall 2009 faculty profile
Total teaching faculty: **125**. Full-time: **58%**; **79%** men, **21%** women, **11%** minorities. Part-time: **42%**; **71%** men, **29%** women, **15%** minorities
Student-to-faculty ratio: **7.3**

SPECIAL PROGRAMS *(as provided by law school)*:
Please see our bulletin and/or website for this information: http://www.law.yale.edu

STUDENT BODY
Fall 2009 full-time enrollment: 613

Men: **52%**	Women: **48%**
African-American: **7.50%**	American Indian: **0.20%**
Asian-American: **11.60%**	Mexican-American: **2.40%**
Puerto Rican: **1.30%**	Other Hisp-Amer: **4.70%**
White: **63.10%**	International: **4.10%**
Unknown: **5.10%**	

Attrition rates for 2008-2009 full-time students
Percent of students discontinuing law school:

Men: 1%   Women: 1%
First-year students: 2%   Second-year students: 1%
Third-year students: 2%   Fourth-year students: N/A

LIBRARY RESOURCES

Total titles: 409,097
Total volumes: 1,254,850
Total seats available for library users: 424

INFORMATION TECHNOLOGY

Number of wired network connections available to students: 1009 total (in the law library, excluding computer labs: 414; in classrooms: 581; in computer labs: 4; elsewhere in the law school: 10)
Law school has a wireless network.
Students are not required to own a computer.

EMPLOYMENT AND SALARIES

Proportion of 2008 graduates employed at graduation: 94%
Employed 9 months later, as of February 15, 2009: 98%
Salaries in the private sector (law firms, business, industry): $160,000 –$160,000 (25th-75th percentile)
Median salary in the private sector: $160,000
Percentage in the private sector who reported salary information: 87%

Median salary in public service (government, judicial clerkships, academic posts, non-profits): $59,631

Percentage of 2008 graduates in:

Law firms: 41%   Government: 5%
Bus./industry: 7%   Judicial clerkship: 35%
Public interest: 8%   Unknown: 0%
Academia : 3%

2008 graduates employed in-state: 6%
2008 graduates employed in foreign countries: 3%
Number of states where graduates are employed: 28
Percentage of 2008 graduates working in: New England: 11%, Middle Atlantic: 27%, East North Central: 5%, West North Central: 4%, South Atlantic: 25%, East South Central: 2%, West South Central: 2%, Mountain: 3%, Pacific: 19%, Unknown: 0%

BAR PASSAGE RATES

Based on 2008 graduates taking Summer 2008 or Winter 2009 exams. Most of the school's first-time test takers took the bar in New York.

97%

School's bar passage rate for first-time test takers

81%

Statewide bar passage rate for first-time test takers

Yeshiva University (Cardozo)

■ 55 Fifth Avenue, 10th Floor, New York, NY, 10003
■ http://www.cardozo.yu.edu
■ Private
■ Year founded: 1976
■ 2009-2010 tuition: full-time: $45,170; part-time: $45,170
■ Enrollment 2009-10 academic year: full-time: 1,020; part-time: 101
■ U.S. News 2010 law specialty ranking: dispute resolution: 8, intellectual property law: 14

3.39-3.75 GPA, 25TH-75TH PERCENTILE

161-166 LSAT, 25TH-75TH PERCENTILE

26% ACCEPTANCE RATE

52 2011 U.S. NEWS LAW SCHOOL RANKING

ADMISSIONS

Admissions phone number: (212) 790-0274
Admissions email address: lawinfo@yu.edu
Application website:
  http://www.cardozo.yu.edu/admissions
Application deadline for Fall 2011 admission: 1-Apr

Admissions statistics:
Number of applicants for Fall 2009: 4,645
Number of acceptances: 1,204
Number enrolled: 268
Acceptance rate: 26%
GPA, 25th-75th percentile, entering class Fall 2009: 3.39-3.75
LSAT, 25th-75th percentile, entering class Fall 2009: 161-166

Part-time program:
Number of applicants for Fall 2009: 625
Number of acceptances: 166
Number enrolled: 102
Acceptance rate: 27%
GPA, 25th-75th percentile, entering class Fall 2009: 3.28-3.71
LSAT, 25th-75th percentile, entering class Fall 2009: 158-161

FINANCIAL AID

Financial aid phone number: (212) 790-0392
Financial aid application deadline: 15-Apr
Tuition 2009-2010 academic year: **full-time: $45,170; part-time: $45,170**
Room and board: $18,400 ; books: $1,200 ; miscellaneous expenses: $4,771
Total of room/board/books/miscellaneous expenses: $24,371
University does not offer graduate student housing for which law students are eligible.

Financial aid profile
Percent of students that received grants for the 2008-2009

academic year: full-time: 58%; part-time 19%
Median grant amount: full-time: $20,000 ; part-time: $6,000
The average law-school debt of those in the Class of 2009 who borrowed: $105,067 . Proportion who borrowed: 75%

ACADEMIC PROGRAMS

Calendar: **semester**
Joint degrees awarded: **J.D./M.S.W.**
Typical first-year section size: Full-time: **49**; Part-time: **49**
Is there typically a "small section" of the first year class, other than Legal Writing, taught by full-time faculty?: Full-time: **no**; Part-time: **no**
Number of course titles, beyond the first year curriculum, offered last year: **156**
Percentages of upper division course sections, excluding seminars, with an enrollment of:
  Under 25: **46%**   25 to 49: **25%**
  50 to 74: **9%**   75 to 99: **10%**
  100+: **10%**
Areas of specialization: appellate advocacy, clinical training, dispute resolution, environmental law, health care law, intellectual property law, international law, tax law, trial advocacy

Fall 2009 faculty profile
Total teaching faculty: **133**. Full-time: **43%**; **65%** men, **35%** women, **11%** minorities. Part-time: **57%**; **67%** men, **33%** women, **7%** minorities
Student-to-faculty ratio: **15.6**

SPECIAL PROGRAMS *(as provided by law school):*
Cardozo is known for intellectual property and dispute resolution programs, and for the Innocence Project, founded by Prof. Barry Scheck. All Cardozo clinics are client-based. Other programs range from human rights studies to constitutional democracy and corporate governance. New short-term international seminars are in countries around the globe. See: http://www.cardozo.yu.edu/info.aspx?cid=266

STUDENT BODY

Fall 2009 full-time enrollment: 1,020

Men: 50%	Women: 50%
African-American: 4.60%	American Indian: 0.30%
Asian-American: 9.10%	Mexican-American: 0.90%
Puerto Rican: 1.30%	Other Hisp-Amer: 4.30%
White: 42.00%	International: 2.70%
Unknown: 34.80%	

Fall 2009 part-time enrollment: 101

Men: 48%	Women: 52%
African-American: 5.00%	American Indian: 0.00%
Asian-American: 9.90%	Mexican-American: 0.00%
Puerto Rican: 1.00%	Other Hisp-Amer: 5.00%
White: 54.50%	International: 1.00%
Unknown: 23.80%	

Attrition rates for 2008-2009 full-time students
Percent of students discontinuing law school:

Men: 2%	Women: 1%
First-year students: 3%	Second-year students: 1%
Third-year students: N/A	Fourth-year students: N/A

LIBRARY RESOURCES

Total titles: 139,069
Total volumes: 560,325
Total seats available for library users: 483

INFORMATION TECHNOLOGY

Number of wired network connections available to students: 39 total (in the law library, excluding computer labs: 39; in classrooms: 0; in computer labs: 0; elsewhere in the law school: 0)
Law school has a wireless network.
Students are not required to own a computer.

EMPLOYMENT AND SALARIES

Proportion of 2008 graduates employed at graduation: 75%
Employed 9 months later, as of February 15, 2009: 94%
Salaries in the private sector (law firms, business, industry): $75,000 –$160,000 (25th-75th percentile)
Median salary in the private sector: $137,500
Percentage in the private sector who reported salary information: 82%
Median salary in public service (government, judicial clerkships, academic posts, non-profits): $53,000

Percentage of 2008 graduates in:

Law firms: 58%	Government: 8%
Bus./industry: 19%	Judicial clerkship: 5%
Public interest: 10%	Unknown: 0%
Academia : 0%	

2008 graduates employed in-state: 81%
2008 graduates employed in foreign countries: 2%
Number of states where graduates are employed: 16
Percentage of 2008 graduates working in: New England: 3%, Middle Atlantic: 88%, East North Central: 1%, West North Central: 0%, South Atlantic: 3%, East South Central: 0%, West South Central: 0%, Mountain: 0%, Pacific: 3%, Unknown: 0%

BAR PASSAGE RATES

Based on 2008 graduates taking Summer 2008 or Winter 2009 exams. Most of the school's first-time test takers took the bar in New York.

92%
School's bar passage rate for first-time test takers

81%
Statewide bar passage rate for first-time test takers

Non-responding Schools

CATHOLIC UNIVERSITY
- 2250 Avenida Las Americas, Suite 584, Ponce, Puerto Rico 00717-0777
- http://www.pucpr.edu
- Private
- Admissions phone number: (787) 841-2000
- Admissions email address: admisiones@pucpr.edu
- 2011 U.S. News Law School Ranking: Unranked

INTER-AMERICAN UNIVERSITY
- PO Box 70351, San Juan, Puerto Rico 00936-8351
- http://www.metro.inter.edu
- Private
- Admissions phone number: (787) 765-1270
- Admissions email address: edmendez@inter.edu
- 2009 U.S. News Law School Ranking: Unranked

LIBERTY UNIVERSITY
- 1971 University Boulevard, Lynchburg, VA 24502
- http://law.liberty.edu
- Private
- Admissions phone number: (434) 592-5300
- Admissions email address: law@liberty.edu
- 2009 U.S. News Law School Ranking: Unranked

PHOENIX SCHOOL OF LAW
- 4041 N. Central Avenue, Suite 100, Phoenix, AZ 85012
- http://www.phoenixlaw.edu
- Private
- Admissions phone number: (602) 682-6800
- Admissions email address: admissions@phoenixlaw.edu
- 2009 U.S. News Law School Ranking: Unranked

SOUTHERN UNIVERSITY LAW CENTER
- PO Box 9294, Baton Rouge, LA 70813
- http://www.sulc.edu/index_v3.htm
- Public
- Admissions phone number: (225) 771-5340
- Admissions email address: Admission@sulc.edu
- 2009 U.S. News Law School Ranking: Tier 4

ST. THOMAS UNIVERSITY
- 16401 N.W. 37th Avenue, Miami Gardens, FL 33054
- http://www.stu.edu
- Private
- Admissions phone number: (305) 623-2311
- Admissions email address: admitme@stu.edu
- 2009 U.S. News Law School Ranking: Tier 4

THOMAS M. COOLEY LAW SCHOOL
- 300 S. Capitol Avenue, PO Box 13038, Lansing, MI 48901
- http://www.cooley.edu
- Private
- Admissions phone number: (517) 371-5140
- Admissions email address: admissions@cooley.edu
- 2009 U.S. News Law School Ranking: Tier 4

UNIVERSITY OF LA VERNE
- 320 E. D Street, Ontario, CA 91764
- http://law.ulv.edu
- Private
- Admissions phone number: (909) 460-2001
- Admissions email address: lawadm@ulv.edu
- 2009 U.S. News Law School Ranking: Unranked

UNIVERSITY OF PUERTO RICO
- PO Box 23303, Estacion Universidad, Rio Piedras, Puerto Rico 00931-3302
- http://www.upr.edu
- Public
- Admissions phone number: (787) 764-0000
- Admissions email address: admisiones@upr.edu
- 2009 U.S. News Law School Ranking: Unranked

Alphabetical Index of Schools

Index of Schools by State

Emory University, 184

Georgia State University, 206

Mercer University (George), 240

University of Georgia, 368

Hawaii

University of Hawaii–Manoa (Richardson), 370

Idaho

University of Idaho, 374

Illinois

DePaul University, 172

Illinois Institute of Technology (Chicago), 220

John Marshall Law School, 226

Loyola University Chicago, 234

Northern Illinois University, 256

Northwestern University, 260

Southern Illinois University–Carbondale, 296

University of Chicago, 352

University of Illinois–Urbana-Champaign, 376

Indiana

Indiana University–Bloomington (Maurer), 222

Indiana University–Indianapolis, 224

University of Notre Dame, 416

Valparaiso University, 462

Iowa

Drake University, 174

University of Iowa, 378

Kansas

University of Kansas, 380

Washburn University, 472

Kentucky

Northern Kentucky University (Chase), 258

University of Kentucky, 382

University of Louisville (Brandeis), 384

Louisiana

Louisiana State University–Baton Rouge, 230

Loyola University New Orleans, 236

Southern University Law Center, 497

Tulane University, 328

Maine

University of Maine, 386

Maryland

University of Baltimore, 342

University of Maryland, 388

Massachusetts

Boston College, 136

Boston University, 138

Harvard University, 214

New England School of Law, 246

Northeastern University, 254

Suffolk University, 312

Western New England College, 482

Michigan

Michigan State University, 242

Thomas M. Cooley Law School, 497

University of Detroit Mercy, 364

University of Michigan–Ann Arbor, 394

Wayne State University, 478

Minnesota

Hamline University, 212

University of Minnesota–Twin Cities, 396

University of St. Thomas, 438

William Mitchell College of Law, 492

Mississippi

Mississippi College, 244

University of Mississippi, 398

Missouri

St. Louis University, 304

University of Missouri, 400

University of Missouri–Kansas City, 402

Washington University in St. Louis, 476

Montana

University of Montana, 404

Nebraska

Creighton University, 168

University of Nebraska–Lincoln, 406

Nevada

University of Nevada–Las Vegas (Boyd), 408

New Hampshire

Franklin Pierce Law Center, 198

New Jersey

Rutgers–Camden, 282

Rutgers–Newark, 284

Seton Hall University, 292

New Mexico

University of New Mexico, 410

New York

Albany Law School, 120

Brooklyn Law School, 142

Columbia University, 164

Cornell University, 166

CUNY–Queens College, 170

Fordham University, 196

Hofstra University, 216

New York Law School, 248

New York University, 250

Pace University, 270

St. John's University, 302

Syracuse University, 314

Touro College (Fuchsberg), 326

University at Buffalo–SUNY, 330

Yeshiva University (Cardozo), 496

North Carolina

Campbell University (Wiggins), 146

Charlotte School of Law, 158

Duke University, 178

Elon University, 182

North Carolina Central University, 252

University of North Carolina–Chapel Hill, 412

Wake Forest University, 470

North Dakota

University of North Dakota, 414

Ohio

Capital University, 148

Case Western Reserve University, 150

Cleveland State University (Clevelandl), 160

Ohio Northern University (Pettit), 264

Ohio State University (Moritz), 266

University of Akron, 332

University of Cincinnati, 354

University of Dayton, 360

University of Toledo, 448

Oklahoma

Oklahoma City University, 268

University of Oklahoma, 418

University of Tulsa, 450

Oregon

Lewis & Clark College (Northwestern), 228

University of Oregon, 420

Willamette University (Collins), 490

Pennsylvania

Drexel University (Mack), 176

Duquesne University, 180

Pennsylvania State University (Dickinson), 272

Temple University (Beasley), 316

University of Pennsylvania, 422

University of Pittsburgh, 424

Villanova University, 468

Rhode Island

Roger Williams University, 280

South Carolina

Charleston School of Law, 156

University of South Carolina, 432

South Dakota

University of South Dakota, 434

Tennessee

University of Memphis (Humphreys), 390

University of Tennessee–Knoxville, 440

Vanderbilt University, 464

Texas

Baylor University (Umphrey), 134

South Texas College of Law, 294

Southern Methodist University (Dedman), 298

St. Mary's University, 306

Texas Southern University (Marshall), 318

Texas Tech University, 320

Texas Wesleyan University, 322

University of Houston, 372

University of Texas–Austin, 442

Utah

Brigham Young University (Clark), 140

University of Utah (Quinney), 452

Vermont

Vermont Law School, 466

Virginia

Appalachian School of Law, 124

College of William and Mary (Marshall-Wythe), 162

George Mason University, 200

Liberty University, 497

Regent University, 278

University of Richmond (Williams), 426

University of Virginia, 454

Washington and Lee University, 474

Washington

Gonzaga University, 210

Seattle University, 290

University of Washington, 456

West Virginia

West Virginia University, 480

Wisconsin

Marquette University, 238

University of Wisconsin–Madison, 458

Wyoming

University of Wyoming, 460

Puerto Rico

Catholic University, 497

Inter-American University, 497

University of Puerto Rico, 497

About the Authors & Editors

Founded in 1933, Washington, D.C.-based *U.S.News & World Report* delivers a unique brand of weekly magazine journalism to its 12.2 million readers. In 1983, *U.S. News* began its exclusive annual rankings of American colleges and universities. The *U.S. News* education franchise is second to none, with its annual college and graduate school rankings among the most eagerly anticipated magazine issues in the country.

Anne McGrath, the book's lead writer, is a deputy editor at *U.S.News & World Report*. She has written about higher education and previously was managing editor of "America's Best Colleges" and "America's Best Graduate Schools," the two *U.S. News* annual publications featuring rankings of the country's colleges and universities.

Robert Morse is the director of data research at *U.S.News & World Report*. He is in charge of the research, data collection, methodologies, and survey design for the annual "America's Best Colleges" rankings and the "America's Best Graduate Schools" rankings.

Brian Kelly is the executive editor of *U.S.News & World Report*. As the magazine's No. 2 editor, he oversees the weekly magazine, the website, and a series of newsstand books. He is a former editor at the *Washington Post* and the author of three books.

Other writers who contributed chapters or passages to the book are Carolyn Kleiner Butler, Kristin Davis, Anna Mulrine, Dan Gilgoff, Betsy Streisand, Jill Rachlin Marbaix, and Samantha Stainburn. The work involved in producing the directory and *U.S. News* Insider's Index was handled by deputy director of data research Sam Flanigan.

Notes

Notes

Notes

Notes

Notes

Notes

Notes

Notes

Notes

Notes

Notes

Notes

CATALOGUE PUBLIC LIBRARY

3 0620 00373 4869

For Reference

Not to be taken from this room